£1-50

THE
DONATZ PROENSALS
OF UC FAIDIT

UNIVERSITY OF DURHAM
PUBLICATIONS

THE
DONATZ PROENSALS
OF UC FAIDIT

EDITED BY

J. H. MARSHALL

LONDON
OXFORD UNIVERSITY PRESS
NEW YORK TORONTO
1969

Oxford University Press, Ely House, London W. 1
GLASGOW NEW YORK TORONTO MELBOURNE WELLINGTON
CAPE TOWN SALISBURY IBADAN NAIROBI LUSAKA ADDIS ABABA
BOMBAY CALCUTTA MADRAS KARACHI LAHORE DACCA
KUALA LUMPUR SINGAPORE HONG KONG TOKYO

© UNIVERSITY OF DURHAM 1969

PRINTED IN GREAT BRITAIN

CONTENTS

INTRODUCTION	1
I. The Manuscripts	3
II. The Editions	9
III. Classification of the Manuscripts	11
1. The Textual Tradition of the *Donatz*	11
2. The Relationship of the Latin Text to the Provençal	16
3. The Relationships of the Manuscripts	24
IV. Characteristics of the Individual Manuscripts	42
V. The Establishment of the Text	48
VI. The Graphy of the Base-Manuscript	53
VII. The Circumstances of the Composition of the *Donatz*	62
VIII. Faidit as Grammarian	66
IX. The Fortunes of the *Donatz*	79
X. Bibliography and Abbreviations	81
CRITICAL TEXT OF THE *DONATZ PROENSALS*	87
NOTES	257
APPENDICES	341
I. *Donatz Proensals*: version of MS. C	343
II. Fragment of list of rhymes from MS. L	371
III. Chapters on prepositions and interjections added to the *Donatz* in MS. L	374
IV. Additions and Corrections to *FEW*	376
ALPHABETICAL LIST OF RHYME-ENDINGS	379
INDEX OF PROPER NAMES	381
GLOSSARY	384

ACKNOWLEDGEMENTS

THE author wishes to acknowledge the help of the many colleagues and institutions whose advice and collaboration have greatly contributed to the preparation of the present edition. In particular, he would like to place on record his debt to Mrs. D. R. Sutherland for her encouragement and counsel freely given over many years and to Professor J. Lough for much helpful advice in the preparation of the manuscript. Tribute should be paid to the staffs of the Library of the Taylorian Institution, Oxford, and of the University Library, Durham, for the many services with which they have facilitated the author's researches. Acknowledgement is due to the Librarians of the Biblioteca Laurenziana and the Biblioteca Riccardiana, Florence, the Biblioteca Ambrosiana, Milan, and the Pierpont Morgan Library, New York, for allowing access to materials in their manuscript collections and for furnishing microfilm. The author wishes also to express his thanks to the Publications Board of the University of Durham for accepting the present work for inclusion among their publications.

INTRODUCTION

I. THE MANUSCRIPTS

THE text published here under the title *Donatz Proensals* is to be found in the following manuscripts:[1]

A. Florence, Bibl. Laurenziana, Aedilium 187. Thirteenth century, Italian.[2] Parchment, 33 ff., consisting of two gatherings of six double leaves (catchwords at the bottom of ff. 12^v and 24^v) and an incomplete gathering of four double leaves, in which f. 28 is geminate with f. 33 (the leaves geminate with ff. 25, 26, and 27 have been removed). Ff. 29-32, two double parchment leaves of somewhat different size and quality from the rest, were clearly an addition to the original MS. The contents are as follows:

ff. 1-28^v (first hand), the *Donatz*;
ff. 29^r-32^r (second hand), three texts in French giving medical information (1, 'Li .iiij. çapitres de garder les dens e les gengies'; 2, 'Li .xv. chapitres choment l'om se doit garder son cors es .iiii. parties dell'an'; 3, 'Esperiment as dens blançir et a les gengives qui sainent volentiers sainement mentenir');
f. 33^v (third hand), further medical information in Italian (incipit: 'A la mingrana e a dolore di testa').
Ff. 32^v and 33^r are blank.

In the part of the MS. which concerns us the page measures 206 × 146 mm., the written portion 152 × 101 mm. The MS. has been rebound since Stengel consulted it in 1872; the trimming of the pages has removed a few letters in the outer margins (cf.

---

[1] For earlier descriptions of the MSS. see Stengel, pp. v-xii; Pillet and Carstens, *Bibliographie der Troubadours*, pp. xx (*P* = our *B*), xxiv-xxv (*a* = our *C*) and the references given there; Brunel, *Bibliographie des manuscrits littéraires en ancien provençal*, nos. 293 (*A*), 290 (*B*), 305 (*C*), 310 (*D*), 332 (*E*), 308 (*L*); Biadene, pp. 335-6 (*L*); C. F. Bühler, 'Another Provençal Manuscript in the Pierpont Morgan Library', *Speculum*, xxv, 1950, pp. 245-6 (*L*); *Mostra di codici romanzi delle biblioteche fiorentine*, Florence, 1957, pp. 71 (*A*), 68-9 (*B*), 170-1 (*C*). My descriptions and transcriptions are based on direct consultation of the MSS., except that I have relied on a microfilm for the readings of *L* and have followed Biadene in my description of that MS.

[2] Brunel's judgement (op. cit., no. 293) that *A* was copied 'en pays catalan' was based on certain graphies in the MS. (cf. op. cit., p. xii, confirmed in a letter to me by M. Brunel), which are not, in my opinion, conclusive. The hand of the MS. is certainly Italian.

1264, 1641, 3161), and the process of rebinding has hidden parts of words written in the inner margins which were visible to Stengel (cf. 850, 2459). The page contains 17 lines of Provençal text, not divided into columns. The interlinear Latin version, in the same hand but in smaller characters and without ruling, is spaced in such a way as to correspond as exactly as possible with the Provençal text; in passages where space was inadequate the interlinear matter forms a double line and occasionally extends somewhat into the margin. In the Provençal text, capitals and other initial letters are touched with red; red and blue large capitals and paragraph marks alternate as far as f. 7^v, after which only red is used for this purpose (a few are omitted in the rhyme-lists, cf. 2408, 2615, 3265). The scribe did not always leave room for the paragraph marks. The three rubrics (the incipit; l. 502; and the explicit) are in the same hand as the text and indicate that the scribe was his own rubricator. The MS. contains no expunctuations but a certain number of erasures, at least one of which (3001–3) was made after the initials of the Provençal text had been touched with red. (2793 also indicates that the scribe continued to correct while rubricating.) Marginal additions are all in the same hand as the text and each is surrounded (as are the catchwords) by a thin red line; the position of marginalia in the text is normally, but not always, indicated by an insertion-mark.

The Provençal text is generally legible, the Latin interlinear version much less so; in both, but particularly in the Latin, distinctions between u, n, i, etc., are not always clear. The first three folios are somewhat damp-stained.

B. Florence, Bibl. Laurenziana, XLI. 42. Early fourteenth century; it is the work of four scribes, the first three Italian, the fourth possibly French. Parchment, 93 ff., constituted as follows:

1, ff. 1–38 (first hand), three gatherings of five double leaves and one of four; f. 38^v has the catchword *La francha captenensa*, which does not correspond to f. 39^r. Anthology of Provençal lyrics.

2, ff. 39–54 (second hand), two gatherings of four double leaves. Ff. 52^v, 53^{r-v}, 54^r blank; f. 54^v ruled but without text. Collection of *vidas* and *razos*, beginning in the middle of a *razo* to a poem of Gaucelm Faidit (Boutière and Schutz, *Biographies des troubadours*, 1st ed., xxxviii C, l. 28; 2nd ed., xviii C, § 8).

THE MANUSCRIPTS

3, ff. 55–83ᵛ, col. 1 (first hand). Ff. 55–66 comprise a gathering of six double leaves, containing a collection of *coblas*; part of f. 66ʳ and all of f. 66ᵛ are ruled but without text. Ff. 67–84 constitute two gatherings of four and five double leaves and contain the *Donatz* (ff. 67ʳ–77ᵛ), a Provençal–Italian glossary (ff. 78ʳ–79ʳ; published by A. Castellani in *Lebendiges Mittelalter, Festgabe für Wolfgang Stammler*, Freiburg, 1958, pp. 1–43) and the *Razos de trobar* (ff. 79ᵛ–83ᵛ, col. 1). At the end of the *Razos* the scribe gives his name: 'Petrus Berzoli de Eugebio fecit hoc opus.' (Parts 1–3 of the MS. constitute the Provençal *chansonnier P*.)

4, ff. 83ᵛ, col. 2, to 84ᵛ (third hand): under the title *Tractatus de bonitate et malitia mulierum*, the French text generally known as *Le Blasme des femmes* (on which see Långfors, *Les Incipit des poèmes français*, pp. 325–6). This was copied in the blank portion at the end of the gathering.

5, ff. 85–92 (fourth hand). A gathering of four double leaves, containing the *Livre des Moralitez* (Bossuat, *Bibliographie*, nos. 2653–5). At the end the scribe gives the date 1310; but this does not constitute evidence for dating the first four parts of the MS.

F. 93 is a blank fly-leaf.

We are concerned here only with the work of the first scribe. The page measures 268 × 193 mm., the written portion 198 × 136 mm. The page contains 43 lines (dry-point horizontal and vertical ruling is visible); the text is copied in two columns per page, except for ff. 71ʳ–79ʳ inclusive (= *Donatz* 931–end, together with the Provençal–Italian glossary), where the page is divided into three columns. In the verb-lists red and blue capitals alternate for the initial of the first word of each alphabetical section; in the rhyme-lists red and blue paragraph marks alternate before the initial of the first word of each rhyme-group. In both lists the Provençal is placed on the left of the column and the Latin on the right, separated by '.i.'; the longer Latin equivalents overflow on to the left-hand portion of the following line, and compound forms in the verb-lists are given on the right-hand side of the column, e.g.:

| Gastar | .i. | vastare. | Gardar | .i. | custodire u*e*l |
| Compost | | degastar. | | | respicere. |

In that part of the rhyme-lists for which Latin equivalents are lacking (3326–3561) the Provençal words are written at the left of the column, one per line. (Thus the Latin must already have been lacking here in *B*'s exemplar, unless—as seems improbable—the scribe of *B* decided deliberately to drop the Latin after 3324.) The other parts of the text in which the Provençal is accompanied by the Latin translation (i.e. 1346–51, 1467–1514, 3105–8, 3115–16, 3173–6, 3220–4) dispose the two languages on alternate lines, the Latin above the Provençal and in red ink. The heading at 775–6 is in red, as are all the headings in the verb-lists, with the exception of ten in black—2654, 2740 var. (*In ons estreit*), 2772, 2789, 2882, 2896, 2907, 2950, 3231, 3433—and two in which the heading is given first in black, then in red (2797, 2816). Marginal indications to the rubricator are visible in all cases except for the two just mentioned and except for 2696 and 2717, where the rubric is written on an erasure. The rubricator followed the marginal indication exactly, even where it was wrong (e.g. 2904, 3078), except where the contrary is noted in the variants (3117, 3128, 3265, 3378). The Latin conclusion (3562–9) is written in black ink on alternate lines.

C. Florence, Bibl. Riccardiana, 2814. Late sixteenth century. Paper, 172 ff. Parts 1 and 2 (ff. 1–132) constitute the Provençal *chansonnier a*; that is, they are part of the copy, made in 1589 by Jacques Teissier of Tarascon for Piero del Nero, of the lost thirteenth-century anthology of Bernart Amoros. Part 3 consists of 40 ff., with an old numbering from 1 to 40 and a modern numbering from 133 to 172. This portion would seem to consist of five gatherings of four double leaves, but there are no catchwords. It contains the *Donatz* (ff. 1–15^r = 133–147^r), the *Razos de trobar* (ff. 15^v–28^v = 147^v–160^v), and some *vidas*, preceded by a copy of Bernart Amoros's preface and followed by a table of contents (ff. 28^v–40 = 160^v–172). All are the work of a single copyist (different from the scribe of Parts 1 and 2), whom Stengel (p. ix) would identify with the author of the signature 'Antonio martelino' on f. 89; this identification seems to me questionable. The page measures 235 × 170 mm., the written portion is variable (approximately 200–10 × 115–25 mm.). The page contains 20 to 24 lines of text, without ruling and without coloured initials or ornamentation. The ink has faded to light brown. Ff. 1^r–2^r (= 133^r–134^r) contain, as does the earlier part of the *Razos de trobar*, underlinings and corrections made in a blacker ink than the rest of the text. The hand is identical with that which wrote, at the top of f. 18^v (= 150^v), the words 'qui manca uedi insu la coperta' (cf. Stengel, p. 71^b, 34–5) and which Stengel identified (p. x) with that of Piero del Nero.

D. Milan, Bibl. Ambrosiana, D. 465 inf. Late sixteenth century, Italian. This is a miscellany of thirty-nine small paper MSS. which belonged to Gianvincenzo Pinelli (cf. S. Debenedetti, *Gli studi provenzali in Italia nel Cinquecento*, Turin, 1911, pp. 57–9). A modern continuous numbering runs from 1 to 347 (with omission of 246 and an unnumbered leaf after f. 242).

No. 35 of the miscellany consists of a fly-leaf added to the original and bearing the title in Italian (f. 308), sixteen numbered leaves (ff. 1–16 = 309–24), and another added fly-leaf, which is blank (f. 325). The original part of the MS. consists of three gatherings of five, one and two double leaves. It contains the text of the *Donatz* 1–1522 (ff. 1^r–12^r = 309^r–320^r), followed by a list of rhymes different from that given by MSS. *ABL* of the *Donatz* (ff. 13^r–15^v = 321^r–323^v); f. 324 is blank. The rhyme-list was printed by Stengel (pp. 105–10) and is not reprinted here. The opening lines of it are in a different hand from the rest; Stengel (pp. xii and 105) recognized here the hand of Piero del Nero. The rhyme-list is arranged in four columns to the page.

Nos. 27 and 36 of this same miscellany (respectively ff. 245–57 and ff. 326–35) consist of two sixteenth-century Italian translations of the *Donatz*; no. 27 is here referred to as d^1, no. 36, which entirely lacks the verb-lists, as d^2. According to Debenedetti (op. cit., pp. 68–70) d^1 may be a copy of a translation made *c.* 1552 by Barbieri and Castelvetro. The relationship of d^1 and d^2 to *D* is examined below (pp. 35–9).

L. New York, Pierpont Morgan Library, 831 (formerly in the library of Sir Horace Landau, Florence). End of thirteenth or beginning of fourteenth century, Italian. Parchment, 17 ff., unnumbered. The MS. is defective at the beginning. It consists of a gathering of six double leaves and an incomplete gathering of four double leaves (f. 16 is geminate with f. 17, while the leaves geminate with ff. 13–15 have been removed). The number iiij, in the bottom right-hand corner of f. 12^v, suggests that at least two gatherings are lacking at the beginning of the MS. The lower half of f. 16^v and the whole of f. 17 are blank. The page measures 320×235 mm. and contains 35 lines. The MS. contains:

1, the end of a rhyming dictionary, not identical with that of the *Donatz* (f. 1^r);
2, the *Razos de trobar* (ff. 1^r–7^r); then, after a gap of six lines,
3, the *Donatz*, 1–2425 (ff. 7^r–16^v).

These five MSS. are the only ones which have textual authority. There exist in addition three *codices descripti*, all containing the *Donatz* and the *Razos de trobar*, which are copies of *B* (cf. Stengel, p. xii):

    E. Vatican, Barberini, lat. 3986. Seventeenth century, copied by F. Ubaldini. Ff. 34–85 contain the two grammars.
    F. Florence, Bibl. Marucelliana, Trib. 2 Scaf. B vol. 17.
    G. Paris, Bibl. Nationale, lat. 7534.

In addition to these, Italian extracts from the *Donatz* and the *Razos de trobar*, made by Benedetto Varchi from MS. *C*, are contained in MS. Ashburnham 1812 of the Laurenziana (cf. Debenedetti, op. cit., pp. 71–2; Biadene, pp. 400–2).

II. THE EDITIONS

THE *Donatz* was first published, together with the *Razos de trobar*, by Guessard in 1840. This edition omitted the verb-lists and the dictionary of rhymes but printed both Provençal and Latin texts for the rest, based respectively on *A* and *B* (more precisely, on copies which he had procured of these MSS.; Guessard was unaware that *A* had an interlinear text throughout, cf. n. 1 to p. 186 of his edition). Guessard knew at this time of the existence of MSS. *C*, *D*, and *G*, but he made no use of *C* and *D*.

Guessard's second edition followed in 1858. In it the lists of verbs and rhymes were printed for the first time. The editor here made use of MSS. *A*, *B*, *C*, and *D*; he printed the Latin text, as in his first edition, at the foot of the page, but arranged the word-lists in columns. The text is somewhat more eclectic than that of the 1840 edition.

Stengel's edition of 1878 had the avowed intention of returning to the readings of the MSS. He printed an interpretative Provençal text of *A* and a more or less diplomatic text of *C* in parallel columns for the main body of the grammar (1–774 and 1467–1522), giving some variants of *D* and some readings of the Latin text (after Guessard's 2nd edition) among the textual notes. For this part of the grammar, Latin renderings of a good proportion of the examples (but not of the grammatical exposition) are incorporated into the Provençal text of *A*; these Latin renderings do not consistently follow either *A* or *B*. For the verb-lists and the dictionary of rhymes, readings of *A* and *B*, for both Provençal and Latin, are given. *B*'s variants are also noted for the Provençal text of 1467–1522 and for the Latin conclusion. It is worth adding that, while Stengel's printing of *C* was based directly on the MS. and is very accurate, his reproduction of the readings of *A* and *B* derives from his own collation of Guessard's second edition against the MSS. and is quite unreliable.

Textual notes, mainly emendations and interpretations, to the last two editions mentioned were published by Galvani, G. Paris, Tobler, Chabaneau, Bauquier, and Bartsch (see Bibliography). Many of these have proved of value in the establishment of the present edition, as they had already proved of value to E. Levy in the compilation of his *SW*. None of the scholars mentioned, with the exception of Levy, knew of MS. *L*, whose text was published in a diplomatic edition by Biadene in 1885.

A number of extracts from the *Donatz* have appeared in various anthologies;[1] all are derived from the printed material so far mentioned.

Although the text has been widely used by lexicographers from Diez onwards—in particular, in *SW* and *FEW*—no re-examination of the manuscript material has been made since Biadene.

[1] Monaci, *Testi antichi provenzali*, Rome, 1888, cols. 1–4, gives the opening of the *Donatz*, after MS. *L*; the same scholar published extracts from the *Donatz* and *Razos de trobar* in *Testi romanzi per uso delle scuole*, no. 30, Rome, 1913. Crescini, *Manuale per l'avviamento agli studi provenzali*, 3rd ed., Milan, 1926, no. 55 (pp. 308–11) is an extract from the *Donatz*, after MS. *A*. The opening of the work is printed in Bartsch, *Chrestomathie provençale* (4th ed., cols. 193–6), and in Meyer, *Recueil d'anciens textes*, pp. 149–52.

III. CLASSIFICATION OF THE MANUSCRIPTS

1. *The Textual Tradition of the* Donatz

A PRE-REQUISITE to the detailed examination of the relationships of the *Donatz* MSS.[1] is some consideration of certain general aspects of the whole textual tradition of the work. The transmission of a grammar is in certain important respects different from that of a literary work. And the transmission of the *Donatz* has certain characteristic features and presents certain characteristic difficulties peculiar to itself.

Four general features of this kind should be mentioned here.

1. A grammar is not merely read but used. It will accumulate marginalia, whose presence or absence in particular MSS. may be the result of individual decisions of scribes, rather than proof of common ancestry.

2. For the same reason a grammar is continually open to correction of real or imagined error. In particular, unusual forms are likely to be 'corrected' to more normal ones or perhaps deleted entirely. Marginal or interlinear correction would present a subsequent copyist with a choice of two forms.

3. In this connection the possibility of continuous interplay between the Provençal text and the Latin translation complicates manuscript relationships. Since, as we shall see, all MSS. go back to a source with interlinear Latin, all were open in various degrees to this process.

4. As a consequence of (1) and (2) it follows that one and the same lost MS. could exist in different 'states', the later states showing new additions and corrections (as well as possible material deterioration). These could be variously mirrored in surviving copies.

---

[1] Attempts at classification have been made by Stengel, pp. xxiii–xxiv, by Biadene, pp. 345–52, and by Avalle, *La Letteratura medievale in lingua d'oc nella sua tradizione manoscritta*, Turin, 1961, pp. 144–7. None of these is sufficiently detailed to merit discussion.

In some measure these processes can actually be observed in the surviving MSS. themselves. *A*'s marginal observation at 464, peculiar to this MS. and dependent on its erroneous reading here (*mo vol* for *per mo vol*), illustrates the first point made above. *B*'s reading in 1232, *vengiar vel veniar*, must stem from a correction made in the form 'vengar' by an earlier reader or scribe for whom *venjar*, not *vengar*, was the normal reflex of vĭndĭcāre. Again, in illustration of point (3), *B* 922 shows the original reading *espirar* (shared with *ADL*) with its first *r* struck through, evidently by a corrector or reader who took note of the Latin translation *inquirere*. Each of the points mentioned would indicate, for the passages in question, a first and a second 'state' of *A* or of *B* (or of the immediate ancestor of each). Again, *B*'s readings for 3117 and 3128 clearly indicate two states of that MS., before and after the intervention of the rubricator.

A further element which limits the quantity of clear evidence for manuscript classification is the fact that a very small proportion of the Provençal text occurs in all five MSS., while the Latin version exists in only two MSS. with fragments in two others. The following table summarizes the position:

Table I

Provençal text		Latin text	
1–774	ACDL	1–1514	AB (and fragmentarily in C and L)
775–1466	ABDL		
1467–99	ABCDL		
1499–1514	ABDL	1515–2580	A
1515–22	ADL	2581–3325	AB
1523–2425	AL	3326–3561	A
2426–2580	A	3562–9	AB
2581–3561	AB	3569–73	A

Thus a strict comparison of all five MSS. would have to depend on a mere 33 lines of the Provençal text; though it should be added that, for 1–774, *B*'s Latin text provides a legitimate element of comparison for at least some features of the transmission of the Provençal text (additions, omissions, order of exposition).

Straightforward comparison of the five MSS. is further complicated by the nature of the text transmitted by MS. *C*. It is demonstrable that *C*'s text is not a copy, but a rehandled version, of the *Donatz* as represented by the other four MSS. And this conclusion has a corollary, important for the classification of the MSS.: the original included inconsequences in the order and manner of exposition which were due to the author—all of which were, of course, open to subsequent correction.

That *C*'s text rehandles a text much like that of *ABDL* can be demonstrated by an examination of a few passages:

1. *C* 413–30 corresponds to 360–7 of the critical text. *C* presents a paragraph on the pluperfect optative of the second, third, and fourth conjugations, which is what one expects at this point in the grammar, but nevertheless includes a paradigm for *amar*. And *C* 431 is totally meaningless in its own context: it is comprehensible only when one realizes that it reproduces the corresponding lines of the critical text (367–8), which, in their own context, have meaning. The passage is far from satisfactory in the critical text, but it is possible to understand its shortcomings (cf. note to 360–7); in *C* the inconsequences of the exposition are explicable only as the result of a partial rehandling of the text, involving only the first part of the paragraph.

2. *C* 235–62 presents a long treatment of the declension of some pronouns, absent from *ABDL*. If this passage was part of the original (and it is hardly in the manner of the rest of the *Donatz*), why should a supposed common ancestor of *ABDL* have omitted it in favour of a different and much briefer note on the pronoun (critical text, 204–19), which *C* also gives, more or less without alteration (*C* 217–32)? The simplest hypothesis is that the author of *C*'s version, having reproduced the paragraph on the pronoun which he found in the original version of the *Donatz*, considered it too brief and added his own much longer exposition.

3. Again, *C* 233–4 makes the point that certain pronouns need no -*s* in the singular. This is an exact observation, and well placed in the exposition. *ABDL* do not have it here, but present a similar observation in 99–104, in the course of the exposition of the case-system in masculine nouns. The placing of the observation in *ABDL*—and hence in the critical text—is illogical, though comprehensible as an inconsequence on the part of the author. It is incomprehensible, on the other hand, that, if *C*'s text be supposed to represent the original, a common ancestor of *ABDL* should have moved this passage from its logical place to one which was less logical. We must suppose, again, an inconsequence of the

original, 'corrected' by the author of the revised version represented by *C*.

These instances could easily be multiplied. Our explanation of them receives further support from the existence of various inconsequences in the exposition of the grammar which the text of *C* shares with the other MSS.:

TABLE II

63 (*C* 55), the ablative case receives no mention.

125–6 (*C* 99–101), present participles are included in the treatment of nouns.

179–80 (*C* 175–7), 182 (*C* 180), 191–2 (*C* 201, if *recors* represents an original *resors*), 197 (*C* 206): past participle forms occur among the nouns.

320–59 (*C* 375–81, 390–412), the passage on the optative (i.e. conditional) of the first conjugation includes lengthy treatment of the verbs of the other conjugations. (Note that, while 695–8 in effect repeats the essentials of this in the proper place, *C* 808–9 substitutes a back-reference.)

344 (*C* 405), there is no mention of the conditional of *saber* in any MS., despite the mention of this verb in 335.

365–8, 375–80 (*C* 414–16, 424–30, 438–44), the paragraph on the pluperfect optative of the first conjugation includes reference to other conjugations and a paradigm of the imperfect subjunctive of *tendre*; this latter is thus duplicated by 719–29 (*C* 829–41), where the imperfect subjunctive of the second and third conjugations is treated in its proper place.

516 (cf. *C* 595), the author admits he has exemplified third conjugation verbs before those of the second conjugation.

532–51 (*C* 602–29), three tenses—the future indicative, the future optative, and the present subjunctive—are mentioned out of order. The last two tenses are repeated in their proper place later (711–18 = *C* 816–28); the future indicative is similarly repeated (685–7), but is omitted in *C* (788).

570 (*C* 658), the singular persons of the preterite of *aver* are the subject of an awkward parenthesis.

603 (*C* 701), the reference to *respondet* is inconsequential, since it has already been cited in the list of verbs here (597; *C* lacks this earlier mention, since it omits, no doubt accidentally, the equivalent of 595–9).

653–5 (*C* 754–7), the paragraph on the imperfect indicative not merely duplicates 534–7 (*C* 604–12) but is out of place, since it should precede the preterite, not come after it.

CLASSIFICATION OF THE MANUSCRIPTS

It follows from this that the revised text represented by *C* was the result of intermittent revision and rationalization on the part of a reviser who was often content to leave unsatisfactory passages unaltered; and that the original itself was not free from inconsequences which must be attributed to the author himself. Thus a more logical, apparently 'better' reading of *C* will commonly be the result of rehandling of an 'illogical' original. And this original may be reproduced with varying degrees of fidelity by *ABDL*: for example, 305–11 (*C* 352–60) and its variants are comprehensible only if one supposes that the author's Provençal original inadvertently omitted all reference to the first plural (perhaps also the third plural) forms of the imperative and that this omission was subsequently made good in the interlinear matter, a fact reflected in different ways in the different MSS.

We are dealing, then, with an 'open' tradition; and, what is more, with a tradition in which the elements from outside the tradition—deriving from the knowledge and the critical intelligence of readers and scribes—may be applied not merely to the correction of scribal errors but also to the elimination of negligences due to the original author and of real or apparent contradictions between the Provençal and the Latin texts.

In these complex circumstances the stemma which seems best to do justice to the variety of the manuscript readings is the following:

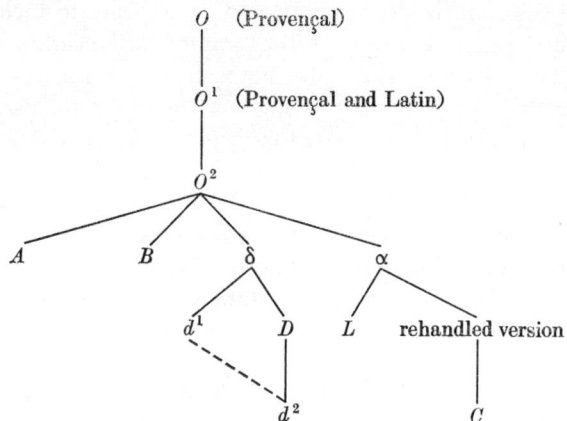

(It is possible that the various direct copies of O^2 were made at different stages, so that O^2 itself may have been somewhat modified meanwhile by accretions and corrections.)

Demonstration of this stemma involves two elements: the relationship of O^2 to O, which depends on our conception of the relationship of the Latin and Provençal texts; and the relationship of O^2 to the surviving copies, which depends predominantly on the comparison of their Provençal readings.

2. The Relationship of the Latin Text to the Provençal

All the surviving MSS. of the *Donatz* go back to a source which contained both the Provençal and the Latin texts. This is clear in the case of A, in which the two versions accompany each other throughout the text. It is clear in the case of B; for where B has only the Latin text (1–774) its defective form presupposes the existence of a vernacular text like that in A (cf. in particular 458–63, 552, and the fragments of the Provençal text embedded in the Latin —through scribal error?—at 336, 516, 705a, 730). L's Provençal text contains extensive fragments of Latin; these involve mainly but not exclusively passages in which the Latin (as represented by AB) gave information not present in the vernacular text, together with Latin renderings of some examples. But the relatively haphazard nature of this Latin material clearly carries its own explanation: it is a selection, partly motivated and partly random, from a fuller body of material which it is reasonable to suppose identical with the Latin of AB. C presents a similar picture, except that here the selection is clearly motivated by a desire to include the Latin renderings of many of the grammatical examples while leaving aside entirely the Latin equivalents for the rest of the grammar. C's position in the stemma (to be established later) makes it impossible to suppose that it goes back to a stage in the history of the text when the grammatical examples were accompanied by a Latin rendering which did not cover the rest of the grammar. (The existence of such a stage is not, in itself, implausible; but nothing in the text of the *Donatz* makes the postulation of its existence necessary.) Moreover, C's text shows two Provençal additions which derive from the Latin version of the *Donatz* (C 539, cf. A 461, Latin; C 590, 592, 594, cf. A 505–7, Latin) and two erroneous expansions suggested by the Latin (C 510–17, 606–12, cf. A 439–44, 536–7, Latin; cf. below, p. 45). That D derives from a source with parallel Provençal and Latin is not easy to prove conclusively. D's variants for 81 and 328–31 show Provençal phrases absent from the other MSS. but equivalent

CLASSIFICATION OF THE MANUSCRIPTS

to the Latin rendering of these passages as given in *AB*; at 686–7 *D*'s *amarai* (against *-rai* in *AL*; *C* omits the passage) corresponds with the Latin *amabo* of *AB*; and at 840 *D*'s *sufflar* (for *bufar*) seems to have been suggested by the Latin *ore insuflare*. It is difficult to explain the provenance of these variants except as the result of consultation of the corresponding Latin phrase. Other positive evidence of this kind is lacking. But the case for a Provençal–Latin source of *D* is supported by two further arguments: firstly, its position in the stemma; secondly, the consistency with which it omits *all* traces of the interlinear material, including vernacular elements which have not yet been mentioned.

In this common source containing text and translation, the translation was interlinear, as it is in *A*. *B* supports this by its arrangement of the Provençal and the Latin on alternate lines in 1346–51, 1467–1514, 2816, 3105–8, 3173–6, 3220–4. Although *B* arranges the verb-lists and the rhyming dictionary in parallel columns, there are scribal errors which indicate that the original arrangement was interlinear: cf. in particular *B*'s variants to 1102–4, 2793–4. *L* supports our hypothesis of interlinear disposition of the Latin text in that Latin equivalents in that MS. for Provençal phrases (as distinct from examples) ordinarily precede the Provençal, cf. *L*'s variants to 304, 311, 416, 464, 542, 667, 701, 702, 720, 1497. And the confused arrangement of the Latin in 413–16, which partly corresponds with a similar confusion in *B*, is explicable only if the Latin was originally disposed as an interlinear gloss (probably overflowing here into the margins). It is not possible to demonstrate from the texts of the *Donatz* given by *C* and *D* that these MSS. go back to a source in which the Latin was interlinear. The demonstration is impossible for *D* because this MS. gives a purely Provençal text, impossible for *C* because the reviser responsible for *C*'s version of the text himself incorporated such Latin elements as he wished to preserve into the text of his revised version. On the other hand, there is no indication that either *D* or the revised version depended on a bilingual source in which the disposition of the Latin was other than interlinear.

The Latin rendering of the *Donatz* contained a certain number of mistakes of translation or interpretation which are of such a kind that they cannot easily be attributed to scribal error.

TABLE III

530, *tenh* must, from the context, be the 1st sg. pr. ind. of *tenher*. The Latin rendering *teneo* (*AB*) shows that the translator misidentified it as 1st sg. pr. ind. of *tener*.

663, the rendering of *escondre* as *excutere* (*AB*) is erroneous: the translator misread or misinterpreted the word as *escodre*. (*Escondre* is the reading of all MSS., including *C* 760.)

690, *de la prima* is rendered *prime persone* (*A*; *B* lacks the whole passage). The context indicates that *prime coniugationis* would be the correct interpretation.

922, *espirar* (common to all four MSS.) is rendered *inquirere* (*AB*). The Latin evidently corresponds to *espiar* and may be explained as a misreading by the translator.

1311, *escondre* is rendered *excutere granum de paleis* (*A*) or *excutere granum* (*B*). The case is identical with 663 above, except that here *D* reads *escodre* and *C* is lacking.

2146, *atens* is rendered *nancisceris* (uantisceris *A*; *B* is lacking). The translator understood this form as the 2nd sg. pr. ind. of *atenher*. The author must have intended the 2nd sg. pr. ind. of *atendre*: not only does it immediately follow *tens*, *destens* (translated *tendis*, *distendis*), but neither in the remaining 71 words in -*ens* nor elsewhere in the rhyming dictionary is there any other example of a confusion on the author's part between [n] and [n']. (Confusions of the graphies *n* and *nh*, on the other hand, are common in MS. *A*.)

It is just possible to regard 663, 922, and 1311 as common scribal errors in the Provençal and 690 as an erroneous scribal addition in the Latin. But 530 and 2146 are not open to this type of explanation: they are necessarily the result of incorrect word-by-word translation. And it is simpler to regard the other four cases as belonging also to the same category of translator's errors.

The Latin text and the Provençal text, then, were not composed *pari passu*. Were they the work of two different hands? Or is it possible to ascribe them to the original author, by supposing that he added the Latin version to his own vernacular text at a later date and with some degree of inattention? No clear decision is possible on this question. The author of the Provençal was capable of inconsequences in the exposition (cf. above, pp. 13-14) and, in one instance, of a straightforward slip in the Provençal (3222, *prima* for *quarta*) which went uncorrected in the Latin. There is nothing impossible in the supposition that Faidit himself occasion-

CLASSIFICATION OF THE MANUSCRIPTS 19

ally mistook the meaning of his own text when translating it at a later date. One mistranslation, however, goes against this:

648, *ai fait*, in an observation made in the first person singular by the author to his readers, is rendered as *fecit* (*AB*).

Unless this is regarded as no more than a scribal error, it is surely an indication that the translator was not identical with the author and reflected this fact—consciously or unconsciously—in referring to the author of the Provençal in the third person. The argument is not absolutely conclusive simply because scribal error remains a possible explanation here. While accepting that the question remains open, I have chosen to refer consistently to the author of the Latin version as 'the translator'.

It follows from all this that the Latin rendering of the *Donatz* was added—by whatever hand—to an already existing complete Provençal text. In the strictest sense, the latter alone is the 'original'. Of what did this interlinear addition to the original consist?

The interlinear matter included a number of elements other than a straightforward rendering of the Provençal text. These may be classified under three headings.

(*a*) Latin observations which add to the substance of the Provençal text an amplification or a restrictive qualification (referred to hereafter collectively as 'glosses'):

Table IV

54, 81*, 95a, 210–11*, 313, 323, 328–31, 340, 367*, 381*, 461, 505–7, 508–10*, 511, 516–17*, 521–2, 527–8, 537, 568, 576, 615*, 670, 705a*, 708*, 710*, 713–14*, 719–20, 737, 740–40a*, 741–6*, 751, 754, 755–60, 763, 767, 770, 771–1a, 1350, 2403: these are amplifications in the interest of greater clarity, i.e. interpretative translations of the Provençal; 708 and 710 were dictated by the fact that Latin had no compound pluperfect;

53, 243–4, 305–8*, 335–6, 413–16*, 564–5, 1468, 3173: these are amplifications which make material additions to the Provençal text;

2, 21–1a*, 25–5a, 119, 259, 259a–60, 261–1a, 287, 419–19a, 501: these are restrictive qualifications of the Provençal text; five cases—21–1a, 25–5a, 119, 259, 287—are concerned with pointing the difference between Latin and the vernacular and thus spring from the nature of the act of translation itself.

(b) Glosses which, while they are of the same kinds as under (a), partially or wholly replace the rendering of the part of the Provençal text to which they are appended. These are listed under (a) above and marked with an asterisk. They are classed below according to the extent of the Provençal text left untranslated as a result of the gloss.

TABLE V

The gloss stands in place of a rendering of some or all of the relevant Provençal examples, which are thus left untranslated: 210–11, 305–8, 413–16, 508–10, 708, 710, 741–6. (81 is a special case in that the three Provençal examples, while not translated, are repeated in the interlinear material.)

A complete sentence or phrase of the Provençal is left untranslated: 413–16 (no equivalent of 416 of the Provençal text), 615 (no equivalent of *In -erc*), 705a (no equivalent of *el cap*, unless *loco avia* is regarded as a paraphrase of the Provençal rather than as an addition to it), 740–40a (no equivalent of *Lo preterit perfeit del conjunctiu*).

The portion of the Provençal text left untranslated is less than a complete sense-group: 21–1a (*cum se fossen masculi*), 367 (*et el preterit perfeit*), 381 (*preterito inperfecto*), 516–17 (*e degra avan dir*), 713–14 (*que fenissen*). In these five passages the Latin combines a gloss on the vernacular text with a partial translation of it and is thus incomprehensible without reference to the Provençal.

It is possible to explain this situation as the result of scribal deficiencies. Under this hypothesis, copyists, faced with the difficulty of fitting into the restricted space above a Provençal phrase both a translation of it and a gloss amplifying or explaining it, would have dropped part of the translation in favour of the gloss. Two of the last five cases in the table above could be attributed to the scribe of *A*, for in 713–14 *B* gives *que desinunt* and in 381 *preterito perfecto* [*sic*] (though with an odd word-order in 381). The other three could be attributed to a scribe earlier in the tradition, for in these instances *B* shares the omissions of *A* (in 21–1a the omission is rather longer in *B*, which lacks *sed sic dicitur*, rendering *an se diçen aici*). The explanation would thus be parallel to that of 37–8, where, in *A*, an erroneous repetition of a phrase of the Provençal text in the Latin so extended the interlinear matter as to leave no room for the translation of the word *Numbres*. And the same explanation might hold good for the other omissions

CLASSIFICATION OF THE MANUSCRIPTS

noted above, in which single examples, sets of examples, and whole phrases of the Provençal are without translation.

The alternative explanation is that some at least of the glosses existed as interlinear additions to the Provençal text before the translation was added. In this hypothesis, it was the translator who failed to translate certain phrases because the space above them was already occupied by a gloss on the text; and in other cases he he must have fitted in the translation with the gloss by making a double line of interlinear matter—a layout of the text found in *A* in many such passages.

The two explanations are equally plausible; but the second receives support from the third element in the interlinear matter, to be mentioned now.

(*c*) Provençal words intended as direct additions to the Provençal text (perhaps also as corrections of it) and not forming part of the syntax of the Latin translation:

Table VI

49, *la* (*A*; *B* omits this and the parallel phrases in 45 and 47) is possibly an addition to the *lo* of the Provençal text (though scribal error is a simpler explanation).

422, *vel es* (*A*) is an addition to *tu est* (note that *DL*, and *C* 495, give *es* as the only form).

458–63, *vel fora*, etc. (*AB*) is a series of additions to *eu seria*, etc. (note that *L* gives *foratz* as an alternative in 462 and that *C* 534–6 has *fora*, *foras*, *fora* as alternatives for the singular persons).

693, *vel amo* (*A*) is an addition to *amon*.

1308, *ante prendere* (*AB*) is an error for *anteprendre*, intended as an addition to the *antreprendre* of the Provençal text. In this case the interlinear addition has supplanted any Latin rendering of the Provençal verb.

1393, *vel eschovir* (*A*), though certainly a corrupt reading, may reflect the addition to *estremir* of a synonymous verb (cf. note).

2071, *telz* (*A*) may be an addition (or alternative) to *telhz*.

2215, *paniers* (*A*) may be an addition to *panatiers*. (Both 2071 and 2215 may be considered as scribal errors of *A*, analogous to those in 3317 and 3388, where the repetition of the Provençal word in the Latin is certainly erroneous.)

2260, *vespo uel* (*A*), a scribal error for *nespoliers*, is an addition to *mespoliers*.

At least five of these (422, 458–63, 693, 1308, 2260) admit only of the explanation advanced here. The two in which *B*'s testimony is added to that of *A* confirm that the additions were interlinear and strongly suggest that they existed before the translation was added (cf. the absence of translation in 1308, the confused disposition of the interlinear text in 458–63).

Whether there were also interlinear corrections of the Provençal text is less certain. A few passages admit of this explanation:

TABLE VII

10, interlinear *Derivatius* (*A*) above Provençal *Dervatius* (*A*).

155, interlinear *da que* (*A*) above Provençal *da quel* (*A*; da quels *D*, daqels que *L*). Interlinear addition of *que* to indicate the correction *d'aquels que* is a possible explanation.

160, interlinear *mescaps* (*A*) above Provençal *mes, caps* (so *AL*; *D* reads *mescaps* and *B* has a Latin rendering corresponding to *mescaps*). Interpretation is uncertain, cf. note.

773, interlinear *si* (*A*; *B* reads *sic*) above Provençal *sia*. Classifiable here on the hypothesis that *A* and *B* were puzzled by an interlinear *si ua*, intended to correct the erroneous Provençal reading (cf. note); for an alternative explanation, see Table VIII.

880, interlinear *condeiare* (*A*) above Provençal *codeiar* may stem from correction of the incorrect Provençal; but *BD* have *condeiar* correctly (*L* omits).

These passages are too few in number and too miscellaneous in character to allow of any sure explanation. In the printed text, 10, 155, and 880 have been resolved on the supposition of simple scribal error in *A*, while 160 and 773 have been left open. But it would not be surprising if, besides additions to the Provençal text, the interlinear matter originally included also a few corrections of errors.

If it is accepted that the interlinear matter surviving in the extant MSS. does show traces of Latin glosses and Provençal additions which existed before the translator added his complete Latin rendering of the text, it becomes likely that the translator worked on a Provençal text which was not the original, but a copy of the original. This is also made likely by the fact that the translation was added at a later date than the composition of the Provençal and perhaps by a different hand. This probability would become a certainty were it possible to demonstrate one of two things: (1) that interlinear corrections to the Provençal existed before the

CLASSIFICATION OF THE MANUSCRIPTS

translation; (2) that the translation was made on an already incorrect Provençal text. The first of these, as we have seen, cannot be demonstrated conclusively. The second is supported by a certain quantity of evidence:

TABLE VIII

188, interlinear *gregnonum* (*A*) above *gregnos* (*A*). No other MS. has this word. If it is accepted that *gregnos* can only be a scribal error for *gergons* (cf. note), then the Latin reading is dependent on an error in the vernacular text.

366 (*C* 415), interlinear *capere* (*A*) above *prendre* (supported by *AL*); *pendre* (given by *CD*) would make much better sense. It is not possible, however, to demonstrate that *prendre* was a scribal error in the copy of the text used by the translator, since the unsatisfactory Provençal could easily be due to the author's carelessness.

773, interlinear *si* (*A*) or *sic* (*B*) above *sia* (*A*; similarly *C* 867–8 and *D*). If the two divergent readings of the Latin are interpreted as errors for an original *sit*, then *sit* would depend on the erroneous Provençal *sia*. (Cf. Table VII for an alternative explanation.)

2435, interlinear *Camleus* or *Canileus* above Provençal *Camleus* or *Canileus* (*A* is sole witness for this passage). The correct Provençal is *Canileus* (cf. note). If the Latin is *Camleus* it would seem to depend on the corrupt Provençal; but interlinear *Canileus* might merely reflect the translator's failure to understand the Provençal word (there is no parallel instance in the text: the use of Provençal instead of—or in addition to—Latin in 180, 182, 876, and 1970 reflects no lack of comprehension on the translator's part).

2437, interlinear *Arueus* above Provençal *Arueus* (*A* again is the sole witness). *Anjeus* is the only possible correct Provençal reading; if this is accepted, then it would seem that the translator merely repeated the erroneous reading of the Provençal text.

These five passages are not conclusive. Four of them are attested only by *A*. One of these (366) is open to more than one explanation. It is possible to explain the three others (188, 2435, 2437) as due, not to a baffled translator, but to a baffled scribe; there is some evidence in *A* of scribal alteration of the Latin in order to make it correspond with an erroneous Provençal reading (1017, 1205, and perhaps 1182), and our three passages may merely be those in which the same scribe's ingenuity was insufficient to produce a passable Latin reading.

There remains the one passage (773) in which *B*'s testimony is added to that of A. Here, as we have seen, two different explanations are possible for the interlinear readings. But, whichever explanation is adopted, this passage necessarily presupposes that the Provençal text existed in a corrupted form before any interlinear matter was added to it.

We must postulate, then, that the Latin translation was added to a copy of the original text of the *Donatz*, a copy which already contained at least one scribal error and in which a certain number of interlinear observations had already been added to the Provençal text. Was this copy ($= O^1$) the archetype of the surviving MSS.? I have postulated that it was not, and that a copy of O^1 ($= O^2$) was the archetype, for reasons which depend on a consideration of the Provençal readings of the MSS.

3. *The Relationships of the Manuscripts*

Direct and conclusive demonstration of the existence of O^2 is difficult. I have postulated that it, and not O^1, was the archetype of the extant MSS. because (1) there are common errors in the Provençal which do not affect the Latin; (2) there are common errors in the Latin.

1. Common errors in the Provençal deriving from error in O^2:

TABLE IX

115-17 (*om. C*), misplaced in *ABDL* (cf. note). This passage was no doubt marginal in O^1 and consequently misplaced in O^2.

167 (*C* 152), *latz* (*ACD*) for *jatz*; *L* has the correct reading, no doubt as the result of intelligent consultation of the Latin. It is not possible to postulate a common source of *ACD* on the strength of this passage. Since the Latin translation corresponds to *jatz*, the error must have arisen later than O^1.

773 (*C* 867-8), *sia* (*AC*), *siaz* (*D*), for *siva* (*L*). The error was inherited by O^2 from O^1 (cf. Tables VII and VIII for the Latin readings. The hypothesis made in Table VII that the interlinear text here had *si ua* would make *L*'s recovery of the correct reading easily explicable; but intelligent conjectural emendation in *L* is not to be ruled out—cf. p. 38 for d^2's similar restoration of the correct sense in this same passage.)

Dubious cases are 1934 (misplacement of *abbas* in *AL*?), 2701 (misplacement of *Santolz* in *AB*?), 3450 (*abranca* for *aranca* in *AB*?). The two MSS. mentioned are the sole witnesses for each passage; error in O^2 is a possible hypothesis in such cases, but cannot be demonstrated.

CLASSIFICATION OF THE MANUSCRIPTS

In addition to these, it is possible to postulate error in O^2 in three passages which we have classed among the errors of the translator (cf. Table III):

TABLE X

663 (C 760), conceivably *escondre* O^2 (followed by $ACDL$) for *escodre* O^1.
922, conceivably *espirar* O^2 (followed by $ABDL$) for *espiar* O^1.
1311, conceivably *escondre* O^2 (followed by ABL but corrected to *escodre* by D) for *escodre* O^1.

The hypothesis of 'translator's error' has been adopted in the text; but error in O^2 is not ruled out.

2. Common errors in the Latin deriving from O^2. These common errors are attested only by A and B; but it is difficult to attribute them to a common source peculiar to AB, since the existence of such a common source is not borne out by any Provençal passage uniting AB in error against the other MSS. We attribute them, therefore, to O^2.

TABLE XI

66 feminini] femini AB.
67 masculinis] masculis AB.
242 ista] istas A, istis B (but B's reading here justifies the plural).
264 brevius] breuis AB.
294 In imperativo] Jnp*e*ratiuo A, Jmp*e*ratiuo B.
455 amamini] amaminor A, ameminor B.
568a sint] sic*ut* AB.
704 pore A, pero B, as renderings of Provençal *pero* (a translator's slip is not inconceivable, however).
815 ocupare vi] ocupauit A, occupauit B.
830 ulnis] uiciis A, brachijs B (assuming B's reading to be a rationalization of *uiciis* suggested by Provençal *braceiar*).
865 tabulas] tibias AB.
891 ocasionem] ocasione A, occasione B.
963 depurare] deputare AB.
1060 ebedare] ebeditare A, ditare B (attempted rationalization in B).
1113 inmunem] jnmune*re* A, i*n*mune*re* B.
1299 conum] conis A, cossas B (assuming B's reading to be a rationalization suggested by Provençal *escoissendre* and by the rendering of 945 *escoissar*).
1471 Ad adverbium] Adu*er*bium A, Aduerbu*m* B.
2720 vectis] uestes A, uectes B.

2775 finduntur] findeitur *A*, fiditur *B* (but *B*'s *lignum* justifies a singular verb).
2886 manser vel spurius] manuu*m* desuri*us A*, manuue*r*suri*us B*.
2913 primus] unus *AB*.
2942 multatio] pe*r*mutatio *AB*.
2943 potes] potest *AB*.
2971 truncate] tracate *A*, tractare *B* (attempted rationalization in *B*).
3171 legerem] legerent *AB*.
3261 scala] sala *AB*.
3566 invidorum] inuide*o*rum *AB*.

A few other passages are better explained as common misinterpretations of O^2, rather than as errors in the latter:

Table XII

180 conreaz] cōrea3 *A*, coream *B* (common misunderstanding of -z as -3).
182 assetaz] assotam *A*, assecta*m B* (as 180; cf. *C* 180 *assettatz*, which suggests that the error was not made in O^2).
930 ad assandum ponere] ad asta*m* ponere *A*, ad assa deponere *B* (for ad assā d'ponere O^2?).
2974, the variants of *A* and *B* suggest that in O^2 *ducs* was written twice, but with the single translation *dux vel quedam avis*.

A few other cases may be explained as deriving from errors or inconsequences of the translator:

Table XIII

4–5, the construction of *cum* with the accusative (*B* substitutes *et* for *cum* and can thus retain the accusative forms).
220, no translation of *es* (*B*'s syntax rationalizes this, cf. 221 *var. B*).
3009 coneris] conaris *AB*; the same error occurs in 2462, where *A* is the sole witness. A grammatical mistake of the translator is possible.

To these we may add the many places in which *A* and *B* agree in giving no translation for Provençal examples. These are best ascribed to the negligence of the translator, though scribal omission or illegibility in O^2 are possible explanations.

The explanations advanced for the cases in Tables XII and XIII may be extended to cover some of the passages in Table XI, but they cannot account for all. There are, therefore, common errors

CLASSIFICATION OF THE MANUSCRIPTS 27

in the Latin which must be attributed to a scribe, not to the translator. These confirm the existence of O^2.

Certain features of O^2 can be deduced from the peculiar and often conflicting testimony of the surviving MSS. In particular, the latter indicate the presence in O^2 of additions, corrections, and errors; but the nature of the textual tradition itself (cf. above, pp. 11–12) means that the testimony of $ABCDL$ is seldom unanimous on such points.

It is clear that O^2 contained marginalia of two kinds: on the one hand, additions to the text; on the other, insertion of words accidentally omitted by the original scribe. The former show, in general, absence of Latin equivalents; the latter do not. The former are reflected in the presence or absence of the relevant phrases in random groupings of the MSS.; the latter in variations in the order of examples in particular passages, again in random groupings. The two classes cannot be rigidly separated in practice and are here classed together. It is important to note that the manuscript-groupings are not consistent and do not allow us to postulate intermediate copies as the sources of particular 'errors' (whether they be additions or omissions).

Table XIV

The Latin heading of the *Donatz*, shared by DL against ABC, should probably be placed here: at some stage in the history of O^2, this adaptation of the concluding paragraph of the text was probably inserted at the beginning of the work to form a title (cf. note to 3569–70).

189–92 (C 193–7), *in ors larg* misplaced in A, omitted in CD, without translation in AB: no doubt marginal and without translation in O^2. L's correctly placed *in ors larg* may well be an independent addition.

518–26 (C 596–601). 524–6 is placed after 520 in BL, omitted by CD. The simplest hypothesis is that 524–6 was marginal in O^2 (C's omission may well be coincidental, since C omits the equivalent of 524–31). This is simpler than supposing coincidental omission in CD and misplacement in A.

576–80 (C 667–72), *in ec estreit* misplaced in A, differently misplaced in DL, without translation in AB: no doubt marginal and without translation in O^2 (C 667 has *estreit*, without *in ec*, correctly placed.)

596–601 (C 696–9 has the end of this passage, after a lacuna corresponding to 595–9 of the critical text). The examples of preterites in *-et* occur in the following order (c. = *compost*; italicized words are additions with respect to *A*'s text):

A: 1. 2. 3. 4. 5. 6. 7. 8. c. 9. c. 10. c. 11. 12. 13. c. 14. 15. 16;
D: 8. c. 9. c. 10. c. 12. c. 13. 1. 2. 3. 4. 5. 6. 7. 14—omitting 11, 15, and 16;
L: 1. *tetendet*. 8. c. 9. c. 10. c. 12. c. 14. 6. 2. 3. 4. 5. 6. 7. 11. 13. 15. *conset*—omitting 16;
B: 1. 8. 2. 4. 5. 6. *vel reprehendit*. 7. 9. 10. *vel reprehendit*. 11. 12. 13. 14. 15. 16. *consuit*—omitting 3;
C (after lacuna): 13. 14. 15. 16.

It is difficult to envisage any explanation other than the presence in the margin of O^2 of at least half a dozen of the examples (possibly augmented at some stage in the history of O^2 by *conset*; for *BL*'s united testimony in favour of this, cf. Table XV below).

612–13 (*C* omits the equivalent of 605–13). *In uis destruis anquara* is given by *AB*, though without translation of *anquara*, and omitted by *DL*: no doubt marginal addition in O^2, with partial translation.

657, *DL* add *vel in etre vel in atre . . . vel in odre* (similarly in *C* 759–60).

659–60, *DL* omit *in ebre decebre* (like *C*, which reorders the whole passage), against *AB*. This and the previous variant suggest marginal additions in O^2 to a passage which was obviously open to expansion.

1065–9. The order of the five words in the MSS. is:

A: 1. 2. 3. 4. 5;
B: 1. 5. 2. 3. 4;
D: 2. 3. 4. 1—omitting 5;
L: 2. 3. 4. 1. 5.

No doubt 5 (= 1069) and probably 1 (= 1065) were marginal in O^2. 1364, placed after 1358 in *B*, omitted by *D*. Conceivably marginal in O^2. 1480–2 (*C* 890–6). The last seven adverbs of time show differences in order:

AL: 1. 2. 3. 4. 5. 6. 7;
B: 3. 4. 2. 5. 6. 7. 1;
D: 3. 4. 1. 2. 5. 6. 7;
C: 1. 3. 4. 2. 5. 6. 7.

1 and 2 (= *adonc* and *mentre*) must have been marginal in O^2. (Did they remain marginal in α, or did *C* coincidentally misplace *mentre*?) 1487–96 (*C* 902–14). The last four classes of adverbs show differences in the order of presentation:

AL: 1. 2. 3. 4;
B: 2. 1. 3. 4;

CLASSIFICATION OF THE MANUSCRIPTS

D: 1. 3—omitting 2 and 4;
C: 3. 2. 4—omitting 1.

One may suppose 2 (= the interrogative adverb) to have been marginal in O^2. (Did it too remain marginal in α?)

The role of coincidence is difficult to assess in these questions. But one cannot attribute *all* of these fluctuations to coincidence, the more so as two features recur: omission by *D*, and absence or partial absence of Latin equivalents. The hypothesis of marginal phrases in O^2 alone explains the variable groupings of the MSS.

This hypothesis, if correct, will serve to explain certain other puzzling features:

689–90 (*C* omits the equivalent of 688–93 in favour of its own 789–806, to be discussed below; *B* omits 688–91). The phrase *que fa sapchas el enperatiu*, present in *ADL* but without translation in *A*, was probably a marginal addition in O^2 (why else the absence of a Latin equivalent?).

690 (*C* 789–99). *C*'s text here is a somewhat expanded version of 690, *var. L.* This passage of *L*, absent from *AD* (and, of course, from *B*, where 688–91 is dropped), cannot be regarded as peculiar to α, since *A*, a few lines later (695), inserts three words of this passage —*trait la prima*—quite out of context and without Latin translation. *L*'s variant must be regarded as a marginal note in O^2 which passed into the text of α and of which *A* unintentionally preserved a trace.

The existence of alterations in O^2 provides an explanation of the great variety of manuscript-groupings in passages which involve alternative forms (sometimes erroneous, sometimes acceptable, sometimes of doubtful standing), mainly for words cited as examples. Some of these are of such a nature as to preclude explanation via intermediate common sources; and they are too numerous to allow of explanation via independent common intention on the part of two (or three) scribes, both (or all) setting out to substitute commoner for less common forms, etc. It is simplest to suppose intervention of a corrector/reviser in O^2—or perhaps a whole series of such interventions—so that O^2 presented copyists with a choice of two readings for certain words. (The 'corrector/reviser' was in all probability no more than an intelligent reader or a succession of intelligent readers.) This would account for the variety of groupings found here, a variety for which neither common intermediate sources nor contaminations provide a satisfactory explanation.

Table XV

596–601, *AD* omit *conset*, against *BL* (cf. Table XIV).
783 anelar *AB*, alleuar *D*, alenar *L*.
798 adempiar *A*, ademprar *B*, adempar *DL*.
837 blesseiar *A*, blesseillar *D*, bleseiar *BL*.
847 calfar *AL*, callar *BD*.
889 deirocar *AD*, derocar *BL*.
908 desaiar *A*, desarrar *B*, desserar *D*, deserar *L*.
909 desflibar *A*, defflibar *D*, desfiblar *BL*.
944 escampar *AD*, escapar *BL*.
974 ferrar *AL*, feirar *BD*.
993 galliar *BL*, *om. AD*.
1022 malevar *A*, mallevar *B*, manlevar *DL*.
1027 messurar *AD*, mesurar *BL*.
1052 nomar *A*, nomnar *B*, nominar *DL*.
1075 pantaiar *AB*, panteiar *D*, pantessar *L*.
1153 sanglentar *A*, sauglentar *L*, sangletar *BD*. (This could also be regarded as (1) sangletar O^2 [scribal error? or acceptable variant form?], corrected independently by *A* and *L*; (2) coincidental error in *B* and *D*.)
1182 sitar *AD*, sugar *B*, suar *L* (the original reading was perhaps *suçar*, cf. note).
1232 vengar *AL*, vengiar vel veniar *B*, veniar *D*.
1234 versificar *AD*, versifiar *BL*.
1256 dechaçer *A*, decazer *B*, descazer *DL*.
1323–4 querer *AL*, querre *BD*.
1343 esdemetre *AL*, esdesmetre *B*, edesmetre *D*. (One could also postulate *esdesmetre* as a scribal error in O^2—if the form is indeed erroneous.)
1389 escrimir *AB*, escremir *DL*.
1400 flechir *AL*, fletir *B*, fleitir *D*.
1401 flebeçhir *A*, flebeizir *D*, febletir *B*, feblezir *L*.
1496 (*C* 914) mens *BL*, *om. AC*; *D* omits 1496 entirely. (Conceivably an addition made independently by *B* and *L*.)
1508 a *AB*, ab *DL*.
1509 sicum *DL*, *om. AB*.

The above table, while including all manuscript-groupings which can reasonably be attributed to additions and corrections in O^2, does not exhaust the examples of groupings which, in my view, it would be illusory to use as evidence of common sources of pairs of MSS. Three further classes may be distinguished among these.

CLASSIFICATION OF THE MANUSCRIPTS

Firstly, groupings which are explicable as showing deliberate modification (usually in more than one MS.) of the text of O^2 and which therefore reflect common purpose on the part of different scribes:

TABLE XVI

84 (*C* 67) nominatiu *AC*, nominatius *DL*;

86 (*C* 70) nominatiu *AC*, nominatius (s *erased in D*) *DL*. Most probably the forms with -*s* were grammatical errors in O^2, independently corrected in *A* and *C*. Note that *D* corrects by erasure in 86, while in 84 *L* alters the construction in the interests of grammar.

220 (*C* 264) Verbes *A*, Verbs *C*, Verbum *DL*. Here, as in 388, *AC* transpose into Provençal (cf. 532–3 below).

225 and *passim*, conjunctius *ACL*, subjunctius *D*, subiunctivus *B*. A modification of the terminology in keeping with Priscian's *subiunctivus*.

293, 450, 543, 769 (= *C* 344, 525, 620, 865). *CD* agree in retaining the 3rd pl. fut. form in -*an* and omitting that in -*au*. *D* does this consistently in the four passages mentioned and in 415 and 500 (for which *C* has no equivalent)—the only exception is *D*'s *vel amarau* in 687 (no equivalent in *C*). These reflect common purpose, not a common source.

366 (*C* 415) pendre *CD*, prendre *AL*. Common correction by *CD* of an inept example (cf. note to 360–87, and Table VIII).

385–7 and *passim*. *DL* sporadically agree in expanding verb-endings into full forms; this process is normal throughout *C*. But the opposite is possible: 266–71 (*C* 313–19), *DL* agree against *AC* in giving endings, not full forms. Similarly, *DL* often agree (e.g. 372–4) in inserting the personal pronoun before verb-forms; again this is general in *C*.

388 (*C* 445) El futur *A*, En lo futur *C*, In futuro *DL*. Cf. 220 above.

532–3 (*C* 602–3). *DL* agree in giving the phrase in Latin, *AC* in Provençal; the interlinear text, as represented by *AB*, omits the latter half of the phrase. In view of this last fact and of the residual Latinisms in the Provençal (imperfec *A*; et futur *AC*; in futur *A*), it is easiest to suppose that *AC* shared the common purpose of translating the original Latin phrase into Provençal. (It is noteworthy that *D*'s Latin is somewhat Provençalized.)

542–3 (*C* 618–20) -rai (etc.) *A*, aurai (etc.) *CDL*. This is a special case of the feature noted above for 385–7. *D* and α expanded the series of six future indicative endings in accordance with the Latin rendering *habebo*. (328–33 [*C*392–8] is exactly parallel, except that here *L* gives endings, not full forms, for all but the first person singular.)

552 (*C* 630) indicativi *A*, del indicatiu *C*, *om*. *DL*. *AC* agree in making the phrase more explicit. (The whole phrase, already in Latin in the

Provençal text, was not rendered in the interlinear version; *C* is alone in translating it into Provençal, a fact which lends support to 532–3 above.)

615 (*C* 704) sofrec *A*, sufrere [error for *sufrerc*] *C*, sofferc *D*, suferc *L*. It is easiest to suppose independent correction in *D* and *L* and—with less intelligence—in *C*. Since the group was headed *In -erc* 'correction' was self-evident.

616 (*C* 707) corec *A*, corre[c] *C*, cucurrit *AB* (Latin), *om. DL*. Again, 'correction' by omitting this word was obvious, since it followed three preterites in *-erc*, with which it was apparently classed by the author.

652 (*C* 753) scenblans *A*, semblan *CDL*. The ungrammatical n. pl. f. form is best explained as an error in O^2, corrected by *A*, rather than as proof of a group *CDL*.

658 (*C* 759) prendre *AC*, prendere *B* (Latin), pendre *DL*. An obvious correction of an inconsequence on the author's part, since *prendre*, unlike *pendre*, does not normally have a p. part. in *-ut*. The correction entailed a further modification in 661: pendre *A*, pendere *B* (Latin), prendre *L*, *om. D* (*C* also omits, perhaps coincidentally). *A*'s Latin readings (658 no translation, 661 prendere) reflect scribal confusion, ultimately attributable to the same motive as the alterations in *DL*.

727–8 (*C* 837–9) agssem, agsetz *A*, aguessem, aguessetz *CDL*. Innovation in *A* is possible. But independent correction to the more usual literary form in *D* and α is more likely.

886 sobradeaurar *A*, sobredeaurare *B*, *om. DL*. Here, as in 975, 996, 1068, *DL* agree in omitting the examples of compound forms, placed in O^2 above the word *compost*, since they agree in copying the main text while, in general, neglecting the interlinear matter.

1180 solheiar *BL*, solleiar *D*, solhelar *A*. If the form in *-eiar* is erroneous, as seems probable, it is best regarded as an error of O^2, corrected by *A*. (The author's form was apparently *solelhar*, cf. 3386 *solelha*.)

1481 (*C* 892) atan *AD*, antan *BL*, autran [*sic*] *C*. This is to be placed here if *atan* is ascribed to O^2, whether as a possible variant form or as a scribal error—otherwise it must be classed as a coincidental scribal error in *A* and *D*.

Secondly, groupings which are readily attributable to coincidence:

Table XVII

64 (*C* 51–4 expresses the passage differently) no *AL*, *om. D*; non *B* (Latin), *om. A* (Latin);

86 (*C* 70) Et *om. DL*, against *AC* and the Latin in *AB*;

105 (*C* 93 expresses this differently) el [= e·l < et lo] *DL*, et *A* (Latin); en *A*, in *B* (Latin);

CLASSIFICATION OF THE MANUSCRIPTS 33

133 (*C* 109) Et *om. AC*, against *DL* and the Latin in *AB*. (These four passages may in fact reflect fluctuating scribal attitudes towards slight discrepancies between the Provençal and the Latin texts.)

132 (*C* 107) [de] declinazos *AL*, against *CD*.

222 (*C* 265–6, rehandled): common omission by haplography in *AL* (*D* has a different omission by haplography in 221–2; the correct Provençal text can be established from *B*'s Latin).

237 (*C* 282 omits) lautras *AD*, against *L*.

348 segria *DL*, seiria *A*.

354 colgaria *D*, colgueria *L*, colria *A*.

364–5 (cf. *C* 424–30) *AD*, against *BCL*, lack the paradigm of *bon fora qu'eu agues tendut*, probably as a result of the confused layout of the passage in O^2 (cf. note to 360–87).

415–16 eundem... vulgari *misplaced in BL* (cf. *L*, var. 416). No doubt the error was encouraged by the layout of the passage in O^2.

421 (*C* 494) fui *AC*, error for *sui* (*DL*).

440–1 (*C* 512–13) -at[z] *A*, amat[z] *D*, against *CL*.

465 [per] mo vol *AL*, against *D* (*C* 543 rehandles the text).

494 (*C* 577) si metez Deus vola en loc de cum *AL*, erroneously, against *BCD*. (The hypothesis of an error in O^2, independently corrected in *BCD*, is not ruled out.)

589 na[c]tus est *BL*, against *A*.

717 (*C* 817–18 rewrites) si cum [cum] eu sia *AL*, against *D* (cf. the same haplography, in *L* alone, in 724, 734, 748, 755).

752 (*C* 856 omits) tendutz *AD*, error for *tendut* (*L*).

883 concagar *AD*, congagar *B*, congegar *L*.

967 eniuragar *AB*, emuragar *D*, enmuragar *L*.

1275 estrenher *om. DL*, against *AB* (but *D*, var. 1268, has *estreingner* for *estenher*, which explains its omission in 1275).

1332 -ire o -ir *AL*, -ir o -ire *BD* (variants to the parallel examples in 1326, 1330, 1331, 1333 are in various ways non-committal as to manuscript-groupings).

1479 (*C* 887–8) deman ja *ACL*, demaia *B*, demain *D*, demaia d^1 (coincidental misinterpretation of *demāia* in *B* and in δ, cf. below, p. 36).

Thirdly, groupings which are explicable as the result of innovation in *A*:

Table XVIII

2–3 (*C* 2–3) names of parts of speech in Provençal *A*, in Latin *CDL*.

7 (*C* 7) numbre cas *A*, numerus casus *CDL*.

10 (*C* omits) Der[i]vatius *A*, Derivativus *DL*.

38 (*C* 28) Numbres *A*, Numerus *CDL*.

1467 (*C* 872) Adverbes *A*, Adverbium *CDL*, Adverbiu [*sic*] *B*.
1497 (*C* 915) Particep *A*, Participium *DL*, Participuis [*sic*] *C*, Participiu [*sic*] *B*. These six passages all involve the transposition into Provençal of grammatical terms which seem to have been given in their Latin form in O^2.
74 (*C* omits) pencheire, fencheire *A*, penheire (peh- *L*), fenheire *DL*. (Also explicable as common substitution of the normal form by *D* and *L*.)
215 (*C* 229) Jacm[e] *A*, Iacobus *A* (Latin), Ugo *L*, N'Uqz *C*. *B*'s variant is irrelevant, since here and in 218 *B* substitutes the name *Petrus* in the examples. *D* omits the phrase, but d^1 (cf. below, p. 36) attests *Uc* here. The agreement of α (= *CL*) and δ (= d^1) points to innovation in *A* or perhaps simply to palaeographical error (i.e. misinterpretation of *Nucz* as *Jac*3).
357 (*C* 410) da quel *A*, da qestz *D*, daqest *L*, da qest *C*.
358 (*C* 410) en *CDL*, *om. A*.
451 Imperativi *A*, Imperativo *DL* (*C* 526 innovates by translating: *El imperatiu*).
456 (*C* 532) sian *A*, sien *CDL* (against 477 [= *C* 557] sien *ADL*, where *C*'s *sian* is an innovation; and against 718 [= *C* 828] sian *ACDL*). The inconsistency must already have been in O^2 and may derive from the original itself.
560 (*C* 638) del *A*, *om. CDL*.

To these may be added those passages in which *A* (no doubt through error) presents examples in an order different from that attested unanimously by the other MSS. (574, 606, 1331–2); those in which *A* presents an unusual but possibly acceptable form, against the united testimony of the other MSS. in favour of a commoner form (e.g. 792, 991, 1014, 1094, 1413, 1417); and all the numerous cases involving graphies individual to *A*. But for the second and third of these groups, the possibility remains that *A* preserved the reading of O^2 against the independent common innovation of the other MSS.

It is very likely that the relation of *B* to O^2 was not that of a direct copy. *B*'s immediate ancestor was incomplete (omission of 1515–2580) and lacked the interlinear Latin for 3326–3561; it must therefore have been a copy of O^2. It is not possible to demonstrate that *A* was or was not a direct copy of O^2. If it was, we must suppose the marginal observation at 464 and the omission of *per* which gave rise to it to have been already present in O^2; and we must suppose that certain corrections reflected only in *A* (cf. notes

CLASSIFICATION OF THE MANUSCRIPTS 35

to 1182, 1223, 1303, 2276) were already in O^2. These suppositions are not open to proof or disproof.

The only intermediate common source which it seems necessary to postulate between O^2 and the extant Provençal MSS. is α, used by L and by the author of the revised version of which C is a copy. The existence of α is indicated (1) by a certain number of variants common to CL and (2) by the utilization, in C's version, of additions preserved also in L.

TABLE XIX

(1)

5 (C 5) generalmen(t) CL, largamen AD, largo modo AB (Latin).
40 (C 30) si cum es CL, si cum AD.
262 (C 309) fei C, sei L, scribal error for *sen*.
319 (C 373) ameran C, -eren L, amaren AD.
424 (C 499) nos sem CL, no sem A, nos em D.
425 (C 500) vos est CL, etz A, vos es D.
620 (C 712–13) aers AD, esit AB (Latin), om. CL.

(2)

L, var. 84 (C 66–9). C's details on the obl. sg. and the plural of *amaire* are a fuller version of the phrase added here by L.

L, var. 149 (C 135). L adds *qe se derivon de las provincias*, C adds *.i. qui derivantur a provinciis*, a gloss on *provincial* which derives from the Latin rendering *que derivantur a provinciis*. CL are alone in incorporating this into the text.

L, var. 230 (C 274–5). The additional remark on the subjunctive is peculiar to CL: *et* (e C) *car vol totas vetz* (ves C) *un autre verbe* (verb C) *ab lui, car non pot esser* (esse L, star C) *per se sol en construction* (en construction om. C).

L, var. 241, 242 (C 287). The additional reference to verbs in *-iure*, with the examples *viure, escriure*, is peculiar to C and L.

L, var. 272 (C 320). The gloss on *perfeit* (.i. conpliz L, zo es complit C) is peculiar to C and L.

L, var. 672 (C 781), the phrase *qe muda* (C; qe mude L) is peculiar to CL; since D omits 672 entirely, however, individual error in A is not excluded as an explanation.

L, var. 690 (C 789–99). See above, p. 29. C presents a much expanded version of a text like that of L, itself derived, via α, from a marginal amplification in O^2.

It remains to examine the relationship of D with the two Italian translations of the *Donatz*. That d^1 and d^2 are closely related to the Provençal tradition represented by D is sufficiently demonstrated by their breaking off at 1522 and by the fact that both Italian versions share with D omissions which are explicitly noted as such, either by a marginal observation (d^1) or by an asterisk (d^2):

Table XX

275–8 manca → d^1, * d^2.
280–5 * d^2; d^1 silently omits 279, as well as 280–5.
309–11 manca → e la terza d^1, * d^2.
315–16 manca la 2ª et la 3ª d^1, * d^2.
330 manca la 3ª → d^1, * d^2.

To these may be added the characteristic error:

140–1 mees maepes Dd^1d^2.

The longer Italian version (d^1) derives, not from D, but from D's source (δ); the shorter Italian version (d^2) derives from D itself.

Table XXI

215–16 *om. D*, eu uc sui uenguz et se io dico eu uei qe (< que) tu es uenguz non mi bisogna dire d^1. (For the name *Uc*, cf. 215, *var. L*, and *C* 229; the reading of d^2 is discussed below, see Table XXIV.)

221–2 significa alcuna causa *D*, significat (fare o patire) alcuna cosa come seu bat io fo alcuna cosa d^1, significa fare ò sofferire alcuna cosa d^2. It is to be noted that d^1 uses brackets elsewhere to indicate suppletion of omissions, e.g. 22 Granz (es), 671 si trahe (ancora). The bracketing of *fare o patire* indicates that δ already lacked *far o soffrir*, an omission compounded in *D* by a haplography. The reading of d^2 shows intelligent conjecture, as is indicated by its omission of any equivalent of *D*'s *seu sui batutz eu soffre alcuna causa*.

375–80 cum eu entendessez cil entendesse uel esso *D*, cum eu entendes (< -dres) tu entendes cel entendes nos entendessem uos entendessez cil entendessen o entendesson d^1, cum en entendes * d^2. The omission, not present in δ, originated in *D*.

561 eu Dd^2, cel d^1.

566 uz Dd^2, iz d^1. In both cases d^2 reproduces *D*'s error.

1479 demain Dd^2, demaia d^1. The error *demaia* (for *demā ia*), shared with *B*, must have been δ's reading, for which *D* attempted a correction.

Thus d^2 shares errors and innovations of *D* which are not present in d^1. Conversely, d^2 avoids errors and peculiarities of translation introduced by d^1:

CLASSIFICATION OF THE MANUSCRIPTS

TABLE XXII

13, etc. omnis Dd^2, totale d^1.
53, 105 el (= et lo) D, et il d^2, nel d^1.
254, 265, 272, 400, 416, 479, 494, 541 el (= en lo) D, nel d^2, il d^1.
116 uocatiu D, uocatiuo d^2, nominatiuo plurale d^1.
30, 38 plurals D, plurale d^2, del piu d^1.
132 declinasons D, declinationi d^2, declarationi d^1.
149 prouincial D, di prouincie d^2, prouenzali d^1.
203 egalmen D, egualmente d^2, singularmente d^1.
232 dels .v. modi D, de i cinque modi d^2, de detti modi d^1.
381 item in preterito imperfecto D, item nel preterito non perfetto d^2, om. d^1.
539 sies pausatz D, il si ui è posto d^2, sia posta d^1.
670 uezer Dd^2, uender d^1.
1508 Coniuncios D, Congiontione d^2, Congiugatione d^1.
1515 expletiuas D, espletiue d^2, riempitiue d^1.

By the same token, d^2 does not have certain innovations of d^1:

TABLE XXIII

370 canteses D, cantesses d^2, cantes d^1.
383 amesses Dd^2, ames d^1 (ames A).
425 es Dd^2, est d^1 (est L, and C 500).
437 fos Dd^2, fost d^1 (fost L).
461 eram Dd^2, serum d^1 (seram L).
466 aguesses Dd^2, agues d^1.
718 sian Dd^2, sien d^1 (to avoid inconsistency with *sien*, D 456, 477).

(The agreement of d^1 with other MSS. of the *Donatz* in some of these passages is to be attributed to coincidental innovation, not to contamination.)

Clearly, then, d^2 cannot derive from d^1. That it in fact derived directly from D itself is shown by the observation added at 1502, after the section on participles: 'Qui parla defettiuo, perche ui sono altre desinentie di particpi come appare a carte 8.' The reference here is to the passage on the pluperfect indicative (656–84), which contains a more detailed treatment of past participles, and which in D falls precisely on ff. 8ʳ and 8ᵛ.

It is possible, however, that d^2 did in fact make some sporadic use of d^1:

Table XXIV

20 no scib [*for* sec lo] uulgaris els neutris substantius D, non sarano uulgari ne neutri sustantiui d^1, non seranno uulgari nel neutrale sostantiuo d^2. It is difficult to believe that d^2 could derive from D without consultation of d^1.

215–16 (for D and d^1, cf. above, Table XXI) eu Joans sui uenguz et se dico tu es uenguz non mi fa bisogno dire d^2. Intelligent conjecture is a possible explanation, but consultation of d^1 is not ruled out.

It is worth noting that there are many instances where an error of D is not shared by d^1 and d^2. In such cases d^2 can as well have derived the correct reading from intelligent correction as from consultation of d^1 (indeed, d^2 may also sometimes have eliminated an error of δ by the same method, as was clearly the case in 22 below).

Table XXV

2 pronomen d^1d^2, *om. D*.
22 Granz D, Granz (es) d^1, Granz es d^2.
64 no *om. D*, non d^1d^2.
84 doz D, der [*sic*] d^1, dor d^2.
90 meillez D, meiller d^1, meiler d^2.
135 emieios D, enueios d^1d^2.
176 guezs D, guers d^1d^2.
226 fai *om. D*, fa d^1, fà d^2.
Etc., etc.

That the translator of d^2 showed considerable critical spirit in his work is indicated clearly by such passages as:

317–19 amaram o amariam amaraz o amariaz amaren ò amerien. (Adunque si può dire ama et ame se ben egli nol dice).
342 (Non pone le 3ᵉ sing. quando sono simili alla prima).
773 siaz D, s'ha d^1, uà d^2 (i.e. d^2 restores the original sense by conjecture).
1522 Non ragiona ne di prepositione, ne di interiettione, et forse il testo è deffettiuo.

The intelligence of the translator of d^2 makes it impossible to demonstrate conclusively that he consulted d^1. His knowledge of Provençal seems also to have been superior to that of the translator of d^1, cf. the second and third entries in Table XXII above. This

CLASSIFICATION OF THE MANUSCRIPTS 39

did not prevent him, however, from sharing an error of translation—coincidentally, no doubt—with d^1:

711 se conte D, si conta d^1d^2.

It follows from this that d^2 has no independent claim to textual authority, whereas d^1 can claim some small interest in that it may sporadically be a better representative of δ than is D. In order to simplify the variants to the critical text, the relevant readings of d^1, in so far as they concern the readings for Provençal examples, are noted here:

TABLE XXVI

90 meiller   130 santatz   135 enueios   176 guers   215–16 eu uc sui uenguz et se io dico eu uei qe (< que) tu es uenguz non mi bisogna dire   216 Peire   231 amar   263 eu dizi o eu dic   268 amaua   271 amauen o amauon   317 amaram o amariam   324 diseraz   328 o in iria   329 dormiras dormirias   333 dormiren o dormirien   335 uoler tener saber hauer conoiser   343 tenria   351 begra   374 cantassen o cantasson   375–80 cum eu entendes (< -dres) tu entendes cel entendes nos entendessem uos entendessez cil entendessen o entendesson   399 donaua   423 cel es amat   442 estat   444 auion   448 serem (< erem)   454 siam   467 amaz   470 aguessen   498 aurem   499 amat   506 tu escriu [sic] o escriues   521 tegra D] tein   539 seria   545 as in a in am   551 escriuo   555 escrissi   566 iz   588 esteis   589 ateis   592 mantenc   595 et   596–601 tendet; battet; fendet (f < u); uendet; conseguet; perdet fotet   617 ers   624 conoc desconoc reconoc   642 affrais   655 a D] ja (< la); as D] jas (< las)   669 ionger   674 eint; ateingner   675 estreingner   679 dit   681 iont   689 saber   693 amem nos   698 rion o rio   701 aguessem aguessez aguessen o aguesson   708 conogut   722 essen o esson   745 aiatz   749–50 tu aias tendut cel aia tendut   752 tendut   759 sentit   765 tu auras tengut   768 tengut   832 bairreiar < barreiar   845 baisar   885 dansar   895 deliurar   909 desflibar   913 dictar   936 enuiar   987 gazaingnar   994 glazar   999 iular o iẑlar [sic]   1019 matar   1020 mandar [sic]   1031 membrar   1034 mesclar   1046 naffrar   1091 et i composti   1092 pregar   1104 et i compt^i 1105 plorar   1118 rasonar   1158 seminar   1209 tricar   1227 vedar   1230 vernissar   1246 asezer   1267 sostraire   1319–20 raire ponre   1385 enriquir   1391 enontir [sic]   1407 fugir   1431 offrir   1474 temerosamen   1479 demaia [sic]   1482 tostemps   1483 ser   1501–2 o ens et in utz o itz o atz   1509 deuem   1516 zo es a saber   1518 ni

In effect, the conception of the manuscript relationships advanced here amounts to an explanation of common errors and common variants without recourse (except for *CL* and for the Italian translations) to the hypothesis of an intermediate common source. This can be acceptable only if this latter hypothesis is seen to be impossible; and this impossibility can be demonstrated only by the multiplicity of 'common sources' for which there is some sort of evidence. The following table gathers together this evidence for various groups of four, three, and two MSS. from all the earlier tables of variants except XIX–XXVI. (Roman figures refer to the earlier tables.)

Table XXVII

(1) *ABDL* 922 (III, cf. X); 115–17 (IX).
(2) *ABDL/AC* 133 (XVII).
(3) *ABDL/C* all innovations in *C* (cf. pp. 13–14).
(4) *ACDL* 663 (III, cf. X).
(5) *BCDL/A* 1467, 1497 (XVIII).
(6) *ABC/DL* 616, 658 (XVI); 86 (XVII).
(7) *ABL/CD* 518–26 (XIV); 366 (XVI, cf. VIII).
(8) *ABL/D* 1311 (III, cf. X).
(9) *ACD/L* 167, 773 (IX).
(10) *ACL/BD* 225 (XVI); 1479 (XVII).
(11) *ACL/D* 690 (p. 29).
(12) *BCD/AL* 494 (XVII).
(13) *BCL/AD* 364–5 (XVII).
(14) *BDL/A* 1180 (XVI).
(15) *CDL/A* 657 (*XIV*); 542–3 [cf. 385–7], 652, 727–8 (XVI); 2–3, 7, 38, 358, 456, 560 (XVIII).
(16) *CDL/AB* 659–60 (XIV).
(17) *AB* 648 (p. 19); 21–21a, 367, 516–17 (V, cf. p. 20); 773 (VII, cf. VIII); all examples in XI and XII; 220, 3009 (XIII).
  AB/CDL, cf. *CDL/AB* (16).
(18) *AB/DL* 612–13 (XIV); 783, 908, 1022, 1256, 1389, 1508, 1509 (XV); 886 (XVI); 967, 1275 (XVII).
(19) *AB/D/L* 1075 (XV).
(20) *AC/BL* 1496 (XV).
  AC/ABDL, cf. *ABDL/AC* (2).
(21) *AC/DL* 84, 86, 220, 388, 532–3, 552 (XVI); 421 (XVII).
  AD/BCL, cf. *BCL/AD* (13).
(22) *AD/BL* 837, 889, 909, 944, 993, 1027, 1234, 1401 (XV); 883 (XVII).

(23) *AD*/*B*/*L* 1182 (XV).
(24) *AD*/*BL*/*C* 1481 (XVI).
(25) *AD*/*CL* 440–1 (XVII).
(26) *AD*/*L* 237, 752 (XVII).
  AL/*BCD*, cf. *BCD*/*AL* (12).
(27) *AL*/*B*/*C*/*D* 1480–2, 1487–96 (XIV); 222 (XVII).
(28) *AL*/*BD* 160 (VII); 847, 974, 1153, 1232, 1323–4, 1343, 1400 (XV); 1332 (XVII).
(29) *AL*/*CD* 293 (XVI); 132 (XVII).
(30) *AL*/*D* 465, 717 (XVII).
  BD/*ACL*, cf. *ACL*/*BD* (10).
  BD/*AL*, cf. *AL*/*BD* (28).
(31) *BL*/*A* 518–26 (XIV); 589 (XVII).
  BL/*AC*, cf. *AC*/*BL* (20).
  BL/*AD*, cf. *AD*/*BL* (22).
  BL/*AD*/*C*, cf. *AD*/*BL*/*C* (24).
  CD/*ABL*, cf. *ABL*/*CD* (7).
  CD/*AL*, cf. *AL*/*CD* (29).
(32) *CD*/*A*/*L* 189–92 (XIV).
  CL/*AD*, cf. *AD*/*CL* (25).
(33) *DL*/*A* 348, 354 (XVII); 10, 74 (XVIII).
  DL/*AB*, cf. *AB*/*DL* (18).
(34) *DL*/*A*/*B* 1065–9 (XIV); 798, 1052 (XV).
  DL/*ABC*, cf. *ABC*/*DL* (6).
(35) *DL*/*A*/*B*/*C* heading (XIV).
  DL/*AC*, cf. *AC*/*DL* (21).
(36) *DL*/*A*/*C* 576–80 (XIV); 615 (XVI); 451 (XVIII).

In fact, all possible groups of three MSS. occur here, with the exception of *ABD*, for which Table XIX would provide some evidence; and all possible groups of two MSS. occur except *BC*, a grouping whose absence is readily explained by the small portion of the text which these two MSS. have in common. Some manuscript-groupings could be supported with stronger evidence than others. But to accept this evidence as proof of a common intermediate source for any group (except *CL*) is to render inexplicable other apparently equally strongly supported groupings. Convergence in error, in innovation, in misinterpretation, and in correction of an already erroneous archetype is the only satisfactory explanation of the apparently random groupings of the *Donatz* MSS.

IV. CHARACTERISTICS OF THE INDIVIDUAL MANUSCRIPTS

A has fewer scribal errors than any of the other MSS.; such errors are markedly more frequent in the Latin than in the Provençal. Omissions by haplography are infrequent (116–17, 222, 737–9). The incorporation of additions into the text is rare (695, cf. above, p. 29; 1854, 2112, 2122, 2974, at least three of which are erroneous repetitions; cf. also pp. 27–8)—the retention of the marginal note at 464 as a marginal note is typical of the scribe's scrupulousness in this respect. He frequently repaired omissions, mainly omissions of examples, by marginal additions (314, 625, 633, 848, 853, 974, 1068, 1081, 1085, 1261–5, 1311, 1351, 1547, 1601, 1638, 1641–3, 2261, 2459, 2511, 2614, 2992–6, 3003, 3077, 3159, 3161—the addition at 1182 is erroneous), sometimes by erasure (2296–7, 3001–3); erasures are found elsewhere, both in the Provençal (691–2, 1237, 1624, 2902–3, 3364) and in the Latin (236–7, 669, 969, 1197, 3008, 3065); words have occasionally been struck through (Provençal: 969, 2955; Latin: 827, 1364, 2793, 2955). Occasionally the expected deletion was not made, though the scribe's awareness of error is shown, either by the presence of the correct reading (1, 54, 658, all in the Latin) or by the relation of the interlinear text to the Provençal (116–17, 494?, 581–2, 825–7, 1550–1); but some omissions passed unnoticed when the interlinear Latin was added (222, 645, 737–9).

Certain types of recurrent scribal error are worth mentioning here. The interlinear disposition of the Latin text resulted in a number of displacements in the renderings of examples (119–20, 146–8, 157–8, 192–3, 584–5, 620, 643, 645–6, 717, 756–7, 825–7, 983, 1102–3, 1135, 1183–5, 1522, 1527–8, 1992–3, 2112–13, 2380–1, 2712–13, 2941–2, 3160–1, 3255–6, 3435–7, 3454–5, 3535–6), sometimes causing one translation to be repeated (581–2, 1320, 1550–1, 1789, 3533), sometimes omitted or partly omitted (303–4, 697, 2653, 3398–9, 3560–1). There are two clear cases where a long Latin translation of an example, written in a double line in *A*'s exemplar, was copied in the reverse order (1970, 3191). The Latin sometimes shows errors derived from the Provençal below it, no

CHARACTERISTICS OF THE INDIVIDUAL MSS. 43

doubt because, in copying the Latin, the scribe repeated to himself the Provençal word (40, 67 [*del*], 84, 155?, 240, 275, 778, 993, 1489, 3317, 3388; 880, 2071, and 2215—cf. above, pp. 22 and 21—are possibly open to the same explanation). The scribe of *A* seems sometimes to have misinterpreted a correction made in his exemplar, perhaps as a result of his ignoring or failing to see an expunctuation. This type of error is rare in the Provençal (1223), but there are a number of examples in the Latin (1060, 1182, 1303, 2276, 3171; two of these—1060 and 3171—are shared with *B*). For some other recurrent errors, see the notes to 930, 2793, 3450.

The scribe's use of abbreviations is generally in accord with the practice of the thirteenth century. His use of the titulus, the Tironian abbreviations, and superscript letters calls for no comment. His use of the apostrophe is occasionally curious. The rare cases of final *d'* = *-dum* (1531, 2403, 3202) are noted in the variants. While *pl'* = *plur-* occurs *passim*, *pl'ral* is used in 53 and 124; *l'r* = *-liter* is found throughout the text, but *pl'r* = *pluraliter* occurs at 323 and 340. Some other uses of *l'* are noted in the variants (38 and 335, Provençal; 75, 1668, 1693, 2506-7, 2556, Latin). Besides the use of *b'* = *ber* or *bre*, one finds it used for *be* (*Cerberus* 201; *saber* 335, 689; *verbe* 1469), *-bis* (*verbis* 1172; *tubis* 1218) and *-bum* (*verbum* 3443). Similarly, besides *h'* = *her*, one finds *onh'r* (669), *estenh'r* (675) and *h'rticus* (2614); in isolation *h'* is used for both *hoc* and *hec*, and also for *he* = *hae* (1470). A certain number of isolated or curious uses of abbreviations are noted in the variants. It is worth remarking that, for obvious practical reasons, abbreviations are much more frequent in the interlinear Latin text than in the Provençal; some abbreviations by suspension (e.g. .$\overset{.}{p}$. or .$\overset{a}{p}$. = *persona*) occur only in the Latin.

It is not possible to say precisely what motives guided the choice of the parts of the Provençal and Latin texts represented in *B*. Two deficiencies of this MS. are explicable as deriving from a defective exemplar, in which the interlinear Latin equivalents for the end of the rhyme-lists (3326-3561) had not been inserted (cf. above, pp. 5-6) and in which a loss of leaves had removed the central part of the grammar (1515-2580). (This loss of leaves probably corresponded to one gathering or to the middle leaves of one gathering.) But the third deficiency of *B*, the absence of the Provençal text for 1-774, is not explicable in this fashion and must have been the result of a deliberate decision. One can only suppose that the copy was made for a reader who already possessed the Provençal text of this part of the grammar, for the Latin would have been useless, indeed incomprehensible, without the Provençal on which it depends.

Throughout *B*'s text an intermittent desire to improve the quality of the Latin is perceptible. This is reflected in the rather more standard orthography, in changes of word-order and syntax (4–5, 21, 62, 221, 225, 235, 265, 398, 602, 714, 854, 1225, 1483, 1485, 1487, 1491, 1495, 2673, 3056, 3272), and in changes of vocabulary (153, 239, 299, 956, 985, 992, 1199, 1375, 1509, 2592, 2969, 3027, 3053, 3103, 3190, 3274, 3286), some of which show a desire to substitute shorter and less circumstantial definitions of single words in the lists of verbs and of rhymes (823, 834, 835, 852, 2602, 3000, 3074; cf. also the abbreviated translations at 801, 825, 827, 845, 850, 999, 1021, 1024, 1087, 1143, 1241, 1247, 1270, 1301, 1311, 1329, 1428, 2603, 2695, 2697, 2751–2, 2802, 2833, 2861, 2866, 2869, 2870, 2926, 3093, 3192, 3196, 3275, 3317). The omission in *B* of many of the longer definitions given by *A* is no doubt explicable palaeographically: the interlinear reading in such cases was necessarily cramped and legible with difficulty (145, 158, 187, 824, 1101, 1183, 2589, 2600, 2613, 2626, 2656, 2713, 2956).

That MS. *C* was copied by a scribe with very little knowledge of Provençal is immediately evident from the nature of the numerous scribal slips corrected in the edition of this text (Appendix I). The scribe was so inattentive as not to notice the misplaced leaves in his exemplar, which caused him to place lines 550–879 of his text before lines 267–549. Omissions and haplographies are particularly frequent.

When these deficiencies have been, so far as is possible, put right, we are left with a rehandled text of the *Donatz* in which certain recurrent features reveal the technique of the author responsible for this revised version. He added a number of passages to make good deficiencies in the original (*C* 42–8, 65–9, 76–87, 102–6, 235–62, 361–3, 382–9, 454–62, 475, 644–8, 800–7, 869–70, 875–6); he expanded (*C* 413–30 [cf. *A* 360–7], 484–9 [cf. *A* 416], 789–99 [cf. *A* 688–94], 816–28 [cf. *A* 713–18]), compressed (*C* 55 [cf. *A* 55–63], 93–106 [cf. *A* 105–31]) and rewrote (*C* 758–88 [cf. *A* 656–84], 810–15 [cf. *A* 699–712]); he removed

CHARACTERISTICS OF THE INDIVIDUAL MSS.

inconsequences and repetitions by omitting (*C* 788 omits the equivalent of *A* 685-7, cf. *C* 616-20), by transposing (*C* 233-4 [cf. *A* 99-104], 455-62 [cf. *A* 381-7]), or by adding a back-reference (*C* 808-9 [cf. *A* 695-8], 855-6 [cf. *A* 740-66]); he expanded verbal paradigms to give all six persons in full, with their Latin equivalents (*C* 292-304, 313-19, etc.; exceptionally, without Latin, 764-9, 818-54, 862-5), though, rather strangely, he often expanded the Latin without the Provençal in the latter part of the text (*C* 432-44, 447-53, 456-62, 467-73, 477-83, 579-85, 627-9, 655-7); he added examples of compound forms (*C* 110-11, 134-5, 691, 693, 695) and occasionally other examples (*C* 14, 15, 49, 90-2, 100, 862-5), but in many of the longer lists of examples he made apparently haphazard omissions (*C* 60-2 [cf. *A* 72-80], 102 [cf. *A* 129-30], 139-40 [cf. *A* 152-61], etc.), and other short passages are dropped without apparent reason (*C* 16 [cf. *A* 20-3], 22 [cf. *A* 30-2], 901 [cf. *A* 1487-8]). But the process of rehandling is intermittent: the work has not been systematically rewritten, and some passages are left virtually unaltered, with awkward joins between old and new (e.g. *C* 431 [cf. *A* 367-8] and the casual use of *Et devetz saber* at *C* 77, 88, 93, 233, etc.). What is more, the author of the rehandled text was guilty of a number of errors: the omission of the imperfect indicative passive (*C* 501, cf. *A* 427-32) and the transposing of the forms of this tense as alternatives for the pluperfect, apparently under the influence of the Latin (*C* 510-17, cf. the Latin at *A* 439-44); the alteration of the pluperfect optative passive forms (*C* 542-9, cf. *A* 464-70); the incorrect imperfect paradigm *eu fingia*, also suggested by the Latin (*C* 606-12, cf. the Latin at *A* 536-7); the unattested and no doubt non-existent compound forms *entenher* and *acenher* (*C* 784-5). To these may be added verb-forms which are wrong (385, 593) or at least dubious (327, 384), including imperfect subjunctive forms of the type *aves* for *agues* (422-3, 425-6, 428-30, 543, 813-14), *prendes* (831, 833, 837, 839, 841), and *tenes* (835). Such forms cast doubt on the reviser's linguistic competence; certainly it is an error to cite his testimony as an authority for the forms *prendes* and *tenes*, as has been done by R. de Dardel, *Le Parfait fort en roman commun*, Geneva, 1958, pp. 77 and 137.

In short, neither the expansions nor the condensations show any great intelligence or any profound understanding of the original text. In all probability the author of the revised version was Italian rather than Provençal. There is no conclusive evidence for the date of this version. It is likely that it belongs to the thirteenth or fourteenth century rather than to the fifteenth or sixteenth: it is hard to envisage in what circumstances and for what purpose such a revision could have been made later than about 1350. Its relation to the *Donatz* is analogous to that of the *Doctrina d'acort* to the *Razos de trobar* and it may well date, like the *Doctrina*, from the latter part of the thirteenth century.

D also contains numerous scribal errors indicating no great understanding of Provençal on the part of the scribe. Haplographies are frequent (26–7, 113, 152–3, 215–16, 221–2, 315–16, 352–3, 375–9, 402–3, 423, 491, 538, 687, 701, 706–7, 749–50, 765, 1294, 1306–9, 1501–2), as are omissions in the lists of examples and of verbs (16–17, 73, 91, 93, 186, 209–10, 268, 275, 278, 280–5, 322, 339, 561, 576, 580, 599–601, 633, 641, 678, 686, 821–2, 839, 848, 857, 860, 961, 969, 1020, 1069–71, 1113–15, 1138, 1210, 1218, 1361, 1364, 1495–6). Graphies are often characteristically Italian. The most obvious traits of the version of the *Donatz* preserved in *D* are the absence of any of the interlinear or marginal matter (cf. above, pp. 27–9; 360–87 is a particularly revealing passage from this point of view), the almost total absence of any additions to the text (exceptions are 81 and 328–31 [adapted from the Latin, cf. pp. 16–17] and the addition of a single example at 582, 609, 637, 817, 921, 1353) and the absence of reformulations of the text (38–9 constitutes a minor exception). One has the impression that *D* derives from a copy whose scribe had systematically neglected everything except the main Provençal text.

It is impossible to guess the date at which the list of rhymes given in this MS. was composed, or the date at which it was substituted for the original rhyming dictionary of the *Donatz*. It is not possible to demonstrate that its compiler made use of the latter; it seems likely, from the number of entries which are longer than single words and from the listing of two separate series in *-iou* and *-ieu*, partly containing the same words, that the compiler derived at least part of his information from one or more Provençal *chansonniers*.

From the point of view of individual scribal errors, *L* is more corrupt than *A* and *B* but less so than the two sixteenth-century

CHARACTERISTICS OF THE INDIVIDUAL MSS. 47

MSS. Its version of the *Donatz* incorporates fragments of the Latin text, but without aiming at any complete reproduction of the latter either for the exposition or for the examples; and it adds to the text a number of expansions in Provençal to make good supposed deficiencies in the original, but without rehandling the latter on the scale of *C*'s version. The Latin elements in *L* consist generally of those phrases which qualified or expanded the Provençal text (21, 52, 259, 261, 304, 364, 416, 419, 537, 567, 703, 710); in some instances the Latin in *L* is merely the equivalent of the Provençal, which it ordinarily precedes (304 [in part], 305, 311, 416 [in part], 464, 542, 590, 606, 667, 701, 702 [treated as rubric], 720, 1497); a few Latin rubrics are added (117, 121, 125, 220, 502, 776, 1244, 1351, 1508); a number of the Provençal examples are followed by their Latin translation, sometimes preceded by *.i.*, though there is no obvious motive behind the selection of words so treated (74, 91, 94, 100, 102, 561, 570, 575–6, 586–9, 606, 626, 628–9, 631, 633, 635, 639, 641–2, 644–5, 681, 710, 1068, 1518, 1522); in a few cases Provençal examples are accompanied by an Italian translation (642, 785?, 802, 806?, 819?, 858, 1357). The additional Provençal phrases in *L* include examples—often inept—added to those of the original text (15, 59, 70, 94, 101–2, 154, 167, 170, 184–5, 188, 212, 242, 252–3, 327, 365–6, 564 [derived from the Latin translation], 1025, 1112, 1122, 1149, 1157, 1277, 1311, 1422, 1466, 1522, 1758, 1768, 1832, 1840, 1902, 2137), explanatory phrases or illustrations added in the interests of greater clarity or explicitness (41, 50, 52, 77, 81, 83–4, 98, 107, 110, 114, 121–2, 125, 136, 148, 149 [derived from the Latin], 181, 184–5, 188, 226 [rubric], 228–30 [rubrics], 235, 236–7 [derived from the Latin], 241–3, 252, 254, 265, 272, 299, 338–42, 364, 657, 672, 690, 723, 1351, 2162), headings supplied for verbal paradigms (426, 432, 438, 444), personal pronouns added to examples of verbs (246–51, 266–71, 273–8, etc.), and some material concerned with Latin grammar and having no possible relevance to the vernacular (123, 126, 1522 [= Appendix III]). As already noted (cf. p. 35), some additional phrases in *L* are shared with *C* and have been ascribed here to an intermediate source α. In general the Provençal additions give the impression of haphazard and casual notes to the text and are not all equally apposite or intelligent: in all probability they represent two or more 'layers' of annotation by different readers of the *Donatz*.

V. THE ESTABLISHMENT OF THE TEXT

It is clear from our examination of the relationship of the MSS. that there is no automatic process by which the text of the *Donatz* may be established. The basis of the critical text presented here is MS. *A*. The overriding argument in favour of *A* is its completeness. This allows the editor to avoid those subjective decisions in the matter of graphies which would be the necessary consequence of a decision to present an eclectic text. The somewhat idiosyncratic usage of *A*'s scribe does not offset this advantage: the editor is at least presenting a text which has a concrete linguistic reality, rather than a confection made according to norms which could hardly be other than arbitrary. An analogous argument has supported the retention of the order of examples in *A*, even where this represented an individual variant opposed to the rest of the manuscript tradition.

A's text is corrected where there is an obvious scribal *lapsus* or an obvious misreading of the exemplar, and where the balance of probability favours the view that *A* presents an incorrect or inadmissible form. This latter class of correction, which depends on the consideration of a wide variety of different types of evidence in each case, is normally discussed in the notes. The present editor's view is that, ideally, a critical edition of a grammar ought not to print—and hence give currency to—elements which there is good reason to believe erroneous. The present edition falls short of this ideal in the sense that inadmissible readings have been allowed to stand where emendation gave no satisfactory solution or where two or more possible emendations of equal weight presented themselves. The majority of the corrections introduced into the present text were already made—usually without comment—in the first or second edition of Guessard. The contribution of other scholars to this collective endeavour is as follows:

Galvani (1871): 891, 930, 1103, 1173, 1550, 1563, 1657, 1659, 1675, 2083, 2112L, 2113, 2226, 2249, 2261, 2267, 2345, 2402, 2552, 3407, 3533 (omission of *sarcina*), 3555;

THE ESTABLISHMENT OF THE TEXT 49

Paris (*Rom.* i, 1872): 1697, 2262P, 2575 (from Diez, *EtWb*), 2653, 2996, 3503;

Tobler (*Rom.* ii, 1873): 856, 1303, 1308, 1412, 1619, 1650, 1718, 1823, 1830, 1991, 2211, 2234, 2243, 2260, 2367, 2380–1, 2414, 2712–13, 2809, 2943, 2971, 3009, 3280, 3353, 3450, 3454, 3509;

Chabaneau (*Rom.* vi, 1877): 1872, 1905, 2112 (omission of *bens*);

Bauquier (*Rom.* vi, 1877): 2071;

Bauquier and, independently, Stengel (1878—cf. Stengel, p. xxvii, n.): 189–90 (in part), 1819, 2137, 2197, 2270, 2648;

Stengel (1878)—many of these corrections are made silently in the index to the edition: 229, 237, 440–1, 465, 626, 673, 695, 792, 812, 850, 1041, 1175, 1181, 1320, 1331L, 1661, 1722, 2190, 2418, 2462, 2636, 2733, 2743, 2873, 2875–81, 3058, 3103, 3171, 3188, 3203, 3388, 3431;

Chabaneau (*RLR* xiii, 1878): 830, 1733 (from Boucherie), 2776, 2811, 3189;

Bartsch (*ZRP* ii, 1878): 127;

Biadene (1885), p. 353, n. 1, following Gröber in *ZRP* viii, pp. 290–3: 3571 (*Coraçhuchii*).

The extent to which I have leaned on the work of these eminent predecessors is abundantly clear. I have added my small contribution to theirs in originating (so far as I am aware) the following emendations: 180, 182, 188, 294, 357, 463 (*r[i]on*), 577, 584, 717, 773, 789, 815, 833, 865, 946, 955 (*pomi*), 993, 999, 1060, 1069, 1102, 1122, 1205, 1213, 1223, 1241, 1299 (*conum*), 1526, 1638, 1668, 1734, 1904, 1919, 1970, 1990, 1993, 2067, 2122, 2166, 2189, 2230, 2276, 2435, 2437, 2458–9, 2518, 2622, 2656, 2678, 2720, 2775, 2793 (*furcando struas*), 2886, 2913, 2923, 2942, 3160, 3219, 3368, 3399, 3424, 3435, 3455, 3484, 3521, 3532, 3536, 3556, 3569–70.

The treatment of the Latin text presents certain special problems. As we have seen, it was added to a Provençal text which was itself already somewhat corrupt and already contained some interlinear glosses; and the translator himself was guilty of omissions and of errors of translation. There can be no question, therefore, of making the Latin translation correspond exactly with the Provençal text: this would amount to confecting a Latin text which certainly never existed. Where there is good reason for thinking that the translator, for whatever reason, did not supply a Latin rendering of a Provençal word or group of words, the lacuna is indicated by: [. . .]. Where there is good reason for thinking that the translator mistranslated the Provençal, his rendering is followed by †. Where an error of Latin grammar or syntax may reasonably be supposed to go back to the translator, it is allowed to remain in the text. These last three aspects of the treatment of the Latin text involve editorial judgements which are necessarily in some measure subjective. In particular, the distinction between a common scribal error of AB (derived from O^2) and an error made by the translator can be drawn only by balancing probabilities. As a general rule, where a case can be made out for leaving A's Latin text unchanged, this has been done.

The material presentation of the two texts, Latin and Provençal, has necessarily had to differ from that found in MS. A itself: to print the Latin as an interlinear gloss would put an intolerable strain on the patience of printers and readers alike. In all cases where the layout of the interlinear matter above the Provençal in MS. A is such that it could not be accurately guessed from a comparison of the two printed texts, the placing of the interlinear words is indicated, as precisely as possible, in the variants to A's Latin text. In cases where interlinear matter has been incorporated into the edited *Provençal* text, this is indicated in the variants to both Latin and Provençal.

The rejected readings of A give the reading of the MS. in all cases where a correction has been introduced into the text, including those in which the correction is indicated in the text with square brackets: it seemed important, even in many relatively trivial cases, to indicate exactly the reading of the base-manuscript. Incorrect word-divisions in A have also been indicated in the rejected readings; where these arose from a desire to space a single Latin word above two Provençal words, this disposition of the interlinear text has been noted.

The Provençal text has been regularized only in the following respects: punctuation and capitalization follow modern practice; the layout of the text is parallel with that found in modern grammars; the distinctions of u and v, i and j are introduced (i is not printed as j in intervocalic position, nor in cases like *camiar*, where the interpretations *camjar* and *camïar* are equally possible); proclitic and enclitic forms follow the scribe's practice (an ambivalent case of the type *alautre* is printed as *a l'autre*). In the presentation of the Latin text, the same principles are followed, except that distinction of i and j is made only for the single case of *conjeries*

(2258); elsewhere *i* is printed. The expansion of abbreviations seldom gives rise to difficulties. The titulus is transcribed as *m*, not *n*, before *p*, *b*, *m*; similarly, 9 = *com-* before the same consonants, and *m̄* = *-mem-* before *b* (1031, 1133); the scribe's usage shows a slight leaning towards *m* rather than *n* when such words are written in full. *q̄*, *q̊*, etc., are rendered *que*, *qua*, etc., in accordance with the scribe's usual practice when writing without abbreviation. *sȝ* is transcribed as *sed* (despite *set* at 1474, 3116), *qȝ* as *quia* (*qȝ* = *que* is noted in the variants, cf. 69, 231a, 569, 572), *grā* as *gracia* (so spelt in full at 45), *m̊* as *michi* (so in full at 23, 96, 240). 7 is rendered *et* in the Provençal (as in the Latin), both before vowels and before consonants; when writing without abbreviation, the scribe fluctuates irregularly between *et* and *e*.

The variants of the other MSS. are selective. They are full for all words or endings cited as examples (i.e. for everything printed in italics, together with the contents of the verb-lists and the dictionary of rhymes) and for all words where *A*'s reading is rejected or modified. Outside these cases, certain orthographical variants are neglected: *q* ∼ *qu* ∼ *c*; *ç* ∼ *çh* ∼ *ch* ∼ *z* ∼ *s* ∼ *ss* (*çh* and *ch* for the reflex of -KJ- -TJ- -D- are peculiar to *A*, except for: 2 prouençhal *D*); *ch* ∼ *c* (< Kᵃ); *aici* ∼ *aisi*; final *tz* ∼ *z* ∼ *ç*; *s* ∼ *sc*; single ∼ double consonants (*s*, *l*, *f*); presence ∼ absence of notation of *n caduc* (final or before final *s*); *l* ∼ *u* before consonant; *lh* ∼ *ill* ∼ *ll* (but the variant *l* ∼ *lh* is noted); *nh* ∼ *gn* ∼ *ign*; presence ∼ absence of *h-* (*om* ∼ *hom*, *a* ∼ *ha*); *con* ∼ *com* ∼ *cum*; *son* ∼ *sun*; *don* ∼ *dun*; *n* ∼ *m* before labial (including *emplural* ∼ *enplural*); *e* ∼ *i* before *n* (*en* ∼ *in*, *endicatiu* ∼ *indicatiu*, *femeni* ∼ *femini*, etc.); *genetiu* ∼ *genitiu*; *adjectiu* ∼ *ajectiu*; *optatiu* ∼ *obtatiu*; *secunda* ∼ *seconda* ∼ *segonda*; *larg* ∼ *larc*; *e* ∼ *et* ∼ 7; numerals in figures ∼ in words; false word-divisions (*aqest* ∼ *a qest*, very common in *D*); *D*'s consistent *subiun(c)tiu* for *conjunctiu* is noted only on its first occurrence (225); *D*'s use of the grave accent is not specially noted (*ò* ∼ *o*; *à quel* ∼ *àquel* ∼ *aquel*; *però* ∼ *pero*). The variants to the Latin text (i.e. the Latin variants of *B*) follow the same principles and are complete for all words cited as examples and for words where *A*'s text has been corrected. Otherwise, the following variant graphies are ignored: double ∼ single consonant; *n* ∼ *m* before labial; *ti* ∼ *ci* (*tertia* ∼ *tercia*, etc.); *set* ∼ *sed*; *pluralis* ∼ *pluraris*; *scire* ∼ *sire*; *optativus* ∼ *obtativus*; presence ∼ absence of initial *h*; certain abbreviations of the types *īpre* = *tempore* and *9iugōis* = *coniugationis*, characteristic of *B* but absent from *A*, are not specially noted; *B*'s consistent *subiun(c)tivus* for *coniunctivus* is noted only on its first occurrence (225). Where the printed Latin text has the reading '[. . .]', it is to be assumed that *B* has the same omission without any lacuna being left in the MS., unless the contrary is expressly indicated. For those parts of the *Donatz* in which *B* has both the Provençal and the Latin text, omission of a word or phrase in both languages is indicated by '*om.*' in the variants for both the Provençal and the Latin. In the verb-lists and rhyme-lists, the cases where *B* has a Provençal reading but lacks a Latin equivalent are indicated in the Latin variants by '*no trans.*'. In those passages in which *B* carries the Provençal and the Latin texts on alternate lines, the omission of a Latin equivalent which leaves a gap in the Latin line is indicated in the Latin variants by '*om. (blank)*'.

Certain matter is relegated to appendices. The text of MS. *C* is treated in this way in order to avoid increasing the bulk of the variants with readings whose interest is much greater when this rehandled version of the *Donatz* is printed complete in a text which attempts, as far as possible, to correct the very numerous errors of transcription made by the sixteenth-century copyist. Appendix I sets out to provide a readable edition of *C*'s text but to avoid eclecticism as far as possible. It is for this reason that the numerous scribal omissions are in general indicated by '[. . .]', not supplied from another MS.; no gap is left by the scribe of *C* at these points. For a similar reason, certain erroneous forms in *C* which seem attributable to the reviser rather than to the scribe are left uncorrected and followed by †.

The fragment of a rhyming dictionary from MS. *L* is published as Appendix II. Though not strictly forming part of the *Donatz*, it is likely that its compiler made use of the latter as one of his sources (cf. particularly the presence of the word *tams*, 45, otherwise attested only by *Donatz* 1689).

The additional chapters on prepositions and interjections which *L* adds to the text of the *Donatz* are published as Appendix III. These clearly represent an unintelligent attempt to make good a deficiency in Faidit's grammar; to that extent their inclusion in the present edition is relevant.

VI. THE GRAPHY OF THE BASE-MANUSCRIPT

THE graphies of MS. *A* are idiosyncratic and far from consistent. The aspects mentioned below do not exhaust the question and are limited to features which present some special interest or difficulty.

1. Reduction of *ei* to *e* is found sporadically: *manera(s)* 12, 133, *mainera(s)* 131, 3196; *esscemen* 674 (cf. *eissemen* 106, *eissa* 604); *escernir* 1394; *pleneramen* 711 (cf. *pleneiramen* 359, *enteiramen* 602); *primera* 772 (cf. *primeira* 105); *cairera* 3194; *soudadera* 3202. With the three exceptions noted, 3182–3206 consistently shows -*eira*.

2. Reduction of *ie* to *e* occurs occasionally in the ending -*ier*: *volunters* 314, *esters* 1522, *lebrers* 2244, *olivers* 2245, *violers* 2257, *palhers* 2226, in one case apparently with palatalization of *l*: *colhers* 2230 = *coliers* (cf. *codonhyers* 2262 = *codoniers*); also *melhz* 173 (cf. *mielhz* 264, *mielz* 2062). The personal pronoun of the first singular is *eu*, *passim*, never *ieu*.

3. Other alternations of vowel with diphthong occur sporadically: *passeria* 350, *quarar* 1112, *manera* ~ *mainera* (see above, § 1), *Paregorzis* 2543; *augues* 465 (against *agues*, *passim*); *estrit* 2063, 2816, 2896, 3177, 3325 (against *estreit*, *passim*); *conosser* 51, *conoseria* 346 (cf. *conoisser* 335), *poria* 344; *conougutz* 3050, *desconougutz* 3051 (cf. *reconogutz* 3071, etc.), *adouzilha* 3415; alternation of *ǫ* ~ *ue* does not occur (cf. *loc* 10 and *passim*, *voilh* 65 and *passim*, *trop* 131, etc.).

4. Initial *an*- for *en*- occurs sporadically: *antremet* 417, *antreprendre* 1308, *antrevalz* 1638, *antepres* 2339–40, *antrebresca* 3509; cf. *ancar* 87, *anquara* 613, *ancara* 3166, against *encar* 99, *encaras* 155. The only example not in the initial position, *Valantines* 2353, is perhaps explicable via assimilation.

5. There is no clear example of *a* ~ *e* apart from the cases just mentioned: *adagar* 786 (with a translation in *A* corresponding to *adegar*) is best regarded as a scribal error in the Latin; *sobradaurar* 886 is no doubt an Italianism; *masdir* 1426, var. *A* (against *mesdir BDL*), is a scribal error suggested by *maldir*; *eissemen* 106, *esscemen* 674, are to be explained via assimilation (see Pfister, *Beiträge*, *Vox*,

xvii, pp. 306–10); for *raspalhz* 1667, *respalhz* 1668, cf. the note to these words.

6. *u* for *o* occurs before nasal in tonic and countertonic syllables: *numbre* 7, 38 (cf. *nombre* 1499, *nombrar* 1051), *Lumbers* 177, 2186, *sumris* 609, *trumbar* 795 (cf. *trombar* 1218), *enunbrar* 942, *umbralhz* 1647, *Lumbarz* 1802, *mundas* 1947, *sumsitz* 2577, *confuns* 2744; some of these forms are no doubt due to Latinizing influence. (For *-un* in 3rd pl. verb forms, see § 31.)

7. Alternation of *o* and *u* in the countertonic syllable is found in *suffrir* 221, *sufri* 615, *sufrens* 1504, *suffrens* 2115 (cf. *sofrec* 615); *ubri, uberc* 615 (cf. *obrir* 1432); *cubri, cuberc* 616 (cf. *cobrir* 1370–2); *culhir* 1373, *aculhir* 1374, *aculens* 2161 (cf. *recolhir* 1375).

8. Pretonic or intertonic *i* for *e* occurs in *giquir* 1416, *giquitz* 2554, *liçers* 2200, *botiliers* 2221, *diniers* 2222. Hesitation between *i* and *e* is marked in grammatical terms adapted from Latin, e.g. *endicatiu* 224–5, *endecatiu* 538, *enfinitiu* 416–17, *segnifien* 1477, against spellings with *i, passim*.

9. Absence of prosthetic *e* is found in *streit* 619, 1995.

10. Latin Kᵃ is represented by Provençal *c* in initial position in the vast majority of cases. The exceptions are: *chant* 226, *chantar* 236, *chanti, chan* 247, *chanta* 296 (elsewhere *can-*); *chavalier* 26, 31 (cf. *cavalier* 28, 35, 59); *chascun* 232 (cf. *quasqus* 357). Within the word, Provençal *c* is still the commonest graphy, but *ch* occurs after *s*: *deschautz* 162, *deschauzar* 899, *moschar* 1040, *peschar* 1080, *dechaçer* 1256 (= *deschaçer*?), *buschalha* 3359, *eschalha* 3363 (but cf. *descaltz* 1634–5, *oscar* 1060, *trescar* 1199, *decaçes, escaçez* 576, *escaçer* 1257, *buscalar* 842, *escalhz* 1648); after *n*: *enchauzar* 951, *ronchar* 1140 (but cf. *encautz* 163, *encaltz* 1632–3); and in final *-char* in infinitives: *ensachar* 960, *machar* 1037, *pechar* 1081, *trichar* 1209 (but cf. *lecar* 1013, *secar* 1157, *tocar* 1217). The graphy *ç* in *trençatz* 1887 is isolated; the use of *ç* in the spelling of a few Latin words where one would expect *c* or *ch* (1749, 2030, 2848) suggests that *ç* here may merely be an alternative for *ch*. And the curious case of *eschrivan* 551, where the scribe added the *h* above the line, as well as the equally isolated *achointans* 1734, suggest that in at least some instances *ch* may simply be a graphy for [k] rather than [tš].

11. Latin Gᵃ consistently appears as *g*: *largamen* 5, *longa* 648, *vergar* 1235 (also *vengar* 1232).

12. Initial [ts] before *a, o, u* shows the graphies *ç*: *ço* 4, 218 (cf.

aiço 1522); z: zo 2, 41, 51, 214, 230, 1516, zocs 2656, zucs 2981, zoira 3557; çh: çho 648, çha 1350; and possibly ch: chuf 2990 (cf. aicho 258, 1499). Before e and i, c is general, except for seis (cĭnxit) 586. (Initial c < Latin s- occurs only in the special case of Cecilias 1959.)

13. For [ts], [dz] ~ [s], [z], intervocalic and initial of syllable, MS. A shows the following graphies (grouped together here are the reflexes of ᴋ^{e,i}, ᴋᴊ, ᴛᴊ, also of ɢ^e in borses 144, borçes 2332, of ᴅᴊ in verçiers 2246 and of ζ in tamboreçar 1189): c (before e and i), s (before tonic a, e, and i), ss (in dissera 320, trissar 1210, vernhissar 1230), tz (only in conjugatzo 3108, 3222), ç, ch, çh, z. Apart from the restrictions mentioned, the graphies appear to be used indifferently (cf. terça 503, etc., terçha 534, terza 125, etc.; plasens 35, plaçens 36, placher 1259, desplaçer 1260, plazenteira 3198; esforchar 939, forçhar 981). They do not show any division consistent either with differences in the etyma of the words concerned or with differences in the Provençal phonemes which precede or follow. Neither the voiced ~ voiceless nor the affricate ~ fricative distinction is clearly reflected in the scribe's usage on this point.

14. Aici occurs in the senses 'here' (20, 21 [second example], 56, 368, 389, 539) and 'thus' (21 [first example], 204, 253, 287, 688, 1514), to the exclusion of aisi, aissi.

15. The graphy ç for the reflex of Latin intervocalic s occurs only in cauçics 2458-9 (if the etymology via ᴄᴀᴜsᴀ̄ʀɪ̄ is accepted) and in içalar 999 (if ᴀsɪ̄ʟᴜs is the etymon); but these are not significant, since both are editorial corrections of scribal errors (cançics, inçatar A).

16. Initial [s] before e shows the graphy sc in: scenblar 55, scenblan 67, 366, 533, 652, 654, 666, 685, 713, scembla 493, scemblan 567, scentit 755 (cf. Avalle, La Letteratura medievale in lingua d'oc nella sua tradizione manoscritta, Turin, 1961, p. 105). Intervocalic [s] shows the same graphy in: esscemen 674, moscidar 1041, escernir 1394; in prescen(s) 689, 694, 695 and prescentar 1091 the same graphy would seem to stand for [z].

17. Intervocalic [s] shows the graphy s in: fenisen 253 [fenis en A], disera 322-3, conoseria 346, e[s] semblans 407, pasius 772. Intervocalic [z] shows the graphy ss in: acussatius 49, messurar 1027, paussar, trapa[u]ssar 1069, pa[u]ssatz 1467, desmessura 3126 (cf. Latin acussativus 49, recussare 1170). At 845 baissar, as the translations indicate, stands at once for the reflexes of ʙᴀ̄sɪᴀ̄ʀᴇ and

*BASSIĀRE. A certain confusion between graphies for [s] and [z] in intervocalic position is suggested by these examples.

18. Reflexes of D intervocalic (also -T- in some words where -T- developed as -D-: METĬPSĬMUM, *CRĀTĀLIS, BAETERRIS). With the exception of forms of *aerdre*, verbs show *ad-*+ vowel: *adirar* 778, *adagar* 786, *adempiar* 798, *adautar* 818, *aderms* 2292, *adira* 3214, *adora* 3233, *adesca* 3514; also *adorns* 2910. Learned words and words open to Latin influence show -*d*-: *paradis* 181, 2516, *odorar* 1058, *odors* 2842, *odora* 3242, *Adams* 5, 1682, *Dedalus* 3099; the single example of *ad aquelh* 407-8 is perhaps also a Latinizing spelling. Apart from these cases, -*d*- occurs < Germanic -D- in: *esfredar* 938, *guidar* 993, *gadanhar* 987; and before Provençal *ei* in: *radeire* 73, *Bedeires* 2355.

The -D- falls between *i* and tonic *a*: *afiar* 814, 975, *fiar* 975, *desfiar* 975; between tonic *i* and *a*: *afia* 3475, *desfia* 3476, *ria* 3479, *aucia* 3480; between *u* and tonic *a*: *suar* 1181; between *u* and tonic *i*: *pruir* 1443; between *e* and tonic *u*: *creütz* 3052-4; in forms of *aerdre* (distinguished from *aderdre*, cf. note to 620): *aers* 179, 620, 2188, *aertz* 2311; and in the isolated example of *meesma* 110 (against *meçeisma* 140, *meçeismes* 209, *meceismes* 209).

Otherwise the graphies show *çh*, *ç*, and *z* before *a*: *areçhar* 812; *lauçar* 1004; *grazals* 1558, *mezalha* 3369; *c*, *ç*, *ch*, *z* before *e*: *meceismes* 209; *meçeisma* 140, *meçeismes* 209, *caçez* 576, *veçer* 670, *dechaçer* 1256, *escaçer* 1257, *fiçels* 2012, *Juçeus* 2426; *secher* 335, *cacher* 1255, *vecher* 1325; *vezer* 368, *Bezers* 177, 2185, *assezer* 1246, *crezens* 2095-6, *jauzens* 2123, *Mozenes* 2374 (here *z* < Italian -*d*-); *c*, *ç*, *ch*, *z* before *i*: *juciatz* 1893; *auçit* 679, 709, *juçiar* 1002, *preçicar* 1090, *auçitz* 1506, *beneçir* 1356, *auçira* 3223; *auchir* 243, 563, 1353; *obezir* 1431; *ç*, *z* before *o*: *meçola* 3338; *pezolhz* 2722; the only example before *u* is the Latinized *Coraçhuchii* 3571, where *çh* < Italian -*d*-. These show the same graphies as in § 13 above, except that *d* and ø are peculiar to the reflexes of -D-, while *s*, *ss*, and *tz* are peculiar to § 13. The rarity of *c* as a graphy for the reflex of -D- (two examples only) is perhaps significant.

19. The treatment of P intervocalic is striking in *arripar* 781, where all MSS. support -*p*-, not -*b*-. No other examples occur in MS. *A* (cf., however, *deripar* 906, var. *B*, *coprir* 1370, var. *B*); the two parallel instances (*laupartz* 1815, *assapora* 3241) are explicable via learned influence (as is *vapors* 2835, var. *B*; *caproletz* 2401, var. *L*, is perhaps an Italianism). This treatment of intervocalic

THE GRAPHY OF THE BASE-MANUSCRIPT 57

p (and pr) has no obvious explanation. The only parallel for any other intervocalic voiceless plosive is *destrica* 3459, which occurs among the rhymes in *-iga* and is open to scribal or etymological explanation, cf. note to 3459(*pezucar* 1086, var. *B*, no doubt shows the influence of the substantive *pezuc*).

20. Palatal *l* shows freely the graphies *lh* and *l* throughout the text, *lh* being somewhat more frequent. At 3378–3403 and 3418–38 the examples consistently show *-elha* and *-olha*, while the four headings show *-ela* and *-ola*. (*Santolz* 2701 may well be misplaced as a result of the graphy *l* for *lh*, cf. note.) The graphy *ilh* occurs in: *voilh* 65, 69, 86, 99, 231 (cf. *volha* 390, 472, 546, 3422, *vola* 494); *oilh* 217 (cf. *olhz* 2703); *meraveilhar* 1033; *trebailhz* 1651 (cf. *-alhz* 1644–50, 1652–68); *ll* occurs only in *fillola* 3323. The graphies *aquelh* (obl. sg.) 408 (cf. *aquel* 493) and *celh* (n. sg.) 766 (cf. *cel*, *passim*) no doubt show *lh* = *l* (for *solhelar* 1180, cf. note).

21. Palatal *n* is commonly rendered as *nh*. The graphy *n* occurs in: *sener* 89, *ensenar* 236, 935, *-onth* (= *-onht?*) 668, *anelz* 2033, *Campanes* 2361, *rossinols* 2661 (for the translator's mistaken interpretation of *atens* as *atenhs*, cf. note to 2146, and p. 18 above); *in* in *ceinth* (= *ceinht?*) 684, *achointans* (achomtans *A*) 1734; *inh* in *-einht* 674, *feinht, peinht, teinht* 683, *enpeinht* 684, *poinht, oinht* 681 (cf. *jonht* 681, *-onhz* 2772–84); *gn* in *significa* 4, 221, 1474, 1483, *segnifien* 1477; *segner* 123 (cf. *senhoreiar* 1161, *senhorils* 2474, *senhorius* 2612); *besogna* 215, 216, 419, 1476 (cf. *besonha* 217); *ign* in *mençoigniers* 2264, *mezoigneira* 3197; *h* in *fehz* 528, *joher* 669 (cf. *ponher, onher* 669)—these perhaps merely show scribal omission of the titulus. Two or three examples (*vernhissar* 1230, *avenhir* 1460, perhaps *codonhyers* 2262) apparently show *nh* for *n*.

22. Preconsonantal *l*. If we leave aside the cases in which the author's classification of forms in the rhyme-lists definitely imposed either the graphy *l* or the graphy *u* on the scribe, the latter's independent usage, where he was under no such constraint, may be resumed as follows:

(*a*) Vocalization of *l* is the rule in the groups [alt, alts, ald, ęlt, ǫlt, ǫlts, ǫlt, ǫld, ülts]: *autre, passim* (15 examples, against six of *altre*), *autretals* 478, *saute* 303, *assautar* 820, *sautar* 1145; *Bautz* 161, *deschautz* 162, *cautz* 162, *encautz* 163, *essauchar* 937, *enchauzar* 951 (cf. *falz* 163); *enribaudir* 1380, *esbaudir* 1381 (cf. *maldithz* 2622, where *l* is final of its morpheme); *beutatz* 129; *mout* 131, 504, *coutelz* 2036; *poutz* 187, *soutz* 187, *douçors* 2848 (cf. *doulz* 186 = [do̞uts] or [do̞lts]?); *voutitz* 2593; *assoudar* 803, *soudadera* 3202; *piuçella* 3275, *despuzela* 3276 (cf. *despulçelar* 901).

(*b*) The *l* is dropped in: *atrestals* 396 (dissimilation), *mot* 560, *des* 771, *descha*[*u*]*zar* 899, *desleia*[*l*]*s* 1561. These last two are clearly scribal slips—possibly *mot* and *des* should be so regarded also.

(*c*) Otherwise, *l* remains in the scribe's graphy.

23. The reflex of -KT-, in the scribe's usage, is always of the type *it*, not of the type *ch* (e.g. *trait*, *perfeit*, *estreit*, *dit* < DĪCTUM, *passim*). Latinisms form an obvious class of exceptions, e.g. *conjunctiu* 225 and *passim*, *interjetios* 3, *ditio*(*n*)*s* 55–6, etc.; *imperfec* 532 is to be regarded as a Latinism (cf. note), as are *pectenar* 1088, *auctors* 2849, and no doubt *Sanc Danis* 182, *Sang Danis* 2527. The only apparent exception to be found outside the rhyme-lists is *flechir* 1400 (cf. note).

The rhyme-lists clearly attest, for the author's language, a reflex of KT other than [i̯t], cf. below, pp. 73–4. The scribe respected this in a large measure, in so far as it affected the rhyme-syllable itself, but with fluctuations which reveal that the rendering of the sound in question was not natural to him: the rhymes in -*athz* (1896–1917) show four -*athz*, fifteen -*ahz*, and two -*atz*; those in -*ethz* (2376–85, 2408–22) show seventeen -*ethz*, one -*ehz*, four -*etz*, and one -*ez* (*thez* 2419, perhaps intended as *tehz*); those in -*ihtz* (2615–22) show four in -*ithz* (cf. below, § 27, for seven examples of -*ithz* for -*itz*), one in -*ilhtz*, and one in -*ilhz* (these last two are corrected in the text); those in -*ohtz* (2761–9) show six in -*ohtz*, two in -*ohz*.

24. N. pl. masc. forms of *tot* show the exclusive use of forms in *t* (*tuit*, thirteen examples; *tut*, twenty-five examples). If my explanation of the two examples of *tu* is correct (cf. note to 535), this would confirm the scribe's unfamiliarity with the spelling *tuh*.

25. *ir* < *rr*; *i* < *r*, *rr*; dissimilatory loss of *r*. The phenomena mentioned occur sporadically in MSS. *A*, *B*, *D*, and *L* of the *Donatz*. They are to be attributed, therefore, not to the scribe of *A*, but to O^2 (or, conceivably, even earlier in the MS. tradition). If the phenomena mentioned are merely scribal errors, then either they already existed in O^2 or the form of the letter *r* in that MS. encouraged misreading as *i*. Certainly, not all the examples grouped below are open to the same explanation. (For convenience, examples from MSS. other than *A* are noted here under the appropriate headings; examples given without further qualification are attested in *A* alone.)

THE GRAPHY OF THE BASE-MANUSCRIPT 59

(a) Scribal error is clear in *nafrai* 1046 (where the last letter is an incomplete *r*).

(b) In certain cases *-ir-* is justified by etymology: *manduirar* 792 (PANDŪRIUM, cf. note), *Novaires* 2373 (NOVĀRIA+-ENSIS), *Beirius* 'Berry' (*AB*) 2614 (*BITURĪVUM), and perhaps *beirius* 'heretic' (*AB*) 2614.

(c) The following clear examples of *-ir-* < *-rr-* occur in the *Donatz*: *bairar* (*AD*; cf. vairar *L*) 824, *baireiaz* (*D*; = *baireiar*) 832, *feirar* (*BD*) 974, *sairar* (*ADL*) 1149, *sosteirar* 1169, *teiralhz* 1650, *eirans* 1739, *Bedeires* 2355, *Mairocs* (*B*) 2647, *veirolhz* 2720, *mairolhz* (*AB*) 2723, *cairera* 3194. We may add to these three instances in which *-ir-* is apparently < *-rr-* < *-sr-* (DĬS+R-): *deirocar* (*AD*) 889, *deirengar* 892, *deirocs* (*AB*) 2653.

(d) Instances of *-i-* < *-r-* or *-rr-* are fewer: *adempiar* 798, *desaiar* 908. It is possible that these would be better regarded as scribal errors, of no more consequence than *geigons* (*D*) 188, *sotteiar* (*D*) 1169, *traveisar* (*B*) 1196.

(e) Instances of ø < *-r-* are fairly frequent: *adempar* (*DL*) 798, *enalbar* (*ADL*) 962, *pejurar* (= *perjurar*) 1094, *anteprendre* (ante prendere *AB*) 1308, *gondir* 1413, *antepres* 2339–40, *antebresca* (*B*) 3509. These cases, all explicable via dissimilation, are regarded as different in kind from *off[r]ens* 2114, *yve[r]ns* 2279, where *A*'s reading has been corrected.

The examples under (c), (d), and (e) are open to phonetic explanation via dissimilation. They are also open to palaeographical explanation, as scribal errors. The first explanation has been preferred to the second here because some support for the existence of the change *rr* > *ir* can be found elsewhere (cf. note to 1650) and because the examples of dissimilatory loss of *r* to some extent lend support to the existence of the other change. It is perhaps worth noting in this connection that MS. *A* of the *Donatz* contains a few forms with intrusive *r* (*prendreire* 76, *sostrar* 1175, *bratrei* 1468) and two examples of metathesis of *r* (*sofrec* = *soferc* 615, *escracs* = *escarcs* 1545). (It is doubtful, however, whether the translator's rendering of *espirar* as if it were *espiar*, 922, has any connection with the phenomena discussed here.)

26. *g* < *k* (initial of word or of syllable—normally initial of morpheme) occurs in: *mesgabar* 1030, *conglus* 3087. (Examples are somewhat more frequent in MS. *B*, cf. *B*'s variants for 883, 905, 1032, 1367–9, 2645, 2938, 2948, 3309, also *L*'s variant for 883.)

27. Final [ts], from whatever source, is written *tz* or *z passim*, rarely *tç* (*-etç* 515), *thz* (*-ithz* 2588–99, seven examples), and *ç* (*gauç* 19, *perfeiç* 396; for *faiç* 225, cf. below).

Reduction to *s* is attested in *podes* (= *podetz*) 1636, in *fes* < FĒCIT 2323 (but this is a feature of the author's language, here respected by the scribe, cf. *fetz* 561), in *descors* 2860–1 (amongst the rhymes in *-ọrtz*), and in *vescons* 41 (cf. *vez-* 41).

Though the language of the author clearly showed [-ns], not [-nts], < NT+S and < N+KJ become final (cf. 1690–1739, rhymes in *-ans*, etc.), the scribe occasionally writes *-ntz* or *-nz*: *lanz* 164 (cf. *lans* 1712), *-henz* 1475, *malamenz* 1476, *-entz* 1501, *plasenz* 1504 (cf. *sufrens* 1504), *presantz* 1503 (cf. *amans* 1503, *-ans* 1501). Again, though the author's language shows [-lts], not [-ls], < LL+S (cf. 1624–35, rhymes in *-altz*, etc.), the scribe commonly writes *-ls*: *els* (IN ILLOS) 61, *dels* (DĒ ILLOS) 66, 99, 107, etc.; but the spelling *-lz* occurs sporadically: *delz* 2405, *aquelz* 69, 152.

Reduction to *-th* is attested in: *venguth* 218, 3068, *amanoïth* 2596 (cf. perhaps the spelling *-ithz* above: was the articulation of [ts] perceptibly more palatal after [i] and [ü]?).

Reduction to *-t* is not clearly attested: the 2nd pl. imperative *entendat* 538 is perhaps open to morphological explanation; the obl. pl. *compost* 134, 671, 673, 675 (cf. *compostz* 148) shows [sts] > [st]; *-at* for *-atz* 440, 441 and *amat* for *amatz* 465 (in each case after *estat*) are to be regarded as scribal slips; similarly *amatz* for *amat* 456, 475 and *tendutz* for *tendut* 752 are regarded as scribal slips, not as inverse graphies; the obl. sg. forms *faiç* 225 and *perfeitz* 397, which could also be regarded as back-spellings indirectly attesting [ts] > [t], are in all probability merely scribal slips (these, falling outside the grammatical examples, have been allowed to stand in the text).

28. Treatment of final consonant + *s*. The scribe hesitated between *-abs* and *-aps* (1523–34), *-ibs* and *-ips* (2438–42); but *-eps* (2163–8), *-obs* (2623–33), *-olbs* (2634–6), and *-orbs* (2893–7) show no such hesitation (cf., however, *cobs* altered from *cops* 2631). Reduction of consonant + *s* to *-s* has been allowed to stand in *baraties* (= *baratiers*) 2242 (the sole example in the *Donatz* of the well-known reduction of *-rs* to *-s*) and in *senescals* 1642 (since *senescal* is attested as an alternative to *senescalc*). Other instances have been considered as scribal errors: *arran[c]s* 1764, *tre[p]s* 2168, *vol[b]s* 2636 (for *s* < *ls*, cf. above, § 22).

THE GRAPHY OF THE BASE-MANUSCRIPT 61

29. Reduction of final *sc* to *s* is attested in *pos* 25, 246, 1476 (cf. *posc* 34).

30. The *n caduc* is not normally written in final position, except for a handful of cases, mainly monosyllables: *non* 11, 61, etc. (also *no* very commonly—9, 18, etc.; the distribution of *no* and *non* is not dependent on following consonant or vowel); *ven* 10, 11, 1472, 1473, *conven* 30, *coven* 238; *un* 18, 654, 1508, *chascun* 232, *alqun* 334; *man* 217, *pan* 227, *vin* 227, *bon* 362, *fin* 702; also *comun* 24, *aperten* 358 (the latter before *al*). Before flexional *s*, the *n caduc* is virtually never written: *ditions* 56 is exceptional. Words whose stem shows alternation between *ns* and *s* commonly have *ns*: *cens* 142, *encens* 143, *censals* 1592 (but *ces* 2328, *ences* 2329-30, where the scribe respected the author's classification of these in -*es*); *consirar* 877, *consirs* 2498-9, *consira* 3219.

31. Apart from the grammatical examples, the 3rd person plural verb-forms, irrespective of their infinitive, most commonly show -*en*. But one finds the present indicatives *volon* 104, *volun* 107, 114, 115, 117, 124, 125, 1742, 1743 (cf. *volen* 53, 54); *declinon* 133, 136, 155, 202; *mudon* 137, 202 (cf. *muden* 667, 671, 674); and the present subjunctive *sion* 121, 137, 240, 242, 567. The reflex of sŭnt is *sun*, *passim*; also *sum* 1347 and *sunt* 3545.

32. Scribal infringements of the case-system are rare. Apart from the obl. sg. forms *faiç* 225 and *perfeitz* 397 (cf. § 27 above) and the n. sg. *chascun* 232 (perhaps due to misinterpretation of *e* as *en*), the examples consist of uninflected n. sg. forms for grammatical terms: *nome*, *pronome* 2, *nom* 4, 9, 10; *verbe*, *adverbe* 2 (cf. *verbes* 220, 702, *adverbes* 1467); *particip* 2, *particep* 1497; *nominatiu plural* 53 (scribal misunderstanding of *el*?); *present* 478, *preterit* ... *perfeit* 493, 704, 740, 761, *futur* 713. *Sanc Danis* 182, *Sang Danis* 2527 show sanctus treated as invariable.

VII. THE CIRCUMSTANCES OF THE COMPOSITION OF THE *DONATZ*[1]

THE grammar published here is entitled *Donatus pro[v]incialis* in *A*, *Donato prodensal* in *D*, *Donatz proensals* in *C*; MSS. *B* and *L* give no title. The present edition adopts the Provençal title, which has gained general currency among modern scholars. The incipit of MSS. *D* and *L* gives the author's name as *Vgo Faiditus* (*D*) or *vgo faidicus* (*L*); the Latin conclusion of the work, in a sentence given only by MS. *A* (3569-70), calls him simply *vgo*. I have attempted to justify palaeographically the correction of *A*'s *cuius vgo* to *Ugo Faiditus* and to indicate that the balance of probability is in favour of the view that the incipit of *DL* results from a transferring to the beginning of the work of part of the Latin paragraph which originally formed the conclusion (cf. note to 3569-70). Despite the corruption of *A* and the absence of testimony from *B* and *C* on this point, there is no reason for questioning the authenticity of the attribution to Uc Faidit.

Of the author nothing is known beyond what can be deduced concerning the dedicatees and the probable date of his grammar. The same passage which names the author (i.e. the incipit in *DL*, the conclusion in *A*) states also that his work was composed *precibus Iacobi de Mora et domini Coraçhuchii de Sterlleto* (3570-1). The identification of these with two Italian noblemen at the Court of the Emperor Frederick II, Giacomo di Mora and Coraduccio di Sterleto, was first made by Gröber and confirmed by Monti's full investigation of the career of Giacomo di Mora.[2] The latter is known as *podestà* of Treviso in 1239, *capitano generale* in the Duchy of Spoleto in 1240, *vicario generale* of the Duchy of Spoleto by 1242, *vicario generale* of the Marca d'Ancona in 1245. In 1246 he was one of the noblemen who unsuccessfully plotted the

---

[1] On this subject see the studies by Gröber, Merlo, and d'Ovidio mentioned in the Bibliography.

[2] Cf. Gröber's articles in *ZRP* viii (see Bibliography); and G. M. Monti's study on 'Giacomino Pugliese e le sue Rime', which constitutes pp. 1-220 of his *Studi letterari*, Città di Castello, 1924; see pp. 24-34 and 182-206 for the documentation relevant here. Monti's identification of Giacomo di Mora with Giacomino Pugliese has not won general acceptance.

assassination of the Emperor. He fled to Rome and remained for some time in the service of the Pope. The date of his death is not known. In October 1243 he had appeared as witness to an Imperial act in favour of *Conradutius de Sterleto*, the other dedicatee of the grammar. Of the latter's career less is known. Whether he is identical with the *Corrado da Sterleto* mentioned in Guittone d'Arezzo's *canzone*, *Se di voi, donna gente*, is uncertain. But the confirmation in 1259 by Percivalle Doria, the Emperor Manfred's *vicario generale* in Spoleto and Romagna, of the act of 1243 clearly indicates that Corraduccio was not implicated in the rebellion of 1246. It is thus impossible to suppose that the two dedicatees of Faidit's grammar could have been associated in any enterprise later than 1246; it is anyway reasonable to assume that Giacomo's interest in the language of the troubadours dates from the period when he was a successful courtier, rather than from the period of political intrigue and exile in Rome. It is usual, on these grounds, to date the *Donatz* from 'c. 1240'. In fact, any date within the period 1225–45 remains possible, though the known association of the two dedicatees in 1243 makes the latter part of this period somewhat more probable.

One piece of evidence—apparently previously unnoticed—would seem to suggest that the Latin conclusion of the work was penned after the disgrace of Giacomo di Mora. It is at least curious that (in MSS. *A* and *D*, though not in *L*) the latter does not have the title *dominus* which is bestowed on his fellow dedicatee. If this detail is really significant, it could be held to demonstrate that the request to compose the grammar was made not long before the conspiracy of 1246 and that, by the time the author had completed it, one of his patrons was already disgraced and in exile. The argument is not entirely conclusive, however, since later deletion of the word *dominus* would, in these circumstances, be readily explicable.

That the *Donatz* was composed in Italy and for Italians is confirmed by a number of indications. All the MSS. are of Italian provenance. There is no indication that the work was known outside Italy. The authors of the *Leys d'Amors* seem not to have known of it; for, if they had, the absence in the *Leys* of any reference to Faidit's dictionary of rhymes would be difficult to explain. The *Diccionari de Rims* of the Catalan Jaume March, written in 1371, has no demonstrable dependence on the *Donatz*, despite the opinion of its editor to the contrary.[1] Nor is it possible to prove that his compatriot Jofre de Foixà made use of the *Donatz* in his *Regles de trobar* (1286–91), again despite its editor's opinion.[2] In both these cases, common subject-matter sufficiently accounts for the parallels which can be established. On the other hand, the *Donatz* continued to be known in Italy after the mid-thirteenth century. The anonymous author of the Provençal–Italian glossary published by Castellani (cf. above, p. 5) made use of it. And from the sixteenth century we have two Italian MSS., two Italian translations, and an Italian abstract (for which cf. pp. 6–8 above).

The content of the *Donatz* reflects in some measure the interests of the Italian readers for whom it was written. The toponyms cited in the rhyme-lists show a marked preponderance of Italian names (cf. Index of Proper Names). The note on the passive mood envisages the needs and difficulties of Italian speakers (cf. note to 413–16). The insistence throughout the *Donatz* on the distinction between close and open *e* and *o* reflects the grammarian's awareness of an aspect of Provençal versification which was found particularly difficult by Italians, as is indicated by occasional confusion of [ẹ] and [ę], [ọ] and [ǫ], in the work of troubadours of Italian origin. It is even possible that occasionally Faidit merely transcribed into Provençal words which were strictly Italian (cf. notes to 1550, 1905, 2680, 2728, 3241), though this last point is not susceptible of proof.

One could argue that it was strange that, in these circumstances, Faidit used Provençal rather than Latin as the language in which his exposition of Provençal grammar was written. We can only suppose that his two patrons already had a sufficient knowledge of Provençal—perhaps acquired simply from contact with troubadour poetry—to make use of the *Donatz*. The presence in the text of so extensive a dictionary of rhymes would suggest that Faidit originally envisaged readers whose knowledge of Provençal justified an ambition to compose verse in that language. But the argument cannot be pursued too far: we know nothing of any literary activity on the part of the grammarian's two patrons; and it is quite possible that

---

[1] See *Diccionari de Rims de Jaume March*, ed. A. Griera, Barcelona, 1921, pp. 9–14.

[2] See *Jofre de Foixà, Vers e Regles de trobar*, ed. E. Li Gotti, Modena, 1952, p. 17, esp. n. 22.

CIRCUMSTANCES OF COMPOSITION

the scope of the finished grammar exceeded the needs and expectations of those who had requested its composition.

Of the author of the Latin version, nothing is known. If he was indeed someone other than Faidit, as seems likely (cf. pp. 18–19), he must clearly have had Provençal for his native speech. And he shared Faidit's preoccupation with the difference between Provençal and Latin (cf. p. 19). His desire in adding the Latin rendering was to expound and clarify, but not to modify, the Provençal text. One may suspect that he belonged to the same circle as Faidit and set out simply to give greater currency and greater utility to the latter's work. Certainly the closeness of the Latin to the Provençal, in letter and in spirit, suggests nearness in time: the manuscript tradition gives no indication of any wide circulation of the *Donatz* before the Latin version was added. And the possibility remains that it was Faidit himself who at a later date added the translation to his vernacular original.

VII. FAIDIT AS GRAMMARIAN

It is clear that Faidit can lay no claim to originality as a grammatical theorist. He accepts, as the natural outline for his exposition of Provençal grammar, the framework of Latin grammar as taught by the standard textbooks current in his time. The title *Donatz*—whether bestowed by Faidit himself or not—characterizes the aim of producing a grammar setting forth the rudiments of the language on a scale comparable with that of the *Ars minor* of Donatus. The provision of verb-lists and a dictionary of rhymes exceeds this limited scope and has no parallel in Donatus. But the grammatical exposition draws widely on the classification and the terminology of elementary Latin grammar.

Thus Faidit finds in Provençal the eight parts of speech and lists them in the same order as Donatus (cf. note to 1–3). And, like Donatus, he defines the parts of speech and their attributes. The definitions, however, are closer to those given by the *Institutiones grammaticae* of Priscian—this is particularly true for the noun, the pronoun, and the verb (cf. notes to 4–7, 204–13, 220–1). In the definition of the participle Donatus is very exactly reproduced, as he was by virtually all medieval writers on Latin grammar (cf. note to 1497–9). The very brief definitions of the adverb and the conjunction are inferior to those given by either of the standard Latin grammarians (cf. notes to 1467, 1508). The most probable explanation of this admixture of sources is that Faidit transcribed into Provençal what he remembered of the Latin material, sometimes adhering closely to his source, sometimes paraphrasing it loosely, once even quoting verbatim a Latin phrase (220); and using each time the well-worn formula of definition by etymological explanation (*Nom es apelatz per ço que*, etc.). Though Faidit lived at a time when grammatical categories were the subject of much discussion, there is no indication that his choice of material here was dictated by any theoretical considerations, or indeed by anything deeper than the hazards of memory.

His treatment of the attributes of the parts of speech shows similar features. Those of the noun are treated at some length and follow Priscian for the enumeration of the attributes themselves (cf. note to 4–7); but the Provençal grammarian shows a curious misconception in his explanation of *species* (cf. note to 8–11), he reduces to five the number of genders (cf. note to 12–13), and he reduces the treatment of *figura* to the barest essentials (cf. note to 40–1). There is no reference to the attributes of the pronoun, and no formal enumeration of those of the verb: for the latter, he mentions only the categories which have some practical importance for his exposition, those of mood, tense, and conjugation. The definitions of the moods are again as brief and elementary as possible; like Donatus and most pedagogic grammars of the Middle Ages, he calls the fourth mood *coniunctivus*, not (as Priscian did) *subiunctivus* (cf. note to 224–44). The three attributes of the adverb follow those of Priscian (cf. note to 1471), but attention is concentrated on the attribute of *significatio*, the only one of practical utility. No attributes are defined for the participle and the conjunction, though Faidit's enumeration of the classes of conjunctions corresponds broadly to the subdivisions of the attribute of *potestas*.

The author's interest in this theoretical side of grammar seems to have been very limited and to have become even more so in the course of his work, for it is only for the noun that he makes any real attempt to reproduce more or less fully the categories of standard Latin grammar. Elsewhere attention is concentrated on the aspects of classification which had some practical utility for the teaching of grammar.

As was natural in his age, Faidit accepted that the terminology and framework of Latin grammar was a fitting mould for the exposition of the grammar of his own language. He was intermittently aware of discrepancies between *gramatica* and *vulgar* (20, 67, 131, 238, 398, 418, 501), as was also the translator (cf. the Latin text at 25, 119, 237, 259, 287). Nevertheless, he admitted the classes of neuter and *omne* among the genders of nouns (18–23, 33–7), with evident embarrassment at finding appropriate examples: he was sufficiently honest to admit that neuter substantives behaved like those of the masculine, but insufficiently radical to deny altogether the existence of neuter substantives in Provençal. Again, he admitted the existence of six cases in the vernacular and gave as illustrations examples which, in our eyes, are merely translations from the Latin (43–50): though he went on to expound, without undue subservience to Latin, the two-case system of Provençal, he was not radical enough to abandon altogether the traditional framework of the six cases. He departs from Latin in finding only three declensions in the vernacular (105–32), but those three are so closely modelled on the first, second, and third declensions of Latin as to obscure the real distinctions relevant to Provençal, namely between masculines and feminines and between masculines which have -*s* in the n. sg. and those which do not (cf. 121–5 for the grouping of *deus* with *segner* and *maestre*).

In the treatment of the noun, then, passages based closely on Latin grammar and passages independent of it exist side by side, often with confusing results. One has the impression that the author's strong practical bias was in conflict with a certain timidity at straying too far from the established categories.

His enumeration of pronouns follows as closely as possible the list given by Priscian (cf. note to 204–13), so that *qui*, mentioned as a pronoun in an earlier passage (101), is left aside here. And he adopted Priscian's term *pronomina demonstrativa* for what we call personal pronouns, giving examples which show that he understood the point of the Latin grammarian's definition (cf. note to 218).

Faidit's division of verbs into four conjugations explicitly departs from those of Latin grammar (237–9), with a formula in which the author seems deliberately to underline his own originality in this matter. Nevertheless, he was unconsciously following Latin more closely than he realized, for his four conjugations are defined, like those of Latin, in accordance with the endings of the infinitive. That this procedure was not entirely satisfactory in Provençal is tacitly admitted by the grammarian when, in the latter part of the exposition of the verb (503–771), he chooses to treat verbs of his second, third, and fourth conjugations together. And the definition of a fourth conjugation in -*ir* concealed the difference between the inchoative and non-inchoative Provençal types, to such an extent that the former receives no proper treatment.

The plan of five tenses and five moods follows Latin grammar very closely. That this led Faidit to class as a future subjunctive what we would call a future perfect (409, 494, 763) is of little importance. Of much more consequence is the fact that adherence to the Latin framework caused him to omit the compound perfect tense altogether: as the equivalent of the Latin perfect tense he he gives always the Provençal preterite.

For the imperative, Faidit sensibly made no attempt to reproduce the present and future imperatives of Latin. But, while all reference to tense is omitted in the first and second passages on this mood (294–311, 451–6), the third ends with the curious observation that the future imperative is the same as that of the present (694).

The optative mood presented considerable problems. The classification which separated optative and subjunctive, which was borrowed from Greek grammar, was not really satisfactory even in Latin, where the sole distinguishing mark between them was that the optatives were preceded by *utinam* and the subjunctives by *cum*, indicating that the former existed in main clauses and the latter in subordinate. Faidit reproduced as best he could the three tenses which Latin grammar admitted for the optative. His use of the two conditional forms of Provençal for the first tense (present and imperfect, in Latin) is reasonable. This seems to have been the optative *par excellence* for him, for it is only on the third mention of this tense (695, against 312 and 457) that he refers to it specifically as the *present* optative. For the other two tenses, Faidit fell back on mere translation from the Latin, hence his *bon fora qu'eu agues amat* (360–4), his *Deus volha qu'eu ame* (388–95, cf. 471–7 and 544–51), and his phrases prefaced—quite inconsequentially —by *si* (706–10). All but the last of these render the Latin forms reasonably well; but they clearly cannot be admitted, for formal reasons, as anything but subjunctives. It is odd that Faidit did not use examples of the type **volunters auria o agra amat*, which would at least have had the virtue of consistency.

The five tenses of the subjunctive presented fewer problems. For Faidit, as for Latin grammar, the present tense was identical with the future optative and the pluperfect with the pluperfect optative (396, 478–9, and 713; 407–8, 493–4, and 761–2). Each tense renders the Latin equivalent exactly. That this was in fact Faidit's procedure here is shown by his observation (396–9, repeated at 538–40) that in the vernacular the imperfect subjunctive may on occasions have the form of the imperfect indicative, which is his way of describing the Provençal use of the indicative in conditional clauses where Latin used the subjunctive. Here, as in many places in the paradigms of verbs, his habit of mental translation from Latin is very clear.

For the infinitive, however, he wisely abandoned the Latin classification of forms, giving only a present and an imperfect and observing that other tenses *hardly* occur in the vernacular (418). This last remark suggests the grammarian's anxiety that his departure from Latin should not be ascribed to mere ignorance.

Faidit's adherence to the order of exposition of Latin grammar is very close in his treatment of the first conjugation, both active and passive, but somewhat less so for the other conjugations. His departure here, however, amounts simply to a decision to mention first, after a brief treatment of the present indicative, those tenses in which the second, third, and fourth conjugations were identical (532–51), a decision then abandoned in favour of a stricter adherence to the Latin order of exposition, with consequent repetition of material already treated (653–5, 685–7, 713–18). Such timid departures from Latin are not to Faidit's advantage, witness his unsystematic and skimpy treatment of the present indicative (505–31) and the quite unsatisfactory paragraph on the imperative (688–94). One could argue that he needed the traditional framework as a support and that he was at his best when working within it, as, for example, in his full treatment of irregular 3rd sg. pret. forms (552–652).

The chapters dealing with the less complicated adverb, participle, and conjunction presented Faidit with fewer difficulties in reconciling Latin and vernacular. The lists of adverbs show some exact recollection of Donatus, some independence in the selection of Provençal examples, some inexactitudes in the classification (cf. note to 1473–96). The brief list of participle forms shows no strict dependence on Latin grammar. But the lists of types of conjunction show the same intermittent reliance on Donatus already noted for the adverb, except that here Faidit's uncertainties of terminology and classification are more marked (cf. note to 1509–22).

Some of the results of Faidit's exposition of his own language on the pattern of Latin grammar are unhappy. It caused him to omit the article, the comparison of adjectives, the compound perfect of verbs, and all reference to syntax. It caused him to deform a considerable number of the facts of Provençal grammar, or to expound them in a way which strikes us as inappropriate to the structure of the vernacular. But in many of the passages which show an uneasy fitting of Provençal into categories originally conceived for Latin, the latter are no more than a formal ground-plan, which is often later abandoned or simply ignored—sometimes explicitly, sometimes silently. We are perhaps unduly struck by these incongruities. Faidit made use of the only framework of grammatical terminology available to him, a framework without which both he and his readers might well have found it impossible to proceed. And he had the virtue of perceiving—even though intermittently —the shortcomings which it had for the vernacular grammarian.

Faidit did not ever indicate that the *vulgar provençhal* (1-2) which was his subject was to be identified specifically with the written or with the spoken language. There is no indication that he was ever conscious of a distinction between the two: Provençal is treated as one and indivisible. From his inclusion of a dictionary of rhymes it is reasonable to suppose that literary usage was his subject and that he assumed in his readers a desire either to compose verse themselves or, at the least, to gain better understanding of the verse of others. But the author never expresses any conscious intention to write a grammar of 'the language of the troubadours', and we should not be justified in assuming the *Donatz* to be such a grammar. The mention of the rare 3rd sg. pret. forms *caçez* (576), *teus*, *preus* (639) suggests a reliance on the chances of personal knowledge rather than any conception of a more or less standardized *koine*. That Faidit did not consciously set up troubadour practice as a linguistic standard is shown by his consistent reference to 3rd pl. fut. forms in *-au* as an alternative to those in *-an*, as well as by certain negative traits: the absence from the grammar of *son* ~ *so* as 1st sg. pr. ind. of *esser*, of *escriure*, of *talan*, etc. Too much weight cannot be given to this argument *ex silentio*, but it does in some measure confirm that, for Faidit, the ordinary linguistic practice of the troubadours was not a criterion—or not the sole criterion— determining the inclusion or omission of grammatical forms. He is at one with troubadour practice in two general respects. Firstly, he is conservative in making no mention of n. sg. m. forms of nouns, adjectives, and pronouns with the analogical *-s* (68-80, 86-94, 99-104, and 206-8)—the newer forms, which were certainly current in his time, are not even mentioned in order to be rejected. The conservatism of the grammarian and the conservatism of literary usage here coincide. Secondly, he is in accord with a well-known feature of the language of the troubadours in admitting a wide range of alternative forms, both morphological and phonetic, almost always without expressing a preference between the two. The one occasion on which he does express a preference (264) shows a leaning towards the commonest literary form (cf. note to

245-64). From this point of view, then, Faidit was as liberal as the troubadours themselves, in striking contrast to the greater dogmatism of Raimon Vidal.

These contacts with the linguistic practice of the troubadours, however, are general rather than specific. Faidit's conservatism does not extend to all elements of the language, nor do the pairs of alternative forms always coincide with those attested by rhyme and scansion as equally current in lyric poetry. Certain verb-forms illustrate these points. Faidit shows a marked preference for 1st sg. pret. forms in *-i*—*dissi, escrissi,* etc. (552-9)—although he also admits the type *dis, escris,* identical with the 3rd person, as correct (610-11). He shows a marked preference for the endings *-e, -es, -e* for the singular persons of the pr. subj. of first conjugation verbs (390-2), though he elsewhere admits 2nd sg. forms of the type *ams* (1684), *cans* (1697), etc., and a whole series of alternatives of the type *chans, chantes* (3105-16). No one could maintain that Faidit's doctrine is here in conflict with troubadour practice: the longer forms are to be found in the poets (cf. notes to 390-2, 552-9), the shorter forms are not rejected by the grammarian. But the difference of emphasis is marked. For Faidit it was the longer, more characterized, forms which were normal, while literary usage favoured the shorter, etymological forms. Here the grammarian was in accord with the language as a whole, rather than with more conservative written practice, as is suggested by the views expressed a century later in the *Leys d'Amors* (cf. ed. Gatien-Arnoult, vol. 2, p. 378, for the preterite forms, and pp. 396-400, for the pr. subj. forms).

If Faidit, therefore, presented in the *Donatz* a personal amalgam of the linguistic tendencies of the spoken and the literary language, was his conception of the spoken language dictated by geographical influences? Did his grammar reflect at all closely the speech of his own native region? And how did the influence of spoken dialect blend with or modify respect for written usage? These questions may be answered, in part at least, on the basis of phonetic traits revealed in the dictionary of rhymes, of morphological traits from the body of the grammar, and of elements of vocabulary.[1]

---

[1] An attempt in this direction was made, using material similar to that used here, by Lienig, p. 22 n. 1, who reached the conclusion that Faidit came from an area including Quercy, central and northern Rouergue, and part of the Cévennes.

FAIDIT AS GRAMMARIAN

On the phonetic side, certain traits are striking.

1. Faidit distinguishes between the Provençal reflexes of -L- and -LL- before final *s*, though not when they occur in intervocalic position in Provençal. This distinction was not in general observed in the rhymes of the troubadours and Faidit could not, therefore, have derived it from literary usage. We may assume that he derived it from the speech of his own region. The phonetic distinction between -L- and -LL- is now found in Languedoc and Gascony; its geographical extension in the Middle Ages is to some extent confirmed by the examples of it which occur in Peire Vidal and in the *Leys d'Amors*. (See notes to 1624–40, 2009–22, 2688–2701.)

2. Faidit admits the vocalization of preconsonantal *l* after *a* and *o*, but not generally to the exclusion of the forms with *l*. After other vowels there is no trace of vocalization: the rhyme-series in *-eus*, *-ius*, and *-ous* (2423–37, 2604–14, 2797–2804) contain no examples. The alternation *-als* ∼ *-aus* is attested, but without comment (see note to 1835–54). The alternation *-alz* ∼ *-autz* is explicitly allowed for all words except those in which the dental element derives from -LL-; thus Faidit admits *altz*—*alt* ∼ *autz*—*aut* but only *cavaltz*—*caval*, not *cavautz—*cavau. The alternations *-ǫlz* ∼ *-ǫutz* and *-ǫlz* ∼ *-ǫutz* are attested by the presence of doublets in the relevant lists. With the exception of *coutz* < COLLIS (2926), these cases are phonetically parallel with *-autz* for *-alz* (see notes to 2916–26, 2927–33). These features correspond broadly with troubadour usage in allowing vocalized and unvocalized forms as equally admissible, though some troubadours went further in admitting rhymes in *-eus* < *-ęls* and *-ius* < *-ils*. But the distinctions depending on the different treatments of L + s and LL + s are, as we have seen, not normally observed by literary usage.

3. The rhyme-series in *-athz* (1896–1917), *-ęthz* (2376–85), *-ęthz* (2408–22), *-ihtz* (2615–22), and *-ǫhtz* (2761–9) group together the reflexes of KT + s, DJ + s, GJ + s, G^e + s, J + s. The rhyme-series in *-atz* (1864–95), *-ętz* (2386–2407), *-itz* (2548–2603), *-ǫtz* (2934–49), *ǫtz* (2950–64), and *-utz* (3022–77) group together the reflexes of T + s, TT + s, D + s, KJ, K^e, TJ. The two classes do not overlap, in the sense that there is no instance of alternative forms of the same word being admitted into two different series. On the other hand, *-athz* overlaps in some measure with *-ais* (*esglahz* 1917, *esglais* 1604; *ensahz* 1908, *assais* 1613; *rathz* 1907, *rais* 1614) and

-*ethz* with -*eis* (*lethz* 2412, *leis* 1996). *Fes* < FĒCIT appears among the rhymes in -*es* (2323), although *ditz* < DĪCIT is classed under -*itz* (2585). And forms in -*oitz* are allowed as alternatives for all words in -*ohtz* (2770–1). The way in which this last point is made, and the absence of any parallel qualification to the series in -*athz*, -*ethz*, and -*ihtz*, indicates that forms with a phoneme rendered as *th* or *h* were normal for Faidit, at least in reflexes of KT + S. He belonged, in short, to the area of the type *fach* < FACTUM, not to the *fait*-area. On the definition of this area, stretching from Périgord to Provence, cf. H. Suchier, *Die französische und provenzalische Sprache und ihre Mundarten*[2], Strasbourg, 1912 (= *Gröbers Grundriss*, i), p. 759 and map VI; Ronjat, ii, pp. 171–8. He knew, however, of the *fait*-forms and did not reject them, hence the admission of -*oitz* beside -*ohtz*. But, for at least some words showing reflexes of DJ + S, GJ + S, and G^e + S, alternations of the type -*athz* ∼ -*ais* were equally acceptable.

As is well known, troubadour usage showed great freedom in these respects. Not only are alternatives of the kinds indicated in the *Donatz* frequently to be found, but rhymes which unite, for example, -*atz* < -ĀTUS with -*atz* < -ACTUS were quite common. The choice offered by the language in this respect seems to have been utilized by poets in the same way as pairs such as *talen* ∼ *talan*. To the extent that he admitted some alternative forms, Faidit was in accord with this tendency, though he did not go nearly so far in this direction as did literary practice. He may well have been held back by his adherence to the speech of the *fach*-area.

4. There are a few apparent signs of the acceptance of -*s* < -*tz*: *fes* < FĒCIT (2323, noted above), *palus* < PALŪDIS (3093), *crus* < CRŪDUS (3095), *malaus* < MALE HABITUS (1849)—though Faidit also has *nutz* < NŪDUS (3036). Although rhymes of -*tz* : -*s* occur sporadically in many troubadours (cf. Lienig, pp. 106–8), it is unlikely that the grammarian was here reflecting this practice. Explanation of *fes* ≠ *dis* < DĪXIT is possible, while the attestation of obl. sg. forms *palu, cru, malau* (*SW* vi. 36–7; i. 422; v. 51–2) suggests that the other forms do not have a purely phonetic explanation.

5. Faidit's language is in accord with troubadour usage (cf. Lienig, p. 31) in distinguishing between -*as larg* (< -ASSUS, etc., 1918–32) and -*as estreit* (< -ĀNUS, etc., 1933–62) but in making no parallel distinction for -*es* (2317–75) and -*is* (2508–47).

FAIDIT AS GRAMMARIAN

6. Equally, he is in accord with troubadour practice in grouping together the Provençal reflexes of -R- and -RR-, cf. the series in -ęrs (2169–86), -ǫrs (2805–15), and -ǫrs (2816–55). In this respect he was closer to the usage of the lyric poets than were the authors of the *Leys* (cf. ed. Gatien-Arnoult, vol. 1, pp. 38 and 156; Lienig, pp. 98–100).

In general, then, Faidit is rather stricter than the troubadours in making certain phonetic distinctions at the rhyme which poetic practice treated with greater freedom or greater licence. In so far as these distinctions have a regional origin, they point towards the area of central Languedoc and Rouergue.

The morphological forms recommended in the *Donatz* include some which can be approximately localized.

7. Verb forms of the 3rd person plural. (*a*) Forms in *-en* and *-on* are presented as alternatives in tenses which show reflexes of Latin -ANT: present indicative (257), imperfect indicative (271, 285, 432, 444, 537, 655), future imperfect (463, 698), conditional (463), present subjunctive (406, 477, 492, 746, 753, 760)—463 and 760 show *-o* for *-on*. The first mention of fut. impf. forms shows only *-en*, as does the first mention of the conditional (319, 325, 333, 342). Present subjunctive forms give only the alternatives *-an* and *-on* in 456, 545, 551, 718.

(*b*) For Latin -ENT, *-en* and *-on* are presented as alternatives for the pr. subj. (395, 693) and impf. subj. (374, 380, 387, 470, 485, 701, 729, 732, 739). The ending *-o* is added to these at 693. At 309–11 and 722, *-en* alone is given for the pr. subj. and impf. subj. respectively.

(*c*) For Latin -UNT, *-en* and *-on* are again alternatives in the preterite (278, 566, 567, 569, 571), with *-o* for *-on* in 438. The pr. ind. shows *-en* and *-on* without distinction for reflexes of -ENT and -UNT (515, 531); and an earlier passage explicitly gives this pair of alternatives for all verbs in all tenses except the future (259).

(*d*) The forms of the future give *-an* and *-au* as alternatives throughout (293, 415, 450, 500, 543, 687, 769).

Thus Faidit shows acquaintance with the speech of the large central area of the Midi, in which *-on* supplanted etymological *-an* and *-en*; with the speech of the area further to the west, in which *-en* supplanted *-on*, including the northern part of that area (Limousin, Périgord), in which *-en* supplanted *-an*; and with the speech of those areas (E. of the Rhône; Comminges, pays de Foix) in which

-an < -ANT survived[1]—though Faidit mentions *-an* only for the present subjunctive, and then not consistently. The consistent presentation of *-au* by the side of *-an* in the future points to the area of Rouergue, Quercy, Albigeois, Gévaudan, Toulouse (see note to 293). And the hypothesis that Faidit was a native of that region is consistent with the linguistic knowledge and linguistic preferences shown by the other 3rd plural forms. It is worth noting, however, that Faidit does not ever recommend a narrowly regional form to the exclusion of a form of more general currency.

8. The admission of 1st sg. pr. ind. forms in *-i* and the absence of any mention of the forms in *-e* again suggest a regional preference, in favour of the speech of a large western and south-western area of the Midi extending as far as Albi and Toulouse (cf. note to 245–64). Again, the expressed preference for the uninflected forms probably shows a respect for the commonest literary usage.

9. The admission of the 3rd pl. pret. forms *dissen* ~ *disson* and the absence of any mention of *disseren* ~ *disseron* suggests the influence of the speech of an area including Toulouse, Moissac, and western Rouergue (cf. note to 571). The absence of the more usual form is striking.

10. The use of the n. pl. m. form *celh* (and *cel*) to the exclusion of *cil* and *cilh* again points to the area including Rouergue, Quercy, Albi, and Toulouse (cf. note to 257). Again, the form most usual in troubadour usage is absent.

Certain morphological features of the *Donatz*, then, point to an area centring on the Albigeois and Rouergue. Local influences in the vocabulary of the text, on the other hand, are rather less clear. A certain number of words confirm the localization indicated by morphological features: *petazar* 1083, *ranqueirar* 1123, *naucs* 1830, *roiols* 2674, *fendalha* 3377, and, in some measure, *calar* 848 and *dorcs* 2792 (see the relevant notes). But others point towards quite different areas: *pistar* 1099, *grobs* and *agrobs* 2629–30 to Provence, *moscidar* 1041 to Limousin, *maials* 1572 to Gascony, *bols* 2680 to Franco-Provençal. There are, however, several good reasons why the picture should appear confused and its interpretation uncertain. Firstly, localizations suggested wholly or partially by modern dialect material may not hold good for the Middle Ages. Secondly, we cannot know whether scribes or readers

[1] See Brunel, *Chartes*, i, pp. xl–xli; ii, p. xiv; P. Meyer, 'Les troisièmes personnes du pluriel en provençal', *Rom.* ix, 1880, pp. 192–215.

of the *Donatz* added their own contributions to the lists of verbs and rhymes. Thirdly, Faidit himself may well have been aware of localized elements of vocabulary which did not belong to his own region. Such elements would readily have been brought to his mind by the act of composing lists of rhymes. If it is possible that he transposed a number of Italian words into Provençal (cf. above, p. 64), it is at least equally possible that he derived genuinely Provençal elements from the speech of regions other than his own.

Nevertheless, the indications given by the vocabulary of the *Donatz* do not in general contradict those given by phonetic and morphological features. The conclusion which best takes account of the evidence is that the speech of the area of Rouergue and the Albigeois had for Faidit a special degree of importance; that he was in all probability a native of that region; but that he was generally aware of the speech of other regions of the Midi.

The willingness to accept alternative forms and thus to reflect in some degree the linguistic variety of Old Provençal is both a virtue and a shortcoming in our grammarian. It is a virtue in that it caused Faidit to avoid the dogmatism of a Raimon Vidal and to approach more closely the spirit of the linguistic usage of the troubadours. It is a shortcoming in that the absence of any criterion for the selection and rejection of forms—even a dogmatic criterion— makes the linguistic basis of the *Donatz* a fluctuating one. It is not a grammar of the language of the troubadours. It is not a grammar of the spoken language of a single area. Rather, it mingles elements of both in a personal amalgam, the exact proportions and composition of which cannot be accurately gauged.

This is perhaps to judge the *Donatz* by too rigorous and too modern a standard. Faidit's manner of exposition precluded the enunciation of general criteria of linguistic correctness or incorrectness, no doubt because he never in fact mentioned a form in order to reject it. It is possible that he was hardly conscious of any such criteria: certainly his principal aim seems to have been inclusiveness, subject only to the chances of accidental omissions and incomplete information.

By the standards of even an elementary modern grammar, of course, the *Donatz* is seriously defective. It concentrates on morphology and vocabulary to the exclusion of any information about pronunciation and syntax. Its treatment of declension and conjugation omits a number of important matters of some difficulty. Its manner of exposition is sometimes confused and inconsequential. Its reliance on the traditional categories of Latin grammar seems to us altogether excessive. But many of these defects derive from the situation in which Faidit was writing and from his somewhat limited original purpose of composing a grammar for two Italian noblemen. He could assume in his readers an acquaintance with the basic elements of Latin grammar, which thus constituted a framework of accepted and unambiguous terminology: if forms were labelled nominative or accusative or optative or subjunctive, it was not necessary to explain or illustrate the syntactical functions of these categories, which were assumed to be the same in Provençal as in Latin. The grammarian had, therefore, a practical as well as a theoretical reason for adhering as closely as possible to the framework of Latin grammar and for explicitly noting his occasional departures from this norm. Again, the fact that Faidit was writing for Italians allowed him to assume a community of syntactical forms between the two vernaculars—an assumption which the translator made explicit in his note on the passive (cf. above, p. 64). And, in all probability, the grammarian could assume that his readers' interest in the Provençal language was stimulated predominantly by contact with lyric poetry—no doubt as much by the performances of jongleurs as by the circulation of manuscript copies—so that a certain (perhaps only approximate) knowledge of pronunciation could be taken for granted. The main needs of Italians with a dilettante interest in Provençal would be for instruction in vocabulary and in morphology, especially the morphology of the two-case system and of those tenses of verbs which showed a high proportion of irregular forms: it is precisely for these needs that the *Donatz* caters most successfully. Within these limits—which are essentially limitations of time and place—Faidit's grammar is reasonably systematic, reasonably complete, and strikingly free from dogmatism.

IX. THE FORTUNES OF THE *DONATZ*

FAIDIT'S grammar seems to have had some degree of currency in Italy up to the early fourteenth century. Not only do we have three copies from this period, but the text was utilized by the anonymous author of the Provençal–Italian glossary in MS. *B* (cf. above, p. 64) and probably by the compiler of the rhyme-list, a fragment of which is preserved in MS. *L* (cf. above, p. 52). It is possibly also in this same period that we should place the compilation of the revised version, now represented solely by MS. *C*; its anonymous author showed no wide acquaintance with the Provençal language and may well have been an Italian (cf. above, pp. 45–6). There is no evidence that the text of the *Donatz* was known outside Italy in this period or that it was known or used anywhere in the course of the following two centuries. But for some of the Italian humanists of the mid-sixteenth century, with their antiquarian curiosity about troubadour poetry, the *Donatz* had a real interest as a source of linguistic information. It is to this interest that we owe, not only MSS. *C* and *D*, but the two Italian translations and the Italian abstract of the work (cf. pp. 6–8). This interest was not totally lost in Italy in the seventeenth and eighteenth centuries: the *Donatz* was known to Federico Ubaldini, to Francesco Redi, to Anton Maria Salvini, to Giovanni Mario Crescimbeni, and to Antonio Bastero. It was in the latter's *Crusca provenzale* (Rome, 1724) that fragments of the *Donatz* were printed for the first time. La Curne de Sainte-Palaye seems to have been the first person outside Italy to have any knowledge of our text. In the nineteenth century Raynouard acknowledged the importance of the *Donatz*, in particular for its statement of the rules of the two-case system in nouns and adjectives. (On all these scholars, cf. Stengel, pp. xiv–xvi.) Raynouard made, however, surprisingly little use of its rich lexicographical material. In the *Lexique Roman* he cited the *Donatz* for a good number of the technical terms of grammar (e.g. *nominatiu*, iv. 320; *accusatiu*, ii. 361; *conjugazo*, iii. 600; *declinazo*, ii. 416; *substantiu*, iii. 211; etc., etc.) but he made very little use of the verb-lists and the dictionary of rhymes (*monestar*, iv. 253, and *organar*, iv. 384, are almost the only words cited).

It was Stichel, in his monograph on the lexicography of the Provençal verb, who was the first to make scientific use of the lexicographical material of the *Donatz* in order to supplement Raynouard's dictionary. Levy pursued the same path and was the first to make full use of Faidit's attestation of numerous *hapax legomena*. Both Stichel and Levy were dependent on Stengel's edition, though Levy made occasional use of the text of MS. *L* in Biadene's transcription. The lexicographical information gleaned in this way passed into Levy's *PD* and, from there and from *SW*, much of it found its way into the relevant articles of *FEW*.

The interest of the text, however, was by no means exhausted by these scholars. Levy utilized all the material available to him—Stengel, Biadene, the various textual and interpretative comments evoked by Stengel and by Guessard's second edition—but was necessarily at the mercy of misprints and errors of transcription in Stengel's text; and, especially in the earlier part of *SW*, he did not always derive from the *Donatz* all the information which it will give. The same is true of the earlier volumes of the *FEW*; and von Wartburg, in his turn, was dependent on Stengel's text and on Levy's interpretations of it. For the last eighty years, in fact, interest in the *Donatz* has been largely limited to lexicographers. It has elicited no response from textual critics—Avalle is a solitary exception, cf. above, p. 11 n. 1—and no new edition has appeared since that of Stengel.

These facts have in a large measure determined the nature of the present edition. Its first aim is evidently that of establishing a critical text. Its second aim is to elucidate the text in the light of the linguistic material now available to students of Old Provençal, a body of material far greater than that which was available to earlier scholars. Its third aim is to apply these elucidations in the lexicographical sphere, both in so far as they serve linguistic history and in so far as they serve the interpretation of literary texts. It is for these reasons that the notes are discursive and the glossary full. They serve the dual purpose of eliciting from the *Donatz* the rich information which it contains and of drawing conclusions from the interpretation of that material.

X. BIBLIOGRAPHY AND ABBREVIATIONS

Aalma = *Recueil général des lexiques français du moyen âge (XIIe–XVe siècle)*, I: *Lexiques alphabétiques*, ed. M. Roques, vol. 2, Paris, 1938.
Abavus = id., vol. 1, Paris, 1936.
Adams = E. L. Adams, *Word-formation in Provençal*, New York, 1913.
AdM = *Annales du Midi*, Toulouse, 1889– .
Anglade = J. Anglade, *Grammaire de l'ancien provençal*, Paris, 1921.
Appel, *Chrestomathie* = C. Appel, *Provenzalische Chrestomathie*, 6th ed., Leipzig, 1930.
Appel, *Inedita* = C. Appel, *Provenzalische Inedita aus Pariser Handschriften*, Leipzig, 1890.
Appel, *Lautlehre* = C. Appel, *Provenzalische Lautlehre*, Leipzig, 1918.
Bartsch = K. Bartsch, [review of Stengel], *ZRP* ii, 1878, pp. 133–6.
Bauquier = J. Bauquier, 'Sur le *Donat proensal*', *Rom.* vi, 1877, pp. 450–3.
Baxter–Johnson = J. H. Baxter and C. Johnson, *Medieval Latin Wordlist from British and Irish Sources*, London, 1934. (Revised by R. E. Latham, London, 1965.)
Biadene = L. Biadene, 'Las Razos de trobar e lo Donatz proensals secondo la lezione del ms. Landau', *Studj di filologia romanza*, i, 1885, pp. 337–402; ii, 1887, pp. 93–5.
Blaise = A. Blaise, *Dictionnaire latin–français des auteurs chrétiens*, Strasbourg, 1954.
Bloch–Wartburg = O. Bloch and W. von Wartburg, *Dictionnaire étymologique de la langue française*, 4th ed., Paris, 1964.
Brunel, *Chartes*, i, ii = *Les Plus Anciennes Chartes en langue provençale*, ed. C. Brunel, Paris, 1926; *Supplément*, Paris, 1952.
Chabaneau (*RLR* xiii) = C. Chabaneau, [review of Stengel], *RLR* xiii, 1878, pp. 138–46.
Chabaneau (*Rom.* vi) = C. Chabaneau, 'Sur les glossaires provençaux de Hugues Faidit', *Rom.* vi, 1877, pp. 136–41.
Chirurgia = U. Cianciòlo, 'Il compendio provenzale verseggiato della Chirurgia di Ruggero da Salerno', *Archivum Romanicum*, xxv, 1941, pp. 1–85.
Croisade = *La Chanson de la Croisade contre les Albigeois*, ed. P. Meyer, 2 vols., Paris, 1875–9. (The edition by E. Martin-Chabot, *La Chanson de la Croisade albigeoise*, 3 vols., Paris, 1931, 1957, 1961, has also been consulted.)

DCELC = J. Corominas, *Diccionario crítico etimológico de la lengua castellana*, 4 vols., Berne, 1954–7.

DEI = C. Battisti and G. Alessio, *Dizionario etimologico italiano*, 5 vols., Florence, 1950–7.

Deux mss. prov. = J. B. Noulet and C. Chabaneau, *Deux Manuscrits provençaux du XIVe siècle*, Montpellier and Paris, 1888.

Dicc. Aguiló = *Diccionari Aguiló. Materials lexicogràfics revisats i publicats sota cura de* P. Fabra *i* M. de Montoliu, 8 vols., Barcelona, 1903–34.

Dicc. Alcover = A. M. Alcover and F. de B. Moll, *Diccionari català-valencià-balear*, 10 vols., Barcelona, 1930–62.

Diez, *EtWb* = F. C. Diez, *Etymologisches Wörterbuch der romanischen Sprachen*, 5th ed., Bonn, 1887.

Donatus = *Donati De Partibus Orationis Ars Minor*, in H. Keil, *Grammatici latini*, 7 vols. and supplement, Leipzig, 1857–70: vol. 4, pp. 355–66. (Reference is by volume, page, and line.)

d'Ovidio, F., 'Che il Donato provenzale sia stato scritto in Italia e nella seconda metà del sec. XIII', *GSLI* ii, 1884, pp. 1–27. (Reprinted, in an extended form, in the author's *Versificazione italiana e arte poetica medioevale*, Milan, 1910, pp. 359–424, and in his *Versificazione romanza: poetica e poesia medioevale*, vol. 2 (= *Opere*, vol. ix. 2), Naples, 1932, pp. 157–215.)

Du Cange = C. Du Cange, *Glossarium mediae et infimae latinitatis*, ed. L. Favre, 10 vols., Niort, 1883–7.

FEW = W. von Wartburg, *Französisches etymologisches Wörterbuch*, Tübingen, then Bâle, 1922– .

Fierabras = *Der Roman von Fierabras, provenzalisch*, ed. I. Bekker, Berlin, 1829.

Flamenca = *Le Roman de Flamenca*, in *Les Troubadours*, ed. R. Lavaud and R. Nelli, Paris, 1960, pp. 619–1063. (Reference is also made to the 2nd ed. of P. Meyer, Paris, 1901.)

Flutre = L. F. Flutre, *Table des noms propres avec toutes leurs variantes figurant dans les romans du moyen âge écrits en français ou en provençal*, Poitiers, 1962.

Galvani = G. Galvani [corrections to Guessard, 2nd ed.], *Opuscoli religiosi, letterarî e morali*, series iii, vol. 3, 1871, pp. 323–37. (This is known to me only through the notes to Stengel.)

Girart = *Girart de Roussillon*, ed. W. M. Hackett, 3 vols., Paris, 1953–5.

Godefroy = F. Godefroy, *Dictionnaire de l'ancienne langue française*, 10 vols., Paris, 1881–1902.

Grandgent = C. H. Grandgent, *An Outline of the Phonology and Morphology of Old Provençal*, Boston, 1905.

Gröber, G., 'Zur Widmung des Donat proensal', *ZRP* viii, 1884, pp. 290–3.

BIBLIOGRAPHY AND ABBREVIATIONS 83

Gröber, G., 'Der Verfasser des Donat proensal', *ZRP* viii, 1884, pp. 112–17.

Gröber, G., 'Gaucelm Faidit o Uc de Sant Circ?' *GSLI* iv, 1884, pp. 203–8.

GSLI = *Giornale storico della letteratura italiana*, Turin, 1883– .

Guessard = F. Guessard, 'Grammaires romanes inédites, du 13ᵉ siècle, publiées d'après les manuscrits de Florence et de Paris', *Bibliothèque de l'École des Chartes*, i, 1839–40, pp. 125–203; id., *Grammaires provençales de Hugues Faidit et de Raymond Vidal de Besaudun*, Paris, 1858. (Unqualified references are to the 2nd ed.)

Jaufré = *Jaufré*, ed. C. Brunel, 2 vols., Paris, 1943. (Reference is also made to the edition by H. Breuer, Göttingen, 1925.)

Lapidaries = G. Contini, 'Due lapidarî provenzali', *Vox*, iii, 1938, pp. 253–74.

Lienig = P. Lienig, *Die Grammatik der provenzalischen Leys d'amors*, Breslau, 1890.

LR = F. Raynouard, *Lexique Roman ou dictionnaire de la langue des troubadours*, 6 vols., Paris, 1836–45.

Merlo, P., 'Sull'autore del *Donato Provenzale*. Postilla', *GSLI* iii, 1884, pp. 218–21.

Merlo, P., 'Sull'età di Gaucelm Faidit', *GSLI* iii, 1884, pp. 386–400.

Mistral = F. Mistral, *Lou Tresor dóu Felibrige ou Dictionnaire provençal–français*, 2 vols., Aix-en-Provence, 1878–86.

Mittellateinisches Wb. = *Mittellateinisches Wörterbuch bis zum ausgehenden 13. Jahrhundert*, Munich, 1959– .

MLN = *Modern Language Notes*, Baltimore, 1886– .

Niermeyer = J. F. Niermeyer, *Mediae latinitatis lexicon minus*, Leiden, 1954– .

Novum Glossarium = *Novum Glossarium mediae latinitatis ab anno DCCC usque ad annum MCC*, Copenhagen, 1957– .

Paris = G. Paris, 'Sur les glossaires du *Donat provençal*', *Rom.* i, 1872, pp. 234–6.

PC = A. Pillet and H. Carstens, *Bibliographie der Troubadours*, Halle, 1933.

PD = E. Levy, *Petit Dictionnaire provençal–français*, 2nd ed., Heidelberg, 1923.

Pfister, *Beiträge* = M. Pfister, 'Beiträge zur altprovenzalischen Grammatik', *Vox*, xvii, 1958, pp. 281–362; id., 'Beiträge zur altprovenzalischen Lexicologie I: abbatem–avunculus', *Vox*, xviii, 1959, pp. 220–96.

Priscian = *Prisciani Institutionum Grammaticarum Libri XVIII*, in H. Keil, *Grammatici latini*, 7 vols. and supplement, Leipzig, 1857- 70: vols. 2–3. (Reference is by book and paragraph.)

Recettes de Montpellier = C. Brunel, 'Recettes médicales de Montpellier en ancien provençal', *Rom.* lxxviii, 1957, pp. 289–327.
Recettes des Pyrénées = C. Brunel, *Recettes médicales, alchimiques et astrologiques du XVe siècle en langue vulgaire des Pyrénées*, Toulouse, 1956.
Recettes médicales = P. Meyer, 'Recettes médicales en provençal, d'après le MS. R. 14. 30 de Trinity College (Cambridge)', *Rom.* xxxii, 1903, pp. 268–99; C. Brunel, 'Recettes médicales du XIIIe siècle en langue de Provence', *Rom.* lxxxiii, 1962, pp. 145–82.
Recettes vétérinaires = C. Brunel, 'Recettes vétérinaires de Fréjus en ancien provençal', *Rom.* lxxxii, 1961, pp. 27–43.
REW = W. Meyer-Lübke, *Romanisches etymologisches Wörterbuch*, 3rd ed., Heidelberg, 1935.
RLR = *Revue des langues romanes*, Montpellier, 1870– .
Roland à Saragosse = *Roland à Saragosse*, ed. M. Roques, Paris, 1956.
Rom. = *Romania*, Paris, 1872– .
Ronjat = J. Ronjat, *Grammaire istorique des parlers provençaux modernes*, 4 vols., Montpellier, 1930–41.
Ronsasvals = M. Roques, 'Ronsasvals', *Rom.* lviii, 1932, pp. 1–28, 161–89; lxvi, 1940–1, pp. 433–80 (text = lviii, pp. 9–28, 161–84).
Schultz-Gora = O. Schultz-Gora, *Altprovenzalisches Elementarbuch*, 5th ed., Heidelberg, 1936.
Souter = A. Souter, *A Glossary of Later Latin to 600 A.D.*, Oxford, 1949.
Stengel = E. Stengel, *Die beiden ältesten provenzalischen Grammatiken, Lo Donatz Proensals und Las Rasos de trobar, nebst einem provenzalisch-italienischen Glossar*, Marburg, 1878.
Stichel = K. Stichel, *Beiträge zur Lexicographie des altprovenzalischen Verbums*, Marburg, 1890.
SW = E. Levy, *Provenzalisches Supplement-Wörterbuch, Berichtigungen und Ergänzungen zu Raynouards Lexique Roman*, 8 vols., Leipzig, 1894–1924.
Thurot, C., 'Notices et Extraits de divers manuscrits pour servir à l'histoire des doctrines grammaticales au moyen âge', *Notices et Extraits de la Bibliothèque Impériale*, xxii, part 2, Paris, 1868.
TL = A. Tobler and E. Lommatzsch, *Altfranzösisches Wörterbuch*, Wiesbaden, 1915– .
TLL = *Thesaurus linguae latinae*, Leipzig, 1900– .
Tobler = A. Tobler, 'Sur quelques passages des *Grammaires provençales*', *Rom.* ii, 1873, pp. 337–47.
Vox = *Vox Romanica*, Zürich, 1936– .
Wildermuth, *Die drei ältesten süd- und nordfranzösischen Grammatiken*, in *Programm des Gymnasiums in Tübingen*, Tübingen, 1857 (pp. 1–39).
ZRP = *Zeitschrift für romanische Philologie*, Halle, 1877– .

BIBLIOGRAPHY AND ABBREVIATIONS

For the troubadour editions cited, see *PC* and I. Frank, *Répertoire métrique de la poésie des troubadours*, vol. ii, Paris, 1957, pp. 89–192. Of editions which have appeared since Frank's *Répertoire*, the following are cited in the notes:

Avalle, d'A. S., *Peire Vidal, Poesie*, 2 vols., Milan and Naples, 1960.
Lavaud, R., *Poésies complètes du troubadour Peire Cardenal*, Toulouse, 1957.
Linskill, J., *The Poems of the troubadour Raimbaut de Vaqueiras*, The Hague, 1964.
Mölk, U., *Guiraut Riquier, Las Cansos*, Heidelberg, 1962.
Mouzat, J., *Les Poèmes de Gaucelm Faidit*, Paris, 1965.
Toja, G., *Arnaut Daniel, Canzoni*, Florence, 1960.

For the abbreviations used for grammatical terms, see the introductory note to the Glossary.

THE
DONATZ PROENSALS
OF UC FAIDIT

CRITICAL TEXT

Incipit Donatus Pro[v]incialis

1a

Las oit partz que om troba en gramatica troba om en vulgar provençhal, zo es: nome, pronome, verbe, adverbe, particip, conjunctios, prepositios et interjetios.

4 Nom es apelatz per ço que significa substantia ab propria qualitat o ab comuna, e largamen totas las causas a las quals Adams pauset noms poden esser noms apelladas. En nom a cinq causas: species, genus, numbre, figura, cas.

8 Speties o es primitiva ɑ es derivativa. Primitivus es apelatz lo nom que es per se e no es venguz d'alqu nome ni d'alqu verbe, si cum es *bontaz*. Der[i]vatius nom es aquel que ven d'altre loc, si cum *bos*, que ven de *bontat*, que bos non pot om esser ses bontat.

12 Genus es de cinq maneras: masculis, feminis, neutris, comus, omnis. Masculis es aquel que aperte a las masclas causas solamen, si cum:

15 *bos, mals, fals.*

1b Feminis es aquel que perte a las causas / feminils solamen, si cum:

bona, bela, mala e *falsa.*

A. *Title* proincialis   4 significa, *with* n *added above* ca, *in same ink as Latin translation*   9 dal qu u*er*be   10 Deruatius

---

DL. *Title* Donato prodensal *D*; Incipit liber quem conposuit Vgo Faiditus precibus Iacobi de mora et domini Conradi de sterleto ad dandam doctrinam uulgaris prouincialis et ad discernendum inter uerum et falsum uulgare *D*, Jncipit liber que*m* co*m*posuit vgo faidicus p*re*cibus d*o*mini Jacobi de mora *et* d*o*mini Cora çuchii (Cora çuchii *split over two lines*) de sterleto ad danda*m* doct*ri*nam uulgaris p*ro*uincialis et ad discernende jnter uerum et falsum uulgare, *in red*, *L*

1 ot *D*, oitz *L*; gramataca *D*   2–3 nome*n* uerbum aduerbium participium coniuncio preposicio interiectio *D*, nome*n* p*ro*nome*n* verbu*m* adu*er*bium participiu*m* co*n*iunctio preposi*ti*o et interiectio *L*   4 Nomen *DL*; preso *D*; que] qar *L*; substancia *D*, substancia*m L*   5 largamen] generalmen *L*; pauser *D*   6 *second* noms] nom *D*; apelatas *L*; El noms *L*   7 numerus *DL*; figura*m L*; casus *DL*   8 ces p. ò d. *D*   8–9 lo noms *D*; apelatz lo nom que es] aqel noms ques *L*   9 dalgun non *D*, dalcun autre nom *L*; dalgun *D*   10 deriuatiuus *DL*; nom es aqels *D*, es aqel noms *L*   11 bons quien da *D*; bonta *L*   12 cinc *L*; maineras *DL*; neutris] .n. et ris *D*; comunis *D*   13 Maschulis *L*; p*er*ten *D*   14 sicum es *L*   15 bons *D*; bos *et* mals e fals et leials *L*   16 aquels *D*; aperten *L*; si cum *om*. *D*, sen sicum es *L*   17 *om*. *D*; bella *L*

Octo partes orationis que inveniuntur in gramatica inveniuntur in 1a
vulgari provinciallis lingue pro maiori parte, videlicet: nomen,
pronomen, verbum, adverbium, participium, coniunctio, prepositio, interiectio. 3a
Nomen ideo dicitur quia significat substantiam cum propriam 4
qualitatem vel comunam, et largo modo omnia quibus Adam
inposuit nomina possunt nomina apellari. Nomini accidunt
quinque.
[. . .] vel est primitiva vel est derivativa. Primitivum [. . .] 8
nomen quod est per se et non derivatur ab aliquo nomine nec ab
aliquo verbo, sicut est *bonitas*. Derivativum nomen est illud quod
venit ab alio loco, sicut *bonus*, quod derivatur a *bonitate*, quia bonus
non potest esse sine bonitate. 11a
Genera sunt quinque: masculinum, femininum, neutrum, 12
comune et omnis. Masculinum est illud quod pertinet [masculinis]
rebus tantum, sicut:

bonus, malus, falsus. 15

Femininum est illud quod pertinet rebus / femininis tantum, sicut: 1b
bona, formosa, mala et *falsa*.

A. 1 in gramatica] i*n*uulgari gramatica; i*n*ueniuntur] ntu *hardly legible*
2 p*r*omaiorip*a*rte *added above* lingue   7 *no trans. above* species . . . cas
8 *no trans. above* Speties; Primitivum] primitiuim *or* primitiium; *no trans. above*
es apelatz   10 Deriuatius   11a *no trans. above* om   13 *no trans.*
above a las masclas

B. 2 provinciallis lingue] prouintiali aliqu*a*ndo   3a *after* prepositio, *et*
added above line   4–5 cum p. q. v. c.] *et* qu*a*litatem propriam u*e*l co*m*u*n*em
7 *after* quinqu*e*, B *adds* speties genus numer*u*s figura *et* casus   8 Speties
uel; *second* est *om.*   9 nom*e*n est illud qu*o*d p*er* se est; nec] u*e*l   11 alio]
aliquo   13 om*n*e; *after* masculinu*m*, B *adds* nomen   15 *after* malus,
et added above line

Neutris es aquel que no perte a l'un ni a l'autre, si cum:

gauç e bes;

20 mas aici no sec lo vulgars la gramatica els neutris substantius,
an se diçen aici cum se fossen masculi, si cum aici:

grans es lo bes que aquest m'a fait
e *grans es lo mals que m'es vengutz de lui.*

24 Comun sun aquelh que perten[en] al mascle et al feme ensems, si
cum sun li particip que fenissen in *-ans* vel in *-ens*, qu'eu pos dire:

aquest chavaliers es presans,
aquesta domna es presans,
28 *aquest cavaliers es avinens,*
aquesta dona es avinens;

mas el nominatiu plural se camia d'aitan que conven a dire:

aqelh chavalier sun avinen,
32 *aquelas donas sun avinens.*

Omnis es aquel que perte al mascle et al feme et al neutri ensems,
qu'eu posc dire:

aquest cavaliers es plasens,
36 *aquesta dona es plaçens*
et *aquest bes m'es plaisens.*

Numbres es singul[a]rs o plurals: singulars quan parla d'una
2a causa solamen, plurals quan parla de doas o de / plusors.

A. 22 los bes   24 p*e*rten   38 singl'rs

DL. 18 aquels *D*; aperten *L*; malautre *D*, ne alautre *L*; sicum es *L*
19 gaugz *D*, gaug *L*; ebens *D*   20 mais *L*; sec lo] scib *D*, set lo *L*; uulgaris
D; la gramatica *om. D*   21 ansen *D*; aisi *L*; *after* masculin, *L* adds Quia
se*cundu*m gramatica*m* non deberet poni .s. in fine sicut hic   22 granz *DL*;
lo bens *D*; qe *L*; aqest *DL*   23 granz *DL*; uenguz *DL*   24 ap*e*rtinen
L; alas femas *D*   25 participi *D*; vel] o *D*; qu'eu] que *L*   26 *om. D*;
cauualiers *L*   27 *om. D*; aqesta *L*   28 a qestz *D*, aqest *L*; caualliers
(r < s) *D*; auinenz *D*   29 a questa *D*; domna *DL*   30 ma sel *DL*;
couen *D*   31 a qeill cauaillier *D*, aquil caualer *L*; son *D*   32 a qellas
D; domnas *DL*; son *D*; auinenz (z < s) *D*, auinen *L*   33 a quels *D*;
aperten *L*; ala fema *D*; esems *D*, emsems *L*   34 pos *DL*   35 a qestz
D, aqest *L*; caualliers *D*; plazenz *D*   36 *om. L*, a questa domna es plazenz
D   37 et *om. DL*; a qestz bens *D*; plazenz *D*, plasens *L*   38 Numerus
est *D*, Numerus es apelaz *L*; o] *et L*; singular quan *L*   38–9 singulars quan
... plusors] qan parla duna causa solamen es singulars qan parla de doas es
plurals *D*

Neutrum est illud quod non pertinet masculino neque feminino, sicut:

> *gaudium* et *bonum*;

sed hic non sequitur vulgare gramaticam in neutris substantivis, sed sic dicitur, quia secundum gramatica non debet poni [*s*] in fine, sicut hic:

> *magnum est bonum quod iste michi fecit*
> et *magnum est malum quod evenit michi per illum.*

Comuna sunt illa que pertinent masculino et feminino simul, sicut sunt participia desinentia in -*ans* vel in -*ens* (et hoc secundum vulgare, quia secundum gramaticam est omnis generis), quia possum dicere:

> *iste miles est laudabillis,*
> *ista domina est laudabillis,*
> *iste miles est aptus,*
> *ista domina est apta*;

sed in nominativo plurali tantummodo mutatur quod oportet dicere ita:

> *illi milites sunt apti,*
> *ille domine sunt apte.*

Omnis est illud quod pertinet masculino et feminino et neutro simul, quia possum dicere:

> *iste miles est placens,*
> *ista domina est placens,*
> *istud bonum est michi placens.*

[. . .] est singularis vel pluralis: singularis quando loquitur de uno verbo tantum, pluralis quando loquitur de duobus vel de pluribus.

A. 20 in neutri siū substantiuus   21 no trans. above first aici; s *om.*
21–21a q*uia* . . . fine *above* cum . . . masculi   22 bo nu*m* (*above* los bes)
25–25a *uel in* ens . . . *omnis generis in double line above* vel in ens   31 illi] isti (*so* B)   34 simul] simillis   37–8 istud bonu*m* es*t* aq*u*est bes mest plasens *above* et aquest . . . plaisens; istud bonu*m* es*t* m*ic*hi placens *above* Numbres

---

B. 21 sed sic dicitur *om.*; gramaticam   23 et *om.*; m*ic*hi euenit   24 Coīa
25–25a et hoc . . . generis *om.*   25a–b possu*n*t   26 laudabilis   27 laudabilis
34 miles < milex *by expunctuation of* x *and addition of abbreviation sign for* s; actus   30a ita *om.*   31 illi] isti; acti   33 est *repeated; first* et *om.*   34⸗possu*n*t   38 Numerus est   39 uno v. t.] uno solu*mm*odo; *second* de *om.*

40 Ffigura o es simpla o composta: simpla si cum *coms*, conposta si cum *vescons*, qu'es partz composta, zo es apostiza, de *vez* e de *coms*.

Li cas sun seis: nominatius, genitius, datius, acusatius, vocatius, ablatius. Lo nominatius se conois per *lo*, si cum:

44 *lo reis es vengutz*;

genitius per *de*, si cum:

aquest destriers es del rei;

datius per *a*, si cum:

48 *mena lo destrier al rei*;

acussatius per *lo*, si cum:

eu vei lo rei armat.

E no se pot conosser ni triar l'acusatius del nominatiu sino per zo 52 que·l nominatius singulars, quan es masculis, vol -*s* en la fi e li autre cas no·l volen, e·l nominatiu plural no [lo] vol e tuit li altre cas volen lo enl plural.

Pero lo vocatius deu scenblar lo nominatiu en totas las ditios que 56 fenissen in -*ors*, et en las autras ditions que·us dirai aici:

deus, reis,
francs, pros,
bos, cavaliers,
60 *cançOs*.

Et els altres locs on lo vocatius non a -*s* en la fi, si es el semblans al nominatiu al menhz en silabas et en letras, que deu aver aitals e tantas cum lo nominatius, trait sol -*s* en la fi.

A. 53 nouol

DL. 40 sempla ò composita *D*   40–1 sicum es (*twice*) *L*   41 uescoms *DL*; ues *L*; uezed e coms *D*; *L adds* qes coinpon uescomes   42 sunt *L* 42–3 -ius] -iuus (*7 times*) *D*   43 *et* ablatius *L*   44 uenguz *DL* 45 lo genitius *D*   46 a questz *D*   47 a] al *D*   49 lo acusatius *D* 50 jeu *L*; *after 50 L adds* El vocatiu o tu segner reis se corme lablatiu eu uau ab lo rei p*er* lo rei ses lo rei del rei   51 conoisser *D*, conoiser *L*; lacusatius *with final* s *apparently expunctuated L*; dal nominatius *D*   52 nominatiu *L*; *after* masculis, *L adds* generis vel comus ou omnis; uole s, *with one letter* (s?) *erased after* uole, *D*; fin de ladiccion *L*   53 uolun *L*; nominatius *D*; plurals *DL*   54 lo uolen el *D*, uolon lo el *L*   55 las] la *D*; dicions *DL* 56 dicions *D*, dicios *L*   58 franceis *D*; pros (s < r?) *D*   59 bons *D*, bos iros *L*; caualliers *D*   60 cansons *D*, canzos *L*   61 en lautres *D* 62 nominatiu] neutro *L*; menz *D*   63 et ai tantas *D*, ententas *L*

Figura vel est simplex vel composita: simplex sicut in hac dicti- 40
one *comes*, composita sicut [in] hac dictione *viscecomes*, que est
pars composita, id est aposita, a *vice* et *comes*. 41a
Casus sunt sex. Nominativus cognoscitur per hanc silabam *lo*,
verbi gracia:
     rex venit; 44
genetivus per *de*, verbi gracia:
     iste destrarius est regis;
dativus per *a*, verbi gracia:
     duc destrarium ad regem; 48
acussativus per *lo*, verbi gracia:
     video regem armatum.

Et non potest conossi neque descerni acusativus a nominativo nisi
per hoc quod nominativus singularis, quando est masculini generis 52
vel comunis vel omnis, vult -*s* in fine dictionis et alii casus singul[ar]i[s] nolunt -*s*, et nominativus pluralis e converso non vult
-*s* in fine et omnes alii casus volunt -*s* in plurali. 54a

Tamen vocativus debet esse simillis nominativo in omnibus
dictionibus que desinunt in hac sillaba -*ors*, et in aliis dictionibus 56
quas dicam hic: 56a
    deus, rex,
    liber vel *curialis, probus,*
    bonus, miles,
    cantio. 60
Et in aliis locis ubi vocativus non habet -*s* in fine, est simillis
nominativo adminus in sillabas vel in literas, quas debet habere
tales et tot quantas nominativus, excepto solummodo -*s* in fine.

A. 40 *first* simplex] simpla   41 in *om*.   42 *no trans. above* nominatius ... ablatius   49 lo] la   52 quando] qu*a*udo   53–4 si*n*guli
54 *after* nolu*n*t .s., *A adds in*plurali

B. 41 uiscomes   41a apostiza; et *om*.   42 *after* sex, *B adds* nomi-
*n*atiuus geniti*uu*s dacti*uu*s acusati*uu*s vocati*uu*s *et* ablati*uu*s   45 genitiuus;
per de *om*.   47 per a *om*.   48 ad regem] regi   49 per lo *om*.
50 ego uidi   51 discerni nec *c*ognosci accusati*uu*ʒ   53–4 singularis *om*.
54 -s et] el; e converso *om*.; vult *om*.   54a omnes *om*.; nolu*n*t   55 simil-
lis] psuralis (ps *is perhaps* p *altered to* s)   56 in ha*n*c sillabam   60 canzio
62 sill's *et* in l'ris

2b Pero de la regla on fo dit desus que·l / nominatius cas no vol -s en
la fi quan es pluralis numeri, voilh traire fors toiz los feminis, que
non es dit mas solamen dels masculis e dels neutris, que sun
scenblan el plural per totz locs, sitot s'es contra gramatica.
E lai on fo dit del nominatiu singular que vol -s pertot a la fi,
voilh traire fors toiz aquelz que fenissen en -*aire*, si cum:

> *enperaire, amaire,*

et en -*eire*, si cum:

> *Peire, beveire,*
> *radeire, tondeire,*
> *pencheire, fencheire,*
> *bateire, foteire,*
> *prendeire, teneire,*

et en -*ire*, si cum:

> *traïre, conssentire,*
> *escarnire, escremire,*
> *ferire, gronire;*

mas *albires* vol -*s* e *conssires* e *desires*.

E devez saber que tut aquelh que·us ai dit, don lo nominatius
singulars fenis en -*aire* et en -*eire* [et en -*ire*], fenissen totz lor cas
singulars en -*dor*, trait lo vocatius, qe semla lo nominatiu, si cum
es dit desus.

Et de la regla del nominatiu singular que vol -*s* a la fi, voilh
ancar traire fors:

A. 76 prendreire   79 Es tremire   81 e c.] es *cons*sires   83 et en ire *om*.

DL. 64 fon dich *D*; no *om. D*   65 quant *D*; numeri] nom *L*; voilh] se uol *D*, uollz *L*; totz *DL*   66 dich *D*; solamentz *L*; des m. *D*   64–7 *to the left of this passage, interlinear and very slightly into the left margin,* qa / proen / gir (*or* guz) *L*   68 fonc *D*, fon *L*; dic *D*   69 totz *DL*; a quels *D*; aquelz noms qe *L*   70 emperaire *DL*; *L adds* edoneiaire   71 sicum es *L*   73 raeire *L, om. D*; doneire *D*   74 pe*n*heire fenheire *D*, peheire .i. perictor fe*n*heire *L*   76 prendere tenire *L*   77 elas rismas qe fenisez en ire si cum es *L*   78 consentire *DL*   79 escarmir *L*; escrimire, *placed after* ferire, *L*   81 mas aquelas rimas que fan in ires sicum es albires *L*; e consires *D*, enconsires *L*; *D adds* a qist iij. son trait dela regola   82 tuit *DL*; a qill *D*; nominatiu *L*   83 lor cas] los cas dels oblics *L*   84 dor] doz *D*; *after* dor *L adds* sicom es adire lemperaire delenperador amaire delamador lobeiuer del beuedor lo ferire del feridor; los uocatius *L*, .v. *D*; sembla lo nominatius *D*, deuon semblar los nominatius *L*   85 es] e *D*   86 Et *om. DL*; reg*u*la *D*; s *erased after* nominatiu *D*, nominatius *L*; voilh] uoluh *L*   87 encar *D*

LATIN TEXT

Tamen de regula ubi fuit dictum superius quod / nominativus 2b
casus [non] vult -s in fine dictionis quando est pluralis numeri, 65
volo excipere omnes dictiones femini[ni] generis, quia non est
dictum nisi de mascul[in]is et de neutris, que sunt similia in plurari
per omnia loca, quamvis sint contra gramaticam. 67a
Et ubi fuit dictum [de] nominativo singulari quod vult -s semper 68
in fine, volo excipere omnia illa nomina que finiunt in -*aire*, verbi
gracia: 69a
> *imperator, amator,*

et en -*eire*, verbi gracia:
> *Petrus, potator,* 72
> *qui radit barbas, tonsor,*
> *pinctor, fintor,*
> *percussor, qui frequenter concubit cum mulieribus,*
> *qui libenter accipit, tenax,* 76

[et in -*ire*,] verbi gracia:
> *traditor, qui consentit,*
> *derisor, cautus cum armis,*
> *percussor, qui frequenter gronit;* 80

sed ab illa [regula] excipiuntur ista tria: *albires, consires* et *desires.*
Et debetis sire quod omnes dictiones supradicte, de quibus
nominativus singularis finit in -*aire* et in -*eire* [et in -*ire*], finiunt
omnes alios casus singularis in -*dor*, excepto vocativo qui est similis 84
nominativo, sicut superius dictum est.
Et de illa regula que dicit quod nominativus singularis vult -s in
fine dictionis, volo adhuc excipere istas dictiones:

A. 65 non *om.*; qua*n*to 66 femini (*so* B) 67 no trans. above
solamen; del masculi*s* (*sim.* B) 67a quantuis 68 de *om.*
69 que] q3 73 qui] q*ue* 75 ml'ib*us* 77 no trans. above et en ire
78 q*u*i co*n*sentire 81 regula *om.* 83 et in ire *om.* (*cf. Prov.*) 84 est
similis] semla 87 istas dict*io*nis

B. 66 femini 67 masculi*s* 67a sint] sit 71 et in hac dictione
eire 74 p*er*itor; fictor 75 cum mulieribus *om.* 76 accepit
77 et in hac dictione ire 79 cantus 80 grorijt 81 albires
... desires *om.* 85 sic*ut* dictum est sup*er*ius 86 uul't

88 *maestre, prestre,*
pastre, sener,
melher, peier,
sordeier, maier,
92 *menre, sor,*
bar, gençer,
leuger, greuger,

e totz los ajectius neutris quan sun pausat senes sustantiu, si cum:

3a *mal m'es, | greu m'es,*
97 *fer m'es, esquiu m'es,*
estranh m'es qu'el aia dit mal de me.

E voilh en traire fors encar dels pronoms alcus, si cum:

100 *eu, tu, el,*
qui, aquel, ilh,
cel, aicel, aquest,
nostre, vostre,

104 que no volon -*s* en la fi, e sun del nominatiu singular.

Tres declinazos sun; e·l nominatius cas de la primeira fenis en -*a*, e tut li altre cas eissemen—del singular devez entendre, car el plurar volun li cas -*s* en la fi trastut. Tut li ajectiu femini dels qals
108 lo nominatius singulars fenis en -*a*, si cum es:

bona, bela, cointa, gaia,

seguen aquella meesma regla. E tut aquelh de la prima declinaço sun feminini, trait:

A. 102 aicel] aitel   104 sun] sim, *with* i *clearly marked*   105 e·l] En
106 eis sem*en*

DL. 88 pestre *D*   89 seingner *D*, senher *L*   90 meillez *D*, meiller, *placed after* maier, *L*   91 sordoier .i. deterior *L*; maier *om. D*   92 mere *L*   93 gencer *L*, *om. D*   94 leugier gresiger .i. grauior *L*; *after* 94 *L adds* et jn enre sicum menre penre tenre   95 tot *D*; qant *D*; substantiu *DL*   96 *first* mes *apparently altered from* mos *L*   97 esquimes *D*, *om. L*   98 estraing *D*; *after 98 L adds* Tug aquist son appellat qe ains vos ai dig desobre agectiu   99 ancara *D*; sicum es *L*   100 eu .i. ego *L*
101-2 qui *om. L*; cui à quell ill cel ai ceill a queste *D*, cel aicel .i. ille aqest aqel ill cill acill *L*   104 uolun *L*; son *D*; n. cas s. *L*   105 nominatiu *L*; primera *D*, primeira declinason *L*   106 tuit *DL*; eissamen *D*, essamen *L*; car] quant *D*   107 enlo plural uolon licas .s. daqesta declinason enlafin *L*; Tuit *DL*; femini *repeated L*; dels] del *L*   108 nominatiu *L*
109 bella *DL*   110 medesima *L*; regula *D*; tuit *DL*; aqill *L*; premeira declinasons *D*, prima declinazon li cas singular qe fenissen in a *L*   111 feminin *D*, femini *L*

> *magister, presbiter,* 88
> *pastor, dominus,*
> *melior, peior,*
> *deterior, maior,*
> *minor, soror,* 92
> *baro, pulcrior,*
> *levior, gravior,*

et omnia nomina adiectiva neutri generis, quando ponuntur sine substantivo, excipiuntur ab illa regla, verbi gracia: 95a

> *malum est michi, | grave est michi,* 3a
> *ferrum est michi, inoportunum est michi,* 97
> *alienum est michi quod ille dixerit malum de me.*

Et volo excipere adhuc aliqua pronomina, verbi gracia:

> *ego, tu, ille,* 100
> *qui, ille, illa* vel *ille,*
> *ille,* [. . .], *iste,*
> *noster, vester,*

que no[n] volunt *-s* in fine dictionis, et sunt nominativi singulari[s]. 104

Tres declinationes sunt; et nominativus casus prime declinationis finit in *-a*, et omnes allii casus similiter—in singulari debetis intelligere, quia in plurali volunt omnes casus *-s* in fine. Omnia adiectiva feminini generis quorum nominativus singularis finit in 108 *-a*, verbi gracia: 108a

> *bona, pulcra, apta, leta,*

secuntur eandem regulam. Et omnes dictiones prime declinationis sunt feminini generis, excepto:

A. 97 jnoponatum 102 no trans. above aitel 104 no; singulari
105 Tres declinationis 110 sectantur

B. 90 prior 95–95a quando p. sine s.] que ponitur sub substantiuo, *placed after* regula 95a regula 97 ferum; inoportunum est michi *om.*
101 qui illi *uel* ille *only* 104 non *om.*; nominativi] numeri (nũi, *as in l. 65*); singulis (= singularis, *as in ll. 86, 127*) 105 et n. c.] in nominatiuo casu
108 femini; quorum] qrum 109 acta 110 secuntur] sequitur; *after* regulam, *B adds* supradictam

112 *propheta, gaita,*
esquiragaita, papa.

Pero *propheta* e *papa* no volun -*s* el nominatiu plural, mas en totz los autres cas lo volun. Celh que fenissen in -*ans* vel in -*ens*, quan
116 s'ajusten [ab femini substantiu, volun -*s*, el vocatiu, a la fi; mas quan s'ajusten] ab masculi substantiu, no lo volun.

De la prima declinatio es:

savieza, cortesia,
120 *dreitura, mesura,*

e tut l'autre que fenissen en -*a*, sion adjectiu o substantiu. [D]e la secunda:

deus, segner, maestre,

124 e tut li nom breumen que no volun -*s* el nominatiu plural et en
3b totz los autres cas lo vo/lun. De la terza sun tut li particip que fenissen in -*ans* et in -*ens*, e tut li nom don lo nominatius singulars e·l nominatius plurals fenissen in -*atz*, e sun femini[ni] generis, si
128 cum:

bontatz, beutatz,
santatz, amistatz,

e mout autre. En vulgar non trop mas d'aquestas tres maineras
132 [de] declinazos qu'eu ai dit desus.

A. 116-17 ab femini ... s'ajusten *om.*   121 fenis sen   121-2 Ela se*cu*nda
127 femini   132 de *om.* (*so L*)

DL. 112 egaita *L*   113 esquiragaita *om. D*; *et* es qergaita epapa *L*
114 uolon *L*; el] enlafin del *L*   115 uolon *DL*   116 saiosten *D*; feminin *D*; uolon *L*; -s *om. D*; *after* vocatiu, *D adds* .s.; fin *L*; mas *om.*
D   117 quant sa uisten *D*; masculins *D*; uolon *DL*, *after which L adds* de *pri*ma declinat*ione*, *in red*   118 premeira *D*; s *erased after* declinason *D*, declinazion *L*   119 sauienssa (ui < iu) *D*   120 mesura *om. L*
121 tuit llautre *D*; lautre nom qe *L*; *after* substantiu, *L adds* de se*cu*nda de., *in red*
122 seconda declinazon es *L*   123 seingner *D*; *after 123 L adds* etug liagectiui qes declinon p*er* tres articles sicum es hic *et* hec *et* hoc felicx
124 tuit *DL*; uolon *L*   125 aures, *with* t *added above* r, *L*; lo] los *L*; uolon *DL*, *after which L adds* de te*r*cia decl'i, *in red*; terza declinazon son *L*; tuit *D*, tug *L*; participi *D*   126 *after* ens, *L adds* sicum es hic *et* hec *et* hoc amans *et* hic *et* hec *et* hoc legens e tug aqill que se declinon p*er* tres dictions sicum es bonus bona bonu*m* malus mala malu*m* lap*ri*miera diccion elatersa sun de laseconda declinason la segonda diccios es dela p*ri*miera declinason; tuit *DL*; nominatiu *L*   127 nominatiu *L*; sum *D*; femenin *D*, femini *L*; generis *om. DL*   128 cum es *L*   129 bontaz *DL*; beutaz *L*   130 sanitatz *or* sanctatz *D*, santaz *L*; amistaz *L*   131 autres *L*; trob *D*; manieras *L*
132 de *om. L*

LATIN TEXT

propheta, speculator, 112
excubie, papa.

Propheta et *papa* non volunt *-s* in nominativo plurali, sed in omnibus aliis casibus volunt. Dictiones finientes in *-ans* vel in *-ens*, quando coniunguntur [cum feminino substantivo, volunt in voca- 116 tivo *-s* in fine; quando coniunguntur cum masculino substantivo, nolunt.] 117a
De prima declinatione est:

sapientia, curialitas (vulgari),
iustitia, mensura, 120

et omnia alia nomina finientia in *-a*, sive sint adiectiva sive substantiva. De secunda sunt ista nomina:

deus, dominus, magister,

et omnia nomina breviter que nolunt *-s* in nominativo plurali in 124 fine dictionis sed in omnibus aliis casibus volunt. / Tercie declina- 3b tionis sunt omnia participia desinentia in *-ans* vel in *-ens*, et omnia nomina quorum nominativus singularis et nominativus pluralis desinunt in *-atz*, et sunt feminini generis, verbi gracia: 128

bonitas, pulcritudo,
sanitas, amicitia,

et plura alia nomina. In vulgari non invenio nisi tres modos declinationum quos dixi superius. 132

A. 114 *no trans. above* Pero 116–117a cum feminino ... nolunt *om.* (*cf. Prov.*) 117–117a *no trans. above* ab masculi ... no lo uolun 119–20 curialitas *above* cortesia; uulgari *iu*stitia *above* dreitura 124 no lunt (*above* no uolun) 131 *no trans. above* daquestas 132 quos] quem

---

B. 112 speculator *om.* 113 excubie *om.* 114 P. et p. non v.] tam*en* uolu*nt* 114–15 in alijs om*n*ibus 118 De *om.* 119 vulgari *om.* 121 et *om.* 123 *et* ma*g*is*t*er 124 breviter *om.*; uolu*n*t 128 atz] as 132 quos] q*ue with abbreviation sign for* s *added*

Sun d'autra manera nom que no se declinon, si cum es *vers*, ab totz sos compost, e tut li adjectiu que fenissen in -*os*, si cum:

amoros, enveios,

136 trait *pros* e *bos*. E tuit aquel que fenissen in -*as* larg no se declinon ni·s mudon, sion substantiu o sion adjectiu, si cum:

nas, pas,
vas, ras;

140 e *cortes* sec aquela regla meçeisma, e

pes, contrapes,
sirventes, cens,
encens, deves,
144   *mes, borses,*
des, bles,
marques, bres,
gles, comes,
148   *escomes* e *pres*, ab totz sos compostz;

e tuit li nom provincial que fenissen in -*es*, si cum:

Fra[n]ces, Angles,
Genoes, Polhes

152 (e tut aquest sobredit fenissen in -*es* estreit); d'aquelz que fenissen in -*es* larg:

confes;

4a encaras, d'aquel[s] in -*as* / larg fenissen, no se declinon:

156   *bas, cas,*
gras, clas,

A.   150 fraces   155 da quel

DL.   133 Et sun *D*, Esun *L*; mainera *DL*   134 tut] tuit *DL*; sicum es *L*   135 emieios *D*   136 a qeill *D*, aquelli diction *L*; o sion adiectiu ò sion substantiu *placed after* larg *D*   137 substatiu *L*   140 regla mees ma *D*, medesma regla *L*   141 econtrapes *D*, contra pes *L*   142 cens siruentes *L*   143 ences *L*   144 borges *D*   145 desbles *D*, bles deues des *L*   146 marqes *L*   146-7 bres *and* gles *interverted L*   148 e *om. D*; compost *DL*, *after which L adds et* aqist sopradit que van aissi seguen aqella meteisma regla   149 e *om. D*; *after* prouincial, *L adds* qe se deriuon delas prouincias   151 jenoes *L*; polles *D*, ponjhes *L*   152 tuit *D*   152-3 estreit ... in -es *om. D*   *after* 153 *L adds* sicum es   154 co*n*fes ades portes *L*   155 ancaras *D*; da quels *D*; daqels que fenissen inas larg *L*; no se] nos sen *D*; *after 155 L adds* sicum es

LATIN TEXT

Et sunt alterius generis nomina que non declinantur, sicut est *versus*, cum omnibus suis compositis, et omnia adiectiva desinentia in *-os*, verbi gracia: 134a

amorosus, invidus,

excepto *probus* et *bonus*. Et omnes ille dictiones que desinunt in hac 136 sillaba larga non declinantur neque mutantur, vel sint nomina substantiva vel sint adiectiva, verbi gracia: 137a

*nasus, passus,
tumulus, rasus;*

et *urbanus* sequitur illam regulam eandem, et 140

*pondus, contrapondus,
cantio facta vituperio alicuius, census,
incensum, locus defensus,
mensis, burgensis,* 144
disscus, qui non potest sonare nisi c,
marchio, lignum quo aves capiunt[*ur*],
*glis animal, provocatus,
provocatus* et *captus,* cum omnibus suis compositis; 148

et omnia nomina que derivantur a provinciis que desinunt in hac sillaba, verbi gracia: 149a

*Francigena, Anglicus,
Genuensis, Apulus*

(et omnia ista nomina supradicta desinunt in hac sillaba stricta); 152 de his que finiunt in hac sillaba larga:

confessus;

adhuc, de his que in hac sillaba / larga desinunt, non declina[n]tur 4a ista: 155a

bassus, casus, 156
pinguis, campanarum concordatio,

A. 136 prob3   142 census] casus   146 lignum quod aues capiunt   147 glis] sl'i; pro uocatus   148 pro uocatus   146–8 trans. misplaced: quod aues capiunt above gles; sl'i animal above comes; first pro uocatus above escomes; second pro uocatus in right margin   151 apulis   153 de his que] da que (above da quel); declinatur   157 caml'anarum only, above clas

B. 134a os] us   135 invidus] surdus   137 sint] sunt   137a sint] sunt   138 passus] pulsus   140 illam et eandem regulam   143 jncensus   145 discus; qui . . . nisi c om.   146 quo] que, with abbreviation sign struck through   147–8 prouocatus once only   153 finiunt] desinunt; after larga, B adds est indeclinabilis   157 concordia campanorum

PROVENÇAL TEXT

	las, mas.
Tals es:	
160	mescaps, Acs,
	fals, Bautz,
	deschautz, cautz,
	falz, encautz,
164	lanz, fars,
	ars, martz,
	latz, glatz,
	jatz, patz,
168	aus, claus (compost),
	laus, raus,
	ais, cais,
	fais, lais,
172	tais, brais,
	Clavais, melhz,
	fems, tems,
	Rems;
176 in -ers larg:	guers, dispers,
	Bezers, Lumbers;
in -ers estreit:	
	ders, aers,
180	aders;
	gris, paradis,
	Sanc Danis, assis,
	Paris, ris,
184	vis, berbiz,
	ops, pols,
	Aiols, doulz,

A. 160 mes. caps (*so L*)   167 jatz] latz (*so D*)   182 damis (i *not marked*)

DL. 160 mes. caps. aics *L*   161 bauz *DL*   162 descauz *D*, descaitz *L*; cauz *D*   163 faltz *L*; encauz *DL*   164 laitz *L*   165 marz *D*   166 laz glaz *D*, laitz glaitz *L*   167 jatz] latz *D*; *after* patz, *L adds* catz   168 clauz *D*   170 ais gais cais *L*   172 brais] bais *D*   173 meillz *D*, melliz *L*   176 guezs despers *D*   177 beiers *D*; lunbers *L*   178 in ers *om*. *D*   179 aers ders *DL*   181 Jnis gris *L*   182 sanzdanis *D*, san daunis *L*   184 uiz berbis *D*, vis Jnitz berbitz ditz contraditz *L*   185 ops] obs *D*, Jnobs gobs lobs Jnols sols *L*   186 doutz *L*, *om. D*

lassus, mansum ubi rustici mane[*nt*].

Tale est istud:

[. . .], *civitas*, 160
falsus, castrum,
discalciatus, pro *calce,*
pro *falce, fuga,*
iactus, farsura, 164
arsus, dies Martis vel *mensis marcii,*
nexus vel *nodus, glacies,*
lectus, pax,
vellus, clausus, 168
pro *laude* vel pro *stagno, arundo,*
tabula, gena,
onus, dulcis cantus,
animal, avium clamor, 172
castellum, melius,
fimus, tempus,
civitas;
strabo, dispersus, 176
civitas, castellum;

in hac sillaba stricta:

erectus, [. . .],
conreaz; 180
[. . .], [. . .],
[. . .], *assetaz* vel *obssessus,*
civitas vel proprium nom[en] viri, *risus,*
facies, ovis, 184
opus, pulsus,
proprium nomen, *dulcis,*

A. 158 ma*n*su*m* ubi co*n*cordatio rustici mane *above* mas 159–60 istud *above* mes; mescaps *above* caps 168 *no trans. above* compost 169 anu*n*do 176 *no trans. above* In ers larg 179 *no trans. above* aers 180 co*n*rea3 181–2 *no trans. above* gris paradis sanc damis 182 assetaz] assotam 183 nom ūı

B. 158 lassus] las; mansum . . . manent *om.* 159 ista 160 . . .] p*r*elium pauco*rum contra* multos; civitas *om.* 162 discaltiatus 164 farse*r*a 165 vel mensis marcii *om.* 166 glaties 167 lectus] lectus. fere 168 *after* clausus, B *adds* prola (1 *uncertain*) 169 laude] laudis; arundo *om.* (*after* stagno, *a space equivalent to about 8 letters*) 171 dulcis. cantus 172 clamor auium 176 strabo *om.* 179 *before* erectus, B *adds* erers (*or* erer *with* x *added above*) 180 coream 182–3 obcessus. assecta*m* uel propriu*m* nom*en* uiri. ciuitas hic risus 184 facies] uisus 185 ͮ pulsus *om.*

       poutz, soutz,
188   *gergons, gergons;*
 in -*ors* larg: *cors, mors;*
       cors, socors,
       ors, sors,
192   *resors, bis,*
       lis, alis,
       crotz, notz,
       potz, Burcs,
196   *plus, reclus,*
       conclus, confus,
       pertus,
       Dedalus, Tantalus,
200   *us, fus,*
       Artus, Cerberus.

E tut aquest qu'eu ai dit desus no se declinon ni·s mudon ni en singular ni en plural, e coren per totz cas egalmen.

204 Pronomen es aici apelatz quar es en loc de propri nome pausatz, e demostra certa persona, si cum:

       eu, tu, el,
       cel, aicel,
208   *aquel, aquest,*
4b   *eu meçeismes, tu meceis/mes, el meçeismes,*
       eu esteus, tu esteus, el esteus,
       eu eis, tu eis, el eis,
212   *meus, teus, seus,*
       nostre, vostre.

A. 188 greg*n*os. gergons 189–90 cors. mors. In ors. larg. cors. socors 203 en eplural

---

DL. 187 pouz solz *D* 188 g. g.] geigons *D*, Jnontz gergomz estronz pontz, *placed after 189, L* 189 in ors larg *om. D* 190 *om. L* 190–2 cors . . . resors *placed after* alis (*193*) *D* 191–2 Jn ors estreg ors sors resors *placed after* alis (*193*) *L* 193 alis, *with* i *added above between* a *and* l, *L* 194 croz noz *D* 195 poz *D*; buris *L* *after* 201 *D repeats* pertus (*198*) 202 E *om. D*; a qist *D*; qu'eu] quio *L*; ni] nien *L* 204 apelatz pronom*en* qar *L*; nom *DL* 205 sicum es *L* 208 àquest *D*; aqest aqel *L* 209 eumez eis *only D*, eumes eismes tu mei eismes el meiseismes *L* 210 eu e. tu e.] tueus *D* 212 tuus *D*; seus *placed after* uostre *D*; *after* seus, *L adds* nos *et* uos

pultes: esca de farina, carnes vel pisses in aceto,
[...], *vulgare trutanorum;* 188
corpus, morsus;
cursus, auxilium,
ursus, de *surgo,*
de *resurgo, quedam color,* 192
levis, azimus,
crux, nux,
puteus, civitas,
[...], *reclusus,* 196
conclusus, confusus,
foramen,
proprium nomen,
usus, instrumentum nendi, 200
proprium nomen, ianitor inferni.

Et omnia ista nomina supradicta sunt indeclinabilia nec mutantur in singullari neque in plurali, et currunt ita per omnes casus equaliter. 203a

Pronomen est ita apellatum quia loco proprii nominis ponitur, 204 et ostendit certam personam, verbi gracia:

ego, tu, ille,
ille, ille,
ille, iste, 208
ego ipse, tu ipse, / ille ipse, **4b**
item alio modo: [...], *tu ipse, ille ipse,*
item alio modo idem,
meus, tuus, suus, 212
noster et *vester.*

A. 187 pultes osca carnes *uel* de farina *above* poutz; pisses *in* aceto *above* soutz   188 ...] gregnonum, *above* gregnos   189 *no trans. above* In ors larg   193 aizmus   192–3 *trans. misplaced:* quedam *above* bis; color *above* lis; leuis aizmus *above* alis   196 *no trans. above* plus   199 proprium nom*en once only, above* Dedalus Tantalus   200 nondi   201 inferu   210 jtem alio modo *above* eu esteus   211 jtem alio modo idem *above* eu eis; *no trans. above* tu eis el eis

---

B. 187 *om.*   188 uulgar trotano*rum only*   190–1 cursus ... desurgo *placed after* azimus (*193*)   191 urser   192 de resurgo *om.;* quedam] quedam < quidam (*or the reverse?*) *by addition of second abbreviation sign*   193 lenis   197 conclusus *om.*   200 instrumentum nendi *om.*   203–203a casus equaliter *om.*   206–8 ille *three times only*   210–11 *om.*   212 meus tuus *om.*

E per zo es ditz 'pausatz en loc de propri nome', que, si eu dic *eu sui vengutz*, no mi besogna dir *eu Jacm[e] sui vengutz*; *eu vei que tu*
216 *es vengutz*, no·m besogna dir *eu vei que tu Peire es vengutz*; s'eu dic *aicel es vengutz* e·l mostri ab la man o ab l'oilh, no·m besonha dir *Joans es venguth*. E per ço sun apelat pronom demostratiu, quar demostren certa persona.

220 Verbes es apelatz quar es cum modis et formis et temporibus e significa alcuna causa far o suffrir, si cum *eu bate, eu sui batutz*. [S'eu bate eu faz alcuna causa, s'eu sui batutz] eu sofre alcuna causa.

224 Cinc sun li modi dels verbes: endicatius, imperatius, optatius, conjunctius, infinitius. Endicatius es apelatz quar demostra lo faiç que om fai, si cum es *eu chant, eu escriu*. Imperatius es aquel que comanda, si cum es *aporta pan, aporta vin*. Obtatius es quar
5a de/sira, si cum *eu volria amar*. Conjunctius es quar ajusta doas
229 raços ensens, si cum en aquest loc: *cum eu ame fortmen, torz es si no sui amatz*. Infinitius es apelatz quar no pausa terme ni fi a zo que ditz, si cum *eu voilh amar*.

232 E chascun dels .v. modi qu'eu ai dit desus deu aver .v. tems: presen, preterit non perfeit, preterit perfeit, preterit plus qe perfeit, e futur.

Quatre conjugaços sun. Tut aquelh verbe, l'infinitius dels quals

A. 215 eu. jacm. sui   222 S'eu bate ... batutz *om.* (*so L*)   226–7 que om comanda   229 ame] amei

---

DL. 214 p*r*opre *L*; nom *DL*; si eu] seu *D*   215 soi *L*; uenguz *DL*; bisogna *D*; eo ugo soi uenguz *L*   215–16 eu Jacme ... besogna dir *om.* *D*   216 uenguz non besona *L*; Petre *D*; uenguz *DL*   217 uenguz *DL*; ablo**l**n non *L*   218 Johans *L*; uenguz *DL*   before 220, Verbum, in red, *L*   220 Verbum *DL*   221–2 far ... alcuna causa *om.* *D* 221 eu bat *L*; soi *L*   222 S'eu bate ... batutz *om. L*; batuz *D*; sufre *L* 224 uerbs *DL*   225 subiunctius *D* (*so passim*); fait *DL*   226 fai *om. D*; es *om. D*; cant *DL*; scriu *L*, *after which L adds* .i. comandar, *in red*   227 uino *D*; *after* uin, *a space* (*for c. 12 letters*) *filled up with a line L*   228 disira *L*; *after* amar, *L adds*. i. desirar, *in red*; Coniunctiuus *L*; auista *D*   229 irizons *D*; ensems *DL*, *after which L adds* .i. aiustar una paraula colaltra, *followed by a space* (*for c. 20 letters*) *filled up with a line*; cum es en *L*; am formen *L* 230 soi *DL*; amaz *D*; *after* amatz, *L adds et* car uol totas uetz vn autre verbe ab lui Car non pot esser per se sol en construction, *then, in red*, Jnfinitiuus soes causa nonfenida car inp*er*latin tan uol dir so es non feniz si com es amar o esser amatz legir o esser legit; termen *D*; ni] ne *L*   231 dix *D*; uoill *D*, uolh *L*; amare *D*   232 cascuns *D*, quascus *L*; dic *D*; .v. tems] temps *D*; *after* tems, *L adds* cio es lo   233 perfet *D*, p*er*fieg *L*; preterit perfet *D*, *om. L*; qe] quam *D*; perfet *D*, perfieg *L*   234 e *om. D* 235 coniugason *D*; sun el verb *L*; Tuit *D*; uerbe don lenfinitius dels cals *L*

Ideo dicitur 'positus in loco proprii nominis', quia, si ego dico *ego veni*, non michi oportet dicere *ego Iacobus veni*; *ego video quod tu venisti*, non oportet dicere *ego video quod tu Petrus venisti*; item si 216 ego dico *ille venit* et illum ostendo cum manu vel cum oculo, non oportet dicere *Iohannes venit*. Et ideo apellantur pronomina demostrativa, quia ostendunt certam personam.

Verbum apelatur quia [. . .] cum modis et formis et temporibus 220 et significat aliquid agere vel pati, verbi gracia: *ego percutio, ego percutior.* [Si ego percutio ego facio aliquid, si ego percutior] ego patior aliquid.

Quinque sunt modi verborum: indicativus, imperativus, obta- 224 tivus, coniunctivus, infinitivus. Indicativus est apellatum quia indicat aliquid quod homo facit, verbi gracia: *ego canto, ego scribo.* Imperativus apellatur ille modus qui imperat, verbi gracia: *afer panem, afer vinum.* Obtativus apellatur quia obtat, / verbi gracia: 5a *ego vellem amare.* Coniunctivus apellatur quia coniungit vel apre- 229 hendit duas rationes simul, sicut in hoc loco: *cum ego diligam fortiter, iniustum est si non diligar.* Infinitivus apellatur quia non ponit terminum neque finem his que dicit, verbi gracia: *ego volo* 231a *amare.* 231b

Et unusquisque de quinque modis supradictis debet habere 232 quinque tempora, silicet: presens, preteritum inperfectum, preteritum perfectum, preteritum plusquamperfectum et futurum.

Quatuor coniugationes sunt. Omnia illa verba infinitivus quorum

---

A. 220 *no trans. above* es   222 Si ego . . . percutior *om.* (*cf. Prov.*)
231a que] q3   233 in p*er*fectum (*above* non p*er*feit)

B. 214 Et ideo   215 michi *om.*; Iacobus] petrus   217 manib*us*
218 Iohannes] petrus   220 et formis *om.*   221 et significat] significatur;
aliq*ui*uid; agere] facere; p. *et* ego   224 *imperatiuus added in margin, with insertion-mark*   225 subiu*n*ctiuus (*so passim*); *et* jnfinitiu*us*; est apellatum]
appellatur   227 modus *om.*; affer   228 afer vinum *om.*   231 diligor
233 silicet *om.*; non pererfectum   235 co*n*iungatio*n*es; quor*um* infinitiu*us*

236 fenis en -*ar*, si cum *amar, chantar, ensenar,* sun de la prima conjugaço. De l[as] autras tres conjugaços sun tan confus l'infinitiu en vulgar que coven a laissar la gramatica e donar autra regla novella; per que platz a mi que aquel verbe que lor infinitiu fan
240 fenir in -*er*, si cum es *aver, tener, dever,* sion de la segonda conjugazo, aquelh que fenissen in -*ire* et aquel que fenissen in -*endre,* si cum *dire, escrire, tendre, contendre, defendre,* sion tuit de la terza,
5b aquelh que fenissen in -*ir*, si cum *sentir,* / *dormir, auchir,* de la
244 quarta.

Lo presens tems del indicatiu de la prima conjugaço se dobla en la prima persona, que pos dir *ami* o pos dir *am,*

248
chanti o *chan,*
plori o *plor,*
soni o *so,*
brami o *bram,*
badalhi o *badalh.*

252 La segonda persona in -*as* fenis, si cum *tu amas*; la terza in -*a*, si cum *cel ama*. Aici fenisen las tres personas el singular del tems presen del indicatiu; et el plural:

256
nos amam,
vos amatz,
celh amen o *amon.*

Et aicho es generals regla que la terza persona del plural se dobla per toz verbes e per totz tems, que pot fenir o in -*en* o in -*on*. E la

A. 237 De lautras (*sim. D*)   253 fenis enlas

DL. 236 sicum es jeu uoill amar *L*; cantar *D*; enseingnar *D*, ensenhar *L*   236–7 coniugazo segon uulgar *L*   237 E lautras *D*, De las autres *L*; tant *D*   238 conuen *L*   239 quel plaz *L*; aqeill *D*, aquelli *L*   241 qeill *D*, aqelli *L*; aqeill que *D*, aqelli qi *L*; *after* endre, *L adds et* in iure; 242 sicom es *L*; escrire] rire *L*; *after* defendre, *L adds* e uiure escriure edeliure; tut *L*; terza coniugazon *L*   243 i qeill *D*; sicum es *L*; durmir *D*; auzir son de la *D*, auzir sion dela*con*iugason *L*   246 eo ami *L*; o] e *D*; ieu am *L* 247 canti ò can *D*, eo chanti o ieu chan *L*   248 eo plori o ieu plor *L* 249 eo soni oiso *L*; so] son *D*   250 eo brami *L*   251 badagli o badagl *D*, eo badalhi oba*d*ailh *L*   252 in -as] mas *D*; *after* amas, *L adds* tu bramas tu clamas; terza fenis in *L*   253 *after* ama, *L adds* cel clama cel brama; Aisi *L*; fenissen *D*; el] del *L*; del] des *D*   254 *after* plural, *L adds* noms uol dir   256 amaz *DL*   257 ceill *D*, celli *L*   258 azo *D*; del] de *L*   259 uerbs *D*; *after* in -on, *L adds* excepto futuro q*u*od desinit in an uel in au; E] De *L*

desinit in hac sillaba, verbi gracia: *amare, chantare, docere,* sunt 236
prime coniugationis, secundum vulgare. De aliis tribus coniugationibus sunt tantum confusi infinitivi modi in vulgari quod
[oportet] dimittere gramaticam et donare aliam regulam novam;
unde placet michi quod illa verba quorum infinitivus desinit in hac 240
sillaba, verbi gracia: *habere, tenere, debere,* sint secunde coniugationis, illa que desinunt in hac sillaba et illa que desinunt in ista,
verbi gracia: *dicere, scribere, tendere, contendere, defendere* et plura
alia, sint omnia tercie coniugationis, illa que desinunt in hac 244
sillaba, verbi gracia: *sentire,* / *dormire, audire,* sint quarte.   5b

   Presens tempus indicativi prime coniugationis duplicatur in 245
prima persona, quia possum dicere sic vel possum dicere sic,

        sic vel sic,
        sic vel [sic],   248
        sic vel sic,
        sic vel sic,
        sic vel sic.

Secunda persona desinit [in hac sillaba], verbi gracia: *amas*; tercia 252
persona in hac, verbi gracia: *amat.* Ita desinunt tres persone in
singullari temporis presentis indicativi; et in plurali:

        nos amamus,
        vos amatis,   256
        illi amant, vel sic.

Et hec est generalis regula quod tercia persona pluralis duplicatur
in omnibus verbis, secundum vulgare, et in omnibus [temporibus],
quod potest finire sic—excepto futuro quod desinit in -*an* vel in 259a

---

A.   236–7 *between* sunt *and* prime, *about three letters* (dela?) *erased*   239 *no*
trans. above couen   240 quorum] que (*above* que); desinit] desirat
242 ista] istas   245 duplicant*u*r   248 *no trans. above* plor   252 desinit
above in; *no trans. above* as fenis   259 temporibus *om.*   259a futuro]
tugran   259a–260 vel in -au] .*in.* *u*elsam

B.   236 sill*a*ba in ar; c*a*ntare *et* d.   239 donare] dare   241 verbi
gracia] sic est   242 in hac . . . desinunt *om.*; in istis   243 verbi
gracia] sic*ut*; *et* defender*e*   243–4 et plura alia *om.*   247–51 uel sic
once only   252 in has desinit   252–3 amas . . . gracia *om.*   253 jlle
amat   255 nos *om.*   256 vos *om.*   257 illi *om.*; amen*t*   259a–260 excepto . . . in -au *om.*

260 prima persona dobla se en totz verbes el tems presen del indicatiu solamen, si cum:

> eu senti o eu sen,
> eu dizi o eu dic;

264 mas mielhz es a dir lo plus cort que·l plus long.

El preterit non perfeit del indicatiu:

>   amava,
>   -vas,
> 268 -va,
>   amavam,
>   amavatz,
>   -aven o amavon.

272 El preterit perfeit:

>   amei,
>   -est,
>   -et,
> 276 amem,
>   -ez,
>   -eren vel ameron.

El preterit plus que perfeit:

> 280   eu avia amat,
>   -ias amat,
> 6a   -ia / amat,
>   -iam -at,
> 284   -iaz -at,
>   -ien vel -ion -at.

El futur sun senblan tuit li verbe en totas las conjugazos, que tut fenissen aici:

A. 262 sen, *with* s. *added above* n, *in same ink as Latin translation*

DL. 260 se dobla *L*; uerbs *D*; presens *D*   261 *after* solamen, *L adds* excepto ai sai qe no*n* duplicantur jmp*r*ima persona; sicomes *L*   262 sen] sei *L*   263 eu dic o eu diczi *D*, eu dic o eu disi *L*   264 meillz *D*, melz *L*; loing *D*   265 perfet *D*; endicatiu uol dire *L*   266 aua *D*, eo aua *L*   267 auas *D*, tu auas *L*   268 *om. D*, cel aua *L*   269 auam *D*, nos auam *L*   270 auaz *D*, vos auaz *L*   271 auem o auo *D*, cel auen o auon *L*   272 perfeit .i. conpliz *L*   273 eo ej *L*   274 amest *D*, tu est *L*   275 *om. D*, cel ec *L*   276 nos em *L*   277 amet *D*, vos etz *L*   278 *om. D*, celli eren uel erun *L*   279 perfet *D*   280 *om. D*, eo ja at *L*   281 *om. D*, tu jas at *L*   282 *om. D*, cel ja at *L*   283 *om. D*, nos jam at *L*   284 *om. D*, vos jaza at *L*   285 *om. D*; ien] celli jen *L*   286 la coniugason *D*; tuit *D*, tug *L*   287 fenissent *D*

LATIN TEXT

-*au*. Et prima persona duplicatur in omnibus verbis omnium 260
coniugationum in tempore presenti indicativi tantum (excepto *ai*,
sai, quia non duplicatur in prima persona): 261a

> *sencio*, vel sic,
> *ego dico*, vel sic;

sed melius est dicere brevi[u]s, silicet monossillabum. 264
In preteritum non perfectum indicativi:

> *amabam*,
> *amabas*,
> *amabat*, 268
> *amabamus*,
> *amabatis*,
> *amabant*, vel sic.

In preterito perfecto: 272

> *amavi*,
> *amavisti*,
> *amavit*,
> *amavimus*, 276
> *amavistis*,
> *amaverunt* vel *amavere*.

In preterito plusquamperfecto:

> *amaveram*, 280
> *amaveras*,
> *amaverat*, / 6a
> *amaveramus*,
> *amaveratis*, 284
> *amaverant*.

In futuro sunt similia omnia verba in omnibus coniugationibus
in vulgari, quia omnia desinunt:

A. 262 vel sic] *uel* sentis   264 breuis (*so* B)   265 Jn*p*reteritu*m*
.s. n*on*; in dicatiui (*above* del indicatiu)   275 amavit] *et* (*above* et)
281 amauerat

B. 260 Et *om*.   260–1 omnium coniugationum *om*.   261 tempore] tp̄r
261a quia] q*uod*   262 *verbi gracia* ego sentio   263 *om*.   264 breuis;
after 264 B *adds* q*uam* dissilabum   265 in *p*reterito in*p*erfecto   266 a
barbaro   284 ratis   286 futuro < futura; sint   287 *after* desinu*n*t,
B *adds* inta *with* n *expunctuated*

288 *amarai,*
-ras,
-ara,
amarem,
292 *-rez,*
-ran vel *amarau.*

El enperatiu tut aquel de la prima conjugaço fenissen in *-a* estreit, si cum:
296 *chanta,*
bala,
viula

—en la seconda persona entendatz, quar imperatius non a prima, 300 que om no pot comandar a si eus. En la terza persona fenis toztems in *-e,* si cum:

dance,
saute,
304 *tombe.*

In plurali fenis in *-atz,* si cum:

cavalghaz,
anaz,
308 *trotaz;*
cavalguen,
anen,
troten.

312 El obtatiu fenissen tuit li verbe de la prima conjugaço in *-era* vel in *-ia* (e de totas las conjugaços comunalmen), si cum:

DL. 288 eo rai *L* 289 amaras *D*, tu ras *L* 290 amara *D*, cel ra *L* 291 nos rem *L* 292 am amarez *D*, uos retz *L* 293 amaran *only D,* celli ran u*e*l rau *L* 294 tuit *D*; aqeill *D*, aquelli *L* 295 sicum es *L* 296 canta *D*, canta tu *L* 297 balla *D*, bala tu *L* 298 uiola *D*, viola tu *L* 299 entendaz (a < e) *D*; l'imperatius *D*; prima persona *DL* 300 eus] eis *L*; toiz tems *D* 302 cel dance *L* 303 cel saute *L* 304 tonbe *D*, cel tombe *L*; *after 304 L adds* Desinit jn hac sill*a*ba .atz. *et* h*a*bet pr*i*ma p*e*rsonam qu*a*m no*n* h*a*b*e*t in singulari 305 az *D*; *after* atz, *L adds* verbi gracia 306 caualcaz *DL* 307 amaz *D*, anatz *L* 308 trotatz *L* 309–11 *om. D,* caualguem anem trotem *L, after which L adds* Jn optatiuo desinu*n*t om*n*ia uerba pr*i*me co*n*iugationis jn hac silaba uel in hac finiunt et duplici modo pronuncia*n*tu*r* in omib*us* co*n*iugatio*n*ibus generali*ter* 313 sicum es *L*

> *amabo,* 288
> *amabis,*
> *amabit,*
> *amabimus,*
> *-itis,* 292
> *amabunt.*

In [im]perativo omnia verba prime coniugationis desinunt in hac sillaba stricta, verbi gracia:

> *canta,* 296
> *salta,*
> *viella*

—videlicet in seconda persona, quia imperativus non habet primam, quia nullus potest percipere sibi ipsi. In tercia persona desinit 300 semper in hac litera, verbi gracia:

> *ducat coream,*
> *saltet,*
> [*cadat*] vel *ludat saltando.* 304

In plurali desinit in hac sillaba; et habet primam personam, quod non habet in singulari: 305a
> *cavalguem,* id est *equitemus,*
> *anem* (*ambulemus*),
> *trotem* (*trotemus*); 308
> *equitent,*
> *ambulent,*
> *trotent.*

In obtativo desinunt omnia verba prime coniugationis in hac 312 sillaba vel in hac sillaba finiunt (duplici modo pronunciantur, in omnibus coniugationibus generaliter), verbi gracia: 313a

A. 294 Jnperatiuo (*sim. B*)   303–4 ca*n*tet *u*el ludere salterio *above* saute tombe   305a habet] lib3   305–6 q*u*od ... singulari *and* caualguem ... eq*u*item*us in double line above* caualghaz   307 anem] ame   307–8 ame trote*m and a*mbulem*us* trotem*us in double line above* anaz trotaz

B. 292 tis   293 *om.*   294 In imperativo] Jmp*er*atiuo   295 sillaba] littera   298 viela   299 non habet primam] caret pr*im*a persona 305–305a q*u*od in singulari no*n* h*a*bet   306–8 u*er*bi gr*a*cia equitatis ambuletis trotatis equitam*us a*mbulemus trotam*us*   311 trottent   313 *second* sillaba *om.*; *et* duplici

       vol[un]ters amera, volunters amaria,
       -ras vel *-rias,*
316   *amera* vel *-ria;*
 in plurali: *amaram* vel *-riam,*
       -aratz vel *-riatz,*
       amaren vel *-rien;*
320 item: *dissera* vel *diria,*
       diceras vel *-rias,*
       disera vel *diria,*
       diseram vel *-riam,*
324   *diceratz* vel *-riatz,*
       -ren vel *-rien.*

Pero aquelh que sun de la quarta conjugaço, don l'infinitius fenis in *-ir* solamen, si cum *dormir,* fan l'obtatiu

328   in *-ira* vel in *-irria,*
6b   *-iras* / vel in *-irias,*
       -ira vel in *-iria,*
       -iram vel *-iriam,*
332   *-iratz* vel *-iriatz,*
       -iren vel *-irien.*

Et sun alqun altre verbe que sun fors d'aquesta regla, si cum *voler, tener, poder, saber, aver, conoisser, dever, secher,* que *voler*
336 fenis la prima persona del obtatiu en

 A. 314 uolters amera, *without trans., added in right margin, with insertion-mark* 334 da questa 335 vol'r *(second time)*

DL. 314 uolontiers amera uolontiers ameria *D,* uoluntiers eo ameria veluntiers amaria *L* 315 *om. D,* tu eras vel jas *L* 316 *om. D,* cel era vel ja *L* 317 amaran uel amarian *D,* nos aram uel rian *L* 318 amaraz uel amariaz *D,* vos raiz uel riatz *L* 319 a. u. amerie*n D,* cil eren vel rien *L* 320 item *om. DL;* disera *L* 321 diseras uel dirias *D,* tu eras vel rias *L* 322 *om. D,* cel era vel ria *L* 323 diriam *D;* nos eram *only L* 324 disiraz uel diriaz *D,* vos eratz vel diriaz *L* 325 diseren uel dirien *D,* celh eren vel diren *L* 326 aqelli *L;* l'infinitiu *D;* fenis] finisser *D* 327 *after* dormir, *L adds* jausir sentir; l'otatiu *D* 328 in ira en la prima persona *D;* jn ira eo dormira uel iria *L* 329 en la segonda in iras uel in irias dormira dormiria dormirias *D,* tu iras vel irias *L* 330 en la terza *only D,* cel ira vel iria *L* 331 in plurali in ram uel in iriam dormiram dormiriam *D,* nos iram vel iriam *L* 332 dormiraz uel dormiriaz *only D,* vos iratz vel iriaz *L* 333 dormirem uel dormiriem *only D,* celh iren vel irien *L* 334 Et *om. D;* algun *D;* sicum es *L* 335 uolez tenez *D;* sabez auez conoissez *D;* secher] sauer (r < z) *D,* sezer *L;* que] I ue *D* 336 del obtatiu *om. D;* en] en, *with* u *added above* n, *D*

       utinam amarem,
       amares,
       amaret,   316
       amaremus,
       amaretis,
       amarent;
       utinam dicerem,   320
       diceres,
       diceret,
et pluraliter: *utinam diceremus,*
       diceretis,   324
       dicerent.

Tamen illa verba que sunt quarte coniugationis, quorum infinitivus desinit in hac sillaba tantum, sicut *dormire*, desinit obtativus in *-ira*:

       utinam dormirem, in prima / persona, 6b
       dormires, in secunda,   329
       dormiret, in tercia,
       utinam dormiremus, in plurali,
       dormiretis,   332
       dormirent.

Et sunt aliqua alia verba que sunt extra istam regulam, verbi gracia: *velle, tenere, posse, sapere, habere, cognoscere, debere, sedere* et plura alia, quia *vole*[*r*] desinit in prima persona presentis obtativi: 336

A. 329 dormiras   336 uole

B. 315 *uel* ita amares   318 tis   319 rent   322 ret   323 dice-*re*mus *only*   325 rent   327-8 in p*ri*ma p*er*sona in iram ut*inam* dormirem 329 in s*ecund*a dormires   330 *in ter*tia dormiret   331 dormirem*us only* 332 tis   333 rent   334 Et *om.*   336 voler] uellem; obtativi] del optatiu *in*

        volgra vel *volria,*
 la segonda *-gras* vel *-rias,*
        volgra vel *-ria,*
340   *volgram* vel *-riam,*
        volgraz vel *-riatz,*
        volgren vel *-rien;*
        tengra vel *tenria,*
344   *pogra* o *poria,*
        auria o *agra,*
        conoseria o *conogra,*
        degra o *deuria,*
348   *segra* o *seiria,*
        plagra o *plairia,*
        pagra o *passeria,*
        begra o *beuria,*
352   *valgra* o *valria,*
        mogra o *mouria,*
        colgra o *colria,*
        nogra o *noçeria,*
356   *vengra* o *venria.*

E quasqus d'aquel[s] sobreditz deu fenir en singular et en plural et personas, de tan cum s'aperten al presen del optatiu, si cum es dit desus pleneiramen de *voler.*

360 El preterit plus que perfeit del obtatiu fenissen tuit in *-es* estreit, si sun de la prima conjugaço, si cum:

      bon fora qu'eu agues amat,

A. 357 da q*u*el 359 pleneira3., *at end of line*

DL. 337 uulgra vel jn uolria *L*; *after* uolria, *D adds* del optatiu 338 la segona *L*; uolgras o uolrias *D*, jngras sicum tu gras vel rias *L* 339 *om. D*, latersa jngra sicum cel gra vel ria *L* 340 in plural u. o uolriam *D*, esen plural la prima p*er*sona ingram sicum nos gram vel riam *L* 341 u. ò uolriaz *D*, la segona jn graz sicum vos gratz velriatz *L* 342 u. ò uolrien *D*, latersa jngren sicum celh gren u*e*l rien *L* 343 t. ò teria *D*, eo t. o t. *L* 344 eo p. *L* 345 eo agra o auria *L* 346 conogra ò conoisseria *D*, eo conogra o conosseria *L* 347 eo d. o douria *L* 348 segra ò segria *D*, eo segro o segria *L* 349 eo p. *L* 350 eo p. *L*; paisseria *D* 351 begra] beura *D*, eo b. *L* 352 *om. D*; eo v. *L* 353 *om. D*; eo m. *L* 354 colgra ò colgaria *D*, eo colgra o colgueria *L* 355 eo n. *L*; noseria *D*, nozeria *L* 356 eo u. *L* 357 chascuns *L*; da qestz *D*, daqest *L*; sobradiz *D* 358 et en personas *DL* 359 pleneramen *L* 360 estreic *D*, estreg *L* 361 si sun ... conjugaço *om. L*; si cum *om. D*, si cum es adire *L* 362 *om. D*; qu'eu] qe *L*

	utinam vellem,	
	velles,	
	vellet,	
et pluraliter:	*utinam vellemus,*	340
	velletis,	
	vellent;	
	utinam tenerem,	
	possem,	344
	haberem,	
	cognoscerem,	
	deberem,	
	sederem,	348
	placerem,	
	passerem,	
	biberem,	
	valerem,	352
	moverem,	
	colerem,	
	nocerem,	
	venirem.	356

Et unusquisque supradictorum debet fenire in singulari et in plurari et in personis, quantum pertinet ad presens obtativi, sicut superius plenius continetur in hoc verbo *velle*.

In preterito plusquamperfecto obtativi desinunt omnia in hac 360 sillaba stricta, si sunt prime coniugationis, sicut:

[. . .],

A. 362 bo*n* fora queu *above* bon fora queu (*sim. B*)   362–4 *no trans. above* agues amat . . . cel agues amat

---

B. 338 les   339 let   340 uellemus *only*   341 tis   350 passcerem   357 finire   358 presente*m*   361 si sunt prime coniugationis *om.*   362–4 bon fora q*u*eu agues amat tu agues amat nos aguessem amat o͞e uos agsem amat cel agsem amat

       tu aguesses amat,
364   *cel agues amat*
7a —et aquelh solamen que fenissen lor enfinitiu in / *-endre* et in *-iure,* si cum *viure, prendre, tendre,* que sun scenblan en aquest loc a la prima conjugazo, et el preterit perfeit et el preterit non perfeit del 368 conjuntiu, si cum podez vezer aici:

      cum eu cantes,
      tu cantesses,
      cel cantes,
372   *cantassem,*
      cantassetz,
      ca[n]tassen vel *cantesson;*
      cum eu tendes,
376   *tu tendesses,*
      cel tendes,
      tendessem,
      tendessez,
380   *tendessen* vel *tendesson;*
item in preterito inperfecto:

      cum eu ames,
      tu ames,
384   *cel ames,*
      -assem,
      -assetz,
      -essen vel *-esson.*

A. 374 catassen

DL. 363–4 *om. D*   *after* 364 *L adds* nos aguessem amat vos aguesses amat cil aguessen amat Epgra hom dire eisamen bon fora queu agues iengut tu aguesses tengut cel agues tengut nos aguessem tengut vos aguessetz tengut cill aguem tengut at mudada in ut videli*cet* indicatiui modi si son dela p*ri*ma coniugaso   365 et *om. L;* aqilli *L; after* endre, *L adds* et jn ire   365–6 et in . . . viure *om. D*   366 si cum es *L;* viure *om. L;* prendre] pendre *D; after* tendre, *L adds* rendre uire ire martire vuire liure deliure   367 et el] del *L;* per feg *L;* et el] edel *L;* preteirit *D;* pe*r*fieg *L*   368 coniunctiu *L;* aici] aia *L*   369 eo *L*   370 canteses *D*   372 nos c. *DL*   373 uos cantassez *DL*   374 cil cantassen *only D;* celli c. *L*   375 cum eu entendessez *D;* eo *L*   376–7 *om. D*   378 *om. D,* nos t. *L*   379 *om. D,* vos tendesses *L*   380 cil entendesse uel esso *D;* celli t. *L*   382 eo *L*   383 amesses *DL*   385 nos amassem *DL*   386 uos amassez *D,* vos amassetz *L*   387 cill amassen uel esso *D,* celli amessen vel amesson *L*

[. . .],
[. . .],
—et illa [. . .] q[uo]rum desinit infinitivus / in hac sillaba et in hac, sicut *vivere, capere, tendere,* que sunt similia hoc loco prime coniugationis, [. . .] (videlicet indicatiui modi) et in preterito inperfecto coniunctivi, sicut potestis videre hic:

> *cum cantarem,*
> *cantares,*
> *cantaret,*
> *cantaremus,*
> *cantaretis,*
> *cantarent;*
> *cum tenderem,*
> *tenderes,*
> *tenderet,*
> *tenderemus,*
> *tenderetis,*
> *tenderent;*

iterum in [. . .] coniunctivi modi:

> *cum amarem,*
> *amares,*
> *amaret,*
> *amaremus,*
> *-tis,*
> *amarent.*

A. 365 qr*um*; illa qr*um above* aquelh; *no trans. above* solamen   367 uide-lic*et* i*n*dicatiui modi *above* et el preterit perfeit   381 J*nconi*u*n*ctiui modi *above* in preterito inperfecto

---

B. 365 et *om.*; infinit*iuu*s desinit; et] u*el*   366–7 sicut . . . coniugationis] bon fora q*ueu* ages te*n*du*n*t tu aguesses ut cel agues ut nos aguessem ut uos agsem ut cel aguessem ut at *et* mutata in ut   369–71 cu*m* cantaret *only*   373 tis   374 rent   375–80 *om.*   381 jter*um* modi *con*iunctiui in preterito perfecto   383 res   384 ret   385 cu*m* a.   387 rent

388 El futur del obtatiu fenissen tut aquelh de la prima conjugaço in -e, si cum aici:

Deus volha qu'eu ame,
tu ames,
392 *cel ame,*
amem,
ametz,
amen vel *amon.*

396 E·l presens del conjunctiu es atrestals. Pero lo preteritz non perfeiç del conjunctiu es semblans al preterit non perfeitz del indicatiu a la vengada, et es contra gramatica, si cum en aquest loc: *S'eu te donava mil marcs, serias tu mos hom?*

400 El preterit perfeit del conjunctiu:

cum eu aia amat,
aias amat,
aia amat,
404 *aiam amat,*
aiatz amat,
aien vel *aion -at.*

7b Lo preteriz plus que perfeitz del con/junctiu e[s] semblans ad 408 aquelh del obthatiu.

El futur del conjunctiu:

cum eu aurai amat,
-ras -at,
412 *-ra -at,*
-rem -at,
auretz amat,
-ran -at vel *aurau amat.*

A. 407 esemblan*s*

DL. 388 In futuro obtatiu *D*, Jnfuturo optatiui *L*; tuit *D*; aqelli *L* 390 uoilla *D*; qeu *DL* 393 Deus uoilla que nos amem (< amen) *D*, nos amem *L* 394 uos amez *DL* 395 qill a. *D*, celli a. *L*; vel] o *D* 396 co*n*iunctius *L*; altre tals *D*, altertal *L*; preterit *DL* 397 es] el *D*; perfet *D*, pe*r*feit *L* 398 uegada *DL* 399 dona *D*; mils mars *L*; homs *L* 401 eo *L* 402 *om. D*; tu a. *L* 403 *om. D*; cel a. *L* 404 nos a. *DL* 405 uos a. *DL* 406 qill a. *D*, celli a. *L*; amat *DL* 407 preterit *DL*; perfeit *D*; semblanz *D* 408 aquel *DL*; optatiu *DL* 410 eo *L* 411 tu auras amat *DL* 412 cel aura amat *DL* 413 nos aurem amat *DL* 414 uos aurez *D*, vos a. *L* 415 qill auran amat *only D*, celli auran uel a. a. *L*

In futuro obtativi desinunt omnia illa verba que sunt prime 388
coniugationis in hac litera -*e*, verbi gracia:

> *utinam amem,*
> *ames,*
> *amet,* 392
> *amemus,*
> *ametis,*
> *ament,* vel sic.

Et presens coniunctivi est simillis illi. Tamen preteritum imper- 396
fectum coniunctivi est simillis preterito inperfecto indicativi aliquando, et est contra gramatica, sicut in hoc loco: *Si ego donarem
tibi mille marchas, esses tu meus homo?*
In preterito perfecto coniunctivi: 400

> *cum amaverim,*
> *amaveris,*
> *amaverit,*
> *amaverimus,* 404
> *amaveritis,*
> *amaverint.*

P[re]teritum plusquamperfectum / coniunctivi est simillis pre- 7b
terito plusquamperfecto obtativi. 408
In futuro coniunctivi:

> *cum amavero,*
> *amaveris,*
> *amaverit.* 412

Inspiciat lector in huius modi modis et temporibus et consideret
qualia verba debet profere in vulgari suo et quod intellectum
habent, quia in vulgare provincialis lingue eundem sensum habent

---

A. 388 obtauiui   396–7 im perfectum (*above* non perfeiç)   397 in perfecto
(*above* non perfeitz)   407 pteritum, *with* m *altered from* o   411 amaueras
412 amauerat   413–16 Jnspiciat... uulgari *above* auretz amat... auer amat

---

B. 391 es   392 et   394 tis   395 ament] ent   396–7 illi...
simillis *om.*   397 preterioto *with first* o *expunctuated*   397–8 aliquado
398 gramatica*m*   398–9 d. t.] tibi donare*m*   400 *co*niuctiui   402 ris
403 rit   405 tis   406 rint   407 *co*niuctiui   *after* 409 B *adds*
dic*it* ita   412 rit amau*er*imus   414 qualia] qua   414–15 suo et...
vulgare *om.*   415 prouintiali   415–16 eundem... vulgari *placed after*
intromittere (*417*)

416 El presen del enfinitiu: *amar*. El preterit non perfeit: *aver amat*.
Dels autres tems del enfinitiu no·m antremet, quar non an loc en
vulgar, se no pauc.

Ni del passiu no·m besogna dir, quar pertot se tria per aquest
420 verbe *sum, es, est*, que vol nominatiu cas denan se et apres, si cum:

        eu sui amatz,
        tu est (vel *es*) *-atz,*
        cel es -atz,
424   *nos em amat,*
        etz -at,
        sun -at;
        eu era amatz,
428   *-ras -atz,*
        -ra -atz,
        nos eram -at,
        eratz -at,
432   *eren* vel *eron amat;*
        eu fui -atz,
        fust -atz,
        fo -atz,
436   *nos fom -at,*
        foz -at,
        foren vel *foro -at;*

A. 420 de nan   421 fui   422 *uel es interlinear*   424 No sem (*sim. L*)   438 foro] ero

---

DL. 416 presens *L*; eu uolria auer amat *D*; *after* amat, *L adds* Jncipiat lector inhui*us*mo*di* modis et te*m*poribu*s et co*nsideret qualia verba debet *p*roferre jnuulgari suo *et* que*m* intellectu h*abent* qu*i*a in uulgari *p*rouincialis lingue de aliis te*m*poribu*s* infinitiui nolo me intromicte*re* qu*i*a eunde*m* senssum h*abe*nt ista ve*r*ba qua*m* sua in suo vulgari silicet ista p*r*olise sicut superius de actiuo s*e*d aliqua*m* ad doct*r*ina*m* simpliciu*m*   417 Dels] Els D; te*m*ps *L*; del] de *L*; nomen tramet *L*   419 dire *L*; *after* dire, *L adds* silicet jta p*r*olixe sicut superius de actiuo sed aliqu*i*d ad doct*r*ina*m* simpliciu$_3$ 420 est *om. D*; cas nominatiu *L*; apres] de dreire se *D*, ap*re*s si *L*   421 amaz *D*   422 tu es amaz (amatz *L*) *only DL*   423 *om. D*, amatz *L*   424 nos sem *L* 425 vos (< nos) es amat *D*, vos est amat *L*   426 qill en amat *D*, celh sun amat *L*; *after 426 L adds* Preterit non p*er*feit del indicatiu sicum 427 amaz *D*   428 tu eras amat (amatz *L*) *DL*   429 cel era amat (amatz *L*) *DL*   430 amat *DL*   431 eraz amatz *D*, vos e. amat *L*   432 eren] qill eran amat *D*, celli eren *L*; *after 432 L adds* preterit p*er*feit   433 eo f. *L*; amaz *D*, amatz *L*   434 tu f. *DL*; amaz *D*, amatz *L* 435 cel fo amaz *D*, cel fu amatz *L*   436 amat *DL*   437 uos fos (fost *L*) amat *DL*   438 qill f. u. f. amat *D*, celli furen u*e*l furon at *L*; *after 438 L adds* Preterit plusqua*m*perfeit

LATIN TEXT

ista verba quem sua in suo vulgari. 416
De aliis temporibus infinitivi nolo me intromittere, quia non habent locum in vulgari nisi parum.
Nec de passivo oportet me dicere ita prolixe sicut superius de activo, sed aliqua ad doctrinam simplicium, quia per hoc verbum 419a *sum, es, est* plene distinguitur, quod vult nominativum casum ante 420 se et post, verbi gracia: 420a

>*amor,*
>*amaris,*
>*amatur,*
>*amamur,* 424
>*amamini,*
>*amantur;*
>*amabar,*
>*amabaris,* 428
>*amabatur,*
>*amabamur,*
>*amabamini,*
>*amabantur;* 432
>*amatus sum* vel *fui,*
>*es* vel *fuisti,*
>*est* vel *fuit,*
>*amati sumus* vel *fuimus,* 436
>*estis* vel *fuistis,*
>*sunt* vel *fuerunt* vel *fuere;*

A. 416 quem sua] q*ue sunt* 419–420a jt*a p*rolixe . . . an*te* se *above* quar pertot . . . denan se 422 *uel* es. amaris 430 amabam*us* 438 sunt vel fuerunt] eri*nt ue*l fueri*nt*

B. 416 quem] q*uam* 418 h*abet* 419 oportet me] no*n* oportet 419a aliq*uam*; ad *om.*; per *om.* 420 sum es est *om.* 422 ris 423 tur 428 baris u*el* amabare 429 batur 436 amati *om.* 438 su*nt* fueru*nt* u*el* ere

                eu avia estat amatz,
440   *avias estat -at*[*z*],
                avia estat -at[*z*],
                nos aviam estat -at,
                vos aviaz estat -at,
444   *cel avien* vel *avion estat -at;*
                eu serai amatz,
                -ras -atz,
                -ra -atz,
448   *-rem -at,*
                -retz -at,
                -ran vel *-rau -at.*
        Imperativi:
452   *sias tu amatz,*
8a   *sia cel amatz,* /
                siam nos -at,
                siatz vos -at,
456   *sian* vel *sion celh amat.*
        Obtatiu:

                per mo vol eu seria (vel *fora*) *amatz,*
                -rias (vel *foras*) *-atz,*
460   *-ria* (vel *fora*) *-atz,*
                -riam vel *-ram* (vel *foram*) *-at,*
                -riatz vel *-ratz* (vel *foraz*) *-at,*
                -rien vel *-r*[*i*]*on* (vel *foren* vel *foro*) *amat.*

A. 439 estat. at. (*sim. D*)   440 estat. at. (*sim. D*)   452 si as tu 453 si acel   456 amatz   458 u*el* fora *interlinear*   459 u*el* foras *interlinear*   460 u*el* fora *interlinear*   461 u*el* foram *interlinear* 462 u*el* fora*m* [*sic*] *interlinear*   463 rien. u*el* ro*n*; u*el* foren u*el* fero [*sic*] *interlinear*

DL. 439 eo *L*; stat amat *D*   440 tu a. èstat amat *D*, tu ias e. amatz *L*   441 cel a. e. amat *D*, cel ia e. amatz *L*   442 estatz *D*; amat *DL* 443 auiatz *L*; amat (t < z *D*) *DL*   444 qill a. *D*, celli a. *L*; vel avion] o uion *D*; amat *DL*; *after 444 L adds* Futur   445 eo *L*; amaz *D* 446 tu seraz amaz *D*, tu seras amatz *L*   447 cel sera amaz (amatz *L*) *DL* 448 nos sirem (serem *L*) amat *DL*   449 vos serez (seretz *L*) amat *DL* 450 qill seran amat *only D*, celli seran uel serau amat *L*   451 Imperatiuo *DL*   452 amaz *D*   453 amaz *D*   454 sian *D*; amat *DL*   455 siaz *D*; amat *DL*   456 sian] sien *DL*; celli *L*   457 En l'optatiu *D* 458 mon *DL*; vol] uoler *D*; vel fora *om. DL*; amaz *D*   459 tu serias amaz (amatz *L*) *only DL*   460 cel seria amaz (amatz *L*) *only DL*   461 nos seriam uel eram (seram *L*) amat *only DL*   462 vos seriatz uel erat (foratz *L*) amat *only DL*   463 qill (celli *L*) serien uel serion amat *only DL*

LATIN TEXT

   amatus eram vel *fueram,*
   eras vel *fueras,*   440
   erat vel *fuerat,*
   amati eramus vel *fueramus,*
   eratis vel *fueratis,*
   erant vel *fuerant;*   444
   amabor,
   amaberis vel *-abere,*
   amabitur,
   amabimur,   448
   amabimini,
   amabuntur.
[. . .]

   amare,   452
   ametur, /   8a
   amemur,
   amamini,
   amantor.   456
[. . .]

   utinam amarer,
   -eris,
   amaretur,   460
   amarem[*ur*] (duplicatur, id est),
   amaremini,
   [*amarentur*].

A. 451 *no trans. above* Imperatiui uos *and repeated above* uel sion celh 455 amaminor (*sim. B*) *above* siatz 456 amantor *above* amatz 457–8 vtinam *above* Obtatiu; amarer u*e*l fora *above* per mo uol eu seria 459 u*e*l foras eris *above* amatz rias atz 460 u*e*l fora amaret*u*r *above* ria atz 461 amare*m* duplicat*u*r .i. u*e*l fora*m above* riam uel ram at 462 u*e*l fora*m* amaremini *above* riatz uel ratz 463 u*e*l foren u*e*l fero *above* at rien uel; *no trans. above* ron amat

B. 446 amabere 447 tur 450 *om.* 453 tur 455 ameminor 456 ame*n*tor 458–63 uti*n*am amare*r* uel fora u*e*l foras rem u*e*l fora amaret*u*r amarem*u*r ter duplicatur ï u*e*l fora*m* u*e*l foras amarem*i*ni u*e*l forem amare*n*t*u*r uel fo*n*ro

464 Preter[it] plus [que] per[feit]:

[per] mo vol eu augues estat amat[z],
-esses -stat -atz,
-es -tat -atz,
468 -essem -stat -at,
-essetz -stat -at,
-essen vel -esson -stat -at.

El futur:
472 Deus volha qu'eu sia amatz,
sias amatz,
sia -atz,
siam amat,
476 siatz -at,
sien vel sion -at.

Lo present del conjunctiu es autretals si metez denan *cum*, lai on ditz *per mo vol*. El preterit non perfeit del conjunctiu:

480 com eu fos amatz,
fosses -atz,
fos -atz,
-em -at,
484 -etz -at,
fossen -at vel fosson.

El preterit perfeit:

cum eu aia estat amatz,

A. 464–5 Preter. plus. per. mo uol (*sim. L*)   465 amat (*so D*) 475 amatz

DL. 464 Preteritz *D*; Preteritoplusqueperfeit amatus essem uel fuissem *L* 465 per *om. L*; pel meu uoler *D*; agues *DL*; amat *D*   466 tu aguesses estat amaz *D*, tu e. estat amatz *L*   467 cel agues estat amat *D*, cel es estat atz *L*   468 nos aguessem (essem *L*) estat amat *DL*   469 uos aguessez (essetz *L*) estat amat *DL*   470 quill aguessem (*with* n *added above* m) *D*, celli esen *L*; o aguesson *D*; estat amat *DL*   472 uoilla *D*, uollia *L*; qeu *DL*; amaz *D*   473 deus uoilla qe tu sies amaz *D*, tu s. a. *L*   474 deus uoilla qe aqels sia amaz *D*, cel sia amatz *L*   475 deus uoilla qe nos s. *D*, nos s. *L*   476 que uos siaz amat *D*, vos s. amat *L*   477 que aqill s. *D*, celli s. *L*; vel] ò *D*; amat *D*   478 presens *DL*; autirtals *L*; deman *D*; lai] lia *L*   479 per mon uoler *D*   480 cum *DL*; eo *L*; amaz *D* 481 cum tu f. amaz *D*, tu f. amatz *L*   482 cum cel f. amaz *D*, cel f. amatz *L*   483 cum nos fossem amat *D*, nos fosem amat *L*   484 cum uos fossez amat *D*, vos fosetz amat *L*   485 cum quill f. ò f. amat *D*, celli f. uel f. amat *L*   487 amaz *D*

Preterito plusquamperfecto: 464

    utinam amatus essem vel *fuissem,*
    esses vel *fuisses,*
    [. . .],
    utinam amati essemus vel *fuissemus,*   468
    essetis vel *fuissetis,*
    essent vel *fuissent.*

[. . .]

    utinam amer,   472
    ameris vel *amere,*
    ametur,
    amemur,
    amemini,   476
    amentur.

Presens coniunctivi est simillis futuro obtativi, posita hac dicione *cum* loco *utinam.* In preterito inperfecto coniunctivi:

    cum amarer,   480
    [*amareris* vel *amarere*],
    amaretur,
    cum amaremur,
    amaremini,   484
    amarentur.

In preterito perfecto:

    cum amatus sim vel *fuerim,*

A.   464 Credo q*uod* uelit dice*re* mo uolges deus qe ages estat amat *added in right margin, with insertion-mark after* plusquamperfecto   467 *no trans. above* es tat atz   471 *no trans. above* El futu*r*   479 in p*er*fecto (*above* non perfeit)   481 amaret*ur above* fosses atz   482 *no trans. above* fos atz

B.   467–9 *om.*   474 tur   475–7 *om.*   478 dictoe   479 p*er*fecto   482 ret*ur*   485 rent*ur*

488 *aias -tat -atz,*
aia -tat -atz,
aiam -stat -at,
aiatz -stat -at,
492 *aien* vel *aion -stat amat.*

Lo preterit plus quam perfeit del conjunctiu scembla aquel del obtatiu, si metez *cum* en loc de *Deus vola.* El futur:

cum eu aurai estat amatz,
496 *auras estat amatz,*
aura -stat -atz,
-rem estat -at,
-rez -at -at,
500 *-ran* vel *aurau estat -at.*/

8b L'enfenitius del passiu non a loc en vulgar.

Explicit prima declinatio.

Li verbe de la segonda e de la terça et de la quarta conjugaço sun 504 mout divers, si cum:

eu escriu o *escrivi,*
tu escrius o *escrives,*
cel escri o *escriu;*
eu dic o *diçi,*
508 *tu dis* o *dizes,*

A. 494 si metez d*e*us uola enloc d*e*cum (*sim. L*) 502 Explici*t* .j. declinat*io*, *in red*

DL. 488 cum aies estat amaz *D*, tu a. estat amatz *L* 489 cum cel a. estat amaz *D*, cel a. estat amatz *L* 490 cum nos a. estat amaz *D*, nos siam estat amat *L* 491 *om. D*, vos siatz estat amat *L* 492 cum cill a. ò aion (i < r) estat a. *D*, celli sien uel sion estat a. *L* 493 preteriz *D*; quam] que *D*, qe *L*; p*er*feitz *L*; coniunctio *L* 494 metez deus uolha en loc de cum *L*; uoilla *D* 495 stat *L*; amaz *D* 496 cum tu a. *D*, tu a. *L*; stat *L*; amaz *D* 497 cum cel a. *D*, cel a. *L*; estat *D*; amaz *D*, amatz *L* 498 cum nos auren *D*, nos aurem *L*; amat (t < z *D*) *DL* 499 cum uos aurez *D*, vos auretz *L*; estat *DL*; amaz *D*, amat *L* 500 cum cill auran e. amat *only D*, celli auran vel a. stat amat *L* 501 Jnfinitius *L*; non *repeated D* 502 *om. DL*; *L has rubric de* u*er*bis 503 sunt *L* 504 sicum es *L* 505 o] vel *L* 506 tu escriues o escriuies *D*; o] vel *L* 507 escri] escrif *D*; estri uel estriu *L* 508 disi *D*, diz *L* 509 tu diz o disis *D*

> sis vel *fueris*, 488
> amatus sit vel *fuerit*,
> cum amati simus vel *fuerimus*,
> sitis vel *fueritis*,
> sint vel *fuerint*. 492

Preteritum plusquamperfectum coniunctivi est similis preterito plusquamperfecto obtativi, silicet posito [*cum*] in loco *utinam*. In futuro: 494a

> cum amatus ero vel *fuero*,
> eris vel *fueris*, 496
> erit vel *fuerit*,
> cum amati erimus vel *fuerimus*,
> eritis vel *fueritis*,
> erint vel *fuerint*./ 500

Infinitivus passivi non habet locum in vulgari, nisi *amari*. 8b

Verba secunde et terçie et quarte coniugationis sunt multum diversa, verbi gracia: 504

> *scribo* (duplicantur enim in prima persona),
> *scribis* (et secunda similiter,
> et tercia) *scribit*;
> et hic similiter duplicatur prima 508
> et secunda,

A. 494 posito in loco vtina*m above* metez deus uola; *no trans. above* en loc de cum   502 *no trans.*   503 verbi

B. 488 tus sis   489 tus sit   490 cum *om.*   494 silicet *om.*; in *om.*   502 *no rubric*   505 duplicatur; in] ipi   506-7 *om.*

> cel ditz;
> eu fenisc o fenis,
512 > tu fenisses,
> cel fenis.

In plurali fan tut:
> -em, -etç, [-en] vel -on.

516 Et aquelh qu'eu ai dit sun de terça, e degra avan dir de la segonda, si cum:

> eu ai,
> tu as,
520 > cel ha;
> eu tenh o teni,
> tu tes o tenes,
> cel te;
524 > eu sai,
> tu saps,
> cel sap;
> eu fenh o fenhi,
528 > tu fehz o fenhes,
> cel fenh;

autretals es *penh, tenh, cenh, estrenh, enpenh*; et en plural:

> -em, -etz, -en vel -on.

532 El preterit imperfec del indicatiu et futur, et in futur del obtatiu et el presen del conjunctiu, sun scenblan tut li verbe de la segonda e de la terçha et de la quarta conjugaço, qu'el preterit non perfeit fan tu:

536 > -ia, -ias, -ia,

A. 515 etç. *u*el o*n*   521 teni *or* tem

DL. 510 diz *D*   514 tuit *D*   515 en em *D*, nos em *L*; etz en en uel o *D*, vos etz celli en vel on *L*   516 aqelli *L*; qu'eu ai] qeriai *D*; dela terza *D*, de terza *co*niugason *L*; avan] enanz *L*, *om. D*   521–3 *placed after* 526 *L*   521 eo *L*; teing (i < s) ò tegra *D*   524–6 *om. D*   527 fenh] feng *L*; eu feing estreingni *D*   528 fenz *L*; tu feingni o feingnes (gn < gr) *D*   529 feing *D*   530 p. t. c.] preing ceing feing *D*, penh cenh *L*; estreing *D*, escrenh *L*; empeing *D*; et *om. D*; en plurali fenis *D*, jmplurali *L*   531 in em in etz et in en uel in o *D*, nos em vos etz celli en uelon *L*   532–3 En preterito inperfecto indicatiu et futuro et in futuro optatiu et in presenti subiunctiu *D*, Jnpreterito in*per*fecto indicatiui *et* futuro et in futuro optatiui *et* in presenti *co*niunctiui *D*   533 tuit *D*, tuti *L*   534 preteirit *D*   535 tuit *DL*   536 in a et in as ia *D*, eo ia tu ias cel ia *L*

tercia vero non;
finio (hic similiter duplicantur),
finis, 512
finit.
In plurali desinunt omnia in hac sillaba:
finimus, finitis, finiunt.
Et illa que dixi superius sunt de tercia, [. . .] (videlicet quia sic 516
ordo postulat), verbi gracia, de secunda:
habeo,
habes,
habet; 520
teneo (duplicatur),
tenes (duplicatur in secunda),
tenet;
sapio, 524
sapis,
sapit;
fingo (duplicatur in prima persona),
(et secunda similliter) *fingis,* 528
fingit;
tales sunt ista: *pingo, teneo*†, *cingo, stringo, inpingo*; et in plurali:
pingimus, pingitis, pingunt. 532
In preterito imperfecto indicativi et futuro indicativi [. . .] sunt
similia omnia verba secunde et tercie et quarte coniugationis,
quia omnia preterita imperfecta desinunt ita:
fingebam, -as, -at, 536

A. 517 ordo postulat] eri*n*t postula7; de sec*u*ndi   516–17 videlicet . . .
postula7 *above* e degra auan dir de la; *no trans. above* segonda; de sec*u*ndi *above*
eu ai   521–2 teneo duplicatur tenes] tenes duplicat*ur* in es, *above* eu tenh
o teni   528 sec*u*nde   533 *no trans. above* et in fut*ur* del obtatiu et el
presen del coniunctiu

B. 511 finit *et* hic; duplicat*ur*   512 fenis   516 de tercia] de la t*er*za
520 bet   521–3 *placed after 526*   529 it   530 talis; isti;
et in plurali *om.*   533 *et* in futuro; *second* indicativi *om.*   535 preteriata *with first* a *expunctuated*   536 bas bat

el plural,   -iam, -iatz, -ien vel -ion

—del endecatiu entendat generalmen, del conjunctiu a la vegada,
540 quan *si* es pausatz denan, si cum aici: *s'eu avia mil marcs, eu seria
9a rics | om.*

El futur del indicatiu:

-rai, -ras, -ra,
-rem, -retz, -ran vel -rau.

544 El futur del obtatiu et el presen del conjunctiu:

-a, -as, -a, -am, -atz, -an vel -on,

si cum: *Deus volha qu'eu escriva,*
tu escrivas,
548   *cel escriva,*
escrivam,
-vatz,
vel *eschrivan* vel *escrivon.*

552 In preterito perfecto indicativi: in prima persona -*i* et in secunda
-*ist*, per la maior part, si cum:

eu dissi, tu dissist,
eu escrissi, tu escrissist,
556   *eu tengui, tu tenguist,*
eu dormi, tu dormist,
eu fezi vel *fi, tu fezist,*
eu feissi, tu feissist.

560 Mas en la terça persona del singular sun mot divers, si cum:

dis, escris, teng, dormi, fetz, feis.

A. 551 escriuan *with* h *inserted above by the scribe*   557 tu. dormisti
---
DL. 537 el plural *om. DL*; et in iam et in iatz et in ien *only D*, nos jam vos iatz cilli jen vel jo *L*; *after* 537 *L adds* Duplicantur jn tercia persona   538 del . . . generalmen *om. D*; indicatiu entendatz *L*   539 deuan *L*; mars *L*; saria *D*   540 hom *DL*   542 aurai auras aura *D*, habebo eo aurai tu auras cel aura *L*   543 aurem aurez auran *D*, nos aurem vos auretz celli auram vel aurau *L*   545 fenissen in a et in as et atz et an uel o *D*, eo a tu as cel a nos am vos atz celli an uel on *L*   546 sicum es *L*; uoilla *D*; qeu *D*, que *L*   547 tu es scriuas *D*   549 nos e. *DL*   550 uos escriuaz *D*, vos escriuatz *L*   551 cil escriuan uel escrio *D*, celli escriuan vel e. *L*   552 indicativi *om. DL*; -i] in i *D*   553 -ist] in ist *D*; parte *D*   554 disi *D*; tu sist *L*   555 eo *L*; scrissi *D*; escrisist *D*, sist *L*   556 eo *L*   557 eo *L*   558 eo fesi *L*   559 eo *L*; feissest *L*   560 Ma *D*; del *om. DL*; mout *DL*; sicum es *L*   561 eu dis eu e. eu teing eu d. *D*; fetz *om. D*; feis *om. D*, frix .i. finxit *L*

fingebamus, -atis, -ant (duplicantur in tercia per[sona])
—indicativi debet intelligi generaliter, de coniunctivo aliquando, quando hec dictio *si* ponitur ante, sicut hic: *si haberem mille marcas, ego essem dives / homo.*

In futuro indicativi:

> *habebo, -bis, habebit,*
> *habebimus, -tis, -bunt.*

In futuro obtativi et in presenti coniunctivi desinit sic, verbi gracia:

> *utinam scribam,*
> *scribas,*
> *scribat,*
> *scribamus,*
> *scribatis,*
> *scribant.*

[. . .]
pro maiori parte, verbi gracia:

> *ego dixi, tu dixisti,*
> *ego scrisi, tu scrisisti,*
> *ego tenui, tu tenuisti,*
> *ego dormivi, tu dormisti,*
> *ego feci, tu fecisti,*
> *ego finxi, tu finxisti.*

Sed in tercia persona singulari sunt multum diversa, verbi gracia:

> *dixit, scripsit, tenuit, dormivit, fecit, finxit.*

A.   537 *no trans. above* el plural; persona] p*er*   544 desinit sic *above* a as; *no trans. above* a am . . . on   552 *no trans. above* In preterito . . . jst

---

B.   537 tis bant; duplicatur   538 coniunctivo] co*n*tinuo   539 ponu*n*tur; marchas   542 ibo ibis it   543 ibim*u*s tis bu*n*t   544 desinu*n*t   547 as   548 at   550 tis   551 ba*n*t   555 ego scripsi sti *only*   556 tenui sti *only*   557 *om.*   558 feci sti *only*   559 fincxi sti *only*   561 fincxit

E tuit aquel don l'infinitius fenis en -*ir* solamen, si cum:

auchir, senthir, cubrir, sofrir,

564 que no se poden doblar (si cum se dobla *dir, dire, escrir, escrire*), fan la prima persona e la terça en -*i* e la segonda en -*ist* el preterit perfet del indicatiu, et el plural -*im*, -*itz*, -*iren* vel -*iron*; e·l autre que no sun d'aquest scemblan fan -*em*, -*ez*, -*en* vel -*on*, sion de la 568 segonda o de la terça conjugaço, si cum:

aguem, aguez, agren vel *agron*

9b (el / singular si cum li autre, trait la terça persona que ditz *ag*),

dissem, dissez, dissen vel *disson.*

572 Tres sun que fan la terça persona del preterit perfeit in -*oc* el singular:

poc, noc, moc,

e·l quarz es *ploc.*

576 *Decaçez, caçez, escaçez.*

In -*ec* estreit:

parec, aparec, crec,
bec, lec, sec,
580 *tec, dec.*

In -*eup*:

deceup, conceup, ereup.

In -*aup*:

584 *saup, caup.*

A. 562 lin finitius   577 Jn. ec. estreit *placed between* crec *and* bec (578–9)

DL. 562 tot *L*; à qill *D*, aqelli *L*   563 auzir (z < s *D*) sentir *DL*; cobrir *L*; soffrir *D*   564 si cum *om. D; after* escrire, *L adds* ausir ausire 566 perfeit *DL*; in im et in uz et in iren uel in iro *D*, nos im vos itz celli iren vel iron *L*   567 *after* semblan, *L adds* jmplurali sicut supradicta duplicata in jnfinitiuo; in em *D*, nos em *L*; vos etz celli en *L*; -on] o *D* 569 nos a. vos aguetz celli a. *L*   570 singular] sin *D*; dicz *D*; ag *om. D*, ag .i. habuit *L*   571 nos d. vos disseiz celli d. u. dison *L*   572 sunt *D*   *after* 573 *L adds* sicum es   574 noc *and* moc *interverted DL* 575 ploc idest pluit *L*   576 *placed after* 577 *DL*   576 decazec *D*, decasetz .i. diuicias amisit *L*; cazec *D*, casec *L*; escasec *L*, *om. D*   578 *placed after* 580 *L*   578 aparec crec *om. D*; cerc *L*   580 tec *om. D*   *after* 582 *D adds* estreup   584 saup *om. L*

LATIN TEXT

Et omnia illa quorum infinitivus desinit in hac sillaba tantum,
verbi gracia: *audire, sentire, copperire, sustinere,* que non possunt
duplicari in infinitivo (sicut duplicantur *dicere, scribere* et *aucir* vel 564
aucire, quod est *interficere*), finiunt primam personam et terciam in
hac litera, et secundam in hac sillaba, silicet in preterito perfecto
indicativi, et in plurali ita; et alia verba que non sunt istis similia
finiunt ita in plurali (sicuti sunt supradicta duplicata in infinitivo), 568
vel sint secunde coniugationis vel tercie, verbi gracia: 568a

habuimus, habuistis, habuerunt vel *habuere*

(in / singulari sicut alia verba, excepta tercia persona que dicit 9b
habuit), 570a
diximus, dixistis, dixerunt vel *dixere.*

Tria sunt que desinunt in tercia persona preteriti perfecti in hac 572
silla[ba] in singulari, silicet:

potuit, nocuit, movit,

et quartum est *pluit.*
In preterito: *amisit divicias, cecidit, contigit.* 576
[. . .]
aparuit, aparuit, crevit,
bibit, licuit, sedit,
tenuit, debuit. 580
Preterita:
decepit, concepit, convaluit.
Preterita:
sapuit, cepit (unde in Evangelio [Iohan]nis: 584
'. . . non capit in vobis'). 584a

A. 562 in finitiuus (*above* lin finitius) 566 hac literam *in* secundam
567 ita *above* im; *no trans. above* jtz . . . iron 568 superdicta
568a sint] sicut (*so B*) 569 que] q3 572 que] q3 573 silla 577 *no
trans. above* Jn ec estreit (*cf. Prov. variants*) 581–2 preterita decepit *above* Jn
eup; deçepit [*sic*] *repeated above* deceup 584 Iohannis] n̄is *or* m̄s
584–584a vnde . . . n̄is (*with* preterita *below, in double line*) *after* cepit, *at end of
line and extending into right margin*; non capit *in* uobis *above* Jn eis

B. 563 cooperire; substinere 564 in *om.*; duplicatur 564–5 et aucir . . .
interficere *om.* 565 prima persona *et* tertia, *last two words being added in margin,
with insertion-mark* 566 littera *et* secunda 568 sicut; duplicato infini-
tiuo 568a sint] sicut; c. u. t.] uel tertie coniugationis 569 stis erunt
uel ere 571 stis erunt 573 sillaba *om.*; silicet *om.* 574 potuit]
ponit; nocuit *and* mouit *interverted* 576 diuitias amisit; cecidit
contigit *om.* 578 *second* aparuit] id apparuit, *placed after* licuit (*579*);
creuit *placed after* debuit (*580*) 581 Preterita in eup 583 *om.*
584–584a unde . . . vobis *om.*

In -*eis*:
>teis, seis, feis,
>peis, empeis, estreis,
>588 destreis, constreiss, esteis,
>ateis.

In -*enc* estreit:
>sovenc, venc, avenc,
>592 mantenc, sostenc.

In -*es* estreit:
>mes (compost), pres (compost), ques (compost).

In -*et* larg:
>596 venquet, seguet, perseguet,
>conseguet, mesquet, respondet,
>perdet, tendet (compost), batet (compost),
>pendet (compost), descendet, fendet,
>600 vendet (compost), fotet, escondet,
>encendet,

que fan tu lo preterit perfeit enteiramen si cum li verbe de la prima conjugaço, et si sun elh de la segonda; e *respondet* e *tondet* seguen 604 aquela eissa regla.

In -*hac*:
>10a plac, pac, mentac, ac. /

In -*is*:
>608 asis, escris, dis,
>ris, sumris, enquis;

A. 604 ei ssa

DL. 586 deis seis idest tingit feis idest finsit *L*   587 peis idest pingressit empeis jdest impingit estreis .i. astringit *L*   588 destreis idest *constinxit L*; c. e.] estreis costreis *D*, costreis idest constrexit *only L*   589 atreis *D*, ateis idest natus est *L*   590 In ec larg *D*; *after* enc, *L adds* preterita sunt 592 matenc *D*   594 p. c. q. c.] ques pres *only L*   595 In er larc *D* 596–601 tender conpost (n < m) bater co*m*post pendet (t < r) co*m*post fender compost uender uenquet seguet (g < q) perseguet consequet mesdet respondet perder foter *D*, venqet tetendet (*or* retendet) tendet compost batet compost pendet compost fendet conpost fotet respondet seguet perseguet co*n*seguet mesquet respondet perdet desendet vendet escondet conset *L*   602 tu] tuit *D*, tot *L*; lo] li *D*; enteramen *L*   603 ill *L*; *second* e *om. D*   605 ac *DL* 606 plac preterita mentat nominauit pac pauit ac habuit *L*; pac *and* mentac *interverted D*   608 assis *D*   609 subris *D*, sunris *L*; enqis *D, om. L*; *D adds* conqis

LATIN TEXT

Preterita:

> tinxit, cinxit, finxit,
> pinxit, impegit, astrinxit,
> constrinxit, constrinxit, exstinxit, 588
> nactus [est].

Preterita:

> recordatus fui, venit, evenit,
> patrocinatus est, sustinuit. 592

Preterita:

> misit, remisit, apprehendit, reprehendit, quesivit, requisivit.

Preterita:

> vicit, secutus est, persecutus est, 596
> consecutus est, miscuit, respondit,
> perdidit, atendidit, percussit,
> suspendit, descendit, divisit,
> vendidit, futuit, abscondit, 600
> incendit,

quorum preteritum perfectum desinit integre sicut verba prime coniugationis, quamvis sint secunde; et *respondit* et *totondit* secuntur eandem regulam. 604

Preterita:

> placuit, pavit, nominavit, habuit. / 10a

[. . .]

> sedit, scripsit, dixit, 608
> risit, subrisit, inquisivit, acquisivit;

A. 588 exstinxit] exstrinxit   589 nactus *only*   598–600 *no trans. above* compost (*4 times*)   602 preteritum < -ta   607 *no trans. above* Jn is   609–10 jnquisiuit *above* enquis; acquisiuit *above* pero; tamen omnia *above* tut

---

B. 585 *om.*   586 tincxit *concessit* fincxit   587 pinxit *om.*; astrincxit 588 *co*nstrincxit idem *co*nstrinxit extendit   589 natus est   592 substinuit   593 *om.*   594 ap*r*ehendit; requisivit *om.*   595 *om.* 596 *after* vicit, B *adds* tetendit; persecutus est *om.*   597 respondit uel reprehendit   598 atendidit *om.*   599 suspendit] suspe*n*dit uel reprehendit   601 *after* incendit, B *adds co*nsuit   602 q*u*orum desinit preteritum p*er*fectum   603–4 sequitu*r*   605 *om.*   606 pauit *and* nominauit *interverted*   609 *et* acquisiuit

pero tut aquist seis sobredit poden esser semblan en prima persona et en terça el preterit perfeit.

612 In -*uis*:

  destruis, anquara.

 In -*erc:*

  sufri o *sofrec*, *ubri* o *uberc*,
616   *cubri* o *cuberc, corec*.

 In -*ers* larg:

  ters, esters.

 In -*ers* streit:
620   *ders, aders, aers*.

 In -*ars*:

  espars, ars.

 In -*oc* estreit:
624   *conoc, desconoc, reconoc*.

 In -*ois* estreit:

  ois, pois, jois.

 In -*olc* larg:
628   *volc, tolc, colc*,
  molc, dolc.

 In -*os* larg:

  fos, apos, despos.

632 In -*os* estreit:

  escos, escos, escos, ros.

 In -*ols* larg:

  sols, absols, vols, revols.

A. 625 ois estreit, *with its trans.*, *added in margin, with insertion-mark*
 633 *third* escos, *with its trans.*, *added in margin, with insertion-mark*

DL. 610 tuit *DL*; seis] .v. *L* 612–13 *om. DL* 615 sofferc soffri *D*; suferc *L*; uberc o obri *D*, ouri ouberc, *placed after* cuberc, *L* 616 cuberc o cobri *D*, cobri ocoberc *L*; corec *om. DL* 617 In es larc *D* 618 ters *and* esters *interverted D* 619 estreit *DL* 620 aers *om. L* 624 conec desconec reconec *D* 626 oix vnxit pois ponxit iois ionxit *L* 627 larc *D* 628 colc coluit *L* 629 molc moluit dolc doluit *L* 630 larc *D* 631 fos fodit apes aposuit dos despos deposuit *L* 633 escos rescos *only D*, escos abscondit predaz ros rosit escos subiecte esconxit *L* 634 larc *D* 635 fols foluit absols absoluit vols voluit reuols *L*; uols < rols *D*

tamen omnia ista sex supradicta possunt esse similes in prima
persona et in tercia in preterito perfecto.
Preterita: 612
>destruxit, [...]

[...]
>(tercia persona preteriti) *passus est* vel *fuit, aperuit*, idem,
>*cooperuit*, idem, *cucurrit*. 616

Hac sillabata:
>*tersit, extersit.*

In hac sillaba:
>*erexit, necessaria dedit, esit.* 620

Hac sillabata:
>*sparsit, arsit.*

Hac sillaba:
>*cognovit, ignoravit, recognovit.* 624

In hac sillaba:
>*unxit, punxit, iunxit.*

Hac sillaba:
>*voluit, abstulit, coluit,* 628
>*moluit, doluit.*

Hac sillaba:
>*fodit, aposuit, deposuit.*

Hac sillaba: 632
>*excussit predam, excussit segues, abs[c]o[n]dit, rodit.*

Hac sillaba:
>*solvit, absolvit, volvit, revolvit.*

A. 611 preterioto   613 *no trans. above* anquara   614–15 tercia persona presentis [*sic*] *above* jn erc   620 erexit necessaria *above* ders *and extending into right margin*; dedit (*or* declit) *above* aders   626 punxit] pinxit   633 segues] *first* e *badly formed and resembling* c *or* o; absodit

B. 610 tamen ... supradicta *om.*   612 *om.*   615–16 persona tertia que passus est idem aperuit idem cooperuit idem cucurit   617 sillaba   618 terxit   621 sillaba   625 In *om.*   626 puncxit iuncxit   627 in hac   629 diluit   633 excusit p. excusit segetem tondit abscondit

636 In -*ors* larg:

    tors, destors, retors.

 In -*eus* estreit:

    teus, preus.

640 In -*ais*:

    conplais, plais, frais,
    refrais, afrais, sofrais,
    trais, atrais, retrais,
644   *contrais, pertrais, sostrais,*
    [*tais*], *atais.*

 In -*aus*:

    claus.

648 E per çho ai fait tant longa paraula de la terça persona del preterit perfeit, quar maier confusios era en aquela que en totas las autras, quar per la maior part la prima persona fenis en -*i* e la
10b segonda in -*ist*—del / preterit perfeit del indicatiu entendatz, on
652 per la maior part la prima e la segonda persona sun scenblans.

 Del preterit non perfeit de la segonda et de la terça et de la quarta conjugaço tut sun d'un scenblan, si cum es dit desus:

    -*ia,* -*ias,* -*ia,* -*iam,* -*iatz,* -*ien* vel -*ion.*

656 El preterit plus quam perfeit, tut aquelh don l'infinitius fenis in -*endre* vel in -*ondre* vel in -*otre*, si cum:

    tendre (compost), *prendre* (compost),

 in -*ebre*:

660   *decebre, fendre* (compost),
    pendre (compost), *metre* (compost),

A. 645 tais *om.*

DL. 636 larc *D* 637 *after* destors, *D adds* restors 639 teus tenuit preus presit *L* 641 conplais conquestus est *L*, *om. D*; plains *L*
642 restrais asfrais soffrais *D*, refrais consolatus est afrais humilat sofrais manca *L* 644 contrais] de bel fe *L*; pertrais valor trase sotrais subripuit *L*
645 tais expediuit atais protinuit *L* 648 fag *L*; tan *DL* 649 confusion *L* 651 segonda persona *D*; perfet *D* 652 semblan *DL*
653 Del] El *D* 654 tuit *D, om. L* 655 in a o en ias o en ia o en iam o en iatz o ien uel io *D*, eo ia tu ias cel ia nos iam vos iaz celli ien vel ion *L*
656 quam] que *D*, qe *L*; tuit *D*; aqelli *L* 657 *after* endre, *DL add* uel in etre uel in atre; *after* ondre, *DL add* uel in odre; *after* otre, *L adds* vel inebre sicum es dessebre com̄post vel endre; sicum es *L* 658 prendre] pendre *DL* 659–60 in ebre decebre *om. DL* 661 pendre compost *om. D,* prendre com̄post *L*; metre compost *om. L*

Hac sillaba: 636
>torsit, distorsit, retorsit.

Hac sillaba:
>timuit, pressit.

Hac sillaba: 640
>conquestus est, planxit, franxit,
>consolatus est, humiliavit, defuit,
>traxit cum arcu, atraxit, naravit,
>debilem fecit, valde traxit, subripuit, 644
>expedivit, pertinuit.

Hac sillaba:
>clausit.

Et ideo fecit† tam prolixum sermonem de tercia persona preteriti 648 perfecti, quia maior confusio erat in illa quam in omnibus aliis personis, quia pro maiori parte prima persona desinit in hac littera et secunda in hac sillaba—de / preterito perfecto indicativi intelli- 10b gatis, ubi [pro maiori] parte prima et segunda persona sunt similles. 652 De preterito inperfecto secunde et tercie et quarte coniugationis omnia verba sunt simillia, sicut dictum est superius.

[. . .]

In preterito plusquamperfecto, omnia illa verba quorum infini- 656 tivus desinit ita:

>tendere (compositum), [. . .],

hac sillaba:

>decipere, sindere (compositum), 660
>pendere (compositum), mitere (compositum),

A. 643 atraxit] atraixit; *trans. misplaced*: traxit *above* trais; cum arcu atraixit *above* atrais   645 traxit *repeated before* expediuit; pertimuit *or* pertunuit   645–6 *trans. misplaced*: traxit expediuit *above* atais; hac sillaba pertimuit *above* Jn aus   652 *no trans. above* per la maior   655 *no trans. above* ja ias . . . uel jon   657 ita *above* in endre; *no trans. above* uel in ondre . . . si cum   658 *no trans. above* prendre compost, *except for* h *above the initial* p   661 prendere

---

B. 639 pressic   640 *om.*   641 planxit *om.*; francxit   643 narrauit   644 debl'e   651 perfecto *om.*   651–2 intelligas   652 secunda   653 ttie   *after* 658 B *adds* prendere compositum   659 *om.*   660 d.] decipere compositum; s. c.] findere   661 mictere

PROVENÇAL TEXT

    batre (compost), *respondre,*
    escondre, fotre,
664 et in -*er*, si cum:
    aver, poder, tener, saber, dever,
sun scenblan a la prima conjugaço, mudat -*at* in -*ut*; et aquelh don l'infinitius fenis in -*ir*, mudat -*at* in -*it*; trait tres que muden -*at* in
668 -*onth*:
    ponher, joher, onher;
e *veçer*, mudat -*at* in -*ist*;
et trait *prendre* et *metre*, ab lo[r] compost, que muden -*at* in -*es*;
672 e trait *escodre*, -*at* in -*os*;
e trait *penher, fenher, empenher, tenher, cenher,* ab totz lor compost, que muden -*at* in -*einht*, et *atenher* esscemen;
11a trait *estrenher*, ab totz sos compost, / que muda -*at* in -*eit*;
676 si cum: *eu avia amat,*
    eu avia saubut, pogut, conogut,
    tengut, degut, agut,
    eu avia auçit, legit, escrit, dit,
680   *eu avia pres, mes,*
    poinht, oinht, jonht,
    estreit, destreit,
    feinht, peinht, teinht,
684   *ceinth, enpeinht.*
El futur del indicatiu sun scenblans totas las quatre conjugaços:
    -*rai,* -*ras,* -*ra,*
    -*rem,* -*retz,* -*ran* vel -*rau.*

A. 667 lin finitius 671 ablo*com*post 673 lor] sos

DL. 662 *om. L* 666 mudar *D*; aqelli *L* 667 mudar *D*; *after* -it, *L adds* Ab illa regula excipiun*tur* tres; etrait treis *L* 668 hont *D*, ont *L* 669 pongner *D*; longer *D*, jonher *L*; honger *D* 670 uezer *DL*; muda *D* 671 *first* et *om. D* 672 *om. D*; traitz escondre qe mude at *L* 673 peingner feingner empeingner tengner teingner ceingner *D*; fener *L*; empenher *placed after* cenher *L* 674 einht] emt *D*, emht *L*; ateingnez *D*; eissamen *D*, esscimen *or* essamen *L* 675 e trait *DL*; estreingnez *D*; co*m*postz *D* 677 sabut *DL* 678 degut *om. D* 679 auzit *DL*; ligit *L*; dit] edic *D* 681 point oint *D*, poinht pinxera*m* oinht vnxera*m L*; lont *D* 683 feint peint teint *D* 684 ceint *D, om. L*; empeint *D*, empeinht *L* 685 sum *D*; semblan *L*; totas *om. D*; quatres *D*; coniugacions *D* 686–7 amarai amara amarem (e < a) uel amarau *only D*

percutere (compositum), *respondere,*
excutere†, *coire,*

et in hac sillaba, verbi gracia: 664
habere, posse, tenere, sapere, debere,
sunt simillia prime coniugationis, mutata hac sillaba -*at* in -*ut*; et
illa quorum infinitivus desinit in hac sillaba, mutata -*at* in -*it*; ab
hac regula excipiuntur tres, ubi loco -*at* ponitur -*onth*: 668

pungere, iungere, ungere;

videre mutat [. . .] (silicet excipitur);
et hoc excepto: *prendere,* et hoc verbo excepto: *mittere,* cum
omnibus suis compositis, que mutant [. . .]; 671a
excepto etiam *excutere,* que mutat [. . .]; 672
exceptis his: *pingere, fingere, inpingere, tingere, cingere,* cum omnibus
suis compositis, que mutant [. . .], *atangere* similliter;
excepto *stringere,* cum omnibus suis compositis, / que mudant 11a
[. . .]; verbi gracia: 675a

amaveram, 676
siveram, potueram, cognoveram,
tenueram, debueram, abueram,
audiveram, legeram, scripsceram, dixeram,
ceperam, miseram, 680
punxeram, onxeram, iu[n]xeram,
strinxeram, constrinxeram,
finxeram, pinxeram, tinxeram,
cinxeram, inpinxeram. 684

In futuro indicativi sunt similia in omnibus quattuor coniugationibus: 685a

amabo, amabis, -bit,
amabimus, -bitis, amabunt.

A. 669 pu*n*gere *on erasure*   670 *no trans. above* at in ist; .s. excipit*ur in
left margin, without insertion-mark*   671a *no trans. above* at in es   672 que
mutat (*followed by a space*) *above* at in os   674 *no trans. above* at in einht
675a *no trans. above* at in eit   681 pinxera*m*; juxera*m*   685–685a quarte
*con*iugationis

B. 663 corre   666 h. s.] sill*a*ba hac   667 at in it *om.*   668 hac *om.*;
ponit onht   670 excipit*ur et* uider*e* m.   671a que*m*   673 *et* exceptis
674 que*m*   674–5 atangere . . . mudant *om.*   677 sciuera*m*   678 habu-
era*m*   679 audieram; scripxera*m or* scripsceram   681 pu*n*cxeram oinxeram
iu*n*cxeram   682 strincxeram; constrinxeram *om.*   683 fincxeram pincxeram
fincxeram   684 cincxeram empe*n*xeram   685–685a *om.*   687 tis bunt

688 E la segonda persona del enperatiu fenis aici cum la terça persona del prescen del indicatiu singular, trait aquest verbe *saber*, que fa *sapchas* el enperatiu. E·l emperatius de la prima fenis in *-a* en segonda persona, en terça in *-e*, sicut:

692 *ama tu, ame cel,*
amem nos, amatz vos, amen cel o *amon* (vel *amo*).

Et es lo futurs del imperatiu tals cum lo prescens.

Lo prescens del optatiu vol en totas conjugaços generalmen 696 fenir en:

-ria, -rias, -ria,
-riam, -riatz, -rien vel *-rion.*

E·l preterit plus quam perfeit fenis in:

700 *agues, aguesses, agues,*
aguessem, aguessetz, aguessen vel *aguesson,*

11b ajustat *-ut* en la fin, en totas personas, si lo verbes es de la segonda / conjugaço o de la terça, si es de la quarta, *-it*. Pero segon que lo 704 preterit plus que perfeit del indicatiu es formatz, sun tuit li preterit plus que perfeit format, ajustat *agues* el cap, si cum:

s'eu agues sabut,
si eu agues tengut,
708 *tendut, perdut, conogut, pogut,*
s'eu agues auçit,
escrit, dormit, delit, aunit,

A. 691–2 sic*ut* ama *on erasure*   693 *uel* amo *interlinear*   695 *after* coni*ugaços, A adds* trait la prima, *without trans.*

DL. 688 E *om. D;* del enperatiu . . . persona *om. L*   689 trat aqueste *D;* sabez *D*   690 sapchaz *D;* E·l e. de la p.] El presen del enperatiu fenissen totas las con*i*ugasos inas dela segonda p*er*sona *et* delatersa in a sicum digas tu diga cel en singular *et* en plural digam nos digatz uos digon cill trait la prima con*i*ugazo del imperatiu qe *L*   691 en terça] ia tercia *D,* et interza *L*; sicum *L, om. D*   693 nos *om. D;* amaz *D;* cill *D,* celli *L;* vel amo *om.* DL 694 futuro *D;* imperatius *L*   695 totas las c. *L*   696 fenire *L* 697 a en rias et en na *D*   698 en na*m* en natz en rien uel no *D* 699 quam] que *D,* qe *L;* p*er*feitz *L*   700 tu aguesses *L;* aguess *D,* cel a. *L*   701 aguessem o aguesson *only D,* nos a. nos a. cill a. *L; after 701 L adds* Addita hac silaba jnfine in omib*us* p*er*sonis   702 auistat *D; after* personas, *L adds rubric* Si u*er*bum est secu*n*de coni*u*gati*on*is (*followed by a space:* Sj lo *begins on a new line, with large capital*); uerbs DL; es] e *D* 703 o] si es *L;* it] addita it *L*   704 tut *L*   705 p*er*feitz *L;* austat *D;* ages *L*   706 *om. D,* eu a. saubut *L*   707 seu DL   708 congut *D*   709 auzit *D,* ausit *L*   710 dormit sic de singu*l*is desit deturpatu*m* aunit uitup*er*atu*m* *L*

Et secunda persona inperativi desinit ita ut tercia persona pre- 688
sentis indicativi singularis, excepto hoc verbo *sapere* [. . .]. Et
inperativus prime persone† desinit sic in secunda persona, et in
tercia in -*e*, verbi gracia:

> *ama tu, amet ille,* 692
> *amemus nos, amate vos, ament.*

Et est futurus inperativi simillis presentis.
Prescens optativi vult in omnibus coniugationibus generaliter ita
fenire: 696
> *utinam amarem, -res,* [-*ret*],
> *amaremus, -tis, -rent.*

In preterito plusquamperfecto:

> *utinam amavissem, amavisses, amavisset,* 700
> *utinam amavissemus, amavissetis, amavissent,*

adita hac sillaba in fine, in omnibus personis, si verbum est
secunde / coniugationis, si est tercie, adita -*ut*, si est quarte, addita 11b
-*it*. [. . .] secundum formationem preteriti plusquamperfecti 704
indicativi formantur alia preterita plusquamperfecti, posita hac
dictione *agues* loco *avia*, verbi gracia: 705a

> *si sivissem,*
> *si tenuissem,*

et sic de singulis addita *agues*: [. . .], *perditum, cognitum,* [. . .], 708

> *si audissem,*

et sic de singulis: [. . .], *dormit*[*um*], *destructum, vituperatum,*

A. 689 *no trans. above* que fa . . . enperatiu   693 ament *u*el amo *above*
amen cel o amon   697 vtina*m* amare*m above* en ria rias; res *above* ria; ret
om.   704 . . .] pore (*above* Pero) (*cf. B*)   708 *et* sic . . . agues *above*
tengut tendut; *no trans. above* pogut   710 *et* sic de*singulis above* escrit;
dormit

B. 688–91 *om.*   692 tu *om.*; ille *om.*   693 ame*n*t amato ame*n*t *only*
694 *om.*   695 Presens; optativi vult *om.*   695–6 g. i. f.] sic*ut*
699 *om.*   700 ses set   701 utinam *om.*; tis sent   703 si est . . .
ut] si prime at si t*er*tie ut; addita *om.*   704 . . .] P*er*o; forma*n*toem
705 plusqua*m*perfecta   705a ages loco ages el cap auia   706 sciuissem
708 addita *om.*; ages   710 sigu*l*is; districtu*m*

si cum se conte plus pleneramen desus el preterit plus que perfeit
del indicatiu.

E·l futur del obtatiu e·l presens del conjuntiu sun scenblan, que
fenissen:

      -a, -as, -a,
      -am, -atz, -an vel *-o,*
si cum: [*cum*] *eu sia, tu sias, cel sia,*
      cum nos siam, vos siatz, cel sian vel *sion.*

El preterit non perfeit del conjunctiu, si es de la segonda o de la
terça:

      -es, -esses, -es,
      -essem, -essetz, -essen,

cum de la prima, si cum:

      cum eu agues,
      tu aguesses,
      cel agues,
      cum nos agssem,
      vos agsetz,
      celh aguessen vel *aguesson;*

si es de la quarta:

      -is, -isses, -is,
      -issem, -issetz, -issen vel *-isson,*

si cum:

      cum eu dormis,
      tu dormisses,
      cel dormis,
      cum nos [*dormissem,*
      vos dormissetz,
      celh] *dormissen* vel *dormisson.*

A. 711 ¶ *marked before* El *preterit*   717 cum *om.* (*so L*)   737–9 nos dormissē. *uel* dormisso*n*

DL. 711 pleneiramen *D*, pleneramen *L*; p*er*feitz *L*   713 coniunctiu *L* 715 *first* a] in a *DL*   716 in am in atz *D*; an uel on *DL*   717 *second* cum *om. L*   718 siaz *D*; cill *D*, cilli *L*   719 p*er*fieg *L* *after* 720 *L adds* cum habere*m*   721 *second* es *om. L*   722 setz *L*; essen] essem *D*, sen *L*   723 prima co*n*iugaçio *L*   724 cum *om. L*; eo *L* 727 aguessem *DL*   728 aguessetz *DL*   729 cill *D*, celli *L*   731 in is in isses in is *D*   732 in issem *D*; issen] issem *D*   734 cum *om. L*; io *L*   737 cum *om. DL*   739 cill *D*, celli *L*; vel] o *DL*

sicut plenius continetur superius in preterito plusquamperfecto indicativi.

Et futurum obtativi et prescens coniunctivi sunt similes in secunda et in tercia et in quarta coniugatione, ita:

>   dicam, dicas, dicat,
>   dicamus, dicatis, dicant,

verbi gracia: cum sim, sis, sit,
>   cum simus, sitis, sint.

In preterito inperfecto coniunctivi, si est secunde (videlicet coniugationis) vel tercie:

>   cum haberem, -res, -ret,
>   cum haberemus, haberetis, haberent;

sicut in prima coniugatione dictum est, verbi gracia:

>   cum haberem,
>   haberes,
>   haberet,
>   cum haberemus,
>   haberetis,
>   haberent;

si est quarte:

>   [. . .],
>   [. . .],

verbi gracia:

>   cum dormirem,
>   dormires,
>   dormiret,
>   in plurari: cum dormiremus,
>   dormiretis,
>   dormirent.

A. 711 *no trans. above* se conte; plen*ius* c*o*ntinet*ur in* p*r*eterito sup*er*ius, *above* plus pleneramen desus; *no trans. above* el preterit   713–15 similes . . . *con*iugatione *above* scenblan . . . a; dica*m* ita. dicas *in double line above* as 717 sis sit *above* tu sias; *no trans. above* cel sia   719 in p*er*fecto (*above* non perfeit)   731–2 *no trans. above* js jsses . . . uel isson   737–9 jnpl*u*rari cu*m* dormirem*us* dor *above* cum nos dormissē; miretis dormire*n*t *above* uel dormisson

B. 711 superius *om.*   713 presens   714 ita] q*ue* desinu*n*t ita   715 dicat] eat   716 tis cant   719 p*er*fecto   722 cum *om.*; tis rent   725 res   726 ret   727 cu*m om.*   728 tis   729 rent   730 quarte] de la qua*r*te   735 res   736 ret   738 tis   739 rent

740 Lo preterit perfeit del conjunctiu:

    aia -ut,
12a   *[a]ias / -ut,*
    aia -ut,
744   *aiam -ut,*
    aiatz -ut,
    aien vel *aion -ut,*

si es de la segonda o de la terça conjugaço, si cum:

748   *cum eu aia tendut,*
    tu aias tendut,
    cel aia tendut,
    nos aiam tendut,
752   *vos aiatz tendut,*
    celh aien vel *aion tendut;*

si es de la quarta, muda *-ut* in *-it,* si cum:

    cum eu aia scentit,
756   *tu aias sentit,*
    cel aia sentit,
    nos aiam sentit,
    vos aiatz sentit,
760   *celh aien* vel *aio sentit.*

Lo preterit plus [que] perfeit del conjunctiu es tals cum del obtatiu.

El futur:

764   *cum eu aurai tengut,*
    tu auras tengut,
    celh aura tengut,

A.   742 ias   752 tendutz (*so D*)   761 p*reterit.* pl*usp*erf.

DL.   740 p*er*fieg *L*   741 eo aia *L*   743 ut *om. D*   745 aitz only *D*   746 ut *om. D*   748 cum *om. L*   749–50 *om. D*   751 aian *L*   752 tendutz *D*   753 cill *D*, celli *L*; vel] ò *D*; aio *L*   754 si] Pi *D*   755 cum *om. L*; sentit *DL*   759 sentitz *D*   760 cill *D*, celli *L*; vel] ò *D*; aion *DL*   761 preteritz plus qe p*er*fieg *L*   after 763 *L* adds cum auro tedu   764 eu *om. L*; arai *L*   765 *om. D*; aras *L*   766 cel *DL*; ara *L*

Hoc duplici modo potest dici, videlicet secunde et tercie con- 740
iugationis: 740a

    prima persona,
    secunda, / 12a
    tercia persona,
    in plurali, 744
    secunda persona,
    tercia persona,

si est secunde vel tercie coniugationis, verbi gracia:

    cum tetenderim, 748
    tetenderis,
    tetenderit,
    in plurari: *cum tetenderimus,*
    tetenderitis, 752
    tetenderint, et sic;

si est quarte (videlicet coniugationis), mutat hanc sillabam *-ut* in
-it, verbi gracia: 754a

    cum scentierim, in singulari, prima persona,
    secunda, *sentieris,* 756
    tercia, *sentierit,*
    in plurari: *cum sentierimus,* prima persona,
    secunda persona, *scentieritis,*
    tercia persona, *scentierint.* 760

Preteritum plusquamperfectum coniunctivi est tale quale obtativi.

Dicit ita in futuro:

    cum tenuero, 764
    tenueris,
    tenuerit,

A. 740–740a *coniug.*   757 sentieris   756–7 *trans. misplaced*: sentieris. ter. sentieris *above* tu aias sentit; *no trans. above* cel aia sentit   759–60 scentieritis. ter. per *above* aiatz sentit; scentierint *above* celh aien; *no trans. above* uel aio sentit

---

B. 742 ut secunda   743 persona *om.*   *after* 744 B *adds* prima persona   745 persona *om.*   746 persona *om.*   751 in plurali prima persona c. t.   752 secunde t.   753 persona tertia tetenderunt; et sic *om.*   754–754a videlicet . . . in it] coniugationis uidelicet mutata hac sillaba at sit   755 sentierim; prime persone   756–60 secunda sentierit tertia sentierimus sentierimus in plurali sentierint *only*   766 rit

> *nos aurem tengut,*
768 > *vos auretz tengut,*
> *celh auran* vel *aurau tengut,*

si es de la segonda o de la terça; si es de la quarta, muda *-ut* in *-it.* Del enfinitiu es dit assatz desus, al come[n]çamen des verbes.

772 Lo pasius de las autras conjugaços, si cum es dit de la primera, si [v]a totz per ordre, fors tan qu'en la segonda et en la terça muda *-at* in *-ut* et en la quarta *-at* in *-it.*

A. 771 começam*en*   773 si va] sia (*sim.* *D*)

DL. 768 aurez *DL*; tengutz *D*   769 cill *D*, celli *L*; vel a.] o auron *D*   770 mada *L*   771 assat de subz *D*; comensamen *DL*; dels *DL*; uerbs *L*   772 O passiun *L*; premera *D*, primiera *L*   773 si va] siaz *D*; orde *DL*; qu'en] quan en *D*

in plurali: *cum tenuerimus,*
tenueritis, 768
tenuerint,

si est secunde, debet ita int[e]lligi, vel tercie coniugationis; si est
quarte, mudat hanc sillabam *-ut* in *-it*. 770a
De infinitivo est dictum satis superius in principio cum cepi
loqui de verbis. 771a
Passivum aliarum coniugationum, sicut dictum est de prima, 772
[. . .] totum per ordinem, excepto hoc quod in secunda et tercia
coniugatione mutat hanc sillabam *-at* in *-ut* et in quarta mutat *-at*
in *-it*. 774a

A. 770 in*t*lligi, *apparently without abbreviation sign* 773 . . .] si *(above* sia)

B. 767 in plurali cum *om.* 768-9 *om.* 770 si e*s*t se*cunde placed after* intelligi   770a mutata hac sill*aba* 772 passiiu*m*; d. e. d. p.] de prima dictum est   773 . . .] sic; hoc] sit   774-774a et in quarta . . . in it *om.*

12b Et aquist sun li verbe de la   Ista sunt verba prime
   prima conjugaço: coniugationis:
   amar   amare
778 adirar   odire
   albergar   hospitari
   ostalar   idem
   arripar   de aqua ad ripam venire
782 aspirar   aspirare
   anelar   anelare
   anar   ambulare
   arar   arare
786 adagar   adaquare
   asclar   findere lingna
   alargar   laxare
   viular   viellare
790 arpar   arpam sonare
   citolar   citariçare
   manduirar   manduiram sonare
   organar   horganiçare
794 cornar   tubam sonare
   trumbar   tubis ereis sonare
   caramelar   [fi]stullis cantare
   assaiar   temptare vel probare
798 adempiar   amicos rogare

Prov. A. 792 mandiurar *rather than* manduirar (*but translation has* manduira*m, with* i *clearly marked*)

BDL. 775 Et a. s.] Aqest son *L, om. B*   776 p*rime B*; *after 776 L adds rubric* Verba pr*ime con*iugationis   778 asirar *L*   780 ostallar *D* 781 aripar *B*, arripiar (*second* i < e) *D*, arpar *L*   783 alleuar *D*, alenar *L* 784 *placed after 797 L*   *after* 785 *L adds* adacquar   788 alegrar *D* 789 violar *BL*, uulgar *D*   790 *om. L* (*cf. 781*)   791 sitular *B*, citola *L*   792 mandurar *BD*, madurar *L*   795 trombar *B*, tronbar *D, om. L* 797–9 *placed after 801 D*   798 ademprar *B*, adempar *DL*

Lat. A. 778 adire   786 equare   789 veillare   791 ti*n*tariçare 796 stullis

B. 775–6 *no trans.*   779 ospitari   780 jde*m* quod ospitari   781 veire 787 ligna   788 lassare   789 violare   792 ma*n*dura*m*   793 organizare   796 cu*m* fistulis (u < t)   797 temptare] tractare

armar	armare	
amblar	plane ambulare	
ajornar	diem assignare, vel clarescere	
acorsar	ad cursum provocare	802
assoudar	stipendiare	
agradar	placere	
auçelar	aves venari	
agulonar	stimulare	806
alongar	prolongare	
abetar	decipere verbis	
abastar	suficere	
aprimar	subtil[i]are	810
aprimairar	ad primos venire	
areçhar	procurare vel ministrare necessaria	
ataïnar	impedire	
afiar	securitatem dare	814
amparar	ocupare vi	
assegurar	securum reddere	
albirar	estimare	
adautar	valde placere	818
avinaçar	vino imbuere	
assautar	provocare ad pugnam	
aprosmar	apropinquare	
badar	os aperire	822
balar	saltare ad vielam vel ad aliquid	
bairar	ponere seram in hostio	

Prov. A. 812 aroçhar

BDL. *after* 802 *L adds* andar uiazo   805 auzelar *B*, ausellar *D*, auselar *L*   806 angulonar *idest* stimular *L*   807 allongair *L*   810 ap*ri*rnar *L*   811 aprimartar *B*, aprimirar *D*   812 arezar *BD*, arizar *L*   *after* 814 *D inserts* 937–50   *after* 817 *D adds* abautar   818 adantar *B*; *after 818 L adds* auinar   819 auinazar *BL*, aumazar *D*   820 asautar *L*   821–2 *om. D*   821 approssimar *L*   823 bolar *B*   824 borar *B*, vairar *L*

Lat. A.   810 subtilare   815 ocupare vi] ocupauit (*sim. B*)

B.   801 diem asignare *only*   802 prouocare a cursu*m*   803 stipendiari   808 decip*erere*   809 sufficere   812 mistrare necc*ess*aria   815 occupauit *only*   819 inbuere   820 pu*n*gnam   823 saltare ad ludu*m only*   824 *no trans.*

baroneiar, baronelar	vel signa baronis hostendere vel iactare se
826 baconar	porcos interficere et ponere in sale
baratar	stulte vel dolose expendere
bateiar	baptiçare
barutelar	farina[m] subtiliare
830 braceiar	cum ulnis mensurare
blanqueiar	candescere
barreiar	impetuose rapere
bellar	ad oves pertinet: bellare
834 bendar	cum victis caput stringere mulierum
bresar	ad capiendum aves sonum facere
bretoneiar	loqui inpetuose
blesseiar	sonare *c* loco *s*
838 bendelar	oculos legare
bullar	bullare
bufar	ore insuflare
brusar	incendere
842 buscalar	ligna parva coligere
brisar	minutatim frangere
biordar	di[s]curere cum equis
baissar	osculari vel d[e]mittere

Prov. A. 825 baroneiar] baronecar   839 buliar

BDL. 825 baronelar *om. BDL*   828 bataiar *L*   829 baratellar *D*; *after* 829 *L repeats* badar (*822*)   830 braciar *B*, brazeiar *D*   831 blanqeiar *BL*   832 baireiaz *D*, bareiar *L*   833 belar *BL*   837 bleseiar *BL*, blesseillar *D*   838 bendellar *D*   839 *om. D*   840 sufflar *D*   841–2 *interverted L*   842 buscallar *DL*, *om. B*   843 *om. B*   843–5 biordar baisar brisar vaissar *L*   844–5 *interverted B*

Lat. A. 825–7 *trans. of* baconar *above* baronelar; *trans. of* baratar *above* baconar; *above* baratar, jmpetuose rapere, *struck through* (*probably not in same ink*)—*this translation belongs to 832, which falls below* baratar *at the end of the following line*   826 et] *uel*   829 farina   830 ulnis] uiciis (*cf. B*)   833 bellare] bella ferre   835 faciens   844 dicurere   845 dmittere *or* dimttere

---

B. 825 s. b. ostende*re only*   827 vel dolose *om.*   828 baptizare   830 cum ulnis] brachijs   832 jnpetuose   833 belare   834 muli*er* bendare *only*   835 bessare *only*   836 impetuose   837 sonar   838 ligare   840 insufflare   842–3 *om.*   844 discurre*re*   845 vel d. *om.*

PROVENÇAL AND LATIN TEXT 155

cantar	cantare	846
calfar	calefieri	
calar	tacere	
caçar	venari	
caminar	equitare per stratas ad inveniendum ho[stem]	850
camiar	mutare	
canbiar	ad monetas pertinet: dare unam pro alia	
castiar	corrigere	
catiglar	digitum ponere sub acella alterius ad provocandum ludere	854
cavar	cavare	
carreiar	portare sarcinas cum asinis	
cembelar	hostendere avem ad capiendum aliam	
classeiar	campanas pulsare	858
clamar	clamare	
cagar	superflua ventris facere	
cremar	incendere	
celar	celare	862
cercar	investigare	
cessar	cessare	
cembar	tabulas valde movere	
cisclar	valde clamare cum voce subtili	866
citar	citare	
cinglar	stringere equum cum cingla	13a
cridar	voce personare	

Prov. A. 848, *with its trans., added in margin, with insertion-mark*   853, *with its trans., added in margin, with insertion-mark*   856 catreiar

---

BDL.   847 callar *BD*   848 *om. D*   849 cazar *BDL*   852 cambiar *BDL*   854 castiglar *B*   856 carcelar *B*, careiar *DL*   857 *om. D*, cenbelar, *placed after 863*, *L*   858 cleseiar *B*; *after 858 L adds* idest sonar campane   860 *om. D*   865 cemblar *D*

Lat. A.   850 *last four letters of* hostem *invisible because of the binding (Stengel read* hos)   854 sub] sub'   865 tabulas] tibias (*so B*)

B.   847 caleficere   850 equitare (*final* e < i); ad i. h. *om.*   852 mutuare *ue*l *mo*netam ca*m*biare *only*   853 castigare   854 abscella; ludum   856 sarcina*m*   857 ostende*r*e; capie*n*de   860 superfluu*m* caga*r*e *only*   865 tibias   868 sti*n*ge*r*e equ*um*   869 personare uoce

156 PROVENÇAL AND LATIN TEXT

870 crivelar   bladum purgare
    conortar   consolari
    confortar   confortare
    coronar   coronare
874 cobeitar   concupisscere
    corolar vel coreiar   coreas ducere
    cobleiar   coblas facere
    consirar   considerare
878 cobrar   recuperare
    colar   colare
    co[n]deiar   valde se in cunctis aptare
    conselar   consilium dare
882 contar   computare
    concagar   cum stercore deturpare
    damnar   damnare
    dançar   ad coreas saltare
886 daurar, compost sobradaurar   deaurare
    devinar   devinare
    descombrar   ab impedimento locum purgare
    deirocar   diruere
890 destorbar   in aliquo facto se op[o]nere
    destrigar   ocasione[m] more dare
    deirengar   de serie militum exire
    desgitar   eicere
894 despolhar   expoliare
    deliurar   liberare

Prov. A. 880 codeiar   886 sobradaurar *interlinear, above* compost

---

BDL. 870 criuellar *D*   875 *om. L*; vel coreiar *om. BD*   876 *om. L*
878 coubrar < conblar *B*   880 *om. L*   881 conselhar *B*, conseillar *D*, comsselliar *L*; *after 881 D repeats* clamar *(859)*   882 comtar *DL*
883 congagar *B*, congegar *L*   885 danzar *BL*, datissar *D*   886 sobradaurar *om. DL*, sobredeaurare, *in column devoted to Latin, B*   887 diuinar *B*, deiunar *D*   888 discombrar *B*, deicombrar *L*   889 derocar *BL*
891 distringar *B*   892 detengar *B*, derrengar *D*, derengar *L*   894 despollar *DL*   895 delliurar (i < e?) *D*

Lat. A. 880 cond*e*iare ualde   888 locum] loco   890 opnere
891 ocasione (*sim. B*)

B. 874 concupisc*ere* (i < u *by expunctuation of second minim*)   887 diuinare   889 dirruere   891 occasione   892 milit*em*   893 cinge*re*
895 deliberare

demandar	requirere	
desmandar	mandata revocare	
dejunar	ieiunare	898
descha[u]zar	discalciare	
desarmar	arma deponere	
despulçelar	corumpere puellam virginem	
desirar	desiderare	902
degolar	decapitare	
desviar	deviare	
descargar	exonerare	
deribar	extra ripam exire	906
desclavar	clavos extraere	
desaiar	aperire, seram aufere	
desflibar	palium deponere	
detirar	valde traere	910
desdejunar	frangere ieiunium	
disnar	prandere	
dictar	dictare	
dissipar	dissipare	914
donar	donare	
domneiar	cum dominabus loqui de amore	
doblar	duplicare	
dolar	dolare	918
doptar	dubitare	
durar	durare	
estar	stare	
espirar	inquirere†	922
esquivar	devitare	

Prov. A. 899 deschazar

BDL. 897 *om.* L   898 deuinar L   899 descauzar BDL   *after*
900 D *repeats 895-6*   901 despouzelar B, despucellar D, despiuzelar L
903 degollar D   904 disuiar B   905 desgargar B   906 deripar B
908 desarrar B, desserar D, deserar L   909 desfiblar BL, defflibar D
911-13 *om.* L   911 dediuinar D   913 dietar D   914 desipar L
916 doneiar BL   *after* 921 D *adds* prestar   922 espirar, *with first* r
struck through with thin vertical stroke, B, esspirar D   923 esquiar B,
esqiuar L

Lat. A. 897 pr*o*uocare

B. 899 discaltiare   901 corru*m*pere; puellam *om.*   903 precipitare
907 claues extrahere   908 se*r*a auferre   910 trahere   921 estare

158 PROVENÇAL AND LATIN TEXT

esperar	sperare
emblar	furari
926 errar	errare
esperonar	calcaribus equum urgere
essugar	sicare
enganar	fallere
930 enastar	in ligno ad assandum ponere
endurar	ie[i]unare
embargar	impedire
enanchar	profichere in aliquo
934 esmaiar	timore deficere
ensenar	docere
enviar	trasmittere
essauchar	probare
938 esfredar	timorem immittere
esforchar	vires colligere
encolpar	inculpare
enpenhar	in pignore mittere
942 enunbrar	propter umbram timere vel sensum amittere
enebriar	inebriare
escampar	evadere
escoissar	per coxas dividere
946 escortgar	excoriare
embotar	utrem implere
essaurar	ad auram exire

Prov. A.   946 escorigare

BDL.   925 enblar *L*   932 enbargar *B*, enbariar *D*   933 enanzar *BDL*   934 elmaiar *L*   935 ensenhar *B*, enseingnar *D*, ensegnhar *L*   936 eni*m*uar *D*, enuiar *L*   937–50 *placed after 814 D*   937 essauzar *BL*, essaiar *D*   938 effredar *B*, effreidar *D*, estredar *L*   939 esforzar *BD*, esforsar *L*   941 enpenar *B*, empegnar *D*   942 enumbrar *BD* enobrar *L*   944 escapar *BL*   945 escoisar (i < r) *B*   946 escortagar *B*, escorgar *DL*   947 embotar (t < r) *B*, enbotar *L*   948 saussar *L*

Lat. A.   930 ad asta*m* ponere   931 jeunare   942 admittere

---

B.   927 equm; urgere *om.*   928 siccare   930 ad assa deponere
931 *no trans., but above the space is written, in the upper margin, faintly,* iegunare
932 inpedire   933 proficere   936 tra*n*smictere   941 mictere
945 *per added above the line;* cossas   948 ad *om.*

PROVENÇAL AND LATIN TEXT

ensanglentar	sanguine poluere	
esmendar	emendare	950
enchauzar	fugare	
enclavar	clavum in pedem figere	
escracar	tusiendo sputum emittere	
essemblar	exemplare	954
entamenar	pannis partem vel pomi vel alicuius rei auferre	
esbudelar	intestina de ventre exire	
enflar	inflare	
enbriar	cresscere	958
estoiar	reponere	13b
ensachar	in sachum mitere	
enborsar	in bursam mitere	
enalbar	erigere duos pedes et in duobus sustentari	962
esmerar	depurare	
enrabiar	in rabiem venire	
escolar	castrare	
enlumenar	inluminare	966
eniuragar	lolio inficere	
far	facere	
fadiar	repulsam pati	
faiturar	maleficiare	970
fade[i]ar	stultitiam facere	

Prov. A. *after* 969 fadiar *repeated and struck through, the translation above it being erased*   971 fadear

---

BDL. 949 ensagneltar *B*, esancretar *L*   950 esmenda'r *B*   951 encausar *BL*, encauzar (z < s) *D*   953 enscracar *D*   954 esemplar *BL*, essemplar *D*   956 esbudellar *D*, esbudarar *L*   957 enfrar *D*   958 embriar *L*   960 ensacar *BDL*   961 *om. D*   962 enarbrar *B*   965 escohar *B*, escollar *D*, escolliar *L*   966 enluminar *D*   967 emuragar *D*, enmuragar *L*   969 *placed after* 971 *B, om. D*   971–2 *interverted L*

Lat. A. 949 sa*nguinem*   952 fi*n*gere   953 tusie*n*de   955 p*arrem ue*l ponu (*or* pomi)   963 deputare (*so B*)

B. 949 polluere   952 pede   953 tussiendo spiritum emictere   955 panis p*artem ue*l pa*n*ni   956 exire] trahere   958 crescere   960 repone*re only, lightly struck through*   961 m*i*ttere*re*   962 substentari   963 deputare   964 rabia*m*   966 illuminare   970 malefitiare

PROVENÇAL AND LATIN TEXT

fabregar — fabricare
fermar — firmare
974 ferrar — ferare
fiar, compost afiar, desfiar — confidere
filar — nere
follar — sub pede calcare
978 afolar — deteriorare
afogar — ignem ponere
ofegar — subfocare
forçhar — vim facere
982 gardar, compost — custodire vel respicere
garar — idem
galopar — inter trotare et curere saltus parvos facere
gastar, compost — devastare
986 gratar — scalpere
gadanhar — lucrari
gaitar — vigilare ad custodiam
gelar — congelare
990 greujar — gravare
grenar — spica post messores coligere
gitar — iactare
guidar — dare conductum
994 glaçar — gelu constringere
governar — gubernare

Prov. A. 974, *with its trans.*, *added in margin, with insertion-mark* 975 afia*r* desfiar *interlinear, above* compost filar

---

BDL. 973 formar *B*   974 feirar *BD*   975 fizar *D,* siar *L*; affiar deffiar *B, om. DL*   977 folar *BL*   978 affolar *B*, afollar *D*   979 affogar *D*   980 offegar *D*   981 forzar *BD,* forsar *L* 984 gallopar *D, placed after* 994 *L*   *after* 985 *B adds* degastar 987 gasanhar *B,* cazaingnar *D,* gasauhar *L*   989 gellar *D*   990 greiuar *B,* gremar *L*   991 glenar *BDL*   993 *om. B,* girdar *D,* gidar *L*; *after* 993, *B adds* galliar .i. fallere, *L adds* galiar   994 glazar *BL*, glazaz *D*

Lat. A.   976 nere *extends into margin, its place being partly occupied by* desfiar (*cf. Prov. var.*).   983 *no trans.*, jdem *being placed above* compost (*982*) 993 dare] guidare

---

B.   973 formare (*cf. Prov. var.*)   977 sub < sup   979 ponere] aponcere   980 suffocare   984 cure*re* intus troctare *et* s. p. f. 985 vastare   991 spicam: colligere   992 iacere   993 *om.*

gotar, compost degotar	stillare	
glotoneiar	ingluviem facere	
intrar	intrare	998
içalar	propter muscam fugere: ad boves pertinet	
jurar	iurare	
jogar	ludere	
juçiar	iudicare	1002
justiciar	iusticiam exibere	
lauçar	laudare	
lavar	lavare	
lairar	latrare	1006
laissar	dimittere	
lassar	fatigare	
laborar	laborare	
latinar	latine loqui	1010
leujar	aleviare	
levar	levare	
lecar	lingere	
listrar	per virgas hornare	1014
liurar, compost	dare	
lipsar	polir[e]	
luitar	luctari	
manjar	manducare	1018
matar	matare	
maridar	maritare	

Prov. A. 996 degotar *interlinear, above* compost   997 gloteneiar
999 inçatar   1017 liurar

BDL. 996 degotar *om. DL*, degotare *B*   999 izalar *BL*, balar *D*
1001 Iogar (I < l) *D*   1002 iutiar *B*, Iustrar (I < l) *D*, uiticar *L*
1003 iustiziar *B*, iustisiar *D*, iustitiar *L*   1004 lauzar *BDL*   1006 latrar *B*   1007 lassar (*with trans.* dimittere) *B*, laisar *L*   1008 *om. B* (*cf. 1007*)   1011 aleuiar *D*   1013 letar *L*   1014 listar *BDL* *after*
1015 *B adds* deliurar   1016 lispar *L*   1017 liuitar *D*   1019 macar *D*   1020 *om. D*

Lat. A. 1016 polir   1017 lucrari (*cf. Prov. var.*)

B. 997 inngluuie*m*   999 ad b. p. *om.*   1003 iustitiam exigere
1008 *om.*   1013 lecare   1014 ornare   1015 libra*m* dare

maçerar	macerare: ad panificat[ionem] pertinet
1022 malevar	fideiubere
mascarar	carbone tingere
menar	conducere vel minare
menaçar	minari
1026 melhurar	meliorare
messurar	mensurare
mechinar	medicinam dare
mendigar	mendicare
1030 mesgabar	infortunio amittere
menbrar, compost remembrar	recordari
mercadar	mercari
meraveilhar	mirari
1034 mesclar	litigare
meitadar	medium facere unius coloris, medium alii
madurar	maturare
machar	percutere
1038 mirar	in speculo inspicere
mostrar	mostrare
moschar	muscas abicere
moscidar	cum naribus insuflare
1042 montar	ascendere
monestar	monere
naveiar	navigare
nadar	natare

Prov. A.   1031 rem*em*brar *interlinear, above* compost   1041 mosciclar

BDL. 1021 mażerar *BD*   1022 malleuar *B*, manleuar *DL*   1025 menazar *BDL*; *after 1025 L adds* maselar   1026 meillurar *D*, mellurar *L*   1027 mesurar *BL*   1028 mezinar *BDL*   1030 mescabar *BDL*   1031 membriar *D*; remembrar *om. BDL*   1032 mergadar *B*   1033 *om. B*, meraueillar *D*, meraueilar *L*   1034 *om. B*, mescollar *D*   1035 *om. B*, meicadar *L*   1037 matar *B*, macar *D*, marcar *L*   1039 mostar *L*   1040 moscar *BDL*   1041 mosidar *L*   1044 nauegar *L*

Lat. A.   1021 panificat, *apparently without abbreviation sign*   1022 fide*m* iubere   1023 ca*r*bonem   1030 admittere

B.   1021 mazerare *only*   1024 minare *only*   1032 mercatari   1033–5 *om.*   1037 p*er*ercutere   1041 *in*sufflare   1045 notare

nafrar	vulnerare	1046
negar	aquis sufocare	
neblar	nebulla perire	
nevar	ningere	
notar	notare	1050
nombrar	numerare	
nomar	nominare	
obrar	operari	
onrar	honorare	1054
orar	orare	14a
ondeiar	undis tumescere	
onceiar	oncias pedum curvare	
odorar	odorare	1058
ocaisonar	ocasiones inquirere	
oscar	ebedare	
ostar	removere	
ostalar	in ospicium intrare	1062
oblidar	obliviscere	
[parar, compost]	[parare]	
passeiar	passus magnos facere	
parlar	loqui	1066
pagar	pecuniam solvere	
passar, compost transpassar	transire	
paussar, compost trapa[u]ssar	requiescere	
pastar	farinam cum aqua miscere	1070

Prov. A. 1046 nafrai, *the* i *resembling an* r *without its final stroke* 1064 *om.* 1068 passar, *with its trans., added in margin, with insertion-mark;* transpassar *interlinear, above* compost 1069 pau*s*/sar, *split over two lines;* trapassar, *interlinear, above* compost

BDL. 1046 naffrar *B*, nastrar *D* 1049 niuar *B* 1051 nonbrar *L* 1052 nomnar *B*, nominar *DL* 1055 *om. L* 1057 onzeiar *B* 1058 odoraiar *L* 1059 ocaissonar *B* *after* 1064 *B adds* reparare 1065 *placed after 1068 DL; after 1065 B inserts 1069* 1068 passare i*dest* transire *L;* transpassar *om. DL* 1069 *om. D, placed after 1065 B;* pausar *BL;* compost *om. B (cf. 1070);* trapaussar *om. BL* 1070 *om. D,* campastar *B*

Lat. A. 1057 oncia*s* pede*s* cu*r*uare, oncias *being added above* pedes 1060 ebeditare (*cf. B*) 1064 *om.*

B. 1047 suffocare 1048 nebla 1054 honorari (h < o) 1056 tumesscere 1057 untiam 1058 odorare (a < e) 1059 occ*asi*oes qu*er*ere 1060 ditare 1062 hospitium 1063 obliuissc*er*e

plaideiar	causari
plantar	plantare
placeiar	per plateas ire
1074 praticar	practicare
pantaiar	so[m]pniare
penar	pena[m] sustinere
penhurar	pignus auferre
1078 peiurar	peiorare
pellar	depillare, vel pilos auferre
peschar	piscari
pechar	peccare
1082 peçeiar	minutatim frangere
petazar	reficere v[e]tera
perilhar	periclitari
pensar	meditari
1086 peçugar	cum digitis duobus aliquid stringere
pesar	ponderare, vel moleste ferre
pectenar	pettinare
pertusar	perforare
1090 preçicar	predicare
prescentar, compost	presentare
pregar	precari
preçar	apreciare
1094 pejurar	periurare

Prov. A. 1081, *with its trans., added in margin, at end of line* 1085, *with its trans., added in margin, with insertion-mark*

BDL. 1071 *om.* D 1073 plaçeiar *B*, plaigiar *L* 1074 practicar *L* 1075 panteiar *D*, pa*n*tessar *L* 1077 pegnorar *B*, peingnorar *D* 1078 peiorar *BD*, peiurar (p < d) *L* 1079 pelar *BDL* 1080 pescar *BDL* 1081 pecar *BD*, peccar *L* 1082 penzeiar *B*, pezeiar *D*, peciar *L* 1083 petezar *L* 1084 perillar *DL* 1086 pezucar *B*, pezugar *D*, pesugar *L* 1087 penzar *B* 1088 petenar *B* 1089 pertussar *D* 1090 presicar *B*, prezicar *D* 1091 presentar *BDL*; compost *om. D (cf. 1092)* 1092 compregar (p *written over another letter, perhaps* r) *D* 1093 prezar *BD*, perzar *L* 1094 periurar *BDL*

Lat. A. 1075 sopinare 1076 pena 1083 vtera

B. 1074 praticare 1076 su*b*stinere 1079 depilare i*d*est p. a. 1083 ue*n*ta 1084 periculare 1085 meditare 1086 cum duobus digitis aliqu*em* s. 1087 vel m. f. *om.* 1088 petenare 1092 precare 1093 apretiare

plegar	plicare	
prestar	mutuare	
pissar	mingere	
picar	picare	1098
pistar	terere	
portar	portare	
ponzilar	ad diruendum muri ligna ponere, vel diruere murum cum ligno	
ponçeiar	inprobare bene[fitia]	1102
podar	putare vineas	
poiar, compost	ascendere	
plorar	flere	
proar	probare	1106
plovinar	frequenter pluere	
pomelar	pomum in aerem proicere	
polsar	valde anelare	
ponhtar	punchare	1110
purgar	purgare	
quarar	quadrare	
quitar	inmunem reddere	
quintar	qu[in]tam partem tollere	1114
quartar	quartam partem tollere	
raubar	rapinam ex[er]cere	
rancurar	conqueri	
raçonar	rationem redere	1118
ramponar	dicere verba contraria derisorie	
rautar	subito de manu auferre	

Prov. BDL. 1097 piscar *D*   1101 pongilar *B*   1102 ponzeiar *BDL*
1104 compost *om. D (cf. 1105)*   1105 co*m*plorar *D*   1106 prohar *B*
1110 pontar *BD*, ponthar *L*   1111 porgar *L*   1112 quarrar *D*, qairar *L*; *after 1112 L adds* qelotar   1113–15 *om. D*   1118 rasonar *BL*, rosonar *D*   1119 ranpoinar *B*, rampoignar *D*, ranponhar *L*   1120 rantar *B*

Lat. A. 1101 ad diru*e*rede muri   1102 inp*r*obare *only*   1103 bene
p. u.   1113 jnmune*r*e *(so B)*   1114 quta*m*   1116 exce*r*e

---

B. 1099 terrere   1101 *no trans.*   1102 pone*r*e benefitia alijs
1103 inp*r*obare *u*el putare *only*   1104 a. uineas   1108 aere*m*m eicere
1110 pu*n*ctare   1113 inmune*r*e   1114 tollere] coll'.   1115 tollere] coll'.   1118 reddere   1120 auferri

rasclar	ligno radere
1122 raiar	radiare
ranqueirar	claudicare
restaurar	restaurare
refiudar	refutare
1126 regardar	respicere
remirar	valde respicere
reparar	reparare
renoelar	renovare
1130 revelar	revellare
respirar	respirare
revelhar	excitare
remembrar	recordari
1134 rimar	rimos facere
ribar, compost	repercutere clavos
rodar	in circuitu ire
romiar	ruminare
1138 rotar	eructare
roflar	turpiter insuflare
ronchar	dormiendo cum gula barrire
rosseiar	rubesscere
1142 roïlhar	rubigine inficere
rogeiar	groco rubescere vel nitescere
rocegar	traere cum equis
sautar	saltare
1146 sadolar	saciare

Prov. A. 1122 raidar 1123 rauqueirar 1142 roilhal

BDL. *after* 1122 L *adds* ranceiar 1123 ranqueiar *BDL* 1125 refudar *L* 1129 renouellar *D* 1130 *om. B*, reuellar *D* 1131 *om. B* 1132 *om. B*, reueillar *D*, reueilar *L* *before* 1133 *B adds* remendar *with trans.* remenendare 1137 rojnar *L* 1138 *om. D*, ructar *B* 1139 rotiar *L* 1140 roncar *BDL* 1141–2 *interverted D* 1142 roglar *D*, roillar *L* 1143 roieiar *BL* 1144 rosegar *L*

Lat. A. 1121 radare 1135 repercutere *above* ribar; clauos *above* compost

B. 1121 cum l. r. 1122 radere 1130–2 *om.* 1133 *no trans., but with a line going up to* remenendare *in the previous line (cf. Prov. var.*) 1134 rimas 1135 clauos repercutere 1137 romicare 1139 insufflare 1140 g. b.] gulabar. 1142 rubiginem 1143 rubescere *only* 1144 trahere 1146 satiare

saborar	saporare	
sanar	sanare	
sairar	claudere vel firmare	
salvar	salvare	1150
saludar	saludare	
sagetar	sagitare	
sanglentar	sanguine poluere	
sacrar	sacrare /	1154
sa/crifiar	sacrificare	**14b**
senhar	signare	
secar	sicare	
seminar	seminare	1158
selar	sternere equum	
segar	resecare	
senhoreiar	dominari	
siblar	sibillare	1162
senblar, compost	similare	
sebrar	separare	
sonar	sonare	
somnhar	somniare	1166
sopar	cenare	
soflar	cum naribus spirare	
sosteirar	sepelire	
sohanar	recussare	1170
sospirar	suspirare	
solachar	verbis ludere	
solar	soleas mitere	
sogautar	super gullam percutere	1174

Prov. BDL. 1147–8 *interverted L* before 1149 *L adds* saciar 1149 sarrar *B* 1150–1 *interverted L* 1152 saietar *L* 1153 sangletar *BD*, sauglentar *L* 1154 sagrar *B* 1156 seingnar *D* 1157 sechar *L*; *after 1157 L adds* serrar 1158 semenar *DL* 1159 sellar *D* 1161 seingnorar *D* 1163 semblar *BDL*; *compositum B* 1166 sonar *B*, somneiar *D*, somnar *L* 1167 soplar *D* 1168 soflar (f < p?) *D* 1169 *om. B*, sotteiar *D*, sosterar *L* 1170 soanar *BDL* 1172 solazar *BDL* 1174–5 *interverted L* 1174 sugautar *B*

Lat. A. 1153 sa*nguinem* 1159 strue*re* 1173 soleras

B. 1148 sana 1149 firmare hostiu*m only* 1151 salutare 1152 sagittare 1153 polluere 1157 siccare 1159 equm 1160 r. he*r*bas 1162 sibilare 1166 so*m*pniare 1169 *om.* 1170 *no trans.* 1171 sospirare 1173 *no trans.* 1174 s*u*b gula

sostar	inducias dare
sobdar	ex improviso prevenire
sobranceiar	superbe se erigere
1178 sobrar	superare
sordeiar	deteriorare
solhelar	ad solem calefacere
suar	sudare
1182 sitar	[...]
taular ⎫ entaular ⎭	⎧invictus manere; utrumque: ⎩ludum ordinare
traïnar	ad caudam equorum traere vel fraudulenter [ad] se traere
1186 travar	duos pedes equi ligare
entravar	idem
trasbucar	ruere
tamboreçar	timpanizare
1190 tauleiar	tabulas parvas sonare
talar	vastare
talhar	resecchare
tabustar	tumultuare
1194 tastar	tangere vel gustare
traucar	perforare
traversar	per traversum ire
entraversar	in oblicum se oponere

Prov. A. 1175 sostrar   1176 soldar   1181 souar   1182 sagitar, *without trans.*, *added in margin with insertion-mark before* sitar

---

BDL. 1177 sobrancar *D*, sobranseiar *L*   1180 solheiar (*with* h *added above the line B*) *BL*, solleiar *D*   1181–2 suar sugar *B*, sitar sudar *D*, suar suar *L*   1185 tramar *D*, rainar *L*   1186 tintiar *or* tinciar *L*   1188 trabucar *D*   1189–94 *given twice D*   1189 tabureiar *B*, taboreiar (*both times D*) *DL*   1191 calar *L*   1191–2 talar *only D* (*first time*), tallar talar *D* (*second time*)   1194 *om. B*   1195 trancar *L*   1196 traueisar *B*

Lat. A. 1177 supe*r*te   1182 sagitare (*cf. Prov. var.*)   1183–4 j*n* uict*us* manere utru*m*que ludu*m* ordinare. *uel* fraudulent*er* se traere, *written in double line above both verbs*   1185 ad c. e. t. *only*   1197 *first* o *of* opone*r*e *on an erasure*

B. 1175 jndutia stare   1179 deteriora.   1182 sciugare (*cf. Prov. var.*)   1183 *no trans.*   1184 ludu*m* ordinare *only*   1185 te*rr*e; trahere   1189 timpanare   1192 resecare   1194 *om.*   1196 tranu*er*su*m*, *with what is possibly* s *added above the line, between* n *and* u   1197 oppone*r*e

tremblar	tremere	1198
trescar	coream intricatam facere	
trencar	secare	
trepar	manibus ludere	
treblar	turbare aquam vel aliquem li-	
	quorem	1202
terçar	terciam partem sumere	
tençar	litigare	
temptar	temptare	
trevar	frequentare	1206
entrevar	treguas facere	
triar	eligere	
trichar	fraudari	
trissar	terere	1210
tribolar	tribulare	
tronar	tonare	
tombar	tombare	
torbar	turbare	1214
tostar	assare	
trobar	invenire	
tocar	tangere	
trombar	tubis sonare	1218
trotar	trotare	
trossar	post se malam ligare	
trolhar	in torculari premere	
trufar	verba vana dicere, vel fallere	1222
vantar	iactare se	

Prov. A. 1203 tereçar 1205 temprar 1223 vanturar

BDL. 1202 trebar *D* 1203 terzar *BDL* 1204 tenzar *BDL*
1205 temtar *D* 1206 trouar *or* treuar *L* 1207 entreuare *D*
1209 *om. B*, tridar *D* 1210 *om. D*, trisar *L* 1212 tornar *D*
1213–14 *interverted L* 1215 toscar *D* 1216 torbrar *D* 1217 toc-
car *B*, tocar, *with* i (?) *added above* ca, *L* 1218 tromba *B, om. D*
1220 troscar *D* 1221 trollar *D* 1222 trutar *L*

Lat. A. 1205 te*m*perare (*cf. Prov. var.*) 1213 dombare 1222 fallere]
facere

B. 1199 facere] ducere 1200 seccare 1201 ludu*m* 1202 liquorem
om. 1203 tertiam 1207 treuguas 1209 *om.* 1210 terrere
1213 tomare 1218 tubas 1219 troctare 1222 vana] uaria
1223 se *om.*

vairar	variare
varar	navem in pellago mittere
1226 ventar	[ad] ventum exponere
vedar	vetare
velhar	vigillare
vergonhar	herubescere
1230 vernhissar	armam post picturam illustrare
vespertinar	in vespere parum gustare
vengar	vindicare
verdeiar	virescere
1234 versificar	versificare
vergar	virgas facere
visitar	visitare
virar	volvere
1238 udolar	ululare
upar	upare
ucar	voce sine verbis aliquem vocare
usclar	pilos comburere, vel ustulare
1242 urtar	frontem contra frontem ponere
usar	usitare
De la segonda conjugaço:	De secunda coniugatione sunt ista:
aver	habere
1246 assezer	sedere
caber	capere ('sermo meus . . .')
saber	sapere

Prov. A. 1237 *first three letters on an erasure*

BDL. 1225 *om. L* 1226 vencar *L* 1227 aiedar *D* 1228 ueillar *D*, velar *L* 1229 uergognar *D* 1230 verniar *B*, uertussar *D*, vernisar *L* 1232 vengiar *uel* ueniar *B*, ueniar *D* 1234 versifiar *BL* 1235 *om. B* 1238 violar *L* 1242 vrar *B*, vurtar *L* 1244 De] En *B*; *after 1244 L adds rubric* Verba secunde coniugationis 1246 asazer, *with second* a *written over another letter* (e?) *D*, asezer *L* 1248 sauer *D*

Lat. A. 1226 ad *om.* 1241 ustulare] cixolare

B. 1225 mittere nauem in pelagum 1228 vigilare 1229 erubescere 1230 vernicare arma prout picturas illustrare 1234 versificari 1235 *om.* 1240 aliquid 1241 pilos buere *only* 1242 ponere *om.* 1244 *no trans.* 1247 capere *only*

dever	debere	
tener	tenere	1250
retener	retinere	
abstener	abstinere	
pertener	pertinere	
mantener	patrocinium dare	1254
cacher	cadere	15a
dechaçer	depauperare	
escaçer	competere	
voler	velle	1258
placher	placere	
desplaçer	displicere	
valer	vallere	
traire	traere	1262
atraire	ad se traere	
pertrair[e]	ad aliquod opus necessaria f[acere]	
retraire	referre	
fortraire	furtim subripere	1266
sotztraire	subtraere	
estenher	extinguere	
penher	pingere	
empenher	impingere vel pellere	1270
fenher	fingere	
cenher	cingere	
tenher	tingere	

Prov. A. 1261–5, *with their trans.*, *added in margins* (*1261–2 in right margin after* desplaçer, *1263–4 in right margin after* empenher, *1265 in left margin, before* fortraire) 1264 *last letter of* pertraire *cut off by binder* (*Stengel read* pertraire)

BDL. 1255 cazer *BDL* 1256 decazer *B*, descazer *DL* 1257 escazer *BDL* 1259 plazer *BDL* 1260–1 *interverted L* 1260 desplazer *BDL*; *after 1260 D repeats* uoler (*1258*) 1267 sostrare *D*, soztraire *L* 1268 estreingner *D* 1269 pinher *B*, peingner *D* 1270–1 *interverted L* 1270 enpenher *B*, empeingner *D* 1271 feingner *D* 1272 ceingner *D* 1273 teingner *D*, thener *L*

Lat. A. 1264 *last five letters of* facere *cut off by binder* (*Stengel read* facere) 1270 pell*is*

B. 1261 valere 1262 trahere 1263 trahere 1264 aliqd'; nec*essari*a trahere 1266 furtu*m* 1267 subtraire 1270 inpingere *only* 1271 *no trans.*

1274 destenher — tincturam removere
estrenher — stringere
destrenher — constringere
creisser — cressere
1278 beure — bibere
moure — movere
viure — vivere
vencher — vincere
1282 percebre — percipere
decebre — decipere
recebre — recipere
concebre — concipere
1286 respondre — respondere
fendre — fi[n]d[e]re
defendre — defendere
encendre — adustionem pati
1290 fondre — fundere vel liquefieri
confondre — ad nichilum redigere
tendre — tendere
estendre — extendere
1294 destendre — arcum vel balistam laxare
contendre — contendere
atendre — expectare vel promissum solvere
vendre — vendere
1298 revendre — iterum vendere
escoissendre — per conum sindere vel panos si[n]dere

prendre — prendere
aprendre — aprendere, adiscere

Prov. A. 1301 apre*n*dere (*cf. Lat. var.*)

BDL. 1274 destreingner *D*   1275 *om.* DL (*cf. 1268 D*)   1276 *om.*
D (*cf. 1274*), destrener *L*   1277 cresser *B*, creiser *L*; *after 1277 L adds*
teisser   1281 vencer *BD*, venzer *L*   1285 *om. L*   1294 *om. D*
1299 escoscendre *B*, escoisendre *L*   1300 perpendre *D*

Lat. A. 1287 fidre   1299 p*er*conis sinder*e* u*e*l panos sidere   1300–1 *above*
prendre *is translation* prendere aprendere adiscere, *with a second* aprendere *added above the first*

B. 1274 ti*n*turam   1276 costringe*re*   1277 cresscere   1290 fo*n*dere
1294 laxare] destendere   1299 p*er*cossas scindere *ue*l pa*n*nos scindere
1301 adisscere *only*

desaprendre	dediscere	1302
mesprendre	delinquere	
sobreprendre	reprehendere vel subito prendere	
enprendre	disponere	
esprendre	accendere	1306
esconprendre	simul accendere vel valde	
antreprendre, anteprendre	[. . .]	
pendre	pendere (media correpta vel producta)	
despendre	a suspendio deponere	1310
escondre	excutere granum de paleis†	
secodre	concuter[e]	
corre	currere	
acorre	succurrere	1314
socore	idem est	
segre	sequi	
persegre	persequi	
consegre	consequi	1318
raire	radere	
ponre	ovum facere	
aponre	aponere	
desponre	deponere	1322
querer	querere	
conquerer	aquirere	

Prov. A. 1308 ante p*rendere*, *interlinear*, *above* antreprendre (*sim. B*) 1311, *with its trans*., *added in margin*, *with insertion-mark*

BDL. 1304 *om*. *L*   1305 emprendre (*second* r *altered from another letter D*) *DL*   1306 *om*. *D*   1307 *om*. *D*, escomprendre *L*   1308 *om*. *D*; anteprendre *om*. *L*, ante prendere *in column devoted to Latin B*   1309 *om*. *D*   1310 desprendre *D*   1311 escodre *D*; *after 1311 L adds* pertondre   1315 socorre *B*, secore *L*   1317 *om*. *B*   1318 conseigre *D*   1319–20 raireponre, *with third* r *altered from another letter* (z?) *D*   1323 querre *BD*   1324 conquerre *BD*

Lat. A.   1303 derelinquere   1308 *see Prov. var*.   1309 pendere] p*rendere*   1312 co*n*cuter   1320 o. f. apone*re*   1323 queroir

---

B. 1303 *no trans*.   1304 reprendere   1307 acendere   1308 *cf*.
Prov. var.   1309 pendere] pode; correcta   1311 de p. *om*.   1314 succurere   1315 est *om*.   1317 *om*.   1318 conseq.   1322 disponere   1324 acquirere

vecher	videre
1326 escrire	scribere
dire o dir	dicere
ploure	pluere
tondre	tondere (media producta)
1330 devire o devir	dividere
[assire o] assir	assedere
auçire o auçir	ocidere
eslire o eslir	eligere
1334 frire	frigere
refrire	resonare
rire	ridere
creire	credere
1338 metre	mittere
prometre	promittere
entremetre	intromittere
sotzmetre	submittere
1342 trametre	transmittere
esdemetre	assultum facere
escometre	provocare
claure	claudere

1346 Tut li verbe sobredit don l'i[n]finitius fenis in -*er* sum 15b de la segonda conjugaço / et tut li altre de la terça,

Omnia verba supradicta quorum infinitivus finit in hac sillaba sunt secunde coniugationis / et omnia alia tercie

Prov. A. 1331 assir *only* 1347 lifinitius

BDL. 1325 vezer *BL*, uezer < ueser *D* 1327 dire u*e*l dir *B*, dire *only D*, dire odire *L* 1328 ploire *B* 1330 deuire *only D* 1331-2 *interverted BDL* 1331 assir o assire *BD*, aissir o aissir *L* 1332 aucir o aucire *B*, auzir (z < s) ò ausire *D*, aucire o aucir *L* 1333 eslir o (ò *D*) eslire *BD*, eslir oeslir *L* 1340 *om*. *B* 1341 *om*. *B*, sozmetre *DL* 1343 esdesmetre *B*, edesmetre *D* 1346 Tuit *BDL* 1347 sun *B*, son *DL* 1349 tuit *BDL*; *after* altre, *B adds* u*e*rbe, *L adds* son

---

Lat. A. 1331 assend*e*re 1349 t*e*rcia

B. 1329 m. p. *om*. 1331 obsid*e*re 1332 occidere 1340-1 *om*. 1348 sillaba] silla er 1349 alia uerba so*n*t tertie

d'aquel loc en çha o fenissen (videlicet coniugationis), ab 1350
celh de la prima. illo loco ubi finiunt verba prime
coniugationis. 1351a

De la quarta sun:	De quarta coniugatione sunt:	
auchir	audire	
aunir	vituperare	1354
abelir	pulcrum esse	
beneçir	benedicere	
bondir	apum est: sonare	
amanoïr	preparare	1358
bandir	per preconem precipere	
brandir	concutere	
blandir	blandiri	
blaçir	marcescere	1362
blanquir	candescere	
bruir	tumul[t]um facere	
causir	eligere	
descausir	vituperare	1366
clocir	gallinarum est	
cropir	super talos sedere	
acropir	idem est	
cobrir	cooperire	1370

Prov. A. 1351 dela prima *in right margin*

BDL. 1350 za *BL*, sa *D*; on *BD*, ou *L*   after 1351 *L* adds *co*niugazo,
followed by rubric Verba quarte *co*niugationis   1352 sum *BL*; *after 1352 L*
adds sicum   1353 auzir *BL*, ausir *D*; *after 1353 D adds* fenir   1355 *om.*
B, abellir *D*   1356 benezir *BDL*   1357 amonir *D*; *above* bondir, *L*
adds sonar   *after* 1358 *B inserts 1364*   1361 *om. D*   1362 *om.*
B, blazir *DL*   1363 blanoir *L*   1364 *om. D, placed after 1358
B*   1366 descauzir *B*   1367 glozir *B*   1368 gropir *B*, clopir *L*
1369 agropir, *with* g *expunctuated and* c *added above the line, B*   1370 coprir
*ue*l cobrir *B*, crobrir *L*

Lat. A.   1360 ca*n*cutere   1361 bamboiri   1364 tumulu*m* eligere,
with eligere *struck through and* face*re added*   1368 tale*s*, *altered from* taleu*s*
by change of abbreviation sign

B. 1350 co*n*iunctionis   1351 verba *om.*   1352 *no trans.*   1355 *om.*
1357 sonare ap*u*d e*s*t   1361 blandirj (j < e)   1362 *om.*   1364 facere
tumultu*m*   1367 galinaru*m*   1370 cope*r*ire

176 PROVENÇAL AND LATIN TEXT

descobrir	descoperire
recobrir	iterum operiri
culhir	colligere
1374 aculhir	recipere aliquem benigne
recolhir	recolligere
escofir	sconficere
delir	destruere
1378 entruandir	mores trutani habere
ensalvatgir	silvestrem facere
enribaudir	more rabaldorum vivere
esbaudir	valde letari
1382 endir	immitere
espelir	avem de ovo exire
enfoletir	stultum facere
enriquir	ditare
1386 enpaubreçhir	ad pauperiem venire
envillanir	pro rustico habere
escarnir	deridere
escrimir	cum ense ludere
1390 escupir	spernere
enantir	ante mittere
envaçir	invadere
estremir vel eschovir	tremefacere
1394 escernir	perficere
falhir	delinquere
fenir	finire
fremir	fremere

Prov. A. 1393 *uel* eschouir *interlinear*

BDL. 1373 cuilhir *B*, cullir *DL*   1374 acuilhir *B*, acuillir *D*, acollir *L*
1375–6 *interverted D*   1375 recullhir *B*, recullir *DL*   1376 esconfir *D*, esocfir *L*   1378 etruandir *D*   1379–81 *om. B*   1383 espellir *D*, expellir *L*   1385 eriquir *or* criquir *D*, enreqir *L*   1386 enpaubrezir *BL*, empaubrezir *D*   1387 enuilanir *BDL*   1389 escremir *DL*   1391 ennantir *B*, inantir *D*   1392 enuazir *BDL*   1393 vel eschovir *om. BDL*   1394 escemir *B*, esscernir *D*, eissetnir *L*   1395 faillir *D*, fallir *L*

Lat. A. 1393 tremefac*ere uel* eschouir

B. 1371 discoperire   1374 a*liqui*d beg*n*ine   1375 fouere *only*   1376 *no trans.*   1378 trutan*n*i   1379–81 *om.*   1382 inire   1383 avem] que*m*   1385 dictare   1386 in pauperem   1390 spuere

ferir	ferire	1398
freiçir	frigescere	
flechir	flectere	
flebeçhir	debilitare	
florir	florere	1402
fornir	necessaria dare	
fronir	inveterare	
fronçhir	rugas facere	
forbir	polire vel tergere	1406
fugir	fugere	
graçir	gracias agere	
gandir	declinare cum fuga	
glatir	in venatione latrare	1410
garir	sanare	
glotir	glutir[e]	
gondir	murmurare	
golir	devorare	1414
engolir	avide sumere	
giquir	relinquere	
grupir	idem	
jauzir	emolumentum habere	1418
jovenir	iuvenescere	
rejovenir	reiuvenescere	
issir	exire	
implir	implere	1422
marrir	tristari	
mentir	mentire	
desmentir	dicere 'mentiris'	

Prov. BDL. 1399 *om.* B, freizir D, freisir L   1400 fletir B, fleitir D 1401–2 *interverted* L   1401 febletir B, flebeizir D, feblezir L   1403 flomir D, formir L   1404 *om.* B, flonir D   1405 fronzir BDL   1407 fuzir D, fogir L   1408 grazir BDL   1411 gazir D   1413 grondir BD, glondir L   1416 gequir, *with* u *expunctuated*, B, giguir L   1417 gurpir BDL   1418 jausir L   *after* 1422 L *adds* lusir laidir lentir languir 1423 martir B, marir L

Lat. A.   1399 fuigescere   1406 poli*gere uel* tin*gere*   1412 glutur

B. 1399 *om.*   1404 *om.*   1408 gratias   1410 in v. *om.*   1411 in uenat*ione* so*n*are   1412 glucire   1417 idem *est*   1419 juuenesscere   1420 reiuuenesscere   1424 me*n*entiri

C 5707   N

1426	mesdir	dicere malum de aliquo
	merir	mereri
	motir	motire vel mutire
	morir	mori
1430	noirir	nutrire
	obezir	obedire
	obrir	aperire
	ofrir	oferre
1434	partir	partire
	departir	dividere
	palueçir	pallescere
	pentir	penitere
1438	perir	perire
	plevir	iurare vel confidere
	polir	polire
	poirir	putrescere
1442	pudir	fetere
	pruir	scalpere
	raubir	rapere
16a	rauquezir	rauqum facere
1446	raustir	assare
	roizir	rubescere
	saçhir	capere contra ius
	salhir	salire
1450	trassalhir	transilire
	assalhir	assultum dare
	sarçir	sarcire
	sentir	sentire

Prov. A. 1426 masdir

BDL. 1429 morrir *B*   1431 obeisir *D*   1433 offrir *B*, osfrir *D*, orir *L*   1436 paluezir *BL*, pallezir *D*   1439 plenir *L*   1440 pollir *D*   1445 ranquezir *B*, raquezir *D*   1447 rotzir *B*, roisir *DL*   1448 satzir *B*, sazir *DL*   1449 saillir *D*, salir *L*   1450 trassalir *B*, trassaillir *D*, trasalir *L*   1451 assalir *B*, assaillir *D*, assallir *L*   1452 sarzire *B*, sazir *D*, sartir *L*

Lat. A. 1427 meriri   1452 sartiire *or* sarture

B. 1428 mutire *only*   1433 offerre   1436 paluesc*ere*   1441 poirir   1443 *no trans.*   1445 raucu*m*   1450 transsalire   1451 assaltu*m* facere

servir	servire	1454
deservir	serviendo offendere	
trahir	tradere	
tendir	tinnire	
venir	venire	1458
revenir	meliorare	
avenhir	evenire	
covenir	expedire	
sovenir	recordari	1462
vestir	vestire	
revestir	iterum vestire	
envestir	investire	
vellzir	villescere	1466

Prov. BDL. 1456 trait *B*, trair *DL*   1460 auenir *BDL*   1461 conuenir *BDL*   1462–4 *om. B*   1466 velzir *BL*, uellir *D*; *after 1466 L adds* vbrir vir

---

Lat. A. 1457 tendere

B. 1457 tunnire   1459 melliorare   1462–4 *om.*   1465 jnuestigare 1466 vilesscere

Adverbes es apellatz quar justa lo verbe deu esser pa[u]ssatz, si cum: *eu dic veramen, se tu no vas tost, eu te batrei malamen.* Dic es verbum, *veramen* adverbium afirmandi; *vas* es verbe, *batrei* verbum, 1470 *tost, malemen,* adverbia qualitatis.

Al adverbe pertenen tres causas: species, significatio et figura. *Malamen* ven de *mal*, e per ço es derivative speciei, quar ven d'autre. *Tost* es primitive speciei, quar no ven d'autre. *Malamen* 1474 significa qualitat, e *bonamen* e *franchamen* e *temerosamen*. Mas saber devez que tut li adverbe que finissen in *-en* poden fenir in *-henz*, si besogna; qu'eu pos dir *malamen* o *malamenz*.

E sun autre adverbe que segnifien tems, si cum:

1478
        oi, er, aras o *ar*,
        l'autrer, deman, ja,
        a la vegada, adonc, mentre, |

16b
        ogan, atan, tart,

1482
        totztems, man.

L'autre significa ajustamen, si cum:

        essems;

l'autre demostramen, si cum:

1486
        veus me, vel vos;

l'autre afermamen, si cum:

        veramen, certamen;

A.   1467 passatz   1468 bratrei

BDL. 1467 Aduerbiu *B*, Aduerbium *DL*; iosta *BL*, iostra *D*; pausatz *B*, paussat *D*, pausaz *L*   1468 se] si *BDL*; non *B*; uais *D*; batrai *L* 1468–70 Dic... qualitatis *om. D*   1469 affirmadi *B*; verbe] uerbum *BL* 1470 malamen *BL*; adu*erbium L*   1471 Al adu*erbum B*, Ala a. *L*; speties *B* 1472 de] del *B*, da *D*; deriuatiua s. *B*, deriuatiua sp*eci*es *D*, sp*eci*ei deriuatiue *L*   1472–3 quar ven... speciei *om. B*   1473 primitiua species *D*, sp*eci*ei p*r*imiti*ue L*   1474 significa *B*; francamen *BDL*; temorosamen *BL*, temosamen (*first* s < r) *D*; Ma *D*   1475 tuit *BD*; au*er*be *BL*; henz] enz *BDL*   1476 qeo *L*   1477 su*n*t *B*; au*er*be *B*; significent *B*, significen *D*, signifien *L*; temps *B*, tempus *D*   1479 lautre *B*; deman ja] demaia *B*, demain *D*   1480 aleuegada *B*; adonc *placed after* mati (*1482*), mentre *after* antan (*1481*) *B*, adonc mentre *placed after* atan (*1481*) *D* 1481 ogam *or* ogani *B*; antan *BL*   1482 toztemps *B*, tosttemps *D*, toz tems *L*; mati *BL*, maiti *D*   1483 sez autre *D*; signifia *BL*, significan *D*; aiostamen *D* 1484 assems *B*, ensems *DL*   1485 l' *om. D*   1486 vel] uei *D*; *after 1486 B adds* alia interogatiua p*er* que, *without translation*   1487 l' *om. D*; affermen *B*   1488 certanamen *DL*

Adverbium dicitur quia iusta verbum debet esse positum et semper innititur verbo, verbi gracia: *ego dico veraciter, nisi vadas cito, percutiam te male.* Hec dictio est verbum, hec adverbium afirmandi; hec dictio est verbum, hec verbum, he due dictiones 1470 sunt adverbia qualitatis. 1470a
[Ad] adverbium pertine[n]t tria: species, significatio et figura. Hec dictio derivatur a *malo*, et ideo est derivative speciei, quia derivatur ab alio. Hec dictio est primitive speciei, quia non derivatur ab alio. Hec dictio significat qualitatem, et hec et hec [. . .]. Set sire 1474 debetis quod omnia adverbia que desinunt in hac sillaba possunt finire in hac sillaba, si necesse est; quia possum dicere sic vel sic.

Et sunt alia adverbia significantia tempora, verbi gracia:

> *odie, eri, modo* vel idem,   1478
> *nuper, cras, iam,*
> *aliquando, tunc, dum,* /   16b
> *hoc anno, alio, sero,*
> *semper, mane.*   1482

Alii significan[t] adiunctionem, verbi gracia:

> *simul;*

alii demostrationem, verbi gracia:

> *ecce me, ecce ille;*   1486

alii afirmationem, verbi gracia:

> *veraciter, certe;*

A. 1468 i*nu*iti*tur*; nisi] ne si (*above* se tu)   1471 Adu*erbium* pertinet (*cf. B*) 1474 *no trans. above* e temerosame*n*   1478 mado   1483 significa*n.*

B. 1467 iusta . . . positum] stat iusta u*er*bu*m*   1468 nititu*r*; vadis   1469 p. te] ego te p.; est *om.*; *second* hec] hec dict*io*   1470 afirmandi *om.* (*blank*); hec v.] *et* h*ec est* u.; he] hec; dictoes   1470a sunt *om.*; qualitatis *om.* (*blank*)   1471 Aduerbuʒ p.; species . . . figura *om.* (*blank*) 1472 spetie   1473 ab *om.*   1473–4 Hec . . . ab alio *om.* (*cf. Prov.*) 1474 . . .] *et* hec   1477 au*er*bia; significantia] que sig*n*ificatiua s*u*nt 1478 hodie   1479 ia   1481 alio] alio a*n*no   8314 Alia sig*n*ificatiua 1485 alia   1487 alia

l'autre interogativa:
1490   *per que*;
l'autre loc, si cum:
                aici, aqui, dins, defors,
                de lai, de çhai, lai, zai,
1494   *amon, aval, sus, jos*;
l'autre comparatio, si cum:
                plus, mais, maormen.

Particep es ditz quar pren l'una part del nome e l'autra del verbe.
1498 Del nom rete cas e genus, del verbe rete tems e significatio, de l'un et de l'autre nombre e figura; e d'aicho ai dit assatz el nome et el verbe.

Mas saber devez que tuit li particip fenissen en *-ans* o en *-entz*
1502 o en *-atz* o en *-utz* o en *-itz*, si cum:

                amans, presantz,
                plasenz, sufrens,
                conogutz, retengutz,
1506   *auçitz, peritz,*
                enganatz, despolhaz.

Co[n]juntios es apellada quar ajusta l'un mot a l'autre, si cum:
17a *eu e tu et el devem disnar ensems*. E las unas / sun copulativas:
1510   *e*;

A. 1489 integratiua   1492 dius *or* dins   1508 Coiuntios

BDL. 1489-90 *om. BD* (*cf. 1486, var. B*)   1489 interogamen *L*; *L adds* sicum   1491 l' *om. D*; a. significan loc *D*   1492 dinz *D*   1493 de çhai] dezai *B*, desai *DL*; zai] sai *D*   1494 auans *B*, à ual *D*   1495 *om. D*; comparatiua *B*, conparatiu *L*   1496 *om. D*; *after* mais, *BL add* mens; ormen *B*, maiormen *L*   *before* 1497 *L adds* Participium *dicitur quia partem capit nominis partemque verbi*   1497 Participiu *B*, Participium *DL*; nom *BDL*; lautre *B*   1498 nom *om. D*; de uerbe *B*; temps *BD*   1499 *after* l'autre *D adds* reten; nomen *B*, nom *DL*; et *om. L* 1501-2 o en entz . . . itz] o ens iz *D*; entz] ens *B*, enz *L*; o en itz *om. B* 1503 presanz *BL*, presans *D*   1504 plasenz, *with one letter erased before z, B*, plazens *D*; suffrens *B*, soffrens *D*, sufrenz *L*   1505 conoguz retenguz *DL*   1506 ausit *B*, auzitz (< ausitz *D*) *DL*; periz *D*   1507 enganaz *D*; despolhat *B*, despollatz *D*, despolatz *L*   1508 Coniunctios *B*, Coniuncios *D*, Coniuncions *L*; aiosta *BD*; *after* l'un, *and filling the rest of the line, L has rubric* De coniuncttione; a] ab *DL*   1509 eu et tu *B*, eu tu *L*; deuenz *D*, deuen *L*; sum *B*; *after* copulativas, *DL add* sicum   1510 *om. B*, e et *L*

alii interogationem, sicut:
> cur, quare, quamobrem;   1490

alii locum, verbi gracia:
> hic, hibi, intus, foris,
> illuc, inde, idem,
> sursum, deorsum, idem;   1494

alii significant comparationem, verbi gracia:
> plus, magis, maxime.

Participium dicitur quia partem capit nominis partemque verbi. A nomine recipit casus et genera, a verbo autem tempora et signi- 1498 ficationes, ab utroque numerum et figuram; et de istis dixi satis in nomine et in verbo.

Sed sire debetis quod omnia participia finiunt in hac dictione vel in hac vel in hac vel in hac vel in hac, verbi gracia: 1502
> diligens, aprecians se vel apreciatus,
> placens, paciens,
> cognitus, retentus,
> auditus, peritus,   1506
> deceptus, spoliatus.

Coniunctio dicitur quia iungit unam dictionem cum alia, verbi gracia: *ego et tu et ille debemus prandere insimul.* Et queda[m] 1509
sunt / copulative, verbi gracia: 17a
> e[t];   1510

A.   1489 integr*amen*   1493 idem] c̄e or c̄e, *above* lai; *no trans. above* zai   1494 jde*m above* sus; *no trans. above* jos   1495 signifīc.   1500 *et* es verbo   1501 dictione] dic*ere*   1503 diligens *with* 1 *altered from* c   1509 queda   1510 e

---

B.   1489-90 *om.* (*cf. Prov.*)   *1491 alia   1492 hibi *om.* (*blank*)   1493 jde*m above* lai; *no trans. above* zai   1494 idem] su*r*sum de*subter*   1495 alia comparatiua; verbi gracia *om.* (*blank*)   1496 plus *om.* (*blank*); *after* magis, B *adds* minus (*above* mens)   1497 p. c.] capit p*artem*   1498 autem] retinet   1499 *first five letters of* figuram *on erasure of black ink*   1502 *third* vel] ul; *fourth* vel in hac *om.* (*cf. Prov.*)   1503 d.] amans; apretia*n*s *uel* apretiat*us*   1504 patiens   1507 dispoliatus   1509 simul   1509a verbi gracia *om.*   1510 *om.* (*cf. Prov.*)

et las autras ordinativas, si cum:

> d'er enan, d'aqui enan, d'aqui en reire;

las autras asimilativas, si cum:

1514   *atressi, aici cum, si cum, quais;*

las autras expletivas, si cum:

> *sivals, zo es a saber, sitot;*

las autras disjunctivas, si cum:

1518   *o, ni;*

las autras racionals, si cum:

> *si, neis, cora,*
> *quan, que, quar,*

1522   *mas, entretan, esters aiço.*

A.   1512 da qui enan. da qui enreire   1522 esters. aiço

BDL.   1512 dez enan *D*, der nan *L*; da qui enan *D*, *om*. *L*; da qi en rere *B*, da qien reire *D*, daqi enriere *L*   1513 si cum *om*. BDL   1514 autresi *B*, atreissi *D*; aisi *B*; quasi *B*, qais *L*, *after which B adds* si cum *followed by 13 blank lines*   1515–2580 *om. B*   1515 lasutras (*corrected from* lautras) *L*; explectiuas *L*   1516 zo] ro *D*; *after 1516 D repeats 1515–16 with variant* zo (< ro) es assaber   1517 lautras *D*; disiuntiuas *D*   1518 ni] tu *D*; *after 1518 L adds* vel neque   1519 rationals *D*   1521 quanque car *D*, qan qe car *L*   1522 esters aizo *D*, esters preterea aizo *L*; *after 1522 L adds* las autras afirmatiuas autras (autras *expunctuated*) auras sicum cais; *this is followed by the passage on prepositions and interjections, for which see Appendix III*

et alie sunt ordinative, verbi gracia:
>de cetero, idem, olim;

alie assimulative, verbi gracia:
>taliter, sicut, sicut, quasi; 1514

alie expletive:
>saltem, videlicet, quamvis;

alie sunt disiunctive, verbi gracia:
>vel, neque; 1518

alie racionales:
>[. . .], [. . .], quando,
>[. . .], [. . .], quia,
>[. . .], interea, preterea. 1522

A. 1515 *no trans. above* si cum   1516 sabre*m*   1519–20 *no trans.*
above si cum si neis   1521 *no trans. above* quan que   1522 *no trans.*
above mas entretan; jnterea preterea *above* esters aiço

B. 1513 alie sunt assimilatiue   1513–14 u*e*rbi grac*i*a *above* autresi; taliter *om.*
1514 *after* quasi, *B adds* u*e*rbi grac*i*a (*above* si cum)   1515–2580 *om. B*

PROVENÇAL AND LATIN TEXT

In -*abs*:

	gabs	laus vel iactes in secunda persona
	naps	cifus
1526	trabs	genus temptorii
	caps	caput
	saps	arbor; sapis
	graps	manus curva
1530	draps	id est pannus
	claps	acer[v]us lapidum
	taps	lutum
	laps	gremium
1534	japs	vox canis

In -*acs*:

	bracs	sanies vel canis
	abacs	abacus
1538	cracs	sanies naris
	dracs	draco
	escacs	ligneus ludus
	flacs	flexibilis
1542	sacs	saccus
	tacs	morbus porcorum
	vacs	vacuus
	escarcs	spuas in secunda persona
1546	ensacs	in saco mittas
	estacs	liges
	abracs	ad saniem venias

In -*af*:

1550	caf	impar
	baf	vox indignantis

Prov. A. 1547, *with its trans.*, *added in margin at end of line*

L. 1525 enaps   1526 traps   1532 *repeated*   1534 saps
1545 escracs

Lat. A. 1526 tempor*um*   1527 cap̄ arbor   1528 sapis *only*
1531 ac*e*rus lapid*e*   1540 lig*n*e*useus*   1550–1 i*m*par *above* af,
vox indignantis *above* caf, vox indignantis *repeated above* baf

In -*aics*:
laics	laicus	
Aics	civitas	1554

In -*als*:
cabals	capitalis vel acceptabilis	
cals	calvus	
grazals	catinum	1558
egals	equalis	
leials	iustus	
desleia[l]s	iniustus	
mals	malus	1562
pals	pallum	
tals	talis	
sals	salvus vel sal	
emperials	inperialis	1566
reials	regalis	
comtals	ad comitem	
vescomtals	ad vescomitem	
venals	venalis	1570
nadals	natale	
maials	maialis	
ivernals	iemalis	
estivals	estivalis	1574
senhals	signum	
generals	generalis	
vidals	vitalis	
mortals	mortalis	1578
comunals	comunis	
cardenals	cardenalis	
peitrals	petorale	
offitials	offitialis	1582
jornals	caput unius diei	
orientals	orientalis	
venials	venialis	

Prov. A.   1561 d*e*sleia*s*., *at end of line*

L.   1575 segnhals   1582 officials

Lat. A.   1563 palium   1573 jenialis *or* jemalis

188 PROVENÇAL AND LATIN TEXT

1586	criminals	criminalis
	infernals	infernalis
	celestials	celestialis
17b	terre/nals	terre/nalis
1590	catedrals	cathedralis
	especials	specialis
	censals	censualis

In *-ais*:

1594	ais	tabula
	bais	osculum
	bais	osculetur
	biais	obliqum
1598	abais	demittat
	fais	onus
	gais	letus
	gais	avis quedam varia
1602	glais	quedam herba vel findecane vel gladius
	esglais	timeas
	esglais	timor
	nais	nascitur
1606	pais	pascitur
	cais	mandibula
	lais	dulcis cantus; dimittat
	eslais	cursus subitaneus
1610	eslais	currat subito
	mais	plus vel mensis
	esmais	desp[er]atio facilis vel desperes
	assais	probatio vel probes
1614	rais	radius
	plais	nemus plicatum
	jais	gaudium

Prov. A. 1601, *with its trans., added in margin, with insertion-mark*

L. 1589 terenals   1596 *om.*   1601 *om.*   1604 *om.*   1611 *repeated*
1612 *repeated*   1613 asais *repeated*

Lat. A. 1586 criminale   1587 infernale   1602 finde cane *or* fina' cane   1608 canis   1612 despatio

savais	iners	
tais	animal: taxus	1618
entais	in luto mitas	
tais	expedivit	
Clavais	castrum	
Roiais	civitas	1622
Cambrais	civitas	

In -*altz*:

altz	altus	
baltz	corea	1626
baltz	letus	
baltz	saltes ad coream	
Baltz	castrum	
caltz	calidus	1630
caltz	calx	
encaltz	fuga	
encaltz	fuget	
descaltz	discalciatus	1634
descaltz	discalciet	

E totz los podes virar in -*autz*, for *baltz* per corola e trait *cavaltz, valz, antrevalz, galz.*

Et omnes que finiu[n]t in -*altz* possunt finire in -*autz*, excepto hoc (ponitur pro *corea*), excepto hoc: *caballus, vallis,* et *intervallum* et *gallus*.   1638

[I]n -*alcs:*

senescals	seneschalcus	1642
auricalcs	auricalcus	

In -*alhz*:

alhz	alium

Prov. A.   1624 n altz *on erasure*   1636 Et otz   1638 galz, *with its trans., added in right margin after* antreualz   1641–3, *with their trans., added in left margin, without insertion-mark;* I *of* In *cut off by binder*

L.   1624 *om.*   1635 *om.*   1636 iurar mautz   1637 carola 1638 ualtz entreualtz galtz   1642 senescalcs   1643 auricals 1644 alliz   1645 alliz

Lat. A.   1619 mitatis   1636 finiut   1638 hoc *est* po*nitur*

190 PROVENÇAL AND LATIN TEXT

1646 bralhz	clamor avium
umbralhz	umbraculum
escalhz	frustum teste
miralhz	speculum
1650 teiralhz	territorium
trebailhz	labor
dalhz	falcs ad secandum fenum
malhz	maleus
1654 sonalhz	parvum ti[n]tinabulum
trebalhz	labores
talhz	secatura
talhz	secces
1658 retalhz	parva pars pani
retalhz	iterum secces
entalhz	scultura
entalhz	sculpas
1662 coralhz	corallium
devinalhz	devinaculum
egalhz	eques
salhz	salis
1666 asalhz	asaltum das
raspalhz	qui remanet de palea
respalhz	coligas residuum de paleis

In -*alms*:

1670 salms	salmus
palms	palmus
calms	planicies sine herba

In -*ams*:

1674 brams	magnus clamor

Prov. L. 1646 bralliz   1647 umbraliz umbralliz   1648 escalliz   1649 miralliz   1650 teraliz   1651 treballiz   1652 dalliz   1653 malliz   1654 sonalliz   1655 treballiz   1656 talliz   1657 talliz   1658 retiliz, *with stroke between* l *and* i (= -illiz *or* -ilhz?)   1659 retalliz   1660 entalliz   1661 entalliz   1662 coralliz *repeated*   1663 deuinalliz   1664 egalliz   1665 salliz   1666 assalliz   1667 rapalliz   1668 *om.*

Lat. A. 1650 te*m*ptorium   1654 titinabulu*m*   1657 sectes   1659 sectes   1661 subpas   1666 dans   1668 pal'as   1672 sine *or* siue

brams	clames	
clams	querela	
clams	conqueraris	
reclams	querela	1678
reclams	caro ad revocandum ancipitrem	
cams	campus	
dams	genus cervi	
Adams	Adam	1682
ams	ambos	
ams	ames	
grams	tristis	
fams	fames	1686
afams	a fame constringas	
lams	fulgur	
tams	par	

In -*ans*:		1690
ans	annus	
ans	ambules; ante	
bobans	inannis gloria	18a
bobans	glorietur	1694
brans	ensis	
blans	blandus	
cans	cantus vel cantes	
avans	antea	1698
cans	cambias	
descans	cantus contra cantum	
encans	incantes	
acans	in latus declines	1702
dans	damnum	
afans	fatigatio; fatiges	
pans	pars vel panus vel gremium	
grans	grandis	1706
glans	glans, glandis	
engans	dolus	

Prov. L. 1677 *om.*   1691–2 ans *four times*   1698 *placed after 1702*
1704 *repeated*   1706 *repeated*   1707 *placed after 1709*

Lat. A. 1675 clanis *or* clauis   1693 jn a*n*nis gl'a   1697 cantes] canite*s*
1702 jn loc*us* declines (*final s not clear*)

engans	decipias
1710 gans	ciroteca
lans	iacias
lans	iactus
eslans	subito iacias
1714 enans	profectus
enans	proficiat
comans	mandatum
comans	mandes
1718 mans	mandatum
mans	mandes
mans	suavis
demans	petitio
1722 demans	petas
desmans	mandes contra mandatum
soans	repudium
soans	respuas
1726 drogomans	interpres
jaians	gigans
aÿmans	adam[a]s
vianans	peregrinus
1730 sans	santus; proprium nomen
truans	trutanus
tans	tantos
tans	tannes, et cortex arboris ad coria paranda
1734 achointans	eloquens
amans	amans
tirans	tirannus vel durus
pesans	gravis
1738 presans	pretio dignus
eirans	errans

Prov. A. 1734 achomtans

L. 1712 *om.*   1715 *om.*   1718-20 mans *four times*   1723 *repeated*   1728 aimans   1733 cans   1734 acontans acoinhtans, *with* i *added above the line*   1736 trans   1738 *om.*   1739 erans

Lat. A.   1718 mandaut   1722 petetas   1728 adams   1733 ta*n*tes

PROVENÇAL AND LATIN TEXT

E tut aquelh que fenissen in -*ans* o in -*ens*, si sun masculi, no volun -*s* el nominatio plural a la fi del mot; si sun femini, volun -*s* per tot lo plural en la fi del mot.

Et omnes finientes in -*ans* vel in -*ens*, si sunt masculini generis, nolunt -*s* in nominativo plurali 1742 in fine dictionis; sed si sunt feminini, volunt -*s* per omnes casus in plurali in fine dictionis.

In -*ancs*:   1746

blancs	candidus	
bancs	scanum	
crancs	crançum	
dancs	color quidam	1750
sancs	sanguis	
sancs	sinistrarius	
francs	mansuetus	
afrancs	mansuescas	1754
mancs	mancus	
esmancs	auferas manum	
fancs	lutum	
afancs	in luto intres	1758
tancs	parvum lignum acutum	
estancs	claudas	
estancs	stagnum aquarum	
rancs	claudus	1762
rancs	saxum eminens super aquas	
arran[c]s	evellas	

In -*ars*:

ars	arsus; arsit	1766
blars	glaucus	
cars	carus	
escars	parcus	

Prov. A. 1764 arra*n*s

L. 1740 tuit aqelli   1741 masculini   1742 uolon; elo nominatiu 1743 uolon   1744 en lo plural p*er* tot; en] a   1747–64 *placed in the following order:* 1748, 1753–9, 1747, 1749, 1760–4, 1751   1750 *om.* 1752 *om.*   *after* 1758 L *adds* atancs   1764 arancs   1766 *repeated* 1767 *om.*   *after* 1768 L *adds* rars

Lat. A. 1765–6 ars*us*. arsit *above* ars. ars

194 PROVENÇAL AND LATIN TEXT

1770	fars	farsura
	afars	factum
	flars	lumen magnum
	esgars	aspectus
1774	esgars	aspicias
	clars	clarus
	disnars	prandium
	mars	mare
1778	amars	amarus
	amars	amare vel amor
	pars	par
	espars	sparsus
1782	espars	sparsit
	joglars	ioculator vel mimus
	vars	varius
1785	avars	avarus
18b	ampars	ocupes vi

In -*arcs*:

	arcs	arcus
	enarcs	flectas vel curves
1790	carcs	oneres
	carcs	onus
	descarcs	exoneres
	enbarcs	inpedimentum
1794	enbarcs	inpedias
	larcs	largus
	alarcs	extendas
	marcs	marcha
1798	Marcs	proprium nomen

In -*artz*:

	bartz	lutum de terra
	enbartz	luto inficias
1802	Lumbarz	Lumbardus

Prov. L. 1773 escars   1774 *om.*   1779 *om.*   1782 *om.*
1785–6 *interverted*   1789 eu arcs   1793 embarcs   1802 lunbartz

Lat. A. 1772 lmn̄ mag^m   1786 uim   1789 cu*r*ues on*us*   1801 lutu*m*

coarz	timidus in bello	
essartz	novale	
essartz	procindas vomere	
dartz	telum	1806
gollarz	ardens in gula	
garz	vilis homo	
pifartz	grossus	
estandartz	vexillum mangnum	1810
penartz	fasanus, avis	
bastartz	spurius	
falsartz	gladius brevis et acutus	
martz	mensis vel dies Martis	1814
laupartz	leopardus	
Mainartz	Mainardus	
partz	pars	
partz	partiris	1818
departz	dividis	
Rainartz	vulpis vel proprium nomen	
Falartz	castellum vel proprium nomen	
artz	ars	1822
artz	ardes	
quartz	quarta pars	

In -*aucs*:

aucs	anser masculus	1826
baucs	qui ponitur supra manica cultelli	
craucs	sterilis	
glaucs	claucus	
naucs	illud [in] quo porci comedunt	1830
paucs	parvus	
traucs	foramen vel perfores	
raucs	raucus	
enraucs	raucus fias	1834

Prov. L. 1803 coartz   1804 ellartz   1805 ellartz   1807 golliartz   1808 gartz   1809 pitartz   1813 fassartz   1818 *om.*   1820 ramartz   1821 talartz   1822 teartz   1823 *om.*   1824 qeartz   1827 paucs   1829 claucs   *after* 1832 L *adds* fraucs

Lat. A. 1819 diuidas   1823 ardens   1830 illud q*uod*

In -*aus*:

braus	inmitis
blaus	bludus vel aereus
1838 aus	vellus
aus	a[u]deat
caus	cavus
claus	clavis
1842 claus	clausus
claus	clausit
enclaus	inclusit vel inclusus
contraclaus	clavis facta contra clavem
1846 laus	laudes
traus	trabes
suaus	suavis
malaus	infirmus
1850 nadaus	natale
paus	pavo
naus	navis
raus	arundo
1854 galengaus	genus speciei, id est galenga

In -*aurs*:

aurs	aurum
tesaurs	tesaurus
1858 saurs	color aureus
laurs	laurus
Vaurs	proprium nomen castri
taurs	taurus
1862 semitaurs	semitaurus
maurs	niger

In -*atz*:

blatz	bladum
1866 emblatz	furatus

Prov. A. 1853 baus   *after* 1854 *A adds* praus, *with trans.* arundo

---

L. *after* 1840 *L adds* faus   1845–8 *om.*   1854 gaiengaus   1866 enblatz

---

Lat. A.   1839 adeat

PROVENÇAL AND LATIN TEXT

catz	catus	
datz	taxillus	
glatz	glacies	
glatz	vox canis venantis	1870
glatz	latras	
fatz	fa[t]uus	
fatz	facies	
fatz	facio	1874
gratz	grates	
jatz	le[c]tus fere	
jatz	iacet	
matz	victus ad schacos	1878
natz	natus	
pratz	pratum	
raubatz	spoliatus	
segatz	secatus	1882
segatz	secate	
secatz	sicatus	
secatz	sicate	
talhatz	scissus ferro vel sindite ferro	1886
trençatz	resecatus vel resecate	
transgitatz	decipite: ad incantatores pertinet	
transgitatz	deceptus	19a
pagatz	pacatus soluta pecunia	1890
pagatz	solvite	
legatz	legatus	
juciatz	iudicatus	
escoriatz	scoriatus	1894
escoriatz	scoriate	

In -*athz*:
bathz   subrufus

Prov. A.   1896 athaz

L.   1876 satz   1878 *repeated*   1879 uatz   1881 *repeated*
1886 tallaz tallatz lalitz   1887 trencatz *repeated*   1888 tragitatz
1889 transaitaz   1893 iusticiatz *repeated*   1896 altz   1897 bathtz

---

Lat. A.   1872 fauus   1876 let*us*

198 PROVENÇAL AND LATIN TEXT

1898	escahz	particula panni
	fathz	factus
	refathz	iterum factus vel impinguatus
	desfahz	destructus
1902	agahz	insidie
	lahz	turpis
	enpahz	inpedimentum
	pahz	pactum vel stultus
1906	enpahz	inpedias
	rathz	radius
	ensahz	probatio vel tentes
	platz	causa inter ostes
1910	trahz	tractus
	alavahz	morbus digiti in radice ungule
	escaravatz	scarabeus cornutus
	retrahz	turpis recordatio benefitii
1914	contrahz	debilis pedibus vel manibus
	pertrahz	aparatus alicuius operis
	fortrahz	sublatus
	esglahz	subitaneus timor

1918	In -*as* larg:	
	bas	demissus
	cas	casus
	cas	cadis
1922	clas	campannarum sonus
	gras	grassus
	las	fatigatus
	ras	rasus vel rasit
1926	vas	tumullus
	mas	mansus rusticorum

Prov. A. 1901 desfahz *with* h *altered from first stroke of* t 1904 enlahz

L. 1898 escathtz 1899 facthtz 1900 refathtz 1901 desfathtz
1902 agathtz; *after 1902 L adds* jatz 1903–4 *placed after 1910*
1903 lathz 1904 ipathtz 1905 *om.* 1906 enparhtz 1907 rathtz
1908 ensathtz 1909 plathtz 1910 trahatz 1911 alauathtz
1912 escarauathtz 1913 retrahtz 1914 contrahtz 1915 p*er*trathtz
1916 fortratz 1917 esglathtz

Lat. A. 1905 pace*m* 1919 dimiss*us* 1926 tumull*is*

nas	nasus	
pas	passus	
pas	transeat	1930
transpas	pertranseat	
transpas	momentum	

In -*as* estreit:

abbas	abas	1934
degas	decanus	
cas	canis	
gras	granum	
vilas	vilicus vel indoctus	1938
baias	insipidus	
nas	nanus	
mas	manus	
pas	panis	1942
cirurgias	cirurgicus	
tavas	musca pongnens equos	
sas	sanus	
umas	umanus	1946
mundas	mundanus	
escrivas	scriba	
Galias	Galienus	
vas	vanus	1950

In -*as* estreit:

nom provincials	nomina sunt provincialia	
Tolsas	Tolosanus	
Marquesas	quilibet de Marchia	1954
Catalas	Catalanus	
Romas	Romanus	
Toscas	Tuscus	
Troias	Troianus	1958
Cecilias	Siculus	

Prov. L. 1931 trapas   1932 tranpas   1933 estreitz   1934 abas
1943 cirorgias   1951 estreitz   1952 prouincial   1953 tolzas
1954 marguesas

Lat. A. 1941 man*uus*

	nom de civitatz	nomina civitatum
	Milas	Mediolanum
1962	Fas	Fanum

In *-hecs* larg:

	becs	rostrum
	cecr	cecus vel signum ad sagittam
1966	decs	terminus
	necs	impeditus lingue
	pecs	insipiens
	tavecs	insultus
1970	bavecs	qui de facili movetur (id est, baveca)
	Grecs	Grecus
	encecs	exeques
	secs	sequeris
1974	persecs	persequeris
	consecs	consequeris

In *-ecs* estreit:

	Becs	proprium nomen viri
1978	decs	vicium
	lecs	lecator
	quecs	quisque
	usquecs	unusquisque
19b	plecs	plica
1983	secs	sicus
	plecs	plices
	secs	sicces
1986	lecs	lambas

In *-eis* larg:

	Eis	civitas
	eis	exit

Prov. L. 1960 ciuitat 1963 ecs 1964–75 *placed in the following*
order: 1968–9, 1964–5, 1970–5, 1966–7   1978 tecs   1984–5 *om.*

Lat. A. 1970 .i. baueca q*ui* d*e* facili moue*tur*   1977 viri] u.   1983 sicas

fleis	parcitas	1990
fleis	sit contentus	
leis	luxus	
seis	numerus sex	
geis	genus petre mollis	1994

In -*eis* streit:

leis	lex	
peis	piscis	
peis	pinxit	1998
feis	finxit	
teis	tinxit	
ateis	nactus est	
meis	miscet	2002
ceis	cinxit	
reis	rex	
neis	etiam	
eis	ipse	2006
el meteis	ille ipse	
creis	cresit	

In -*els* larg:

Abels	Abel	2010
cels	celum	
fiçels	fidelis	
Jezabels	proprium nomen mulieris	
Micaels	Michael	2014
Gabriels	Gabriel	
Rafaels	Rafael	
Misaels	Misael	
mels	mel	2018
fels	fel	
gels	gelu	
Bordels	civitas Burdegala	
escamels	scabelum	2022

Prov. L. 1995 estreit   2012 fizels   2013 sesabels   2020 *om*.
2022 escanels

Lat. A. 1990 paratas   1991 fit *contentus*   1992 lux*us* nu*mer*us
1993 sex *only*   1994 petro

In -*els* estreit:

camels	camelus
pels	pilus
2026	cels	cautela
cels	celes

In -*elz* larg:

cabrelz	edus parvus
2030	belz	pulçer
flagelz	flagellum
flagelz	flagelles
anelz	anulus vel agnus
2034	porcelz	porcellus
meselz	leprosus
coutelz	cultellus
tortelz	parvus panis
2038	pomelz	parvum pomum
cairelz	pilum baliste
panelz	parvus panis vel barda
escavelz	alabrum
2042	maçelz	macellum
portelz	parva porta
barutelz	stamina ad purgandum farinam
cantelz	ora panis
2046	isnelz	velox
cantarelz	qui cantat frequenter
Otonelz	proprium nomen viri
Ospinelz	nomen unius viri
2050	caramelz	fistula
cardonelz	avis
Rudelz	proprium nomen viri
budelz	intestinum
2054	tonelz	parvum dolium
Sordelz	nomen viri
mantelz	mantellus

Prov. L. 2028 eltz 2029–31 -eltz 2032 flagltz *with* e *added above* g 2033 anheltz aneltz 2034–9 -eltz 2040 paueltz 2041 escaluetz 2042 mazeltz 2043–53 -eltz 2053 *placed after 2044* 2054 tomeltz 2055–6 -eltz

Lat. A. 2043 porca 2048 auri

Verçelz	civitas quedam	
pelz	pellis	2058
apelz	appelles	

In *-ielz* larg:

vielhz	senex	
mielz	melius	2062

In *-elhz* estrit:

cabelhz	capillus	
vermelhz	rubicundus	
conselhz	consilium vel consulas	2066
aparelz	aparat[us] vel prepares vel preparatus	
desparelhz	paria dividas	
solelhz	sol	
solelhz	ad solem ponas	2070
telhz, telz	arbor quedam	
calelhz	lucerna ferea ubi oleum ardet	
artelhz	articulus	
velhz	vigiles	2074
espelhz	speculum	
ventrelhz	ventriculum vel stomachus	
somnelhz	somno seducaris	20a
semelhz	asimilles	2078

In *-ems* larg:

Jerusalems	civitas

In *-ems* estreit:

fems	fimus	2082

Prov. A. 2071 telz *interlinear*

L. 2057 verseltz   2058–9 -eltz   2060 eitz   2061 uieliz   2062 *et* mielhz   2063 Jneltz estreit   2065 uermeliz   2066 conseliz consellitz   2067 auarellitz aparellitz   2068 desparellitz   2069 solessitz   2070 sollellitz, *added in margin*   2071 tellitz *only*   2072 callellitz   2073 arcellitz   2074 vellitz   2075 espellitz   2076 ventrellitz   2077 sonnellitz   2078 semellitz   2080 jesuralems

---

Lat. A. 2067 aparat   2071 telz a*r*bor

PROVENÇAL AND LATIN TEXT

sems	semis vel minuas
ensems	insimul
nems	nimis
2086 Rems	civitas quedam
temps	tempus
tems	times
per tems	tempestive

2090 In -*ens* estreit:

brens	furfur
coçens	urens
calens	providus
2094 nocalens	inprovidus
crezens	credens
descrezens	recedens a fide
creissens	cressens
2098 descreissens	dissipans
dens	dens
dolens	dolens
fazens	facie[n]s
2102 desfazens	destruens
fendens	findens
defendens	defendens
fo[n]dens	liquesens
2106 confondens	consumens
encendens	adurens
escondens	absconder.s
esconprendens	incendens
2110 avinens	aptus vel apta
gens	pulcer vel pulcra
grens	barba iuxta labia
lens	le[n]tus

Prov. A.   2090 ems   2105 fodens   *after* 2112 A *adds* bens, *without trans.*

L.   2087 *om.*   2092 cozens   2095–6 *om.*   2097 creizens
2098 descreizens   2102 destazens   2104 desfendens   2109 escomprendens   2111 *repeated*

Lat. A.   2083 munia*s*   2101 facies   2112 barba *only*   2113 let*u*s iux*ta* labia

PROVENÇAL AND LATIN TEXT 205

off[r]ens	offerens	2114
suffrens	paciens	
dolens	dolens	
covinens	conveniens	
sovinens	recordans	2118
mordens	mordens	
sens	sensus	
tenens	tenens	
mantenens	fovens	2122
jauzens	gaudens	
olens	olens	
pudens	fetens	
conoissens	cognossens	2126
desconoissens	ignorans	
parens	consanguineus	
prendens	prendens	
reprendens	reprehendens	2130
penedens	penitens	
contenens	continens	
garens	custodiens vel p[ro]tegens	
sens	sentis	2134
vens	vincit	
mens	mentiris	
prens	aprehendis	
apprens	adiscis	2138
reprens	reprehendis	
escomprens	incendis	
pens	pendis	
pens	cogito	2142
despens	expendis	
tens	tendis	

Prov. A. 2114 offens *after* 2122 *A repeats* souinens (*2118*), *with trans.* recordans

---

L. 2114 ostrens   2115 sufrens   2117 conuinens *with first* n *expunctuated*   2126 conoisens   2127-8 *interverted*   2127 desconoisens   2132 cotenens   2135 *repeated*   *after* 2137 *L adds* gens 2138 aprens   2140 *placed after* 2130

Lat. A. 2124 oleus   2125 fet/tens, *split over two lines*   2133 ptegens 2137 aprehendit

destens	distendis
2146 atens	nancisceris†
rens	reddis
covens	pactum
fens	findis
2150 defens	defendis
ardens	ardens
luçens	lucens
sabens	sapiens
2154 avens	adventus ante natale
bulens	buliens
resplandens	resplendens
maldizens	maledicens
2158 fenhens	fingens
penhens	pingens
talens	voluntas vel appetitus
aculens	lete recipiens
2162 jaçens	iacens

20b In -*eps* estreit:

ceps	stipes, -tis
seps	sepes, -pis
2166 greps	[su]perbus
treps	ludus
tre[p]s	ludas

In -*ers* larg:

2170 cers	cervus
sers	servus
sers	servis
guers	strabo
2174 vers	versus

Prov. A. 2168 tres

L. 2152 lucens   2154 nauens   2159 *om.*, *leaving gap for about five letters*   2162 iasens; *after 2162 L adds* Tuit aqeli qe fenissen inens uel inans si son masculin sun general sisum femenin volun .d. p*er* tot enlo plural mas el singular sun del general

---

Lat. A. 2146 ua*n*tisceris   2166 paruus

vers	ver	
envers	inversus	
travers	obliqus	
convers	conversus	2178
pervers	perversus	
revers	reversus	
pers	genus panni	
fers	ferrum	2182
fers	ferus	
fers	feris	
Bezers	civitas Biteris	
Lumbers	proprium nomen castri	2186

In -*ers* estreit:

aers	aderens vel adhesit	
sabers	sapere (nominaliter positum)	
poders	posse (nominaliter positum)	2190
avers	abere	
devers	debere (nominaliter posita)	
espers	speres vel spes	
ders	erectus	2194
ders	erexit	
aders	procuratus	
a[d]ers	procuravit	
sers	sero	2198
vers	verum	
liçers	licentia	

In -*iers*:

cavaliers	miles	2202
escudiers	scutifer	
trotiers	cursor	
parliers	loquax	
lausengiers	bilinguis	2206

Prov. A. 2197 aers

L. 2193 *repeated*   2199 ver   2200 lezers

Lat. A. 2189 p⁹st' (= po*sstum*?)   2190 positum] possu*m*   2200 licen-tia*m*

208 PROVENÇAL AND LATIN TEXT

bergiers	qui custodit oves
porquiers	custos porcorum
formiers	formarius
2210 forniers	fornarius
mo[l]iniers	molinarius
saumiers	mullus vel asinus vel iumentum ferens honus
saumaliers	custos saumerii
2214 paniers	canistrum
panatiers, paniers	qui dat panem ad mensam
carceriers	carceratus
monestiers	monasterium
2218 mestiers	mestarium
celiers	celarium
seliers	faciens sellas
botiliers	pincerna
2222 diniers	denarius
encombriers	inpedimentum
destorbiers	turbatio
feniers	cumulus vel acervus feni
2226 palhers	acervus palearum
fumiers	fumarius
terriers	terratorium
semtiers	semita
2230 colhers	collarius
cloquiers	campanile
boviers	bubulcus
oliers	figullus
2234 sab[a]tiers	calciamenta faciens
graniers	oreum
noveliers	qui libenter recitat nova
traversiers	qui in oblicum vadit

Prov. A.   2211 moiniers (*cf. L*)   2215 paniers *interlinear*   2234 sabtiers

L.   2207 bergieres   2208 porgiuiers   2209 *om.*   2211 moniers
2212 saumieres   2215 paniers *om.*   2216 carcereis   2217 mostiers
2220 *om.*   2221 *placed after 2215*   2222–3 *om.*   2225 finiers
2226 palliers   2229 sentiers   2230 culliers   2233 ouiers
2235 grauiers   2236–8 *om.*

Lat. A.   2215 paniers q*ui*   2225 acervus] anicum*us or* amcum*us (second* m *unclear)*   2226 pallarii   2230 colloquear

PROVENÇAL AND LATIN TEXT

pesquiers	locus ubi pisces mituntur	2238
arquiers	qui cum arcu trait	
balestiers	balistarius	
borsiers	faciens bursas	
baraties	baratator	2242
ronciniers	miles qui non habet nisi unum roncinum	
lebrers	canis capiens lepores	
olivers	oliva vel proprium nomen viri	
verçiers	viridarium	2246
periers	pirus	
pomiers	pomus	
pruniers	arbor faciens prunas	
figuiers	ficus	2250
mandoliers	amigdalus	
noguiers	arbor nucis	
avelaniers	avellanarius	
ciriers	cirarius vel citarista	2254
sorbiers	sorbarius vel corbellarius	
rosiers	rosetum	
violers	violetum	21a
lenhiers	conjeries lignorum	2258
moriers	morus	
mespoliers, nespoliers	esculus	
poliers	[pul]larius	
codonhyers	cotanarius	2262
soliers	solarium	
mençoigniers	mendax	
destriers	destrarius	
talhiers	catinus in quo carnes ponuntur	2266

Prov. A. 2243 rainiers 2260 mespoliers *only (cf. Lat. var.)* 2261, *with its trans., added in margin, with nsertion-mark* 2262 condonhyers

L. 2242 baratiers 2243 rontiniers, *with first* n *apparently altered from* ti 2244 libriers 2245 oliuiers 2246 uergiers 2247 perriers 2249 primiers 2250 figiers 2252 nogiers 2254 cerisiers 2256 roseiers, *with first* e *apparently expunctuated* 2257 uioliers 2259–62 *om.* 2264 mensogniers 2266 talliers

Lat. A. 2238 mite*r*untur 2249 brinas 2260 vespo *ue*l esculus 2261 lari*us* 2262 cocanari*us*

C 5707 P

210　PROVENÇAL AND LATIN TEXT

teliers	illud in quo tela texitur
maçeliers	macelarius
caronhiers	qui cadavera sequitur, vel homicida
2270 esperoniers	qui facit calcaria
taverniers	caupo
senestriers	sinistrarius
loguiers	merces
2274 tesauriers	tesaurarius
entiers	integer
petiers	qui frequenter bumbinat
rotiers	eructuator

2278 In -*erns*:

yve[r]ns	iems
esquerns	derisio
quazerns	quaternio
2282 esterns	vestigium
enferns	infernus
verns	arbor quedam
Salerns	civitas quedam: Salernum

2286 In -*erps*:

serps	serpens
verps	luppus

In -*erms*:

2290 verms	vermis
erms	incultus
aderms	inhabitabilem facis

In -*ertz* larg:

2294 covertz	coopertus

Prov. A. 2279 yuens

L. 2267 *om.*　　2268 mazeliers　　2273 logiers　　2275 etiers
2277 ratiers　　2278 ernes　　2279 uiernes　　2280 esquernes
2281 quazernes

Lat. A. 2267 in quo] q*uod in*　　2270 fecit　　2276 bu*m*bicinat

descovertz	discopertus	
desertz	desertum	
offertz	oblatus	
certz	certus	2298
overtz	apertus	
espertz	propinqus	
apertz	providus	
Imbertz	proprium nomen	2302
Robertz	proprium nomen	
tertz	tercius	
tertz	terge	
merz	mercimonia ad vendenda	2306

In *-ertz* estreit:

vertz	viridis	
dertz	erigit	
adertz	procura vel procurat	2310
aertz	ineret	

In *-es* larg:

pes	pes, -dis	
confes	confessus vel confiteatur	2314
ades	cito	
pres	prope	

In *-es* estreit:

pes	pondus	2318
contrapes	contrapondus	
bes	bonum	
fes	fides	
fes	fenum	2322
fes	fecit	
des	discus	
ades	tangat	
mes	mensis	2326
mes	misit	

Prov. A. 2296–7 desertz offe *written in rather small characters on erasure*

L. 2297 ostertz 2302 unbertz 2306 mertz 2320 ves

ces	census
ences	incensum
2330 ences	incences
deves	locus defensus
borçes	burgencis
marques	marchio
2334 pres	aprehensus
pres	cepit
mespres	reprehensus vel deliquit
repres	reprehensus
2338 repres	reprehendit (preteriti)
antepres	interceptus
antepres	intercepit
bres	lignum fixum propter aves
2342 les	levis
fres	frenum
gles	glis, -ris
bles	qui utitur *c* loco [*s*]
2346 benapres	bene doctus
nom provincial:	nomina provincialia:
Frances	Francigene
Angles	Anglici
2350 Genoes	Genuenses
21b Bordales	Burdegalenses
Vianes	Vienenses
Valantines	Valentinenses
2354 Carcasses	Carcasonensses
Bedeires	Biterences
Agades	Agatences
Marsselhes	Marssilienses
2358 Brianzones	[. . .]
Poles	Appulli
Toes	Alamanni

Prov. L. 2329 encens, *added in margin, with insertion-mark*   2330 encens
2332 borgues   2333 magues   2336 *repeated*   2338–40 *om.*
2351 bordales (d < τ)   2353 valentines   2354 cartases   2356 acades
2357 marselies   2359 pollies

Lat. A. 2345 c̄ loco., *at end of line*   2358 *no trans.*

Campanes	a Campania dicuntur	
Bolonhes	Bononienses	2362
Verceles	Vercellensses	
Paves	Papienses	
Cremones	Cremonenses	
Tertones	Tertonenses	2366
Saones	Savonenses	
Pontremoles	Pontremulenses	
Luques	Luquences	
Senes	Senenses	2370
Verones	Verronenses	
Rimenes	Rimenenses	
Novaires	Novairenses	
Mozenes	Mutinenses	2374
e moutz d'autres.	et multa alia.	

In *-ethz* larg:

lethz	lectus	
cadalethz	lectus ligneus altus	2378
vethz	veretrum	
methz	medius	
despethz	despectus, -tus, -ui, vel contemptus	
respethz	inducie vel expectatio	2382
pethz	pectus	
pethz	peius	
delethz	delectatio	

In *-etz* estreit: 2386

Bretz	proprium nomen vel homo lingue impedite
detz	digitus
petz	bombus

Prov. L. 2362 milanes   2363 vetreles   2375 montz   2376 elthtz
2377 lethtz   2378 cadelethtz   2379 uethtz   2380 methtz
2381 despethtz   2382 respethtz   2383 pethtz   2384 pethtz;
after 2384 L adds sethtz vethtz (*cf. 2389–93*)   2385 *placed after 2389*

Lat. A.   2367 sansones   2380 medi*us* *uel* *contem*ptus   2381 d*espectus* tus ui *only*

2390 petz	[...]
setz	sitis
vetz	vicium
vetz	vicis
2394 quetz	parum loquens
escletz	purus
soletz	solus
tosetz	puerus
2398 fadetz	fatuus
anheletz	agniculus
aneletz	anulus
cabroletz	capreolus
2402 foletz	faunus vel stultus

E totas las segondas personas del plural del presen del conjunctiu delz verbes de la prima 2406 conjugazo e tuit li nominatiu singular dels noms diminutius.	Et notandum est quod omnes secunde persone pluralis numeri presentis coniunctivi verborum prime coniugationis et omnes nominativi singularis nominum diminutivorum.

[I]n [-*ethz*] estreit:

frethz	frigus vel frigidus
2410 drethz	ius vel rectus
adrethz	aptus
lethz	lex
espletz	supelectile vel usufructus
2414 esplethz	habeas usumfructum
plethz	plica
aplethz	instrumenta
nelethz	culpa

Prov. A. 2402 soletz   2407 diminiatius   2408 n. estreit (*red capital* I *omitted, but* i *still visible in margin*)

L. 2390 *om.*   2391 *placed after 2398*   2393 *om.*   2397 toletz 2399 *om.*   2401 caproletz   2405 deltz uerbs   2407 del; deminutius   2408 ethtz   2409 frethtz   2410 drethtz   2411 adre thtz, *separated by a space sufficient for three letters, in the middle of which the scribe has written two strokes, resembling a* u   2412 lethtz   2413 espletz, *with* t *perhaps altered from* c *and* i *apparently added above*   2414 esplethtz 2415 plethtz   2416 aplethtz   2417 nelethtz

---

Lat. A. 2390 *no trans.*   2403 nota*nd*e   2414 habe*n*s

PROVENÇAL AND LATIN TEXT

cortehz	coloquium militum cum d[omi]-	
	nabus	2418
thez	tectum parvum	
estretz	constrictus	
destretz	districtus	
corretz	corrigia vel çona	2422

In -*eus*:

breus	brevis vel carta	
Ebreus	Ebreus	
Juçeus	Iudeus	2426
deus	deus	
feus	feodus	
seus	suus	
meus	meus	2430
greus	gravis	22a
leus	levis	
romeus	peregrinus	
teus	tuus	2434
Canileus	Canileus	
Andreus	Andreus	
Anjeus	[. . .]	

In -*ibs*: 2438

macips	puer parvus	
tribs	tribus	
rips	acumen clavi	
derips	abstraas clavos	2442

In -*ics*:

brics	miser	
abrics	locus sine vento; protectio	
abrics	protegas vel operias	2446
fics	ficus, morbus	

Prov. A. 2418 correhz   2435 canileus *or* camleus   2437 arueu*s*
2447 sics

L. 2418 corthtz   2419 tethtz, *placed after 2422*   2420 estreithtz
2421 destreithtz   2422 corethtz   2426–end *om.*

Lat. A. 2418 dnab*us*   2419 rectu*m*   2435 canileus *or* camleus
2437 arueus   2442 claues

216 PROVENÇAL AND LATIN TEXT

pics	avis perforans lignum rostro
pics	varius
2450 pics	percutias
trics	intricatio
antics	anticus
mendics	mendicus
2454 amics	amicus
enemics	inimicus
enics	inicus
fenics	avis que dicitur fenix
2458 cauçics	increpatio
[c]auçics	increpes
rics	dives
afics	vis
2462 afics	coneris
espics	spica
colerics	collericus
flecmatics	fleumaticus

2466 In -*ils*:

fils	filum
fils	neas
anafils	parva tuba cum voce alta
2470 abrils	aprilis
badils	locus ubi speculator manet
humils	humilis
Nils	Nilus
2474 senhorils	dominabilis
femenils	feminilis
subtils	subtilis
camzils	pannus lini subtilissimi
2478 jovenils	iuvenilis
priorils	ad priorem pertinet
abadils	ad abatem pertinens
mongils	monacalis

Prov. A. 2458 cançics   2459 cançics, *with its trans., added in margin, with insertion-mark; initial* c *now hidden in binding (Stengel read* cançics*)*

Lat. A. 2462 conaris   2464 colloricus   2467 *no trans.*   2468 filum *uel* neas   2477 pa*n*nis

In -*ims*: 2482
crims	crimen	
cims	sumitas arboris	
vims	vimen	
raçims	racemus	2486
prims	acutus vel subtilis	
aprims	subtilies	
noirims	nutrimentum	
Caïms	Caym	2490

In -*ins*:
quins	quintus	
esquins	scindat	
tins	timpus	2494
ins	intus	
lins	lignum maris	

In -*irs*:
consirs	consideratio	2498
consirs	consideres	
albirs	estimatio	
desirs	desiderium	
sospirs	suspirium	2502
safirs	safirus	
Tirs	Tyrus, civitas	
sospirs	suspires	
mirs	speculeris	2506
remirs	iterum speculeris	

In -*is*:
bis	color	
robis	lapis	2510
Robis	proprium nomen viri	
clis	inclinatus	
aclis	inclines	
roncis	roncinum	2514

Prov. A. 2511, *with its trans.*, *added in margin, with insertion-mark*

Lat. A. 2495 jncus   2506 specul'is   2507 specul'is

gris	color
paradis	paradisus
fis	valde bonus
2518 latis	latine[s] vel latinus
Longis	Longinus
lis	lenis
alis	azimus
2522 molis	molendinum
mis	missus
sothzmis	submissus
mesquis	miser
2526 fenis	debilis
Sang Danis	Sanctus Donissius
pis	pinus
albespis	albor spinosa
2530 ris	risus
Paris	Parisius
matis	mane
vis	vinum
2534 vis	facies
devis	devinus
devis	divisus
Folis	civitas
2538 Forlis	civitas
Assis	civitas

22b nom provincial:	nomina provincialia:
Peitavis	Pictavensis
2542 Anjavis	Andegavensis
Paregorzis	Petragorisensis
Faentis	Faventinus
Spoletis	Spoletanus
2546 Caersis	Caturcensis
Lemozis	Lemov[i]censis

In -*itz*:

garitz	curatus
2550 garnitz	munitus

Lat. A. 2518 latines] latine 2546 cacur*c*ensis 2547 lemouce*n*sis

PROVENÇAL AND LATIN TEXT 219

graziz	graciosus	
ganditz	festinans timore	
gurpitz	derelictus	
giquitz	dimissus	2554
criz	clamor	
causitz	electus vel curialis	
aibitz	morigeratus	
cabritz	edus	2558
delitz	destructus	
adormitz	sopitus	
coloritz	coloratus	
escoloritz	palidus	2562
esperitz	spiritus	
esditz	negat	
esconditz	denegat	
descausitz	rusticus vel iniuriosus	2566
acrupitz	sedens super talos	
saziz	occupatus	
implitz	impletus	
conplitz	completus	2570
aunitz	vituperatus	
fugitz	fuga lapsus	
fugiditz	fugitivus	
escaritz	solus	2574
escarnitz	derisus	
formitz	formatus vel abens necessaria	
sumsitz	mersus in mare vel aquis	
sebelitz	sepultus	2578
senthiz	sentitus	
traïtz	traditus prodictione	
transitz	semimortuus	
tritz	minutus	2582
finitz	finitus vel mortuus	
peritz	peritus (a pereo, peris)	

Prov. B. *B resumes with* 2581 *preceded by rubric* De las rimas en itz 2583 fenitz

---

Lat. A. 2552 destina*n*s   2556 el'ctus   2557 mo*n*rigerat*us*
2575 densus   2582 munit*us*

B. 2584 peritus (u < z); peris] is

PROVENÇAL AND LATIN TEXT

ditz	dicit
2586 raubitz	raptus
berbitz	ovis
freisithz	refrigeratus
espelitz	avis de ovo procede[n]s
2590 issithz	qui exiit
noirithz	nutritus
samithz	pannus sericus
voutitz	volubilis
2594 polithz	politus
poiritz	putrefactus
amanoïth	promtus
falitz	qui deliquid vel fallit
2598 salithz	saliens
vestithz	vestitus
desvestitz	qui redit investicionem unde fuit investitus
envestitz	investitus
2602 aveneditz	aliunde veniens
tortitz	tortitium: multe candele simul iuncte
In -*ius*:	
brius	inpetus
2606 caitius	miser vel captus
solorius	solitarius
rius	rivus
vius	vivus
2610 aurius	amens
grius	quedam avis
senhorius	dominium
esquius	homo austerus vel delicatus (a vitando dictus)

Prov. B. 2588 freisitz   2589 esperitz   2590 issitz   2591 noiritz   2592 samitz   2594 politz   2596 amanoitz   2597 fallitz   2598 salhitz   2599 vestitz   2605–8 *om.*

Lat. A. 2589 proced*es*   2613 ui*n*ta*n*do

B. 2586 rap.   2589 *no trans.*   2590 exit   2592 examitu*m* p. s.   2597 deli*n*quid   2598 *no trans.*   2600 *no trans.*   2602 auena *only*   2603 tortitium *only*   2605–8 *om.*   2613 *no trans.*

PROVENÇAL AND LATIN TEXT

Beirius	provincia quedam vel hereticus	2614

[I]n -*ihtz*:

fihtz	fixus	
frihz	frixus	
dithz	dictus	2618
afrithz	calidus amore	
aflithz	aflictus	
escrithz	scriptus	
maldithz	maledictio vel maledictus	2622

In -*obs* larg:

obs	opus
clobs	claudus
galobs	medium inter curere et trotare 2626
trobs	invenias

In -*obs* estreit: 23a

grobs	nexus vel nodus	
agrobs	nodes	2630
cobs	testa capitis	
lobs	lupus	
globs	plenum os alicuius liquoris	

In -*olbs* larg: 2634

colbs	ictus
vol[b]s	vulpis

Prov. A. 2614, *with its trans.*, *stretches into right margin*   2615 *red initial omitted*   2616 filhtz   2617 frilhz   2631 cobs < cops   2636 uols

---

B. *after* 2614 B *adds* beirius, *with trans.* hereticus   2615 Jn hitz   2616 fitz   2617 fritz   2618 dihitz   2619 afritz   2620 aflitz   2621 escrihtz   2622 malditz   2623 In obs u*el* obz *only*   2625 *om.*   2626 galobz   2628 ops   2629 grops   2630 *om.*

Lat. A. 2614 h'rtic*us*   2622 maledictio] maledic*us*   2633 loqu*e*us

---

B. 2614 prouintia q. *only* (*cf. Prov. var.*)   2619 amore *with* a *apparently expunctuated*   2622 maledict*us* u*el* maledicto   2625 *om.*   2626 *no trans.*   2627 *no trans.*   2630 *om.*   2631 t. campis

In -*ocs* larg:

2638	jocs	iocus vel ludus
	brocs	vas testeum
	brocs	curas
	ocs	etiam
2642	focs	ignis
	flocs	vestis monaci
	cocs	coccus
	crocs	croceus
2646	grocs	ferrum curvum
	Marrocs	quedam civitas
	badocs	parum siens
	locs	locus
2650	locs	conducas
	rocs	rochus: ludus ligneus
	Enocs	Enoc
	deirocs	[precipites]

2654 In -*ocs* estreit:

	bocs	ircus
	zocs	pes ligneum propter ludum
	mocs	sanies naris
2658	tocs	tangas

In -*ols* larg:

cabrols	capreolus
rossinols	filomena

Prov. A. 2655 locs

B. 2640 biocs   2643 flocs < floxs *by expunctuation of* x *and addition of* c *above, perhaps in different ink*   2645–6 crocs grocs, *but with the translations interverted*   2647 mairocs   2648 baudocs   2649 lecs   2650 *om.*   2651 jocs   2653, *with its trans., placed after 2647*   2654 hocs estreitz   2660 cabreols   2661 rossinhols

---

Lat. A. 2648 parisienses   2653 pes ligneu*m* propte*r* ludu*m* (*cf. 2656*) 2655–8, *the translations are somewhat misplaced, the correct alignment being shown by thin lines*   2656 ligneus   2657 neraris

---

B. 2640 curtas   2643 manici   2644 coctus   2645 ferru*m* curuu*m*   2646 croccus   2648 sciens   2650 *om.*   2651 rochus *om.*   2655 yrcus   2656 *no trans.*

vols	voluntas vel vis vel volvit, preterea voles (de volo, -las)	2662
auriols	avis aurei coloris	
sols	solum	
sols	soles	
sols	solvit	2666
moyols	cifus vitreus	
aiols	avus	
Peirols	proprium nomen viri	
Micols	proprium nomen mulieris	2670
cols	colis	
arestols	extrema pars lancee	
rofiols	cibus de pasta et ovis	
roiols	genus piscis	2674

In -*ols* estreit:

sols	solus	
pols	pulsus	
pols	pulset	2678
pols	pulvis	
bols	equs nimis pulsans	
cols	colles	
princols	primum vinum	2682
escols	exaurias	
mols	mulsus	
mols	mulsit lac	
Aiols	proprium nomen viri	2686
Rainols	proprium nomen viri	

In -*olz* larg:

folz	stultus

Prov. A. 2678-9 pol o pols

B. 2662 vols *four times, with trans.* uoluntas, uis, uolat*us*, uolu*i*t preterita 2663-6 *om.* 2667 moiols 2678 *om.* 2687 Raiols

---

Lat. B. 2662 cf. Prov. var. 2663-6 *om.* 2669 proprium *om.* 2670 nom*en* uiri *only* 2673 *et* de ouis 2674 piss*cis* 2678 *om.* 2681 coles 2684-5 *translations interverted* 2686 proprium *om.* 2687 proprium *om.*

2690 colz   collum
tolz   aufers
molz   molis
solz   solidus, denarius
2694 solz   solutus
acolz   amplectaris ad collum

In -*olz* estreit:

solz   carnes vel pisces in aceto
2698 polz   pultes
polz   pullus
volz   ymago ligni
Santolz   proprium nomen viri

2702 In -*olhz* larg:

olhz   ocullus
brolhz   locus plenus arboribus
folhz   folium vel carta
2706 colhz   coligis
acolhz   bene recipis
trolhz   torcular
recolhz   patrocinaris
2710 escolhz   color
capdolhz   capitolium vel arces
molhz   illud ubi rota figitur
molhz   perfundas vel aqua umectes
2714 despolhz   expolies
rolhz   lignum cum quo furnus tergitur
Cardolhz   nomen castri

Prov. B. 2694 *om.*   2696 *rubric on erasure*   2702 oilhz   2703 oilhz   2704 broilhz   2705 folz   2708 etrolhz   2713 melhz   *after* 2716 B *adds* Rantolhz *and* Marolhz, *each with the trans.* nom*en* castri

Lat. A.   2712 figitur *u*el aqua   2713 p*er*fundas vmectes *only*

B.   2690 collum] aufers < auferz, *by expunctuation of z and addition of abbreviation sign for* s   2691 *no trans.*   2692 mollis   2694 *om.*   2695 amplectari *only*   2697 vel p. *om.*   2698 pulices   2701 proprium *om.*   2703 oculus   2704 *after* arboribus, *and stretching into right margin,* B *adds* domesticis   2706 colligis   2707 bene recept*us* *u*el recipis, *with last two words stretching into right margin*   2712 fingitur   2713 *no trans.*   2715 furt'i t'g'.

PROVENÇAL AND LATIN TEXT

In -*olhz* estreit:

colhz	testiculus	2718
tolhz	genus pisis	
veirolhz	vectis ostii	
genolhz	genu	
pezolhz	pediculus	2722
mairolhz	marubium: herba est	23b
dolhz	dolium vel foramen dolii	

In -*oms* larg:

coms	comes	2726
vescoms	vicecomes	
doms	domus comunis	

In -*oms* estreit:

coloms	columbus	2730
coms	equs abens cavum dorsum	
noms	nomen	
soms	som[n]ium	
ploms	plumbum	2734
roms	genus pisis	
roms	rumpis	
poms	pomum tentorii	
toms	casus vel cadas	2738
doms	dominus	

In -*ons* larg:

cons	vulva	
fons	fons	2742

Prov. B. 2717 *rubric on erasure*   2720 uerolhz   2724 colhz, *placed after 2721*   2727 uiscoms   2738 toms *twice, with trans.* casus *and* cadas   2739 *om.*   *after* 2740 B *adds* dons .i. do*m*inu*s* (*cf.* 2739), amons .i. nom*en* uiri, gions .i. fluui*us* qu*i*dam, fizons .i. nom*en* fluuij (*for the last two, cf.* 2746–7), *followed by the heading* In ons estreit

---

Lat. A. 2720 uestes (*cf.* B)   2733 somium *or* sonnum

B. 2718 testiculi   2719 piscis   2720 uectes   2722 pediculo
2730 columba*s*   2731 h*a*bens   2733 su*m*mum   2735-6 *translations interverted*   2735 piscis   2739 *om.*

226 PROVENÇAL AND LATIN TEXT

fons	liquefacis
confuns	confundis
mons	mons vel acervus
2746 Gions	fluvius quidam
Fisons	nomen fluvii
segons	secundus
Trons	nomen fluvii vel ebetatus
2750 pons	pons, -tis
estrons	stercus, -ris
frons	frons, -tis
sons	sopor
2754 gergons	vulgare trutanorum
rons	ruga
rons	facias rugas
fons	fundus
2758 afons	ad fundum venias
escons	abscondis
preons	profundus

In -*ohtz* larg:

2762 bohtz	fundus dolii
vohtz	vacuus
mohtz	modius
cohtz	coctus
2766 recohtz	recotus
bescohz	panis biscotus
dohtz	doctus
pohz	podium vel mons

2770 E tuit poden fenir in -*oitz*, si
cum *coitz, voitz*.

Prov. B. 2744 confons   2746–7 *om.* (*cf. 2740*)   2749 trons *twice, with trans.* nomen fluuii *and* ebetatus   2758 affons   2759 ascons   2761 hotz   2762 bothz   2763 uohz   2764 mothz   2766 rechotz   2767 bescohtz   2769 pohtz   2770 oithz   2771 coihtz uoihtz

Lat. A. 2743 liqu*e*facias   2770–1 *no trans.*

B. 2743 liqu*e*facit   2745 mon   2746–7 *om.*   2751 ris *om.*   2752 tis *om.*   2753 *no trans.*   2754 uulgar' trutam*n*orum   2756 fatias   2757 fundu*m*   2758 ad f.] affundu*m*   2759 absconditu*s*   2762 fundu*m*   2766 recoctus   2767 biscocts panis   2770–1 *no trans.*

In -*onhz* estreit:

onhz	ontus	
onhz	ungis	2774
conhz	cuneus cum quo ligna finduntur	
conhz	cum cuneo cudas	
ponhz	manus clausa	
ponhz	punctus	2778
ponhz	punctum; pungis	
perponhz	vestis armandi grossa et valde puncta	
Gronhz	proprium nomen viri	
gronhz	rostrum animalis	2782
besonhz	opus	
lonhz	prolonges	

In -*orcs* larg:

porcs	porcus	2786
orcs	quedam herba	
Austorcs	proprium nomen viri	

In -*orcs* estreit:

borcs	vicus	2790
reborcs	obtusus vel hebes	
dorcs	anfora	
forcs	dicitur a furca: vel bivium vel furcando struas	
estorcs	evellas	2794
gorcs	gurges	
engorcs	ingurges	

Prov. B. 2772 onhtz   2774 onz   2778–9 *om.*   2794 enforcs
2795 grocs

Lat. A. 2775 find*e*itur (*cf. B*)   2776 cudas] claudas   2793 di*c*itur a furca *u*el biniu*m* *u*el fu*r*ca*m* d*e*struas. euellas, *with last word struck through in red ink*

B. 2773 unctu*s*   2775 c*un*c c*um* quo fiditur lignu*m*   2776 cudas *om.*
2778–9 *om.*   2780 grossa *et* valde pu*n*cta uestis ad a*r*ma*n*de   2781 proprium *om.*   2788 proprium *om.*   2791 hebes] hn*s*.   2793 di*c*itur afurci *only*
(*without the usual idest*)   2794 euella *u*el biuiu*m* (< biñiu3)   2796 ingurgites

228 PROVENÇAL AND LATIN TEXT

  In *-ous* lar[g] o estreit: In hoc ritimo largo vel stricto:
2798 ous   ovum
  bous   bos
  nous   novus
  renous   usura
24a annous   annus novus vel Circumcisio
2803 mous   moves
  plous   pluis

  In *-ors* larg: In hoc ritimo largo:
2806 cors   corpus
  ors   ora panni
  mors   morsus
  pors   porrus
2810 tors   pars pisis
  fors   foras vel perfores
  tors   torsit
  Elienors   proprium nomen mulieris
2814 mors   momordit
  mors   morsus

  In *-ors* estrit: In hoc ritimo stricto:
  labors   labor
2818 tabors   timpanum
  cors   cursus
  cors   cucurrit
  acors   subvenit
2822 socors   idem: subvenit

Prov. A. 2797 lar

B. 2797 *heading in black, repeated in red on next line*; o en estreit, *both times*
2807–8 *interverted*   2816 Jn ors estret, *in black, followed on next line by* Jn ors estreit, *in red*   2821 *om.*

Lat. A. 2799 hos   2809 portus   2811 p*re*forsit

B. 2797 *no trans.*   2801 renouus *only*   2802 vel C. *om.*
2804 pluit   2805 *no trans.*   2807 orapam.   2809 porus
2810 pisis] parsi   2811 perfores] pu*nctus*   2813 proprium *om.*
2815 morsus aura   2816 Jdest in hoc r. s.   2818 ty*m*panu*m*
2820 currit   2821 *om.*   2822 idem *om.*

colors	color	
socors	auxilium	
flors	flos	
amors	amor	2826
ors	ursus	
ardors	ardor	
pudors	fetor	
calors	calor	2830
sabors	sapor	
freidors	frigiditas	
rasors	rasor (de rado, -is)	
valors	valor	2834
vabors	vapor	
umors	umor	
verdors	viror	
tors	turris	
bestors	parva turris	
comtors	parvus comes	
austors	ancipiter	
odors	odor	2842
legors	ocium	
honors	honor	
deshonors	dedecus	
paors	timor	2846
ricors	divicie	
douçors	dulçor	
auctors	auctor	
tristors	tristicia	2850
albors	albedo diei	
sors	surrexit	
sors	susitatus vel elevatus	
resors	resusitatus	2854
resors	resurrexit	

Prov. B. 2835 vapors   2840 contors   2845 desonors   2848 douzors

---

Lat. B. 2833 de rado is *om.*   2847 diuitie   2848 dulzor
2850 tristitia   2851 diei albedo   2852 s. *uel* eleua*tus*   2853 suscitatus *only*   2854 resuscita*tus*

In -*ortz*:

ortz	ortus
2858 acortz	concordia
acortz	concordes
descors	discordes
descors	discordia, vel cantilena habens sonos diversos
2862 conortz	consolatio
fortz	fortis
esfortz	conamen
confortz	confortatio
2866 confortz	pars corii in corio aposita causa confortandi, sicut in sotularibus
sortz	sors
tortz	vis illata
tortz	tortus vel torquet
2870 retortz	iterum torquet: ad filum pertinet
retortz	retortus
estortz	liberatus a periculo aliquo
estortz	liberat
2874 estortz	denodatus in vinctura aliqua
portz	portus
portz	portes
aportz	deferas
2878 deportz	ludus in spaciando
deportz	ludas
mortz	mors
mortz	mortuus

Prov. A. 2875–81 *placed after* 3561

B. 2856 ortz larg   2860 discortz   2861 descortz   2862 conort 2865 *om*.   2866 contrafortz   2870 recortz   *after* 2874 *B adds* estortz, *without trans*.   2878 *om*.

Lat. A. 2866 scl'arib*us*   2873 liberatus

B. 2861 discordia vel *om*.   2865 *om*.   2866 apposita; causa c. s. in s. *om*.   2869 vel torquet *om*.   2870 ad f. p. *om*.   2872 l. ab aliquo periculo   2874 desnodatus ab aliqua ui*n*ctura   2878 *om*. 2879 liudas *or* luidas

In -*ortz* estreit: 2882

cortz	curia
cortz	curtus
bortz	ludus
bortz	manser vel s[p]urius 2886
sortz	surdus
tortz	quedam avis
lortz	p[a]rum audiens
gortz	rigidus infirmitate 2890
biortz	cursus equorum
sortz	surgit

In -*orbs* larg:

| corbs | corvus 2894 |
| orbs | orbus |

In -*orbs* estrit:

| corbs | curvus 2897 |

In -*orns* larg: 24b

borns	pomum temptorii
corns	cornu
corns	tuba vel bucina
corns	buccines 2902
magorns	tibia sine pede

In -*orms* larg:

| vorms | [. . .] |
| dorms | [dormis] 2906 |

Prov. A. 2902–3 corns ma *on erasure*

B. 2888 bortz   2896 In orbs *om.*; estreit   2902 *om.*   2904 Jn oms larg (*both rubric and indication to rubricator*)

Lat. A. 2886 manuu*m* desurius (*sim. B*)   2889 pru*m*   2903 pedu*m*   2905 *no trans.* (*so B*)   2906 *no trans.*

B. 2886 manuu*er*surius   2889 raru*m*   2890 rigida firmitate   2899 te*n*torij   2902 *om.*   2905 *no trans.*

232   PROVENÇAL AND LATIN TEXT

In -*orns* estreit:

alborns	quedam arbor
dorns	mensura manus clause
2910 adorns	aptus
torns	instrumentum tornatile, vel revertaris
morns	subtristis
contorns	primus sulcus aratri
2914 retorns	redeas
forns	furnus

In -*outz* larg:

Moutz	quidam fluvius
2918 moutz	in molendino tritus
voutz	versus vel revolutus
revoutz	idem est
desvoutz	extentus: ad filum pertinet
2922 arcvoutz	arcus lapideus
esmoutz	gladius ad molam ductus
toutz	ablatus
soutz	solutus
2926 coutz	cultus vel paries

In -*outz* estreit:

voutz	ymago ligni
soutz	carnes vel pisses in aceto
2930 moutz	multos
moutz	mulget lac
doutz	dulcis
estoutz	de facili irascens, vel stultus

Prov. A.   2911 gorns

B. 2907 oms   2911 torns *twice, with the two translations separately*
2916–33 *placed in the following order: 2916–17, 2925–6, 2918, 2932–3*
2917 voutz   2919–24 *om.*   2927–31 *om.*

Lat. A.   2913 primus] un*us* (*so* B)   2923 cladi*us*

B. 2912 substrictus   2913 primus] unus   2918 tritus] i̇t.^{o} *or* i̇t.^{a}
2919–24 *om.*   2926 vel p. *om.*   2927–31 *om.*   2933 facl'a

In -*otz* larg: 2934
botz   ictus
escotz   lignum parvum acutum
escotz   precium pro prandio
clotz   locus cavus   2938
lotz   lentus
rotz   erutuatio
potz   labium
cotz   mu[l]tatio   2942
potz   potes
trotz   inter passum et cursum
regotz   recurvitas capillorum
arlotz   pauper   2946
galiotz   pirata
cabotz   genus piscis
notz   nocet

In -*otz* estreit: 2950
botz   nepos
botz   uter
brotz   teneritudo herbe
cotz   lapis ad acuendum   2954
cogotz   cuius uxor eum adulterat
glotz   gulosus
motz   verbum
totz   omnis vel totus   2958
rotz   ruptus
potz   puteus
sotz   locus ubi porci comedunt
sotz   subtus   2962

Prov. A. *after* 2955 *A adds* colotz, *with trans.* gulosus, *both words being struck through*

B. 2938 glotz   2948 gabotz   2949 noz   *after* 2954 *B adds* cotz, *with trans.* paruus canis   2961 *om.*   *after* 2962 *B adds* soptz, *without trans.*

Lat. A. 2941 labiu*m* permutatio (*cf.* 2942, var. B)   2942 *no trans.*
2943 potest (*so B*)

B. 2937 pretiu*m*   2940 eructuatio   2942 p*er*mutatio   2943 potest
2946 paup*er* uilis   2947 *no trans.*   2955 eum *om.*; adultera   2961 *om.*

notz	nux
fotz	cois

In [-*ucs*]:

2966	ucs	clamor sine verbis
	ucs	clames
	bucs	brachium sine manu
	sambucs	arbor
2970	saüc[s]	idem
	trebucs	calige truncate
	trasbucs	precipites
	claücs	clausis
2974	ducs	dux vel quedam avis
	calucs	curtum habens visum
	astrucs	fortunatus
	desastrucs	infortunatus
2978	pezucs	strictura facta cum duobus digitis
	pezucs	stringas cum duobus digitis
	sucs	succus
	zucs	testa capitis
2982	malastrucs	infortunium passus
25a	paorucs	timidus
	palhucs	parva palea
	festucs	festuca
2986	devertucs	apostema extrinseca
	pesucs	onerosus

In -*uf*:

	buf	vox indigna[ntis]
2990	chuf	pili super frontem
	buf	insuflatio

Prov. A. 2965–7 vcs *twice only*   2970 sauc   *after* 2974 *A repeats* ducs, *with trans.* auis

B. 2963 nupz *with* p *expunctuated*   2964 fortz   2966 vics   2967 *om.*   2969 sabucs   2973 *om.*   2979 *om.*   2983 paurucs   2990 cuf

Lat. A. 2971 tracate (*cf. B*)   2989 in*d*igna

B. 2964 cors   2966 *no trans.*   2967 *om.*   2969 sambuc*us* quedam   arbor sterilis   2971 tractare   2973 *om.*   2974 avis *om.*   2979 *om.*   2986 intrinseca   2987 honerosus   2989 indign*n*antis   2991 insufflatio

PROVENÇAL AND LATIN TEXT

In -*uls*:

muls	mulus	
culs	culus	2994
coguls	[. . .]	
Saüls	Saul	

In -*ums* estreit:

fums	fumus	2998
lums	lumen	
agrums	res acerba, sicut fructus recentes	
alums	alumen	
escums	spumam auferas	3002
betums	bitumen	

In -*urs*:

agurs	augurium	
segurs	securus	3006
asegurs	securum facias	
aturs	conamen	
aturs	coneris	
durs	durus	3010
endurs	ieiunes	
purs	purus	
murs	murus	
escurs	obscurus	3014
tafurs	homo parvi precii	
Surs	nomen civitatis	

Prov. A. 2992–6 *form the end of a line and are cramped together,* 2996 *being in right margin*   3001–3 lums escums b *on erasure (made after the initials were touched with red, since the parchment is slightly reddened);* 3003 *is in right margin*

B. 2994 guls; *after* 2994 B *adds* culs, *without trans.*   2996 *om.* *after* 3001 B *adds* alhums, *with trans.* illumines   3006 *om.*   3007 assegurs   3008–9 *interverted*   3009 acurs

Lat. A. 2995 *no trans.* (*so* B)   2996 sanu: 3007 secur*us* 3008 coname*n with* m̄ *on erasure* (< conaris?)   3009 conaris (*so* B)

B. 2994 cal*us* *uel* anus   2995 *no trans.*   2996 *om.*   3000 agrume*n only*   3001 a. *uel* illumines   3002 auferas spuma*m*   3005 agurium 3006 *om.*   3007 fatias   3009 conaris   3011 *no trans.*   3015 pretij

perjurs	periurus vel periures
3018 rancurs	conqueraris
In *-urcs*:	
Turcs	Partus, genus Saracinorum
Burcs	nomen civitatis
3022 In *-utz*:	
cambutz	habens longas tibias
alutz	plenus alis
agutz	acutus
3026 cutz	vilis persona
drutz	qui intendit in dominabus
grutz	farrum
glutz	glutinum
3030 lutz	lux
lutz	lucet
salutz	salus
salutz	salutes
3034 salutz	sanitas
mutz	mutus
nutz	nudus
putz	fetes
3038 romputz	ruptus
cosutz	consutus
pelutz	pilosus
menutz	minutus
3042 canutz	plenus canis
descosutz	desconsutus
fendutz	fissus
perdutz	perditus
3046 saubutz	scitus
receubutz	receptus
ereubutz	ereptus

Prov. B. 3017 periurs *twice, with trans.* periurus *and* periures   3020 urcs .i. partus, turcs .i. genus saracenor*um*   3031 *om.*   3033 *om.* 3044 fendutz (t < z)   3048 *om.*

Lat. A. 3017 periurus] p*er*iurius

B. 3020 *cf. Prov. var.*   3024 alijs   3027 procus qui; in *om.*   3028 *no trans.*   3029 glutiniu*m*   3031 *om.*   3032 s. *u*el salute*s*   3033 *om.* 3034 *no trans.*   3048 *om.*

PROVENÇAL AND LATIN TEXT

aperceubutz	promtus	
conougutz	cognitus	3050
desconougutz	incognitus	
creütz	creditus	
descreütz	incredibilis	
recreütz	a bono opere cessans	3054
deceubutz	deceptus	
espatlutz	habens magnos humeros	
pendutz	suspensus	
despendutz	a suspendio [liberatus], vel expensus	3058
sospendutz	suspensus	
mogutz	motus	
esmogutz	commotus	
tendutz	tensus	3062
atendutz	expectatus	
destendutz	distensus	
estendutz	extensus	
tengutz	tentus	3066
sostengutz	sustentatus	
venguth	qui iam venit	
revengutz	melioratus	
esperdutz	stupefactus	3070
reconogutz	recognitus	
cregutz	auctus	
descregutz	diminutus	
enbutz	illud cum quo mittit vinum vel aquam in vase	3074
batutz	percussus	
combatutz	preliatus	
taütz	feretrum	

Prov. A.   3077, *with its trans.*, *added below 3076, at bottom of page*

B. 3050 conogutz   3051 desconogutz   3056 espalhutz   3058 *twice*,
with trans. a suspendio liberatus *and* expen*sus*   3059 suspendutz
3063 *om.*   3065 extendutz   3068 vengutz   3073 descreutz
after 3075 B *adds* abatutz, *with trans.* prostratus   3076 conbatutz

---

Lat. A.   3058 a suspendio. *u*el expensus   3065 *on erasure*

B. 3053 ille cui n*on* creditur   3056 magnos habens h.   3063 *om.*
3067 s*u*bste*n*tatus   3068 ille qui   3074 embutus *only*

25b In -us:

3079	lus	die[s] lune
	l'us	unus
	us	unus
3082	us	hostium
	us	usus
	brus	fuschus
	grus	granulum uve
3086	reclus	reclusus
	conglus	conclusus
	negus	nullus
	jus	deorsum
3090	dejus	ieiunus
	fus	lignum cum quo femine filant
	confus	confusus
	palus	palus, -ludis
3094	pertus	foramen
	crus	crudus
	enfrus	homo insaciabilis
	plus	plus
3098	Cerberus	ianitor inferni
	Dedalus	proprium nomen viri
	Tantalus	proprium nomen viri
	Artus	proprium nomen viri
3102	sus	sursum
	Jhesus	Iesus
	comus	comunis

E devetz saber que la segonda 3106 persona del presen del conjunctiu se dobla en la prima conjugatzo, si cum:

Et debetis sire quod secunda persona presentis coniunctivi duplicatur in prima coniugatione, verbi gracia:

Prov. B. 3078 us dics (*both rubric and indication to rubricator*)   3083 *om.*   3087 conclus   3108 coniugazo

Lat. A. 3079 die   3103 aesus

B. 3079 lum*en only*   3082 ostiu*m*   3083 *om.*   3084 fuscu*s*
3091 lignum e*st* q*uo* ueru*nt only*   3093 ludis *om.*   3096 i*n*satiabili*s*
3099 proprium *om.*   3100 proprium *om.*   3101 proprium *om.*
3103 filius dei *only*   3104 co*m*munis   3106 presetis coniuctiui
3107-8 *co*niugazo

chans o chantes	cantes	
enbarcs o enbargues	inpedias; idem	3110
estancs o estanques	idem	
ensais, ensaies	probes; idem	
bais, baises	osculeris; idem	
lais, laisses.	dimittas; idem.	3114

Et aquesta regla es generals per la maior part, mas non de tot. Et hec regula est generalis pro maiori parte, set non ex toto.

In -*ura*:

cura	cura	3118
pura	pura	
rancura	querimonia	
rancura	conqueritur	
jura	iurat	3122
perjura	degerat	
mesura	mensura	
desmesura	superfluitas	
desmessura	facit contra mensuram	3126
amesura	facit ad mensuram	
dura	dura	
dura	durat	
endura	ieiunium	3130
melura	meliorat	
peiura	peior efficitur	
atura	conatur	
falsura	falsitas	3134
dreitura	iustitia	
adreitura	iusticiat	

Prov. B. 3109 cans   3111 estanqes   3115 regu*l*a   3117 *rubric* Jn ura larg, *but marginal indication to rubricator reads* Jn ura   3121 *om*. 3126 desmesura   3127 *om*.   *after* 3128 B *adds rubric* Jn ura estreit (*but marginal indication to rubricator reads* Jn ura), *followed by* calura, *without trans*.   3129–30 *om*.   3131 melhura   3134 *om*.   3136 *om*.

Lat. A.   3111 *no trans. above* estancs, jdem *above* estanques   3131 melioret

B.   3109 ide*m only*   3110 jmpedias; jdem (m < o)   3111 liges jdem 3113 obscules   3114 dimictas   3115 proro   3121 *om*.   3127 *om*. 3129–30 *om*.   3134 *om*.   3136 *om*.

conjura	adiurat
3138 pastura	pascua
pastura	pascitur
aventura	fortuna
desaventura	infortunium
3142 centura	çona
escura	obscura
peintura	pinctura
agura	auguratur
3146 segura	secura
asegura	reddit securum
ambladura	planus et velox incessus
pura	pura
3150 mura	facit murum
natura	natura
desnatura	facit contra naturam
cosdura	sutura

3154 In -*ara*:

cara	cara
amara	amara
rara	rara
3158 clara	clara
para	parat
ampara	ocupat vi
desa[m]para	derelinquit
3162 gara	custodit
esgara	aspicit
regara	respicit
ara	modo
3166 ancara	aduc

Prov. A. 3147 asegeura 3153 condura 3159, *with its trans.*, *in right margin at end of line* 3161 desapara, *with its trans., added in margin, with insertion-mark*

B. 3138 *om.* 3140 *om.* 3147 assegura 3163 *om.*

Lat. A. 3160 ocupat *only* 3161 u derelinquit (*the first letter is partly cut off by the binder and is probably a relic of* ui)

B. 3138 *om.* 3140 *om.* 3142 zona 3144 pictura 3145 augitatur 3160 occupauit 3161 derelin*qu*id 3163 *om.* 3166 adhuc (h < u)

PROVENÇAL AND LATIN TEXT

In -*era*:   26a

fera	fera
bera	feretrum
esmera	depurat	3170
lesquera	legerem
cantera	cantarem

Et totas las primas personas del presen del obtatiu de la prima conjugazo fenissen in -*era* o en -*ia*.   Et omnes prime persone et tercie presentis obtativi prime con- 3174 iugationis finiunt in -*era* vel in -*ia*.

In -*era* estrit:

cera	cera	3178
pera	pirum	
vera	vera	
apodera	subpeditat	

In -*eira*:   3182

cadeira	catedra	
feira	nundine	
feira	feriat	
teira	series	3186
enteira	integra	
ateira	per seriem [ponit]	
a teira	seriatim	
ribeira	planicies super aquas	3190
sobreira	superba vel exuperans	
arqueira	fenestra vel fissura ad sagitandum	

Prov. A. 3185 feirat

B. 3171 lesqera   3177 estreit   3182 eira, *with the* i *added above*
3188 areira   3189 *om.*   3192 arqeira

Lat. A. 3171 legerent (*so* B)   3188 ponit *om.*   3189 seriatu*m*
3191 exup*er*ans sup*er*bali*s*

B. 3169 fe*r*retru*m*   3171 legerent   3174–5 coiugatoi*s*   3181 supeditat
3183 chathedra *with first* h *expunctuated*   3189 *om.*   3190 planities
iux*t*a aq*u*as   3191 superba] sup*er*a   3192 vel fissura *om.*; sagittandu*m*

lebreira	canis leporina
3194 cairera	strata vel via publica
saleira	ubi sal reponitur
mainera	modus, vel ad manum cito veniens
mezoigneira	mendax mulier
3198 plazenteira	placens mulier
corseira	discurrens mulier
enqueira	inquirat
requeira	requirat
3202 soudadera	mulier accipiens solidum
derreira	ultima
presenteira	mulier audacter loquens
peteira	mulier bumbos faciens
3206 meira	mereatur

In *-ira*:

ira	ira
mira	aspicit
3210 remira	valde aspicit
tira	tirat
sospira	suspirat
desira	desiderat
3214 adira	odio habet
vira	volvit
revira	revolvit
gira	idem quod super
3218 regira	idem quod supra
e consira	considerat

Prov. A. 3203 detreira   3219 econsira

B. 3194 carreira   3196 maneira   3197 mezongeira   3198 plasenteira   3199 *om.*   3200 enqeira   3201 reqeira   3202 soudadeira   3208 *om.*   3219 escosira

---

Lat. A. 3202 solid*e*

B. 3193 carnis   3196 modus *only*   3199 *om.*   3204 audaciter   3205 mul*i*er (u < l') bubos fatiens   3208 *om.*   3211 trait   3217 supra

E totas las primas personas e las terças del presen del obtatiu de la prima conjugatzo, si cum:	Et omnes prime persone et tercie presentis obtativi prime coniugationis finiunt in -*ira*, 3222 sicut: 3222a
auçira	audirem vel audiret
dormira	dormirem vel dormiret

In -*ora* larg:	In hac ritima:	
nora	nurus	3226
Flora	proprium nomen mulieris	
demora	moratur vel ludit	
fora	foras	
devora	devorat	3230

In -*ora* estreit:	In hac stricta:	
ora	ora	
adora	adorat	
aora	modo	3234
labora	laborat	
plora	plorat	
mora	morum	
fora	esset	3238
cora	quando	
onora	honorat	
assapora	gusta quid sapit	
odora	odorat	3242

In -*aura*:	In hac:	
aura	aura	
laura	color laureus	
maura	nigra	3246
saura	crisea	
daura	deaurat	

Prov. B.   3220 E *om.*   3222 las primas coniugazo jn ira fenissen aisi sicum   3223 auzira

---

Lat. B.   3220 Et *om.*   3222–2a finiunt . . . sicut] jn ira finiu*n*t ita u*e*rbi gra*cia*   3223 audire*m* u*e*l audir*e*., *stretching into margin at end of line* 3224 dormirem] dormire   3225 *no trans.*   3227 proprium *om.* 3229 forat   3231 *no trans.*   3241 gustat   3243 *no trans.* 3245 laureu*m*   3247 grisea   3248 daurata

sobredaura	idem
26b essaura	ad aerem ponit
3251 restaura	restaurat

In -*ala*:

ala	ala
3254 sala	aula
pala	pala ad extrahendum panem
tala	devastacio vel detrimentum
tala	devastat
3258 cala	tacet
mala	mala
mala	mantica
escala	s[c]ala
3262 escala	ordinat exercitum
sala	salem mittit
dessala	salem tolit

[I]n -*ela* larg: In hac larga:

3266 bela	pulcra
noela	novella
noela	novum verbum
renovela	renovat
3270 maissela	maxilla
mamella	mamma
cembela	ostendit avem ad capiendum aves
apela	vocat vel apellat
3274 caramela	fistula cantat
piuçella	virgo vel pulcella

Prov. A. 3265 *red initial om.*

B. 3257 cala   3258 *om.*   3264 desala   3265 lar (*but* larg *in marginal indication to rubricator*)   3271 mamela   3275 punzella

---

Lat. A. 3255 pale *only*   3256 d. *uel detrimentum* ad exte*n*de*n*dum pane*m*   3261 sala (*so* B)   3262 ordinat. exc*antur*

B. 3249 jdem est   3255 pala ad extraendum ponit   3256 deuastio   3258 *om.*   3260 mancia   3261 sala   3264 s. dedit   3265 no *trans.*   3272 capiendas   3273 app*e*llat   3274 canit   3275 puella *only*

PROVENÇAL AND LATIN TEXT

despuzela	coru[m]pit virginem	
sela	sella	
sela	sellam mittit	3278
desella	sellam tolit	
acantela	[in] latus declinat	
mantela	velat	
canela	species quedam	3282
revela	revella vel rebellat	
capdella	ducatum prebet	
aissella	acella	
pustella	morbus	3286
padela	patella vel sartago	

In -*ela* estreit:

cela	illa	
cela	celat	3290
vela	velum	
pela	pilos aufert	
tela	tella	
estela	stella	3294
donzela	domicella	
candela	candela	

In -*ila*:

vila	vila	3298
ila	insula	
pila	lapis cavus; pes pontis	
pila	terit	
fila	net	3302

Prov. A. 3282 cantela   3299 pila

B. 3276 dispunzella   3279 dessella   3284 capdela   3285 aisela
3286 pustela

Lat. A. 3276 corupit   3280 in *om.*   3287 sarrago *or* sartago

B. 3276 corru*m*pit   3277–8 *translations interverted*   3279 tollit
3282 speties   3283 revella] reuelat   3284 *dicitur* p.   3286 fistule
3287 patena   3293 tela   3294 stela   3298 villa   3299 in-
sula*m*, *with stroke through abbreviation sign*   3300 lapis cauus *terris*
3301 pes po*n*tis

PROVENÇAL AND LATIN TEXT

guila	decepcio
desfila	extrait filum
anguila	anguilla
3306 afila	acuit
apila	inititur
esquila	parva campana
crila	cribat

3310 In -*ola* larg:

stola	stola
fola	stulta
degola	precipitat
3314 mola	molis vel mola
dola	dolat
escola	scola
acola	ampletitur ad collum
3318 percola	valde amplectitur
sola	soleas consuit
desola	dissuit solas
viola	viola
3322 vola	vola
fillola	que habet patrinum
afola	destruit

In -*ola* estrit:

3326 sadola	satura
gola	gula
agola	in gula mittit
esgola	foramen facit in veste unde caput intrat

Prov. A. 3316 eescola

B. 3306 affila   3308 esquila (s < x)   3309 grila   3320 dessola
3323 filhola   3324 affola   3325 estreit

Lat. A. 3304 ex*tert* (*the third character is smudged and could be read as* f *or* l')
3317 acolla a. ad c.   3323 q*ui*

B. 3303 dece*t*io   3304 ex*tra*hit   3312 sculta   3317 ampleti-
tur only   3320 soleas dissuit   3322 volat   3323 patruu*m*
3326–3561 *no trans.*

PROVENÇAL AND LATIN TEXT 247

cola	colat	3330
escola	exaurit	
sola	sola	
sadola	saturat	
grola	solea vetus	3334
fola	sub pede calcat	
bola	meta	
bola	metas ponit	27a
meçola	medulla	3338
ola	olla	

In -*ula*:

mula	mulla	
recula	retrograditur	3342
acula	cullum ponit in terra	

In -*alha*:

malha	amus lorice	
desmalha	spoliat	3346
malha	facit ammos in lorica	
malha	macula in oculo	
malha	maleo percutit	
malha	[. . .]	3350
trebalha	labor	
trebalha	laborat	
nualha	inercia	
anualha	vilescit vel ad pigriciam venit	3354
batalha	prelium	
sarralh[a]	illud ubi clavis mittitur	
moralha	quod pendet in vecte	
palha	palea	3358
buschalha	colligit ligna minuta	
talha	secat vel tributum	

Prov. A.   3353 anualha   3356 sarralh

B.   3338 mezola   3340–3 *om.*   3345 malha *with the* h *added above*
3348–50 *om.*   3356 seralha

Lat. A.   3337 pan*em*   3338 mud*u*lla   3341 mull*is*   3350 *no*
trans.   3354 vilesc*t*

rethalha	iterum secat
3362 entalha	sculpit
eschalha	frangit
baralh[a]	contentio
valha	valeat
3366 salha	saliat
assalha	assaltum det
tartalha	loquitur frequenter et ociose
mezalha	obulum
3370 falha	facula
falha	delinquat
falha	quidam ludus tabularum
falha	[...]
3374 toalha	mantille
ventalha	pars lorice que ponitur ante faciem
badalha	oscitat, id est aperit os
fendalha	fissura

3378 In *-ela* estreit:

vermelha	rubicunda
semelha	similat
somnelha	frequenter sonniatur, vel dormitat
3382 velha	vigilat
revelha	excitat
esvelha	evigilat
ovelha	ovis
3386 solelha	ad solem siccat
conselha	consulit
botelha	vas aquatile
aparelha	preparat vel equat

Prov. A. 3364 baralh, *after which one letter has been erased*

B. 3361 retalha   3363 escalha   3367 asalha   3368 tartailha
3369 mesalha   3371–3 *om.*   3374 coalha   3377 *om.*   3378 elha
(*but* ela *in marginal indication to rubricator*)   *after* 3384 B *adds* deuelha
reuelha   3385 *om.*   3386 sonelha   3387 sonselha   3389 aparelha
(lh < ll)

Lat. A.   3368 preciose   3373 *no trans.*   3388 botelha u. a.

PROVENÇAL AND LATIN TEXT 249

despar[e]lha	dispares facit	3390
pendelha	frequenter pendit	
aurelha	auricula	
pelha	vetus pannus	
relha	ferrum aratri	3394
selha	vas aquatile	
telha	cortex tilie	
abelha	apis	
estrelha	ferrum, instrumentum proprium [ad] equos tergendos	3398
est[r]elha	[. . .]	
trelha	vitis in altum elevata	

In -*ela* larg:
velha	veterana	3402
Amelha	proprium nomen mulieris	

In -*ilha*:
filha	filia	
miravilha	mirum vel mirabile	3406
roïlha	rubigo vel rubigine tingitur	
desroïlha	aufert rubiginem	
bilha	lign[e]us ludus	
essilha	in exilium mittit	3410
cornilha	cornix	
canilha	vermis comedens dura	
ponzilha	ponit ligna supra muros	
ilha	ilia	3414
adouzilha	spinam in dolio mittit	
asotilha	subtiliat	27b
afilha	adoptat in filium vel in filiam	

Prov. A.   3390 desparlha   3399 estelha   3413 pouzilha

B. 3396 delha   3400 *om.*   3401 elha   3406 merauilha
3408 desfroilha   3410 esilha   3415 aduzilha   3416 asoutilha

---

Lat. A. 3398–9 f. i. *proprium.*, *above* estrelha; *equos tergendos above* estelha
3407 uergitur   3409 lignus   3415 dolio *with the* i *added above*

3418 In -*ola* larg:

molha	umecta vel aqua perfunde
remolha	ad umiditatem venit
despolha	expoliat
3422 volha	velit
tolha	auferat
destolha	deviet
dolha	doleat
3426 acolha	bene recipiat
recolha	patrocinetur
orgolha	superbit
capdolha	asendit
3430 brolha	pullulat
trolha	exprimit torculari
folha	equivocum: folium, vel folia producit

In -*ola* estreit:

3434 colha	pellis testiculorum
dolha	foramen quo asta in ferrum ponitur
Polha	provincia quedam
solha	poluit
3438 verolha	vecte firmat

In -*amba*:

camba	tibia

In -*enga*:

3442 lenga	linga
lausenga	adulatio vel verbum bilinguis
fenga	fingat
tenga	tingat
3446 estrenga	stringat

Prov. A. 3436 pholha

B. 3418 olha   3426 aicolha   3431 tolha   3433 olha

Lat. A. 3424 deruet   3431 to*r*culam   3435 foram*en* q*uo* asta inserit *only*   3436 poni*tur only*   3437 p*r*ouincia q*uedam* poluit 3438 ugre f.

In -*anca*:

branca	frondes	
blanca	candida	
abranca	capit vi	3450
tanca	firmat	
estanca	retinet aquam	
anca	nates	
manca	mulier amissa manu	3454
sanca	sinistra	

In -*iga*:

figa	ficus	
triga	moram facit	3458
destrica	inpedit	
eniga	iniqua	
enemiga	inimica	
antiga	antica	3462
mendiga	mendica	
diga	dicat	
esdiga	neget	

In -*ia*:   3466

embria	proficit	
cambia	permutat	
tria	eligit	
lia	ligat	3470
deslia	solvit	
tria	discernit	
mia	mea	
sia	sit	3474
afia	fideiubet	
desfia	diffidit vel minatur	
dia	die[s]	
mia	amica	3478

Prov. B.   3449 *om.*   3459 destriga   3467 embraia   3476 desfja
(j < e)   3478 amia

Lat. A.   3450 cap*it* (*or* cap*ut*) ui*m*   3454 mulier amissa *only*
3455 manusinistra   3477 die

PROVENÇAL AND LATIN TEXT

    ria   rideat
    aucia   occidat

In -*ica*:
3482 pica   picat
     fica   figit
     afica   afirmat vel conatur
     desfica   evellit
3486 rica   dives mulier

In -*ega*:
     lega   leuga
     ega   equa
3490 pega   insipida
     sega   segat
     sega   sequatur
     cega   ceca
3494 trega   treuga
     encega   excecat
     persega   persequatur
     consega   consequatur

3498 In -*auca*:
     pauca   parva
     auca   anser
     mauca   venter grossus
3502 rauca   rauca
     crauca   terra sterilis

28a In -*esca*:
     lesca   particula pannis
3506 sesca   arundo secans, incisa
     fresca   recens

Prov. A.   3486 bica   3503 erauca

B. 3484-5 *interverted*   3492 *om.*   3503 grauca   *after* 3505 B
adds iesca   3507 *om.*

Lat. A.   3484 uinci*tur*, *with first* u *not clear*

bresca	favus	
antrebresca	intermiset	
mesca	propinet	3510
pesca	piscatur	
cresca	crescat	
esca	illud cum quo ignis accendi-t[ur], vel esca cara cani	
adesca	inescat	3514
tresca	correa intricata	
tresca	coream facit ve ludum intricatum	

In -*aira*:

laira	latrat	3518
vaira	variat	
quaira	quadrat	
escaira	quadrando strue	
esclaira	claresit	3522
repaira	repa[t]riat	
aira	area	

In -*ossa* larg: In hac sillaba:

fossa	cavea	3526
grossa	grossa	
trasdossa	mantica, vel quicquid portat homo in dorso equi	
ossa	collectio ossium	
desossa	carnes ab ossibus removet	3530

In -*ossa* estreit:

rossa	rubra	
mossa	que in veteri arbore nasitur super corticem	
trossa	sarcina	3534

Prov. B. 3509 antebresca   3516 bresca   3525 larg *om.*   3528 transdossa

---

Lat. A. 3509 inte*r*misit   3513 acce*n*dit   3521 quadru*m* destrue   3523 repariat   3528 q*ui*cq*ui*d'   3529 assiu*m*   3532 ruta*m*   3533 sa*r*cina q*ue* i*n*uen*it* arbore

trossa	ligat sarcinam
detrossa	solvit sarcinam
escossa	excussa
3538 rescossa	excussa

In -*osa* larg:

rosa	rosa
osa	ocrea de corio
3542 glosa	glosa
prosa	prosa

In -*osa* estreit fenissen tuit li femini que sunt dels ajectius 3546 que fenissen in -*os* estreit.	[. . .] finiunt omnia feminina adiectivorum nominum finientium in -*os*.

In -*assa*:

grassa	grassa
lassa	fatigata
3550 passa	transit
massa	nimis alicuius rei
amassa	congregat

In -*oira*:

3554 foira	fluxus
esfoira	ventris polluit fluxu
loira	lutra
zoira	vetus canis

3558 In -*iscla*:

giscla	pluit simul et ventat
ciscla	alta voce clamat
3561 iscla	[. . .]

Prov. A. *after* 3561, *and continuing on the same line, A places 2875–81, followed, after a gap of one line, by 3573, in red, which ends f. 28a.*

B. 3535 *om.*   3536 destrossa   3540 tosa   3544–6 *on alternate lines, leaving room for translation*   3445 son   *after* 3547 B *adds* lassa *after* 3550 B *adds* traspassa   3559–60 giscla *three times*

Lat. A. 3535 l. s. solu*it* (*or* solu*m*)   3536 sarcina*m only*   3544 *no trans. above* In osa estreit   3555 flux*us*   3556 liccier   3560 alta *only*   3561 voce clamat

LATIN TEXT 255

Et hec de ritimis dicta sufficiant, non quod plures adhuc nequeant 28b
inveniri, sed ad vitandum lectoris fastidium. Finem operi modo
volo imponere, sciens procul dubio librum meum emulorum voci-
bus lacerandum, quorum est proprium reprehendere que ignorant.
Sed si quis invidorum in mei presentia hoc opus redarguere pre- 3566
sumpserit, de scientia mea tantum confido quod ipsum convincam
coram omnibus manifeste; sciens quod nullus ante me tractavit
ita perfecte super his nec ad unguem ita si[n]gula declaravit. Ugo
Faiditus nominor qui librum composui, precibus Iacobi de Mora 3570
et domini Coraçhuchii de Sterlleto, ad dandam doctrinam vulgaris
provincialis et ad dissernendum verum a falso in dicto vulgare.

Explicit liber Donati Provincialis.

A. 3566 inuide*orum* (*so B*); *one letter* (t?) *erased after* presentia
3568 tractatu*m*   3569 nec] ue*ro*; sig*u*la   3569–70 Ugo F.] Cui*us* vgo
3571 corā çhuchij   3573 *rubric placed after 3561*

B. 3562 hoc; rittimis satis dicta susfitiant   3563 set   3565 lacta*n*dum
3566 inuid*e*orum   3568 hominib*us*   3569–73 Ugo *to end om.*

NOTES

NOTES

1–3. The translator modified the statement that Provençal contains all the eight parts of speech of Latin grammar by adding the phrase *pro maiori parte*, no doubt simply because Faidit did not finally treat the preposition and interjection. The order in which the parts of speech are enumerated (and, in the body of the grammar, expounded) is the same as that of the *Ars minor* of Donatus (iv. 355. 2–3); Priscian's *Institutiones grammaticae* follows a different order.

4–7. The definition of the noun is based on a partial recollection of Priscian's two definitions (ii. 18 and 22), cf. the *substantiam et qualitatem* of the first and the *communem vel propriam qualitatem* of the second. On Adam's naming of things as the origin of language see J. J. Bäbler, *Beiträge zu einer Geschichte der lateinischen Grammatik im Mittelalter*, Halle, 1885, p. 78. The five attributes of the noun (the vague *causas*, which recurs in 1471, reflects Faidit's difficulty in expressing in Provençal the Latin formula *Nomini accidunt quinque*) follow those of Priscian (ii. 22), for Donatus (iv. 355. 6–7) gave *qualitas* and *comparatio* in place of *species*.

8–11. The treatment of *species* does not accurately follow Priscian's classification into *species principalis* and *derivativa* (ii. 22). Firstly, Faidit substitutes *primitivus* for the first of these terms, probably by confusion with Priscian's use of *primitiva* in his parallel classification of the *species* of adverbs (xv. 5). Secondly, Faidit's use of the examples *bontaz* and *bos* indicates a fundamental misconception of the nature of *species*—all the more striking in that his later treatment of the same concept with reference to the adverb (1472–3) is entirely orthodox. For the noun, however, Faidit turns Priscian's classification upside down: by using a philosophical instead of a grammatical argument he manages to use as an example of the 'primitive' *species* a word which was, from the point of view of its form, clearly 'derivative'. The ultimate source of Faidit's remark here would seem to be Aristotle, *Topica*, vi. 4. Faidit was not the only Provençal grammarian to be aware of this dichotomy between grammatical and philosophical arguments: the author of the *Leys d'Amors* (ed. Gatien-Arnoult, vol. 2, p. 30) knew that Aristotle and *li antic natural phylozophe* had argued that *bel* derived from *beleza*, though the Toulouse grammarian, unlike Faidit, avoided incorporating this point into his exposition of grammar.

12–13. In admitting five genders, Faidit was reducing the number indicated by both Donatus (iv. 355. 14–18) and Priscian (v. 1–2). Both Latin grammarians give *epicoenon* (words where one gender covers both sexes, e.g. *hic passer, haec aquila*), and Priscian adds *dubium* (words where usage admitted either of two genders). Both of these might have been readily illustrated from Provençal—with far less difficulty, indeed, than the neuter and *omne* genders.

12–37. The definitions of the five genders which Faidit admits for Provençal are, from the Latin point of view, orthodox (cf. Priscian, v. 1–2). But the examples are unorthodox in various ways: only adjectives are used to illustrate masculine and feminine; the neuter is exemplified merely by translating the Latin neuters *gaudium* and *bonum* (despite Faidit's later admission of a genuine neuter adjective at 95–8); and the common and *omne* genders are illustrated by present participles, which in Faidit's classification of the parts of speech have no place here (adjectives like *grans* could have adequately represented the common gender). The author's embarrassment, stemming predominantly from the admission of a neuter gender in Provençal, is reflected, not only in the choice of examples, but in the curious observation at 20–3 (cf. 66–7), which effectively denies the existence of a vernacular neuter gender.

21. *An* for *ans*, a form absent from the OPr. dictionaries, is not uncommon, cf. G. Riquier, *Cansos*, ed. Mölk, iv. 34; vii. 21; viii. 43; xi. 20; *Leys d'Amors*, ed. Gatien-Arnoult, vol. 2, pp. 134, 154, 188, 206, 228, etc.

38–9. Number receives the brief treatment usual in Latin grammar (cf. Donatus, iv. 355. 18–19; Priscian's treatment is much fuller, v. 46–55).

39. The rendering of *una causa* by *uno verbo* is curious. *B*'s omission of *verbo* is possibly correct.

40–1. The treatment of *figura* is limited to the essential classes of simple and compound, as in Donatus (iv. 355. 20–1). Priscian's third class of *decomposita* (v. 56) is omitted, as are the subdivisions explaining the ways in which compounds are formed (Donatus, iv. 355. 22–5; Priscian, v. 58–9).

41 *apostiza*. *Apostitz* is not otherwise attested in the sense 'joined together, put together' (cf. *LR* iv. 611, where the word is taken as a feminine noun; *SW* i. 73; *PD*). One may suspect that the author meant *aposta* (cf. *LR*, ibid., s.v. *aponher* [sic]).

42–63. The cases are enumerated in the order usual in med. Latin grammar. The omission of the ablative from the subsequent treatment (made good by *L*, cf. var. to 50) is probably the result of chance, as the manner of the passage grew more discursive and Faidit moved towards treatment of the two-case system of the vernacular. There is no indication, however, that Faidit had any misgivings about the existence of six cases in Provençal. The awkward use of *lo* as the distinguishing mark of both nominative and accusative cases (43–4, 49–50) is immediately qualified by the statement of the real distinction between the two cases in masculine nouns (51–4). *A*'s *la* (49 Lat., var. *A*) was perhaps originally intended as an addition to the *lo* of the text, made with the intention of providing a reference to feminine nouns.

NOTES

53–4. *Singuli* for *singularis* is partly explicable as the result of the use of the abbreviation *l'*, cf. *B*'s *singl'is* = *singularis* in 86, 104, 127.

55–63. The rule given for the vocative singular does not correspond exactly with OPr. practice, in which the presence or absence of *-s* in the voc. sg. seems not to have been subject to any rule. One may suspect that Faidit in fact admitted *-s* as correct in words which occurred particularly frequently in the vocative: in this hypothesis the inclusion of *canços* would be due to literary usage and the reference to words in *-ors* to the vocative *Amors*, frequent in lyric poetry. This would suggest that in this passage Faidit was laying down a rule where none existed. But voc. sg. forms occur too rarely at the rhyme for us to be certain about troubadour practice on this point.

65. *Toiz* for *totz*, though unattested by the OPr. dictionaries and grammars, is retained in the text because it recurs in 69 (also in 300, var. *D*). But the form may well be merely a scribal slip.

67. Both *A* and *B* give Latin *mascul'*, perhaps intending *masculinis* (cf. note to 53–4), perhaps from common error.

72. *Peire* owes its presence here to the well-known tendency of anthroponyms to show a preference for a single declensional form; cf. Brunel, *Chartes*, i, p. xiv, for the nominative *Peire*.

73 *radeire—qui radit barbas*. Sole example of this sense in *SW* vii. 57.

74 *pencheire, fencheire*. These are the only examples of the forms with *-ch-*, for usual *penheire, fenheire*, in *SW* vi. 212 and iii. 438–9. They are explicable via the influence of the p. part. forms *pench, fench*; for *tencheire* beside *tenheire* see *LR* v. 343 (and cf. *SW* viii. 167).

76 *teneire—tenax*. Sole example in *SW* viii. 139 for the sense 'tenacious'.

79 *escremire—cautus cum armis*. Stengel, who printed *cum armis percussor* as the translation of *ferire* (80), here gave *cautus* only; this passed into *SW* iii. 193 (where it is the sole example), whence *PD*'s 'défiant, circonspect'. As the origin of the word suggests, the translator no doubt intended the sense 'prudent fighter'.

80 *gronire*. Sole example in *SW* iv. 201.

81. The presence here of *albires, conssires*, and *desires* is, from a modern point of view, inconsequential. Faidit knew also the forms in *-irs*, cf. 2498, 2500–1.

92. The inclusion of the feminine *sor* is illogical, the more so as Faidit has already noted (64–6) that the n. sg. of f. nouns lacks *-s*.

105–32. The three declensions admitted by Faidit clearly show again his reliance on the framework of Latin grammar.

112-15. Of the four nouns in -*a* given here as masculine, *propheta* and *papa* are attested in both genders, cf. *SW* vi. 582 and 51-2, where one example each of the n. pl. *li propheta, li papa* is given. (The phrase *totz los autres cas*, 114-15, means 'the other *plural* cases', i.e. the obl. pl., as in 124-5.) But *gaita* and *esquiragaita* are attested only in the feminine (*LR* iii. 416; *SW* iv. 8-9 and iii. 282-3, respectively). The author seems to have been in some doubt here, since, despite the alleged gender of these words, he seems deliberately to have avoided mentioning n. pl. forms *li gaita, *li esquiragaita. Probably he was in error here in grouping with two words of genuinely fluctuating gender two others which, though masculine in sense, were grammatically feminine. The hypothesis that *gaita* and *esquiragaita* were interpolated receives insufficient support from the absence of their Latin equivalents in *B* (whose reading here may well represent an intelligent correction).

It is worth noting that the form *esquiragaita*, with -*a*-, accepted by *SW*, loc. cit., and by *PD* but not given in *FEW* xvii. 103-4 *SKARWAHTA (where no form with -*a*- or -*e*- occurs), is attested solely by *A*. If it is not merely a scribal slip, it could be held to continue the etymon *SKARAWAHTA (cf. OItal. *scaraguaita* and *FEW*, loc. cit.). The form given by *A* could, of course, be explained as an Italianism.

115-17. The remark about words in -*ans* and -*ens*, though given here by *ABDL*, is clearly misplaced. It would seem to have been a marginal observation intended to qualify and amplify 125-8. The same point is made in 30-2 and recurs in 1740-5 and in 2162, var. *L*.

119. The translator's *vulgari* calls attention to the fact that, though *cortesia* is of the first declension in OPr., its translation *curialitas* is not of the first declension in Latin.

133-203. On indeclinable nouns and adjectives in OPr. see A. Bergh, *La Déclinaison des mots à radical en s en provençal et en catalan*, Göteborg, 1937.

142 *cens*. *PD* admits only *ces*, cf. *LR* ii. 387 (*ces, ses*), and this is the only form given in the dictionary of rhymes (2328). But cf. Brunel, *Chartes*, i and ii, for *sens* and *cens*.

144 *borses*. For the form cf. *borçes* 2332; Appel, *Lautlehre*, pp. 56, 59; *LR* ii. 237; Ronjat, ii, p. 203. Cf. also note to 2246.

145 *bles—qui non potest sonare nisi c*. For the form of the definition cf. 837.

147 *gles*. *SW* iv. 137 cites only two examples from the *Donatz*; *FEW* iv. 155 GLĪS gives the OPr. form as if it were OFr.

147-8. *Comes, escomes*, and *pres* ought strictly not to have been classed among the nouns.

160. The inclusion of *mescaps* 'misfortune, mishap' among invariable nouns is odd: *SW* v. 245 and *LR* ii. 276 show the word declining normally. This must be an authorial error, if we can accept the text as reliable. The

latter is not entirely free from suspicion, however. *B* alone gives the translation *prelium paucorum contra multos* (i.e. 'military disaster', a specialized use of the normal sense of *mescap* and not, as doubtfully given in *SW*, loc. cit., a separate word). The interlinear text in *A* gives *mescaps*, not the expected Latin equivalent, while the Provençal, in *A* and in *L*, shows *mes* and *caps* as two separate words. The original perhaps had *mes* ('messager, mets' *PD*) and a second word of which *caps* is a misreading, perhaps *capras* 'with shaven head' (*SW* i. 206)—*ras* occurs earlier, at 139; a scribe or reader could then have 'corrected' by the interlinear addition of *mescaps*, which in turn suggested the Latin translation in *B*. This is too uncertain to be accepted into the printed text; but it does cast some doubt on the authenticity both of indeclinable *mescaps* and of *B*'s Latin rendering of it.

160. *Acs—civitas*, despite Stengel (p. 146, *Namenregister*), is not the same as *Aics* (1554): the latter is Aix, the former Dax.

164 *fars—farsura*. Guessard's first edition, though not his second, printed *farcitus*, a reading which remained in Stengel, whence it passed to *SW* iii. 416, to *PD* ('farci'), and to *FEW* iii. 415 FARCIRE. No MS. has this reading and *fars*, adj., seems to be a ghost-word in OPr. (though not in OFr., cf. Godefroy, iii. 725; *TL* iii. 1640). The translation *farsura* reappears in 1770, these two passages being the sole examples in *SW*, loc. cit.

167 *jatz—lectus*. The translation is acceptable as an approximation, though the agreement of *BC* here (cf. *C* 152) and *A* in 1876 suggests that the original had the more accurate *lectus fere*.

169 *laus—pro laude vel pro stagno*. Both *lau* and *laus* 'praise' are attested as obl. sg. forms, cf. *SW* iv. 333-5. For *laus* 'lake' as an obl. sg. cf. *SW* iv. 295, s.v. *lac*, second example; Ronjat, iii, p. 4.

170 *ais—tabula*. The sole example in *SW* i. 39 is from *Donatz* 1594.

170 *cais*. Though *LR* ii. 287 and *PD* give the senses 'joue' and 'mâchoire', only the translations in the *Donatz* attest them without possible ambiguity (here *gena*, cf. 1607 *mandibula*).

171 *lais*. Both *lais* and *lai* are attested as obl. sg. forms, cf. *SW* iv. 307-8.

172 *tais*. For *tais* 'badger' as an obl. sg. form cf. *LR* v. 310; *PD*'s '*taisọn*, cas suj. *tais*' is therefore misleading.

183 *brais*. *PD* gives only *brai*. The examples in *LR* ii. 248 and *SW* i. 161 do not show the obl. sg. or n. pl. *Girart* 9350 has *brait*, obl. sg., at the rhyme, but this is not quite the same word (*brai* on *braire* < *BRAGĔRE, *brait* on *braidar* < *BRAGĬTĀRE, cf. *FEW* i. 490-2 *BRAG-, where *brai* is misplaced). But Faidit was not mistaken in listing *brais* as indeclinable: Gaucelm Faidit, ed. Mouzat, xxv. 72, attests the obl. sg. *brais* at the rhyme.

173. *Clavais* (cited again in 1621) is the Italian town of Chivasso. Our grammarian counted the word as indeclinable, as did Gaucelm Faidit (ed.

Mouzat, xxii. 47); P. Vidal, on the other hand, used the obl. *Clavai* at the rhyme (ed. Avalle, xxxv. 47).

173. The adverb *melhz* (like *plus*, 196) no doubt owed its inclusion among indeclinable nouns to the existence of *lo melhz, lo plus*.

180 *aders*. *A*'s *cōreaʒ* and *B*'s *coream* are explicable only as misinterpretations of Provençal *conreaz* by scribes who, expecting a Latin word, took -*z* as the abbreviation for -*m*. The same error occurs in 182, where *assotam* (*A*) and *assectā* (*B*) are misreadings of Provençal *assetaz* (correctly given by *C* 180). The translator was presumably at a loss for a Latin equivalent, as perhaps for 179 *aers*, left untranslated. For the sense of *aders* and the distinction between it and *aers* cf. note to 620.

182 *Sanc Danis*. Correction of *A*'s *damis* to *Danis* (with *D* and 2527) is perhaps slightly preferable to *Daunis* (with *L* and Bartsch, *ZRP* ii, 1878, p. 135).

186 *Aiols*, indeclinable. For *Aiolz*, obl., cf. G. de Cabrera, *Cabra joglar*, l. 61 (ed. Riquer, *Les Chansons de geste françaises*, p. 344). Cf. Brunel, *Chartes*, i, p. xiii, for *Raols*, obl.

187 *poutz*. *SW* vi. 437 quotes only the *Donatz* (here and 2698); *FEW* ix. 549 PŬLS cites this as *pouç* [*sic*] without a further example. *PD* gives the word as '*s. m. pl.*': the translation *pultes* suggests the word may have been used only in the plural, but the gender is uncertain (cf., for OFr., Godefroy, vi. 358, s.v. *pous*; and *FEW*, loc. cit.).

187 *soutz*. *SW* vii. 793 quotes only the *Donatz* (here, 2697 and 2929); *FEW* xvii. 269 *SULTJA cites a 14th-century example of *sols*.

188–93 (cf. Introduction, p. 27). The variants suggest that *in ors larg* was a marginal addition whose position in the text was unclear, perhaps because an insertion-mark was placed before the wrong *cors*. This seems preferable to supposing (with Stengel, p. xxvii, n. to 8, 27) that *in ors larg* simply belongs to the words which *precede* it, an arrangement found nowhere else in the *Donatz*. The variants further suggest that the words in -*is* originally preceded those in -*ǫrs* (*A* alone has the opposite arrangement) and that *L* has somewhat rationalized the passage by the addition of *in ors estreg*.

188. Before *gergons* 'thieves' slang', *A* alone has *greg̊s*, with the translation *gregnonū*. Guessard dropped the word without comment in both editions, Stengel (8, 23) printed 'gregors' [*sic*] and listed the word as a proper name, without comment. However, *gregnos* is the only possible transcription (*g̊* = *gno* occurs a number of times elsewhere in *A*), perhaps confirmed by the Latin rendering *gregnonum*. If there were no translation, one would most readily suppose the word to be an erroneous anticipation of *gergons*, of the kind which an alert scribe would have erased or expunctuated. But if this were the case, how did such a form acquire a Latin (or pseudo-Latin) equivalent? Rather than assume that a copyist invented

a Latin word to render a non-existent Provençal word (*gregnos* and *gregnonum* are equally unattested), I have preferred to suppose that the Provençal at least is a scribal error for a real word. The only possibility here is *gergons* 'jacinth, a precious stone'; the fact that this word was followed by its homonym would sufficiently explain its omission from the other MSS. The dictionaries do not give *gergons* 'jacinth': *SW* iv. 115–16 knows only *gergonsa, jar-*, sb. f., to which *PD* adds *gergonci*, sb. m.; similarly *FEW* iv. 520–1 HYACINTHUS. However, apart from P. Cardenal, ed. Lavaud, lxxi. 71, where *gergonse* should surely be emended to *e gergons* (the word is n. pl.), there is one certain example of *jergons*, obl. sg., in the first of the OPr. lapidaries (ed. Contini, *Vox*, iii, p. 264, § xiv; cf. *iargonci*, ibid., p. 263, § iii). This example shows that the word was indeed indeclinable. Since *gregnonum* cannot be emended to any med. Latin word for 'jacinth', I have considered this among the cases where the translator was working on an already corrupt Provençal text (cf. Introduction, p. 23).

188 *gergons—vulgare trutanorum*. *LR* iii. 468 has a single 14th-century example of *girgo*, obl. sg. *SW* iv. 115 adds the two examples from the *Donatz* (here and 2754), apparently without noticing that the word is indeclinable here and that 2754 shows the *n* not to be *n caduc*, for *PD* merely lists *gergọn, gir-*, but not *gergons*. That the word was indeclinable in OPr. is suggested by OSpan. *girgonz*, apparently a loan-word, on which see *DCELC* ii. 1049–51, s.v. *jerga* 2. *FEW* iv. 59 GARG-, following *PD*, registers only *gergon* for OPr., noting it incorrectly as a *hapax*. While it is unnecessary to subscribe to Spitzer's etymon *GARGONICE (*MLN* lxxi, 1956, 385–6; cf. *DCELC* iv. 1030), it seems likely that *gergons* was formed under the influence of *romans*. It is worth noting that Faidit's two examples of this word contradict von Wartburg's statement (*FEW* iv. 62) that all Romance forms in *ger-* are attested much later than the French forms and depend on MidFr. *jergon*. The *Donatz* also attests the sense 'thieves' slang' earlier than the French examples known to von Wartburg (*FEW* iv. 59: 'seit 1426'; similarly Bloch–Wartburg, s.v. *jargon*), though in fact *TL* (iv. 1586) has clear examples of this sense. The history of the whole word-family needs further clarification; cf. the doubts expressed by Meyer-Lübke (*REW* 3685) about the etymon GARG.

191–2 *sors, resors*. Stengel, following Guessard's editions, printed *desurgo, deresurgo*; his index classifies *sors* as 1st sg. pr. ind. and *resors* as 3rd sg. pr. ind., with the translation noted as *deresurgere*! Clearly both are intended as past participles; cf. 147–8.

193 *lis—levis*. The translation (i.e. *lēvis* 'smooth') is perfectly acceptable, cf. 2342, where it recurs as a rendering of *les*; correction to *lenis* is unnecessary.

193 *alis—azimus*. Levy's only examples (*SW* i. 51) are from the *Donatz* (here and 2521); *PD* omits the word. Cf. *FEW* i. 72 ALLISUS and, for OCat., *Dicc. Aguiló*, s.v. *alís*, 1.

204–13. Faidit's definition is appreciably closer to Priscian's first definition (ii. 18, especially *certas significare personas*) than to his second (xii. 1) or to that of Donatus (iv. 357. 2–3). Priscian's conception of the pronoun, which excluded from this class indefinites like *quis* and *qualis*, prevailed amongst Latin grammarians in the 13th century, cf. Thurot, *Notices et Extraits de la Bibliothèque Impériale*, xxii, part 2, Paris, 1868, p. 171. The examples of Provençal pronouns follow as closely as possible the list of fifteen given by Priscian, who listed eight *primitiva* (*ego, tu, sui, ille, iste, ipse, hic, is*) and seven *derivativa* (*meus, tuus, suus, noster, vester, nostras, vestras*) (xii. 1); Faidit, however, omits the reflexive (accidentally?) and the translation does not use *hic* or *is* to render any of the Provençal forms. Following Priscian's conception of the pronoun, he makes no mention here of relative, interrogative, or indefinite forms; it is worth noting that earlier he did mention *qui* as a pronoun (101).

218. In referring to *eu, tu*, and *aicel* as *pronom demostratiu*, Faidit is still following Priscian (xii. 1 and 3), for whom *ego, tu, hic*, and *iste* were *pronomina demonstrativa*. And it is clearly true that, in OPr. as in Latin, a personal pronoun used emphatically as subject of a verb did have a certain demonstrative force.

220–1. Faidit's definition of the verb is closest to Priscian's first definition (ii. 18, especially *cum modis et formis et temporibus*); Priscian's second definition (viii. 1) and that of Donatus (iv. 359. 4–5) formulate much the same thing in different words, and it is possible that Donatus's *agere aliquid aut pati* suggested the Provençal formulation *alcuna causa far o suffrir*.

224–44. Faidit gives no formal treatment of the attributes of the verb. He mentions only those features which have practical importance: mood, tense, conjugation. In giving five moods Faidit is closer to Priscian (viii. 63), for Donatus (iv. 359. 7–9) counted the impersonal as a sixth mood. Again, Donatus does not define the moods; Priscian does, and the definitions of the *Donatz* correspond, though in a much simplified form, to those of the *Institutiones* (viii. 63–9). In calling the fourth mood *conjunctius*, however, Faidit followed Donatus and most pedagogic grammars of the Middle Ages; Priscian used *subiunctivus* and was followed in this by the *Grecismus* (Book xxvi. 32) and by MSS. *B* and *D* of the *Donatz* (cf. 225, var.). Faidit's five tenses are the standard ones. The plan of four conjugations may reflect the four of Priscian (viii. 93) rather than the three mentioned by Donatus (iv. 359. 12–33). But here Faidit was already explicitly abandoning the pattern of Latin grammar (cf. 238).

241–2. The definition of a Provençal third conjugation consisting of verbs in *-ire* and *-endre* (*L* adds *-iure*) is not altogether satisfactory. Faidit presumably meant verbs in *-re*; but neither here nor in two later passages (365–6, 656–63), parallel but not identical, did he admit this simple formulation.

NOTES

243–4. Similarly, the definition of fourth-conjugation verbs should no doubt exclude those where *-ir* alternated freely with *-ire*, as is done in two later passages (326–7, 562–4).

245–64. Faidit knew 1st sg. pr. ind. forms in ø and *-i* but not in *-e* (cf. his further examples in 505, 508, 521, 527). He admitted them for all verbs (260). And he expressed a preference for the shorter form (264). On the first point, it is worth noting that the *i*-forms were current in the whole of the west and south-west of the Midi, as far as Albi and Toulouse, and in S. Provence; Faidit no doubt came from that area, since he made no mention of the *e*-forms, current in the whole central part of the Midi (cf. B. Müller, *Die Herkunft der Endung -i in der 1. Pers. Sing. Präs. Ind. des provenzalischen Vollverbs*, Erlangen, [1956], esp. p. 68). Faidit's third observation indicates a preference for the commonest literary form over a widely current alternative (cf. Müller, op. cit., p. 63). Faidit's second remark is not to be taken too literally: the translator observed that *ai* and *sai* constituted exceptions (261–261a); the grammarian was no doubt aware that verbs whose stem required a supporting vowel were also outside his rule; and it seems likely that he did not accept forms in *-i* for inchoative verbs, since he later mentions only *fenisc* and *fenis* (511).

257. Here and throughout the *Donatz* the n. pl. form of the demonstrative used as a 3rd person pronoun is *celh* (for which *cel*, 444, 693, 718, is no doubt to be regarded as a graphy), never *cil* or *cilh*. The 12th-century charters show forms of this type in an area including Rouergue, Quercy, Albi, and Toulouse, cf. Brunel, *Chartes*, i, pp. xxviii (*eil, eill*) and xxxv (*aqueil, aqueill*), ii, pp. xxi (*eil, eill*) and xxv (*aizel, ceil*). Certainly forms in *-il* and *-ilh* were generally more common in literary usage; cf. W. Bohnhardt, *Das Personal-pronomen im Altprovenzalischen*, Marburg, 1888, p. 33. H. Kjellman, *Étude sur les termes démonstratifs en provençal*, Göteborg, 1928, p. 59, attributes n. pl. forms of the type *cel(h)* to the influence of the obl. pl. *cels*; he gives no information on the localization of this morphological feature.

293. The 3rd pl. fut. ending *-au*, which Faidit consistently gives as an alternative to *-an* (415, 450, 500, 543, 687, 769), occurred in Rouergue, Quercy, and the Albigeois, and sporadically in Gévaudan and the Toulouse area (cf. Brunel, *Chartes*, i, p. xlii). It is reasonable to assume that Faidit consistently stressed this form because he came from the area where it was current. It did not form part of the language of the troubadour lyric (cf. C. F. Wolff, *Futur und Conditional II im Altprovenzalischen*, Marburg, 1885, pp. 12–16).

294–5. By *-a estreit* Faidit must have meant 'unstressed final *a*'. This use of *estreit* does not occur elsewhere in the *Donatz*.

300–4. Faidit mentions only a 3rd sg. imperative in *-e* (as also in 692), just as he gives only the endings *-e*, *-es*, *-e* for the 1st–3rd sg. pr. subj. of first-conjugation verbs, not ø, *-s*, ø (390–2).

305–11. The variants clearly indicate that the Provençal original omitted the 1st pl. forms, which were supplied in the interlinear matter. *C* alone (345–60) has all five persons of the imperative in the normal order.

312. By 'optative', here and in 457, Faidit meant 'present optative' (as he calls it, more precisely, in 695), distinguished from a pluperfect tense (360, 464, 699) and a future (388, 471, 713).

317–19. For the plural persons of the conditional (< Latin plpf. ind.), the *Donatz* has *amaram, amaratz, amaren,* not the commoner forms in *amęr-*; the MSS. are unanimous for the 1st and 2nd pl. (except *C* 372, *vos ameras*), but *L* gives *-eren* (= *amęren*) for the 3rd pl. and *C* 373 has *ameran*. Forms of the type *amára* for *amęra* certainly existed (Anglade, pp. 275–6; Schultz-Gora, p. 91; Ronjat, iii, p. 197, § 582). Faidit's combination of these in the plural with *amęra*-forms for the singular is perhaps connected with his use in the impf. subj. of *amęs*-forms in the singular and *amassem*, etc., in the plural (369–74).

319, 325, 333, 342. For the 3rd pl. fut. impf., only forms of the type *amarien*, not *amarion*, are given here. That Faidit knew the forms in *-on* is shown by 463 (-*r[i]on* = *serion*) and 698 (-*rien* vel *-rion*). Their omission from the present passage is no doubt fortuitous.

320–59. It is, of course, an inconsequence that the optative forms of the 2nd, 3rd, and 4th conjugations should be mentioned here. All MSS. (including *C* 374–81, 390–409) place this development here, where it is prepared by the remark in 313 and confirmed by the brief treatment of the same tense in 695–8.

360–87. The exposition is somewhat confused. After the passage on the present optative, i.e. the conditional (312–59), which deals with verbs of all types and not merely with the 1st conjugation, the author seems to have set out to do something similar for the plpf. optative, i.e. the plpf. subj. As the text stands, this departure from the normal order of exposition is strikingly unsuccessful. The author presumably intended an exposition like this:

(α = 360–1) In the plpf. optative all verbs end in *-ęs* (i.e. the tense consists of *aguęs* + p. part.).

(β = 362–4) Ex. 1: *bon fora qu'eu agues amat*.

(γ) And similarly, with change of *-at* to *-ut*, ex. 2: *bon fora qu'eu agues tendut*.

(δ = 365–7) This last point applies only to verbs in *-endre* and *-iure* (in fact it applies to all verbs with p. part. in *-ut*).

(ϵ = 367–8) And this last class of verbs is like the 1st conjugation in the pret. (i.e. *tendei* is like *amei*) and in the impf. subj. (i.e. *tendes* is like *ames*; this last point is made again at 719–23).

(ζ = 369–80) Ex. 3, illustrating the second point under (ϵ): paradigms of *cum eu cantes* and *cum eu tendes*.

(η = 381–7) Ex. 4, paradigm of *cum eu ames*, no doubt an afterthought dictated by the fact that *amar*, not *cantar*, was the author's usual 1st-conjugation model.

A has only part of (β) and lacks (γ) altogether; *BL* have both (as has *C* 417–30), *D* lacks both entirely; there is no Latin equivalent for 362–4, since *B*, which normally has only the Latin, here gives the Provençal paradigms, while *A* began to repeat *bon fora qu'eu* as the equivalent of a translation and then left the rest blank. These facts suggest that the two paradigms (*bon fora qu'eu agues amat | tendut*) were interlinear in O^2 (though they seem essential to the sense). Certain other phrases are suspect: *si sun de la prima conjugaço* (361), omitted by *B* and misplaced in *L* (cf. *C* 413–14), is inessential, indeed misleading; *solamen* (365) is also misleading and is omitted in the Latin—did the translator 'correct' this, just as he (or an attentive reader?) avoided the potential ambiguity of *preterit perfeit* (367) by the gloss *videlicet indicativi modi*? Clearly one cannot introduce these speculations into the text, which follows *A* with all its faults here; but the passage is comprehensible only if one makes allowance for the textual corruption it may well have suffered. The author, however, is not guiltless here: it is difficult, for example, to free him from blame for *prendre* (366—*D* has *pendre*, as has *C* 415), which is an inept example in the context.

369–74, 382–7. The two paradigms for the impf. subj. of the 1st conjugation differ somewhat. In the 2nd sg., both *cantesses* (370) and *ames* (383; *amesses DL*) are possible. Grammars give only the longer form (Anglade, p. 276; Schultz-Gora, p. 84; Grandgent, p. 146) but the charters most frequently use the shorter (Brunel, *Chartes*, i, p. xlvi). Both paradigms give 1st and 2nd pl. forms in *-assem*, *-assetz*, not *-essem*, *-essetz*; the former are not uncommon (cf. Schultz-Gora, p. 89; Appel, *Chrestomathie*, p. xxiv; K. F. T. Meyer, *Die provenzalische Gestaltung der mit dem Perfectstamm gebildeten Tempora des Lateinischen*, Marburg, 1884, p. 31). For the 3rd pl., the paradigms again diverge, showing *cantassen* (374) but *amessen* (387)—*D* alone avoids the inconsistency by giving *amassen*. Again, the rarer forms in *-assen* do occur (cf. Brunel, *Chartes*, i. 13. 53 [*avogassun*] and 97. 4 [*tocasan*], from Gévaudan and Comminges respectively; Appel, *Chrestomathie*, p. xxiv). Emendation for the sake of consistency is unnecessary here, therefore. (See also note to 317–19.)

390–2 *ame, ames, ame*. For these longer forms of the pr. subj., cf. Anglade, p. 276; Schultz-Gora, pp. 88–9; Grandgent, p. 130; Brunel, *Chartes*, i, p. xliii. It is odd that Faidit omitted to mention here the forms *am, ams, am*; both types are given for the 2nd sg. in 3105–16. Apart from this latter passage, the rhyme-lists do not mention the longer forms; but this is explicable by the absence of the appropriate rhyme-endings there. The rarity of the longer forms in the rhymes of the troubadours may be explained in a similar way.

396–9. This point, repeated in 538–40, clearly reveals the degree to which Faidit classified Provençal forms by a process of mental translation into Latin. The absence here of any paradigm for the impf. subj. is explained by the inclusion of that tense in the digression a little earlier (367–87, esp. 375–80).

398 *a la vengada*. The form with *-n-* seems otherwise unattested (*SW* viii. 601–2, s.v. *vegada*) but is conceivable (influence of *a l'aventura*?).

409. The classification of what we call a future perfect indicative as a future subjunctive, here and in 494 and 763, follows the normal practice of Latin grammar in the Middle Ages, from Donatus (iv. 361. 2–3) and Priscian (viii. 55, 57) onwards.

413–16 (Latin). These lines, containing a general comment on the passive mood, were clearly intended to introduce l. 419 of the Provençal text. They are somewhat misplaced in all the three MSS. (*ABL*) which contain them. This is comprehensible only if one supposes that the Latin accompanied ll. 413–18 of the Provençal text and was partly interlinear and partly marginal. The observation made here is apt. The reader—in the first instance the Italian reader—is advised to consider the forms of his own vernacular, rather than those of Latin, as a guide to the passive forms in Provençal. And it is true that, compared with the forms of any Romance vernacular, Latin forms like *amor* and *amatus sum* were, respectively, useless and misleading as a means of understanding Provençal *sui amatz*.

422. *A* gives both 2nd sg. forms, *est* and *es*. *CDL* (*C* 495) offer only *es*, which was not uncommon (cf. Brunel, *Chartes*, i. 102. 5; Appel, *Chrestomathie*, 6. 54; 106. 11).

424. For the 1st pl. *D* offers *em*, *CL* (*C* 499) *sem*; *A*'s *no sem* is open to either interpretation. Both forms were possible; although Anglade, p. 314, regards *sem* as very rare, it is rather commoner than *em* in the charters.

458–63. *Vel fora* and the parallel forms for the other persons were clearly interlinear additions to *seria, serias*, etc. *AB* have them complete, *DL* lack them entirely, except that *L* gives *foratz* for the 2nd pl.; *C* (534–6) has them as alternatives for the three singular persons. There is nothing surprising in Faidit's omission here: though in the earlier passage on the optative (312–59) he remembered to give paradigms of both Provençal conditional tenses, later in the text (695–8) he mentioned only the forms in *-ria*, etc. The omission was repaired in the second of the three passages but not in the third. It is natural that these interlinear forms are irregularly disposed in both *A* and *B* and that both MSS. have a number of scribal errors. The phrase *duplicatur id est* is placed in *A* in such a way as to apply to the 1st pl.; this makes sense, in that this person was the first for which two forms were given by the Provençal text (as distinct from the interlinear additions), and I have accepted *A*'s reading. *B* places the phrase similarly but with the addition of the word *ter*; this can be taken as the adverb *ter* ('there are *three* forms [in the 1st pl., as against two each for the sg. persons]') or as *tercia* ('the 3rd person [pl.] has two forms [i.e. *foren* and *foro*, as distinct from the single form in *for-* in the other five persons]'). This second explanation is not ruled out, though the placing of the words in both MSS. goes against it, as does the fact that *C* (539) places a similar observation after the 1st pl., not after the 3rd.

461–2 *-ram, -ratz*. These present something of an enigma. The obvious interpretation of them is that they stand for *seram* and *seratz*; L opted for the former in 461 but gives *foratz* in 462, while *D* gives *eram* and *erat*. First and 2nd pl. conditionals of this kind are not inconceivable: one could readily suppose, for example, that *serám* for *seriám* was due to the influence of *forám*. But forms of this kind are not attested in the standard grammars, nor does C. F. Wolff (*Futur und Conditional II im Altprovenzalischen*, Marburg, 1885, pp. 21–3) know of them. Admittedly Brunel (*Chartes*, i, p. xlvii) lists a number of 1st and 2nd pl. cond. forms of the type *cantaram, cantaratz*; but in vol. ii, pp. xxix–xxx, all these are listed as futures, and there is no doubt that Brunel's second thoughts were best here (for the references see his glossaries to the two volumes). In these circumstances it seems better to suppose that *-ram, -ratz* were intended for *foram, foratz*; that they were misunderstood by *D* and, partly at least, by *L*; and that, when *vel fora* and the other parallel forms were added, *vel foram* and *vel foraz* were added also, superfluously, for the 1st and 2nd pl.

464. The marginal note, with its interpretation of the Provençal as *mo volgues Deus*, would seem to be the work of an Italian; cf. Rohlfs, *Historische Grammatik der italienischen Sprache*, iii, pp. 78–9 and 157. This interpretation of *mo* was first made by d'Ovidio (*GSLI* ii, p. 19 n. 1).

501. It was, of course, untrue that the passive infinitive did not occur in the vernacular. Was the translator's *nisi amari* intended as a qualifying reference to *esser amatz*?

502. *A*'s rubric may well have originated with the rubricator himself. *Declinatio* was used of verbs as well as nouns in Latin grammar (cf. *TLL* v. 1. 190. 11–40), though not in quite the same sense as here.

505, 511. *Duplicantur* can be taken as a plural *ad sensum* ('verbs of this kind are . . .'); *B*'s singular forms may be 'corrected'.

506 *escrives* (cf. 509 *dizes*, 512 *fenisses*, 522 *tenes*, 528 *fenhes*). The longer 2nd sg. pr. ind. forms are consistently mentioned here as alternatives, even to the exclusion of the shorter form *fenis*. However, in 525 *sabes* (attested at the rhyme in P. Cardenal, ed. Lavaud, lv. 109) is not listed, but only *saps*. In general, these longer forms are hardly to be found in the lyric poetry of the troubadours. Cf. A. Harnisch, *Die altprovenzalische Praesens- und Imperfect-bildung*, Marburg, 1886, pp. 13–15.

507 *escri*. This rare 3rd sg. pr. ind. form, attested in *Girart* 3731, was no doubt dependent on the infinitive forms *escrire* and *escrir*, which Faidit mentions to the exclusion of the commoner *escriure* (242, 564, 1326).

528 *fehz.* This form has been allowed to stand in the text on the strength of *joher* (669). But correction of both forms is tempting.

530. *Tenh* can only be a form of *tenher* < TĬNGĔRE in this context: *tenh* < TĔNEO has already occurred (521), and *tener* was not conjugated on the model of *fenher*. The error must be attributed to the translator.

532. The linguistic oddity of this line (*imperfec*, and the repeated use of *futur* without the article) probably indicates that it was originally in Latin and was turned into Provençal in *A* word by word (cf. p. 31). It is likely that *imperfec* reflects the abbreviation *ip̄fc̄*., which is used elsewhere in the interlinear text of *A*.

535. The n. pl. m. form *tu* has been allowed to stand, here and in 602, though it seems unattested elsewhere (*Girart* 744, 8500, 8711 attests *tui*). Was *tu* the result of a misinterpretation of *tuh*?

552–9. The mention of the 1st sg. pret. forms *dissi, escrissi, tengui, fezi, feissi*, to the exclusion of the strong forms *dis, escris, tinc, fis, feis*, is striking—the more so as Faidit later allows *dis* and *escris*, together with four other forms in -*is*, as admissible in the 1st sg. as well as the 3rd (607–11). The forms in -*i*, whose object was evidently a better characterization of the 1st sg. by contrast with the 3rd, seem not to have been regional (cf. Anglade, pp. 307, 310; Brunel, *Chartes*, i, p. xlv) and are rarely to be found in the troubadours (cf. K. F. T. Meyer, *Die provenzalische Gestaltung der mit dem Perfectstamm gebildeten Tempora des Lateinischen*, Marburg, 1884, *passim*—see pp. 8, 9–10 and 20 for *fezi, dissi, vengui*).

561 *teng* < TENUIT. Faidit later notes *tec* also (580).

571. The 3rd pl. pret. form *dissen* ~ *disson* is given to the exclusion of the usual *diron* and *disseron*. Forms without -*r*- in reflexes of Latin -SERUNT and -UERUNT are attested in charters of the region of Toulouse, Moissac, and western Rouergue (cf. Brunel, *Chartes*, i, p. xlv; ii, p. xv).

576 *decaçez, caçez, escaçez. L*'s *decasetz* confirms these unusual 3rd sg. pret. forms, for which the much commoner forms in -*ec* have been substituted in *D* (for all three verbs) and in *L* (for the last two only). Weak 3rd sg. pret. forms in -*ez* and -*es* (also in -*est* and -*ezt*), for usual -*et* and -*ec*, are sporadically attested: cf. *Girart* 159 (*dones*), 6651 (*manes*, at the rhyme), 8732 (*trencez*), and, more dubiously, 148 (*montez*) and 9555 (*amanest*); an early 13th-century Limousin version of a French poem to the Virgin (ed. P. Meyer in *Rom.* xx, 1891, pp. 455–62), 9 and 47 (*cardez* = *gardet*), 28 (*esauchez*), and 57 (*arbergezt*); Brunel, *Chartes*, i. 48 (*acaptez*) and 348. 5 (*des*), respectively from Rouergue and from Bouzin (*c.* 70 km. south-west of Toulouse); *Vie de Ste Enimie*, ed. Brunel, 1520 (*detz*, cf. p. viii n. 6; Brunel's text corrects to *det*). The *Regles de trobar* of Jofre de Foixà seems to be acquainted with *ametz* as an alternative to *amet*: 'E axi matex ha lo temps passatz tres persones, axi com *amey, amest, amet*; es aquell verb qui en aquest loch fan -*etz* [en MS.], poden axi matex fenir en -*et*' (ed. Li Gotti, 680–3, following MS. β^1 = Bar-

celona, Bibl. central, 239), cf. the reading of the other MS. (*C* = Barcelona, Arxiu de la Corona d'Aragó, Ripoll 129): 'aysi matex ha lo temps passat .iii. persones, aysi con *amey, amest, ametz* o *amet*; car aquel verbs qui en aquel loch fenex en *-etz* poden atressi fenir en *-et*' (ed. J. Rubió y Balaguer, in *Revista de bibliografia catalana*, v, 1911, p. 319). Brunel's explanation of these forms via analogy with *fez* ∼ *fes* < FĒCIT (*Chartes*, i, p. xlv) is convincing. Further contamination with *-et* would explain *-est* and *-ezt*. It is difficult to say whether these forms were localized, nor can one guess why it was only for *cazer* and its compounds that Faidit mentioned them. Was there an area in which *-ez* succeeded in supplanting *-ec* (Faidit has no reference to 3rd sg. preterites in *-ęc*)?

582 *ereup—convaluit*. The sense 'to regain health (after illness)' is not admitted in *PD*, which gives only 'réchapper' for intransitive *erebre*. *SW* iii. 118 (s.v. *erebre*, 2) has one example with the sense 'to have better luck (after a period of poverty)'.

584 *caup*. The Biblical quotation in the Latin (not printed in Guessard or in Stengel), like the parallel phrase in 1247 (dropped by Guessard but given by Stengel without comment), has remained unexplained. In both passages the reference is to Ev. Io. 8: 37, *sermo meus non capit in vobis* ('my word hath no place in you', AV). The quotation is intended to justify or explain the rendering of *caber* as *capere*. In fact this use of *capit* in the Vulgate is apparently quite isolated (cf. *TLL* iii. 333; Blaise, s.v. *capio*, 11); in the OPr. version of St. John's Gospel printed by Gilly (*The Romaunt Version of the Gospel according to St. John*, London, 1848, p. 38) the Dublin MS. has *non cap en vos*, while the Paris MS. has *non pren en vos*. Besides the linguistic point of this gloss, the translator may have intended some cryptic personal reference to the slowness of pupils— the phrase can be taken as a specimen of schoolmasterly humour.

588 *esteis—exstinxit*. Neither *B*'s *extendit* (accepted by Stengel without comment, cf. his index, s.v. *estendre*) nor *A*'s *exstrinxit* is possible.

591 *sovenc*. Since *sovenir* was used impersonally in OPr., the translation *recordatus fui*, which seems bizarre in a list of 3rd sg. forms, can be accepted on the assumption that the translator was rendering *me sovenc*.

596–601. The variety in the order and contents of this list of preterites in *-et* suggests that some of them were marginal or interlinear additions. It is possible that *AD* are in error (cf. *BL*) in omitting *coset* after *encendet* (601), and that *A* is in error (cf. *DL*) in placing *compost* after *vendet* (600) instead of *fendet* (599). But the corrections are too uncertain to be accepted into the text.

597 *mesquet—miscuit*. The same translation recurs in 2002. Since *meisser* seems not to be attested in OPr. with the general sense 'to mix' (*SW* v. 163–4), it is preferable to interpret here 'to mix or prepare a drink', a sense clearly indicated at 3510.

600 *escondet.* Faidit admits both the weak pret. of *escondre* (one example in *LR* iii. 153) and the strong form *escos*, 633.

603. The mention of *respondet* here, after its occurrence in 597, is no doubt an inconsequence of the author, for all MSS. agree in both passages.

609. *Acquisivit* (*AB*) must be taken as a second rendering of *enquis* (*aquis* can hardly have dropped out, since 610 refers to *six* verbs). This passage thus confirms *PD*'s 'procurer?', based on two examples in *SW* iii. 18–19, s.v. *enquerre*, 3.

610–11. Cf. note to 552–9.

612–13. The phrase *In -uis: destruis, anquara*, which *DL* lack, was no doubt a marginal addition. That *anquara* belongs here and not with 614 (contrary to Stengel, 22, 33, who was following Guessard's two editions) is shown by the punctuation in *A* (paragraph-marks before 612 and 614) and by the extent of the omission in *DL*.

615. *Sofrec* for *soferc* is explicable by metathesis, cf. 1545 *escarcs* = *escracs*.

616. The placing of *corec* here is hardly logical.

620 *aders, aers.* Raynouard separated *aderdre, aerdre* 'attacher, lier' (*LR* ii. 25) from *aderdre* 'élever' (*LR* iii. 137). *SW* has no entry for these forms, but *PD* gives only a single transitive verb with the meanings 'élever; établir, marier; attacher', which passed without comment into *FEW* i. 30 *ADERIGERE. The *Donatz* is certainly correct in making a distinction which later lexicographers have obscured. Here *aerdre* consistently has the sense 'to be attached, to be fixed, to adhere' (620, 2188, 2311; untranslated in 179) and is no doubt to be regarded as intransitive; in A. de Mareuil, ed. Johnston, xii. 26 (which is Raynouard's sole example for 'attacher, lier'), the p. part. has the sense 'joined (to s.o.)' (cf. 2188 *aers—aderens*) and could be regarded as transitive. And *aderdre* consistently has the sense 'to make provision for (sthg. or s.o.)' (620, 2196–7, 2310; cf. the Provençal translation in 180); this is the basic meaning behind *PD*'s 'établir, marier', cf. Brunel, *Chartes*, i and ii, Glossaries, s.v. *aderzer*. The two verbs, then, were separate for Faidit—the only confusion is in 2197, where *A* has *aers* against *L*'s *aders*. (That troubadour MSS. confuse the two words is hardly surprising, cf., for example, the variants in A. de Mareuil, loc. cit.; F. de Marseille, ed. Stroński, iv. 2; vi. 11.) The words have different etymologies: *aerdre* < *ADĔRĬGĔRE, *aderdre* < *AD-DĒRĬGĔRE (on the latter, cf. the etymology *ades* < *ADDERSUM proposed by G. Tilander, 'Vieux français, provençal, catalan *ades*, italien *adesso*, ancien espagnol *adieso*', *Mélanges de philologie offerts à M. Johan Melander*, Uppsala, [1943], pp. 109–12). Semantically, of course, *aerdre* continues ADHAERĒRE (which itself, however, had no popular reflex, cf. *FEW* i. 30 ADHAERERE). But it is false to maintain, with Corominas (*DCELC* ii. 313, s.v. *erguir*, n. 3), that OPr. shows [ẹ] in the reflexes of ERIGERE and its compounds: all good poets, like the *Donatz*, rhyme these words in [ę]. (See also J. Engels,

'L'étymologie de l'afr. *aerdre*: ADHAEREO ou *ADERIGO? (L'origine de l'afr. *erdre*)', *Mélanges de linguistique romane et de philologie médiévale offerts à M. Maurice Delbouille*, Gembloux, 1964, vol. 1, pp. 173-89, for an attempt to disprove the etymology *ADERIGERE for OFr., without reference to the OPr. material.)

631 *despos*. One would expect the translation *disposuit*, but *ABL* all have *deposuit*; cf. 1322, where *desponre* is rendered *deponere* in *A*, *disponere* in *B*. This may be a translator's error, corrected in the second passage by *B* alone. But the sense 'to depose' is possible for *desponre*, for Raynouard has a single example of the p. part. *despost*—wrongly classed under *desposezir* (*LR* iv. 616)—in what is apparently this sense. Levy noted this dubiously in *SW* ii. 164 but accepted the sense 'déposer' in *PD* only for *deponre* (of which *LR* iv. 613 has a single example). The fact that *desponre* 'to expound, explain' was a relatively common verb, while *deponre* 'to depose' is hardly attested, makes the hypothesis of a translator's error rather less likely.

637 *retors*—*retorsit*. *SW* vii. 296, s.v. *retorser*, refers only to Stichel, p. 72; the latter cites *Donatz* 2870-1 but not this example.

639 (*C* 730-1) *teus*—*timuit*, *preus*—*pressit*. Short of supposing (with K. F. T. Meyer, *Die provenzalische Gestaltung der mit dem Perfectstamm gebildeten Tempora des Lateinischen*, Marburg, 1884, p. 15) an error for *tens*, *prens* in the source of *ACDL* (i.e. in our O^2), these forms must be accepted as correct. Levy (*SW* viii. 111-12, s.v. *temer*) cites a single example of *teus* and refers to the variant *teuses* ~ *teusses* in F. de Marseille (ed. Stroński, xiii. 2, var. *ABR*). To this may be added *teuses* in G. de Bornelh, ed. Kolsen, xx. 32, var. *C*. For *preus*, Levy (*SW* vi. 505, s.v. *premer*, 1) notes a single 14th-century example of *prieussa* = *premsa*, supported by Mistral's *priéusso* (cf. *SW* vi. 506-7; see also *FEW* ix. 362 PRĔSSĀRE, with n. 13, and 367 *PRESSIARE). It is not clear that these forms have any connection with the development *-eussa* < -ENTIA, on which see A. Grafström, *Étude sur la graphie des plus anciennes chartes languedociennes*, Uppsala, 1958, pp. 103-11; E. Nègre, 'A propos de Caramancio-Carmaux', *Actes et Mémoires du IIe Congrès International de Langue et Littérature du Midi de la France*, Aix-en-Provence, 1961, pp. 191-5.

642 *afrais*—*humiliavit*. Sole example for the sense 'to humble' in *SW* i. 29; the verb was commonly used reflexively, however, in the sense 'to humble oneself' (e.g. F. de Marseille, ed. Stroński, xix. 67).

658, 661. The inclusion of *prendre* and *metre* among the verbs which have a p. part. in -*ut* is probably an oversight on the author's part; cf. 671 and 680 (*pres*, *mes*). *Metut*, however, is attested (*SW* v. 269-70, s.v. *metre*, 6 [2nd example] and 12 [3rd example]). Cf. Ronjat, iii, p. 218; P. Mann, *Das Participium Praeteriti im Altprovenzalischen*, Marburg, 1886, p. 24 (*remetutz*).

663 *escondre*. The translation *excutere* renders *escodre* 'to thresh; to carry off, steal'; cf. 633 for more precise renderings of this verb. This is best

regarded as a translator's error, repeated in 1311, for *ADL* are unanimous here, as *ABL* are unanimous against *D* in 1311. *Escondre* is correctly translated in 600, 633, 2108, 2759. The partial identity of forms in the pret. and p. part. explains the confusion of the two verbs. For the p. part. *escondut* cf. *LR* iii. 153.

669 *joher*. See note to 528.

670. The words *silicet excipitur* were intended as a gloss (presumably marginal) on the inexplicit *et* which introduces *videre*.

672. *Escodre* (*A*), with the translation *excutere* (*AB*), is acceptable. In view of *CL*'s *escondre*, however, it is possible that this is a third example of the translator's error found in 663 and 1311, 'corrected' here by *A* as it was in 1311 by *D*; cf. note to 663. *SW* iii. 175 has an example of the p. part. *escos* (cf. also *Donatz* 3537–8).

688–90. Faidit ought to have excepted from his rule, not only *saber*, but *aver*, *esser*, and *voler*; cf. Anglade, p. 260.

690–4. The reference here to imperative forms of the 1st conjugation is inconsequential. So is the quite isolated reference to a *future* imperative, identical with the present; this last remark shows the influence of Latin grammars (cf. Donatus, iv. 360. 26–7; Priscian, viii. 40–1).

690. The rendering *prime persone* is here regarded as a lapse on the translator's part; it could rather less plausibly be explained as a scribal slip.

695. *A*'s meaningless *trait la prima*, which is lacking in all other MSS. and for which *A* itself provides no translation, is certainly to be rejected. The phrase must have been part of a gloss on the passage dealing with the imperative (688–93), intended to explain why this mood had no 1st sg., for *C* (789–90) has a similar observation and so does *L* (var. 690, with an erroneous expansion to *trait la prima conjugazo*—the inverse, incidentally, of the error in *A*'s Latin in 690). A marginal gloss in *O²*, incorporated into α (= *CL*) but rejected by *B*, *D*, and—in principle—*A*, has survived vestigially in the latter.

706–10. The use of phrases introduced by *si* to illustrate the optative mood is quite incorrect. From the point of view of medieval grammatical categories these forms could only be classed as plpf. subjunctives. Faidit's difficulties in setting up an OPr. optative separate from the subjunctive are very clear here.

727–8. For the syncopated forms *agssem*, *agsetz* cf. Grandgent, p. 146; Brunel, *Chartes*, i, p. xli; *aguessem*, *aguessetz* are given earlier (701).

773. The subjunctive *sia*, though supported by all MSS. except *L*, is not acceptable. The sentence is a straightforward statement and the indicative mood is essential, hence the correction to *si va*, identical with *L*'s reading. For the use of *si* reflexive here cf. W. S. Lipton in *Romance Philology*, xiv, 1960–1, pp. 126–8; the sense is 'The passive of the other conjugations ... goes, for its part, entirely regularly ...'.

781. *Arripar*, for *arribar*, is unknown to *LR*, *SW*, or *PD*. All MSS. attest the *-p-* here; cf. *deripar* (906, var. *B*), which Levy admitted, rather inconsequentially (*SW* ii. 108; *PD*).

783 *anelar*. Sole example in *SW* i. 64 for the sense 'to breathe', well attested for the variant *alenar* (*LR* ii. 84). It is possible to take Latin *anelare* in the sense 'to strive, aspire' (Blaise, s.v.), a sense also attested for OPr. *anelar* (*LR* ii. 84; cf. *SW* i. 64).

786 *adagar—adaquare*. In face of the unanimous Provençal reading, it is difficult to regard this as a scribal form of *adegar*, which alone would justify *A*'s translation *equare*. *B*'s *adaquare* can be rendered 'to water, irrigate' or 'to mix with water'. The latter sense is absent from *PD*, though attested in *SW* i. 19 (to which may be added *Recettes médicales*, ed. Brunel in *Rom.* lxxxiii, p. 171 (§ 316); *Recettes de Montpellier*, ed. Brunel in *Rom.* lxxviii, pp. 301 (§ 5c) and 312 (§ 74)).

792 *manduirar*. The form *manduiram* in *A*'s Latin supports *-ui-* rather than *-iu-* in the Provençal. *Manduirar*, an otherwise unattested variant of *mandurar*, is parallel with OFr. *mandoire* (< PANDŌRIUM) and requires the etymon PANDŪRIUM (attested in Cassiodorus, cf. Blaise, s.v.); see *FEW* vii. 540–1 PANDŪRA, where *A*'s form should be added and n. 5 (attributing to a *Donatz* MS. the variant *mandurcar*) corrected. Neither *manduira* nor *mandura* seems to be attested in med. Latin; no doubt the translator was here simply Latinizing a vernacular word, although neither is in fact attested in OPr.

793 *organar—horganiçare*. The sense of both Provençal and Latin is rather uncertain: some form of singing is no doubt meant, perhaps of a particularly ornate and decorated kind. Cf. the only other OPr. example (Marcabru's starling) in *SW* v. 518; the examples in Du Cange, s.vv. *organizare, organare, organisare* (= *organum* 1, *in fine*); and *FEW* vii. 410 ORGANUM.

794–5. The different Latin renderings are no doubt intended to make a distinction between intr. *trumbar* and tr. (but also intr.) *cornar*.

801 *ajornar—diem assignare*. For a second example of this sense, not given for OPr. in *FEW* iii. 105 DIURNUM, cf. *LR* iii. 589.

802 *acorsar—ad cursum provocare*. This is Levy's sole example (*SW* i. 17) for any part of this verb except the p. part. *acorsat* 'swift'; presumably the sense was 'to spur on'.

803 *assoudar*. *SW* i. 92 cites only Stichel, p. 17, whose sole example is this passage (the verb is to be distinguished from *assoltar*, as Levy noted in *ZRP* xv, pp. 533–4); cf. also Dicc. Aguiló, s.v. *assoldar*. For *stipendiare* (instead of the more usual deponent) cf. Baxter–Johnson, Niermeyer, s.v.

812 *areçhar—procurare vel ministrare necessaria*. For *arezar* 'to provide for (s.o.)' cf. *Jaufré* 5442; this meaning is not clearly brought out in *LR* v. 82 or in *PD*. It is confirmed by *arezadamens* 'necessities of life',

which *SW* i. 82 and *PD* misinterpret and which should be added to *FEW* xvi. 699 *RĔPS.

819 *avinaçar*. *SW* i. 114 cites only Stichel, p. 19, who has no other example; cf. *FEW* xiv. 482 VĪNUM for mod. *avinachar* 'imbiber de vin (un tonneau)'.

825 *baroneiar*. Sole example in *SW* i. 127, from Stichel, p. 21. *A*'s *baronecar* cannot be retained against *BDL*; correction to *-eçar* is possible (cf. 1189 *tamboreçar*), though there is no other case of *c* for *ç* in MS. *A*. On the other hand, the alternative form *baronelar*, despite its absence from *BDL*, is acceptable if one interprets *l* as *lh*; cf. Adams, p. 350 n. 4, for confusion of *-eiar* and *-elhar*. This form, absent from the dictionaries, is otherwise unattested. Whether the verbs are intr. (as in *PD*) or refl. is impossible to decide—mod. dialects appear to have both (*FEW* i. 255 BARO).

826 *baconar*. Sole example in *SW* i. 118, from Stichel, p. 20. Is it tr. (as in *PD*) or intr.?

827 *baratar*. For *stulte expendere* cf. the OFr. example in *TL* i. 832. 36–8; is this the sense in B. de Born, ed. Appel, xxxix. 40 (*ses baratar* 'without paying heavily')? For *dolose expendere* (*A* alone has *vel dolose*), cf. the senses 'deceive, exchange, lend money' (*LR* ii. 183; *SW* i. 126; *FEW* ix. 330–1 PRATTEIN): the intended meaning is perhaps 'to make a profitable deal through cunning'.

830 *braceiar*. Sole example in *SW* i. 160, from Stichel, p. 22. Chabaneau's correction to *ulnis* (*RLR* xiii, p. 140) is preferable to *B*'s *brachiis*, which looks like a rationalization of *uiciis*.

833 *bellar*. *A*'s translation *bella ferre*, against *B*'s *belare*, has brought into the dictionaries (Stichel, p. 22; *SW* i. 137; *PD*; whence *FEW* i. 317, sole entry under BELLARE) a verb *belar* 'to wage war'. No second example of the latter has been found (surprisingly, in view of its supposed meaning) apart from *Flamenca* 1039, for which *PD* hesitantly accepts the figurative sense 'être très agité'; but on the latter cf. Meyer's 2nd ed., Corrections, p. 415, accepted in Lavaud and Nelli's ed., with the translation 'qui a ce regard béant'. Clearly, *belar* in these senses, literal or figurative, is a ghost-word. *A*'s reading is adequately explained if one supposes the translation *bella/re* split over two lines. No doubt the translator's *ad oves pertinet* was intended precisely to eliminate possible misunderstanding.

836 *bretoneiar—loqui inpetuose*. Levy (*SW* i. 164; *PD*), accepting G. Paris' emendation to *impedite* (*Rom.* i, p. 235), interprets 'to stammer, stutter'. The correction, suggested by the translation of *bretz* (2387), is unnecessary: the verb, of which the *Donatz* furnishes the sole example, may well have meant 'to gabble', cf. *FEW* i. 539 BRĬTTUS for some semantic parallels.

837 *blesseiar*. BL provide the sole OPr. attestation of the form with *-s-* = [z]; both forms exist in mod. dialects (*FEW* i. 392 BLAESUS).

838 *bendelar*. Sole example in *SW* i. 139, from Stichel, p. 22.

839 *bullar*. Cf. *LR* ii. 271 and *PD*; omitted in *FEW* i. 613 BULLA.

842 *buscalar*. The other example in the *Donatz* (3359; *SW* i. 175 has only these, from Stichel, p. 23) shows this to be a spelling for *buscalhar*; this is confirmed by mod. dialect forms (*FEW* i. 648 *BŪSCA). *PD* is therefore wrong in admitting the form with -*l*-. Cf. also *Dicc. Alcover*, s.v. *buscallar* (example of 1470).

844 *biordar—discurere cum equis*. The translation is no doubt an approximate rendering of the notion 'to joust'.

845 *baissar*. The translations correspond to both *baisar* with [z] and *baissar* with [s]; *L* alone gives the two verbs separately. The translator may well have been responsible for the confusion.

847 *calfar—calefieri*. *PD* gives the verb as tr. only. The Latin suggests that the translator was rendering the intr. sense of the verb used reflexively (cf. Raynouard's second example, *LR* ii. 290 = G. de Poitiers, ed. Jeanroy, v. 41).

848 *calar—tacere*. Modern dialect evidence indicates localization mainly in an area comprising Gascony and part or all of the départements of Haute-Garonne, Tarn, Aveyron, Lozère, Hérault, Aude, Ariège; cf. *FEW* ii. 1. 61 CALARE, also xiii. 1. 28 TACĒRE.

850 *caminar—equitare per stratas ad inveniendum hostem*. The translation renders the notion 'to pursue (a fleeing enemy)', attested in a figurative use in Raynouard's second example (*LR* ii. 302 = R. de Vaqueiras, ed. Linskill, vi. 8). *FEW* ii. 1. 145 CAMMĪNUS lacks our verb.

854 *catiglar*. The unanimity of *ADL* against *B*'s *castiglar* makes the latter suspect, nor can one seriously accept Levy's proposed correction to *cassiglar* (*SW* i. 228, where the *Donatz* provides the sole example; *PD*). *Catiglar* is acceptable, cf. *FEW* ii. 1. 511 KAT-Ł for mod. forms with -*g*- (the doubts expressed there [p. 512 n. 1] about *ADL*'s reading are exaggerated); the graphy -*gl*- for [l'] does not occur in our text and cannot be supposed here.

865 *cembar—tabulas valde movere*. Sole example in *SW* i. 240, from Stichel, p. 25, whence *PD* 'jouer des cymbales' and *FEW* ii. 2. 1611 CYMBALUM. The sense is confirmed by the existence of *cembas* 'cymbals' (*SW*, loc. cit.); but the correction of *tibias* to *tabulas*, not made by Stichel or Levy, is essential.

870 *crivelar—bladum purgare*. Sole example of the form with -*v*- in *SW* i. 417; add *Rom.* xl, p. 361, § 9 (crimelat MS.). *Purgare* 'to sieve' is a Provençalism (cf. *FEW* ix. 614 PŪRGARE).

875 *corolar vel coreiar*. Sole example for both words in *SW* i. 368–9, from Stichel, p. 28; cf. *SW* i. 372–3 for *corola*. If *coreiar*, given by *A* alone, is not merely a scribal hesitation over reading *corolar*, it is no doubt

a formation on *cor* < CHŎRUS; it exists in Catalan (cf. *Dicc. Alcover,* s.v. *corejar*), but *FEW* (ii. 1. 644 CHORAULA and 651–3 CHORUS) has neither the OPr. word nor any modern analogue.

879 *colar—colare.* The sense 'to strain (liquid)', though absent from *PD,* is clear in Raynouard's first example (*LR* ii. 437), to which may be added *Recettes médicales,* ed. Meyer in *Rom.* xxxii, pp. 280, 281, 282, 283, 286; *Recettes de Montpellier,* ed. Brunel in *Rom.* lxxviii, pp. 299 (§§ 1b, 2a), 300 (§§ 2e, 4a), etc.

880. *A*'s *condeiare,* which is unattested in med. Latin, may have arisen from an interlinear *condeiar* intended as a correction of the reading *codeiar.*

886. *Sobradaurar* shows the Italianism *sobra* for *sobre,* on which cf. *SW* vii. 695.

892 *deirengar—de serie militum exire.* In the sense 'to step forward (from the ranks of soldiers), to advance' the verb is not only intr. (as in *PD,* from R. de Vaqueiras, ed. Linskill, xviii. 81, to which may be added *Ronsasvals* 65, 716, 750, 1071, 1278), but also refl. (cf. the third example in *SW* ii. 107; also *Roland à Saragosse* 1249). *B*'s reading, with *militem,* is not inconceivable if *exire* is taken in a transitive sense (for which cf. note to 948).

906 *deribar—extra ripam exire.* Sole example of this sense in *SW* ii. 108; cf. *Dicc. Alcover,* s.v. *derivar* 1, a.

910 *detirar—valde traere.* The sense 'to pull forcefully', absent from *SW* ii. 186 and *PD,* is common in OFr. (cf. *FEW* vi. 403 MARTYRIUM, etc.). Stengel printed *A*'s reading as *valde detraere* (i.e. 'to pull downwards').

922. It is difficult to suppose that the unanimous *espirar* of the MSS. (*B*'s deletion of the *r* was clearly made later than the copy itself and may not be by the scribe) is an error for *espiar* which arose after the translation was made. A simpler explanation is that the translator misread *espirar* as *espiar* and mistranslated accordingly.

930 *enastar—in ligno ad assandum ponere.* Sole example of this sense in *SW* ii. 422. For the correction, which supposes misinterpretation in *A* and in *B* of *assād*', cf. the examples of erroneous *-de* for *-dum* in 1101, 1531, 2403, 3202; for *lignum* 'wooden implement' (here, a spit) cf. 1101, 1121, 2715.

937 *essauchar—probare.* Sole example of this sense ('to approve of') in *SW* ii. 332; cf. ibid. for a single example of *eisausamen* 'approbation'.

942 *enunbrar—propter umbram timere vel sensum amittere.* The intended sense is 'to take umbrage, to shy (of a horse)', cf. *SW* iii. 16; *sensum amittere* is a literal rendering of *perdre lo sen* (*SW* vii. 561, s.v. *sen,* 14)— it is conceivable that *vel* is an error for *et.*

944 *escampar* (*AD*), *escapar* (*BL*). The latter form seems somewhat commoner; cf. the variants to G. de Bornelh, ed. Kolsen, xxx. 5; xlii. 80; A. de Peguilhan, ed. Shepard and Chambers, xii. 10.

945 *escoissar—per coxas dividere*. Sole example in *SW* iii. 176, from Stichel, p. 50; add *Jaufré* 2206, 2638, 2980, 4324, 8494 (*esquisar*), also 7825, var. *c* (*eisscoissar*). The Latin rendering here seems to have been suggested—in part at least—by etymological considerations; the verb's normal meaning is 'to tear', though it is not impossible that 'to dismember' also existed and was intended here by the translator.

946. For the spelling *escortgar* cf. *Croisade* 1958 (noted by Stengel, note to 30b, 19).

947 *embotar*. Sole example in *SW* ii. 360, from Stichel, p. 39; cf. *Dicc. Alcover*, s.v. (15th-century Catalan example), and, for mod. dialects, *FEW* i. 662 BŬTTIS.

948 *essaurar—ad auram exire*. Sole example in *SW* ii. 331 of the sense 'to take the fresh air' (v. refl.), similarly in *PD* and in *FEW* iii. 262 *EXAURARE. This is very unlikely: the most natural sense for the Latin is 'to soar (of birds)', a meaning attested in the *Auzels cassadors*, ed. Schutz, 1075, and found also for OFr. *essorer* (*TL* iii. 1318). It is possible, however, that *exire* is to be taken transitively, as in 1383 (cf. also note to 892), hence 'to put out in the air (to dry)', a sense rendered more explicitly in *Donatz* 3250.

952 *enclavar*. Sole example in *SW* ii. 439; add *Recettes vétérinaires*, ed. Brunel in *Rom*. lxxxii, p. 36 (§ 36), and *Recettes des Pyréneés*, § 429 (p. 57).

954 *essemblar—exemplare*. It is not clear which of the various senses of the Latin verb (on which cf. *TLL*, Blaise, Niermeyer, Du Cange, s.v.) is intended. The translation tentatively advanced here, 'to form according to a (real or imagined) model', like *PD*'s 'modeler', takes account of Raynouard's examples of *exemplar* (*LR* iii. 240). MS. *A* of the *Donatz* alone has the form with -*b*-.

955 *entamenar—pannis partem vel pomi vel alicuius rei auferre*. It is possible to regard *A*'s *ponu* or *pomi* as a misreading of *pani* = *panni* (cf. *SW* iii. 43 for an example of this verb applied to cloth). But in fact *pomi* makes perfectly acceptable sense; for *entamenar* applied to fruit cf. Cerveri de Girona, ed. Riquer, ci. 21.

961 *enborsar*. Sole example in *SW* ii. 359, from Stichel, p. 41.

962 *enalbar* [enarbrar *B*]—*erigere duos pedes et in duobus sustentari*. The correction to *in duabus* [*manibus*], proposed originally by Bauquier (*ZRP* ii, p. 83) and given wider currency by Chabaneau (*RLR* xiii, p. 140), was accepted by Levy (*SW* ii. 412, where this is the sole example), whence the sense 'to do a hand-stand' passed to *PD* and to *FEW* i. 125 ARBOR. As already noted by G. Paris (*Rom*. vii, p. 467), the emendation is quite wrong: the verb is identical with OFr. *s'enarbrer* 'to rear up on the hind-legs (of a horse)', cf. *Li Fet des Romains*, ed. Flutre, glossary (vol. ii, p. 266), and the same editor in *Rom*. lxv, p. 489.—Correction to *enalbrar* (*SW*, loc. cit., and *PD*) is hardly necessary.

963 *esmerar.* Correction to *depurare,* despite *AB*'s agreement on *deputare,* is supported by *Donatz* 3170.

971 *fadeiar.* Stengel misprinted *faduiar* as *A*'s reading; this ghost-word was accepted into *SW* iii. 377 and *PD,* whence it passed into *FEW* iii. 437 FATUUS.

991 *grenar.* *A*'s reading (against *glenar BDL*) is conceivably correct (? × *gran* < GRĀNUM). *SW* iv. 137 and *PD* admit it, but *FEW* iv. 152–4 GLENNARE has no form in *gr*-.

993 *guidar.* *A*'s *guidare conductum* is impossible: one may suppose a haplography (*g.* [*vel dare*] *c.*) or—as preferred in the text—a scribal *lapsus* provoked by the OPr. word. The sense 'to give safe-conduct to' is well attested (cf. *SW* iv. 210–11, s.v. *guidar,* 5).

999 *içalar.* Sole example in *SW* iv. 240–1. Given the etymology (*FEW* i. 153 ASĪLUS) and the evidence of *BDL* (*D*'s *balar* is no doubt from *izalar,* cf. *d¹*'s reading, p. 39), *A*'s *inçatar* cannot be defended.

1002 *juçiar.* *A*'s reading, supported by 1893 *juciatz,* needs no emendation, despite its absence from the OPr. dictionaries and from *FEW* v. 58 JŬDĬCARE. It is to be regarded as a semi-learned form, cf. *jutzia* 'droit de justice' in Brunel, *Chartes,* ii. 352. 1.

1015 *liurar—dare.* The Latin is a poor approximation to the sense 'to hand over', preferable, however, to *B*'s *libras dare,* which is no doubt etymologically motivated.

1016 *lipsar—polire.* Sole example in *SW* iv. 406. The verb is registered, very dubiously, in *REW* 5081 *LĪSIUS. It clearly belongs in *FEW* v. 374 LISPOS 'smooth', where it should be added to the few mod. dialect forms, none of them with -*ps*-, which are mentioned. *L*'s variant *lispar* is not, therefore, merely a scribal *lapsus*.

1017 *luitar.* On the basis of *A*'s *liurar—lucrari,* Chabaneau (*RLR* xiii, p. 140) conjectured *luirar* 'gagner', which passed into *SW* iv. 442 and *PD* but not *FEW* (which registers only OPr. *logre* < LŬCRUM, v. 438). In fact **luirar,* phonetically difficult as a reflex of LŬCRĀRĪ (cf. *REW* 5145), is a ghost-word: *BDL* confirm the obvious emendation. An analogous error is committed by *A* at 1205, where there is the same misreading of *t* as *r* and the same 'correction' of the Latin in conformity with the Provençal.

1029 *mendigar.* Though *PD* gives the verb as tr., both examples in Raynouard (*LR* iv. 194), like that in *Ronsasvals* 285, are intr.

1035 *meitadar—medium facere unius coloris, medium alii.* Sole example of this precise sense in *SW* v. 165; but *Dicc. Alcover,* s.v. *meitadat,* cites three medieval examples.

1040 *moschar.* Sole example in *SW* v. 325, from Stichel, p. 64. Is it intr. (as in *PD*) or tr. and refl. (like Fr. *émoucher*)?

NOTES 283

1041 *moscidar.* Sole example in *SW* v. 326, from Stichel, p. 64; cf. *FEW* vi. 3. 268 MŬSSĬTARE—the modern examples are restricted to Limousin.

1043 *monestar.* Lacking in *PD* and *SW*, but cf. *LR* iv. 253, to which one may add *Ronsasvals* 1643.

1048 *neblar—nebulla perire.* The sense of the Latin is not clear. *PD*'s 'être gâté par le brouillard', which derives from Mistral, s.v. *nebla*, is accepted by *FEW* vii. 69 NĔBŬLA with the addition '(des plantes)'; Levy's earlier 'durch Nebel zu Grunde gehen' (*SW* v. 373-4) is more noncommittal. It is quite possible that the translator intended 'to be lost in the mist' (cf. Blaise, s.v. *pereo*)—indeed, this seems the most natural rendering of the Latin. Without a second example of the verb, however, its sense must remain dubious.

1057 *onceiar.* Sole example in *SW* v. 495, from Stichel, p. 65; cf. *FEW* xiv. 28 *ŪNCIA.

1060 *oscar.* *A*'s *ebeditare* (for which *B*'s *ditare* is a misguided correction) must have arisen from an original *ebedare* corrected to *ebetare* (i.e. *ebedare*). For the -*d*-, cf. 1151 *saludare*; Du Cange cites an example of *hebidus* for *hebes*.

1065 *passeiar.* Sole example in *SW* vi. 126, from Stichel, p. 65—Levy also cites Mistral's *passeja*; cf. *Dicc. Alcover*, s.v. *passejar*, 1.

1069 *trapa[u]ssar.* Despite the existence of a few examples of pretonic and intertonic *a* for *au* (cf. Pfister, *Beiträge*, *Vox*, xvii, pp. 302-3), it seems preferable to regard this as a scribal confusion of *passar* and *pauzar*, as in 1467. *SW* viii. 393 attests only *traspauzar* ('to carry over'), but the alternation *tras-* ~ *tra-* was common in other verbs with this prefix.

1076 *penar—penam sustinere.* It is not clear whether the intended sense is 'to suffer pain or punishment' (*PD* has only 'être en mal d'enfant' = *SW* vi. 202, s.v. *penar*, 2) or 'to expiate', as in Raynouard's last example (*LR* iv. 488 = P. Cardenal, ed. Lavaud, lv. 139).

1083 *petazar.* On the geographical distribution of the forms in *pet-* and *ped-*, cf. *FEW* viii. 615-18 PITTACIUM and von Wartburg, *Von Sprache und Mensch*, Berne, 1956, pp. 104-6.

1086 *peçugar,* cf. 2978-9, *pezucs.* *PD* registers only *pesugar* and *pesuc.* The graphies in the *Donatz* (*L* alone has *pesugar* here) indicate [-ts-], in accordance with the etymology *PĬTS- (*FEW* viii. 541-8 *PĬNTS-, p. 547); cf. *SW* vi. 296 for an example of *peçuc* in Sordello (= ed. Boni, xix. 30).

1088 *pectenar.* Sole example of this form (for usual *penchenar*) in *SW* vi. 203-4; *FEW* viii. 105-8 PECTINARE has neither this nor any other learned form.

1094 *pejurar.* This form, for *perjurar*, is conceivable (cf. Introduction, p. 59) but not clearly attested; cf., however, R. d'Orange, ed. Pattison, x. 44, var. *C* (*peiurs* = *perjurs*), and G. de Bornelh, ed. Kolsen, xxviii. 44, var. *Sg* (id.).

1099. The form *pistar* (as distinct from *pestar*) belongs to Provence in the narrower sense; cf. *FEW* viii. 598 PISTARE; *DCELC* iii. 808–9.

1101 *ponzilar* [*l* = *lh*, cf. 3413]—*ad diruendum muri ligna ponere, vel diruere murum cum ligno*. *PD*'s translation 'étayer, étançonner' is derived ultimately from Mistral, s.v. *pounsiha*, via Stichel, p. 67, and *SW* vi. 455, whence it passed to *FEW* ix. 582 *PŬNCTIARE. This sense is very questionable for OPr., for which the *Donatz* furnishes the only two examples of the word. The translation here, together with 3413 *ponzilha—ponit ligna supra muros*, does not bear out the contention of Galvani (p. 326) that the translator was envisaging the excavation of soil under fortifications, which were then supported on wooden props and made to collapse by setting fire to the wood. This interpretation forced Galvani to correct *supra* (3413) to *subter* and *ponere* (1101) to *supponere*. But the translation given by the *Donatz* yields a perfectly acceptable sense: 'to set up a wooden contrivance against a wall, to destroy a wall by this method'— for *lignum* in the sense of 'wooden construction or implement' cf. note to 930. This contrivance was evidently some kind of siege-engine which could be hooked on to the top of the enemy walls (hence *supra muros*) in the same manner as scaling-ladders (on which cf. W. Giese in *ZRP* lii, 1932, p. 388, esp. n. 13 on two passages in the *Prise de Damiette*). Despite *FEW*, loc. cit., our verb is clearly connected with the *pontel* and *pontil* 'étai, étançon' registered by *PD* (cf. *SW* vi. 457; the sense of *pontelhs* [so spelt] in Levy's example is not certain, as is noted in *FEW* ix. 172 PONTĬCŬLUS, n. 1; the *pontils* of his second example are clearly 'tent-poles'; cf. also the Latinized verb (*ap*)*pontellare* 'stützen' in *SW*, loc. cit.). A few modern forms of similar sense are cited, with the present verb *ponsilhar*, in *FEW* ix. 582 under *PŬNCTIARE. They would be better placed with those already mentioned, under PONTĬCŬLUS: both there and s.v. PŌNS (ix. 168–72) the semantic development to 'scaffolding' occurs often enough to support this etymology. *Ponsilhar* was formed on **ponsilh*, a blend of *ponsel* < *PONTICĔLLUS and *pontilh* < *PONTĬCŬLUS; whether the verb was tr. or intr. cannot be decided.

1102 *ponçeiar*. The translations for 1102–4 are somewhat misplaced in both MSS., no doubt because of the unusual length of the translation in 1101. *B*'s *ponere* (1102) belongs to 1101, which *B* leaves untranslated; *B*'s *inprobare* (1103) belongs to 1102; *B*'s *vineas* (1104) belongs to 1103. Similarly, *A*'s *bene* (1103) belongs to 1102. For *podar* and *poiar*, which are well attested, there is no difficulty. *Ponçeiar*, however, is a *hapax* and, in the state of the text, presents an insoluble problem. With the restorations already noted, *A* presents *inprobare bene* for this word, while *B* has *benefitia alijs inprobare*. Chabaneau (*RLR* xiii, p. 141) proposed *pungere vel beneficia aliis improbare*; the first translation derived from a misapprehension about Languedocien *pounchejá* (*FEW* ix. 579 PŬNCTA; cf. 584 *PŬNCTIARE, n. 1) and is clearly unacceptable; the second prompted Levy's guess 'um Kleinigkeiten streiten, missbilligen?' (*SW* vi. 455), which passed into *PD* as 'pointiller, désapprouver?' and thence, without the question-mark, into *FEW* ix. 582, where *ponsejar* stands in striking isolation at the head of the article *PŬNCTIARE. But it is highly unlikely that B's reading could mean this, nor is *aliis* likely to be right, for nowhere else does the translator indicate a verb's indirect object in this fashion (he normally uses some form of *aliquis*). We must assume, then, either that *aliis* was B's attempt to improve on his exemplar (like *vel* in 1103)—in which case *improbare benefitia* would be the right reading—or that it represents a misreading of some other word. The latter case—inherently less probable, since it presupposes that A dropped a word and a half—gives possibilities for emendation too wide for any correction to be other than arbitrary (e.g. *i. b. alodii* 'to refuse to grant the right to feudal dues on an inherited domain'). In the former case the obvious interpretation is 'to reject a favour' (*benefitium* in this sense recurs in 1913), though other renderings are possible. Only a second example or a certain etymology could decide the question—is the verb simply a formation on the proper name *Pons*?

1107 *plovinar—frequenter pluere*. The translation of this, the sole OPr. example of the word, gave *PD*'s 'pleuvoir fréquemment' (similarly *SW* vi. 396–7, from Stichel, p. 67). From both OFr. and mod. Provençal (Godefroy, vi. 232; Mistral, s.v. *plouvina*; *FEW* ix. 81 PLŬĔRE) one would expect the sense 'to drizzle' (though the noun *pluvina* is attested with, apparently, the sense 'heavy rain', *SW* vi. 396). And in fact 'to drizzle' is no doubt what the translator intended: two parallel cases (3381 *somnelha—frequenter sonniatur*; 3391 *pendelha—frequenter pendit*), where 'frequently' is impossible, show the same imprecise use of *frequenter*, which was perhaps motivated by a vague recollection of Latin frequentative verbs. (Elsewhere *frequenter* is used in its usual sense, e.g. 75, 80, 2047, 2276; in 3368 either sense is possible.)

1108 *pomelar—pomum in aerem proicere*. *Pomum* can be 'apple' or 'ball' (for the latter sense cf. Du Cange); the same ambiguity recurs with 2038 *pomelz—parvum pomum*. Levy renders 'apple' in both cases (*PD*; *SW* vi. 441 and 440–1, respectively). It is inherently more probable that 'ball' was intended by the translator; cf. G. de Calanso's 'E paucs pomels / Ab tres coutels / Sapchas gitar e retenir' (cited in *SW* vi. 440, s.v. *pomel*, 1), where the context would suggest juggling with balls. 'Knob' is the commonest sense of *pomel* (*LR* iv. 594; *SW*, loc. cit.); *pomelar* is attested only in the *Donatz*.

1109 *polsar—valde anelare*. The Latin indicates that the sense was something more than *PD*'s 'respirer': rather 'to pant'.

1110 *ponhtar—punchare*. A's Latin (for *punctare*, as in B) may well be a scribal slip or even the result of an interlinear note adding *punchar*; but *puncherium*, which Du Cange attests from Nîmes in 1227, justifies its retention in the text.

1119 *ramponar*. Sole example in *SW* vii. 21 (from Stichel, p. 68), where there is, however, a single example of *ramponador*, to which one may add *ranproners* (= *-iers*) 'querelleur', unknown to the dictionaries, in *Girart*

7686. It is uncertain whether *A*'s reading is a graphy for *ramponhar*, which is otherwise unattested (but cf. Italian *rampognare*, attested in the 14th century, and the OFr. forms in *-ogne* in Godefroy, vi. 585–6); the spellings in *D* and *L* suggest, at least, that the form with palatal *n* existed, as it still does in mod. Provençal dialects (cf. *FEW* ix. 479 PROTHYRUM).

1120 *rautar* < RAPTARE (*REW* 7060); the sense is borne out by R. de Vaqueiras, ed. Linskill, v. 36. *FEW* seems to lack this word.

1121 *rasclar—ligno radere*. For *lignum* cf. note to 930; *A*'s *radare* is clearly unacceptable. It is doubtful whether the translation really means 'to strickle (a measure of corn)', as once supposed by Levy (*SW* vii. 38, s.v. *rasclar*, 2; not repeated in *PD*) and accepted by *FEW* x. 82 *RASCLARE. This translation is possible (cf. the other examples in *FEW*, loc. cit.) and *radere* was used in this sense in med. Latin (cf. Niermeyer). But there is no other attestation of just this sense in OPr., and 'to scrape with a wooden implement' is sufficient here.

1122 *raiar*. *A*'s *raidar*, dubiously accepted in *SW* vii. 8 but not included in *PD*, can hardly be correct. *FEW* x. 15–16 RADIARE omits it and shows no comparable form.

1123 *ranqueirar* [rauqueirar *A*]—*claudicare*. The form *ranqueirar*, though depending on a correction and isolated against *BDL*'s *ranqueiar*, may be correct. It was admitted by Levy (*SW* vii. 32 and *PD*) and placed by *FEW* xvii. 621 *WRANKS with a few mod. dialect forms (Gascony, Aveyron) which presuppose an OPr. *ranqueira 'lameness'.

1125 *refiudar—refutare*. Tobler's emendation to *refiuidar* (*Rom.* ii, pp. 338–9), accepted by Stengel, by *SW* vii. 163–4, and by *FEW* x. 198 REFUGIUM, is difficult to maintain against the united reading of *ABD* (*L* has *refudar*). *Refiudar* can be explained as an Italianism or conceivably as an example of metathesis. It is also possible to take *refutare* in the sense 'to renounce possession of (a fief, in another's favour)', for which cf. Niermeyer, s.v. *refutare*, 1, and Du Cange; the sense is unattested in OPr. but perhaps supported by *refiuzamen* and *refiu* (*SW* vii. 147, 146). Our verb would then belong in the family of *FEHU. But, short of the discovery of a second example of the word, this will remain an uncertain interpretation of the translator's Latin.

1129 *renoelar*. Though *SW* vii. 334, like *LR* iv. 340, gives only *renovelar* (*PD* lacks both forms), the form without *-v-* does exist outside the *Donatz* (cf. the variants to P. d'Auvergne, ed. del Monte, xv. 5 and 6; G. de Bornelh, ed. Kolsen, xl. 10).

1130 *revelar—revellare*. For *revellare* = *rebellare* see Niermeyer; cf. also 3283 *revela—revella vel rebellat*, where this interpretation is assured by the rhyme in [ę].

1134 *rimar—rimos facere*. For *rimus* cf. the single example of 1198 in Du Cange, s.v. *B*'s *rimas* is Provençal rather than Latin.

1135 *ribar—repercutere clavos.* Sole example in *SW* vii. 339, from Stichel, p. 73; cf. *FEW* x. 413 RĪPA. For *repercutere* 'to rivet' cf. the single example of 1296 cited by Baxter–Johnson.

1138 *rotar.* *B*'s *ructar*, accepted in *SW* vii. 384 and *PD* (but not in *FEW* x. 539 RŬCTARE) and conceivable as a Latinism, is otherwise unattested.

1139 *roflar.* Guessard interchanged (accidentally?) the *turpiter* of 1139 and the *dormiendo* of 1140, an error perpetuated, for *roflar*, in Stengel (33b, 3); thence the translation 'to snore', which passed from Stichel (p. 63) to *SW* vii. 367, *PD* ('ronfler' only) and *FEW* x. 471 RONFL- ('ronfler; râler'). Since neither *A* nor *B* has *dormiendo*, it is questionable whether *roflar* really had this sense in OPr. The other examples of the word (*Jaufré* 771, 2556, MS. *A*; MS. *B*, followed by Breuer, has *renflar*; cf. *LR* v. 111 and *SW* vii. 367) show the sense 'to sob' or 'to rattle in the throat' ('gémir, râler', Brunel; 'röcheln', Breuer). Either sense is possible for the *Donatz*, depending on the meaning attached to *turpiter*.

1141 *rosseiar.* Sole example in *SW* vii. 383, from Stichel, p. 73.

1144 *rocegar—traere cum equis.* This seems to be the sole attestation of the spelling with *-c-* (*SW* vii. 382–3; Stichel, p. 73); for the etymology cf. *FEW* x. 579 *RŬPTIARE.

1153 *sanglentar.* *BD*'s *sangletar* is not necessarily erroneous, cf. *ensangle[n]taz* in *Girart* 3308; both forms are readily explicable by dissimilation.

1159 *selar—sternere equum.* *SW* vii. 535 cites only two examples from the *Donatz* (here and 3278), from Stichel, p. 75; cf. *FEW* xi. 422 SELLA.

1168 *soflar—cum naribus spirare.* In fact the verb was not limited to blowing through the *nostrils*; cf. *LR* v. 246, also *SW* vii. 742, s.v. *soflation.*

1172 *solachar—verbis ludere.* The translation, which brings out the frivolous nature of the activity, is more precise than *PD*'s 'entretenir, causer avec' (similarly *SW* vii. 771–2).

1174 *sogautar.* Sole example in *SW* vii. 755, from Stichel, p. 77; cf. *FEW* iv. 7 *GABA, where the word is quite isolated. *B*'s *sugautar* is no doubt merely a graphy (cf. *tabureiar*, 1189, var. *B*), unworthy of being recorded in *PD*.

1175 *sostar.* *A*'s *sostrar* is hardly acceptable. *FEW* xii. 357–9 SUBSTARE does not admit it and has nothing comparable. Chabaneau's argument (*RLR* xiii, p. 141) from a mod. Provençal *soustrous* 'paresseux' is not valid: the latter (which I have not located in any dictionary) must belong with OPr. *sostre* 'litière' (i.e. with *SUBSTRĀRE for SUBSTĔRNĔRE). It should be added, however, that *REW* 8394 SUBSTARE registers 'lomb. *sost(r)a*, romagn. *zbsostra*'.

1180 *solhelar.* This form, given by *A* alone, may not be merely a bizarre graphy (despite 2070 *solelhz* and 3386 *solelha*), for the sb. *solhel* is well enough attested (*SW* vii. 780–1). *BDL* are unanimous in giving an otherwise unattested form in *-eiar*. This may reflect an error in O^2 (cf. Introduction, p. 32), though it is possible to suppose an early shift of [l′] > [j] in a word which specially favoured the change for reasons both morphological (the suffix *-eiar*) and phonetic (dissimilation of [l — l′]).

1181 *suar*. Despite Chabaneau (*Rom.* vi, p. 136), *sovar* < SŪDARE, hesitantly accepted in *FEW* xii. 391 (cf. 395 n. 1), is hardly possible; the correction to *suvar* is scarcely more convincing and equally unattested (Limousin *-v-* < *-D-* seems to be attested only after countertonic *au*; cf. Appel, *Lautlehre*, p. 63).

1182 *sitar*. *A*'s marginal *sagitar* was clearly a scribal attempt to 'correct' the oddity of a text in which *sitar* was accompanied by the translation *sagitare*. But *sitar* (*AD*), even if one corrects the Latin to *sitare*, can hardly be right: it does not account for the readings of *BL*; it does not explain *sagitare*; and one would expect here a word in *su-*. The possibilities are: 1, *sugar* 'to wipe dry', as in *B*; the translation might then be *siccare* (*SW* vii. 872–3 has one certain example of the verb). 2, *suçar* 'to suck' (*SW* vii. 882); the obvious translation would be *sugere*.

The first of these does not explain *AD*'s *sitar* or *A*'s *sagitare*, nor is it clear why *B* should have replaced Latin *siccare* with Italian *sciugare*. The second possibility would account for *sitar* as a misreading of *suçar*, and for *B*'s *sugar* as a misreading of *suzar* or *suçar* (cf. 1101, var. *B*, *pongilar*). *B*'s translation would then be an attempt to replace a reading which no longer corresponded with the (erroneous) Provençal; similarly, *A*'s *sagitare* would be the result of the 'correction' of *sugere* to *sitare*—to accord with the (erroneous) Provençal—in the form *su͡gere*. In this hypothesis erroneous translations are consequential on scribal errors in the Provençal; but this reconstruction is too uncertain to be admitted into the text.

1183–4 *taular, entaular*. Of the translations placed above both verbs in *A*, the last (*vel fraudulenter* [*ad*] *se traere*) clearly belongs to 1185 *traïnar*, as in *B*; for the sense 'to draw (s.o.) on by wiles, to lure on' cf. *SW* viii. 353; *LR* v. 398. In the rest of the translation as given by *A*, *utrumque* indicates that what follows (*ludum ordinare*) applies to both verbs; hence *invictus manere* was intended to apply only to *taular*. The sense 'to set up (a game on a board)' is well attested for *entaular* (*SW* iii. 44; *LR* v. 308), less so for *taular* (*SW* viii. 82–3: *Donatz* and *Flamenca* 6480 only); for both cf. also *FEW* xiii. 1. 14 TABULA. Despite its absence from Levy (*SW* notes it hesitantly only s.v. *entaular*, iii. 44), the sense 'to remain the winner (i.e. at the end of a game)' is attested for *taular* in G. de Poitiers, ed. Jeanroy, vi. 47, where, despite the editor and despite *SW* viii. 82–3, the reading *Tro fuy taulatz* 'until I was left the winner' (of the *joc grossier*) alone gives a satisfactory sense. It would also be possible to interpret *invictus manere* as 'to be equally matched, to have the same score (of two players at a game)', a sense which fits the passage from G. de Poitiers less well but receives support from some mod. dialect forms (*FEW*, loc. cit.;

NOTES 289

note in particular *tablâ* 'avoir le même nombre de points qu'un autre (au jeu de quilles, de cartes)').

1189 *tamboreçar*. Despite its isolation (*BDL* all have *-eiar*), this reading of *A* must be accepted, as it was by Stichel, p. 78, *SW* viii. 3 and *PD*. In a text which shows *verçier* < vĭrĭdiārium (2246), *-eçar* < -ĭzāre cannot be rejected as necessarily a scribal error (cf. Ronjat, ii, pp. 132–4).

1201 *trepar—manibus ludere*. The translation 'jouer des mains' (*SW* viii. 444, s.v. *trepar*, 4; *PD*; *FEW* xvii. 364 *trippōn) is unconvincing and otherwise unattested. Tobler (*Rom.* ii, p. 339) already considered *manibus* suspect and Chabaneau (*Rom.* vi, p. 136) emended to *pedibus*. Since a passage in R. de Cornet (*Deux mss. prov.* xx. 49, cited in *SW*, loc. cit.) castigates *trepar de mas* as a reprehensible activity which goes beyond *solasar*, it is probable that the sense intended by him and by the *Donatz* was 'to caress'; OFr. *tripot* (Godefroy, viii. 78; *FEW* xvii. 367) shows a similar semantic development.

1203 *terçar*. Sole example in *SW* viii. 195 for the sense 'to take a third part of'. The verb, given as intr. in *PD*, may well be tr. (cf. *quintar, quartar* 1114–15).

1205 *temptar*. In view of the parallel error at 1017 (see note), it is difficult to defend *A*'s *temprar* against the united reading of *BDL*.

1206 *trevar*. Despite *PD*, the verb is almost always intr.; cf. *SW* viii. 455–6.

1207 *entrevar*. Sole example in *SW* iii. 82–3 of the form with *-v-*; cf. *treva* beside *trega*.

1222 *trufar—verba vana dicere, vel fallere*. The senses 'to speak frivolous or empty words' and 'to deceive' are not admitted by *PD*: *SW* viii. 512 (where the *Donatz* is not cited) and *LR* v. 437 attest meanings close to these; cf. also *trufa* 'frivolité' (*PD*; *SW* viii. 511) and *trufairitz* 'trompeuse' (*PD*; *SW* viii. 511–12). *A*'s *facere* (for *fallere*) can be retained only by omitting *verba*.

1223 *vantar*. *A*'s *vanturar*, accepted in *SW* viii. 588, in *PD* and in *FEW* xiv. 156 vanitare, is quite isolated (cf. also Adams, who has no example of verb-formation in *-urar*). In view of this, together with the unanimity of *BDL* in favour of *vantar* and the absence of the word from the relatively frequent rhyme-series in *-ura*, the reading is better regarded as a scribal error, perhaps the result of misinterpretation of a correction in the form *vaůrar*, perhaps simply influenced by *aventurar*.

1231 *vespertinar*. Sole example in *SW* viii. 704, from Stichel, p. 82; cf. *FEW* xiv. 348–9 vĕspĕrtīnus.

1235 *vergar—virgas facere*. Levy opted for the interpretation 'to cut rods', for which the *Donatz* was his only source (*SW* viii. 667–8 and *PD*, followed by *FEW* xiv. 494 vĭrga). Much more probable, in view of the

1239 *upar—upare*. The sense of both Provençal and Latin is uncertain. *PD*'s 'chanter aussi longtemps que l'haleine le permettra?' is a conjecture suggested by Godefroy, iv. 529, s.v. *huper*, 'pousser un cri aussi long que l'haleine peut s'étendre' (*TL* iv. 1231, s.v., gives only 'schreien, rufen'). The only other OPr. example of *upar*, in G. de Cabrera's *Cabra joglar*, l. 211 (ed. Riquer in *Les Chansons de geste françaises*, p. 351), refers to some form of singing, as is the case in the single example of *uppatura* cited by Du Cange (med. Latin *upare* seems unattested elsewhere). In these circumstances, no sure translation of *upar* is possible. It is not mentioned in *FEW* iv. 515 HUP-, which is presumably where it belongs.

1241 *usclar—pilos comburere vel ustulare*. This is the only clear attestation in OPr. of the sense 'to singe (hair)', not specially noted in *PD* and *SW* viii. 545, but attested for OFr. *usler* (Godefroy viii. 123, cf. *FEW* xiv. 75–6 ŪSTŬLARE).

1246 *assezer—sedere*. The translator clearly intended the refl. and intr. sense 'to sit', quite well attested elsewhere (cf. *LR* v. 219; Appel, *Chrestomathie*, glossary) but oddly omitted by *PD*, where the verb is only mentioned as transitive.

1247 *caber*. See note to 584.

1256 *dechaçer—depauperare*. The tr. sense 'to impoverish' is absent from *PD*, from *SW* ii. 24–5, and from *LR* ii. 346; cf. in P. Cardenal, ed. Lavaud, xviii. 15, the adj. *decazei* 'ruiné, appauvri'.

1264 *pertraire—ad aliquod opus necessaria facere*. Sole example of this sense in *SW* vi. 282 (*PD*: 'faire les préparatifs nécessaires'). It is possible that the translator intended *opus* as 'work of construction' (Niermeyer, s.v. *opus*, 2); cf. the senses of *pertrach* (*SW* vi. 279–80. 3) and *pertrachura* (ibid. 282. 2).

1290 *fondre*. The intr. sense 'to melt', rendered here by *liquefieri*, is omitted in *PD*, though Raynouard has one clear example (*LR* iii. 355 = G. Magret, ed. Naudieth, vi. 48) and *Donatz* 2105 provides another.

1299 *escoissendre—per conum sindere*. *B*'s *per cossas* was apparently suggested by 945 *escoissar*. But neither Stengel's acceptance of *A*'s *per conis* nor Chabaneau's correction (*RLR* xiii, p. 141) to *per cuneis* is acceptable: *per* + abl. does not occur elsewhere in the translator's Latin. On the other hand *per conum* 'through the top of a helmet' (which is palaeographically more likely than *per coxas*) gives a sense in which *escoissendre* was commonly used. Raynouard and Levy happen not to have any example of it in this context, but cf. *Girart* 5270, 6617; *Roland à Saragosse* 668, 991; *Ronsasvals* 67, 723, in all of which the object of the verb is a hauberk.

1303 *mesprendre—delinquere.* A's *derelinquere* is no doubt another example of a misinterpreted correction (i.e. *de̊linquere*).

1308 *antreprendre.* I have accepted Tobler's explanation (*Rom.* ii, p. 339) of the *ante prendere* which figures as the translation of this word in *AB* as a misinterpretation of an interlinear *anteprendre* intended as an alternative form (cf. 2339–40, *antepres*).

1311 *escondre—excutere granum de paleis.* For the translation cf. note to 663.

1322 *desponre—deponere.* For the translation cf. note to 631.

1329 *tondre—tondere* (*media producta*). The last two words of the translation, indicating *tondĕre*, are strictly unnecessary, though *tondĕre* did exist in med. Latin (cf. Du Cange). It is possible, however, that *media producta* is misplaced and belonged originally in 1331 (indicating *assidēre* 'to besiege', not *assidĕre* 'to sit').

1335 *refrire—resonare.* Despite the doubts of Tobler (*Rom.* ii, p. 339) and Levy (*SW* vii. 160), the translation is acceptable. OPr. does not apparently offer a second example of this verb. But *TL* iii. 2269 has an example of OFr. *frire* 'to resound'; and *FEW* iii. 789 FRĪGĔRE has a number of mod. dialect forms with the meaning 'bruire'. The semantic change no doubt started from the sense 'frissonner', attested for OPr. *frir(e)* (*LR* iii. 400; *SW* iii. 603), which itself arose from a fusing of FRĪGĔRE with FRĪGĒRE (*FEW* iii. 797). For *refrire*, the influence of *refrinher* was clearly important.

1343 *esdemetre—assultum facere.* The existence of the form *esdesmetre*, admitted by Levy (*SW* ii. 462–3; *PD*), seems to depend solely on *B*'s reading here (with some support from *D*); it may well be a scribal error. For the sense 'to charge (in battle)' cf. *SW*, loc. cit., and *Girart* 5236.

1357 *bondir—apum est: sonare.* This is Levy's sole example (*SW* i. 155) in the sense 'to buzz (of bees)'; but cf. *FEW* i. 429 *BOMBITIRE, where the OPr. attestation of this sense should be added.

1362 *blaçir—marcescere.* *LR* (ii. 226) has no example of this form, for commoner *blezir*; cf. *FEW* i. 401–2 *BLAS-. It is impossible to tell whether the verb was used in this sense intransitively (as supposed in *PD*) or reflexively.

1363 *blanquir—candescere.* The translation indicates an intr. sense not given by *PD* and not clearly exemplified in *LR* ii. 223; for OFr. *blanchir*, tr. and intr., cf. Godefroy, viii. 328–9.

1367 *clocir.* Sole example in *SW* i. 264 (from Stichel, p. 26) of the form in *cl*-, for which *FEW* iv. 159 GLŌCĪRE cites also a 15th-century example.

1372 *recobrir—iterum operiri.* The verb is normally tr. (*LR* ii. 425; *SW* vii. 102; *PD*). If *operiri* is correct, one can only suppose that the translator envisaged a refl. use of the verb, perhaps with reference to the sky.

1378 *entruandir—mores trutani habere.* Sole example in *SW* iii. 97, from Stichel, p. 47. The verb may have been intr. or—perhaps more probably—refl.

1379 *ensalvatgir—silvestrem facere.* Sole example in *SW* iii. 29, from Stichel, p. 46. One may doubt whether such a verb was really used other than reflexively or in the p. part.—the only example of OFr. *ensauvagir*, other than the p. part., is intr. (*TL* iii. 508–9); cf., however, *Dicc. Alcover*, s.v.

1380 *enribaudir—more rabaldorum vivere.* Sole example in *SW* iii. 28, from Stichel, p. 46. Despite *PD*, it is not necessarily intr., cf. note to 1378. *A*'s *rabaldorum* may be merely a scribal *lapsus*; but Niermeyer, s.v. *ribaldus*, attests *rebaldus*, which may justify *A*'s spelling here.

1382 *endir—immitere.* This, with *B*'s translation *inire* = *hinnire*, is Levy's sole example of *endir* 'to neigh' (*SW* ii. 471, from Stichel, p. 43). Though there is no doubt of the existence of *endir* in this sense (cf. *FEW* iv. 427 HĬNNĪRE, where a second example is noted), it is unlikely that this is what we have in the *Donatz*. *A*'s *immitere* is acceptable if one allows it to have the sense 'to impose (a tax or payment)'; for this meaning, which is non-Classical (*TLL* vii. 1. 472), cf. Blaise and Niermeyer, s.v. *immissio*. This is precisely the sense of *endir* < ĬNDĪCĔRE (cf. *SW* ii. 471, s.v. *endire*, 2; *FEW* iv. 644). For the form *endir* without *-e*, cf. 1426 *mesdir*.

1386 *enpaubrechir.* This, like 1378 and 1380, may conceivably be (as in *PD*) intr. or refl. *LR* iv. 461 has three examples, all indecisive from this point of view.

1389 *escrimir—cum ense ludere.* The translation clearly indicates the meaning 'to fence', curiously absent from *PD*. Most passages in which the word occurs would admit the more general senses 'to fight', 'to defend oneself' (*LR* iii. 156–7; *SW* iii. 194); but Raynouard (*LR* iii. 157) has one example of the sb. *escrima* referring definitely to a game, not a battle. Cf. also 79 *escremire*.

1390 *escupir.* *A*'s *spernere* makes good sense as a rendering of the tr. meaning 'to spit on'; it is not necessarily a scribal error for the more obvious *spuere*, given by *B*.

1393 *estremir vel eschovir—tremefacere.* This is the only certain example of *estremir* in *SW* iii. 344–5, from Stichel, p. 56 (cf. *Dicc. Alcover*, s.v. *estremir*, 2); in *FEW* iii. 334 *EXTREMESCERE, 'trembler' is an error for 'faire trembler'. *Eschovir*, given only by *A*, is an enigma: Tobler's proposed corrections (*Rom.* ii, pp. 339–40)—*estobir, escharir, eschausir*—are unconvincing. *SW* iii. 164 registers the verb hesitantly, but it is dropped in *PD*. It may merely reflect a scribe's uncertainty in deciphering a hardly legible *estremir*. If it is authentic (and its absence from *BDL* proves nothing against its authenticity), it must be a scribal error for some OPr. verb meaning *tremefacere*. There are three possibilities: (1) *estonir* 'to stun, amaze', unattested in OPr., but cf. modern *estouni* 'étourdir' in *FEW* iii. 330 *EXTONARE; (2) *estornir* 'to stun'—for this type in mod. Franco-Provençal dialects cf. *FEW* xii. 322 STŪRNUS; there is an OPr. example in *Fierabras* 1175 (*estornit*; *SW* iii. 331, following Hofmann and Stichel, would emend to *estonat*); (3) *estormir* ~ *estornir* 'to assail, attack' (*LR* v. 380; *SW* iii. 332; *FEW* xvii. 266 *STŪRM)—the p. part. *estormit* 'taken aback' is clear in *Girart* 9244 (glossary: 'agiter') and *estornit* 'id.' in *Fierabras* 4097 (despite *LR*, loc. cit.: 'combattus'). Semantically, none of these corresponds exactly with *tremefacere*, though the distance between 'stunned' and 'terrified' is not great. Correction to *esthonir* is slightly preferable palaeographically, but *esthornir* has the merit of medieval attestations. In view of the uncertainty, *A*'s reading has been left in the text.

1397 *fremir—fremere*. The normal sense is 'to tremble', cf. *LR* iii. 394, and *tremere* would be a better Latin rendering; cf., however, *Abavus*, iii. 2777: 'fremere—tranbler *uel* fremir'.

1399 *freiçir—frigescere*. The intr. sense 'to grow cold' is omitted in *PD*, despite Raynouard's second example (*LR* iii. 390).

1400 *flechir*. Sole example cited by Levy (*SW* iii. 504), who was dubious about *B*'s *fletir*; this latter must surely be a mis-spelling either of *fleitir* (which is given by *D*) or of a learned *flectir*, otherwise unattested. It is doubtful, therefore, whether *fletir* has any real existence or any claim to be cited independently in *FEW* iii. 618 FLĔCTERE, where it is separated from *flechir*, classed under *FLĔCTICARE (iii. 618–19). This latter etymology is certainly correct, for MS. *A* nowhere shows *ch* as the reflex of KT. It is possible that *D*'s *fleitir* (and *B*'s *fle*[*i*]*tir*?) is a mistaken 'translation' of *flechir* in accordance with the equation *ch* = *it*.

1404 *fronir—inveterare*. Guessard printed the translation as *inventare* and was followed, inadvertently no doubt, by Stengel; Levy (*SW* iii. 605) registered the verb with puzzlement, not unnaturally. In fact *A*'s reading is quite clear. The translation corresponds with the adj. *fronit* 'brisé' registered by *PD*; the latter is the p. part. of our verb and is attested twice (*LR* iii. 393–4; *SW*, loc. cit.): *Croisade* 2142, *fronia* 'broken, shattered (of lances in battle)' and *Girart* 7759, var. *P, frunitz* 'worn out, weary (of a person)'. The translator renders the basic sense 'to wear out' which underlies these two uses of the word. The etymology of the word occupied Diez (*EtWb*, p. 591), who, rejecting *frunisci* as semantically too difficult, thought of med. Latin *frunire* 'to tan' (itself of unknown origin), but later etymologists seem to have neglected it: Corominas (*DCELC* ii. 584 n. 6, s.v. *fruncir*) notes the obscurity of its relation with *froncir*; *REW* and *FEW*, so far as I know, do not register the word. I would propose *fronit* < FRUNĪTUS, p. part. of FRUNĪSCĪ 'to enjoy, have the use of' (*TLL* vi. 1422–3, *frūnīscor*). The semantic development 'used' → 'worn out' is straightforward (cf. Fr. *usé*); the *ū* given in *TLL* is difficult, but one example, from an inscription, shows the spelling *froniti*. If *fronir* is independent of *froncir*, as this etymology would indicate, its influence may nevertheless explain why in Provençal *froncir*, unlike parallel forms in other Romance languages, developed the sense 'to break in pieces'.

1413 *gondir*. *A*'s reading may be accepted as a dissimilated form of *grondir*, though this is otherwise unattested in OPr., on the strength of OFr. *gondre*, for which see *TL* iv. 695. 22–4 and *FEW* iv. 290 GRŬNDĪRE (= *Roman de Renart*, ed. Martin, *ib*. 2734, var. *C*; ed. Roques, i. 2790, var. *a*—i.e. *gondre* is attested in two different MSS., if the editions are to be trusted).

1414 *golir*. Sole example in *SW* iv. 145, from Stichel, p. 60; *FEW* iv. 321 GŬLA, n. 14, incorrectly denies that the word is attested.

1417 *grupir*. *A*'s reading, for the commoner *gurpir* of *BDL*, is paralleled by a 3rd sg. pr. ind. form *grup* cited by Raynouard (*LR* iii. 516 = P. Cardenal, ed. Lavaud, ii. 50, var. *CT*).

1419 *jovenir*. Sole example in *SW* iv. 278, from Stichel, p. 61.

1420 *rejovenir—reiuvenescere*. Though given as tr. by *LR* iii. 595 and by *PD*, the translation here suggests an intr. sense parallel with that attested for OFr. *rejovenir* and *rajeunir* (Godefroy, vi. 757; x. 477): *reiuvenescere* seems to have been used intransitively (cf. Du Cange).

1422 *implir*. The alphabetical placing of the word, as well as the agreement of *ABDL*, clearly attests the countertonic *i*; this form is not in *SW* or *PD*, but *LR* iv. 570 attests *adimplir*. For the phonetic point involved cf. G. Millardet in *RLR* lvii, pp. 189–208, resumed in his *Linguistique et dialectologie romanes*, p. 157.

1424 *mentir*. *A*'s translation *mentire* is no doubt scribal (cf. 1425, 2136 *mentiris*), but none the less perfectly acceptable, cf. *TLL* viii. 776.

1428 *motir—motire vel mutire*. If *A*'s alternative translations have any point, the second must mean 'to utter (a word)', cf. Blaise, s.v. *mutio*, the first 'to designate', cf. Du Cange, s.v. *motire* (*PD* has 'indiquer', from Raynouard's single example, *LR* iv. 276).

1436 *palueçir—pallescere*. The OPr. reading was rejected by Galvani (p. 327), by Tobler (*Rom*. ii, p. 340), and by Levy (*ZRP* xv, p. 541; *SW* vi. 26); the *Donatz* furnishes the sole example, under the heading *palezir*, in *SW*, whence this latter form passed to *PD* and to *FEW* vii. 505 PALLIDUS. *D* alone attests *pallezir*, however, for *ABL* agree on the form with -*u*-. That one should read *palueçir* rather than *palveçir* is suggested by the existence of OFr. *paloïr* (Godefroy, v. 705) and *empaluïr* (*TL* iii. 85; cf. also F. Lecoy in *Rom*. lxxxviii, 1967, p. 430), possibly to be explained by the influence of liturgical *impalluit* (*FEW* vii. 506 n. 3); our verb should take its place beside these. There is at least one parallel OPr. form, unknown to the dictionaries. The second of the two lapidaries published by G. Contini has 'Calcedoynes es peyra d'espalva e reborca color' (*Vox*, iii, p. 271, § vi), translating the Latin words *hebeti pallore refulgens*. Contini (loc. cit., p. 262) was unable to explain *espalv*. It is no doubt preferable to read *espalua* (masc. *espalue), a back-formation on *espaluezir (*LR* iv. 401 has one example of *espalezir* = G. de Cabestanh, ed. Långfors, iii. 39).

1443 *pruir*. *Scalpere* 'to scratch' is merely a bad translation for 'to itch'; cf. 986, where *scalpere* is used correctly.

1445 *rauquezir*. Sole example in *SW* vii. 49, from Stichel, p. 68.

1447 *roizir*. Sole example in *SW* vii. 370, from Stichel, p. 73. *B*'s *rotzir*, accepted by *SW* and *PD* (though not by *FEW* x. 534 RŬBEUS) and used by Pfister (*Beiträge, Vox*, xvii, p. 325) as an example of pretonic *o* for *oi*, is simply a scribal error, paralleled in 1006 (*latrar* for *lairar*).

1451 *assalhir—assultum dare*. *B*'s *facere* is better Latin (Niermeyer, s.v. *adsaltus*; cf. 1343 *assultum facere*), but *A*'s *dare* is allowable as a literal rendering of *dar batalha* (*SW* ii. 8, s.v. *dar*, 3).

1457 *tendir—tinnire*. *Tendir* is unattested as a subsidiary form of *tendre*. *A*'s *tendere* is therefore to be rejected, as hesitantly suggested in *SW* viii. 137: the influence of the vernacular word sufficiently explains the scribal error in the Latin, encouraged also perhaps by the preceding *tradere*.

1467. The definition of the adverb is much briefer than those of Donatus (iv. 362. 15–16) and Priscian (ii. 20; xv. 1)—too brief, in fact, to be linked with any single source. In particular Faidit omits all mention of the function of the adverb.

1468–9 *batrei*. The 1st sg. fut. in *-ei* is noteworthy. Only *L* has the form in *-ai*, and that only in 1468.

1471. The three attributes of the adverb are those listed by Priscian (xv. 5); here, as for the noun (cf. note to 4–7), Faidit preferred Priscian's *species* to the *comparatio* of Donatus (iv. 362. 16–17). The explanation of *species*, unlike that given for the noun (cf. note to 8–11), is orthodox. *Figura* receives no further mention, no doubt because, in Provençal as in Latin, its subdivisions overlapped with those of *species*.

1473–96. In the enumeration of the types of adverb, Faidit uses categories selected from those given by Donatus (iv. 362. 17–32). He does not reproduce them all, nor does there seem to be any rational ground for his omissions. Medieval Latin grammars differ widely in the types of adverb they list; but Faidit's selection does not correspond with any of those listed by L. Jeep, *Zur Geschichte von den Redetheilen bei den lateinischen Grammatikern*, Leipzig, 1893, pp. 277–9. The adverbs of quality correspond with the *adverbia qualitatis* of Donatus (iv. 362. 27) and Priscian (xv. 35); the latter in fact cites *bene* and *male* as his examples. The fourteen adverbs of time include equivalents for the three examples of Donatus (iv. 362. 23–4: *hodie, nuper, aliquando*); the erroneous inclusion here of *mentre* seems not to be due to any Latin model. Priscian's classification (xv. 28–9) is more complex. The term *ajustamen* (Latin *adiunctionem*), covering the single example *essems*, is Faidit's own; the Latin grammarians classified *simul* and *una* as *adverbia congregandi* (Donatus, iv. 362. 31) or *congregativa* (Priscian, xv. 36). The demonstrative adverbs, exemplified by *veus me* and *vel vos*, correspond to the *adverbia demonstrandi* of Donatus (iv. 362. 25) and the *demonstrativa* of Priscian (xiii. 32; xv. 39); *en* and *ecce* are the only two examples, which Faidit's Provençal rendered as best it could. The adverbs expressing *afermamen* (*veramen* and *certamen*) were perhaps suggested by Donatus's *adverbia affirmandi* (iv. 362. 24–5: *etiam*, *quinni*); Priscian (xvii. 86) classed *etiam* as an *adverbium confirmativum*. The single interrogative adverb corresponds with the class of *adverbia interrogandi* of Donatus (iv. 362. 26) and the *interrogativa* of Priscian (xv. 39); the threefold translation of *per que* (*cur*, *quare*, *quamobrem*) in fact reproduces the three examples given by both Latin grammarians. The first six of the adverbs of place correspond exactly, in their order and in their Latin translations, with the six given by Donatus (iv. 362. 22–3), except that where the latter gives *illic* the *Donatz* has *illuc* (cf. note to 1493). The comparative adverbs correspond to the *adverbia comparandi* of Donatus (iv. 362. 32) and Priscian's *comparativa* (xv. 36) but do not precisely reproduce the former's *magis, tam* nor the latter's *magis, minus*.

1481. *AD*'s *atan* for *antan*, though it may be merely scribal, is explicable as an otherwise unattested dissimilated form, cf. Ronjat, ii, p. 369 for *tatecant, quatecant, atau* (= *altal). *A*'s *alio* for *alio anno* is admissible after the immediately preceding *hoc anno*.

1482. *A* alone has *man*, which is not necessarily to be regarded as an error for *mati*. Though *PD* registers the word only as a noun, Faidit was justified in classing it as an adverb, since its use seems to have been limited to adverbial phrases (cf. *LR* iv. 132; *FEW* vi. 181–2 MĀNĔ).

1493. The translation *idem*, intended to cover *lai* and *zai*, is correct in the sense that these can have the same meanings as *de lai* and *de çhai* respectively (cf. *SW* iv. 301. 4; vii. 425. 10). But the meanings actually attached to these last two expressions by the translator are bizarre: *illuc* 'to that place' does not fit *de lai*, nor is *inde* 'from there' quite right for *de çhai*. The errors can hardly be scribal and are best regarded as mere carelessness on the translator's part.

1496. *A*'s *maormen* for usual *maiormen* is not attested in *SW* v. 39–40 (nor ibid. 37, s.v. *major*), but Appel, *Lautlehre*, p. 62, attests *maer* and *maor*.

1497–9. The definition of the participle closely follows that of Donatus (iv. 363. 13–15), which is reproduced by virtually all medieval writers on grammar; Priscian (xi. 8) has a rather different formulation. Faidit gives no attributes of the participle, no doubt because the definition included mention of all of them.

1503 *presantz*. *A*'s *aprecians se*, against *B*'s *apretians*, is a *lectio difficilior*. *SW* vi. 533 has a single example of *prezan* 'arrogant', which Levy regarded as dubious. But *se prezar* 'to value oneself too highly', which is unknown to the dictionaries, occurs in *Girart* 9896; *FEW* ix. 372 PRĔTIUM notes *soi prisier* for OFr. and refl. *prezá* for Toulouse. The translator's Latin was no doubt suggested by this refl. use of the verb.

1508. The definition of the conjunction seems to derive from Donatus's equally brief but more precise formulation (iv. 364. 33); those of Priscian (ii. 21; xvi. 1) are much more circumstantial. Faidit mentions no attributes of the conjunction. Of the three given by Donatus (iv. 364. 34), *ordo* had no application to Provençal and *figura* could have little relevance, while the classes of conjunction listed by Faidit fulfil the same functions as the various subdivisions of the third attribute, *potestas*.

1509–22. The classes of conjunctions do not correspond with those given by any single Latin grammarian, cf. Jeep, op. cit. [note to 1473–96], pp. 284–8, though there are a number of parallels with the *Ars minor*. Faidit follows Donatus (iv. 364. 36–7) in counting *e* alone as a *copulativa*; Priscian (xvi. 2) included *sed* and *autem* also, but Faidit places *mas* in another class. The class of *ordinativas* was suggested by nothing in either Donatus or Priscian. The erroneous classification of *d'er enan, d'aqui enan, d'aqui en reire* as conjunctions seems to be independent of any Latin model. The *asimilativas* likewise correspond to nothing in Donatus or Priscian. Of the four examples, *atressi* and *quais* are not strictly conjunctions; it is possible that Faidit was thinking of *atressi cum* and *quais que*, though the translations *taliter* and *quasi* do not confirm this. The *expletivas* follow Donatus (iv. 364. 37–9), whose list includes *saltem, videlicet*, and *quamvis*; the first of these explains the inclusion here of the adverb *sivals*. The *disjunctivas* follow Donatus (iv. 364. 37), for Priscian's *disiunctivae* (xvi. 7) include no equivalent of Provençal *ni*. No doubt through a lapse of memory, the *racionals* reproduce, not Donatus' *rationales* (iv. 365. 3–5), but his *causales* (iv. 364. 39–365. 3), which include, among others, *si, etiamsi, quando, nam, sed, interea, praeterea*. These correspond exactly, even in the order of their occurrence, with the examples in the *Donatz*. The inclusion here of the adverbs *entretan* and *esters aiço* is justified by Donatus' classification of their Latin equivalents. And the presence in the Provençal list of the adverb *neis* (untranslated here but equivalent to *etiam*, as in 2005) is no doubt due to an inexact recollection of the Latin grammarian's *etiamsi*. (It is worth noting that neither Priscian's *rationales* nor his *causales* [xvi. 11–12 and 4–5] show any similarity with Faidit's *racionals*.)

1512. The *Donatz* provides the sole example of *d'aqui en reire* in *SW* i. 75; there are two examples of *d'aqui a d'en reire* in Brunel, *Chartes*, i. 264. 12 and 14 (the glossary, s.v. *reire*, mistranslates 'désormais').

1525 *naps*. Levy cited this form dubiously in *SW* ii. 418, s.v. *enap*, but did not include it in *PD*; *FEW* xvi. 214 *HNAPP omits it. It is, however, perfectly admissible: for a second example cf. the *coblas PC*. 393. 3 in *Archiv*, l, p. 263, no. VII, where *nap* in l. 12 is attested by the scansion; cf. also *Dicc. Alcover*, s.v. *nap*¹, and *Dicc. Aguiló*, s.v. *nap*, 4.

1529 *graps—manus curva*. Sole example in *SW* iv. 170; *PD* renders 'main crochue?' The sense is no doubt 'hooked claw'; cf. *Novum Glossarium*, s.v. *manus*, II. For the sense 'griffe' cf. *FEW* xvi. 358 and 361 *KRAPPA.

1532 *taps—lutum.* Sole example in *SW* viii. 57, where, however, Mistral's *tap* is noted; cf. *FEW* xxi. 38–9.

1533 *laps—gremium.* Sole example in *SW* iv. 322 of this word, to which Levy attributed the sense 'sein, giron' (*PD*). This is improbable. The translation of 1705 *pans* shows *gremium* in the sense 'flap or skirt of a garment' (cf. *TLL* vi. 2320), and that is no doubt what the translator intended here. *Laps* is part of the family of *LABBA (*FEW* xvi. 431–4). Von Wartburg—misled by Levy's interpretation—does not include it and observes (ibid. 433) that the simplex of the type LAB- (his i. 1) is not preserved while that of the type LAP- (his ii. 1) is only attested much later than its derivatives. The attestation in the *Donatz* fills in this lacuna. Semantically, it continues the basic sense 'loosely hanging piece of material'—the closest of *FEW*'s mod. dialect forms is *lap* 'trouser-flap' at Châtenois (Belfort) (ibid. 432). (*FEW* xxi. 305 may thus be corrected.)

1537 *abacs—abacus.* The translation was no doubt intended in the sense 'arithmetic' (cf. Du Cange, Niermeyer, s.v.), attested for the OPr. word in *LR* ii. 10 (*SW* and *PD* omit it).

1538 *cracs—sanies naris.* Sole example in *SW* i. 399; cf. *FEW* ii. 2. 1267 KRAKK-, where the word is inadvertently given as OFr.

1540 *escacs—ligneus ludus.* For *ligneus ludus* in the sense 'chess-man', 'gaming-piece (made of wood)', cf. 2651 (where 'game played with wooden pieces' is impossible), 3409 and probably 2656. In the sense 'game of chess' the translator used *schacos* in 1878.

1543 *tacs—morbus porcorum.* Sole example in *SW* viii. 5; mod. Languedocien *tac* 'maladie qui se manifeste par des taches rousses' is classed by *FEW* xvii. 294 under TAIKNS, which is no doubt where the OPr. word should also be placed.

1544 *vacs—vacuus.* Sole example in *SW* viii. 554 for the sense 'empty'. *PD* rightly has 'oisif, inoccupé' only, an interpretation of *vacuus* borne out by *SW*'s second example of *vac.*

1548 *abracs.* Sole example of *abragar* in *SW* i. 7, to which should be added *Recettes des Pyrénées*, §§ 590, 597 (pp. 100, 102); cf. *FEW* i. 489 *BRACU.

1550 *caf—impar.* Sole example in *SW* i. 184; cf. *FEW* xix. 75–6 QAFĀ, where this is the only example for Provençal of any period. The word is possibly to be regarded as a mere adaptation of Italian *caffo.*

1551 *baf.* Levy's sole example of this exclamation (*SW* i. 172, s.v. *buf*), omitted from *PD* and from *FEW* i. 203 *BAFF.

1556 *cabals.* The translation *acceptabilis* confirms Levy's 'agréable, aimable?' (*PD*), for which cf. *SW* i. 176, s.v. *cabal*, 2 and the references given there, especially At de Mons, ed. Bernhard, ii. 1180 ('Lauzors non es cabals, / S'us avols homz la da').

1563 *pals—pallum.* For *pallum* 'fence' cf. *Abavus*, iv. 6027.

NOTES

1572 *maials—maialis.* Sole example in *SW* v. 17 'Schwein' (and *PD*: 'cochon'). Despite Levy, the Latin is to be taken in its normal sense 'castrated pig'. *FEW* vi. 52 MAIALIS notes that all southern French reflexes of this word belong to the Gascon area.

1573 *ivernals—iemalis.* The sense 'pertaining to winter', not given in *PD* and not clearly attested in *LR* iii. 577, is certainly intended here (cf. *estivals,* which follows). *FEW* iv. 419 HĪBĔRNUS lacks *ivernal* in any sense.

1583 *jornals—caput unius diei.* The translator envisaged the use of *jornal* as a unit of land measurement ('area which could be ploughed in one day'). It is unnecessary, however, to follow Guessard, Stengel, and Levy (*SW* iv. 273, s.v. *jornal,* 6) in emending to *campus;* cf. Niermeyer, s.v. *caput,* 21, and Du Cange, s.v. *caput,* 1, for the use of this word as a land measure.

1589 *terrenals.* The translator's *terrenalis* (for *terrenus*) seems to be absent from the dictionaries of classical or med. Latin.

1602 *glais.* The sense of the translation *findecane* is obscure: the reading is uncertain and resists attempts at emendation. Stengel printed 'fina cane?' for which Chabaneau (*RLR* xiii, p. 141) proposed *fina canna* 'reed'; but *glai* is not attested in this sense, and the translator does not elsewhere use *finus* (cf. 2517 *fis—valde bonus*).

1603 *esglais—timeas.* This is Levy's sole example for *esglaiar,* v. tr., 'to fear' (*SW* iii. 228; *PD*). Since *timere* is intr. as well as tr., it is preferable to suppose that the translator intended *esglaiar,* v. refl., 'to be afraid' (which is attested elsewhere, cf. *SW,* loc. cit.).

1607 *cais.* Cf. note to 170.

1619 *entais—in luto mitas.* Sole example of *entaiar* in *SW* iii. 42, from Stichel, p. 46. Cf. *thai* (conjectured) 'mud' in P. Vidal, ed. Avalle, xxxv. 84, and OFr. *tai* (Godefroy, vii. 623) and *entaiier* (*TL* iii. 544).

1621 *Clavais.* Cf. note to 173.

1622 *Roiais,* for usual *Roais.* This form, on which *AL* agree here, is attested also in B. de Born, ed. Stimming (1879), ix. 23, var. *B.*

1624–40. The rhymes in -*altz* are distinguished from those in -*als* (1555–92): the present series shows etyma in LT + S, LD + S, LKJ, LK^e, and LL + S, while those in -*als* show only L + S. For Faidit there was a real phonetic difference between the reflexes of, for example, -LUS and -LLUS, a fact which is borne out by the later rhyme-series in -*elz* (2028–59; cf. note to 2009–22) and -*olz* (2688–2701, cf. note). A similar distinction is made by the *Leys d'Amors* (ed. Gatien-Arnoult, vol. 1, p. 38; ed. Anglade, vol. 2, p. 44), though the 14th-century text, unlike the *Donatz* (3252–3343), makes it for feminine rhymes as well as for masculine. The practice of the troubadours does not in general show an observance of this distinction (cf. Lienig, pp. 87–90); it would seem to depend on the preservation of the double articulation of -LL- (as against the usual Provençal reflexes

[l] and [l']), a feature attested in mod. dialects in Languedoc and Gascony (cf. Lienig, pp. 86–7; Ronjat, ii, pp. 148–52). The *Donatz* makes a further distinction within the rhymes in *-altz*, in that forms in *-autz* are considered permissible for all words except those where *-altz* < ALL + S. Again, some troubadours provide exceptions to this, e.g. B. de Born, ed. Appel, xxii. 3, 18, 42 (*chavaus, vassaus*); A. Daniel, ed. Toja, xiii. 2 (*vaus* < VALLES); cf. Lienig, pp. 91–2, where there are also a few examples of *-au* < -ALLUM. But these rhymes are much less frequent than those showing *-aus* < -ĀLIS and perhaps never became a standard part of literary usage.

1642. *A*'s *senescals*, though it is clearly scribal here, is perfectly admissible (cf. *LR* v. 200; *PD*).

1643 *auricalcs*. The translator's *auricalcus* (for usual *-um*) seems to be absent from dictionaries of classical and med. Latin.

1646 *bralhz*. The *Donatz* makes it clear that *brail*, admitted (like *brailar*) in *PD*, is merely a graphy for *bralh* (cf. the examples in *LR* ii. 248); *FEW* i. 490–1 *BRAG- (§ ii *BRAGULARE), which follows *PD*, should be modified in consequence.

1648 *escalhz—frustum teste*. Sole example of this sense in *SW* iii. 141; the translator indicates a more precise meaning than *PD*'s 'écaille, éclat' or *FEW*'s 'petit éclat' (xvii. 90 *SKALJA).

1650 *teiralhz—territorium*. Sole example of this sense in *SW* viii. 186, s.v. *terralh*, 2, 'Gebiet'. The form shows a further example of *-ir-* < *-rr-* (cf. Introduction, p. 59). In this instance, however, there is a parallel outside the *Donatz*: Brunel, *Chartes*, i. 159 (ll. 3, 7, 8, and 9) attests *teiral* 'earth-bank' four times in a document of 1177, from Rouergue. Pfister, *Beiträge* (*Vox*, xvii, p. 318) classed this among his examples of alternation of *e* and *ei* in the pretonic syllable but subsequently (*Vox*, xviii, p. 296), following a suggestion of P. Nauton, attached *teiral* to the family of *TĔRĪ. Neither explanation seems to me satisfactory. The etymology via TĔRĪ, even if conceivable for *teiral*, is surely impossible for *teiralhz* unless one is to suppose the secondary influence of TĔRRA; cf. *FEW* xvii. 325–7, where neither word is included. For the *Donatz*, at least, the explanation of *-ir-* < *-rr-* is well supported by the other examples of the same feature. This is not to deny possible secondary influence of TĔRRA on the family of *TĔRĪ, cf. in particular Puisserguier (Hérault) *counteiral* 'compatriote' (*FEW* xvii. 326).

1662 *coralhz*. *PD* wrongly admits only *coral*, despite Raynouard's two examples of *coralh* (*LR* ii. 479), to which may be added *Recettes de Montpellier*, ed. Brunel in *Rom*. lxxviii, p. 308 (§ 39b). These reflexes of CORALLIUM should be added to *FEW* ii. 2. 1178, where OPr., like OFr., is credited only with forms continuing late Latin CORALLUM.

1667–8 *raspalhz—qui remanet de palea*; *respalhz—coligas residuum de paleis*. The substantive is attested once in OPr. outside this passage, cf.

LR v. 44–5 = B. de Venzac, *PC*. 71. 1 (Appel, *Inedita*, pp. 50–2), l. 40, *raspalh*; the verb occurs only here (*SW* vii. 39, from Stichel, p. 71; cf., for Catalan, *Dicc. Alcover*, s.v. *raspallar*, 2). The variation *ras-* ~ *res-* is preserved in *PD*, whence also in *FEW*: vii. 499 PALEA gives *respalhar* in complete isolation; but xvi. 670 RASPÔN has *raspalh* surrounded by a sizeable family of dialect forms. No doubt the OPr. verb would be better included in this second family, where the types ⌜*raspalhar*⌝ and ⌜*respalhar*⌝ both occur. It is not necessary, therefore, to explain *respalhz* as merely a graphy, though this remains a possible explanation.

1687 *afams—a fame constringas*. The Latin is odd and it would perhaps be better to emend by omitting *a*, as suggested by Stengel (p. xxvii, additional note to 42a, 17). Emendation to *afams—afame[s]*, [*liams*]—*constringas* is not unthinkable.

1689 *tams—par*. Emendations to *Cams* 'the Great Cham' (Tobler, *Rom*. ii, p. 340; Chabaneau, *Rom*. vi, pp. 136–7) and to *lams—pareas* (Stengel, n. to 42a, 19) have been proposed; but the former is irreconcilable with the translation *par* and the latter gives a bizarre rendering for *lampar*, which anyway seems unattested in OPr. (for modern reflexes of Greek LAMPEIN, cf. *FEW* v. 145). It is preferable to accept the text without correction and to see in *tam* the antonym of *caf—impar* (1550). Both words are *hapax legomena*, but, while *caf* is supported by other reflexes of Arabic QAFĀ (cf. *FEW* xix. 75–6), *tam* seems to be without analogues in other Romance languages. It is possible that it is an isolated reflex of Arabic TĀMM 'complete'.

1696 *blans—blandus*. Sole example in *SW* i. 148; a second example, noted by Schultz-Gora (*Provenzalische Studien*, ii, p. 117, n. to 46) in Bermon Rascas, is more probably a verb-form. Cf. *FEW* i. 394 BLANDUS and *Dicc. Aguiló*, s.v. *bla*, which justify the rejection of the simple emendation to *blandiris*.

1698 *avans—antea*. *PD* admits only *avan*, but cf. *Flamenca* 2478 for an example of *avanz* at the rhyme.

1699 *cans—cambias*. The translator clearly intended this as 2nd sg. pr. subj. of *cam(b)iar*. It is the only instance in the rhymes in *-ans* where $n < M$ (1703 *dans* < DAMNUM is not strictly parallel) and is possibly to be regarded as a translator's error.

1700 *descans—cantus contra cantum*. It is not clear whether the intended sense is 'descant' or 'song composed against (i.e. as an attack or satire on) an existing song'. The only other example of the word (*LR* ii. 314 and *SW* ii. 118 = A. Catalan, ed. Blasi, iv. 11 and 15) is equally unclear: Blasi interprets 'descant, accompaniment in song', though the context would also permit 'song imitating the form and melody of another song'.

1702 *acans—in latus declines*. Sole example of *acantar* in *SW* i. 11, from Stichel, p. 7. *PD* interprets 'poser de chant, sur le côté'. It may be either v. tr. 'to turn (sthg.) on its side' or v. refl. 'to lean sideways' (cf. *TL* i. 80–1 for OFr. *achanter*). The interpretation of *acantelar* (*Donatz* 3280) poses a similar problem.

1704 *afans—fatigatio; fatiges*. *Afan* and *afanar* do not seem to be attested in the senses 'weariness', 'to weary' (*LR* ii. 31; *SW* i. 24–5; *PD*), which, however, are obvious extensions of the basic idea of 'trouble, pain'; cf. also *Dicc. Aguiló*, s.v. *afany*, 2. (*PD*'s 'se fatiguer' for refl. *afanar* derives from Raynouard's weak translation of B. de Ventadour, ed. Appel, xxxvii. 50.)

1705 *pans—pars vel panus vel gremium*. The second translation is best rendered 'piece of cloth'; 'banner' is also possible (cf. Niermeyer, s.v. *pannus*, 2; Du Cange, s.v. *pannus*, 5), but there is no clear OPr. example of this sense: B. de Born, ed. Appel, xvii. 22, permits of other interpretations (cf. *SW* vi. 40). The third translation is 'flap or skirt of a garment' (cf. note to 1533).

1720 *mans—suavis*. Sole example in *SW* v. 113; cf. *Dicc. Aguiló*, s.v.

1723 *desmans—mandes contra mandatum*. Levy's correction to *contramandatum* (*SW* ii. 147) is unnecessary; one would anyway expect *contramandamentum* or *contramandum* (cf. Du Cange).

1733 *tans—tannes, et cortex arboris ad coria paranda*. *A*'s *tantes* was presumably induced by *tantos* (1732); one would expect *vel* rather than *et*, however.

1734 *achointans—eloquens*. This is the sole example in *SW* i. 14 for *acomtan* 'eloquent' (similarly *PD*). In view of the existence of *mal acoindan* (Appel, *Chrestomathie*, 97. 46) and *gen aconhdan* (G. de Bornelh, ed. Kolsen, vii. 64), the correction of *m* to *in* is clear and receives some support from *L*. The adj. derives from *acointar*, not *acomtar*; *FEW* ii. 2. 995 COMPUTARE needs correction in consequence.

1739 *eirans*. No doubt to be taken as a further example of *-ir-* < *-rr-*, rather than as a reflex of ĬTĔRARE, which would be highly unlikely in OPr., cf. *FEW* iv. 824–5.

1749 *crancs*. Med. Latin *crançum*, for *crancus*, seems otherwise unattested.

1750 *dancs—color quidam*. Neither from this nor from the other OPr. example (P. Vidal, ed. Avalle, xv. 36) is it possible to ascertain the precise colour called *danc*; *PD*'s 'brun?' (from *SW* ii. 7) is a guess.

1752 *sancs—sinistrarius*. This and *Donatz* 3455 are the only examples in *SW* vii. 456. The word seems to have no parallel in other Romance languages; cf. *FEW* xxi. 309. For *sinistrarius*, absent from dictionaries of med. Latin, cf. a second example in 2272.

1755 *mancs—mancus*. The interpretations 'crippled' and 'one-handed' are equally possible; though no absolutely clear OPr. example is cited by Levy (*SW* v. 84) for the latter sense, it is unambiguously indicated for *manca* (3454).

1756 *esmancs—auferas manum.* Sole example of *esmancar* in *SW* iii. 237, from Stichel, p. 52; cf. also *Dicc. Alcover*, s.v. Omitted in *FEW* vi. 139 MANCUS (i. 1. b).

1758 *afancs—in luto intres.* The intr. sense indicated by the translator must belong to *afangar* used reflexively, for it is otherwise attested only in the tr. sense 'embourber' (*LR* iii. 259; *PD*).

1759 *tancs—parvum lignum acutum.* Sole example in *SW* viii. 52 for the sense 'splinter'. It is perhaps more likely that the sense intended here and in the second of Levy's examples (where he translates 'tree-stump') was 'thorn', though this is not substantiated by the material in *FEW* xii. 233–4 *STANTICARE. Cf. also note to 2936, where the same Latin words are used to translate *escotz*.

1767 *blars—glaucus.* Sole example in *SW* i. 148; cf. *FEW* i. 401 *BLĀROS.

1772 *flars—lumen magnum.* *SW* iii. 501 cites this example and *Flamenca* 7496, where the meaning seems rather more specific. For another example in the same sense as in the *Donatz* cf. *Vida de Sant Frances*, ed. Arthur, iv. 4. 2.

1789 *enarcs.* *SW* ii. 419–20 cites only one other example of *enarcar*, in which the sense is uncertain.

1801 *enbartz—luto inficias.* Sole example of *embartar* in *SW* ii. 356, from Stichel, p. 41. The examples grouped in *FEW* i. 264 *BARRUM suggest that the infinitive may in fact have been *embardar*.

1805 *essartz—procindas vomere.* Sole example in *SW* ii. 331 for the literal sense of this verb.

1807 *gollarz—ardens in gula.* The correction to *goliarz*, recommended by Tobler (*Rom.* ii, p. 340) and Stengel and hesitantly accepted by Levy (*SW* iv. 144, 145; cf. *PD*: '*golart*, v. *goliart*'), is not essential, though it is supported by *L*'s *golliartz*. *Goliart* 'impostor' is attested by Raynouard's second example (*LR* iii. 421 = *Sant Honorat*, ed. Suwe, 1435); *goliart* 'glutton' seems to be attested solely by MS. *L* of our text (supported by OCat. *goliart*, cf. *Dicc. Alcover, Aguiló*, s.v.), while *golart* 'id.' depends solely on MS. *A*. *FEW* iv. 318 GŬLA follows Levy in including *L*'s reading and neglecting that of *A*. But there is in fact nothing to choose between the two readings and *golart* should be added to the forms with -*l*- (as distinct from -*li*- or -*lh*-) in *FEW*, loc. cit.; our example considerably antedates those cited by von Wartburg, whose French forms with -*l*- go back no further than 1596 and whose Provençal forms draw exclusively on mod. dialect material. The translator's *ardens in gula* is at once a translation and an 'etymology'; *gula* is of course to be taken in the sense of 'gluttony'.

1811 *penartz—fasanus avis.* Sole example in *SW* vi. 202. The only parallel formation in *FEW* viii. 527 PĬNNA is mod. Picard *pennard* 'canard à longue queue'.

1813 *falsartz—gladius brevis et acutus*. This seems to be the sole attestation, in either OPr. or OFr. (cf. *SW* iii. 404–5; *TL* iii. 1643; for the sense in *Croisade* 4894 cf. Martin-Chabot's ed., vol. 2, p. 191 n. 11), of *falsart* in the sense of 'sword' or 'dagger'; but cf. Du Cange, s.v. *falsarius*, 1, where the med. Latin form of the word seems to refer to some sort of dagger.

1816 *Mainartz—Mainardus*. This is to be taken as a proper name which the translator Latinized instead of providing his more usual *proprium nomen*.

1820 *Rainartz—vulpis vel proprium nomen*. This is Levy's sole example (*SW* vii. 8; *PD*) for *rainartz* 'fox', and this is accepted in *FEW* xvi. 688 REGINHART. In view of its isolation in OPr. it seems preferable to suppose that by *vulpis* the translator simply intended the hero of the *Roman de Renart*.

1821 *Falartz—castellum vel proprium nomen*. *Talartz*, given by *L*, is perhaps the correct reading, cf. the name *Taillar* in Flutre and the modern surname *Taillard*. Is the place-name then *Tallard* (Hautes-Alpes)?

1826 *aucs*. Sole example in *SW* i. 101; cf. *FEW* i. 169 AUCA.

1827 *baucs—qui ponitur supra manica cultelli*. This is Levy's only example in precisely this sense, cf. *SW* i. 134; in his second example (from the *Chanson d'Antioche*) the word apparently denotes 'rings' or 'ferrules' round a trumpet. Cf. also *FEW* i. 300 *BAUG. For Alart's erroneous identification of the word with Catalan *bavech* see note to 1970.

1829 *glaucs*. *A*'s *claucus* for *glaucus* is acceptable Latin, cf. *TLL* vi. 2038–40.

1830 *naucs*. The OPr. examples of this word seem to be limited to Rouergue and the départements of Tarn and Tarn-et-Garonne (*FEW* vii. 59 *NAVĬCA).

1834 *enraucs—raucus fias*. Sole example in *SW* iii. 25, from Stichel, p. 45.

1835–54. Two of the nineteen words in *-aus* show vocalization of *l*: *galengaus* 1854 and *nadaus* 1850, against *nadals* 1571. The fact that only one of the thirty-seven rhymes in *-als* (1555–92) is repeated in the later series suggests that the pronunciation with [u̯], though known to Faidit, was regarded by him as not entirely standard or that he felt it correct to maintain a distinction which was perhaps in the process of becoming obscured in the spoken language as he knew it. His hesitation over *nadals* ∼ *nadaus* no doubt reflects the uncertainties of a period of transition; in *galengaus* the change *-als* > *-aus* may well have been hastened by a tendency to dissimilation. It is well known that the rhymes of the troubadours admitted forms with vocalized *l* after *a* from the beginning. Vocalization was and is attested over a wide area of the Midi; cf. Lienig, pp. 90–2; Ronjat, ii, pp. 205–9.

1837 *blaus—bludus vel aereus*. Neither Tobler's *lividus* (*Rom.* ii, p. 341) nor Chabaneau's *blundus* (*Rom.* vi, p. 137) are convincing emendations. Baxter–Johnson cites an example of *bludus* 'blue' for 1249, cf. also *blodus* in Du Cange.

1854 *galengaus*. Apart from this example, Levy and Raynouard attest only *guareng(u)al* (*SW* iv. 19; *LR* iii. 516); cf. also *galengar* in the *Recettes de Montpellier*, ed. Brunel in *Rom.* lxxviii, p. 309 (§ 42), and *galenguar* in *Recettes des Pyrénées*, § 490 (p. 75). The *-l-* is supported by med. Latin *galenga* ~ *galanga* (Niermeyer, Du Cange), by OCat. *galengal* (cf. *Dicc. Aguiló*, s.v.), and by the etymology (cf. *FEW* xix. 61–3 ḤALANǦĀN).

1862. While *semitaurs* is attested a second time in OPr. (*LR* v. 309), *semitaurus* seems to be absent from dictionaries of Classical and med. Latin.

1863 *maurs—niger*. This and *Donatz* 3246 are the only examples of *maur* 'black' in *SW* v. 147; cf., however, *FEW* vi. 547 MAURUS and n. 17 (p. 556).

1888 *transgitatz—decipite: ad incantatores pertinet* (cf. 1889 *transgitatz— deceptus*). The sense 'to deceive', absent from *LR* iii. 471, *SW* viii. 386–7, and *PD*, is supported by *trasgitamen* 'deceit' (*SW* viii. 386) and suggested by Raynouard's second example s.v. *trasgitaire* (*LR*, loc. cit.); cf. also *Dicc. Alcover*, s.v. *tragitar*, 1, and *Dicc. Aguiló*, s.vv. *tragitador*, *tragitayre*. The connection with mountebanks and conjurers is clear in most of Levy's and Raynouard's examples for the verb and the related nouns; cf. also *FEW* v. 21 JĀCTĀRE. The meaning intended by the translator in 1888 may well have been 'to perform tricks by sleight of hand'; the phrase *ad incantatores pertinet* was possibly intended to apply to 1889 as well as 1888.

1893 *juciatz*. Cf. note to 1002.

1900 *refathz—impinguatus*. Sole example of the sense 'fattened up' in *SW* vii. 142, s.v. *refaire*, 3; cf. Godefroy, x. 515 for OFr. *refait* 'id.'.

1904 *enpahz—inpedimentum*. With *A*'s reading *enlahz* uncorrected, this constitutes Levy's sole example of *enlach* (*SW* iii. 6; *PD*). The emendation is self-evident; *enlach is a ghost-word.

1905 *pahz—pactum vel stultus*. Sole example in *SW* vi. 3 for both senses; *PD* has *pach* only in the second sense. *FEW* vii. 461–3 PACTUM has no popular reflex other than *pacha* < PACTA: von Wartburg does not cite the present example, which clearly belongs there, though he gives a number of OPr. learned forms from the 13th century on. As already noted by Chabaneau (*Rom.* vi, p. 137), *pahz* 'stupid' is evidently a reflex of PATIE(N)S parallel with Italian *pazzo*; since it is otherwise unattested in OPr., it may simply be adapted from the Italian. *FEW* viii. 16–17 PATIENS omits the OPr. word, as does *REW* 6292.

1911 *alavahz*. Sole example in *SW* i. 47.

1913 *retrahz—turpis recordatio benefitii*, i.e. 'expression of ingratitude, undeserved reproach'. The sense indicated by the translator is a specialized use of the general meaning 'reproach' (*SW* vii. 297–8, s.v. *retrach*, 4; *PD*).

1919 *bas*. *A* shows *dimissus* for *demissus*, a frequent confusion, cf. *TLL* v. 1. 488, s.v. *demitto*.

1934 *abbas—abas*. Chabaneau's correction to *albas* [< *ALBĀNUS]—*albus* (*Rom.* vi, p. 137) is tempting, since it would explain the presence of the word in the rhymes in *-as estreit* (< -ĀNUS, etc.). The correction was accepted by von Wartburg (*FEW* i. 62 ALBUS, cf. 64 n. 1) but reproduced with an error, so that *albe*—a ghost-word—stands at the head of the relatively few reflexes of ALBUS which retain the original meaning; the same *albe* has been given wider currency by Pfister (*Beiträge, Vox*, xviii, p. 254, no. 48). In fact Chabaneau's correction is not absolutely necessary: n. sg. *abáz* (for *ábas*) is attested by scansion in *Girart* 265, 366, and n. sg. *abás* is equally conceivable; the quality of the *a* is explicable by the influence of *capelas, degas*. Correction by placing *abbas* after 1932 would presuppose a common error of *AL* or an error of O^2.

1938 *vilas*. The translation *vilicus* is no doubt intended as 'rustic', though this sense seems not to be given in Latin dictionaries.

1943 *cirurgias—cirurgicus*. This is Levy's sole example in the adjectival sense 'surgical' (*SW* i. 255; *PD* lacks the word). The intended meaning is evidently the substantival one 'surgeon'; for med. Latin cf. Niermeyer, Du Cange, Baxter–Johnson; for OPr. cf. the examples in the Provençal *Chirurgia*, 24, 597, 889, and 1177 (*Archivum Romanicum*, xxv, pp. 7, 29, 41, and 52), also *FEW* ii. 1. 641 CHIRURGIA.

1944 *tavas*. *PD*'s *tavan* is an error for *tavaṇ*.

1960. The Latinism *civitat*, absent from *PD*, is confirmed by a second example, from an act of 1040, in *LR* ii. 399.

1965 *cecs—signum ad sagittam*. Sole example in *SW* i. 238 of *cec* 'target', tenuously supported by Italian *azzeccare* 'hit (a target)' (Galvani, p. 329; cf. *DEI*, s.v.; *REW* 9610 ZECKEN does not mention *cec*, perhaps rightly). It is possible that the words *vel signum ad sagittam* belong with *decs* (1966), which seems to be used with the sense 'goal' in A. Daniel, ed. Toja, ix. 74, and perhaps in G. Faidit, ed. Mouzat, xxi. 32 (cf. *SW* ii. 22; Mouzat renders 'torts'). But this is too uncertain to justify emendation. Correction to *sagittandum*, as in Guessard, is tempting, cf. 3192.

1969 *tavecs—insultus*. *SW* viii. 89 proposed emendation to *insulsus* and hesitantly interpreted 'insipid, foolish' (as also in *PD*), an interpretation which is possible in his other example, from Lantelm (= Branciforti's edition of L. Cigala, p. 187, l. 19: 'juge tavec'). This, though accepted without comment by Branciforti, is quite unconvincing: *insulsus* does not occur elsewhere in the *Donatz* in the sense 'foolish', for which the translator uses a number of other words, nor is there any real indication that 'foolish' is the right meaning in Lantelm. If one is to emend arbitrarily, there is rather more to be said for *iniustus* or *incultus*. But in fact *insultus* 'an affront, an insult' defines the force of *tavec*—which is clearly used pejoratively by Lantelm—without, strictly speaking, translating it. The word is attested also for med. Catalan—in a sense which is again pejorative but impossible to define—in Llull's *Concili*, 667 (*Poesies*², *ENC*, Barcelona, 1928, p. 130; cf. *DCELC* iv. 323, s.v. *tábano*, n. 6, and *Dicc. Alcover*, s.v.). Cf. also *FEW* xiii. 1. 1 TĀBĂNUS and n. 1 (p. 6), where Levy's *insulsus* is rejected—though the text still includes the translation 'insipide'—and an unacceptable interpretation of Lantelm's text is put forward.

1970 *bavecs—qui de facili movetur* (*id est, baveca*). The translation given in *A* is comprehensible only if one takes .*i. baveca* as a gloss on *qui . . . movetur* and interprets *baveca* as 3rd sg. pr. ind. of the OPr. verb *bavecar* 'to weigh, to balance'. For *bavec* 'a balance' cf. *SW* i. 135–6; for *bavecar* cf. *SW* i. 136 and Stichel, p. 21. It is worth noting that Alart (*Documents sur la langue catalane*, Paris, 1881, p. 143 n. 1) is quite wrong in associating our word with *bauc* (*Donatz* 1827) and that, in the Catalan document of 1301 which he was attempting to interpret, *bavech* clearly means 'balance (for weighing coins)' and *bavechejar* 'to weigh (coins)'. Alart's erroneous interpretation is followed by *Dicc. Aguiló, Alcover*, s.vv. *bavech, bavequejar*.

1972 *encecs—exeques*. The translation is acceptable if *encegar* for *eisegar* 'to share, divide equally' (*SW* ii. 333–5: note the possibility, ibid. 333, that *ensegnar* in *Flamenca* 7156 is an error for *eisegar*) is allowed as a possible form. Otherwise one must take *encecs* either as a form of *ensegre*, emending to *exsequeris* as in Guessard (inadvertently reproduced as the MS. reading by Stengel), or as a form of *encegar*, emending to *exceces* as recommended by Bauquier (*Rom*. vi, p. 451). Neither correction imposes itself, though the second receives some support from 3495 *encega—excecat* and the first from the occurrence elsewhere in MS. *A* of *nc* = *ns* (e.g. 2330, 2332, 2355–6, 2369, all in the Latin; cf. also Introduction, p. 55, § 15).

1978 *decs—vicium*. Neither our form (*SW* ii. 21–2) nor *dech* (cf. R. d'Orange, ed. Pattison, xvii. 59 and—with an interesting semantic development—R. de Vaqueiras, ed. Linskill, xiii. 15) is cited in *FEW* ii. 1. 29 CADĚRE. *PD*—wrongly, in my opinion—separates *dec* 'défaut, vice' from *dech* 'qualité'.

1987–2008. Faidit distinguishes between [ęis] and [ęis]. Troubadours did not always rigidly respect this distinction, cf. Lienig, pp. 43–6.

1988 *Eis—civitas*. Stengel (note to 45b, 44) apparently considered this an alternative form of 1554 *Aics*, which is clearly impossible. Though not, so far as I know, otherwise attested in OPr., *Eis* must be the Italian town Iesi (Latin *Aesis*), in the province of Ancona, the birthplace of the Emperor Frederick II.

1990 *fleis—parcitas*. Guessard silently corrected *A*'s *paratas* to *paratus*, a reading inadvertently retained by Stengel and registered with puzzlement by Levy (*SW* iii. 505). The emendation to *parcitas* 'restraint, moderation' is confirmed by Levy's first example (ibid. = P. Duran, *PC*. 234. 8, ed. Sakari in *Mélanges Frank*, pp. 595-613): in l. 43 (ibid., p. 602) it is necessary to read, with Levy, 'Pus lo fleis no m'es grazitz' ('Since my restraint is not appreciated')—Sakari's argument against *grazitz* (p. 611) is without foundation and hence his text and interpretation are erroneous. The present example of *fleis*, in short, confirms Levy's conjecture 'retenue, abstinence?' (*PD*), accepted in *FEW* iii. 619 FLĔXARE and supported by *se fleisar* 'to refrain (from doing sthg.)' (*SW* iii. 505-6); cf. also *Dicc. Alcover*, s.vv. *flixar*, 2 and *flix*¹, 2, and *Dicc. Aguiló*, s.v. *flixar*.

1991 *fleis—sit contentus*. Levy cites this, with 1990, s.v. *fleis* (*SW* iii. 505), without attempting an interpretation; for *fleisar*, v. refl., *PD* admits only 'se détourner, se dérober', the only senses attested in *SW* iii. 505-6. With Tobler's correction (*sit* for *fit*, *Rom*. ii, p. 341), however, the interpretation 'to be satisfied, to content oneself' is clear and was made already by Mussafia (*Die catalanische metrische Version der Sieben Weisen Meister*, Vienna, 1876, p. 83, s.v. *flixar*); l. 1227 of Mussafia's text provides a Catalan example, cf. *Dicc. Alcover*, s.v. *flixar*, 2a, and *Dicc. Aguiló*, s.v. *flixar*, for others. The *Donatz* seems to provide the sole OPr. example in this sense, which should be added to *FEW* iii. 619 FLĔXARE.

1992 *leis—luxus*. Guessard printed *lectus*, for which Tobler proposed *legis* (*Rom*. ii, p. 341), while Chabaneau (*Rom*. vi, p. 138) interpreted *lectus* as p. part. of *legere*. Stengel (note to 45b, 44) hesitantly proposed *lectus* 'bed', pointing to the existence in the *Donatz* of doublets in *-ais* ~ *-athz* (1604, 1613, 1614 = 1917, 1908, 1907) and *-eis* ~ *-ethz* (*leis* 1996, *lethz* 2412). Chabaneau later proposed *seis—sexus* (*RLR* xiii, p. 141). None of these is satisfactory: even *lectus* 'bed' is open to the objection that none of the pairs of doublets in the *Donatz* includes an etymon in -CTUS, so that *leis* < LĔCTUS, if accepted, would be quite isolated. The word remains an enigma.

1994. *Geis* is correctly placed under *-eis larg*; *PD*'s *geis*, following Stengel (note to 45b, 46), is erroneous. For the open vowel, cf. *FEW* iv. 356-8 GYPSUM.

2002 *meis*. Cf. note to 597.

2009-22. The rhymes in *-els larg* are distinguished from those in *-elz larg* (2028-59) in deriving from etyma with -L-, not -LL- (cf. note to 1624-40). A few troubadours observe this distinction; cf. most notably P. Vidal, ed. Avalle, xxxvi, where eighteen rhyme-words in [-ęl] consistently exclude words with etyma in -ĚLLUM. Vidal's rhymes, like Faidit's, include a good proportion of Biblical proper names. The majority of troubadours, however, make no distinction of this kind in their rhyme-series in [-ęl]. On this question see Lienig, pp. 84-90. It is likely that the inclusion among these rhymes of *escamels* (2022) < SCAMĔLLUM (*FEW* xi. 274) is an error; since the word is the last of the series, it was possibly an addition not due to Faidit himself.

2022 *escamels.* Sole example of this form in *SW* iii. 138.

2024 *camels.* Despite our example, classed under *-els estreit*, *PD* admits only *camęl.* In fact Raynouard's single example (*LR* ii. 301 = P. Vidal, ed. Avalle, xxxvi. 69) does show [ę]. That both were possible is indicated by *FEW* ii. 1. 129 CAMĒLUS.

2028–59. The rhymes in *-elz larg* all show etyma in -ĕLL + s. For the distinction involved cf. note to 2009–22.

2038 *pomelz.* See note to 1108.

2040 *panelz—parvus panis vel barda.* Sole example in the sense 'small loaf' in *SW* vi. 46; cf. *FEW* vii. 546 PANIS, where the form is quite isolated. For *panel* 'a type of saddle' cf. *SW* vi. 46 and *FEW* vii. 558 PANNUS (cf. 564 n. 23, on the geographical distribution).

2041 *escavelz—alabrum.* Sole example in *SW* iii. 162; cf. *FEW* xi. 259 SCABELLUM.

2045 *cantelz—ora panis.* Levy quotes no example in precisely this sense (*SW* i. 200); Raynouard's single example for this meaning (*LR* ii. 316 = P. d'Auvergne, ed. del Monte, xi. 7) is a misquotation. *PD*, however, has 'chanteau de pain', no doubt from the *Donatz*; cf. *FEW* ii. 1. 229 CANTHUS for reference to a further example, and, for Catalan, *Dicc. Aguiló*, s.v. *cantell.*

2047 *cantarelz—qui cantat frequenter.* Sole example in *SW* i. 200; cf. *FEW* ii. 1. 221 CANTARE.

2051 *cardonelz—avis.* Sole example in *SW* i. 213; cf. *FEW* ii. 1. 369 CARDUUS.

2064 *cabelhz—capillus.* *PD* gives only *cabęl*, despite the examples in *SW* i. 179, *LR* ii. 323, and Lienig, p. 88.

2066 *conselhz—consulas.* The translation indicates the intr. sense of *conselhar* 'to deliberate', which, though omitted in *PD*, is attested in Raynouard's third example (*LR* ii. 460 = B. de Ventadour, ed. Appel, vii. 20), to which may be added *Girart* 4102, 6939, 6940, as well as a second example in the *Donatz* (3387).

2068 *desparelhz—paria dividas.* The translation indicates the sense 'to separate (things which belong together)' somewhat more accurately than *PD*'s 'séparer'. The verb is erroneously given as a *hapax* in *FEW* vii. 649 PARĬCŬLUS; cf. a second example in Raynouard (*LR* iv. 417 = R. de Vaqueiras, ed. Linskill, i. 71). *Donatz* 3390 attests the verb in a different sense.

2072 *calelhz.* This is the only genuinely OPr. example in *SW* i. 187; *PD* gives *calęl, -ęlh.* That *calęlh* is correct is shown by the *Donatz* and confirmed by the etymology, cf. *FEW* ii. 1. 86 CALĬCULUS, where references to other OPr. examples are given.

2075 *espelhz—speculum.* That this is correctly classed in *-elhz estrit* is shown by other OPr. examples at the rhyme (*LR* iii. 170; *SW* iii. 253; Lienig, p. 46). It confirms the etymology *SPĬCŬLUM given by Meyer-Lübke for Sardinian (but not for OPr.) in *REW* 8133. *FEW* xii. 162 SPECULUM has no comment on this point.

2078 *semelhz—asimilles.* That the sense is 'to resemble' is indicated by *Donatz* 3380 and by Levy's first example (*SW* vii. 553, from Peire de Corbiac). Correction to *similles* (cf. 3380 *similat*) or to *asimilleris* (cf. Blaise, s.v. *adsimilo*, 3) is not essential: it is possible to take *asimilles* as bad Latin (*TLL* ii. 898 cites a single example, of the 6th century), and this is certainly preferable to attributing to *semelhar* the sense 'to cause to resemble, to compare' simply on the strength of this passage. The verb was rare in OPr.: *FEW* xi. 628 *SIMILIARE notes that the only examples come from a Gascon text and from a text written in Italy. Whether the verb is tr. (*PD*) or intr. (*FEW*, loc. cit.) cannot be determined: the example from P. de Corbiac is inconclusive.

2080 *Jerusalems.* Though the *Donatz* notes this as having [ẹ], as is normal in learned words, the troubadours normally rhymed it in [-ẹm] (Lienig, p. 35; cf. P. d'Auvergne, ed. del Monte, xviii. 76; A. Daniel, ed. Toja, xii. 37 and 45).

2083 *sems—semis vel minuas.* For *sem* 'incomplete, half-full' cf. *SW* vii. 535–6 and *FEW* xi. 440 SĒMIS; more usual med. Latin in this sense would be *semus* (cf. Niermeyer). For *semar* 'to diminish' cf. *SW* vii. 539 and *FEW* xi. 425 SĒMĀRE.

2093 *calens—providus.* This is Levy's sole example for the sense 'far-sighted, provident' (*SW* i. 188, s.v. *caler*, 3); *FEW* ii. 1. 82–5 CALĒRE omits it.

2098 *descreissens—dissipans.* The precise sense 'to destroy, disperse' is not given by the dictionaries but is akin to the sense 'to bring low', cf. Raynouard's second example (*LR* ii. 512 = Marcabru, ed. Dejeanne, xi).

2105 *fondens.* Cf. note to 1290.

2111 *gens—pulcer vel pulcra.* The normal f. form is *genta*; Grandgent, p. 96, § 103. 1, admits *gens*, but this is no doubt on the strength of the present passage. Tobler (*Rom.* ii, p. 342) proposed *pulcret*: the emendation is tempting, although *gensar* does not occur elsewhere in the *Donatz* nor *pulcrare* in the translation. *Pulcra* would then be a scribal error induced by the preceding *aptus vel apta*; or it may be regarded as a translator's error due to the same cause. But *gens* may have been a real feminine form on the analogy of *avinens.* It seems better, therefore, not to emend.

2146 *atens—nancisceris.* The translator took this as 2nd sg. pr. ind. of *atenher* (cf. *ateis—nactus est* 589, 2001); its presence among the rhymes in *-ens estreit* indicates that it was intended as 2nd sg. pr. ind. of *atendre.* The rhyme-lists show no other example of confusion of dental and palatal *n*, though interchange of the graphies *n* and *nh* is relatively frequent in

MS. *A*. This is not to deny that forms such as *atendre* for *atenher* may occur in texts; cf., in a poem wrongly attributed to R. de Vaqueiras (ed. Linskill, xxxiii. 15, 49), *atendre* and *empendre*, apparently for *atenher*, *empenher*; *SW* iii. 318–19, s.v. *estenher*, for an example of *estendre*, which Levy attributes to the Italian poet's ignorance of Provençal; and *SW* ii. 388, s.v. *empenher*, where two possible examples of *empendre* are considered.

2166 *greps—superbus* [paruus *A*]. *SW* iv. 185 cites only 'grep, gripus', from the *Floretus*, and the present example from the *Donatz*, with a hesitant correction to *parvus* [*canis*]. The translation 'petit chien?' passed into *PD* and is noted, with some doubt, in *FEW* xvi. 368 *KRAPPA, n. 52. That *gripus* could mean 'small dog' is not in doubt, but its basic meaning was 'haughty, stubborn', cf. Du Cange, s.v., to which may be added 'gripus: supervus, cervicosus' in the *Glossarium Ansileubi* (*Glossaria Latina*, vol. 1, 1926, p. 272b; dubiously cited in *TLL* vi. 2. 2341, s.v. *gryps*). This last example suggested my emendation. It is curious that both OPr. examples of *grep* and all Latin examples of *gripus* occur in glossaries. The only parallel in *FEW* xvi. 357–68 *KRAPPA is (p. 364) Igé (Saône-et-Loire) *græpe*, adj. 'agressif, hargneux' (Provençal and Franco-Provençal forms derive from East Germanic KRĚPP-, ibid., p. 366).

2175 *vers—ver*. The [ẹ] indicates the word's learned origin. *FEW* xiv. 273 VĒR, n. 9, notes that both OPr. examples (the other is from Cerveri, ed. Riquer, cx. 2) occur in texts written outside the Midi.

2188 *aers*; 2196–7 *aders*. Cf. note to 620. For the senses of *procurare* cf. Niermeyer, s.v.

2192. The words *nominaliter posita*, though placed above *devers*, are clearly intended to refer to *avers* as well; correction to *positum* (Guessard) is therefore unnecessary.

2204 *trotiers—cursor*. The sense 'messenger' (cf. Niermeyer, s.v. *cursor*, 1) is attested by a second example in *SW* viii. 504 but omitted from *PD*.

2209 *formiers—formarius*. Sole example for *formier* 'last-maker' in *SW* iii. 549; the word is attested in Catalan from 1378, cf. *Dicc. Alcover*, s.v. *former*[1], 1. There is no doubt of the sense intended here, though *formarius* 'last-maker' is not given by dictionaries of med. Latin. The word is attested much later in French (1680, cf. *FEW* iii. 714 FORMA).

2215 *panatiers, paniers*. *A*'s interlinear *paniers* was no doubt originally an addition to the well-attested *panatiers*; it may well be erroneous. Though accepted by Levy (*SW* vi. 47, s.v. *panier*, 4; *PD*), it does not occur elsewhere in the sense 'pantler', nor does *FEW* provide any mod. parallel s.vv. PANIS and PANARIUS.

2218 *mestiers—mestarium*. 'Loom' is the most likely sense, cf. *SW* v. 263, s.v. *mestier*, 8, and Du Cange, s.v. *mestarium*, 2. Note, however, that for *teliers* (2267) the translator expressed the same meaning in a different way.

2227 *fumiers—fumarius*. Bad Latin for *fumarium* 'chimney' (cf. Niermeyer; Du Cange has a single example of *fumerius*).

2228 *terriers—terratorium.* The sense 'domain', absent from *PD*, is attested in *SW* viii. 192.

2230 *colhers—collarius.* *A*'s bizarre *colloquear*, for which—no less bizarrely —Guessard printed *collo ferens* and Stengel proposed **colloquiarium* [*sic*], must have been induced by the following word *cloquiers*.

2236 *noveliers.* Sole example in *SW* v. 430; cf. *FEW* vii. 204 NŎVĔLLUS.

2241 *borsiers.* Sole example in *SW* i. 158 for the sense 'purse-maker'; cf. also *Dicc. Aguiló*, s.v. *bosser*, 2, and *Dicc. Alcover*, s.v. *bosser*[1], 1.

2242 *baraties—baratator.* For the Latin cf. Du Cange, Niermeyer. The sense 'trickster', not admitted by *PD*, is possible in Raynouard's first example (*LR* ii. 184 = *vida* of Uc de Pena) and is supported by parallel senses for *barat, baratar*, etc., as well as by med. Catalan examples (cf. *Dicc. Aguiló, Alcover*, s.v. *barater*).

2246 *verçiers—viridarium.* For the form *verzier* (absent from *SW* viii. 660–1 and *PD*) cf. *Jaufré*, ed. Breuer, 10723, 10888, and *FEW* xiv. 506 VIRIDIARIUM. On the development of -DJ- after consonant $> z \sim g \sim j$ cf. *targar* (P. Cardenal, ed. Lavaud, lv. 58; *SW* viii. 64) = *tarzar*; Appel, *Lautlehre*, p. 89; Ronjat, ii, p. 253. Note that the *Donatz* attests *borses* 144 and *borçes* 2332, not *borges* (cf. note to 144).

2251 *mandoliers—amigdalus.* Sole example in *SW* v. 95; cf. *FEW* i. 91 AMYGDALA.

2254 *ciriers—cirarius vel citarista.* This is Levy's sole example of the form *cirier* 'cherry-tree' (*SW* i. 246), for in his second example (= B. de Ventadour, ed. Appel, p. 279, l. 38) no MS. has this form. For a genuine second example cf. A. de Peguilhan, ed. Shepard and Chambers, xix. 25, var. *M*; the form *cirier* should be added to *FEW* ii. 1. 600 CERASEUM. The Latin *cirarius* should perhaps be corrected to *cerasus* or *ceresarius* (cf. Niermeyer) or *cerisarius* (cf. Baxter–Johnson); but it is possible to regard it as bad Latin induced by the form of the Provençal word. For *ciriers* 'cithern-player', unattested elsewhere and omitted by *SW* and *PD*, cf. *FEW* ii. 1. 717 CITHARA and 719 n. 2.

2255 *sorbiers—sorbarius vel corbellarius.* Both of the Latin words seem to be absent from dictionaries of med. Latin. Du Cange, however, attests *sorberius* and *corberius*; *corbellarius* is acceptable as a Latinization of a vernacular—probably Italian—form (cf. *FEW* ii. 2. 1188–9 *CORMA). There is no reason for supposing that the alternative Latin renderings were other than synonymous, both meaning 'service-tree, rowan'.

2256 *rosiers—rosetum.* The sense 'rose-garden', absent from *PD*, is not unambiguously attested elsewhere. In Raynouard's second example (*LR* v. 114 = R. Buvalelli, ed. Bertoni, i. 9), however, Bertoni translates 'roseto'; *rosier* is attested once in this sense in 13th-century French (Godefroy, vii. 241; *FEW* x. 477 RŎSA, where our example should be added).

2257 *violers—violetum*. Sole example, without translation, in *SW* viii. 793. *PD*'s 'bed of violets' is the most likely interpretation, though *violetum* does not occur in this sense in dictionaries of med. Latin (it was perhaps simply coined ≠ *rosetum*, which immediately precedes); this sense is attested for Fr. *violier* from 1372 (Godefroy, viii. 255; *FEW* xiv. 485 VIOLA, where the OPr. should perhaps be added). Other conceivable but less likely interpretations are (1) 'path' (Du Cange, s.v. *violetum*, and, for a few parallel mod. dialect forms, *FEW* xiv. 372 VĬA); (2) 'violet cloth' (Baxter-Johnson, s.v. *violetum*)—cf. Fr. *violier* attested in this sense at Tournai in 1476 (*FEW* xiv. 485; Godefroy, viii. 255). In the first of these senses, however, OPr. had *viol* and *violet* (*SW* viii. 789-90, 792) and in the second *violat*, *violet*, and *violeta* (*SW* viii. 791, 792, 793). No certainty is possible here without a second example of *violier* 'bed of violets'.

2260 *mespoliers, nespoliers—esculus*. *A*'s *vespo uel* is explicable as a misreading of the alternative form *nespoliers* added between the lines (Tobler's correction, *Rom.* ii, p. 342). For *esculus* 'medlar-tree' cf. *Mittellateinisches Wb.*, s.v. *aesculus*, 1, c, also *Abavus*, s.v. *esculus*.

2261 *poliers—pullarius*. The correction of *A*'s *larius* is clear and was made first by Galvani (p. 330) and independently by G. Paris (*Rom.* i, p. 235). It is worth noting, however, that the normal med. Latin for 'poulterer' was *pulletarius* (cf. Niermeyer, Baxter-Johnson).

2262 *codonhyers—cotanarius*. The normal medieval form was *cotanus* (cf. Du Cange); *cotanarius* is not attested in dictionaries of med. Latin.

2266 *talhiers*. Sole example in *SW* viii. 39 for the sense 'meat-dish, trencher'.

2269 *caronhiers—qui cadavera sequitur*. The translation is clearly 'carrion-eating (of birds)', not merely 'carnivorous', cf. the examples in *SW* i. 218 and *LR* ii. 341.

2276 *petiers—qui frequenter bumbinat*. Correction of *A*'s *bumbicinat* is essential, unless one supposes that the translator inadvertently thought of *bombicinare* 'to make silk'. Both *bombinare* and *bombizare* are possible in the sense 'to break wind', cf. Du Cange, s.vv., and *Abavus*, iii. 840-1, iv. 901-2—the hexameter quoted in *Abavus* iv indicates a preference for *bombinare*. If the error is, as I have supposed, scribal, it can be explained as a misunderstanding of *bumbĭnat* (or *bumbĭṇat*).

2277 *rotiers—eructuator*. Sole example in *SW* vii. 384; cf. *FEW* x. 539 RŪCTARE, where this is the only formation in *-ier*. Dictionaries of med. Latin seem not to attest *eructuator*.

2288 *verps—luppus*. Tobler (*Rom.* ii, p. 343) proposed *guerps—linquis*; Chabaneau (*Rom.* vi, p. 138) supposed *verps* to mean 'werewolf', arguing from Limousin *le-berou* (for which, however, see *REW* 9524b WERWULF). Neither proposal is worth serious consideration: Levy registered the word without any comment of his own (*SW* viii. 682) but omitted it from *PD*. In fact the word is an enigma. *Luppus*—if it is not a corrupt reading—

may be interpreted as 'wolf', 'lynx', 'bass, a fish', 'lupus, a skin disease' (*Novum Glossarium*, s.v. *lupus*). *Verps*—if it is not an error of *AL* or of O^2—might be supposed to be identical with *verpus* 'middle finger', 'Jew' (Du Cange, s.v.; cf. *Aalma* 13095 and *Abavus*, iv. 9041), though this would entail a considerable emendation to *Iudeus* or to *verpus*. But without a second example the sense really remains impenetrable.

2294 *covertz*; 2295 *descovertz*; 2299 *overtz*. Such p. part. forms with *-v-* for usual *-b-* seem hardly attested elsewhere (*Girart* 9713, *covert*, is quite isolated). No mention of them is made by P. Mann, *Das Participium Praeteriti im Altprovenzalischen*, Marburg, 1886, p. 5, cf. pp. 72–3, nor by the standard grammars of OPr.

2300 *espertz—propinqus*. This provided Levy with one of his two examples of the sense 'near' (*SW* iii. 262, s.v. *espert*, 3), the other being A. Daniel, ed. Toja, xi. 39. But in this second passage Toja interprets 'ready'— a better translation would be 'eager'; at all events, no sense of Latin *propinquus* fits the context. Thus the interpretation given by the *Donatz* is really isolated; *PD* maintained it ('proche?') but it is not given in *FEW* iii. 309–10 EXPERTUS, where no modern reflex has this sense either. Emendation to *properus* 'swift' would give an acceptable sense but is difficult to justify palaeographically. Other conceivable senses for *espertz* are (1) 2nd sg. pr. subj. of *espertar*, (2) p. part. of *espereisser*, (3) 2nd sg. pr. ind. of *esperdre*; but none of these suggests any convincing correction of the MS. reading, which has been allowed to stand in the text.

2301 *apertz—providus*. This provides the only clear attestation of *apert* 'farsighted, prudent' in *SW* i. 69–70, though the latter is semantically close to the well-attested sense 'intelligent, skilful'. Cf. *FEW* iii. 309 EXPERTUS (note Swiss *apers* 'fin, clairvoyant').

2310–11 *adertz, aertz*. Cf. notes to 620 and 2188, 2196–7.

2332 *borçes*. Cf. note to 144.

2342 *les*. For the translation *levis* (Guessard and Stengel printed *lenis*) cf. note to 193.

2366 *Tertones—Tertonenses*. Correction to *Tort-* in both words (Tobler, *Rom.* ii, p. 343) is possible but hardly essential, though I know of no OPr. attestation of the form *Tertona*. It is possible to argue for a reading *Tartona* in R. de Vaqueiras, ed. Linskill, vi. 43, cf. ibid. iv. 4, var. *DIKNR*.

2378 *cadalethz—lectus ligneus altus*. Sole example in *SW* i. 183; cf. *FEW* ii. 1. 488 *CATALĔCTUS, where a 15th-century example of *chaliech* is noted; cf. also *SW* vii. 733, where the fourth example s.v. *soc*, 1, attests the form *cadelheyt* (cf. *L*'s reading *cadelethtz*).

2382 *respethz—expectatio*. Cited in *SW* vii. 266, s.v. *respech*, 3, with the erroneous reading *expectatum* (given by Guessard and Stengel), as sole example of the sense 'Erwartetes'; but this sense is absent from *PD*.

2387 *bretz—homo lingue impedite*. Sole example in *SW* i. 164 for the sense 'stammerer'; cf. *FEW* i. 539 BRITTUS.

2390 *Petz*, without translation, was no doubt intended in the sense 'pitch' (*LR* iv. 524; *SW* vi. 299).

2392 *vetz—vicium*. The word is otherwise attested in OPr. only with the neutral sense 'habit, manner, conduct' (*SW* viii. 718–19); for 'vice, bad character' one finds *mal vetz*. It is therefore reasonable to suppose that this last expression was in the mind of the translator, who was also perhaps influenced by the etymology.

2395 *escletz—purus*. Sole example in *SW* iii. 172; cf. *FEW* xvii. 141 SLAÍHTS, also *Dicc. Alcover*, s.v. *esclet*. *PD* is wrong in printing *esclęt*.

2399 *anheletz—agniculus*. Sole example in *SW* i. 66; cf. *FEW* i. 54 AGNELLUS, where our example should be added.

2401 *cabroletz—capreolus*. Sole example in *SW* i. 182; cf. *FEW* ii. 1. 304 CAPREOLUS.

2402 *foletz—faunus vel stultus*. For the first sense cf. *LR* iii. 349 and *FEW* iii. 692 FŏLLIS. For the second, omitted from *PD* and not definitely indicated in *SW*, Levy's first example (*SW* iii. 521, s.v. *folet*) seems to provide confirmation of the *Donatz*; *folet* 'foolish' should be added to *FEW* iii. 689.

2413 *espletz—supelectile*. The collective sense of the Latin (cf. Baxter–Johnson) suggests that the translator envisaged *espletz* as an obl. pl. form: Raynouard's examples in this sense (*LR* ii. 104) all show the plural.

2416 *aplethz—instrumenta*. The Latin plural seems to indicate a collective meaning; this is possibly the sense in A. de Peguilhan, ed. Shepard and Chambers, xlvii. 1, cf. some parallels in *FEW* i. 109 APPLICTUM. Alternatively, *aplethz* may be taken as obl. pl., or emendation to *instrumentum* may be introduced.

2435 *Canileus—Canileus*. Raynouard (*LR* ii. 307) attests *canineu* (cf. *SW* i. 199). For the form with -*l*- by dissimilation (normal in OFr., cf. P. Meyer in *Rom*. vii, pp. 441–4), cf. P. Vidal, ed. Avalle, xxxviii. 53, var. *DRf*, and *Girart* 1500, 7328. The translation is best regarded as a mere repetition of the Provençal; it seems not to be attested in med. Latin as a form of *Cananaeus*.

2437 *Anjeus*. *A*'s *arueus* (which Guessard omitted and Stengel placed without comment among the proper names) can only be a scribal error for *Anjeus* 'Angers'; cf. A. de Belenoi (?), ed. Dumitrescu, xviii. 51 (*Angeus*:-*ęus*) and B. de Born, ed. Appel, xiv. 19 and xxvii. 21 (*Angieus*). The repetition of the erroneous Provençal reading in the guise of a Latin rendering no doubt reflects the translator's bewilderment when faced with an already corrupt reading. (It is striking that 2435–7 all have interlinear renderings identical with the Provençal words, in the first and third of which the MS. has respectively an uncertain and a corrupt reading.)

2442 *derips—abstraas clavos*. Sole example in *SW* ii. 108; *Donatz* 1135 (*ribar, compost*) constitutes indirectly a second example. Cf. also *FEW* x. 413 RĪPA.

2444 *brics—miser*. *SW* i. 165–6, s.v. *bricon*, noted that this is the only example of this sense, although Raynouard (*LR* ii. 258) already gave 'misérable'. There is no reason to suspect the accuracy of the translation, which should be added to *FEW* i. 521 *BRICCO.

2451 *trics—intricatio*. *SW* viii. 465 hesitates over whether this is the same word as *tric* 'deceiver, deceit' or *tric* 'delay' (*FEW* xiii. 2. 260 *TRĬCCARE and 258 TRĪCARE respectively). The sense given here seems otherwise unattested and is omitted from *PD* and *FEW*. For *intricatio* 'entanglement, difficulty' cf. Baxter-Johnson; the translation shows awareness of the etymology and is perhaps not to be taken too literally.

2458–9 *cauçics* [cançics MS.]—*increpatio*; *increpes*. Tobler's unhappy series of emendations to *cauçics* (on *caussa* < CALCEA), *increpidatio*, and *increpides* (supposedly formed on *crepida* 'slipper') (*Rom.* ii, p. 343) has been universally accepted: silently by Stengel (index), explicitly by *SW* i. 229–30 and *PD*, whence *causic* 'coup de pied' passed into *FEW* ii. 1. 73 *CALCICARE. Despite the existence of *causigar* (*LR* ii. 289; *FEW*, loc. cit.), *causic* is unattested, as are *increpidare* and *increpidatio*. Tobler's emendation of *n* to *u* is correct, though accidentally so, but the Latin readings of the MS. must be retained: *cauçics* is thus comparable in form and identical in meaning with OFr. *choser* 'to blame, reproach, chide' (*TL* ii. 419–20). Despite *FEW* ii. 1. 543–4, CAUSĀRĪ does have an OPr. reflex *cauzar* 'to blame, reproach' (*LR* ii. 359; P. Cardenal, ed. Lavaud, xlv. 62; *REW* 1782), omitted by *PD*. Our present words are clearly derivatives on the same stem, no doubt influenced by the synonymous *castigar* and *castic*. Both noun and verb are *hapax legomena*, unless *caussicx* is the correct reading in Arnaut Plagues, *PC.* 32. 1 (ed. Appel, *P. Rogier*, pp. 84–7), l. 26, where Appel prints *cambicx* (cf. *SW* i. 192, s.v. *cambigar*).

2461 *afics—vis*. The sense 'force, violence', absent from *LR* iii. 321, *SW* i. 26, and *PD*, is attested also in *Girart* 3488, 6961; *FEW* iii. 509 *FĪGĬCARE has only the senses given by Levy.

2471 *badils*. Sole example in *SW* i. 119; cf. *FEW* i. 285 BATARE, where this is the only formation in *-il*.

2474 *senhorils—dominabilis*. *SW* vii. 588 is dubious about the sense intended, classing this with a single example of *senhoril dia* 'the Lord's day'; *PD* has 'du seigneur'. In general 'pertaining to a lord' is the most acceptable interpretation (cf. Du Cange, s.v. *dominabilis*); see also *Dicc. Alcover*, s.v. *senyoril*, for a 13th-century Catalan example in this sense.

2475 *femenils—feminilis*. The sense would seem to be 'female, womanish, womanly', cf. *LR* iii. 302 and *SW* iii. 431–2 (also *Dicc. Aguiló, Alcover*, s.v.); *PD* has 'féminin', which is somewhat non-committal. *Feminilis* seems otherwise unattested in med. Latin and was no doubt suggested by the Provençal word.

2477 *camzils.* For the more usual *cansil* cf. *LR* ii. 310, to which may be added *Girart* 3310, 3822, 9883. For a second example of *camsil* (the only form admitted in *PD*) cf. *Jaufré* 5231, var. B.

2479 *priorils.* Sole example in *SW* vi. 561; cf. *FEW* ix. 394 PRIOR, where this is the only formation in *-il*.

2480 *abadils.* Sole example in *SW* i. 1; *FEW* i. 3 ABBAS omits the word. Pfister, *Beiträge, Vox*, xviii, p. 233 (no. 1) cites a mention of a *pratum Abadil*.

2489 *noirims—nutrimentum.* This is Levy's sole example (*SW* v. 404) for the sense 'nourishment'; those cited by him as dubious admit one of the senses attested elsewhere: 'nurseling, young animal; offspring, brood'. *FEW* vii. 249 NŬTRĪMEN accepts the sense 'nourriture' and adds a reference to B. Marti (ed. Hoepffner, ii. 39), where, however, despite the editor, the sense is certainly 'offspring, brood'. Since *nutrimentum* is attested in med. Latin as 'brood, cattle, young animals' (cf. Du Cange, Niermeyer, s.v.), it is likely that this was the sense intended by the translator. At the best, the existence of *noirim* 'nourishment' is dubious.

2494 *tins—timpus.* For the form *timpus*, no doubt used by the translator in the interests of clarity, cf. Du Cange; the *Floretus* provides a further example (*SW* viii. 118, s.v. *templa*).

2496 *lins—lignum maris.* For the form *lin* cf. *SW* iv. 365; *FEW* v. 332 LĬGNUM wrongly dates this as 14th-century. The Latin, a not very clear rendering of 'boat', is influenced by etymological considerations.

2507 *remirs—iterum speculeris.* This is Levy's sole attestation (*SW* vii. 219) of the sense 'to gaze again at', which is omitted from *PD*. In view of the translations elsewhere in the *Donatz* (1127, 3210), which indicate that *remirar* was more intense than *mirar*, it is perhaps better to regard the rendering here as mechanical and not altogether accurate.

2526 *fenis—debilis.* Despite Chabaneau (*Rom.* vi, p. 139), Stengel (index), and *FEW* iii. 557 FĪNĪRE, this is not a reflex of FĪNĪTUS; cf. *SW* iii. 443 and the derivative *afiniatz* in *Jaufré* 5048.

2529 *albespis—albor spinosa.* The form *albor*, absent from dictionaries of med. Latin, may be justified by *alboratus* (Du Cange) and *alborosus* (Souter). The translator's rendering is partly motivated by etymological considerations.

2537 *Folis—civitas.* If this is Foligno, in Umbria (Latin *Fulginium*)—and what else can be intended?—the Provençal form is surprising. (The identification with Foligno was first proposed by d'Ovidio, *GSLI* ii, p. 8.)

2561–2 *coloritz*; *escoloritz*. *PD* admits *colorir* (and *descolorir*), but only *escolorit*, adj. The existence of the infinitives is dubious; Raynouard (*LR* ii. 441) attests only the p. part. for all three verbs.

2573 *fugiditz—fugitivus.* Sole example in *SW* iii. 612; cf. *FEW* iii. 838 FŬGĔRE and *Dicc. Alcover,* s.v. *fugidís.*

2598 *salithz—saliens.* The translation is odd. It is difficult to believe that the translator intended an otherwise unattested adjectival use of the p. part. in the sense 'leaping'. More probably he was trying to render its force in compound tenses (*sui salithz,* etc.).

2603 *tortitz—tortitium.* The usual med. Latin form was in *-us* (cf. Du Cange, s.v. *tortisius*).

2607 *solorius—solitarius.* This is Levy's sole example for the sense 'lonely' (*SW* vii. 791), a rendering repeated in *PD* and in *FEW* xii. 80 SŌLUS. The sense 'unique', attested by Levy's other example (= P. Vidal, ed. Avalle, xxxvi. 11), is certainly what is intended here, cf. Blaise, Souter, s.v. *solitarius.*

2614 *Beirius—provincia quedam vel hereticus.* In the sense 'province of Berry', *Beiriu* is also attested in *Flamenca* 375, cf. the forms *Beriu* in P. Vidal, ed. Avalle, xxxvi. 51, and *Berriu* in *Girart* 2360, 3335. If the etymology is *BITURĪVUM ≠ PICTĀVUM, as these forms suggest, then the *-ir-* of the *Donatz* (both MSS.) is not merely a scribal graphy for *-rr-*. Did *beiriu* 'heretic' fluctuate similarly between *-ir-* and *-rr-*? Levy's only other example (*SW* i. 137) has *beriu*; *PD* admits both spellings. Even if it were possible to establish that *beiriu* 'heretic' is a graphy for *berriu,* this would prove nothing about Faidit's own spelling of the word: since the two homonyms are given separately in *B,* one cannot argue that *A*'s single *beirius* necessarily represents the original (the more so as the scribe seems to have crowded this word into a limited space).

2616 *fihtz—fixus.* Sole example in *SW* i. 479, but *fichamen* is attested in *Jaufré* 7260 (cited by *SW* i. 478-9) and Raynouard has an example of *ficamen* (*LR* iii. 320); cf. also *Dicc. Alcover,* s.v. *fix. FEW* iii. 586-7 FĪXUS omits the OPr. form.

2620 *aflithz—aflictus.* Sole example in *SW* i. 27; omitted in *FEW* i. 50 AFFLIGERE.

2629-30 *grobs—nexus vel nodus; agrobs—nodes.* Sole examples in *SW* iv. 201 and i. 35; cf. *FEW* xvi. 420 *KRUPPA, also 421, where it is noted that the Provençal forms belong to the eastern part of the Midi, adjoining Upper Italy.

2631 *cobs—testa capitis.* Sole example for the sense 'skull' in *SW* i. 355; cf. *FEW* ii. 2. 1556 CŬPPA, where a 15th-century example with the meaning 'helmet' and OFr. *cop* 'head' (also a *hapax*) are noted.

2633 *globs—plenum os alicuius liquoris.* To Levy's second example of *glop* (*SW* iv. 139) may be added *globs* in *Recettes médicales,* ed. Brunel in *Rom.* lxxxiii, p. 152 (§ 41).

2636 *volbs—vulpis. PD* gives only *vǫlp,* although *SW* viii. 831-2 defends the [ǫ] indicated in the *Donatz* by reference to Raynouard's attestation of *vuolp* (*LR* v. 567). The point is not discussed in *FEW* xiv. 645-6 VŬLPES.

2640 *brocs*. *Curas* (= *curras*), given by *A*, is acceptable as an approximate translation (the translator elsewhere used *currere* in this sense, e.g. 2626): *brocar*, v. intr., 'to ride fast' is well attested (*LR* ii. 262), but I know of no example in which the verb means 'to run (on foot)'. *B*'s reading gives a possible sense with correction to *biocs*—*curtes* (Diez, *EtWb* iic, s.v. *bioc*, already accepted *biocar* 'curtare'), though *biocar* is otherwise attested only in the p. part., as a technical term of versification used in the *Leys d'Amors* (*LR* ii. 220; *PD*, s.vv. *bioc*, *biocat*). Emendation is possible but not essential.

2646 *grocs*—*ferrum curvum*. Sole example in *SW* i. 417-18 of this form, for usual *croc*; for a second example cf. G. Ademar, ed. Almqvist, ii. 46, var. *U*. *B*'s inversion of the translations for 2645-6 gives the commoner forms for both words (*groc* 'yellow', *croc* 'hook'), but *A*'s reading is a *lectio difficilior* which might well invite scribal alteration.

2647 *Marrocs*—*quedam civitas*. *B*'s *Mairocs*, which seems otherwise unattested in OPr., is paralleled in *Cligès*, ed. Micha, 6249, var. *S* (*Mairoc*). Flutre cites also *Marioch* in *Le Chevalier du Papegau*. The translator seems to have thought Morocco a city.

2656 *zocs*—*pes ligneum propter ludum*. Diez (*EtWb* iic, s.v. *soc*) proposed the reading *p. ligneus* [with the MS.] *p. lutum*, accepted by G. Paris (*Rom.* i, p. 236), by Stengel, and, hesitantly, by Levy (*SW* vii. 733-4, s.v. *soc*, 6). This would identify *zocs* with *soc* 'clog', for which Levy cites a further example. *FEW* xii. 13 sŏccus accepts this without comment. The form of the word makes no difficulty: both the *z*- and the [ǫ] are explicable via the influence of Gaulish *TSŬKKA (*FEW* xii. 15; similarly *DCELC* iv. 870-1, s.v. *zueco*, though Corominas, p. 871 n. 2, regards the [ǫ] as an error on Faidit's part); and *çoch* is attested in the same sense in 15th-century Catalan (*Dicc. Alcover*, s.v. *soc*[1], 2, and *Dicc. Aguiló*, s.v. *soch*, 1). But there are two objections to the interpretation 'clog': (1) *ludum*, not *lutum*, is attested twice, since *A* gives this same translation, erroneously, in 2653. Levy envisaged this difficulty (*SW*, loc. cit.) and wondered if, keeping *ludum*, one could interpret 'stilt', a sense otherwise unattested. (2) The use of *pes* to denote 'footwear' is at the very least odd. The natural sense of *pes ligneus* is 'foot of something constructed in wood (e.g. table, stool, bench)', cf. 3300 *pes pontis* 'pillar of a bridge'. It is difficult, then, to feel sure that 'clog' was the sense intended here, nor is it easy to attach any other plausible sense to the words which *A* gives above *zocs*. Since, when the scribe first copied the phrase (in 2653, erroneously), he wrote *ligneum*—for which *ligneus*, after *pes*, would be a very natural 'correction'—I have supposed that the translator intended the rendering 'base of a chess-man'; for *ligneus ludus* 'chess-man' cf. note to 1540. Our word would then be a specialized instance of *soc* 'block of wood' (*SW* vii. 732-3, s.v. *soc*, 1—Levy's last example under this heading shows *soc* referring to the base of a candlestick). I know of no attestation of the precise sense proposed here for *zoc*, unless the word be admitted as an emendation for *lox* in R. de Cornet's *Cirventes d'escax* (*Deux mss. prov.* xlvii. 5): 'Escax ni lox pres ni tocatz no sia'—*loc* 'square of the chessboard', the editors' interpretation (cf. *SW* iv. 418, s.v. *loc*, 7), is hardly possible, and the other MS. of the poem (*Sg*; ed. Massó Torrents in *AdM* xxvii–xxviii, 1915–16, pp. 29–30, no. XVI) has *rochs*, which gives a possible but not very satisfactory sense.

2657 *mocs—sanies naris.* Sole example in *SW* v. 287; cf. *FEW* vi. 3. 179 MŬCCUS, also *Dicc. Alcover*, s.v. *moc*[1], 1, and *Dicc. Aguiló*, s.v. *moch*.

2668 *aiols—avus.* Levy's only example for this form (*SW* i. 45), to which may be added *Girart* 9003.

2672 *arestols—extrema pars lancee.* The translation clearly indicates 'hilt' or 'haft' rather than 'shaft', despite *PD*'s 'fût de lance', inherited from *LR* ii. 119. The available examples bear this out: *Jaufré* 831, 3341, 8420 (Brunel, glossary: 'partie de la lance opposée au fer'); *Philomena*, l. 2294, var. *P*. Cf. *TL* i. 520, s.v. *arestuel*, 'Handhabe der Lanze'.

2673 *rofiols—cibus de pasta et ovis.* Sole example in *SW* vii. 367, where Levy mentions Mistral's *raviolo, roujolo* as well as G. Paris's emendation (*Rom.* i, p. 236) to *rosiols* (= OFr. *roisole*). *PD* prudently omits the word. It is dubious whether the OFr. or the mod. Provençal words are the same or related. Neither emendation nor conjecture on the exact sense is possible here.

2674 *roiols—genus piscis.* Sole example in *SW* vii. 370; cf. *FEW* x. 533 RŬBEUS—the mod. examples are limited to Aveyron and indicate 'small gudgeon' as the sense (*PD*'s very precise 'espèce de petit goujon à teintes rougeâtres' is lifted bodily from Mistral, s.v. *roujau*).

2680 *bols—equs nimis pulsans.* Sole example in *SW* i. 154; cf. *FEW* xiv. 646–7 VŬLSUS. All other Gallo-Romance examples are Franco-Provençal: von Wartburg observes that Faidit may simply have adapted the word from Italian.

2682 *princols—primum vinum.* Sole example in *SW* vi. 560; cf. *FEW* ii. 2. 878 COLARE.

2688–2701. The rhymes in -*olz*, with [ǫ] and with [ọ], show etyma in LL + S, LT + S, LD + S and are distinguished from the preceding series in -*ols*, which show etyma in -L-. Cf. 2671 *cǫls* < CŎLIS (CŎLĔRE), 2681 *cǫls* < CŌLES (CŌLĀRE), 2690 *cǫlz* < CŎLLUM + S. For this distinction, not observed in the rhymes of the troubadours (cf., for example, B. de Born, ed. Appel, xxxiii; A. Daniel, ed. Toja, vi), see the notes to 1624–40 and 2009–22. For *Santolz*, which is an apparent exception, see note to 2701.

2692 *molz—molis.* This is the adj. *mol* (*molis* = *mollis*, as in 3314), not, as supposed in Stengel's index, the 2nd sg. pr. ind. of *molre*. In the language of the *Donatz* MŎLIS > *mols*, not *molz*.

2701 *Santolz*. This proper name, the last of the words in *-olz estreit*, may well belong properly with the following group in *-olhz larg*; cf. the troubadour *Pons Santolh* and the family name *Santeuil*.

2710 *escolhz—color*. The intended sense is presumably 'sort, kind', cf. *SW* iii. 177-8. The ambiguous translation was no doubt suggested by a false etymology.

2712 *molhz—illud ubi rota figitur*. Sole example in *SW* v. 297. Levy translates 'hub of a wheel'; the Latin would also permit the interpretation 'axle'.

2715 *rolhz—lignum cum quo furnus tergitur*. Sole example for this sense in *SW* vii. 371; our example should be added to *FEW* x. 511 RŎTŬLUS. For *lignum* 'wooden implement' cf. note to 930.

2720 *veirolhz—vectis ostii*. The reading *vectes ostii* (Guessard, approved by Stengel) is possible only if one supposes that the translator, for no good reason, took *veirolhz* as an obl. pl. Correction to *vectes* [2nd sg. pr. subj.] *ostium* is also possible; but for rendering *verolhar* in 3438 the translator avoided using *vectare* (for which cf. Du Cange).

2723 *mairolhz—marubium*. Sole example in *SW* v. 26. So far from showing the influence of *maire* < MATER (*FEW* vi. 378 MARRŬBIUM, n. 9), this is simply a scribal graphy for *marrolhz*. For other examples of the word cf. *Recettes de Montpellier*, ed. Brunel in *Rom*. lxxviii, p. 315, § 106 (*marulh*), § 107 (*marjuelh*), and p. 316, § 117 (*morjulh*). The uncontaminated reflex of MARRŬBIUM (not in *LR*, *SW*, or *PD*) was *marog* or *maroi*. For the former cf. *FEW* vi. 377, from *Recettes des Pyrénées*; the same text attests *malrog* and *malrot* (× *mal*). For the latter, not noted by *FEW*, cf. *Recettes médicales*, ed. Brunel in *Rom*. lxxxiii, pp. 160 (§§ 166, 170), 164 (§ 222), 169 (§ 288); the same text also attests *maror* (p. 161, §§ 179, 186; × *amaror* 'bitterness'?). The word was evidently open to various forms of contamination. The forms with *-j-* show the influence of *jolh*, *juelh* < LŎLIUM. The ending *-ǫlh* so far lacks a satisfactory explanation: influence of *ROBĪCŬLU (supposed by *FEW*) is unacceptable for OPr., where *ROBĪCŬLU > *ro(v)ilh*. Can one postulate *-ǫlh* < *-ǫi* (*maroi*) + *-ǫlh* (*jolh*)?

2724 *dolhz—dolium vel foramen dolii*. Sole attestation of the second sense in *SW* ii. 270. *FEW* iii. 119 DOLIUM, n. 1, separates *dolh* 'cask' from *dolh* 'bung-hole' and supposes the latter to be derived from *adolhar*. The [ǫ] of the verb makes this unlikely, however, as is tacitly admitted in *FEW* xv. 1. 80 *DULJA, where *dolh* 'bung-hole' is now classed.

2726-8. The distinction between these three words in *-oms larg* and the longer series in *-oms estreit* (cf. note to 2730-9) is not borne out by troubadour practice, cf. Erdmannsdörfer, *Reimwörterbuch*, p. 57 n. 1; Lienig, pp. 59-60. Ronjat, i, p. 187, notes the conservation of [ǫ] before implosive nasal in a small area of Gascony.

2728 *doms—domus comunis*. Sole example in *SW* ii. 271; the sense must be 'cathedral', though the Latin rendering is odd (*domus* alone, in this sense, is attested from the 8th century, cf. Niermeyer, s.v. *domus*, 8—the earliest example, of 760, has *ad domum publicum*). If OPr. *dom* is borrowed from Italian, as seems to be supposed in *FEW* iii. 135–6 DOMUS, it strikingly antedates Fr. *dôme*, not attested until the 15th century.

2730–9. The ten words in *-oms estreit* show seven with etyma in ō or ŭ and three with ŏ, namely SŎMNUS, RHŎMBUS, and DŎMINUS (2733, 2735, 2739). It is worth noting, however, that the first and third of these are differently interpreted in MS. *B* and that ŏ in the second depends on the assumption that Latin preserved the vowel of Greek ῥόμβος (ῥύμβος is also attested). Moreover, these three are not identical phonetically with the etyma of the words in *-oms larg* (CŎMES, DŎMUS). This may be the basis of Faidit's distinction.

2731 *coms—equs abens cavum dorsum*. Sole example in *SW* i. 291; Levy, here and in *PD*, interprets the word as a noun and is followed by *FEW* ii. 2. 1526 *CŬMBOS. That it was in fact an adj. is indicated by a second example, in the *Recettes vétérinaires*, ed. Brunel in *Rom.* lxxxii, p. 31 (§ 9).

2733 *soms—somnium*. Palaeographically this is the most natural correction of *A*'s *somium* or *sonnum*. For *som* 'dream' cf. *SW* vii. 798, s.v. *som*, 3, and *FEW* xii. 95 SOMNUS. (*PD* wrongly separates *sǫm* 'songe, rêve' from *sǫm* 'sommeil', erroneously listing the latter as feminine.) But in fact there is no entirely reliable attestation of the sense 'dream' in OPr. Levy's other examples (= G. de Bornelh, ed. Kolsen, xl. 14, 21, 33, 39, var. *M*) are variants in a single MS. for *somnhe*; in von Wartburg's other example (= A. de Belenoi (?), ed. Dumitrescu, xx. 30), one may interpret *entre sons* as 'in my dreams' or 'in my sleep' (cf. 2753 *sons—sopor*). Even the Latin rendering in the *Donatz* is uncertain, for *B* has *summum*, which is conceivably the correct reading.

2735 *roms—genus pisis*. For the precise type of fish intended cf. *SW* vii. 373; *PD*; *FEW* x. 381–2 RHOMBUS.

2739 *doms—dominus*. *A* attests *dǫm*, *B* attests *dǫn*. There seems to be no example of *dom* at the rhyme; *dǫn*, equally unconfirmed, is omitted from *PD*, no doubt rightly.

2740–60. The disposition of the rhymes in *-ons* in the text follows *A*. It is possible, however, that *B* is right in placing under a separate heading (*-ons larg*) the Biblical rivers *Gions* and *Fizons* and the proper name *Amons*, which is no doubt the Biblical Amnon (2 Sam. 3: 2) or Amon (2 Kings 21: 18). As is well known, learned words, including proper names of Hebrew origin, normally have an open vowel in OPr. usage. The fact that no rhymes in [ǫns] are attested in the troubadours is not necessarily significant: the available rhyme-words would have been too few and too unusual. Though *B* is probably wrong in including *dons* here, the original text may well have given a series of three proper names in *-ons larg* before the longer series in *-ons estreit*. This in its turn could explain why in *A* the whole series is listed as *larg*, an error which can hardly be scribal (though it could, of course, be regarded as a *lapsus* on the author's part). Alternatively, one may suppose that the short series in -*ons larg* was a marginal addition misunderstood in an ancestor of *A*— this would explain why, in *A*, *Gions* and *Fisons* do not occur at the beginning of the series.

2749 *trons—ebetatus*. This must be a reflex of *TRŬNCEUS (*REW* 8954), not of TRŬNCUS (*REW* 8956), which would appear as *troncs*; *SW* viii. 491–2 is therefore probably wrong in classing this word with *trǫn* ('plat, camus; affligé?' *PD*). The word seems unattested elsewhere; but *tronc* 'blunt', despite the absence of this sense from *PD*, is attested once (*SW* viii. 493). OFr. *trons* is attested only as a noun (Godefroy, viii. 88). The OPr. form should be added to *FEW* xiii. 2. 337–9 TRŬNCEUS, for which it provides the sole Gallo-Romance attestation of a continuation of the original adjectival force.

2754 *gergons*. Cf. note to 188.

2755 *rons—ruga*. Sole example in *SW* vii. 379; cf. *FEW* xvi. 255 *HRUNKJA.

2762 *bohtz—fundus dolii*. Sole example in *SW* i. 152; *PD* lists also the form *bǫtge*.

2772–84. On the phonetic interpretation of the graphy -*onhz* here cf. Ronjat, ii, p. 181.

2776 *conhz—cum cuneo cudas*. Precisely this sense—'to strike with a wedge (or a die?)'—is not attested by Levy (*SW* i. 324–5, cf. i. 294, s.v. *comar*; *PD*); it should be added to *FEW* ii. 2. 1531 or 1533 CŬNĚUS.

2784 *lonhz—prolonges*. For *prolongare* 'to remove (sthg.) to a distance' cf. Baxter–Johnson (also Blaise, s.v. *prolongatio*, 2, 'éloignement').

2787 *orcs—quedam herba*. Sole example in *SW* v. 510. Despite the speculations of Tobler and Meyer (*Rom.* ii, p. 344), the precise sense remains unknown; cf. *FEW* xxi. 210.

2791 *reborcs—obtusus vel hebes*. Sole example in *SW* vii. 77; a second example occurs in the OPr. lapidary quoted in the note to 1436. Cf. the verb *emborcar* 'to blunt', used figuratively in Gavaudan, ed. Jeanroy, vi. 49–50 (*Rom.* xxxiv, p. 522)—Jeanroy's 'encombrer', adopted by *PD*, is certainly erroneous. *Reborc* is not cited in *FEW* i. 508–9 BRECHA, where OPr. *bercar* 'ébrécher' is given, nor in i. 543–8 BROCCUS, where the type ⌈*ébroquer*⌉ 'émousser, ébrécher' (ibid. 544, 547, cf. 548 n. 28) shows the same semantic development. Both *reborc* and *emborcar* would seem to show the influence of *berc* and *bercar* on reflexes of BROCCUS.

2792 *dorcs—anfora*. Modern dialect evidence suggests localization in a relatively limited area centring on Castres and covering part or all of the départements of Gers, Haute-Garonne, Tarn, Ariège, Aude, Hérault, Gard, and Cantal; cf. *FEW* vii. 392 ŏRCA. The [ǫ] attested by the *Donatz* and confirmed by Gavaudan, ed. Jeanroy, vi. 13 (*Rom.* xxxiv, p. 522), is presumably due to the influence of *dǫrna* and *dǫlh*.

2793 *forcs—dicitur a furca: vel bivium vel furcando struas.* The first of the two renderings provides Levy's sole example of *forc* 'bifurcation (of a road)' (*SW* iii. 538; for parallels cf. *FEW* iii. 891 fŭrca). *B*'s reading, which attaches *bivium* to *enforcs*, is suspect because it leaves *forcs* without any real translation; despite this, *enforc* was admitted as a *hapax* in *SW* ii. 494, whence it passed to *PD* and to *FEW* iii. 892, with the somewhat inaccurate translation 'crossroads'. For *A*'s 'furcam destruas', omitted in *B*, Guessard and Stengel printed *furca destruas*, which Levy noted with puzzlement (*SW* iii. 539); nevertheless, *forcar* was accepted into *PD* with the translation 'percer d'un coup de fourche?' but is not given in *FEW* iii. 885 (where mod. Provençal *fourca* 'donner un coup de fourche' is the closest analogue). The emendation adopted here gives *forcar* 'to pile up with a fork', a *hapax* in OPr. but supported by med. Latin *furcare* 'to load with a fork' (Du Cange, Baxter–Johnson) and by an exactly parallel scribal error in *A* (3521; these two, together with 953 *tusiende* for *tusiendo*, suggest that *A* derived from a copy in which *-d'* was used as an abbreviation for *-do*, cf. note to 930 for a similar use of *-d'* for *-dum*).

2794 *estorcs* [enforcs *B*]—*evellas*. This remains an enigma: *estorcar* or *-gar* is unattested, *enforcar* occurs only in the sense 'to hang from a gibbet' (*LR* iii. 363; *PD*). Neither *escorgar* nor *estorser* is possible here because of their [ǫ]; **esforcar*, which is just conceivable in the sense 'to pull up (weeds, etc., with the aid of a fork)', is unattested in OPr. and unparalleled elsewhere.

2796 *engorcs—ingurges. Ingurgare* seems otherwise unattested in med. Latin: one would expect *ingurgites*, as in *B*. However, it is possible to regard *A*'s reading as bad Latin induced by the form of the Provençal.

2797. Though classed as *-ous larg o estreit*, all seven examples show [ǫu]. For the troubadours there seems to have been only one type of rhyme in *-ou*—to that extent the heading in the *Donatz* is justified.

2802 *annous—annus novus vel Circumcisio*. The alternative translations were intended to indicate both the general sense 'new year' and the particular sense 'New Year's Day'. Guessard and Stengel printed only *annus novus*, and the second sense was not specially noted in *PD* or in *SW* i. 66, where, however, the three examples suggest that *annou* referred to a specific date. This sense should be added to *FEW* vii. 211 nŏvus, with which one should compare the examples cited in i. 99 annus.

2809 *pors—porrus*. Despite *B*'s *porus*, *porrus* is palaeographically a better emendation of *A*'s *portus*. For *por* 'pore' *LR* iv. 603 provides only two 14th-century examples, to which *SW* vi. 459 added the *Donatz*; *por* 'leek' is well attested (*SW*, loc. cit.).

2810 *tors—pars pisis*. This is a particular instance of the general sense 'piece, slice, fragment'; *SW* viii. 315 has one example where *tors* refers to fish and another (viii. 499, s.v. *tros*) referring to a serpent cut in pieces.

2811 *fors—perfores*. The emendation of *A*'s *preforsit* presupposes scribal misinterpretation of *pforS*. *SW* iii. 536 has no clear example of *forar* 'to pierce' (omitted from *PD*), whose existence is not necessarily established by *forat* 'hole' (ibid.). Cf. *FEW* iii. 698-9 FORARE, where our example should be added to those from OFr. and mod. Provençal.

2815 *mors—morsus*. *A*'s reading is retained on the supposition that *morsus* was intended here as a noun and in 2808 as a p. part.; *B*'s variant is no doubt a misreading of *morsus, -sura*.

2835 *vabors—vapor*. The form with *-b-*, absent from *LR* (v. 468), *SW*, and *PD*, should be added to *FEW* xiv. 166 VAPOR, where a number of modern forms with *-b-* are listed. (*LR* iii. 414 has a single example of *gabor*.)

2839 *bestors*. Not masculine, despite *PD*: cf. *SW* i. 142 and *LR* v. 374.

2849 *auctors—auctor*. *SW* i. 105 attests, as a n. sg. form, only *autre* (cf. *PD*, s.v. *autor*); for another example of *autors* cf. *Girart* 331.

2856 *In -ortz*. One would expect *larg*, as in *B*; cf., however, 3167, where both *A* and *B* omit the expected *larg*.

2866 *confortz* (*A*), *contrafortz* (*B*)—*pars corii in corio aposita causa confortandi, sicut in sotularibus*. *B*'s reading provides Levy's sole example for the sense 'leather stiffening (in shoes, etc.)' (*SW* i. 345; cf. *PD*). *A*'s reading is not noted by Levy—Stengel already gave only *contrafortz* in his index. While the existence of parallel forms in other Romance languages supports *B*'s reading against that of *A* (which could be explained palaeographically as a misreading of $\overset{a}{g}$ as 9), there is hardly a sufficiently strong case for emending *A*'s reading. *Confort* in this sense, though isolated, is conceivable semantically; in fact *contrafort* is not much less isolated, for Fr. *contrefort* is not attested in this sense before the 16th century (*FEW* iii. 733 FORTIS) and Sp. *contrafuerte* is attested in the same period (*DCELC* ii. 590, s.v. *fuerte*); for Catalan cf. *Dicc. Aguiló, Alcover*, s.v. *contrafort*.

2870-1 *retortz—iterum torquet: ad filum pertinet*; *retortus*. Sole examples of *retorser* in *SW* vii. 296, from Stichel, p. 72.

2885 *bortz—ludus*. The *Donatz* separates this word from *biortz—cursus equorum* (2891); in this Faidit is a better lexicographer than Raynouard (*LR* ii. 211-12) and Levy (*PD*), who confuse the two word-families. *PD* lists *bort* as a form of *beort*, *baordir* as a form of *bordir*, and is led by this confusion to mistranslate *bordei* and *bordeiar*. *Beordar* 'to joust' and *beort* 'joust' have always a disyllabic stem; cf. *FEW* i. 357-8 *BIHURDAN, where the only relic of Levy's confusion is the translation 'jeu' (ultimately from the translator's *ludus*) attached to OPr. *beort*. To the family of *bort* (cf. *FEW* i. 440-1 *BORDA) belong *bordir* 'to frolic' (*LR* ii. 212, to which may be added J. Rudel, ed. Jeanroy, iii. 10; Cercamon, ed. Jeanroy, ii. 39; *Girart* 914, 4244, 7739; P. Cardenal, ed. Lavaud, li. 48, where 'joûter' is a mistranslation); *bordre* 'id.' (*SW* i. 156 = R. d'Orange, ed. Pattison, iv. 2—apparently a *hapax*); *borda* 'tall story' (*LR* ii. 237); *bordei* 'frolic' (*LR* ii. 211, with a mistranslation which passed into *PD* as 'behourd, sorte de joute?'); *bordeiar* 'to frolic' (*SW* i. 156, mistranslated;

cf. *PD* 'combattre au *bordei*'); and possibly *bordeitz* 'toy' (J. Rudel, loc. cit., var. *C*; cf. Bertoni in *AdM* xxvii–xxviii, 1915–16, p. 218, and *FEW* i. 441 n. 4). The pr. part. *baorden* (*Jaufré*, ed. Breuer [= MS. *B*], 3079), which misled Raynouard and hence Levy into admitting the ghost-word *baordir*, is an error for *burden* (so Brunel's ed. = MS. *A*). There is no clear instance in OPr. of confusion between the two word-families. The substantive *bort* is little attested. Apart from the *Donatz*, the only certain example (already in *LR* ii. 211) is A. Daniel, ed. Toja, xv. 36—'Anc mais . . . no'm plac tant treps ni bortz'—where Toja mistranslates 'jousts'. A probable third example is R. d'Orange, ed. Pattison, xxi. 12, where the editor, still using Raynouard's confusion of *bort* and *beort* as an argument, interprets *dreich bort* as 'bastard justice', hence 'unjust'; but the only satisfactory interpretation is 'a mere game, a mere frolic'.

2886 *bortz—manser vel spurius*. For *manser*, which is the only possible emendation of *AB*'s corrupt readings, cf. Blaise, Niermeyer, *Novum Glossarium*, s.v. *manzer*. That *bort* had [ǫ] is confirmed by Raynouard's last example (*LR* ii. 238 = A. Daniel, ed. Toja, xv. 29) and by *Deux mss. prov.* xxvi. 45 (R. de Cornet); *PD*'s *bǫrt* is erroneous.

2889 *lortz—parum audiens*. The sense 'hard of hearing' is confirmed by examples of ⌈*lort*⌉ 'sourd' in mod. dialects, mainly of Franche-Comté, cf. *FEW* v. 468 LŪRĬDUS, where the present example should be added. *SW* iv. 439–40 and *PD* admit only the sense 'slow-witted'.

2890 *gortz—rigidus infirmitate*. *SW* iv. 151, s.v. *gort*, 2, emended to *r. frigiditate* and interpreted 'stiff with cold', as also in *PD*. This is quite unnecessary. *FEW* iv. 327–8 GŬRDUS shows a number of examples expressing stiffness from causes other than the cold; our example, for which *FEW* iv. 327 accepts Levy's translation, belongs with these. It is confirmed by *Deux mss. prov.* xxvi. 49 (R. de Cornet), which Levy (*SW*, loc. cit.) found unclear, where the sense 'stiff with infirmity' is the most satisfactory.

2899 *borns—pomum temptorii* (cf. 2737, where the same translation renders *poms*). Sole example of *born* 'knob on top of a tent' in *SW* i. 156 (and *PD*). Tobler (*Rom.* ii, p. 345) proposed the emendation *nomen territorii*. The word is something of an enigma. Raynouard registers *born* 'bord' (*LR* ii. 239, also *PD*) with a single 15th-century example in which *de born en born*, however, seems rather to mean 'from one boundary to another'. The word is registered under *BŎTINA in *REW* 1235 but not in *FEW* i. 465–6; *FEW* i. 436 BORD registers a modern *born* 'edge', from Bazas (Gironde). If *born* 'boundary(-stone)' really existed in OPr.—and this is not clear— one might suppose *born* 'knob' to be due to the semantic influence of *bola* 'ball; boundary(-stone)' (*LR* ii. 233–4; *PD*). Or one might consider the possible correction to *borna territorii*; for *borna* cf. Du Cange.

2905 *vorms*, without translation. As Chabaneau noted (*RLR* xiii, p. 143), the intended sense must have been 'glanders'; cf. *SW* viii. 844–5, to which may be added *Recettes vétérinaires*, ed. Brunel in *Rom.* lxxxii, pp. 31 (§ 2) and 35 (§ 32), and *Recettes des Pyrénées*, §§ 488, 494, 501 (pp. 74, 76, 79).

NOTES 327

2911 *torns—instrumentum tornatile.* The interpretation 'lathe' (*SW* viii. 287), of which there is a second example, is preferable to 'winch, reel' (*PD*).

2913 *contorns—primus sulcus aratri.* Sole example in *SW* i. 343; cf. *FEW* xiii. 2. 74 TORNARE. The sense must clearly be 'the first furrow made round a field when beginning to plough'—*PD*'s 'lisière d'un champ' (accepted in *FEW*, loc. cit.) is an approximation. More startling is Levy's emendation of *AB*'s *unus* to *ultimus* (*SW*, loc. cit.); *primus* is the only satisfactory correction, cf. the use of *.j.* for *prima* in 502 (MS. *A*).

2916–26. With the possible exception of 2917, all ten words in -*ǫutz* show vocalization of -*l*-. Only one of the ten is listed by Faidit in both forms (*soutz* 2925, *solz* 2694). Relevant rhymes are rare in the troubadours; in A. Daniel, ed. Toja, xii, however, the rhymes in -*outas* are parallel with the present series. Leaving aside 2917, all words here show etyma in -LTUS except for 2926 *coutz* 'wall'. The case is parallel but not quite identical with the words in -*altz* ~ -*autz* (see note to 1624–40). It is worth remarking, however, that the rendering of *coutz* as *paries* stems from the translator and could conceivably be regarded as a misrepresentation of Faidit's original intention. At all events, the condemnation of *cavautz* < CABALLUS is hardly consistent with the acceptance of *coutz* < CŎLLIS.

2917 *Moutz* (*A*), *Voutz* (*B*)—*quidam fluvius.* I have not succeeded in identifying either of these forms.

2922 *arcvoutz—arcus lapideus.* Raynouard has two examples of *arcsvoltutz* and *arc-vout* (*LR* ii. 113 = *Girart* 7820, 1595), for which, however, Miss Hackett's edition offers *arvoluz* and *arvol* (the latter form, absent from the dictionaries, occurs a number of times in *Girart*). Does the *Donatz* provide the only example of the spelling with *arc*?

2926 *coutz—paries.* *SW* i. 397 has a single passage attesting *cou* five times in the sense 'wall' and indicating its feminine gender. *PD* gives *colt, cout, cou* (for *o* read *ǫ*), the first two presumably derived from the *Donatz*. In the orthography of *PD* the word would be better written *cǫl*; it is a reflex of CŎLLIS, as the gender shows. In *FEW* ii. 2. 917 COLLUM (para. *f*), where some modern representatives of the same family are given, the OPr. forms are entirely omitted; they resolve the question (ibid. 919 n. 47) of whether the whole group—described (ibid. 918) as 'ganz vereinzelt'—belongs under CŎLLUM or CŎLLIS. Thus both articles require some modification.

2927–33. All six rhymes in -*ǫutz* show vocalization of -*l*-. Two of the words concerned are listed in both forms (*soutz* 2929, *solz* 2697; *voutz* 2928, *volz* 2700). None of the six has an etymon in LL + s: Faidit gives, for example, *polz* < PŬLLUS (2699) but not *poutz.

2933 *estoutz—de facili irascens.* This is to be regarded as a rendering of the sense 'proud, haughty' (*PD*; cf. *LR* iii. 220 and *SW* iii. 333–4). *FEW* xvii. 245 *STOLT admits 'qui s'irrite facilement' for OFr. *estout*.

2935 *botz*—*ictus*. This suggests that *bǫt* should be added to the *bọt*, but of *PD* (cf. *SW* i. 159). The [ǫ] is confirmed by *Girart* 6541, if the editor's emendation of *boc* for *broc* is admitted. *FEW* i. 455–63 BŌTAN does not discuss the quality of the vowel, which seems otherwise to be [ǫ] in OPr. and OFr.

2936 *escotz*—*lignum parvum acutum*. 'Splinter', according to *SW* iii. 192 and *PD*. But 'thorn' fits Levy's other example rather better; and this is confirmed by *Girart* 6611 ('partie du corps', hesitantly advanced in the glossary, is erroneous) and perhaps by the use of the same Latin translation for (*tancs* 1759). *FEW* xvii. 128–30 *SKŎT has no example of this sense; cf., however, the single mod. dialect example of *écoter* 'to tear a garment' (ibid. 128) and OFr. *escoter* 'to tear' (on which cf. *Rom.* lxxxvi, p. 428).

2940 *rotz*. The *Donatz*, alone of OPr. examples of *rot* and *rotar*, attests the [ǫ], explained for French (Bloch–Wartburg, s.v. *rot*) as expressive in origin. OPr., however, shows the open vowel much earlier than French (cf. *FEW* x. 539 RŬCTARE, RŬCTUS).

2942 *cotz*—*multatio*. The translation *permutatio* given by *B* and attached in *A* to the previous word is clearly wrong. Chabaneau (*Rom.* vi, p. 140) suggested *percutatio* 'a blow', dubiously accepted in *SW* i. 395 and *PD* ('coup?'). The Latin word is quite impossible, though *cot* 'blow' is not in itself inconceivable (*FEW* ii. 2. 1155–7 KOPTEIN, however, has nothing parallel). The word cited by the *Donatz* is certainly *cot* 'a fine for damage to the fields' (*PD*, from *LR* ii. 503–4; cf. *FEW* ii. 2. 1547 QUŎT). It suffices to emend to *multatio*; the *per-* of *AB*, if it is not merely the result of an attempt to make sense of a corrupt *mutatio*, may be a relic of a word or words which, in the original, followed *multatio* and amplified it.

2948 *cabotz*—*genus piscis*. Sole example in *SW* i. 181; cf. *Dicc. Aguiló, Alcover*, s.v. *cabot*. Thomas, *Mélanges d'étymologie française* (*première série*)[2], Paris, 1927, p. 68 n. 5, cites *cabos* in a Latin document of 1181 from Toulouse and maintains, against *SW* and *PD*, that the n. sg. was *cabotz*, not *cabot*. If the etymon were certainly *CAPŎCIUS (Bloch–Wartburg, s.v. *chabot*) this would be true (cf. *FEW* ii. 1. 335 CAPUT, where the nature of the suffix is not discussed).

2951 *botz*—*nepos*. There is no example of *botz*, n. sg., in *SW* i. 158–9 and v. 374 or in *LR* iv. 313, but Brunel, *Chartes*, attests the form a number of times (i. 151. 2; 190. 13; 243. 16; 270. 1 and 4; ii. 510. 2; 527. 21).

2954 (var. *B*) *cotz*—*parvus canis*. Sole example of this form (for usual *gotz*, *gos*) in *SW* i. 397, cf. *LR* iii. 488 and *FEW* ii. 2. 1591–2 KŬŠ. Is the form an Italianism?

2955 *cogotz*—*cuius uxor eum adulterat*. For the form in -*otz*, admitted in *PD* but whose existence was queried in *SW* i. 274, cf. *Girart* 1465, 4689 (two examples of *cogoz* at the rhyme).

2968 *bucs—bracchium sine manu.* Sole example in *SW* i. 171 for this sense; *FEW* i. 600–2 *BŪK provides no semantic parallel.

2971 *trebucs—calige truncate.* The basic sense appears to be 'leggings', cf. *SW* viii. 340; *FEW* xvii. 383 TUBRUCUS; Du Cange, s.vv. *trebucus, tubrucus, trabucus.* For the use of *truncatus* in this context cf. Du Cange, s.v. It is unclear why *PD* gives the word as feminine; its masculine gender is suggested, not only by the med. Latin forms, but by the n. pl. *trabuc* in P. Cardenal, ed. Lavaud, xviii. 37. It is noteworthy that the n. sg. or obl. pl. OPr. form is here translated by a Latin n. pl.

2973 *claücs—clausis.* Emendation to *cazucs—caducus* (Tobler, *Rom.* ii, p. 345) is hardly possible: OPr. attests only *caduc*, a learned loan-word (*LR* ii. 286: two examples from the *Elucidari*); there is no indication that CADŪCUS had any popular reflex (cf. *FEW* ii. 1. 32). Chabaneau (*RLR* xiii, pp. 143–4) accepted Guessard's emendation to *clausus* and explained *claüc* as a form of (or scribal error for) *cluc* ~ *cuc* 'closed (of eyes)'; *claüc* was hesitantly admitted in this sense into *PD*, s.v. *cluc* (cf. *SW* i. 264), but is not listed in *FEW* ii. 1. 798–9 *CLŪDICARE, where there is nothing comparable. Besides the difficulty of admitting *claüc* as a possible form and the equal difficulty of explaining it as a scribal error, *clausus* would be an improbably vague translation. Med. Latin *clausis* 'rabbit-warren' is a *hapax* (cf. Du Cange, s.v.) and sheds no light on our word, which remains an enigma.

2974 *ducs—quedam avis.* This is Levy's only certain example (*SW* ii. 307) for the sense 'horned owl'; to it may be added R. d'Orange (?), ed. Pattison, p. 209, l. 13.

2981 *zucs—testa capitis.* Sole example of this form in *SW* vii. 870, for the more frequent *suc.* But *SW*, loc. cit., s.v. *suca*, has a single example of *çuca* and *LR* v. 284 attests *zuquet* for *suquet* (the latter is oddly omitted in *PD*, despite the cross-reference s.v. *zuquet*); the forms in *ç-* and *z-* are both from Daude de Prades. Cf. also *FEW* xiii. 2. 399–400 *TŪKKA.

2984 *palhucs—parva palea.* Sole example in *SW* vi. 29; cf. *FEW* vii. 497 PALEA, where this is the only form in -*uc*. Levy's 'chopped straw' is the most likely interpretation of the Latin, though 'a small straw' or 'fine straw' is not impossible; cf. *Dicc. Aguiló, Alcover*, s.v. *palluc(h)*.

2986 *devertucs—apostema extrinseca.* Sole example in *SW* ii. 195; cf. *FEW* xiv. 318 VĚRTĚRE for a single mod. example of [devertüt] 'boil', from Dégagnac (Lot), to which the OPr. form should be added.

2989 *buf—vox indignantis.* Sole example in *SW* i. 172 (omitted in *PD*); omitted in *FEW* i. 597 BUFF-, PUFF-.

2990 *chuf* (*A*), *cuf* (*B*)—*pili super frontem.* Sole example in *SW* i. 252; there, as in *PD*, both forms are admitted. It is impossible to say whether *A*'s graphy represents [ts] or [tš] or even [k], nor can one be sure that *B*'s reading is an error for *çuf* or even *tuf*. Chabaneau (*RLR* xiii, p. 144) discussed these matters inconclusively; cf. *REW* 9632a ZUPPFA (where no

OPr. form is noted) and, for a different etymology, *DEI*, s.v. *ciuffo*. The presence in *FEW* xvii. 405 pūfa of Aude *cufelhado* 'crested lark' is possibly relevant. A form **tuf*, if such existed, might conceivably find its place in *FEW* xiii. 2. 397 tūfa. It is noteworthy that here, as in 2991, an OPr. obl. sg. form is rendered by a Latin nominative.

2996 *Saüls—Saul*. *Saulus* (Acts 7: 58) or *Saullus* are equally possible emendations.

2997 *In -ums estreit*. The qualification *estreit* is strictly unnecessary.

3000 *agrums—res acerba, sicut fructus recentes*. Sole example in *SW* i. 35; cf. *FEW* i. 18 ACER. The sense of *agrum* would seem to have been wider than *PD*'s 'fruit aigre'.

3001 (var. *B*) *alhums—illumines*. Since 3001–3 are compressed into a limited space in *A*, this may well be a scribal omission of *A* rather than an addition in *B*.

3009 *aturs—coneris*. The *conaris* of *AB* repeats the error found in 2462.

3023 *cambutz—habens longas tibias*. Sole example in *SW* i. 193; cf. *FEW* ii. 1. 111 CAMBA.

3024 *alutz—plenus alis*. Sole example in *SW* i. 54; cf. *FEW* i. 56 ALA.

3026 *cutz—vilis persona*. That this form, attested only in the *Donatz*, is the n. sg. of *cuson* (*LR* ii. 533) was already supposed by Levy (*SW* i. 431; *PD*) and is confirmed by the spelling *cuczun* in *S. Foi* 574 and by *cucon, cucos* (-*c*- = *ç*) in *Girart* 5389, 3522. Cf. also *FEW* ii. 1. 832 cŏctio, n. 1.

3028 *grutz—farrum*. Sole example in *SW* iv. 205; cf. *FEW* xvi. 96 **grût and, for a second example, *Recettes des Pyrénées*, § 488 (p. 74). For the form *farrum* cf. Du Cange, s.v.; for the sense 'gruel' cf. *TLL* vi. 1. 276 (ll. 37 and 47), s.v. *far*.

3050–1 *conougutz, desconougutz*. On pretonic *ou* for *o* cf. Pfister, *Beiträge, Vox*, xvii, p. 326 (§ 26).

3074 *enbutz—illud cum quo mittit vinum vel aquam in vase*. *Mittit* is admissible in the sense 'one puts'; cf. 11a, where *potest* translates *pot om*. Guessard corrected to *mittitur* and *aqua*; Stengel erroneously reproduced *aqua* as the MS. reading.

3085 *grus—granulum uve*. *LR* iii. 497 has two examples which confirm this sense; *PD*'s 'grain'—no doubt intended for 'grain (de raisin)'—is misleading.

3105–16. This note on alternative forms for the 2nd sg. pr. subj. of first conjugation verbs finds its place here as a sort of link between the masculine rhymes which precede and the feminine ones which follow: the verb-forms in question will give rhymes of either kind.

3111 *estancs o estanques—idem*. *A*'s reading is acceptable if one takes 'to hinder' (*idem* referring to *inpedias*) as an approximation to the sense 'to dam, hold back' (cf. 3452). *B*'s *liges* is possible only with emendation to *estacs o estaques* (recommended by Tobler, *Rom.* ii, p. 346; cf. 1547 *estacs—liges*). Conceivably the original had both *estancs* and *estacs*, as supposed by Bauquier (*Rom.* vi, p. 452), though this involves an excessive amount of conjectural emendation. It must be conceded that *A*'s reading, which I have accepted, is strikingly asymmetrical, since in 3110 and 3112–14 *idem* is used to render only the second verb-form of each pair.

3117 sqq. *B*'s erroneous division of the rhymes in *-ura* into *larg* and *estreit* is due solely to the rubricator (cf. var. to 3117, 3128), who must have been puzzled by the marginal indication for two rubrics *Jn ura*. The second of these may have derived from a blank line in *B*'s exemplar, the result of a failure to decipher 3129–30.

3123 *perjura—degerat*. For the Latin cf. Niermeyer, s.v. *dejerare*.

3127 *amesura—facit ad mensuram*. The translation indicates *s'amesurar* 'to act with moderation' (*LR* iv. 201 has two examples), a sense omitted by *PD*, which registers the verb as tr. only.

3139 *pastura—pascitur*. *PD* has only *pasturar*, v. tr., 'to drive to pasture', cf. *SW* vi. 135 and *LR* iv. 450. For another example of the intr. sense 'to graze' cf. *Girart* 1009. *FEW* vii. 764 PASTŪRA has the intr. sense only.

3167 *In -era*. Cf. note to 2856.

3171 *lesquera—legerem*. *AB*'s *legerent* is explicable as a misunderstanding of *legerē^t*, i.e. the addition of a 3rd sg. form to the original 1st sg., paralleled in the words *et tercie* of the Latin (3173). In a text which originally mentioned *-era* for the 1st person alone, the addition would be an obvious one.

3181 *apodera—subpeditat*. Sole example in *SW* i. 72 for the sense 'to put (s.o.) in possession of (sthg.)', accepted by *PD* and hence by *FEW* ix. 235 PŎSSE. It is hardly likely that this is the sense intended. *Suppeditare* was commonly used in med. Latin in the sense 'to trample on, subjugate', cf. Du Cange, Baxter–Johnson, s.v., the translation 'metre souz pié' in *Abavus*, iii. 5244, and the injunction 'Nunquam suppedito ponas pro sub pede pono' in *Abavus*, iv. 8389. And the most common meaning of *apoderar* was precisely 'to subjugate, vanquish', cf., besides *LR* iv. 584, the glossaries to *Croisade*, *Jaufré* (ed. Breuer), G. de Bornelh (ed. Kolsen), B. de Ventadour (ed. Appel), A. de Belenoi (ed. Dumitrescu), F. de Marseille (ed. Stroński), etc. This is the natural interpretation here.

3188 *ateira—per seriem ponit*. Sole example in *SW* i. 97, to which may be added *Chartes*, i. 119. 9; cf. *FEW* xvii. 326 *TÊRĪ.

3219 *consira—considerat*. Guessard printed *esconsira* (a conflation of *A* and *B*), which is given as if it were *A*'s reading by Stengel (who, however, notes the MS. reading *econsira* on p. xxviii, n. to 61b, 26). From here *esconsirar*, *escos-* passed to Stichel, p. 50, whence it was accepted by *SW* iii. 188, by *PD*, and by *FEW* ii. 2. 1067 CONSĪDĔRARE, where *esconsirar* is noted as 'rare' (!) and has no parallel. Clearly this is a ghost-word, for which MS. *B* and Guessard are jointly responsible. *A*'s text needs no correction, beyond the word-division *e consira*.

3222. *Prima conjugatzo* is a simple slip on Faidit's part, uncorrected by the translator. He meant the fourth conjugation, i.e. verbs in *-ir*.

3226 *nora—nurus*. The [ǫ] is confirmed by Raynouard's first example (*LR* iv. 327 = Raimon de Tors, ed. Parducci in *Studj romanzi*, vii, 1911, pp. 38–9, iv. 10, 20, 30, 36, 40, 42), cf. *FEW* vii. 246 NŪRUS. *PD*'s *nǫra* is erroneous.

3241 *assapora—gusta quid sapit*. *LR* v. 129, and hence *PD*, attest only the form with *-b-*. Is the present form learned, or an Italianism?

3245 *laura—color laureus*. Sole example in *SW* iv. 336, interpreted as a f. noun 'the colour of laurels', a sense repeated in *PD* and in *FEW* v. 208 LAURUS, where our word is noted as a *hapax*, without analogues. In fact the Latin rendering no more indicates *laura* as a noun than in the exactly parallel *saurs—color aureus* (1858). Two other examples show that it is simply the f. form of the adj. *laur*: *Deux mss. prov.* xxvi. 27 (R. de Cornet), which *SW*, loc. cit., already noted separately without translation, and *Girart* 6530. In these the adj. is applied respectively to a bull and a horse; cf. *FEW* v. 209 for a number of mod. parallels, to which the OPr. attestations should be added. Corominas (*DCELC* iii. 135, s.v. *loro*, 2) notes that most early Romance examples of this colour-adjective apply to cattle and horses and that the translation given in the *Donatz* may well depend on considerations of etymology. This is certainly true; as a result, it is impossible to say precisely what colour was denoted by *laur*.

3264 *dessala—salem tolit*. Sole example in *SW* ii. 112, from Stichel, p. 35; cf. *FEW* xi. 81 SAL and *Dicc. Alcover*, s.v. *dessalar*.

3280 *acantela—in latus declinat*. Sole example in *SW* i. 11, from Stichel, p. 7; for the interpretation cf. note to 1702.

3281 *mantela—velat*. Sole example in *SW* v. 115, from Stichel, p. 62; cf. *FEW* vi. 275 MANTUS.

3300 *pila—lapis cavus*. This is Levy's sole example (*SW* vi. 316) for the sense 'trough?', reproduced in *PD* but not in *FEW* viii. 474–5 PĪLA. Though this sense is well attested in mod. dialects (*FEW*, loc. cit.), it is unnecessary to suppose it here: the translator's Latin merely indicates 'a hollowed-out stone receptacle'.

3309 *crila* (*A*), *grila* (*B*)—*cribat*. Sole example in *SW* iv. 195 for both forms, which are admitted together in *PD*, as in Stichel, p. 29; cf. *FEW* ii. 2. 1333 CRĪBRARE. Latin *cribare*, given here by both *A* and *B*, is attested from the 5th century (*TLL* iv. 1189; cf. *FEW* ii. 2. 1334).

3311 *stola—stola*. *LR* iii. 221 attests only *estola*, but both forms are admitted into *PD*; *FEW* xii. 279 STOLA provides a second example of *stola* (Aude, 1504) but omits the present one.

3314 *mola—molis vel mola*. *AB*'s *mol'* can be interpreted only as *molis* (= *mollis*), not, as by Guessard and Stengel, as *molat*. That *mola* existed as f. of *mol* is shown by the adv. *molamen* (*LR* iv. 248).

3320 *desola—dissuit solas*. Sole example in *SW* ii. 154, from Stichel, p. 34; cf. *FEW* xii. 41 SŎLEA, *Dicc. Alcover*, s.v. *dessolar*, and *Recettes des Pyrénées*, § 501 (p. 78). For *sola* = *solea* cf. Du Cange, s.v. *sola*, 1.

3328 *agola—in gula mittit*. Sole example in *SW* i. 33, from Stichel, p. 11; cf. *FEW* iv. 309 GŬLA.

3329 *esgola—foramen facit in veste unde caput intrat*. Sole example in *SW* iii. 229, from Stichel, p. 51; cf. *FEW* iv. 308 GŬLA. *LR* ii. 437 has a single example of the p. part. *escolat* 'décolleté', which is omitted from *PD*.

3334 *grola—solea vetus*. Sole example in *SW* iv. 199; cf. *FEW* iv. 271 *GROLLA. *Recettes des Pyrénées*, § 366 (p. 39), confirms the Latin rendering.

3343 *acula—cullum ponit in terra*. Sole example in *SW* i. 18, from Stichel, p. 9; cf. *FEW* ii. 2. 1512 CŪLUS.

3347 *malha—facit ammos in lorica*. Sole example in *SW* v. 65 for the sense 'to make (a hauberk) in chain-mail'; cf. *FEW* vi. 14 MACULA.

3363 *eschalha—frangit*. Sole example in *SW* iii. 141, from Stichel, p. 49; the word is omitted in *PD* and in *FEW* xvii. 88–94 *SKALJA, where none of the verbs cited has so general a sense as is indicated here by the translator. The latter may well have envisaged some specific meaning or meanings, such as that of mod. Provençal *escayá* 'casser (des œufs pour les cuire à la poêle)' (ibid. 89).

3368 *tartalha—loquitur frequenter et ociose*. *A*'s *preciose*, despite Stengel's opinion (n. to 63b, 24), is impossible, as are the corrections to *precise*, proposed by Galvani (p. 334), and to *precipitose* or *impetuose*, proposed by Tobler (*Rom.* ii, p. 346). *SW* viii. 69 dubiously accepts the last of these and hesitates between 'to stammer' (accepted in *PD*, without question-mark) and 'to chatter noisily'. *FEW* xiii. 1. 108 TAR- accepts the former without comment, though the second receives rather more support from the mod. dialect forms. *Ociose* is the only emendation which satisfies sense and palaeographical probability; for the sense cf. Blaise, s.v. *otiose*. On a possible interpretation of *frequenter* see note to 1107. This is the only example of *tartalhar* in this sense: the other cited in *SW—tartalha, favelare spesso* in the Provençal–Italian glossary (Stengel, 91b, 24; ed. Castellani, 255 = *Lebendiges Mittelalter*, p. 42)—derives from the *Donatz*.

3372 *falha—quidam ludus tabularum*. Sole example in *SW* iii. 399. The game seems not to be attested in French before the 15th century (cf. Godefroy, iii. 699, to which may be added Charles d'Orléans, ed. Champion, *rondeau* 178. 11 = vol. 2, p. 392), unless the expression *joer a totes failles* (*TL* iii. 1560–1, s.v. *faille* = *Bible Guiot*) can be held to presuppose *faille* as the name of a game. Cf. also *Dicc. Aguiló*, s.v. *falla*, 3, and *Dicc. Alcover*, s.v. *falla*³, 2 (b), where the translation given for *joch de falles* is certainly incorrect for the medieval example cited. On the game itself see

H. J. R. Murray, 'The Medieval Game of Tables', *Medium Aevum*, x, 1941, pp. 57–69, especially pp. 59–60, 67.

3373 *falha*, without translation. No doubt intended in the sense 'buttocks (of a horse)', a sense not registered by the dictionaries; for an example cf. *Recettes vétérinaires*, ed. Brunel in *Rom.* lxxxii, p. 31 (§ 11)—the word belongs with *FEW* iii. 391 *FALLIA, where there are some analogues in mod. dialects.

3377 *fendalha—fissura*. Sole example in *SW* iii. 436; it should be added to *FEW* iii. 551 FĬNDĔRE, where the mod. analogues suggest localization in Gascony, Béarn, Aveyron.

3381 *somnelha—frequenter sonniatur, vel dormitat*. If the two translations were not intended as synonymous, then the former means 'to dream (about sthg.)' and the latter 'to doze' (cf. *SW* vii. 802 for other attestations; *PD* omits the first sense). For *frequenter* cf. note to 1107; rather than merely modifying *sonniatur*, the word applies generally to the whole sense of *somnelha* and would perhaps be better followed by a colon.

3387 *conselha—consulit*. Cf. note to 2066.

3388 *botelha—vas aquatile*. Cf. 3395, where the same Latin words render *selha*. On *aquatilis* 'for holding water' cf. *Mittellateinisches Wb.*, s.v., where a similar but not identical sense is noted.

3390 *desparelha—dispares facit*. The sense 'to make unlike, to match (two things) badly' is not registered by *PD* (cf. *LR* iv. 417), where the only meaning is that attested in *Donatz* 2068; this is also the case in *FEW* vii. 649 PARĬCŬLUS.

3391 *pendelha—frequenter pendit*. *LR* iv. 493 attests *pendelhar*, v. intr., with a single example; it is given only as intr. by *PD* and *FEW* viii. 177 PENDĔRE, cf. *SW* vi. 205. Unless one corrects *pendit* to *pendet* (cf. 1309, which shows that the translator was aware of the distinction between *pendĕre* and *pendēre*), the present example must be accepted as an attestation of a transitive sense. For *frequenter* cf. note to 1107.

3396 *telha—cortex tilie*. Sole example in *SW* viii. 108. *B*'s *delha*, accepted in *SW* ii. 62, in *PD*, and (to the exclusion of *telha*) in *FEW* xiii. 1. 328 TILIA (cf. 331 n. 7: 'Warum sonorisierung des *t-*?'), is no doubt a scribal error.

3399 *estrelha*, without translation. The word is untranslated in *A*, since the translation of *estrelha* 'curry-comb' (*SW* iii. 342) is erroneously split in two in such a way as to cover both words. *B*'s reading supports the correction to *estrelha*, 3rd sg. pr. ind. of *estrelhar* 'to curry (a horse)'; *LR* iii. 231–2 and *SW* iii. 350 attest only *estrilhar*, with two examples of its use in a figurative sense, but cf. *FEW* xii. 303 STRĬGĬLIS for the frequent occurrence of ⌈*estrelhar*⌉ in mod. dialects.

3403 *Amelha—proprium nomen mulieris*. Brunel, *Chartes*, i and ii, attests the masculine *Amelh*.

3408 *desroïlha—aufert rubiginem*. Sole example in *SW* ii. 167, from Stichel, p. 35; cf. *FEW* x. 428–9 RŌBĪGO.

3409 *bilha—ligneus ludus*. *SW* i. 146 cites this as the sole example in a literal sense; *PD*, following Mistral, s.v. *biho*, interprets 'game of tip-cat', which is accepted in *FEW* i. 365 *BILIA. The Latin rendering more probably expresses the object used in the game, rather than the game itself (cf. note to 1540); 'skittle' is the most likely interpretation (cf. *FEW*, loc. cit., and *Dicc. Alcover*, s.v. *bitlla*[1], 1) and would account for the figurative use of *juar de la bilho* in an obscene sense, in Levy's other example.

3412 *canilha—vermis comedens dura*. Sole example in *SW* i. 199. The interpretation 'woodworm', also given in Diez, *EtWb*, ii c, s.v. *chenille*, in *PD* and in *FEW* ii. 1. 188 CANĪCULA, seems the only possible one.

3413 *ponzilha*. See note to 1101.

3414 *ilha—ilia*. Sole example in *SW* iv. 226, cf. *FEW* iv. 545 ĪLIA; OFr. *illes* (Godefroy, iv. 542) is also a *hapax*.

3415 *adouzilha—spinam in dolio mittit*. Normally *adozilhar* (cf. *LR* iii. 76; *PD*; *FEW* iii. 172 DUCĪCULUS); on *ou* for *o* cf. note to 3050–1.

3416 *asotilha—subtiliat*. *PD*, following *LR* v. 284, registers only *asotilar*. Our form should be added to the other reflexes of *ASSŬBTĪLIARE in *FEW* xii. 366 SŬBTĪLIS (cf. 367 n. 6).

3420 *remolha—ad ŭmiditatem venit*. This is Levy's only example (*SW* vii. 220, s.v. *remolhar*, 2; omitted in *PD*) for the intr. sense 'to become damp'. It is impossible to say whether the verb was intr. (cf. the single example of OFr. *remoiller* in Godefroy, vii. 7) or refl.

3424 *destolha—deviet*. Neither *A*'s *deruet* nor Guessard's correction to *diruat*, approved by Stengel, is acceptable; *deviet* alone gives a possible sense, either v. tr. 'to turn (s.o.) aside from his path' or v. intr. 'to turn aside from the road' (cf. Blaise, Du Cange; *deviare* occurs in 904 in the first of these senses). Neither of these meanings is given for *destolre* by the OPr. dictionaries; but the former is presupposed by the refl. sense 'to refrain, to desist' (*PD*; *LR* v. 370), while *SW* ii. 169, s.v. *destoler*, contains a clear example of the latter (Guiraut d'Espanha, l. 2 of Levy's quotation). Cf. *FEW* xiii. 2. 19 TŎLLĔRE, where the sense attested in the *Donatz* belongs with OFr. *destolir* 'détourner, empêcher, prévenir'.

3435 *dolha—foramen quo asta in ferrum ponitur*. Sole example in *SW* ii. 270; cf. *FEW* iii. 177 *DULJA, where a 15th-century *dolis* (Avignon) is also noted, and *Dicc. Aguiló, Alcover*, s.v. *dolla*. The simple correction to *inserit[ur]*, made by Guessard and accepted by Chabaneau (*RLR* xiii, p. 144) and Levy (*SW*, loc. cit.), does not account for the *ponitur* which the MS. erroneously gives as the translation for 3436. The correction to *in ferrum* postulates that the scribe at once misread and misinterpreted *inferr̄*. It is worth noting that virtually all examples of OFr. *doille* (Godefroy, ix. 402; *TL* ii. 1988) do in fact refer to weapons with an iron point or blade fixed in a wooden haft.

3437 *solha—poluit*. This seems to be the sole example which attests [ǫ] in this word (cf. *SW* vii. 787), though *PD* lists also *sulhar* (following the single example of the 3rd sg. pr. ind. *sulha* in *LR* v. 288). This could be held to support the etymology *sŭcŭlare (*REW* 8418; cf. *FEW* xii. 66 sŏlium and 67, n. 14); the omission of OPr. *solhar* in *FEW* (xii. 63) is the more unfortunate.

3438 *verolha—vecte firmat*. Sole example in *SW* viii. 685; cf. *FEW* xiv. 284 vĕrĭcŭlum, where the present attestation should be added.

3448 *branca—frondes*. The Latin plural is striking. It is possible to accept it as a rendering of a collective sense of *branca* (parallel with *fuelha*), a sense which is possible in Raynouard's first example (*LR* ii. 249) but for which I know of no certain attestation. Alternatively, correction to *frondet* or *frondescit* can be envisaged (Stengel's index, which classes *branca* as 3rd sg. pr. ind. of *brancar*, silently assumes this emendation); or one could read *frons, -dis* (cf. 2752 *frons, -tis*).

3450 *abranca—capit vi*. Guessard printed *capit vimen*, for which Stengel (index) and Tobler (*Rom*. ii, p. 346) hesitantly proposed *capit vimine* or *vi*. Levy (*SW* i. 7) was undecided between these and omitted the verb from *PD* (it is apparently a *hapax*). The emendation to *vi* is supported by the occurrence of the same scribal error elsewhere in the *Donatz* (1786; *vi* gave rise to difficulties in 815 and 3160 also); the sense 'to take hold of (sthg., s.o.) by force' would then be related to the meanings 'entourer de ses bras; enlacer, embrasser' attested by *FEW* i. 497 branca for some mod. dialects and by *SW* (loc. cit.) for OCat. (cf. also *Dicc. Alcover*, s.v. *abrancar*). Emendation to *aranca*, 3rd sg. pr. ind. of *arancar* 'to pull up by the roots' (*LR* v. 82; *PD*) is possible; it would presuppose a common error of *AB* or an error of *O*².

3454 *manca*. Cf. note to 1755.

3455 *sanca—sinistra*. Clearly the *manu* which *A* places here—and which, if kept, would entail correction to *manus*—is required by the sense in 3454 (where Tobler, *Rom*. ii, p. 346, already proposed *mulier* [*manu*] *amissa*). Cf. note to 1752.

3459 *destrica—inpedit*. The rhyme requires *destriga*, as in *B*. But *destricar*, though it seems otherwise unattested, is perhaps a conceivable form (× *tricar*?; or was the semantic divergence between trīcare and *trĭccare not absolutely clear-cut?—cf. *FEW* xiii. 2. 258–9, 259–61, especially 259 on the type ⌜*estricar*⌝).

3476 *desfia—diffidit*. The sense 'to mistrust', though clearly attested by a second example in *SW* ii. 142, is omitted from *PD* and from *FEW* iii. 500 *fīdare.

NOTES

3478 *mia—amica.* Sole example of *mia* for *amia* in *SW* v. 278; cf. *FEW* i. 87 AMICA.

3479–80 *ria, aucia.* For such forms at the rhyme in the troubadours see Harnisch, *Die altprovenzalische Praesens- und Imperfect-bildung*, Marburg, 1886, p. 265; they seem rather more frequently attested than forms in *-iza* (ibid., p. 275).

3484 *afica—afirmat vel conatur.* For *aficar*, v. tr., 'to affirm, declare', unattested in the dictionaries and absent from *FEW* iii. 508 *FĪGĬCARE, cf. *Girart*, glossary. For the emendation *conatur* for *uincitur* cf. 2462 *afics—coneris*; Guessard's *vincit*, approved by Stengel, is not acceptable.

3485 *desfica—evellit.* Sole example in *SW* ii. 141, from Stichel, p. 33; cf. *FEW* iii. 507 *FĪGĬCARE. For a second example cf. *Girart* 5809.

3487 *In -ega.* All ten words in fact show [ę].

3490 *pega—insipida.* *Insipiens* would be better Latin; but cf. Niermeyer, s.v. *insipidus*, 2 ('ignorant, illiterate') and Baxter–Johnson ('dull').

3503 *crauca* (*A*), *grauca* (*B*)*—terra sterilis.* Sole example for both forms in *SW* i. 401 and iv. 174; cf. *FEW* ii. 2. 1295 *KRAW-.

3504 *In -esca.* All twelve examples show [ę].

3506 *sesca—arundo secans, incisa.* Guessard and Stengel omit *incisa*, which, however, is important for the sense: four of Levy's examples (*SW* vii. 629–30) in fact refer to cut or gathered bulrushes. The translator's use of *secans* once again suggests his etymologizing tendency.

3513 *esca—illud cum quo ignis accenditur, vel esca cara cani.* The first sense, 'tinder', though omitted in *PD*, is attested also in Raynouard's second example (*LR* iii. 142 = R. d'Orange, ed. Pattison, i. 67; the editor mistranslates 'spark'); cf. also *Dicc. Alcover*, s.v. *esca*, 2. One would expect the second sense to be 'bait' (cf. *LR* iii. 142; *PD*; *FEW* iii. 244–5 ESCA), but this would entail the bold but not unthinkable emendation to *esca causa piscandi*. Tobler's *esca data cani* (*Rom.* ii, p. 346) and Chabaneau's *esca: caro cani* (*Rom.* vi, p. 141) are hardly convincing, although the sense 'food for dogs', otherwise unattested, is conceivable.

3521 *escaira—quadrando strue.* Guessard, followed silently by Stengel, printed *quadrum distrue*. Tobler (*Rom.* ii, p. 346) conjectured *in quadrum distribue*, which is semantically unlikely. In fact *A*'s reading shows the same error as in 2793 (cf. the note there): correction to *quadrando strue* (cf. *quadrare* in 1112) gives a satisfactory sense, not absolutely identical with those attested by Raynouard and Levy, but a natural extension of the basic meaning 'to square (timber, stone)' (cf. *LR* v. 11; *SW* iii. 138; *FEW* ii. 2. 1395 QUADRARE). Precisely this sense is attested for *acairar* 'to make square (a construction)' (*LR* v. 11).

3530 *desossa—carnes ab ossibus removet.* Sole example in *SW* ii. 230, from Stichel, p. 34; cf. *FEW* vii. 429 ŏs and *Dicc. Aguiló, Alcover*, s.v. *desossar*.

3532 *rossa—rubra.* Palaeographically, *rubra* is a more likely correction of *A*'s *rutā* than Tobler's *rubida* (*Rom.* ii, p. 346), which Stengel also accepted.

3536 *detrossa—solvit sarcinam.* Sole example in *SW* ii. 180 for *detrossar*; *B* gives the more common form in *des-*. Cf. *FEW* xiii. 2. 94 TŏRQUĒRE, where the present form should be added.

3538 *rescossa—excussa.* This is Levy's only example for *rescodre* 'to thresh?' (*SW* vii. 258), a translation not maintained in *PD* or noted in *FEW* iii. 288 EXCUTERE (where, however, a few dialect reflexes of RE + EXCŭTĕRE show the sense 'to scutch (hemp)'). It is possible but not certain that 'to thresh' was the sense intended by the translator, who had just rendered *escossa* in the same way. The only other sense of OPr. *rescodre* is 'to take away' or 'to take back, recover', attested in Levy's third example (= *Croisade* 2687) and confirmed by OFr. *rescorre* (Godefroy, vii. 88–90) but omitted in *PD* and in *FEW* iii. 289. The other sense supposed by *SW* is 'to deliver, save'; but this, the only rendering admitted in *PD*, depends solely on a corrupt passage of R. de Vaqueiras, ed. Linskill, xx. 44 (the editor rightly emends *rescos* to *secor*), and should be deleted. If, therefore, we reject 'to thresh' as the sense here, we are forced to accept 'to carry off (booty, etc.)'; cf. the more precisely defined uses of *excutere* in 633. Either of the meanings is possible for *escossa* (3537).

3555 *esfoira—ventris polluit fluxu.* Sole example in *SW* iii. 216, from Stichel, p. 51. Whether *esfoirar* really meant 'to have diarrhoea', as Levy supposed, or 'to soil with diarrhoea', as the Latin suggests, is not clear. If Levy is right, one would expect *se polluit.* Cf. *FEW* iii. 712 FORIA, where the mod. dialect examples mostly show the type ⌜*s'esfouira*⌝ in the intr. sense (cf. also *Dicc. Alcover*, s.v. *esfoirar-se*); this could be held to confirm *esfoirar* as a tr. verb.

3556 *loira—lutra.* Guessard assumed this to be the river Loire and emended to *Liger.* Stengel, while retaining *A*'s meaningless *liccier*, apparently made the same assumption, for *Loira* appears in his index of proper names. In OPr., however, LĭGER > *Leire* (cf. *Girart* for eight examples); *Loira is clearly impossible. Correction to *lutra* is palaeographically simple: *lutā* misread as *liccī.*

3557 *zoira—vetus canis.* This is Levy's only example for the form in *z*- and for the literal sense of the word (*SW* vii. 756); his other example shows *soyra* used figuratively as a term of abuse.

3559 *giscla—pluit simul et ventat.* Levy's other example of *gisclar* in this sense (*SW* iv. 123, s.v. *gisclar*, 2) = R. d'Orange, ed. Pattison, x. 2, var. *CE*; cf. *FEW* ii. 1. 713–14 *CĪSCŭLARE.

3560 *ciscla* (*A*), *giscla* (*B*)—*alta voce clamat.* Sole example of *cisclar* in this sense in *SW* i. 255, to which may be added *Donatz* 866 and *S. Foi* 384; cf. *FEW* ii. 1. 711–12 *CĪSCŭLARE. *B*'s reading provides Levy's only example of *gisclar* 'to cry out' (*SW* iv. 123); cf. *FEW* ii. 1. 712–13.

3561 *iscla*, without translation (*A*), *giscla, iscla* (*B*). If *B* is right in giving *giscla* a third time, it was presumably intended in the sense 'to whip'; cf. *SW* iv. 124, s.v. *gisclar*, 3, and *FEW* ii. 1. 714. *A*'s reading may be taken as *iscla* < INSŬLA (but cf. 3299 *ila*). Or 3560-1 may be read as *ciscla*, [*g*]*iscla*, with a single Latin rendering applying to both words (for *gisclar* 'to cry out' cf. the previous note; for translations applying to two consecutive Provençal words in the *Donatz* cf. 199, 1183-4).

3569-70. It has been universally recognized that the *cuius Ugo nominor* of *A* is not possible Latin. The following emendations have been suggested: Guessard (1st ed.), *civis Ugo*; Guessard (2nd ed.), *cuius* [*auctor*] *Ugo*; Galvani (p. 335), *Faiditus Ugo*; Stengel, *cuius* [. . .] *Ugo*; Merlo (in *GSLI* iii, pp. 218-21, 386-400), *Faiditus ego* or *G. Faiditus ego*; Gröber (in *ZRP* viii, pp. 112-17, cf. *GSLI* iv, pp. 203-8), *Santcircus Ugo*. All are unacceptable, if only because of the absence of credible palaeographical explanation of the error.

Clearly the incipit given by *DL* and this concluding sentence given by *A* have a common source: it is unlikely that the author named himself and his patrons twice, in identical terms, once at the beginning and once at the end of the text. This being so, the sentence giving the three names must have belonged originally at the end of the text, not at the beginning, for three reasons. Firstly, of the three early MSS., the two which give the end of the rhyming dictionary (*A* and *B*) both attest the existence of a Latin conclusion, in which the author's name and those of his patrons would find their natural place. Secondly, it is perfectly comprehensible that two MSS. (*D* and *L*), perhaps independently, should transfer part of this concluding paragraph to the beginning to give an incipit to the whole work; but the contrary procedure would be quite unmotivated. The third argument is the converse of the second: if we were to suppose that the author named himself and his patrons at the beginning, why should that passage have been omitted by the oldest MS., *A*, which is notable precisely for giving a text free from omissions? If these arguments are accepted, it follows that *Ugo Faiditus* is the author's name and that it occurred in the original text in the final sentence: *D* alone gives it in this form; *L* has the simple scribal error *Faidicus*; *A* has the more complex error *cuius Ugo*.

How did the error occur? Palaeographically, it is not inexplicable. One must suppose a first error, like that in *L*: *ugo faidi* / *c⁹ nominor*, split over two lines. A second error consisted of omitting the apparently meaningless *faidi* and interpreting *c⁹* in the usual way: *ugo cuius nominor*. The third error was the 'correction' of the phrase by moving the relative pronoun to its normal position at the beginning of the phrase, giving the text which stands in *A*. It is possible to conceive of the second and third errors occurring together: one and the same scribe could reject *faidi* and transfer *cuius* to make a semblance of sense. Two details support this argument. Firstly, errors arising from words split over two lines occur elsewhere in *A* (786?, 796, 833, 2261). Secondly, the name of Faidit's second patron gave rise to a precisely similar error in *A*: *corā çhuchij* (3571) evidently arose from a misunderstanding of *cora* / *çhuchij* split over two lines, the first element being interpreted as Latin *coram* just as the second element of *faidi* / *c⁹* was interpreted as *cuius*. It is worth noting, in passing, that *L*'s incipit does in fact so split the word; and that *D*'s incipit, with the reading *Conradi*, shows a different misinterpretation of *cora*, coupled with a rejection of *çhuchij* which is exactly parallel with *A*'s rejection of *faidi*.

APPENDICES

APPENDIX I

Donatz Proensals: *version of MS C*

Aquest es le Donatz Proensals, faitz per la raizo de trobar. **1a**

Las oit partz que hom troba en gramatica ditz hom en vulgar proensal, zo es: nomen, pronomen, verbum, adverbium, participium, coniunctio, prepositio, interiectio.

Nomen es appellatz per zo significa substancia ab propria qualitat **4** o ab comuna, e generalment totas las causas a las cals Adamus pauzet noms podon esser noms appelladas. E·l noms a sinc cauzas: species, genus, numerus, figura, casus.

Species zon en doas maneiras: o es primitiva o es dirivativa. Primi- **8** tius es appellatz lo noms qe es per se e non es vengutz d'alqu nom ni d'alqu verbe, si con es *bontats* [. . .] qe bons non pot hom esser senz bontat.

Genus es de sinc maneiras: masculinus, femininus, neutrus, comunis, **12** omnis. Masculinus es aqel qe aperte a las masclas causas solament, si cum: *bons, mals, Petrus, Martinus*. Femininus es aqel qe aperte a las cauzas feminils solamen, si con: *bona, bella, Na Maria*. Neutrus es aqel qe non perten ni a l'un ni al altre, si con: *gaugz e bes*. Comunis es aqel **16** qe perten al mascle et al femel ensems, si cun son li adjectiu qe fenisson en *-anz* o en *-ens*, si cun: *presans, avinens*, q'eu posc dire:

o	aquest cavaliers es prezanz	
	aquest cavaliers es avinens	**20**
et	aquesta dompna es prezans /	
et	aquesta donna es avinens.	**1b**

New paragraphs begin at 1*, 12*, 28, 29 (plurals), 30 (Figura), 30 (simpla si cum), 32*, 47 (Et sum), 88, 93, 97, 99, 103 (Aqil), 107, 109, 111 (Etuit), 118 (E cortes), 139, 190 (Gergonz), 191 (Cors pro corpore), 217*, 240, 241 (Notq), 249, 256, 264, 268, 587, 595, 602, 613* (Del indicatiu), 616, 662, 703, 789, 812 (Si es), 867*, 872, 879* (De specie), 883, 915*; *those marked with an asterisk have the initial capital in the margin*.

Rejected Readings of C.

3 propositio   5 comu*n*na   6 podon] pron (r *and* n *underlined*); esser] osset; *after* cauzas, *C adds* quall. (ll *underlined*)   8 Specias (a *underlined*)   9 dal qu   10 dal qu; esset   13 ap*e*rtet   15 bella] besta (e *underlined*)   18 posc dire] porse due (s *and* u *underlined*)   20 caualienz (n *underlined*)

Omnis es aqel qe perten al mascle et al femel et al neutri ensems, qu'eu
puesc dire:

> aqest cavaliers es plazens,
> aquesta donna es plaizens,
> bes m'es plazens.

Numerus o es singulars o es plurals; singulars qan parla d'una causa solamen, plurals qan parla de doas o de plusors.

Figura o es simpla o es composita: simpla si cum es *coms*, composita [...] zo es apostiça de *ves* e de *coms*.

Li cas del nom son seis: lo nominatius e·l genetius e·l datius e·l accusatius e·l vocatius e·l ablatius. Lo nominatius si conois per *le*, si cun:

> le reis es vengutz;

genetius per *de*, si cun:

> aquest destrers es del rei;

datius per *al*, si cun:

> mena lo destrier al rei;

accusatius per *lo*, si cun:

> eu vei lo rei armat.

E no se pot conoiser ni triar l'acusatius del nominatiu, si non per zo que l'accusatius vol lo verbe denan se e·l nominatius vol lo verbe derer se, si con *Joans ama Martin*, per qe *Martin* es cas accusatius. Et ancara se pot conoiser l'accusatius del nominatiu per zo qe·l nominatius fa e l'accusatius soste, si cum *Peire fer Martin*: *Peire*, per zo q'el fer, zo es q'el fa, es nominatius cas, et *Martin*, per zo q'el soffre qe Peire lo bata, es accusatius cas. Et *sum, es, est* vol nominatiu cas et denan se et derer se, si con *Arpulins es bos homs*. E deves saber / qe·l nominatius singularis, cant es masculins si com es *auzels* o neutris si com es *castels* e *bes* e *gaugs*, vol -*s* en la fi e li autre cas no volun. E·l nominatius plurals no vol -*s* en la fi e tuit li autre cas volon lo em plural. E tuit li femenin qe fenissen en -*a* non volon -*s* el singular, e son endeclinabel, zo es qe non se

---

24 puesc] prouest (u, e, *and* t *underlined*) 26 plauzens 28 es singularis, *with second* i *apparently struck through* 31 *second* a *of* apostiça *underlined*; u *of* ues *underlined* 33 e *of* le *underlined* 36 aqueest; es] el 42 de nan; deter 44 por; l·accusatius 45 soste] soffe *with* ff *struck through and* st *added above*; Petre; petre 46 es] el; soffre *rather than* softre; petre 47 de nanse; de ret 49 cant es] cait el (i *and* l *underlined*); *originally* gau-/ges, *split over two lines, altered to give* gauges *on one line* 50 la fi] *originally* bast, *struck through, with* la fi *added above, the latter having also been struck through and* bast (*with* a *underlined*) *added above*; e li] eb (b *underlined*); autte (*first* t *underlined*); nominatiuns 51 *first* tuit] au*n*t

APPENDIX I

declinon, car finissen tuit li cas en -*a* en lo singular; mas en lo plural volun -*s* per totz los cas en la fi, e finissen tuit en -*as*.

Et deves saber qe cascuns vocatius es semblans al seu nominatiu.

E lai on fon dit del nominatiu singular qe vol -*s* per totz a la fi, voil traire fors totz aqels qe finissen en -*aire*, si cum: 56

emperaire, amaire,

et en -*eire*, si cun:

Peire, beveire, 60

et en -*ire*, si cun:

traïre,

qe non volon -*s* el nominatiu singular. Mas *albires* vol -*s* et *consires* et *desires*. 64

E tuit aquel que·us ai dit que fenissen en -*aire* et -*eire*, si cun *Peire, beveire*, et en -*ire*, fenissen totz lor cas singulars en -*dor*, si cun: *amaire, amador*—trait lo vocatiu, qe sembla nominatiu, si con es dig desus—e·l nominatiu plural fan tuit en -*dor*, si con *li amador*, et en totz los autres 68 cas en -*dors*, si cun *dels amadors, als amadors*.

E de la regla del nominatiu singular que vol -*s* a la fi, vol encar traire fors:

maistre, p[r]estre, pastre, 72
et *signer, meilher, peier,*
sordeier, maier, sebren†,/
genser, leuger, greuçer, 2b

qe podon haber -*s* a la fin et podon esser sens -*s*. 76

Et devetz saber qe tuit li nom son o ajectiu o sustantiu; e tuit aqil que per se solamen non se podon entendre ni non portan complida sententia son ajectiu, si con *bons, mals, pros, valens*: non se pot entendre de cui, et aissi non portan dreita sentencia. Mas si eu dic *Martins es valens* 80 *cavaliers* o *Joans es pros*, adons es complida sentenza per aqel nom, zo es *Martins*, et per aquel nom, zo es *Joans*, que son substantiu. Et per zo son dit adjectiu, zo es ajustantiu, car ajustan las soas signifiazons ab lor sustantius. E tuit aqill nom qe per se solam[en] portan perfetta sentenza 84 e qe se podon entendre per se son substantiu, si con es *Peire, Na Maria,*

---

55 cacscunl (*second* c *and* l *underlined*)   57 traue (u *underlined*); a qels
60 beuerze (r *and* z *underlined*)   62 traue (a *underlined*)   63 confiteres   65 a qu*e*l; si] li   67 de fus   69 dels] deis; all'amadors   70 regla] re gfa; en car   72 pestre; paistre
73 tigner; meillier   75 greuçer] grençer   77 aiectiui; a qil
78 entefidre   80 et] el; portairan dreira   81 a qel   83 a iustantiu; a*n* iustan   84 sustantiuis; solam   85 petre

homs, dompna; et per [zo] son dit substantiu car per se solamen podon star e portan perfetta sentenza en construction.

88 Et devetz saber qe tuit li adjectiu qan son pauzat sens substa[n]tiu non volon -*s* en la fin, si cun:

> *bo m'es emparar,*
> *estrain m'es partir d'aisi,*
> 92 *greu m'es car Peire no·m ama, pueis eu l'am tan finamens.*

Encara devetz saber qe·l noms ha tres declinazons. E tuit aqill nom qe finissen el nominatiu singular en -*a*, si cun *dompna, bella, gaia, gaita, papa, propheta,* tuit son de la prima declinazon; mas *propheta* et *papa* 3a non volon -*s* el nominatiu plural et en totz los autres / cas lo volon.

97 Della segonda declinazon es *deus, segner, maestre,* e tuit li nom breumen que non volon -*s* el nominatiu plural et en totz los autres cas lo volon.

Della terza declinazon son tuit li nom e li particip qe finissen el 100 nominatiu singular en -*ans* et en -*ens*, si cun *prezans, amans, avine*[*n*]*s, valens*. Et tuit li nom qe finisson in -*atz* sun feminini, si cun *bont*[*at*]*z, amistatz,* qe·l nominatiu e·l vocatiu fant en -*az* el singular, e·l plural eissamen fan en -*az* et no·s declino ni se mudant. Aqil qe finissen en 104 -*uz*, si con es *saluz* et *venguz,* fan lo nominatiu e·l vocatiu en -*uz*, totz los autres cas en -*ut* in singular; el plural fan lo nominatiu e·l vocatiu in -*ut*, los autres cas en -*uz*.

En vulgar non trob mais se non aqestas tres maneiras de declinazons 108 que·us ai dit desus.

Son d'autras maneiras de noms que non se declinon, si con es *vers* ab totz sos compotz, si con *pervers, devers, envers, revers, advers, convers, travers;* e tuit li adjectiu qe finissen en -[*o*]*s*, si com *amoros, enveios,* 112 trait *pros* e *bos,* qe se declinon. Et non se declinon ni se mudon tuit aqil qe finissen en -*as*, sion adjectiu o sustantiu, si cun:

> *nas* .i. nasus,
> *pas* .i. passus,
> 116 *vas* .i. tumulus,
> *ras* .i. rasus;

e *cortes* sec aqella regola mezeisma, et

> 3b *pes* .i. pondus,/
> 120 *contrapes, sirventes,*
> *cens* .i. census,

86 zo om.   88 substatiu   90 bos   91 parut   92 non ania pueil; fina mens   93 En cara; aqilli   94 gaita] gaira   99 3ᵃ
100 anines   101 bontz   103 eissameri; no·s declino] mon deditio; mundant   104 faluz   107 a qestas   111 en .s.
112 ni < in   113 si on   114 natus   119 pes] apes
120 contra pes

APPENDIX I

encens .i. incensus,
defes .i. defensus,
mes .i. mensis,
borses,
des .i. discus,
bles .i. qui non potest sonare [. . .],
marqes,
bres .i. lignum quo capiuntur aves,
gles .i. glis animal,
comes .i. [pro]vocatus,
escomes .i. provocatus,
pres .i. captus,

ab totz sos compotz, si con *empres, apres, repres, compres, sorpres, sotz-pres*; et tuit li nom provensal† (.i. qui derivantur a provinciis) qe finissen in *-es*, si con:

Frances, Engles,
Genoes e *Loges*†.

Encara non se declinon:

Baus .i. castrum,
fals,
Acs .i. civitas,
descauz,
[. . .] .i. vilis fuga,
fals pro falce,
lanz .i. iactus,
fartz .i. farsura,
ars .i. arsus,
martz .i. mensis vel dies Martis,
latz .i. nodus,
glas .i. glacies,
jatz .i. lectus fere,
patz .i. pax,
aus .i. vellus,
claus .i. clausus,
laus .i. pro laude et pro stagno,
raucs† .i. raucus,
ais .i. tabula,

126 decus   128 marqes] q*ui* arqes   130 gles] bles   131 uocatus
132 est comes   134–5 sotz pres   135 q*ue*   137 englos   138 eloges
139 En cara   142 aes   143 des caum *with* z *added above* m
146 raccus   147 farez   149 marez   150 latet   152 latz
153 partl   157 **Raues**

APPENDIX I

        cais .i. gena,
160   *fais* .i. honus,
        lais .i. dulcis canticus,
        tais .i. animal,
        brais .i. clamor avium,
164   *Clavais* .i. castellum,
        meils .i. melius,
        fems .i. fimus,
        temps .i. tempus,
168   *Rems* .i. civitas;

    in -*ers* (.i. larg):

        guers .i. strabo vel guerzus,
        desper[*s*] .i. dispersus,
172   *Bezers* .i. civitas,
        Lumbers .i. castellum;

    in -*ers* (.i. estreit):

        aers .i. erens,
176   *ders*,
        aders .i. erectus,
        gris, paradis,
        San Danis,
180   *assis* .i. assettatz (.i. obsessus),
        Paris .i. civitas et proprium nomen viri,
        ris .i. risus,
        vis .i. visus vel facies,
184   *berbis* .i. ovis,
        obs,
        pols .i. pulsus,
        Aiols .i. proprium nomen,
188   *douç* .i. dulcis,
        pouç .i. pultes: esca de farina,
        gergonz .i. vulgare trutannorum—

4a *cors* pro corpore est indeclinabile; *cors* pro corde facit in / nominativo
192 et vocativo [. . .] in -*or*, in reliquis in -*ors*—

    cors .i. corpus,
    mors .i. morsus,
    bis .i. quidam color,
196 *lis* .i. lenis,

    159 E ais   166 fenis .i. fumus   168 tenis   169 iners i largz
    170 buers .i. stra*m*bo   171 desper   172 berz ers   177 arders
    178 gris] bris   186 pullis   188 douç .i. dauç .i. dulcis

APPENDIX I 349

et   *alis* .i. azimus,
     curs .i. cursus,
     secors .i. auxilium,
     ors .i. ursus,   200
     recors,
     croz .i. crux,
     notz .i. nux,
     potz .i. puteus,   204
     plus, reclus,
     conclus, confus,
     pertus .i. foramen,
     Dedalus .i. proprium nomen viri,   208
     Tantalus .i. proprium nomen,
     us .i. [u]sus,
     fus est instrumentum quoddam,
     Artus .i. proprium nomen,   212
     Cerber[*us*] .i. ianitor inferni.

Et tuit aquist q'eu ai dit desus non se declinon, zo es non se varian ne se mudon, ni en singular ni en plural, mas corron per totz cas singulars e plurals engalmen.   216

   Pronoms es appellatz car es en luec de propri nom pauzatz et demostra certa persona, si cun:

     eu, tu, cel,
     el, aicel, aqel,   220
     aquest, qui, il,
     eu mezeimes .i. ego ipse,
     tu mezeimes .i. tu ipse,
     el meteismes .i. ille ipse,   224
     meus, teus,
     seus .i. suus,
     nostre, vostre.

Et per zo es ditz 'pausatz en luec de propri nom' qe si eu dic *eu sui* 228 *vengutz* no mi besoigna dir *eu N'Uqz sui vengutz*; *tu es vengutz,* no mi besoigna dir *tu Peire es vengutz*; s'eu dic *aicel es vengutz* e·l mostri ab la man o ab l'oill, no·m besoigna dir *Johanz es venguz.* E per zo son appelat pronom demostratiu car demostran certa persona.   232

   202 Eroz   203 mux *struck through before* nux   210 sus   213 celer
214 de sus   216 en galmen   220 aqel < aqueel (*abbreviation sign struck through*)   222 Eumez eimes   224 mete ismes   227 n̄r, ūr
228 ditz e pausatz; dic] dit   229 tu] eu   230 dir] der   231 lo hanz
232 demostratiui; de mostran

E deves saber qe tuit aqist pronom, si cum es *eu, tu, el, qui, aqel, il,*
4b *cel, aicel, aquest, nostre, vostre,* no volon -*s* a la fi / en lo singular.

E devetz saber aquest pronoms *eu* es de prima persona et aissi si
236 declina: nominativo, *eu*; genetivo, *de me*; dativo, *a me*; accusativo, *m*;
vocativo non a, car nuls non clama se meteus; ablativo, *a me*; et pluraliter:
nominativo, *nos*; et aissi per totz los cas plurals, si cum *de nos, a nos,
nos, ab nos*.

240 E devetz saber qe aqest pronoms *tu* es de la segunda persona et aissi
declina: nominativo, *tu*; genetivo, *de te*; dativo, *a te*; accusativo, *te*;
vocativo, *o tu*; ablativo, *a te*; et pluraliter: nominativo, *vos*; et aissi per
totz los cas plurals, si cun *de vos, a vos, vos, o vos, ab vos*.

244 Et deves saber qe tuit li pronom [son] della terza persona, trait *eu*, qe
es de la prima, et *tu*, qe es de la segunda si cun es ditz desus, et tuit li
vocativi, qe tuit li vocativi son de la segunda persona, si cun: *O Arpulins,
danza*; vezetz cun aqel *Arpulins,* qe es vocatius, car es de la segunda
248 persona, s'ajusta ab aqel verbe, zo es *danza,* qe es de la segonda persona.

Nominativo, *el*; genetivo, *de lui,* dativo, *a lui*; accusativo, *lo*; vocativo
non a, car es demonstratius de la terza persona et aisi non pot aver
vocatiu, car lo vocatius es de la segonda persona, si cum es dig desus;
252 ablativo, *ab lui*; et pluraliter: nominativo, *ill*; genetivo, *d'els*; dativo,
a els; acusativo, *los*; ablativo, *ab els.* Eissamen declino *aqel, cel, aicel,*
5a estier que fan en l'accusatiu si cun / els autres cas, zo es genetiu, datiu
et ablatiu.

256 E aquest pronom si cun *nostre, vostre,* sun endeclinabel el singular, et
en lo plural fan si cun li autre adjectiu nom, car en lo nominatiu plural
non vol[on] -*s* ni en lo vocatiu, et en totz los autres lo volon, si cun:
pluraliter, nominativo, *li nostre*; genetivo, *dels nostres*; dativo, *als nostres*.
260 Aqest *meus, teus, seus* seguen aqella metesma regola dels noms, car en
lo vocatiu singular volon -*s* et en los autres cas singulars non lo volon,
et en lo nominatiu plural non lo volon et en totz los autres cas lo volon.

Sequitur de Verbo

264 Verbs es appellatz car es cum maneiras et formas et tempus e significa
alcuna causa fa[r] o sufrir, si cun *eu bate Martin*: s'eu bate eu faz alcuna
causa, si Martis es batutz el sufre alcuna causa.

233 aqiste; a qel   240 a qest   244 cre *struck through after
saber*; son *om*.   245 de sus   247 a qel   248 sa iusta
250 aisi] al si   253 a qel   254 astier; l·accusatiu; auttels   256 a
quest   258 uol   260 A qesti; se guen a qella   265 fa; *first* eu] cu
266 si] seu; *after* causa, *and continuing on the same line without punctuation,
C inserts 550–879*

Modi Verborum (10a)

Li modi del[s] verbs son cinc: indicativus, imperatius, optatius, conjunctius, infinitius. Indicatius es appellatz car demostra lo fait que hom fa, si cun *eu cant, escriu,* o qe demanda, si cum *qe fas tu? m'amas tu o qe fas tu?* Imperatius es aqel qe comanda, si con es *aporta pan, aporta vin.* Optatius es qar desira, si cun es *eu volria amar.* Conjunctius es car ajusta doas razons ensems, si cun en aqest loc: *cum eu ame fortmen, es tortz si no soi amatz,* e car vol totas ves un autre verb ab lui car non pot star per se sol. Infinitius es appellatz car non pauza terme ni fin a zo que ditz, si cum: *eu voil amar.*
Et quascu dels cinc moz que ai dig desus deu aver .v. tempus, zo es prezent, preterit non perfeit, preterit perfeit, preterit plus quam perfeit et futur.
Li verbi o son de la prima conjugazon o de la segonda o de la terza / **10b** o de la quarta. Tuit li verb, l'infinitiu del[s] ca[l]s finissen en *-ar,* si cun *amar, cantar, ensenhar,* son de la prima conjugazon. [. . .] en sun tan confus l'infinitiu en vulgar qe conven a laissar la gramatica e donar autra regla novella, per qe plaz a me aqell verb qe lor infinitiu fan fenir en *-er,* si cun es *aver, tener, dever,* sion de la segonda conjugazon; aqill qe finisson en *-ire,* si cun *dire,* et aqell qe finissen en *-endre,* si cum *tendre, contendre, defendre,* et in *-iure,* si cum *viure, scriure,* sion tuit de la terza conjugazon; et aqell qe finissen en *-ir,* si cum *sentir, dormir,* sion de la quarta conjugazon.
Lo prezens tempus del indicatiu de la prima conjugazon se dobla en la prima persona, q'eu pos dir

> *eu ami* o *eu am* .i. ego amo,
> *eu canti* o *eu can* .i. ego canto.

La seconda persona fenis en *-as,* si cun:

> *tu amas* .i. tu amas;

la terza in *-a,* si cun:

> *cel ama* .i. ille amat.

Aissi fenissen las tres personas en singular del temps prezent del indicatiu. El plural finis la prima persona in *-am,* si cum:

> *nos amam* .i. nos amamus;

268 del   270 tant; cu*m* added above the line   273 a qest;
es] et   277 El; de sus   281 del cas   284 regla < reg*u*la
(*abbreviation sign struck through*)   286 aqelle   288 a qell   290 indiaziu
298 femilen

in *-atz,* si cum:

> *vos amatz* .i. vos amatis;

la terza in *-en* o in *-on:*

304   [. . .] .i. illi amant.

11a Et aisso / es generals regla qe la terza persona del plural se dobla per totz verbs et per totz temps, que pot [fenir] o in *-en* o in *-on.* Et la prima persona dobla se en totz verbs el temps prezent dell'indicatiu solamen, 308 si cum:

> *eu senti* o *eu sen,*
> *eu diçi* o *eu dic;*

mas meils es a dir lo plus cort que·l plus lonc.

312   El preterit non perfeit, zo es non complit:

> *eu amava* .i. ego amabam,
> *tu amavas* .i. tu amabas,
> *cel amava* .i. ille amabat;

316 et pluraliter:

> *nos amavam* .i. nos amabamus,
> *vos amavatz* .i. vos amabatis,
> *ill amaven* o *amavon* .i. illi amabant.

320   El preterit perfeit, zo es complit:

> *eu amei* .i. ego amavi,
> *tu amest* .i. tu amavisti,
> *cel amet* .i. ille amavit;

324 et pluraliter:

> *nos amem* .i. nos amavimus,
> *vos ametz* .i. vos amavistis,
> *ill ameren* o *amaron* .i. illi amaverunt vel amavere.

328   El preterit plus quam perfeit:

> *eu avia amat* .i. ego amaveram,
> *tu avias amat* .i. tu amaveras,
> *cel avia amat* .i. ille amaverat;

332 et pluraliter:

> *nos aviam amat* .i. nos amaveramus,

---

305 q̄ē (= qu*ee* or q*en?*)   306 fenir *om.*   307 dell·indicatiu
309 sen] fei   311 mas] uras; a dir] ader; que·l] qua*m*; lonc] lane
313 ego amaba*m* .i. eu amaua

vos avias amat .i. vos amaveratis,
cill avian amat .i. illi amaverant.

El futur son semblan li verbi tuit en totas las conjugazons, qe tuit finissen aissi:

eu amarai .i. ego amabo,
tu amaras .i. tu amabis,
cel amara .i. ille amabit;

et pluraliter:

nos amarem .i. nos amabimus,
vos amares / .i. vos amabitis,
cel amaran .i. illi amabunt.

El imperatiu del temps prezent tuit aquell de la prima conjugazon finissen en -*a*, si cum:

canta, balla

—e de la segonda persona entendatz, qar imperatius non ha prima persona en singular, que hom non pot comandar se meteus. En la terza persona fenissen en -*e*, si cum:

ame .i. amet ille.

Et pluraliter, zo es en lo plural, finis la prima persona in -*em*, si cun:

cavalguem .i. equitemus,
amem nos .i. amemus nos;

la segonda persona in -*atz*, si cum:

anatz .i. eatis,
amatz vos .i. amate vos;

la terza finis in -*en*, si cun:

cavalguen .i. equitent,
ill amen .i. ament illi.

Et devetz saber qe tuit aqill verbe que finissen en l'infinitiu in -*ar* [et] podon finir in -*aire*, si cun: *far, faire*; *trar, traire*, fan en l'emperatiu en la prima persona del plural in -*am*, si con: *fezam, tragam*.

En l'optatiu finissen tuit li verb de la prima conjugazon del temps prezent el singular la prima persona in -*era* o in -*ria*—et de totas conjugazos generalmen—si cun:

---

336 totas] totz   345 imperatius   349 meteu*er*t   352 en *added above the line*; si *repeated*   361 q̄e (= q*uee or* q*en?*); a q*ill*; l·infinitiu; et *om.*   363 sezam   365 totz

O 5707   A a

APPENDIX I

   volenters amera, volenters amaria .i. ego libenter amarem,
368 *tu ameras* .i. tu amares,
   cel amera .i. ille amaret;

et pluraliter:

   nos amaram .i. nos amaremus,
372 *vos ameras* .i. vos amaretis,
   ill ameran .i. illi amarent;

item:

375 *eu dissera* o *diria* .i. dicerem,
12a *tu disseras* o *dirias* [.i.] tu diceres,
   cel dissera o *diria* .i. ille diceret;

et pluraliter:

   nos disseram o *diriam* .i. nos diceremus,
380 *vos disseratz* o *diriatz* .i. diceretis,
   ill diceren o *dirien* .i. illi dicerent.

Encara finissen li ottatiu el temps prezen aisi, si cum:

   Deus volgues qu'eu ames .i. utinam ego amarem,
384 *Deus volgues qe tu amasses* .i. utinam tu amares,
   Deus volgues qe cel amasset† .i. utinam ille amaret;

et pluraliter:

   Deus volgues que nos amassem .i. utinam nos amaremus,
388 *Deus volgues qe vos amasses* .i. utinam vos amaretis,
   Deus volgues q'ill amessen .i. utinam illi amarent.

Pero aquell que son de la quarta conjugazon, don l'infinitius fenis in *-ir* solamen, si cum *dormir*, fan l'optatiu en *-ira* o in *-iria*, si cum:

392 *eu volenters dormira* o *dormiria* .i. ego libenter dormirem,
   tu dormiras o *dormirias* .i. dormires,
   cel dormira o *dormiria* .i. ille dormiret;

et pluraliter:

396 *nos dormiram* o *dormiriam* .i. nos dormiremus,
   vos dormiraz o *dormir[i]atz* .i. vos dormiretis,
   ill dormiren o *dormirien* .i. illi dormirent.

Et sun alcun autre verbe qe sun fors d'aquesta regla, si cun *voler, tener,*
400 *poder, saber, aver, conoiscer*, qe finissen la prima persona del optatiu in *-gra* o in *-iria*, si cun:

  376 .i. om. 382 En cara; arsi 388 qe < ql 389 uolgues qe qill
  390 a quell 396 dormiran o dormirian 397 dormiratz 399 da questa

eu [...
...] *volgram* o *volriam* .i. / nos vellemus, **12b**
vos volgras o *volriatz* .i. velletis, 404
ill volgren o *volrien* .i. illi vellent;
segra o *seiria* .i. sederem,
colgra o *colria* .i. colerem,
nogra o *noçeria* .i. nocerem, 408
vengra o *venria* .i. venirem.

Et cascus d'aqest supradiz deu finir en singular et en plural et en personas, de tan com s'aperten al prezent del optatiu, si cum es dit desus pleneiramen de *voler*. 412
El preterit plus quam perfeit del optatiu fenissen tuit aqell de la prima conjugazon et aquell qe finissen lor infinitiu en -*endre* et in -*iure*, si cum *pendre, tendre*, que sun semblan en aquest luec a la prima conjugazon, finissen tuit aissi, si cun: 416

    be fora qu'eu agues amat .i. ego amavissem,
    tu agesses amat .i. tu amavisses,
    el agues amat .i. ille amavisset;

et pluraliter: 420

    nos aguessem amat .i. nos amavissemus,
    vos avesset[*z*] *amat* .i. vos amavissetis,
    ill avesson amat .i. illi amavissent;
e   *ben fora qu'eu agues tendut,* 424
    tu avesses tendut,
    cel aves tendut;

et aissi fan em plural:

    nos avessem tendut, 428
    vo[*s*] *avess*[*e*]*z tendut,*
    ill avessen tendut.

Et el preterit non perfeit del conjunctiu, si cum podetz vezer aissi:

    cum eu cantes .i. cum ego cantarem, 432
            tu cantares,
            ille cantaret;

et pluraliter: cum nos cantaremus,
            vos cantaretis, 436
            illi cantarent;

402-3 eu uolgran o uolriam   410 da qest; den; *first* en < el   411 sa
p*er*ten; de sus   413 a qell   414 a q*u*ell; in uinure   415 luce
417 fore; angues   418 agesset   419 amatz   421 aguessen
422 auesset   428 auessen   429 uo auessz   431 vezer] uez et

APPENDIX I

13a   *cum eu tendes* .i. cum ego tenderem,
                    tu tenderes,
440   ille tenderet;
   et pluraliter:
      nos tendessem .i. nos tenderemus,
                     vos tenderetis,
444   illi tenderent.

En lo futur del optatiu finissen tuit aquil de la prima conjugazon aissi, si cum:

      Dieus voilha q'eu ame .i. utinam ego amem,
448   tu ames,
                    ille amet;
   et pluraliter:
      Deus voilha qe nos amem .i. utinam nos amemus,
452   vos ametis,
                  illi ament.

E·l present del conjunctiu est [...] que lai on es *utinam* deu esser *cum*. El preterit non perfeit:

456   *cun eu ames* .i. cum ego amarem,
                tu amares,
                ille amaret;
   et pluraliter:
460   *cum nos amassem* .i. cum nos amaremus,
                     vos amaretis,
                     illi amarent.

Pero lo preterit non perfeit de conjunctiu [es semblanz] al preterit non 464 perfeit del indicatiu a la vigada, si tot es contra gramatica, si cun en aquel loc: *S'eu te donava mil, serias tu mos hom?* (.i. *s'eu te dones*). El preterit perfeit del conjunctiu:

      cum aia amat .i. cum amaverim,
468   tu amaveris,
               ille amaverit;
   et pluraliter:
      nos aiam amat .i. cum nos amaverimus,
472   vos amaveritis,
                illi amaverint.

447 uoillja   451 uoillia   454 esset   460 amare mus   463 es
semblanz *om*. (*cf.* 466 *var*.)   465 a quel; mil] nul; mes   466 el
semblanz *struck through after* coniunctiu (*cf.* 463)   467 ara   471 aram

APPENDIX I

Lo preterit plus quam perfeit del conjunctiu es sembla[n]z ad aqel / **13b**
del optatiu, estier que lai on es *utinam* el optatiu, el conjunctiu vol *cum*.
El futur del conjunctiu: 476

 cun eu aurai amat .i. cum amavero,
        tu amaveris,
        ille amaverit;

et pluraliter: 480

 cum nos aurem amat .i. cum nos amaverimus,
        vos amaveritis,
        illi amaverint.

E present del infinitiu e·l non perfeit an solamen una determinazon 484 en singular et en plural et en totas las personas, zo es *amar*, si cum: *eu voil amar, tu voles amar, cel vol amar, nos volem amar*. Et per zo es ditz infinitius, zo es non finitius, car, si cun es dit desus, non fenis ni termina certa persona ni nombre, qu'e[s] aissi la prima cum la segonda 488 e cum la terza e aissi en plural cum en singular. Dels autres temps del infinitiu no m'entramet, car non an gaire luec en vulgar.

Del passiu no·m besoinha dir aissi con del actiu qu'e[s] dit desus, que per tot se tria per aqest verbe, zo es *sum, es, est*, que vol nominatiu cas 492 denan se et der[er] se, si cum:

 eu sui amatz .i. ego amor,
 tu es amatz .i. tu amaris vel amare,
 cel es amatz .i. ille amatur. 496

Aissi finissen las tres personas singulars del temps prezent del indicatiu, mas en lo plural finissen aissi:

 nos sem amat .i. nos amamur,
 vos est amat .i. vos amamini, 500
 ill sun amat .i. amantur.

El preterit perfeit: **14a**

 eu fui amatz .i. ego amatus sum vel fui,
 tu fust amatz .i. tu es vel fuisti amatus, 504
 cel fo amatz .i. ille est vel fuit amatus;

et pluraliter:

 nos fom amat .i. nos sumus vel fuimus amati,
 vos fos amat .i. vos estis vel fuistis amati, 508
 ill foren o *foron amat* .i. illi sunt, fuerunt, vel fuere amati.

474 en semblaz   475 estrer; eu*m*   485 totz   486 nos uolen   487 de sus   488 nombre] nomer; q*ue*   490 men tramet; gatte luce   491 non besoinlia; q*ue* dit de sus   493 de nan; der   494 fui   497 ailli   504 amatus] amatz   508 amat] amati   509 ill] illi

APPENDIX I

El preterit plus quam perfeit:

eu era o *avia estat amatz* .i. ego eram vel fueram amatus,
512   *tu eras* o *avias estat amatz* .i. tu eras vel fueras amatus,
cel era o *avia estat amatz* .i. ille erat vel fuerat amatus;

et pluraliter:

nos eram o *aviam estat amat* .i. nos eramus vel fueramus amati,
516   *vos eratz* o *aviatz estat amat* .i. vos eratis vel fueratis amati,
ill eren o *eron, avien* o *avion estat amat* .i. illi erant vel fuerant amati.

El futur:

eu serai amatz .i. amabor,
520   *tu seras amat*[*z*] .i. amaberis vel amabere,
cel sera amatz .i. ille amabitur;

et pluraliter:

nos serem amat .i. nos amabimur,
524   *vos seres amat* .i. vos amabimini,
ill seran amat .i. illi amabuntur.

El imperatiu:

527   *sias tu amatz* .i. amare tu,
14b   *sia cel amatz* .i. ametur / ille;

et pluraliter:

siam nos amat .i. amemur nos,
sias vos amat .i. amamini vos,
532   *sien* o *sion ill amat* .i. amentur illi.

El optatiu:

per mo voler eu seria o *fora amatz* .i. utinam ego amarer,
tu serias o *foras amatz* .i. tu amareris vel amarere,
536   *cel seria* o *fora amatz* .i. ille amaretur;

et pluraliter:

nos seriam amat .i. amaremur
(et dobla se en vulgar, e cal vol pot hom dir),
540   *vos serias amat* .i. vos amaremini,
ill serien amat .i. illi amarentur.

514 et] El   516 e stat amat .i. < amatz   520 tu s. a.] .i. tu seratz amat   530 sian; 531 sian; uos *struck through before* uos amat   535 ferias; foras < foratz   536 foratz

APPENDIX I

El preterit perfeit et plus quam perfeit:

Deus aves volgut q'eu fos estat amat[z] .i. utinam ego essem vel fuissem amatus,
tu fosses estat amat[z] .i. esses vel fuisses amatus,   544
cel fos estat amat[z] .i. esset vel fuisset amatus;

et pluraliter:

Deus agues volgut qe nos fossem estat amat .i. utinam essemus vel fuissemus amati,
vos fosses estat amat .i. essetis vel fuissetis amati,   548
ill fossen estat amat .i. illi essent vel fuissent amati.

El futur: (5a)

Deus voilha que sia amatz .i. utinam amer,
tu sias amatz .i. ameris vel amere,   552
cel sia amatz .i. ille ametur;

et pluraliter:

Deus voilha qe nos siam amat .i. utinam nos amemur,
vos sias amat .i. amemini,   556
ill sian amat .i. amentur.

Lo presenz del conjuncti[u] es atretals si cun lo futurs del obtatiu si metets denan *cum* lai on ditz *utinam*.

El preterit non perfeit del conjunctiu: 560

cum eu fos amatz .i. cum ego amarer,
tu fosses amatz .i. tu amareris vel amarere,
cel fos amat[z] .i. ille amaretur;

et pluraliter: 564
    5b
cun nos fossem amat .i. cum nos amaremur,
vos fossetz amat .i. amaremini,
cil fossen o *fosson amat* .i. illi amarentur.

El preterit perfeit: 568

cum eu aia estat amatz .i. cum ego amatus sim vel fuerim,
tu aias estat amatz .i. amatus sis vel fueris,
cel aia estat amatz .i. ille amatus sit vel fuerit;

et pluraliter: 572

cum nos aiam estat amat .i. cum simus vel fuerimus amati,
vos aias estat amat .i. vos sitis vel fueritis amati,
cil aio estat amat .i. illi sint vel fuerint amati.

543 auer; amat   544 amat   545 amat; esses   550–879 *placed after 266*   551 uoillia   552 fias   555 uoilli a   557 illi
558 coniuncties attetuls   559 meteis   560 p*er*fart   563 fossem amat

576 Lo preterits plus quam perfeit del conjunctiu sembla aqel del optatiu si metetz *cum* en loc de *Deus voilha*.

El futur del [conjunctiu]:

cum eu aurai estat amatz .i. cum ero vel fuero amatus,
580   tu eris vel fueris amatus,
          ille erit vel fuerit amatus;
et pluraliter:

nos aurem estat amat .i. cum amati erimus vel fuerimus,
584   vos amati eritis vel fueritis,
          illi amati erint vel fuerint.

Infinitius de verbi passiu non a luec en vulgar.

Li verb della seconda e de la terza e de la quarta coniugatio sum
588 mout divers, si cum:

eu scriu o *eu scrivi*
(e dobla se en la prima persona),

tu escrius o *tu escrives*
592 (e dobla se en la segonda eissamen),

cel escriu, cel escrive†
(et aisi se dobla en la terza).
Ancara vol dir de la segonda conjugazon:

596 *eu ai* .i. ego habeo,
    tu as .i. tu habes,
    cel ha .i. ille habet;
6a *eu tein* o *teni* .i. ego teneo,
600 *tu tes*,
    cel [. . .] .i. ille tenet.

El preterit non perfet de l'indicatiu et futur e·l futur del optatiu e·l prezent del conjunctiu son semblan tuit verbe de la seconda et de la
604 terza e de la quarta conjugazon, q'el preterit non perfeit fan tuit la prima persona in -*ia*, si cum:

eu fingia† .i. ego fingebam,
tu fingias† .i. tu fingebas,
608 *cel fingia*† .i. ille fingebat;

---

576 p͞tit.ᵃ   577 meteiz; uoillia   578 conjunctiu *om*.   583 auiem
586 passiui   588 mout] ero,ut   589 en seriu oue scriui   594 et] ut
605 in ia] mia

el plural, la prima persona tuit en -*iam*, si cum:

> *nos fingiam*† .i. nos fingebamus,
> *vos fingias*† .i. vos fingebatis,
> *cill fingion*† .i. ill[i] fingebant 612

—del indicatiu entendatz generalmen, del conjunctiu a la vigada, can *si* es pauzatz denan, si cum aissi: *S'eu avia mil marchs, eu seria rics hom* .i. si haberem mille marchas, ego essem dives.

El futur del indicatiu finissen tuit en -*ai*, si cun es dit desus del futur 616 del indicatiu de la prima coniugatio, si cum:

> *eu aurai, tu auras, cel aura*;

et pluraliter:

> *nos aurem, vos aures, cill auran.* 620

El futur del optatiu e·l present del conjunctiu tuit finissen la prima persona en -*a*, si cum:

> *Dieus voilha qu'eu escriva* .i. utinam ego scribam,
> *tu escrivas* .i. tu scribas, 624
> *cel escriva* .i. ille scribat;

e pluraliter:

> *Deus voilha qe nos escrivam* .i. nos scribamus,
>   vos scribatis, 628
>   illi scribant.

El preterit perfet del indicatiu la prima persona finis en -*i*, / la segonda 6b en -*ist*, per la maior part, si cun:

> *eu dissi* .i. ego dixi, 632
> *tu dissist* [.i.] tu dixisti;
> *eu dormi* .i. ego dormivi,
> *tu dormist* .i. tu dormisti;
> *eu feçi* o *fi* .i. ego feci, 636
> *tu feçist* .i. tu fecisti.

Mas en la terza persona singular son mout divers, si cum:

> *dis* .i. dixit,
> *escris* .i. scripsit, 640
> *feis* .i. finxit;

et tuit aqil don l'enfinitius fenis en -*ir* solamen, si cun *auzir* .i. audire,

610 *first* nos] non   612 ill   613–14 can fies pauz atz   614 auira; feria rios   616 El] E il   623 uoillja (j < i)   627 uoillja   632 eu dissi] en dixi   633 tu dixist. tu dissisti   642 len finitius

sentir .i. sentire, *cubrir* .i. coperire, *sofrir* .i. substinere, qe non se podon doblar si cun se dobla *dir* e *dire*, fan la prima e la terza del singular in *-i* et la segonda in *-ist*, si cun:

  eu soffri .i. substinui,
  tu sofris .i. sustinuisti,
648   *cel sofri* .i. sustinuit;

el plural fan la prima persona en *-im*, si cum:

  nos sofrim .i. sustinuimus,
  vos sufritz .i. sustinuistis,
652   *cill sufriren* o *sufriron*, id est illi sustinuerunt vel sustinuere.

E li autre que non son d'aqest semblan fan en plural la prima persona in *-em*, si cum:

  nos aguem .i. nos habuimus,
656   vos habuistis,
    illi habuerunt vel habuere

(el singular si cun li autre, trait la terza persona qe diz *ac* .i. habuit),

  nos dissem .i. diximus,
660   *vos disses* .i. dixistis,
  ill dissen o *disson* .i. dixerunt vel dixere.

Tres sunt qe fan en la terza persona del singular in *-oc*, si cun:

  poc .i. potuit,
664   *moc* .i. movit,
  noc .i. nocuit,

e·l quart es *ploc* .i. pluit.
In pret[erit]o perfetto [. . .] estreit:

668   *bec* .i. bibit,
  lec .i. licuit,
  sec .i. sedit,
  tenc .i. tenuit,
672   *dec* .i. debuit.

7a In / *-eup*, si cum:

  deceup .i. decepit,
  conceup .i. concepit,
676   *ereup* .i. convaluit.

  643 sofris   653 da qest   658 trait] tuit; diz] biz; ac] Ae
  661 illi   666 quart es] qu*a*tres   667 p*r*eto

APPENDIX I

In -*aup*, si cum:
    saup .i. sapuit,
    caup .i. cepit.

In -*eis*, si cum:
    teis .i. tinxit,
    seis .i. cinxit,
    feis .i. finxit,
    peis .i. pinxit,
    empeis .i. impinxit,
    estreis .i. strinxit,
    destreis .i. constrinxit,
    ateis .i. nactus est.

In -*es* estreit, si cun:

    mes .i. misit
(compost, si cun *remes* .i. remisit),

    pres .i. prendit
(compost, si cum *apres* .i. apprehendit, *repres* .i. reprehendit),

    qes .i. quesivit
([. . .], si cum *reqes* .i. requisivit);

    vendet .i. vendidit,
    fotet .i. fotuit,
    escondet .i. ascondit,
    encendet .i. encendit,

qe fan tot lo prete[ri]t perfeit enteiramen si cum li verbe de la prima conjugation, e si son ill de la segonda, e *respondet* .i. respondit e *tondet* .i. totondit seguen aqella meteisma regola.

In -*erc*, si cum:
    sufri o *sufrerc* .i. passus est,
    obri o *uberc* .i. aperuit,
    cubri o *cuberc* .i. cooperuit,
    corri o *corre*[*c*] .i. cucurrit.

In -*ers* larc, si cum:
    ters .i. tersit,
    esters .i. estersit.

---

682 conci*n*xit   700 pretet   701 cogniugation; si] li   702 a qella
704 sufrere   705 ubere   706 cubere   707 corre   708 larc] lans

APPENDIX I

In -*ers* estret, si cun:

712   *ders* .i. esit,
      adhers .i. adhesit.

In -*ars*, si cun:

       espars .i. exparsit,
716   *ars* .i. arsit.

In -*os* estreit, si cun:

       escos .i. excussit,
       ros .i. rodit,
720   *escos* .i. abscondit.

In -*ols* larg, si cun:

       sols .i. solvit,
       absols .i. absolvit,
724   *vols* .i. volvit,
       revols .i. revolvit.

In -*ors* larg, si cun:

       tors .i. torsit,
728   *destors* .i. destorsit.

In -*eus*, si cum:

       teus .i. timuit,
       preus .i. pressit.

732 In -*ais*, si cun:

       complais .i. conquestus est,
       plais .i. planxit,
7b   *frais* .i. / franxit,
736   *refrais* .i. refransit,
       afrais .i. humiliavit,
       sofrais .i. defuit,
       trais .i. traxit,
740   *atrais* .i. atraxit,
       retrais .i. narravit,
       contrais .i. debilem fecit,
       pertrais .i. valde traxit,
744   *sostrais* .i. subripuit,
       tais .i. espedivit,
       atais .i. pertinuit.

715 exparsit (x < s)   721 lirgz   726 ers   727 ters   728 destors]
dexteters   732 *placed after 733*   733 complans   742 conurais;
facit   745 dais   746 p*er*timuit

APPENDIX I

In -*aus*, si cun:

claus .i. clausit. 748

E per zo ai fait tan longa paraula de la terza persona del preterit perfeit qar maiers confuzions era en aquella qu'en totas las autras, qar per la maior part la prima persona fenis en -*i* e la segonda en -*ist*—del preterit perfeit del indicatiu entendatz, o per la maior part la prima e la 752 segonda persona sun semblan, si cum es dit desus.

Del preterit non perfeit de la segonda e de la terza e de la quarta conjugazon tuit sun d'un semblan, si cum es dig desus, si cun:

eu avia, tu avias, cel avia, 756
nos aviam, vos aviatz, ill avien o *avion*.

El preterit plus quam perfeit tuit aquill don l'infinitius fan in -*endre*, se cun *prendre*, o en -*etre*, si cum *metre*, o in -*atre*, si cum *batre*, o in -*ondre*, si cun *escondre*, o in -*otre*, si cun *fotre*, o in -*er*, si cun *aver*, 760 *poder*, son semblan a la prima conjugazon, mudat -*at* in -*ut*, si cun:

eu avia agut .i. ego habueram,
eu avia fotut .i. ego fotueram,
tu avias agut o *fotut,* 764
cel avia agut o *fotut;*

et pluraliter:

nos aviam sabut,
vos avias sabut, 768
ill avian sabut;

et aqill don / l'infinitius finis in -[*i*]*r*, mutat -*at* in -*it*, si cum: 8a

eu avia dormit, tu avias dormit, cel avia dormit,
nos aviam, vos avias, cil avian amat; 772

trait tres qe mudant -*at* in -*hoint*, zo es *poigner, joigner, hoigner*, si cum:

eu avia point, eu avia joint, tu avias joint;

e trait *vezer*, qe muda -*at* in -*ist*, si cun:

eu avia vist; 776

e trait *prendre* e *metre*, ab lor compost, si cum *comprendre, sometre*, que muden -*at* in -*es*, si cum:

[*eu*] *avia pres, tu avias pres,*
eu avia mes, tu avias mes; 780

749 Emp*er*; 3ª 750 a quella; *second* qar] qan 752 entendaiz 757 illi illi *struck through after* auiatz 758 in endre] mendre 761 pŕima; at] ac 767 auian 769 subut 770 a qill; in r. mutar 772 aviam] auian 773 trait] Trais; joigner] loigner 777 prendre] pitore; so metre 778 es] ens 779 eu *om*.

APPENDIX I

e trait *escondre*, qe muda *-at* in *-os*, si cun:

eu avia escos, tu avia[s] escos;

et trait *peigner, feigner, teigner, ceigner*, ab totz lor compostz, si cun
784 *enfeigner, enteignher*†, *acenher*†, qe mudent *-at* in *-eint*, si cum:

eu avia enteint, eu avia e[n]feint,

et *atener* eissamen;
et trait *estrenher*, ab totz sos compost, qe muda *-at* in *-eit*, si cun:
788   *eu avia estreit, tu avias estreit.*

El prezen de l'imperatiu fenissen totas las conjugazos, trait la prima persona, la segonda persona del singular in *-as*, si cun:

digas .i. dic tu,

792 la terza in *-a*, si cum:

diga cel .i. dicat ille;

el plural, la prima in *-am*, si cun:

digam .i. dicamus nos,

796 la segonda in *-az*, si cun:

digatz .i. dicite vos,

la terza in *-on*, si cun:

799   *digon* .i. dicant illi.

8b Mas aissi faill / la regla en la seconda persona del singular per la maior
801 part, si cun:

pren, repren, penh, oinh, streinh,

e generalmen tuit finissen si cun en l'enfinitiu, trait la ultima sillaba, si
804 cun *batre* qe fai *bat* et *audir* qe fa *au* et *escondre* qe fa *escon* et *legir* qe fa *leg*. En la terza persona fan tuit en *-a*, si cun es dit desus, si cun *bata, auia, lega, faza*. El futur de l'imperatiu de totas las conjugazos fan tuit aissi con lo futur del indicatiu, si cun es dit desus.
808   Del prezen de optatiu de totas las conjugazos fon dit pleneiramen lai on fo dit del optatiu de la prima conjugazon.
[. . .] o de la terza fan aissi con lo preterit plus quam perfet de la prima, mutat *-at* in *-ut*, si cun: *Deus volgues qu'eu agues agut* o *qu'eu*
812 *agues volgut* o *qu'eu agues entendut*; si es de la quarta conjugazo, si cun

782 eu] en; tu auia   785 efeint   787 enstrenher   789 coniuga
zos   795 digan   797 dicatz   799 dicunt   802 penh] peitz
803 generalm*e*nen   804 et ilegir   806 limperaziu; totas] totz
812 coniugazon *with* n *struck through*

auzir, servir, mutat *-at* in *-it,* si cun: *Deus volgues qu'eu aves servit* o *qu'eu aves audit.* Et aissi mudon si con es dig pleneiramen del preterit plus quam perfeit de l'indicatiu.

E futurs optatius e·l prezens del conjunctiu son semblan, que finissen en la prima persona en *-a,* si cum:

Deus no voilla qu'eu aia o *cum eu aia* o *cum eu scriva* o *cum eu diga;*

la segonda in *-as:*

tu scrivas o *que tu aias* o *sias;*

la terza si cum:

Deus voilha qu'el sia o *qu'el scriva* o / *cum el escriva* o *qu'el sia;*

el plural, la prima persona in *-am,* si cun:

Deus voilha que nos aiam o *siam* o *scrivam* o *cum nos voillam* o *tengam;*

la segonda in *-az,* si cum:

Deus voilha que vos aiaz, qe vos siaz o *cum vos voilhaz;*

la terza in *-an* o in *-on,* si cun:

Deus voilha qe ill aian o *sian* o *cun ill bevan.*

El preterit non perfeit del conju[n]ctiu, si es de la segonda e de la terza conjugazon, fenis la prima persona de singular in *-es,* si cum:

eu agues, cum eu prendes, cum eu fotes;

la segonda in *-esses,* si cum:

tu aguesses o *tu prendesses;*

la terza in *-es,* si cum:

cel agues o *tenes;*

e plural fan la prima in *-em,* si cum:

nos aguessem o *cum nos prendessem;*

la segonda in *-es,* si cun:

vos aguesses, vos prendesses;

la terza in *-en,* si cun:

ill aguessen o *cum ill prendessen.*

818 *second* aia] ara   822 uoillia   824 uoillja (j < i)   826 uoillia; uoilliaz   828 uoillia   829 coniuctiu   834 3^a

Si es de la quarta conjugazon, finis la prima persona del singular in -*is*, si cum:

844   [*eu*] *dormis, cum eu servis*;

la segonda in -*isses*, si cun:

tu dormisses;

la terza in -*is*, si cum:

848   *cel dormis, cun cel servis*;

el plural fan la prima in -*issem*, si cum:

nos dormissem, cum nos servissem;

la segonda in -*issez*, si cum:

852   *vos dormissez*;

la terza in -*issen* o en -*isson*, si cun:

ill dormissen o *dormisson*.

El preterit perfeit del conjunctiu fan aissi cum lo preterit perfeit del
856 conjunctiu / [...]
9b   [...] fan aissi con el preterit plus quam perfeit del optatiu, ajustat *cum* en loc de *utinam*.

El futur fan aissi con lo futurs de la prima conjugazon, mutat -*at* in
860 -*ut*, si es de la segonda o de la terza conjugazon, si es de la quarta mutat -*at* [in] -*it*, si cum:

[*eu*] *aurai, tu auras, cel aura tengut, fotut, servit*;
nos aurem rendut, servit,
864   *vos aures volgut, auzit*,
ill auran rendut, servit.

Del infinitiu es dit assatz desus al comensamen del[s] verbs.

Lo passius de las autras conjugazos, si cun es dit de la prumeira, si
868 [v]a totz per orde, fors tan q'en la segonda et en la terza conjugazon muta -*at* in -*ut* et en la qarta -*at* in -*it*, e trait aqel que se mudan si con es dit el preterit plus quam perfeit del indicatiu del actiu.

Sequitur de Adverbio

872   Adverbium es appellatz que josta lo verbe deu esser pauzatz, si cum:
eu dic veramen, si tu non vas tost, eu te battrai malamen .i. ego dico, nisi

---

844 eu *om.*   849 el] Et   853 issen] issem   857 auistat   861 at in it] at ut   862 eu *om.*   863 prendut   865 auran en rendut   866 de sus; del   867–8 si atotz   868 q'en] qan; et *added above the line*   869 muta] mutat   873 non *repeated*; batterai

vadas cito, percutiam te male. Veetz cun aquella dicios, zo es *dic*, es verbs et aqella dicios, zo es *veramen*, es adverbium, car es pauzada 875 justa / aqella dicion, zo es *dic*, que es verbs. **10a**
A l'adverbi pertenon tres cauzas, zo es species, significazons et figura. 877 Tuit li adverbi sun de specie derivativa o primitiva. Derivativa son tuit aqel que venon d'autre loc, si cum *malamen*, que ven de *mal*. / De specie **(14b)** primitiva es aqel [que] no ven d'alcun, si cum *tost*, que no ven d'autre. 880 Et devez saber qe tuit aquell que finisson in -*en* podon finir in -*enz*, et significant qualitat, si cun *malamen* o *malamenz*, *bonamen* o *bonamenz*.

Et sun autre adverbe que signifian temps, si cun: **15a**

    oi .i. hodie, 884
    her .i. heri,
    l'autreir .i. nuper,
    deman .i. cras,
    ja .i. iam, 888
    a la vegada .i. aliquando,
    adoncs .i. tunc,
    ogan .i. hoc anno,
    antan .i. alio anno, 892
    mentre .i. dum,
    tart .i. sero,
    tostemp[*s*] .i. semper,
    mattin .i. mane; 896

et autre significa ajustamen (.i. adiunctionem), si cum:

    ensems .i. simul;

l'autre demostramen, si cum:

    veus me .i. ecce me, 900
    vel vos .i. ecce ille;

l'autre luec, si cum:

    aissi .i. hic,
    aqui .i. ibi, 904
    dins .i. intus,
    defors .i. deforis,
    de lai, sai,
    amon .i. sursum, 908

---

874 Veectz; a q*u*ella   875 *second* es] Et   876 *an* qella   877 *perte* non   879 malamer; *after* mal, *and beginning on the following line,* C *inserts* 267–549, *after which* De specie *begins a new line*   880 *first* que *om.*; *second* que] q*u*am   881 deuem   888 .i.] et   890 adonos   892 autran 895 tostemp   898 ens ems   900 veus] meus   902 luec] Luce 904 a qui

aval .i. deorsum,
sus, *jos*;

l'autre interrogazion, si cum:

912   *per qe*;

e l'autre comparation, si cun:

plus, mais, maiorme[n].

Participius es ditz quar pren l'una part del nom e l'autra del verbe:
916 del nom reten cas et genus, del verbe reten temps et significazons, dell'un et del autre ten numerus et figura. Et d'aysso ai dit assaz.

Il fine

909 au al   914 maior me   915 Participuis; quan

APPENDIX II

Fragment of list of rhymes from MS. L

fortrais verais   1a

-aus:

aus aus aus braus
blaus bairaus caus claus   4
claus forclaus enclaus entreclaus
contreclaus esclaus faus fraus
naus paus paus paus
repaus raus traus laus   8
laus aus

-aucs:

baucs craucs naucs paucs
glaucs raucs traucs   12

-aics:

Aics laics Ebraics

-autz:

autz cautz cautz encauz   16
sautz asautz bautz faus
bauz ribautz Raembautz adauz
blizaus

-aurs: 20

saurs maurs laurs aurs
taurs Vaurs tesaurs

-als:

sivals sals mals sals   24
anals anoals nadals airals
batrals cals rals tals
aitals canals cabals carnals

Readings of *L*.   2 aus   4b = ?   ¶ before 5b   9b = -aucs?
¶ before 13   ¶ before 15   ¶ before 20   ¶ before 23   26a = bar-
rals?

APPENDIX II

28 corals contals criminal[s] comunals
dedals destrals espiritals egals
enfernals eminals emperials estivals
fenals fals fivals fogals
32 gazals jornals ivernals juvenals
maestrals mortals maials naturals
nizals ostals orials organals
orientals pals portals peitrals
36 principals reials senhals vals
venals venials

-ams:

ams ams brams brams
40 cams clams clams reclams
reclams cizams coirams dams
Adams estrams erams essams
estams fams afams aflams
44 forams grams lams rams
tams

-ans:

ans ans abans avans
48 afans brans bolans bobans
cans descans dans gans
engans enans enans grans
garans escans glans Joans
52 joans lans lans mans
comans demans vans olifans
pans pesans tans destans
—usque mille;
56 Tristans talans tirans truans
semblans vians soans
—et omnia participia prime coniugationis desinunt in *-ans*, sicut *amans,
cantans,* et cetera.

60 *-anhz:*

banhz Galvanhz gazanz estranz

28c criminal	31c = fevals?	34a = nazals?	¶ before 34b
34c = orinals?	¶ before 35b	¶ before 38	¶ before 39c
39d brabms	¶ before 40a	41b cizamrs; = ?	¶ before 41d
¶ before 43b	¶ before 46	46 aus	47a aus 47b aus
48c = blans? bobans?	52a = jaians?	54d destaus *rather than*	
destans; = descans?	¶ before 56a, *which begins a new line*		57b =
vianans?	58 ¶ before et, *which begins a new line*	¶ before 60	

manhz museranhz tanhz estanhz
planhz planhz, compost flanhz, compost sanhz
fanhz gilfanhz   64

-ars:

ars ars celars bars
autars avars azars baisars
bacal[a]rs cars escars clars   68
culars culars calamars

62b = masanhz eranhz?   63c = franhz?   ¶ *before* 65   68a bacalrs
68c escars *or* estars   69a–b = cujars colars?   69c *after* calamars, *the remainder of the line is left blank; the text of the* Razos de trobar *begins, without heading, on the following line*

APPENDIX III

Chapters on prepositions and interjections added to the Donatz in MS. L

14b   De prepositione

    Preposicions es apellada car es denan pa[u]ssada a las autras partz, per apositio, so es per regimen de cas, o per conposicio, so es car se
4 conpon; qe las prepositions no serven si no al cas acusatiu et al ablatiu—las unas al ablatiu et las autras al acusatiu e las autras serven ad amdos los cas.

    A l'acusatiu serven *at, apud, ante, adversum, cis, citra, contra, erga,*
8 *infra, intra, op, pone, prope, post, trans, ultra, preter, supra, circiter, usque, secus, penes.* Aqestas .xxiij. prepositios serven al cas acusatiu.

    Al cas ablatiu serven aqestas: *a, ab, abs, cum, coram, clan, de, ex, pro, pre, sine, absque, tenus.* Aqestas .xiij. prepositios serven al ablatiu cas.
12   E aqestas .iiij. prepositios serven ad ambsdos cas, al acusatiu et a l'ablatiu: *in, sub, super,* et *subter.*

    E devetz saber qe las preposicios qe serven a l'acusatiu cas significant aionzimen et aqelas qe serven al ablatiu significan despartimen, si cum
16 es *vauc m'en a la maison de Peire* e *vign da la maison d'Albert.*

    E devetz saber qe la prepositio *in* tal vez es serven a l'acusatiu et tal vez es a l'ablatiu: can si met cum verbe significan movimen, serf *in* a l'acusatiu, si cum es *va[u]c m'en in maison, vau m'en in la glesia*; et can
20 se met cum verbe significan stagamen serf al ablatiu, si cum es *sui in maison, vau m'en in la gleisa.*

    E devetz saber qe aqesta prepositio *super,* can se met cum causa animada racional o inracional e sensibel o non sensibel, serf a l'acusatiu,
24 si cum es *som subra aqest ostal* e *sobra·l lenga.* Et atresi can se pon cum causa animada, si cum es *sientia* et *arz* et autras semblantz causas, serf
15a [a l']ablatiu, si cum / es *studui sobra aqesta lesion et sobra aqesta qestion.* Et de *super* et *supra* es un aital vers: *super* tang[it ad] rem, sed *supra*
28 distat ab illa.

Readings of *L.*   1 *rubric* De pre positione *after* denan (2), *at end of line*
2 passada   8 cir. citer   15 aionzimen = ajostamen? movimen?
16 *before first* maison, *in expunctuated*   19 uacmen   23 esen sibel;
sen sibel   25 = inanimada?   25–6 serf ablatiu   27 un] um; taingn. rem

De interiectione

Interjetions es apelada car se met et pausa entre las autras partz d'oration, e non a se no signification de dolor, si cum es *ai! Deus! e! q'en volon dir?; las! q'eu mor desiran; oi! eu! a!* Et aisi fenis tota aqesta obra complidamen.

29 *rubric*   *after* 33, Donatz *1523 begins on following line*

APPENDIX IV

Additions and Corrections to FEW

LISTED below are the articles of the *FEW* to which examination of the *Donatz* suggests additions and corrections. Reference is made here to the relevant volume of *FEW* and to the relevant note in the present edition. Many of the notes merely correct errors and omissions of minor importance, but some involve questions of classification or word-history of some consequence.

I. ABBAS, 2480; *ADERIGERE, 620; AFFLIGERE, 2620; AGNELLUS, 2399; ALBUS, 1934; ARBOR, 962; *BAFF, 1551; BELLARE, 833; *BIHURDAN, 2885; *BILIA, 3409; *BOMBITIRE, 1357; BŌTAN, 2935; *BRAG-, 172, 1646; BRANCA, 3450; *BRICCO, 2444; BROCCUS, 2791; BULLA, 839.

II. 1. CADĔRE, 1978; *CALCICARE, 2458–9; CALĒRE, 2093; CAMMĪNUS, 850; CAPUT, 2948; KAT-Ł, 854; CAUSARI, 2458–9; CERASEUM, 2254; CHORUS, 875.

II. 2. COLLIS, 2926; COLLUM, 2926; COMPUTARE, 1734; CONSĪDĔRARE, 3219; CORALLIUM, 1662; KRAKK-, 1538; *CŬMBOS, 2731; CŬNĔUS, 2776.

III. DIURNUM, 801; DOLIUM, 2724; *EXAURARE, 948; EXCUTERE, 3538; *EXTREMESCERE, 1393; *FALLIA, 3373; FARCIRE, 164; FATUUS, 971; *FEHU, 1125; *FĪDARE, 3476; *FĪGĬCARE, 2461, 3484; FĬNDĔRE, 3377; FĪNĪRE, 2526; FĪXUS, 2616; FLĔCTERE, 1400; FLĔXARE, 1991; FŎLLIS, 2402; FORARE, 2811; FRĪGĔRE, 1335; FŬRCA, 2793.

IV. GARG-, 188; GLĪS, 147; GŬLA, 1414, 1807; GŬRDUS, 2890; HĪBĔRNUS, 1573; HUP-, 1239; HYACINTHUS, 188.

V. JŪDĬCARE, 1002; LAURUS, 3245; LĬGNUM, 2496; LISPOS, 1016; LŪRĬDUS, 2889.

VI. MANCUS, 1756; MARRŬBIUM, 2723.

VII. NŎVUS, 2802; NŬTRĪMEN, 2489; PACTUM, 1905; PALEA, 1667–8; PALLIDUS, 1436; PANDŪRA, 792; PARĬCŬLUS, 2068, 3390; PASTŪRA, 3139.

VIII. PATIENS, 1905; PECTINARE, 1088.

IX. PONTĬCŬLUS, 1101; PŎSSE, 3181; PŬLS, 187; *PŬNCTIARE, 1101, 1102.

X. *RASCLARE, 1121; RONFL-, 1139; RŎSA, 2256; RŎTŬLUS, 2715; RŬCTARE, RŬCTUS, 2940.

APPENDIX IV 377

XII. sŏccus, 2656; sŏlium, 3437; sōlus, 2607; speculum, 2075; stola, 3311; sŭbtīlis, 3416.

XIII. 1. tăbănus, 1969; tabula, 1183-4; tar-, 3368; tilia, 3396.

XIII. 2. tŏllĕre, 3424; tŏrquēre, 3536; trŭnceus, 2749.

XIV. vanitare, 1223; vapor, 2835; vĕrĭcŭlum, 3438; vĕrtĕre, 2986; viola, 2257; vĭrga, virgatus, 1235; vŭlpes, 2636.

XVI. *hnapp, 1525; *krappa, 2166; *labba, 1533; raspôn, 1667-8; Reginhart, 1820; *rēþs, 812.

XVII. *skalja, 1648, 3363; *skarwahta, 112-15; *skŏt, 2936; taikns, 1543; *trippōn, 1201.

XXI, p. 305, 1533.

—. *ad-derigere, 620; frunītus, 1404; raptare, 1120; tămm, 1689.

ALPHABETICAL LIST OF RHYME-ENDINGS

THIS list, though intended primarily as an index to the dictionary of rhymes, includes also references to parallel material in the rest of the grammar.

a estreit 294–5
abs 1523
ac, see hac
acs 1535
af 1549
aics 1552
aira 3517
ais 1593 (cf. 640)
ala 3252
alcs 1641
alha 3344
alhz 1644
alms 1669
als 1555
altz 1624
amba 3437
ams 1673
anca 3447
ancs 1746
ans 1690
ara 3154
arcs 1787
ars 1765 (cf. 621)
artz 1799
as estreit 1933
as larg 1918 (cf. 136, 155)
assa 3547
athz 1896
atz 1864
auca 3498
aucs 1825
aup 583
aura 3243
aurs 1855
aus 1835 (cf. 646)

ec estreit 577
ecs estreit 1976
ecs larg, see hecs
ega 3487
eira 3182

eis larg 1987
eis streit 1995 (cf. 585, eis)
ela estreit 3288
ela larg 3265
ela [= elha] estreit 3378
ela [= elha] larg 3401
elhz estrit 2063
elhz larg, see ielz
els estreit 2023
els larg 2009
elz larg 2028
ems estreit 2081
ems larg 2079
enc estreit 590
enga 3441
ens estreit 2090
eps estreit 2163
era [sc. larg] 3167
era estrit 3177
erc 614
erms 2289
erns 2278
erps 2286
ers estreit 2187 (cf. 178, 619)
ers larg 2169 (cf. 176, 617)
ertz estreit 2307
ertz larg 2293
es estreit 2317 (cf. 149, 152, 593)
es larg 2312 (cf. 153)
esca 3504
et larg 595
ethz estreit 2408
ethz larg 2376
etz estreit 2386
eup 581
eus [sc. larg?] 2423
eus estreit 638

hac [= ac] 605
hecs [= ecs] larg 1963

ALPHABETICAL LIST OF RHYME-ENDINGS

ia 3466
ibs 2438
ica 3481
ics 2443
ielz [= ielhz] larg 2060
iers 2201
iga 3456
ihtz 2615
ila 3297
ilha 3404
ils 2466
ims 2482
ins 2491
ira 3207
irs 2497
is 2508 (cf. 607)
iscla 3558
itz 2548
ius 2604

obs estreit 2628
obs larg 2623
oc [sc. larg] 572
oc estreit 623
ocs estreit 2654
ocs larg 2637
ohtz larg 2761
oira 3553
ois estreit 625
ola estrit 3325
ola larg 3310
ola [= olha] estreit 3433
ola [= olha] larg 3418
olbs larg 2634
olc larg 627
olhz estreit 2717
olhz larg 2702
ols estreit 2675
ols larg 2659 (cf. 634)
olz estreit 2696
olz larg 2688

oms estreit 2729
oms larg 2725
onhz estreit 2772
ons estreit 2740 (var. B)
ons larg 2740
ora estreit 3231
ora larg 3225
orbs estrit 2896
orbs larg 2893
orcs estreit 2789
orcs larg 2785
orms larg 2904
orns estreit 2907
orns larg 2898
ors estrit 2816
ors larg 2805 (cf. 189, 636)
ortz [sc. larg] 2856
ortz estreit 2882
os estreit 632 (cf. 134, os)
os larg 630
osa estreit 3544
osa larg 3539
ossa estreit 3531
ossa larg 3525
otz estreit 2950
otz larg 2934
ous larg o estreit 2797
outz estreit 2927
outz larg 2916

ucs 2965
uf 2988
uis 612
ula 3340
uls 2992
ums estreit 2997
ura 3117
urcs 3019
urs 3004
us 3078
utz 3022

INDEX OF PROPER NAMES

BESIDES proper names of persons, places, rivers, etc., this list includes ethnic adjectives. All forms are of the nominative singular unless otherwise indicated; names specifically cited as indeclinable in the text are noted as *indecl.*

Abels 2010, Abel
Acs 160, *indecl.*, Dax
Adams 5, 1682, Adam
Agades 2356, *adj. m., n. pl.*, of Agde
Aics 1554, Aix
Aiols 186, 2686, *indecl.*, man's name
Amelha 3403, woman's name
Amons 2740 (*B*), Amnon (2 Samuel 3: 2) (?); or Amon (2 Kings 21: 18) (?)
Andreus 2436, Andrew
Angles 150, *n. pl.* Angles 2349, *adj. m. indecl.*, English
Anjavis 2542, *adj.*, Angevin
Anjeus 2437, Angers (*conjectured*)
Artus 201, 3101, *indecl.*, Arthur
Assis 2539, Assisi
Austorcs 2788, man's name

Baltz 1629, Bautz 161, *indecl.*, Les Baux
Becs 1977, man's name
Bedeires 2355, *adj. m., n. pl.*, of Béziers
Beirius 2614, Berry
Bezers 177, 2185, *indecl.*, Béziers
Bolonhes 2362, *adj. m., n. pl.*, of Bologna
Bordales 2351, *adj. m., n. pl.*, of Bordeaux
Bordels 2021, Bordeaux
Bretz 2387, family name
Brianzones 2358, *untranslated*; = *adj. m., n. pl.*, of Briançon
Burcs 195, 3021, *indecl.*, Burgos

Caersis 2546, *adj.*, of Cahors
Caïms 2490, Cain
Cambrais 1623, Cambrai
Campanes 2361, *adj. m., n. pl.*, of the Campagna
Canileus 2435, *adj.*, Canaanite

Carcasses 2354, *adj. m., n. pl.*, of Carcassonne
Cardolhz 2716, Carlisle
Catalas 1955, *adj.*, Catalan
Cecilias 1959, *adj.*, Sicilian
Cerberus 201, 3098, *indecl.*, Cerberus
Clavais 173, 1621, *indecl.*; Chivasso, in Montferrat
Coraçhuchius de Sterlleto 3571 (*A*), Coraçuchius de Sterleto *title* (*L*), Conradus de Sterleto *title* (*D*), one of the author's two patrons
Cremones 2365, *adj. m., n. pl.*, of Cremona

Danis, *see* Sanc Danis
Dedalus 199, 3099, *indecl.*, Daedalus
Donatus Provincialis *title* (*A*), liber Donati Provincialis 3573 (*A*), Donato prodensal *title* (*D*), Donatz proensals *title* (*C*)

Ebreus 2425, *adj.*, Hebrew
Eis 1988, Iesi, in Italy
Elienors 2813, Eleanor
Enocs 2652, Enoch

Faentis 2544, *adj.*, of Faenza
Falartz 1821 (*A*), name of a town (= ?); *cf.* Talartz
Falartz 1821 (*A*), man's name or family name (?); *cf.* Talartz
Fas 1962, Fano, in Italy
Fisons 2747, the river Pison (Vulgate: Phison), one of the four rivers of Paradise (Genesis 2: 11)
Flora 3227, Flora
Folis 2537, Foligno, in Umbria (?)
Forlis 2538, Forli, in Italy
Frances 150, *n. pl.* Frances 2348, *adj. m. indecl.*, French

INDEX OF PROPER NAMES

Gabriels 2015, Gabriel
Galias 1949, Galen
Genoes 151, *n. pl.* Genoes 2350, *adj. m. indecl.*, Genoese
Gions 2746, the river Gihon (Vulgate: Gehon), one of the four rivers of Paradise (Genesis 2: 13)
Grecs 1971, *adj.*, Greek
Gronhz 2781, man's name

Iacobus de Mora 3570 (*A*), *title* (*DL*), one of the author's two patrons
Imbertz 2302, man's name

Jacme 215, James
Jerusalems 2080, Jerusalem
Jezabels 2013, Jezabel
Jhesus 3103, Jesus
Joans 218, John
Juçeus 2426, *adj.*, Jewish

Latis 2518, *adj.*, Latin
Lemozis 2547, *adj.*, Limousin
Longis 2519, Longinus
Lumbarz 1802, *adj.*, Lombard
Lumbers 177, 2186, *indecl.*, Lombers (cant. de Réalmont, arr. d'Albi, Tarn)
Luques 2369, *adj. m., n. pl.*, of Lucca

Mainartz 1816, family name
Marcs 1798, Mark
Marolhz 2716 (*B*), Mareuil
Marquesas 1954, *adj.*, of the March (of Ancona?)
Marrocs 2647, Morocco
Marsselhes 2357, *adj. m., n. pl.*, of Marseille
Micaels 2014, Michael
Micols 2670, Michal (Vulgate: Michol) (1 Samuel 14: 49)
Milas 1961, Milan
Misaels 2017, Misael
Moutz 2917 (*A*), name of a river (=?); *cf.* Voutz
Mozenes 2374, *adj. m., n. pl.*, of Modena

Nils 2473, the Nile
Novaires 2373, *adj. m., n. pl.*, of Novara

Olivers 2245, Oliver

Ospinelz 2049, man's name
Otonelz 2048, man's name

Paregorzis 2543, *adj.*, of Périgord
Paris 183, 2531, *indecl.*, Paris (the city)
Paris 183, *indecl.*, Paris (the Greek name)
Paves 2364, *adj. m., n. pl.*, of Pavia
Peire 72, 216, Peter
Peirols 2669, man's name
Peitavis 2541, *adj.*, Poitevin
Polha 3436, Apulia
Polhes 151, *n. pl.* Poles 2359, *adj. m. indecl.*, Apulian
Pontemoles 2368, *adj. m., n. pl.*, of Pontremoli

Rafaels 2016, Raphael
Rainartz 1820, man's name; Renard the fox (?), *cf. Glossary*
Rainols 2687, man's name
Rantolhz 2716 (*B*), *no doubt an error for* Nantolhz, Nanteuil
Rems 175, 2086, *indecl.*, Reims
Rimenes 2372, *adj. m., n. pl.*, of Rimini
Robertz 2303, Robert
Robis 2511, Robin
Roiais 1622, Edessa
Romas 1956, *adj.*, Roman
Rudelz 2052, man's name

Salerns 2285, Salerno
Sanc Danis 182, Sang Danis 2527, *indecl.*, St. Denis
Sans 1730, family name
Santolz 2701, man's name
Saones 2367, *adj. m., n. pl.*, of Savona
Saüls 2996, Saul
Senes 2370, *adj. m., n. pl.*, of Siena
Sordelz 2055, man's name
Spoletis 2545, *adj.*, of Spoleto
Surs 3016, Tyre

Talartz 1821 (*L*), name of a town (=?), conceivably to be identified with Tallard (Hautes-Alpes); *cf.* Falartz
Talartz 1821 (*L*), man's name or family name (?); *cf.* Falartz
Tantalus 199, 3100, *indecl.*, Tantalus
Tertones 2366, *adj. m., n. pl.*, of Tortona
Tirs 2504, Tyre

Toes 2360, *adj. m., n. pl.*, German
Tolsas 1953, *adj.*, of Toulouse
Toscas 1957, *adj.*, Tuscan
Troias 1958, *adj.*, Trojan
Trons 2749, name of a river, no doubt the Tronto, in Italy
Turcs 3020, Turk, Saracen

Ugo 215 (*L*), Hugh
Ugo Faiditus 3569–70 (*A*), *title* (*D*), vgo faidicus *title* (*L*), the author of the *Donatz Proensals*

Valantines 2353, *adj. m., n. pl.*, of Valence
Vaurs 1860, Lavaur (arr. de Castres, Tarn) (?); or Vaour (arr. d'Albi, Tarn) (?)
Verceles 2363, *adj. m., n. pl.*, of Vercelli
Verçelz 2057, Vercelli
Verones 2371, *adj. m., n. pl.*, of Verona
Vianes 2352, *adj. m., n. pl.*, of Vienne
Voutz 2917 (*B*), name of a river (= ?); *cf.* Moutz

GLOSSARY

The glossary lists all examples cited in the verb-lists and the dictionary of rhymes, in the lists given in the body of the grammar (e.g. indeclinable nouns, adverbs), and in the paradigms of verb-forms. For words cited in phrases or sentences used as exemplifications in the grammar, the glossary is selective. References are exhaustive unless followed by 'etc.'. Forms from MSS. other than *A* are noted only where there is some special reason for doing so. Translations reflect as closely as possible the Latin equivalents of the text. Verbs are noted as transitive, intransitive, etc., in accordance with *PD*, except where there is reason to challenge the accuracy or the completeness of Levy's classification. The same is true for the gender of substantives, except that substantives and adjectives are to be taken as masculine unless the contrary is expressly indicated. All forms of substantives and adjectives are nominative singulars when not otherwise described; only those classed in the *Donatz* as indeclinable are noted as such. Verb-forms are listed under the infinitive form; the latter is followed by no line-reference when it is not cited as an example in the text of the *Donatz*.

Words absent from the standard Old Provençal dictionaries are printed in heavy type, as are their translations. Forms (other than those merely involving graphies of MS. *A*) and meanings not registered by the dictionaries are also indicated by heavy type, as are such classifications as **adj.** and **v. intr.** when the latter are absent from *PD*.

The following abbreviations are used: *adj.* adjective; *adv.* adverb; *art.* article; *comp.* comparative; *cond.* conditional; *def.* definite; *dem.* demonstrative; *f.* feminine; *fut.* future; *imper.* imperative; *impers.* impersonal; *impf.* imperfect; *ind.* indicative; *indecl.* indeclinable; *indef.* indefinite; *inf.* infinitive; *interj.* interjection; *intr.* intransitive; *lit.* literally; *m.* masculine; *n.* nominative; *num.* numeral; *obl.* oblique; *p.* past; *part.* participle; *pers.* personal; *pl.* plural; *poss.* possessive; *pr.* present; *prep.* preposition; *pret.* preterite; *pron.* pronoun; *refl.* reflexive; *sb.* substantive; *sg.* singular; *s.o.* someone; *sthg.* something; *subj.* subjunctive; *tr.* transitive; *v.* verb.

a 47, 48, *prep.*, to (*presented as sign of dative in Provençal*)
abacs 1537, *sb.*, arithmetic
abadils 2480, *adj.*, pertaining to an abbot or *abbé*
abaissar, *pr. subj.* 3 abais 1598, *v. tr.*, to lower
abastar 809, *v. intr.*, to suffice
abatre, *p. part.* abatutz 3075 (*B*), *v. tr.*, to strike down
abbas 1934, *sb.*, abbot, *abbé*

abelha 3397, *sb. f.*, bee
abelir 1355, *v. intr.*, to be pleasing or agreeable
abetar 808, *v. tr.*, to deceive with words
abragar, *pr. subj.* 2 abracs 1548, *v. intr.*, to suppurate
abrancar, *pr. ind.* 3 abranca 3450, *v. tr.*, take hold of (sthg., s.o.) by force
abrics 2445, *sb.*, place sheltered from the wind; protection

GLOSSARY

abrigar, *pr. subj.* 2 abrics 2446, *v. tr.*, to protect; to cover up
abrils 2470, *sb.*, April
absolver, *pret.* 3 absols 635, *v. tr.*, to absolve
abstener 1252, *v. refl.*, to abstain
acantar, *pr. subj.* 2 acans 1702, *v. tr.*, to turn (sthg.) on its side (?); or *v. refl.*, **to lean sideways** (?)
acantelar, *pr. ind.* 3 acantela 3230, *v. tr.*, to turn (sthg.) on its side (?); or *v. refl.*, **to lean sideways** (?)
achointans 1734, *adj.*, ready of speech, eloquent
aclinar, *pr. subj.* 2 aclis 2513, *v. intr.* and *refl.*, to bow down
acolar, *pr. ind.* 3 acola 3317, *pr. subj.* 2 acolz 2695, *v. tr.*, to embrace
acordar, *pr. subj.* 2 acortz 2859, *v. refl.*, to agree
acorre 1314, *pret.* 3 acors 2821, *v. intr.*, to come to the aid of, succour
acorsar 802, *v. tr.*, to spur on
acortz 2858, *sb.*, agreement, concord
acropir 1369, *p. part.* acrupitz 2567, *v. refl.*, to squat
acular, *pr. ind.* 3 acula 3343, *v. refl.*, to sit down on the ground
aculhir 1374, *pr. ind.* 2 acolhz 2707, *pr. subj.* 3 acolha 3426, *pr. part.* aculens 2161, *v. tr.*, to welcome
adagar 786, *v. tr.*, to water, irrigate; to mix with water
adautar 818, *v. intr.*, to delight
adempiar 798, *v. tr.*, to request (from one's friends)
adermir, *pr. ind.* 2 aderms 2292, *v. tr.*, to lay waste
aderzer, *pr. ind.* 3 adertz 2310, *imper.* 2 adertz 2310, *pret.* 3 aders 620, 2197, *p. part.* aders 180, 2196, *v. tr.*, **to make provision for (sthg. or s.o.)**
ades 2315, *adv.*, straightaway
adesar, *pr. subj.* 3 ades 2325, *v. tr.*, to touch
adescar, *pr. ind.* 3 adesca 3514, *v. tr.*, to entice with bait
adirar 778, *pr. ind.* 3 adira 3214, *v. tr.*, to hate
adonc 1480, *adv.*, then
adorar, *pr. ind.* 3 adora 3233, *v. tr.*, to adore

adormir, *p. part.* adormitz 2560, *v. tr.*, to put to sleep
adorns 2910, *adj.*, suitable
adozilhar, *pr. ind.* 3 adouzilha 3415, *v. tr.*, to broach (a cask)
adreiturar, *pr. ind.* 3 adreitura 3136, *v. tr.*, to pass judgement on
adrethz 2411, *adj.*, suitable, appropriate
aerzer, *pr. ind.* 3 aertz 2311, *pret.* 3 aers 620, 2188, *p. part.* aers 179, 2188, *v. intr.*, **to be attached, adhere, cling**
afamar, *pr. subj.* 2 afams 1687, *v. tr.*, to starve
afanar, *pr. subj.* 2 afans 1704, *v. tr.*, **to weary, fatigue**
afangar, *pr. subj.* 2 afancs 1758, *v. refl.*, to stick in the mud
afans 1704, *sb.*, **weariness**
afars 1771, *sb.*, business, deed, domain
afiar 814, 975, *pr. ind.* 3 afia 3475, *v. tr.*, to guarantee
aficar, *pr. ind.* 3 afica 3484, *pr. subj.* 2 afics 2462, *v. tr.*, **to declare, affirm** 3484; *v. refl.*, to endeavour 2462, 3484
afics 2461, *sb.*, **force, violence**
afilar, *pr. ind.* 3 afila 3306, *v. tr.*, to sharpen
afilhar, *pr. ind.* 3 afilha 3417, *v. tr.*, to adopt (child)
aflithz 2620, *adj.*, afflicted
afogar 979, *v. tr.*, to set fire to
afolar 978, *pr. ind.* 3 afola 3324, *v. tr.*, to damage 978, to ruin 3324
afondar, *pr. subj.* 2 afons 2758, *v. refl.*, to sink to the bottom
afrancar, *pr. subj.* 2 afrancs 1754, *v. tr.*, to make gentle
afranher, *pret.* 3 afrais 642, *v. tr.*, to humble
afrithz 2619, *adj.*, burning with love
agahz 1902, *sb.*, ambush
agolar, *pr. ind.* 3 agola 3328, *v. tr.*, to swallow
agradar 804, *v. intr.*, to please
agropar, *pr. subj.* 2 agrobs 2630, *v. tr.*, to knot
agrums 3000, *sb.*, something sour or sharp in taste (unripe fruit, etc.)
agulonar 806, *v. tr.*, to goad on, incite

386 GLOSSARY

agurar, *pr. ind.* 3 agura 3145, *v. tr.*, to foretell
agurs 3005, *sb.*, augury, portent
agutz 3025, *adj.*, sharp, pointed
aibitz 2557, *adj.*, pleasing
aicel 102, 207, 217, *dem. pron.* and *adj.*, that, that one
aici 1492, *adv.*, here
aici cum 1514, *conj.*, just as
aiols 2668, *sb.*, grandfather
aira 3524, *sb. f.*, threshing-floor
ais 170, 1594, *sb. m. indecl.*, plank
aissella 3285, *sb. f.*, armpit
ajornar 801, *v. intr.*, to appoint a day (i.e. for judicial proceedings); *v. impers.*, to break (of day)
ala 3253, *sb. f.*, wing
alargar 788, *pr. subj.* 2 alarcs 1796, *v. tr.*, to loosen 788, to enlarge 1796
alavahz 1911, *sb.*, whitlow, paronychia
albergar 779, *v. intr.*, to lodge, take a lodging
albespis 2529, *sb.*, hawthorn
albirar 817, *v. tr.*, to estimate, judge
albires 81, albirs 2500, *sb.*, opinion, judgement
alborns 2908, *sb.*, laburnum
albors 2851, *sb. f.*, dawn, first light
alhz 1645, *sb.*, garlic
alis 193, 2521, *adj. m. indecl.*, unleavened
alongar 807, *v. tr.*, to lengthen
altz 1625, *adj.*, high
alumar, *pr. subj.* 2 alums, alhums 3001 (*B*), *v. tr.*, to illuminate
alums 3001, *sb.*, alum
alutz 3024, *adj.*, winged
amaire 70, *sb.*, lover
amanoïr 1358, *p. part.* amanoïth 2596, *v. tr.*, to prepare
amar 228, 231, 236, 777, *used as sb.* amars 1779, *fut.* 1 amarai 288, 2 amaras 289, 3 amara 290, 4 amarem 291, 5 amarez 292, 6 amaran, amarau 293, *fut. impf.* 1 amaria 314 2 amarias 315, 3 amaria 316, 4 amariam 317, 5 amariatz 318, 6 amarien 319, *pr. ind.* 1 ami, am 246, 2 amas 252, 3 ama 253, 4 amam 255, 5 amatz 256, 6 amen, amon 257, *impf. ind.* 1 amava 266, 2 amavas 267, 3 amava 268, 4 amavam 269, 5 amavatz 270, 6 amaven, amavon 271, *pr. subj.* 1 ame 229, 390, 2 ames 391, ams 1684, 3 ame 392, 4 amem 393, 5 ametz 394, 6 amen, amon 395, *imper.* 2 ama 692, 3 ame 692, 4 amem 693, 5 amatz 693, 6 amen, amon, amo 693, *pr. part.* amans 1503, 1735, *pret.* 1 amei 273, 2 amest 274, 3 amet 275, 4 amem 276, 5 amez 277, 6 ameren, ameron 278, *cond.* 1 amera 314, 2 ameras 315, 3 amera 316, 4 amaram 317, 5 amaratz 318, 6 ameren 319, *impf. subj.* 1 ames 382, 2 ames 383, 3 ames 384, 4 amassem 385, 5 amassetz 386, 6 amessen, amesson 387, *p. part.* amat 280–5, 362–4, etc., *v. tr.*, to love, like
amars 1778, *f.* amara 3156, *adj.*, bitter
amassar, *pr. ind.* 3 amassa 3552, *v. tr.*, to bring together
ambladura 3148, *sb. f.*, canter
amblar 800, *v. intr.*, to canter
amesurar, *pr. ind.* 3 amesura 3127, *v. refl.*, to act with moderation
amics 2454, *f.* amia 3478 (*B*), mia 3478, *sb.*, friend
amistatz 130, *sb. f.*, friendship
amon 1494, *adv.*, up
amoros 135, *adj. m. indecl.*, amorous
amors 2826, *sb. f.*, love
amparar 815, *pr. ind.* 3 ampara 3160, *pr. subj.* 2 ampars 1786, *v. tr.*, to take possession of by force, to seize
ams 1683, *adj. m.*, *obl. pl.*, both
anafils 2469, *sb.*, small high-pitched trumpet
anar 784, *pr. ind.* 2 vas 1468, 1469, *pr. subj.* 2 ans 1692, *imper.* 4 anem 307 (Lat.), 5 anaz 307, 6 anen 310, *v. intr.*, to go
anca 3453, *sb. f.*, rump
ancara 3166, *adv.*, still
anelar 783, *v. intr.*, to breathe, strive, aspire
aneletz 2400, *sb.*, little ring
anelz 2033, *sb.*, ring
anelz 2033, *sb.*, lamb
anguila 3305, *sb. f.*, eel
anheletz 2399, *sb.*, little lamb
annous 2802, *sb.*, new year; Feast of the Circumcision (New Year's Day)
ans 1691, *sb.*, year
ans 1692, *adv.*, before
antics 2452, *f.* antiga 3462, *adj.*, ancient

GLOSSARY 387

antrebrescar, *pr. ind.* 3 antrebresca 3509, *v. tr.*, to mingle
anteprendre 1308, **anteprendre** 1308, *pret.* 3 antepres 2340, *p. part.* antepres 2339, *v. tr.*, to seize
antrevalz 1638, *sb.*, interval
anualhar, *pr. ind.* 3 anualha 3354, *v. refl.*, to become lazy, to lose one's worth
aora 3234, *adv.*, now
aparelhar, *pr. ind.* 3 aparelha 3389, *pr. subj.* 2 aparelz 2067, *v. tr.*, to prepare 2067, 3389; to make equal, match together 3389
aparelz 2067, *sb.*, preparation, equipment
aparer, *pret.* 3 aparec 578, *v. intr.*, to happen
apelar, *pr. ind.* 3 apela 3273, *pr. subj.* 2 apelz 2059, *v. tr.*, to call
aperceubutz 3049, *adj.*, prepared, ready (of persons)
apertz 2301, *adj.*, far-sighted, prudent
apilar, *pr. ind.* 3 apila 3307, *v. refl.*, to lean
aplethz 2416, *sb.*, **tools** (*collective*)
apoderar, *pr. ind.* 3 apodera 3181, *v. tr.*, to subjugate, vanquish
aponre 1321, *pret.* 3 apos 631, *v. tr.*, to join, add
aportar, *pr. subj.* 2 aportz 2877, *imper.* 2 aporta 227, *v. tr.*, to bring
aprendre 1301, *pr. ind.* 2 apprens 2138, *v. tr.*, to learn; see also benapres
aprimairar 811, *v. refl.*, to come to the front, to come forward
aprimar 810, *pr. subj.* 2 aprims 2488, *v. tr.*, to refine
aprosmar 821, *v. refl.*, to approach
aquel 101, 208, *dem. pron.* and *adj.*, that, that one
aquest 22, 26, 28, 35, 37, 102, 208, *f.* aquesta 27, 29, 36, *dem. pron.* and *adj.*, this, this one
aqui 1492, *adv.*, there; d'aqui enan 1512, from now on; d'aqui en reire 1512, formerly
ar 1478, ara 3165, aras 1478, *adv.*, now
arar 785, *v. tr.*, to plough
arcs 1788, *sb.*, bow (weapon)
arc-voutz 2922, *sb.*, archway
ardors 2828, *sb. f.*, heat, ardour
ardre, *pr. ind.* 2 artz 1823, *pr. part.* ardens 2151, *pret.* 3 ars 622, 1766, *p. part.* ars 165, 1766, *v. tr.* and *intr.*, to burn
areçhar 812, *v. tr.*, to furnish with necessities, to provide for
arestols 2672, *sb.*, **hilt or haft of a lance**
arlotz 2946, *sb.*, beggar
armar 799, *p. part.* armat 50, *v. tr.*, to arm
arpar 790, *v. intr.*, to play the harp
arqueira 3192, *sb. f.*, loop-hole (for shooting arrows)
arquiers 2239, *sb.*, archer
arrancar, *pr. subj.* 2 arrancs 1764, *v. tr.*, to pluck out
arripar 781, *v. intr.*, to disembark
artelhz 2073, *sb.*, toe
artz 1822, *sb. m.* and *f.*, art
asclar 787, *v. tr.*, to split (wood)
asotilhar, *pr. ind.* 3 asotilha 3416, *v. tr.*, to make finer or more subtle
aspirar 782, *v. tr.* and *intr.*, to blow, blow on, inspire
assaiar 797, *pr. subj.* 2 assais 1613, *v. tr.*, to attempt 797; to test 797, 1613; see also ensaiar
assais 1613, *sb.*, test; see also ensahz
assalhir 1451, *pr. ind.* 2 asalhz 1666, *pr. subj.* 3 assalha 3367, *v. tr.*, to attack
assaporar, *imper.* 2 assapora 3241, *v. tr.*, to try the taste of, to savour
assautar 820, *v. tr.*, to attack
assegurar 816, *pr. ind.* 3 asegura 3147, *pr. subj.* 2 asegurs 3007, *v. tr.*, to make secure, to assure
assezer 1246, assire 1331, assir 1331, *pret.* 1 asis 610–11, 3 asis 606, *p. part.* assis 182, *v. tr.*, to put down, place 182, to besiege 182, 1331; *v.* **refl.**, to sit 606, 1246
assoudar 803, *v. tr.*, to employ in one's service
astrucs 2976, *adj.*, lucky
ataïnar 813, *v. tr.*, to impede
atan 1481, *adv.*, last year, formerly
atanher, *pret.* 3 atais 645, *v. intr.*, to belong, pertain
ateirar, *pr. ind.* 3 ateira 3188, *v. tr.*, to put in a line
atendre 1296, *pr. ind.* 2 atens 2146, *p. part.* atendutz 3063, *v. tr.*, to

GLOSSARY

atendre (*cont.*)
await 1296, 3063, to keep (a promise) 1296; mistranslated as *v. tr.*, to obtain (= atenher) 2146
atenher 674, *pret.* 3 ateis 589, 2001, *p. part.* -einht 674, *v. tr.*, to reach, obtain
atraire 1263, *pret.* 3 atrais 643, *v. tr.*, to draw on, attract
atressi 1514, *adv.*, in the same way
aturar, *pr. ind.* 3 atura 3133, *pr. subj.* 2 aturs 3009, *v. refl.*, to endeavour
aturs 3008, *sb.*, effort, endeavour
auca 3500, *sb. f.*, goose
auçelar 805, *v. intr.*, to hunt birds
auchir 243, 563, 1353, *cond.* 1 and 3 auçira 3223, *p. part.* auçit 679, 709, auçitz 1506, *v. tr.*, to hear
aucir 564 (Lat.), auçir 1332, aucire 564 (Lat.), auçire 1332, *pr. subj.* 3 aucia 3480, *v. tr.*, to kill
aucs 1826, *sb.*, gander
auctors 2849, *sb.*, author, witness
aunir 1354, *p. part.* aunit 710, aunitz 2571, *v. tr.*, to dishonour, revile
aura 3244, *sb. f.*, wind
aurelha 3392, *sb. f.*, ear
auricalcs 1643, *sb.*, brass
auriols 2663, *sb.*, oriole
aurius 2610, *adj.*, mad
aurs 1856, *sb.*, gold
aus 168, 1838, *sb. m. indecl.*, fleece
ausar, *pr. subj.* 3 aus 1839, *v. tr.*, to dare
austors 2841, *sb.*, goshawk
autrer, *see* l'autrer
aval 1494, *adv.*, down
avans 1698, *adv.*, before, previously
avars 1785, *adj.*, avaricious
avelaniers 2253, *sb.*, hazel
aveneditz 2602, *sb.*, stranger
avenhir 1460, *pret.* 3 avenc 591, *v. intr.* and *refl.*, to happen
avens 2154, *sb.*, Advent
aventura 3140, *sb. f.*, fate, fortune
aver 240, 335, 416, 665, 1245, *used as sb.* avers 2191, *fut.* 1 aurai 495, 764, 2 auras 496, 765, 3 aura 497, 766, 4 aurem 498, 767, 5 aurez 499, auretz 768, 6 auran, aurau 500, 769, *fut. impf.* 1 auria 345, *pr. ind.* 1 ai 518, 2 as 519, 3 a 22, ha 520, *impf. ind.* 1 avia 439, 2 avias 440, 3 avia 441, 4 aviam 442, 5 aviaz 443, 6

avien, avion 444, *pr. subj.* 1 aia 401, 487, 748, 755, 2 aias 402, 488, 749, 756, 3 aia 403, 489, 750, 757, 4 aiam 404, 490, 751, 758, 5 aiatz 405, 491, 752, 759, 6 aien 406, 492, 753, 760, aion 406, 492, 753, aio 760, *pret.* 3 ag 570, ac 606, 4 aguem 569, 5 aguez 569, 6 agren, agron 569, *cond.* 1 agra 345, *impf. subj.* 1 agues 362, 700, 705–7, 709, 724, augues 465, 2 aguesses 363, 466, 700, 725, 3 agues 364, 467, 700, 726, 4 aguessem 468, 701, agssem 727, 5 aguessetz 469, 701, agsetz 728, 6 aguessen, aguesson 470, 701, 729, *p. part.* agut 678, *v. tr.*, to have
avinaçar 819, *v. tr.*, to imbue or soak with wine
avinens 28, 29, 2110, *n. pl. m.* avinen 31, *n. pl. f.* avinens 32, *adj. m.* and *f.*, comely 28–32, suitable 2110
aÿmans 1728, *sb.*, lodestone

baconar 826, *v. tr.* (or ***intr.*?**), to kill and salt pigs
badalhar, *pr. ind.* 1 badalhi, badalh 251, 3 badalha 3376, *v. intr.*, to gape, yawn
badar 822, *v. intr.*, to open the mouth
badils 2471, *sb.*, watchtower
badocs 2648, *adj.*, foolish, stupid
baf 1551, *interj.* expressing indignation or displeasure
baias 1939, *adj.*, insipid, tasteless
bairar 824, *v. tr.*, to bolt (door)
bais 1595, *sb.*, kiss
baissar 845, *pr. subj.* 2 bais, baises 3113, 3 bais 1596, *v. tr.*, to kiss
baissar 845, *v. tr.*, to lower
balar 823, *pr. subj.* 2 baltz 1628, *imper.* 2 bala 297, *v. intr.*, to dance (to the viol or another instrument)
balestiers 2240, *sb.*, cross-bowman
baltz 1626, *sb.*, dance
baltz 1627, *adj.*, joyful
bancs 1748, *sb.*, bench
bandir 1359, *v. tr.*, to proclaim (through a herald or crier)
bar 93, *sb.*, baron
baralha 3364, *sb. f.*, dispute
baratar 827, *v. tr.*, **to spend foolishly** (i.e. **extravagantly**?); **to spend deceitfully** (i.e. **to make a profitable deal through cunning**?)

GLOSSARY 389

baraties 2242, *sb.*, **trickster, impostor**
baroneiar 825, **baronelar** 825, *v. intr.* (*or* ***refl.***?), to pass oneself off as a baron; to make an ostentatious display
barreiar 832, *v. tr.*, to carry off by force
bartz 1800, *sb.*, mud
barutelar 829, *v. tr.*, to sift (flour)
barutelz 2044, *sb.*, bolting-cloth for sifting flour, bolter
bas 156, 1919, *adj. m. indecl.*, low
bastartz 1812, *adj.*, bastard
batalha 3355, *sb. f.*, battle
bateiar 828, *v. tr.*, to baptize
bateire 75, *sb.*, one who beats
bathz 1897, *adj.*, bay (colour of horse)
batre 662, *fut.* 1 batrei 1468, 1469, *pr. ind.* 1 bate 221, *pret.* 3 batet 598, *p. part.* -ut 666, batutz 221, 3075, *v. tr.*, to beat
baucs 1827, *sb.*, ring or ferrule on a knife-handle
bavecs 1970, *sb.*, balance (for weighing)
becs 1964, *sb.*, beak
beirius 2614, ***sb.***, heretic
bellar 833, *v. intr.*, to bleat
belz 2030, *f.* bela 17, 109, 3266, *adj.*, beautiful
benapres 2346, *adj.*, skilled, well versed
bendar 834, *v. tr.*, to bind (a woman's head)
bendelar 838, *v. tr.*, to bind (the eyes)
beneçir 1356, *v. tr.*, to bless
bera 3169, *sb. f.*, bier
berbitz 2587, berbiz 184, *sb. f. indecl.*, sheep
bergiers 2207, *sb.*, shepherd
bes 19, 22, 2320, *sb.*, that which is good
bescohz 2767, *sb.*, biscuit
besonhz 2783, *sb.*, need
bestors 2839, *sb. f.*, turret
betums 3003, *sb.*, bitumen
beure 1278, *fut. impf.* 1 beuria 351, *pret.* 3 bec 579, *cond.* 1 begra 351, *v. tr.*, to drink
beutatz 129, *sb. f.*, beauty
beveire 72, *sb.*, drinker
biais 1597, *sb.*, crookedness
bilha 3409, *sb. f.*, **skittle** (?), **game of skittles** (?)

biocar, *pr. subj.* 2 biocs 2640 (*B*), *v. tr.*, **to shorten** (*conjectured*)
biordar 844, *v. intr.*, to joust
biortz 2891, *sb.*, joust
bis 192, 2509, *adj. m. indecl.*, greyish-brown
blaçir 1362, *v. intr.* (or ***refl.***?), to wither
blancs 1747, *f.* blanca 3449, *adj.*, white
blandir 1361, *v. tr.*, to flatter, blandish
blanqueiar 831, *v. intr.*, to become white
blanquir 1363, *v. intr.* or ***refl.***, to become white
blans 1696, *adj.*, flattering
blars 1767, *adj.*, bluish-grey, glaucous
blatz 1865, *sb.*, corn
blaus 1837, *adj.*, blue, sky-blue
bles 145, 2345, *adj. m. indecl.*, lisping (*lit.*, pronouncing *c* for *s*)
blesseiar 837, *v. intr.*, to lisp (*lit.*, to pronounce *c* instead of *s*)
bobans 1693, *sb.*, empty boasting, ostentation
bobansar, *pr. subj.* 3 bobans 1694, *v. refl.*, to brag
bocs 2655, *sb.*, he-goat
bohtz 2762, *sb.*, bottom of a cask
bola 3336, *sb. f.*, boundary-stone
bolar, *pr. ind.* 3 bola 3337, *v. tr.*, to fix the boundary of
bols 2680, *adj.*, broken-winded (horse)
bonamen 1474, *adv.*, well
bondir 1357, *v. intr.*, to buzz (of bees)
bontatz 129, bontaz 10, *obl. sg.* bontat 11, *sb. f.*, goodness
borçes 2332, borses 144, *sb. m. indecl.*, citizen
borcs 2790, *sb.*, country-town
borns 2899, *sb.*, knob on top of a tent (?)
borsiers 2241, *sb.*, purse-maker
bortz 2885, *sb.*, game
bortz 2886, *adj.* and ***sb.***, bastard
bos 11, 15, 59, 136, *f.* bona 17, 109, *uninflected neuter* bon 362, *adj.*, good; bon fora que 362, would that
botelha 3388, *sb. f.*, bottle
botiliers 2221, *sb.*, butler, cup-bearer
botz 2935, *sb.*, blow
botz 2951, *sb.*, nephew, grandson
botz 2952, *sb.*, leather bottle, wineskin
bous 2799, *sb.*, ox

boviers 2232, *sb.*, one who ploughs with oxen
braceiar 830, *v. tr.*, to measure with one's arms
bracs 1536, *sb.*, pus, discharge (from wound)
bracs 1536, *sb.*, hound
brais 172, *sb. m.* **indecl.**, twittering of birds
bralhz 1646, *sb.*, twittering of birds
bramar, *pr. ind.* 1 brami, bram 250, *pr. subj.* 2 brams 1675, *v. intr.*, to cry out
brams 1674, *sb.*, loud noise
branca 3448, *sb. f.*, **branches** (*collective*)
brandir 1360, *v. tr.*, to shake, brandish
brans 1695, *sb.*, sword
braus 1836, *adj.*, rough, harsh
brens 2091, *sb.*, bran
bres 146, 2341, *sb. m.* indecl., fixed wooden trap for catching birds
bresar 835, *v. intr.*, to lure birds into a trap, by imitating bird-calls
bresca 3508, *sb. f.*, honeycomb
bretoneiar 836, *v. intr.*, **to gabble** (?)
bretz 2387, *adj.*, stammering
breus 2424, *adj.*, short
breus 2424, *sb.*, document, charter
brics 2444, *adj.*, wretched
brisar 843, *v. tr.*, to break in pieces
brius 2605, *sb.*, impetuosity, vigour
brocar, *pr. subj.* 2 brocs 2640, *v. intr.*, to run (*more exactly*: to ride fast, gallop forward)
brocs 2639, *sb.*, jug
brolhar, *pr. ind.* 3 brolha 3430, *v. intr.*, to sprout (of a plant)
brolhz 2704, *sb.*, copse, grove
brotz 2953, *sb.*, shoot (of a plant)
bruir 1364, *v. intr.*, to make an uproar
brus 3084, *adj.*, dark (in colour)
brusar 841, *v. tr.*, to burn
bucs 2968, *sb.*, stump (of arm after loss of hand)
budelz 2053, *sb.*, intestine
buf 2989, *interj.* expressing indignation or displeasure
buf 2991, *sb. m., obl. sg.*, breath, puff
bufar 840, *v. tr.*, to blow on
bulir, *pr. part.* bulens 2155, *v. tr.* and *intr.*, to boil
bullar 839, *v. tr.*, to place one's seal on

buscalar 842, *pr. ind.* 3 buschalha 3359, *v. intr.*, to gather sticks

cabals 1556, *adj.*, pre-eminent; agreeable, pleasing
cabelhz 2064, *sb.*, a hair
caber 1247, *pret.* 3 caup 584, *v. intr.*, to find a place (in), to be contained (in)
cabotz 2948, *sb.*, sort of fish (chub?)
cabrelz 2029, *sb.*, kid
cabritz 2558, *sb.*, kid
cabroletz 2401, *sb.*, small roe-deer
cabrols 2660, *sb.*, roebuck
caçar 849, *v. tr.* and *intr.*, to hunt
cacher 1255, *pr. ind.* 2 cas 1921, *pret.* 3 caçez 576, *v. intr.*, to fall
cadalethz 2378, *sb.*, high wooden bed
cadeira 3183, *sb. f.*, chair
caf 1550, *adj. m., obl. sg.*, odd (of numbers)
cagar 860, *v. intr.*, to defecate
cairelz 2039, *sb.*, bolt of cross-bow
cairera 3194, *sb. f.*, street, public road
cais 170, 1607, *sb. m.* indecl., cheek 170; jaw 1607
caitius 2606, *adj.*, wretched; captive
calar 848, *pr. ind.* 3 cala 3258, *v. intr.* and *refl.*, to be silent
calelhz 2072, *sb.*, oil-lamp made of iron
calens 2093, *adj.*, provident
calfar 847, *v.* **refl.**, to grow warm
calms 1672, *sb. f.*, bare plain
calors 2830, *sb. f.*, warmth
cals 1557, *adj.*, bald
caltz 1630, *adj.*, warm, hot
caltz 1631, cautz 162, *sb. f.* indecl., lime, chalk
calucs 2975, *adj.*, short-sighted
camba 3440, *sb. f.*, leg
cambutz 3023, *adj.*, long-legged
camels 2024, *sb.*, camel
camiar 851, *pr. subj.* 2 cans 1699 (?), *v. tr.*, to change 851; to exchange 1699
caminar 850, *v. tr.*, to pursue (a fleeing enemy, on horseback)
cams 1680, *sb.*, field
camzils 2477, *sb.*, fine linen cloth
canbiar 852, *pr. ind.* 3 cambia 3468, *v. tr.*, to change or exchange (money) 852; to change 3468
canços 60, *sb. f.*, song
candela 3296, *sb. f.*, candle
canela 3282, *sb. f.*, cinnamon

GLOSSARY

canilha 3412, *sb. f.*, woodworm (?)
cans 1697, *sb.*, song
cantar 846, chantar 236, *pr. ind.* 1 chant 226, chan 247, chanti 247, *pr. subj.* 2 cans 1697, chans 3109, chantes 3109, *imper.* 2 chanta 296, *cond.* 1 cantera 3172, *impf. subj.* 1 cantes 369, 2 cantesses 370, 3 cantes 371, 4 cantassem 372, 5 cantassetz 373, 6 cantassen, cantesson 374, *v. tr.* and *intr.*, to sing
cantarelz 2047, *adj.*, one who sings frequently
cantelz 2045, *sb.*, hunk of bread cut from the side of a loaf
canutz 3042, *adj.*, white-haired
capdelar, *pr. ind.* 3 capdella 3284, *v. tr.*, to govern, command
capdolhar, *pr. ind.* 3 capdolha 3429, *v. intr.*, to rise
capdolhz 2711, *sb.*, citadel, keep
capras 160 (*conjectured*), *adj. m. indecl.*, with shaven head
caps 1527, *sb.*, head
caramelar 796, *pr. ind.* 3 caramela 3274, *v. intr.*, to play the reed-pipe
caramelz 2050, *sb.*, reed-pipe
carceriers 2216, *sb.*, prisoner
carcs 1791, *sb.*, burden
cardenals 1580, *sb.* and *adj.*, cardinal
cardonelz 2051, *sb.*, goldfinch
cargar, *pr. subj.* 2 carcs 1790, *v. tr.*, to load
caronhiers 2269, *adj.*, **carrion-eating** (of birds); bloodthirsty
carreiar 856, *v. tr.*, to transport (baggage, with asses)
cars 1768, *f.* cara 3155, *adj.*, dear
cas 156, 1920, *sb. m. indecl.*, accident, (grammatical or legal) case
cas 1936, *sb.*, dog
castiar 853, *v. tr.*, to punish, blame
catedrals 1590, *adj.*, cathedral
catiglar 854, *v. tr.*, to tickle
catz 1867, *sb.*, cat
cauçics 2458, *sb.*, **reproof**
cauçigar, *pr. subj.* 2 cauçics 2459, *v. tr.*, **to reprove**
caus 1840, *adj.*, hollow
causir 1365, *v. tr.*, to choose; *p. part.* causitz 2556, polite, courteous
cavalgar, *imper.* 4 cavalguem 306

(Lat.), 5 cavalghaz 306, 6 cavalguen 309, *v. tr.* and *intr.*, to ride
cavaliers 28, 35, 59, 2202, chavaliers 26, *n. pl.* chavalier 31, *sb.*, knight
cavaltz 1638, *sb.*, horse
cavar 855, *v. tr.*, to hollow out
cecs 1965, *f.* cega 3493, *adj.*, blind
cecs 1965, *sb.*, target (in archery) (?)
cel 102, 207, 253, 364, etc., celh 766, *n. pl.* celh 258, 456, etc., cel 444, 693, 718, *f.* cela 3289, *dem. pron.* and *adj.*, that, that one, he
celar 862, *pr. ind.* 3 cela 3290, *pr. subj.* 2 cels 2027, *v. tr.*, to hide
celestials 1588, *adj.*, celestial
celiers 2219, *sb.*, cellar
cels 2011, *sb.*, sky, heaven
cels 2026, *sb.*, circumspection, secrecy
cembar 865, *v. intr.*, to play the cymbals
cembelar 857, *pr. ind.* 3 cembela 3272, *v. tr.*, to catch (birds) with the aid of a decoy
cenher 673, 1272, *pr. ind.* 1 cenh 530, *pret.* 3 ceis 2003, seis 586, *p. part.* ceinth 684, *v. tr.*, to gird
cens 142, ces 2328, *sb. m. indecl.*, rent, quit-rent
censals 1592, *adj.*, subject to pay an annual quit-rent called *cens*
centura 3142, *sb. f.*, girdle
ceps 2164, *sb.*, trunk (*more exactly*: vine-stock)
cera 3178, *sb. f.*, wax
cercar 863, *v. tr.*, to seek
cers 2170, *sb.*, stag
certamen 1488, *adv.*, certainly
certz 2298, *adj.*, certain
cessar 864, *v. intr.*, to cease
chuf 2990, *sb. m.*, *obl. sg.*, tuft of hair over the forehead
cims 2484, *sb.*, top of a tree
cinglar 868, *v. tr.*, to girth (a horse)
ciriers 2254, *sb.*, **cithern-player**
ciriers 2254, *sb.*, cherry-tree
cirurgias 1943, **sb.**, **surgeon**
cisclar 866, *pr. ind.* 3 ciscla 3560, *v. intr.*, to shriek
citar 867, *v. tr.*, to summon to court
citolar 791, *v. intr.*, to play the citole (a plucked stringed instrument)
clamar 859, *pr. subj.* 2 clams 1677, *v. intr.*, to cry out 859; *v. refl.*, to complain 1677

clams 1676, *sb.*, complaint at law
claps 1531, *sb.*, heap of stones
clars 1775, *f.* clara 3158, *adj.*, clear
clas 157, 1922, *sb. m. indecl.*, peal of bells
classeiar 858, *v. intr.*, to ring bells
claücs 2973, *meaning uncertain*
claure 1345, *pret.* 3 claus 647, 1843, *p. part.* claus 168, 1842, *v. tr.*, to shut
claus 1841, *sb. f.*, key
clis 2512, *adj.*, inclined, bowed
clobs 2625, *adj.*, lame
clocir 1367, *v. intr.*, to cluck
cloquiers 2231, *sb.*, bell-tower
clotz 2938, *sb.*, hollow
coarz 1803, *adj.*, cowardly
cobeitar 874, *v. tr.*, to covet
cobleiar 876, *v. intr.*, to compose *coblas*
cobrar 878, *v. tr.*, to regain
cobs 2631, *sb.*, skull
cocs 2644, *sb.*, cook
codonhyers 2262, *sb.*, quince-tree
cogotz 2955, *sb.*, cuckold
coguls 2995, *untranslated; no doubt* = *sb.*, cuckoo
cointa 109, *adj. f.*, comely
colar 879, *pr. ind.* 3 cola 3330, *pr. subj.* 2 cols 2681, *v. tr.*, **to strain** (liquid)
colbs 2635, *sb.*, blow
colerics 2464, *adj.*, choleric
colha 3434, *sb. f.*, scrotum
colhers 2230, *sb.*, porter (who carries loads on his back)
colhz 2718, *sb.*, testicle
coloms 2730, *sb.*, pigeon
coloritz 2561, *adj.*, coloured
colors 2823, *sb. f.* and *m.*, colour
colre, *fut. impf.* 1 colria 354, *pr. ind.* 2 cols 2671, *pret.* 3 colc 628, *cond.* 1 colgra 354, *p. part.* coutz 2926, *v. tr.*, to venerate
colz 2690, *sb.*, neck
comandar, *pr. subj.* 2 comans 1717, *v. tr.*, to command
comans 1716, *sb.*, command
combatre, *p. part.* combatutz 3076, *v. tr.* and *refl.*, to fight
cometre, *p. part.* comes 147, *v. tr.*, to provoke, challenge
complanher, *pret.* 3 conplais 641, *v. refl.*, to complain
complire, *p. part.* conplitz 2570, *v. tr.*, to complete, finish
coms 40, 41, 2726, *sb.*, count
coms 2731, **adj.**, hollow-backed (of a horse)
comtals 1568, *adj.*, pertaining to a count
comtors 2840, *sb.*, rank of nobility below viscount
comunals 1579, *adj.*, common
comus 3104, *adj.*, common
concagar 883, *v. tr.*, to soil with excrement
concebre 1285, *pret.* 3 conceup 582, *v. tr.*, to conceive
concluire, *p. part.* conclus 197, conglus 3087, *v. tr.*, to conclude
condeiar 880, *v. refl.*, to deck oneself out
confes 154, 2314, *adj. m. indecl.*, shriven
confesar, *pr. subj.* 3 confes 2314, *v. tr.*, to confess
confondre 1291, *pr. ind.* 2 confuns 2744, *pr. part.* confondens 2106, *v. tr.*, to destroy, annihilate
confortar 872, *v. tr.*, to console, encourage
confortz 2865, *sb.*, comfort, aid
confortz 2866 (contrafortz *B*), *sb.*, **leather stiffening or reinforcement (as in shoes)**
confus 197, 3092, *adj. m. indecl.*, confused
conhar, *pr. subj.* 2 conhz 2776, *v. tr.*, to strike with a wedge (or a die?)
conhz 2775, *sb.*, wedge for splitting wood
conjurar, *pr. ind.* 3 conjura 3137, *v. tr.*, to beseech
conoisser 335, *fut. impf.* 1 conoseria 346, *pr. part.* conoissens 2126, *pret.* 3 conoc 624, *cond.* 1 conogra 346, *p. part.* conogut 677, 708, conogutz 1505, conougtz 3050, *v. tr.*, to know, be acquainted with
conortar 871, *v. tr.*, to console
conortz 2862, *sb.*, consolation, encouragement
conquerer 1324, *v. tr.*, to acquire
cons 2741, *sb.*, vagina
consegre 1318, *pr. ind.* 2 consecs 1975, *pr. subj.* 3 consega 3497, *pret.* 3 conseguet 597, *v. tr.*, to reach, attain

GLOSSARY

conselar 881, *pr. ind.* 3 conselha 3387, *pr. subj.* 2 conselhz 2066, *v. tr.*, to advise 881; *v. intr.*, to deliberate 2066, 3387
conselhz 2066, *sb.*, advice
consirar 877, *pr. ind.* 3 consira 3219, *pr. subj.* 2 consirs 2499, *v. tr.* and *intr.*, to consider
conssentire 78, *sb.*, one who consents or approves
conssires 81, consirs 2498, *sb.*, consideration, reflection
constrenher, *pret.* 3 constreiss 588, *v. tr.*, to constrain
contar 882, *v. tr.*, to count
contendre 242, 1295, *v. intr.*, to dispute, contend
contener, *pr. part.* contenens 2132, *v. tr.*, to contain
contorns 2913, *sb.*, the first furrow made round a field when beginning to plough
contraclaus 1845, *sb. f.*, skeleton key
contrafortz 2866 (*B*), *see* confortz
contranher, *pret.* 3 contrais 644, *p. part.* contrahz 1914, *v. tr.*, to cripple in feet or hands
contrapes 141, 2319, *sb. m. indecl.*, counterweight
convers 2178, *sb.*, lay brother
cora 1520, 3239, *conj.*, when
coralhz 1662, *sb.*, coral
corbs 2894, *sb.*, raven
corbs 2897, *adj.*, bent
coreiar 875, *v. intr.*, to dance a round-dance
cornar 794, *pr. subj.* 2 corns 2902, *v. tr.*, to blow (a trumpet)
cornilha 3411, *sb. f.*, crow
corns 2900, *sb.*, horn (of animal)
corns 2901, *sb.*, horn, trumpet
corola 1637, *sb. f.*, dance
corolar 875, *v. intr.*, to dance a round-dance
coronar 873, *v. tr.*, to crown
corre 1313, *pret.* 3 corec 616, cors 2820, *v. intr.*, to run
corretz 2422, *sb.*, strap; belt
cors 189, 2806, *sb. m. indecl.*, body
cors 190, 2819, *sb. m. indecl.*, running, course
corseira 3199, *adj. f.*, swift-running
cortehz 2418, *sb.*, conversation of knights with ladies, courtly dalliance
cortes 140, *adj. m. indecl.*, courtly
cortesia 119, *sb. f.*, courtly behaviour
cortz 2883, *sb. f.*, court
cortz 2884, *adj.*, short
cosdura 3153, *sb. f.*, seam
cotz 2942, *sb.*, a sort of fine
cotz 2954, *sb. f.*, grindstone
cotz 2954 (*B*), *sb.*, little dog
coutelz 2036, *sb.*, knife
coutz 2926, *sb. f.*, wall
covenir 1461, *pr. part.* covinens 2117, *v. intr.*, to be advantageous or expedient 1461; to be suitable 2117
covens 2148, *sb.*, agreement, covenant
cozer, *pr. part.* coçens 2092, *p. part.* cohtz 2765, coitz 2771, *v. tr.*, to cook 2765; to burn 2092
cozer, *p. part.* cosutz 3039, *v. tr.*, to sew
cracs 1538, *sb.*, mucus
crancs 1749, *sb.*, ulcer, canker
crauca 3503, *sb. f.*, infertile land
craucs 1828, *adj.*, infertile
creire 1337, *pr. part.* crezens 2095, *p. part.* creütz 3052, *v. tr.*, to believe
creisser 1277, *pr. ind.* 3 creis 2008, *pr. subj.* 3 cresca 3512, *pr. part.* creissens 2097, *pret.* 3 crec 578, *p. part.* cregutz 3072, *v. intr.*, to grow
cremar 861, *v. tr.*, to burn
cridar 869, *v. intr.*, to cry out loudly
crilar, *pr. ind.* 3 crila 3309, *v. tr.*, to sift, sieve
criminals 1586, *adj.*, criminal
crims 2483, *sb.*, accusation, crime
crivelar 870, *v. tr.*, to pass (corn) through a sieve
criz 2555, *sb.*, shout
crocs 2645, *adj.*, yellow
cropir 1368, *v. intr.*, to squat
crotz 194, *sb. f. indecl.*, cross
crus 3095, *adj.*, raw
cubrir 563, cobrir 1370, *pret.* 3 cubri, cuberc 616, *p. part.* covertz 2294, *v. tr.*, to cover
culhir 1373, *pr. ind.* 2 colhz 2706, *v. tr.*, to gather, collect
culs 2994, *sb.*, anus
cum 229, 369, 375, etc., com 480, *conj.*, since, as (*introducing phrases exemplifying the subjunctive*); *see also* aici cum, si cum
cura 3118, *sb. f.*, care

GLOSSARY

cutz 3026, *sb.*, good-for-nothing, worthless fellow

dalhz 1652, *sb.*, scythe
damnar 884, *v. tr.*, to condemn
dams 1681, *sb.*, sort of deer
dançar 885, *imper.* 3 dance 302, *v. intr.*, to dance
dancs 1750, *adj.* expressing a colour—possibly brown
dans 1703, *sb.*, harm, damage
dartz 1806, *sb.*, dart, javelin
datz 1868, *sb.*, die
daurar 886, *pr. ind.* 3 daura 3248, *v. tr.*, to gild
de 45, 46, *prep.*, of (*explained as sign of genitive case*)
decebre 660, 1283, *pret.* 3 deceup 582, *p. part.* -ut 666, deceubutz 3055, *v. tr.*, to deceive
dechaçer 1256, *pret.* 3 decaçez 576, *v. tr.*, **to impoverish** 1256; *v. intr.*, to become poor, lose one's wealth 576
decs 1978, *sb.*, defect, vice
decs 1966, *sb.*, boundary, limit
decs 1966, *sb.*, **target** (in archery)(?), *cf. note to 1965*
defendre 242, 1288, *pr. ind.* 2 defens 2150, *pr. part.* defendens 2104, *v. tr.*, to defend, forbid
defors 1492, *adv.*, outside
degas 1935, *sb.*, dean, deacon
degolar 903, *v. tr.*, to decapitate
degolar, *pr. ind.* 3 degola 3313, *v. tr.*, to cast down
degotar 996, *untranslated*; = *v. intr.*, to drip
deirengar 892, *v. intr.* and **refl.**, to step forward (from the ranks of soldiers), to advance
deirocar 889, *pr. subj.* 2 deirocs 2653, *v. tr.*, to demolish 889; to knock down 2653
dejunar 898, *v. intr.*, to fast
dejus 3090, *sb.*, fast
delethz 2385, *sb.*, delight
delir 1377, *p. part.* delit 710, delitz 2559, *v. tr.*, to destroy
deliurar 895, *v. tr.*, to set free
deman 1479, *adv.*, tomorrow
demandar 896, *pr. subj.* 2 demans 1722, *v. tr.*, to ask for
demans 1721, *sb.*, request, legal suit

demorar, *pr. ind.* 3 demora 3228, *v. intr.*, to delay; *v. refl.*, to amuse oneself
dens 2099, *sb. m.* and *f.*, tooth
departir 1435, *pr. ind.* 2 departz 1819, *v. tr.*, to divide
deportar, *pr. subj.* 2 deportz 2879, *v. refl.*, to amuse oneself, to play
deportz 2878, *sb.*, distraction, diversion
derenan, *see* er
deribar 906, *v. intr.*, to overflow the banks
deribar, *pr. subj.* 2 derips 2442, *v. tr.*, to unrivet
derreira 3203, *adj. f.*, last
derzer, *pr. ind.* 3 dertz 2309, *pret.* 3 ders 620, 2195, *p. part.* ders 179, 2194, *v. tr.*, to erect
des 145, 2324, *sb. m. indecl.*, table
desaiar 908, *v. tr.*, to open, to unbolt
desamparar, *pr. ind.* 3 desampara 3161, *v. tr.*, to abandon
desaprendre 1302, *v. tr.*, to unlearn, forget
desarmar 900, *v. refl.*, to lay down one's arms
desastrucs 2977, *adj.*, unlucky
desaventura 3141, *sb. f.*, misfortune
descaltz 1634, deschautz 162, *adj. m. indecl.*, barefoot
descans 1700, *sb.*, **descant** (?); song composed as an attack or satire on an already existing song (?)
descargar 905, *pr. subj.* 2 descarcs 1792, *v. tr.*, to unload
descausir 1366, *v. tr.*, to revile
descausitz 2566, *adj.*, rough, coarse, injurious
descendre, *pret.* 3 descendet 599, *v. intr.*, to descend
deschauzar 899, *pr. subj.* 3 descaltz 1635, *v. tr.*, to take off (shoes)
desclavar 907, *v. tr.*, to unnail
descobrir 1371, *p. part.* descovertz 2295, *v. tr.*, to uncover
descombrar 888, *v. tr.*, to clear (a place) of rubbish or obstacles
desconoisser, *pr. part.* desconoissens 2127, *pret.* 3 desconoc 624, *p. part.* desconougutz 3051, *v. tr.*, not to know
descordar, *pr. subj.* 2 descors 2860, *v. refl.*, to disagree

GLOSSARY

descors 2861, *sb.*, disagreement; type of song characterized by the use of different tunes for the various stanzas

descozer, *p. part.* descosutz 3043, *v. tr.*, to unsew

descreire, *pr. part.* descrezens 2096, *p. part.* descreütz 3053, *v. tr.*, to abandon one's faith in 2096; to disbelieve 3053

descreisser, *pr. part.* descreissens 2098, *p. part.* descregutz 3073, *v. tr.*, to diminish 3073; **to destroy, disperse** 2098

desdejunar 911, *v. intr.*, to break one's fast

desellar, *pr. ind.* 3 desella 3279, *v. tr.*, to unsaddle

desertz 2296, *sb.*, desert

deservir 1455, *v. tr.*, to serve (s.o.) badly

desfar, *pr. part.* desfazens 2102, *p. part.* desfahz 1901, *v. tr.*, to destroy

desfiar 975, *pr. ind.* 3 desfia 3476, *v. tr.*, to mistrust; to defy, challenge

desficar, *pr. ind.* 3 desfica 3485, *v. tr.*, to tear out

desfilar, *pr. ind.* 3 desfila 3304, *v. tr.*, to unravel, fray

desflibar 909, *v. tr.*, to take off (cloak)

desgitar 893, *v. tr.*, to throw out

deshonors 2845, *sb. f.*, dishonour

desirar 902, *pr. ind.* 3 desira 3213, *v. tr.*, to desire

desires 81, desirs 2501, *sb.*, desire

desleials 1561, *adj.*, unjust, unlawful

desliar, *pr. ind.* 3 deslia 3471, *v. tr.*, to untie, set free

desmalhar, *pr. ind.* 3 desmalha 3346, *v. tr.*, to demolish

desmandar 897, *pr. subj.* 2 desmans 1723, *v. tr.*, to revoke (an order)

desmentir 1425, *v. tr.*, to contradict, give the lie to

desmesura 3125, *sb. f.*, excess, superfluity

desmesurar, *pr. ind.* 3 desmessura 3126, *v. intr.* and *refl.*, to act immoderately

desnaturar, *pr. ind.* 3 desnatura 3152, *v. intr.*, to act against one's nature

desolar, *pr. ind.* 3 desola 3320, *v. tr.*, to remove the soles from (shoes)

desossar, *pr. ind.* 3 desossa 3530, *v. tr.*, to bone (meat)

desparelhar, *pr. ind.* 3 desparelha 3390, *pr. subj.* 2 desparelhz 2068, *v. tr.*, to separate (things which belong together) 2068; **to make unlike, to match (two things) badly** 3390

despendre 1310, *p. part.* despendutz 3058, *v. tr.*, to take down from the gibbet

despendre, *pr. ind.* 2 despens 2143, *p. part.* despendutz 3058, *v. tr.*, to spend

despethz 2381, *sb.*, contempt, scorn

desplaçer 1260, *v. intr.*, to displease

despolhar 894, *pr. ind.* 3 despolha 3421, *pr. subj.* 2 despolhz 2714, *p. part.* despolhaz 1507, *v. tr.*, to strip, despoil

desponre 1322, *pret.* 3 despos 631, *v. tr.*, **to depose** (*possibly an error of translation*)

despulçelar 901, *pr. ind.* 3 despuzela 3276, *v. tr.*, to deflower (virgin)

desroïlhar, *pr. ind.* 3 desroïlha 3408, *v. tr.*, to remove the rust from

dessalar, *pr. ind.* 3 dessala 3264, *v. tr.*, to remove the salt from

destendre 1294, *pr. ind.* 2 destens 2145, *p. part.* destendutz 3064, *v. tr.*, to unbend 2145, 3064; to unbend (bow or ballista), i.e. to release (the arrow or missile) 1294

destenher 1274, *v. tr.*, to remove the dye from

destolre, *pr. subj.* 3 destolha 3424, *v. intr.*, **to turn aside from the road**; *v. tr.*, **to turn (s.o.) aside from his path**

destorbar 890, *v. tr.*, to interrupt

destorbiers 2224, *sb.*, disorder, disturbance

destorser, *pret.* 3 destors 637, *v. tr.*, to twist, wring

destrenher 1276, *pret.* 3 destreis 588, *p. part.* destreit 682, destretz 2421, *v. tr.*, to restrain

destriers 46, 2265, *obl. sg.* destrier 48, *sb.*, charger

destrigar 891, *pr. ind.* 3 destrica 3459, *v. tr.*, to hinder

destruire, *pret.* 3 destruis 613, *v. tr.*, to destroy

desvestir, *p. part.* desvestitz 2600, *v. refl.*, to relinquish possession of
desviar 904, *v. tr.*, to turn (sthg., s.o.) aside
desvolver, *p. part.* desvoutz 2921, *v. tr.*, to unwind (thread)
detirar 910, *v. tr.*, **to pull vigorously**
detrossar, *pr. ind.* 3 detrossa 3536, *v. tr.*, to untie a pack
detz 2388, *sb.*, finger
deus 57, 123, 2427, *sb.*, god; Deus volha que 390, 472, 546, Deus vola que 494, would that (*introducing phrases exemplifying the optative*)
dever 240, 335, 665, 1249, used as *sb.* devers 2192, *fut. impf.* 1 deuria 347, *pr. ind.* 4 devem 1509, *pret.* 3 dec 580, *cond.* 1 degra 347, *p. part.* degut 678, *v. tr.*, to owe, to be obliged to
devertucs 2986, *sb.*, abscess
deves 143, 2331, *sb. m. indecl.*, private land, preserve
devinalhz 1663, *sb.*, prophecy, enigma
devinar 887, *v. tr.*, to guess
devire 1330, devir 1330, *p. part.* devis 2536, *v. tr.*, to divide, share out
devis 2535, *adj.*, divine; *sb.*, soothsayer
devorar, *pr. ind.* 3 devora 3230, *v. tr.*, to devour
dia 3477, *sb. m.* and *f.*, day
dictar 913, *v. tr.*, to dictate, compose
diniers 2222, *sb.*, denier, a coin
dins 1492, *adv.*, within
dire 242, 564, 1327, dir 564, 1327, *fut. impf.* 1 diria 320, 2 dirias 321, 3 diria 322, 4 diriam 323, 5 diriatz 324, 6 dirien 325, *pr. ind.* 1 dic 263, 508, 1468, dizi 263, diçi 508, 2 dis, dizes 509, 3 ditz 510, 2585, *pr. subj.* 3 diga 3464, *pret.* 1 dissi 554, dis 610–11, 2 dissist 554, 3 dis 561, 608, 4 dissem 571, 5 dissez 571, 6 dissen, disson 571, *cond.* 1 dissera 320, 2 diceras 321, 3 disera 322, 4 diseram 323, 5 diceratz 324, 6 disseren 325, *p. part.* dit 679, dithz 2618, *v. tr.*, to say
disnar 912, 1509, used as *sb.* disnars 1776, *v. refl.*, to breakfast
dispers 176, *adj. m. indecl.*, scattered, dispersed
dissipar 914, *v. tr.*, to disperse, destroy
doblar 917, *v. tr.*, to double

dohtz 2768, *adj.*, learned, skilled
dolar 918, *pr. ind.* 3 dola 3315, *v. tr.*, to adze (wood)
doler, *pr. subj.* 3 dolha 3425, *pr. part.* dolens 2100, 2116, *pret.* 3 dolc 629, *v. intr.*, to be painful
dolha 3435, *sb. f.*, hole through which handle is fitted into iron, i.e. socket (of an axe, spear, etc.)
dolhz 2724, *sb.*, cask; bung-hole of cask
domna 27, dona 29, 36, *n. pl.* donas 32, *sb. f.*, lady
domneiar 916, *v. intr.*, to speak with ladies about love, to pay court, woo
doms 2739, dons 2740 (*B*), *sb.*, lord
doms 2728, *sb.*, cathedral
donar 915, *impf. ind.* 1 donava 399, *v. tr.*, to give
donzela 3295, *sb. f.*, damsel
doptar 919, *v. tr.* and *intr.*, to doubt
dorcs 2792, *sb.*, pitcher
dormir 243, 327, *pr. ind.* 2 dorms 2906, *pret.* 1 dormi 557, 2 dormist 557, 3 dormi 561, *cond.* 1 and 3 dormira 3224, *impf. subj.* 1 dormis 734, 2 dormisses 735, 3 dormis 736, 4 dormissem 737, 5 dormissetz 738, 6 dormissen, dormisson 739, *p. part.* dormit 710, *v. intr.*, to sleep
dorns 2909, *sb.*, hand's breadth
douçors 2848, *sb. f.*, sweetness, gentleness
doulz 186, doutz 2932, *adj. m. indecl.*, sweet, gentle
dracs 1539, *sb.*, dragon
draps 1530, *sb.*, cloth
dreitura 120, 3135, *sb. f.*, justice
drethz 2410, *adj.*, straight, right; *sb.*, what is right or just
drogomans 1726, *sb.*, interpreter
drutz 3027, *sb.*, lover
ducs 2974, *sb.*, duke; horned owl
durar 920, *pr. ind.* 3 dura 3129, *v. intr.*, to last
durs 3010, *f.* dura 3128, *adj.*, hard

e 1509, 1510, et 1509, *conj.*, and
ega 3489, *sb. f.*, mare
egalhar, *pr. subj.* 2 egalhz 1664, *v. tr.*, to make equal
egals 1559, *adj.*, equal
eis 2006, *adv.*, self, even; eu eis 211, I myself

GLOSSARY

el 98, 100, 206, 209-11, 1509, 2007, *obl. sg.* lui 23, *pers. pron.*, he
embargar 932, *pr. subj.* 2 enbarcs 1794, 3110, enbargues 3110, *v. tr.*, to hinder
emblar 925, *p. part.* emblatz 1866, *v. tr.*, to steal
embotar 947, *v. tr.*, to pour into a leather bottle
empenher 673, 1270, *pr. ind.* 1 enpenh 530, *pret.* 3 empeis 587, *p. part.* enpeinht 684, *v. tr.*, to strike against
emperials 1566, *adj.*, imperial
enalbar 962, *v. refl.*, **to rear up on the hind legs** (of a horse)
enanchar 933, *pr. subj.* 3 enans 1715, *v. intr.* and *refl.*, to advance
enans 1714, *sb.*, advantage
enantir 1391, *v. tr.*, to put forward
enarcar, *pr. subj.* 2 enarcs 1789, *v. tr.*, to bend, curve
enastar 930, *v. tr.*, to put on a spit for roasting
enbarcs 1793, *sb.*, obstacle
enbardar (*or* enbartar?), *pr. subj.* 2 enbartz 1801, *v. tr.*, to soil with mud
enborsar 961, *v. tr.*, to put in a purse
enbriar 958, *pr. ind.* 3 embria 3467, *v. tr.*, to profit 3467; *v. refl.*, to increase 958
enbutz 3074, *sb.*, funnel (for pouring liquid)
encaltz 1632, encautz 163, *sb. m. indecl.*, pursuit
encantar, *pr. subj.* 2 encans 1701, *v. tr.*, to bewitch
encegar, *pr. ind.* 3 encega 3495, *pr. subj.* 2 encecs 1972 (?), *v. tr.*, to blind
encegar (= eisegar) (?), *pr. subj.* 2 encecs 1972, *v. tr.*, to divide equally
encendre 1289, *pr. part.* encendens 2107, *pret.* 3 encendet 601, *v. tr.*, to set fire to 601, 2107; *v. intr.*, to burn, catch fire 1289
encens 143, ences 2329, *sb. m. indecl.*, incense
encesar, *pr. subj.* 2 ences 2330, *v. tr.* and *intr.*, to cense, burn incense
enchauzar 951, *pr. subj.* 3 encaltz 1633, *v. tr.*, to put to flight, pursue
enclaure, *pret.* 3 enclaus 1844, *p. part.* enclaus 1844, *v. tr.*, to enclose

enclavar 952, *v. tr.*, to prick (a horse, when shoeing)
encolpar 940, *v. tr.*, to accuse
encombriers 2223, *sb.*, obstacle
endir 1382, *v. tr.*, to impose (a tax or payment)
endir 1382 (*B*), *v. intr.*, to neigh
endura 3130, *sb. f.*, fast
endurar 931, *pr. subj.* 2 endurs 3011 *v. intr.*, to fast
enebriar 943, *v. tr.*, to make drunk
enemics 2455, *f.* enemiga 3461, *sb.*, enemy
enferns 2283, *sb.*, hell
enflar 957, *v. tr.*, to inflate
enfoletir 1384, *v. tr.*, to drive mad
enfrus 3096, *adj.*, insatiable, greedy
enganar 929, *pr. subj.* 2 engans 1709, *p. part.* enganatz 1507, *v. tr.*, to deceive
engans 1708, *sb.*, deceit
engolir 1415, *v. tr.*, to consume greedily
engorgar, *pr. subj.* 2 engorcs 2796, *v. tr.*, to cram, stuff with food
enics 2456, *f.* eniga 3460, *adj.*, hostile, unjust
eniuragar 967, *v. tr.*, to mix with tares or darnel
enlumenar 966, *v. tr.*, to illuminate
enpachar, *pr. subj.* 2 enpahz 1906, *v. tr.*, to hinder, prevent
enpahz 1904, *sb.*, obstacle, impediment
enpaubreçhir 1386, *v. intr.* (or *refl.*?), to become impoverished
enpenhar 941, *v. tr.*, to pawn
enperaire 70, *sb.*, emperor
enprendre 1305, *v. tr.*, to agree on, decide on
enquerer, *pr. subj.* 3 enqueira 3200, *pret.* 1 enquis 610-11, 3 enquis 609, *v. tr.*, to seek for, inquire 609, 3200; to procure 609
enrabiar 964, *v. intr.* and *refl.*, to become enraged
enraucar, *pr. subj.* 2 enraucs 1834, *v. intr.* (or *refl.*?), to become hoarse
enribaudir 1380, *v. intr.* (or **refl.**?), to live like a vagabond, lead a dissolute life
enriquir 1385, *v. tr.*, to enrich
ensachar 960, *pr. subj.* 2 ensacs 1546, *v. tr.*, to put in a sack
ensahz 1908, *sb.*, test, examination; *see* assais

GLOSSARY

ensaiar, *pr. subj.* 2 ensais 3112, ensahz 1908, ensaies 3112, *v. tr.*, to test 3112; to attempt 1908; *see* assaiar
ensalvatgir 1379, *v. tr.*, to render wild
ensanglentar 949, *v. tr.*, to cover with blood
ensegre, *pr. ind.* 2 encecs 1972 (?), *v. tr.*, to pursue, carry out
ensems 1509, 2084, essems 1484, *adv.*, together
ensenar 236, 935, *v. tr.*, to teach
entaiar, *pr. subj.* 2 entais 1619, *v. tr.*, to put in the mud
entalhar, *pr. ind.* 3 entalha 3362, *pr. subj.* 2 entalhz 1661, *v. tr.*, to carve
entalhz 1660, *sb.*, carving
entamenar 955, *v. tr.*, to take a part of (a loaf, an apple, etc.)
entaular 1184, *v. tr.*, to set out the board for (a game)
entiers 2275, *f.* enteira 3187, *adj.*, whole, complete
entravar 1187, *v. tr.*, to hobble (a horse)
entraversar 1197, *v. refl.*, to place oneself athwart something (blocking the way)
entremetre 1340, *v. refl.*, to intervene
entretan 1522, *adv.*, meanwhile
entrevar 1207, *v. intr.*, to make a truce
entruandir 1378, *v. intr.* (or *refl.*?), to live like a beggar or vagabond
enunbrar 942, *v. refl.*, to take umbrage, to shy (of a horse)
envaçir 1392, *v. tr.*, to attack, enter by force
enveios 135, *adj. m. indecl.*, envious
envers 2176, *adj.*, turned upside down
envestir 1465, *p. part.* envestitz 2601, *v. tr.*, to put in possession of, invest
enviar 936, *v. tr.*, to send
envillanir 1387, *v. tr.*, to treat like a peasant, i.e. to insult
er 1478, *adv.*, yesterday
er, *adv.*, now; d'er enan 1512, from now on
erebre, *pret.* 3 ereup 582, *p. part.* ereubutz 3048, *v. tr.*, to set free 3048; *v. intr.*, **to regain health** (after illness) 582
erms 2291, *adj.*, uncultivated (of land)
errar 926, *pr. part.* eirans 1739, *v. intr.*, to wander, err

esbaudir 1381, *v. refl.*, to rejoice
esbudelar 956, *v. tr.*, to disembowel
esca 3513, *sb. f.*, **kindling, tinder, touchwood; food for dogs** (?)
escaçer 1257, *pret.* 3 escaçez 576, *v. intr.*, to happen, to fall to someone's lot 576; to belong to (s.o.) as his due 1257
escacs 1540, *sb.*, chess-man
escahz 1898, *sb.*, small piece of cloth
escairar, *imper.* 2 escaira 3521, *v. tr.*, to make square (e.g. the construction of a building, beams, etc.)
escala 3261, *sb. f.*, ladder
escalar, *pr. ind.* 3 escala 3262, *v. tr.*, to draw up (army)
escalhar, *pr. ind.* 3 eschalha 3363, *v. tr.*, to break to pieces
escalhz 1648, *sb.*, fragment of pot
escamels 2022, *sb.*, stool
escampar 944, *v. intr.*, to escape
escaravatz 1912, *sb.*, stag-beetle
escaritz 2574, *adj.*, alone
escarnir 1388, *p. part.* escarnitz 2575, *v. tr.*, to mock
escarnire 79, *sb.*, mocker
escars 1769, *adj.*, parsimonious
escavelz 2041, *sb.*, reel, bobbin
escernir 1394, *v. tr.*, to complete, accomplish
eschovir 1393; *probably scribal error for esthonir or esthornir, q.v.*
esclairar, *pr. ind.* 3 esclaira 3522, *v. intr.* and *refl.*, to shine, grow light
escletz 2395, *adj.*, pure
escodre 672, *pret.* 3 escos 633, *p. part.* -os 672, *f.* escossa 3537, *v. tr.*, to thresh 633, 672, 3537; to carry off (booty) 633
escofir 1376, *v. tr.*, to vanquish
escoissar 945, *v. tr.*, to dismember (?), to tear
escoissendre 1299, *v. tr.*, to cut through (the top of a helmet); to cut or tear (pieces of cloth)
escola 3316, *sb. f.*, school
escolar, *pr. ind.* 3 escola 3331, *pr. subj.* 2 escols 2683, *v. tr.*, to empty
escolar 965, *v. tr.*, to castrate
escolhz 2710, *sb.*, sort, kind
escoloritz 2562, *adj.*, pale
escometre 1344, *p. part.* escomes 148, *v. tr.*, to challenge, provoke, summon

GLOSSARY

escondire, *pr. ind.* 3 esconditz 2565, *v. tr.*, to refuse

escondre 663, 1311, *pr. ind.* 2 escons 2759, *pr. part.* escondens 2108, *pret.* 3 escondet 600, escos 633, *p. part.* -ut 666, *v. tr.*, to hide; mistranslated as *v. tr.* to thresh (= escodre) 663, 1311

esconprendre 1307, *pr. ind.* 2 escomprens 2140, *pr. part.* esconprendens 2109, *v. tr.*, to set on fire, burn up

escoriar, *imper.* 5 escoriatz 1895, *p. part.* escoriatz 1894, *v. tr.*, to skin

escortgar 946, *v. tr.*, to skin

escotz 2936, *sb.*, **thorn** (?), splinter (?)

escotz 2937, *sb.*, price (of a meal), reckoning

escracar 953, *pr. subj.* 2 escarcs 1545, *v. intr.*, to spit

escremire 79, ***sb.*, a prudent fighter**

escrimir 1389, *v. refl.*, **to fence**

escrire 242, 564, 1326, escrir 564, *pr. ind.* 1 escriu 226, 505, escrivi 505, 2 escrius, escrives 506, 3 escri, escriu 507, *pr. subj.* 1 escriva 546, 2 escrivas 547, 3 escriva 548, 4 escrivam 549, 5 escrivatz 550, 6 eschrivan, escrivon 551, *pret.* 1 escris 610–11, escrissi 555, 2 escrissist 555, 3 escris 561, 608, *p. part.* escrit 679, 710, escrithz 2621, *v. tr.*, to write

escrivas 1948, *sb.*, scribe

escudiers 2203, *sb.*, squire

escumar, *pr. subj.* 2 escums 3002, *v. tr.*, to skim

escupir 1390, *v. tr.*, to spit on; *v. intr.*, to spit (*B*)

escurs 3014, *f.* escura 3143, *adj.*, dark, obscure

esdemetre 1343, *v. refl.*, to charge (in battle), to rush to the attack

esdire, *pr. ind.* 3 esditz 2564, *pr. subj.* 3 esdiga 3465, *v. tr.*, to deny

esfoirar, *pr. ind.* 3 esfoira 3555, *v. tr.*, **to soil with diarrhoea** (?)

esforchar 939, *v. refl.*, to collect one's strength

esfortz 2864, *sb.*, effort

esfredar 938, *v. tr.*, to terrify

esgarar, *pr. ind.* 3 esgara 3163, *pr. subj.* 2 esgars 1774, *v. tr.*, to look at

esgars 1773, *sb.*, glance

esglaiar, *pr. subj.* 2 esglais 1603, *v. refl.*, to be afraid

esglais 1604, esglahz 1917, *sb.*, fear, terror

esgolar, *pr. ind.* 3 esgola 3329, *v. tr.*, to cut out the neck of (a garment)

eslais 1609, *sb.*, sudden running, rush forward

eslaissar, *pr. subj.* 3 eslais 1610, *v. refl.*, to rush forward

eslansar, *pr. subj.* 2 eslans 1713, *v. tr.*, to hurl

eslire 1333, eslir 1333, *v. tr.*, to choose

esmaiar 934, *pr. subj.* 2 esmais 1612, *v. refl.*, to be terrified 934; to despair 1612

esmais 1612, *sb.*, thoughtless or ill-considered despair

esmancar, *pr. subj.* 2 esmancs 1756, *v. tr.*, to maim by cutting off the hand

esmendar 950, *v. tr.*, to improve, correct

esmerar 963, *pr. ind.* 3 esmera 3170, *v. tr.*, to purify

esmolre, *p. part.* esmoutz 2923, *v. tr.*, to grind, sharpen (sword-blade)

esmoure, *p. part.* esmogutz 3061, *v. tr.*, to excite, move

esparser, *pret.* 3 espars 622, 1782, *p. part.* espars 1781, *v. tr.*, to scatter

espatlutz 3056, *adj.*, broad-shouldered

especials 1591, *adj.*, special, particular

espelhz 2075, *sb.*, mirror

espelir 1383, *p. part.* espelitz 2589, *v. tr.*, to hatch out (egg)

esperar 924, *pr. subj.* 2 espers 2193, *v. tr.*, to hope, hope for

esperdre, *p. part.* esperdutz 3070, *v. refl.*, to be bewildered

esperitz 2563, *sb.*, spirit

esperonar 927, *v. tr.*, to spur on (horse)

esperoniers 2270, *sb.*, spurrier

espers 2193, *sb.*, hope

espertz 2300, *adj.*, near (?); quick (?)

espics 2463, *sb.*, ear of corn

espirar 922; mistranslated as *v. tr.*, to inquire into (= espiar)

esplechar, *pr. subj.* 2 esplethz 2414, *v. tr.*, to have the use and enjoyment of

espletz 2413, *sb.* (possibly *obl. pl.* in the first sense), tool, utensil; use, profit

esprendre 1306, *v. tr.*, to set on fire

esquerns 2280, *sb.*, mockery

esquila 3308, *sb. f.*, small bell

GLOSSARY

esquinsar, *pr. subj.* 3 esquins 2493, *v. tr.*, to tear

esquiragaita 113, *sb. m. (correctly?)*, guard-patrol, watch

esquius 2613, *uninflected neuter* esquiu 97, *adj.*, harsh, disagreeable 97, 2613; fastidious (*more exactly*: shy, unwelcoming) 2613

esquivar 923, *v. tr.*, to avoid

essartar, *pr. subj.* 2 essartz 1805, *v. tr.*, to break up (land) with the ploughshare

essartz 1804, *sb.*, land cleared for cultivation

essauchar 937, *v. tr.*, to approve of

essaurar 948, *pr. ind.* 3 essaura 3250, *v. tr.*, to expose to the air 3250, 948 (?); *v. refl.*, **to soar into the air** 948 (?)

essemblar 954, *v. tr.*, to form according to a (real or imagined) model (?)

esser, *fut.* 1 serai 445, 2 seras 446, 3 sera 447, 4 serem 448, 5 seretz 449, 6 seran, serau 450, *fut. impf.* 1 seria 458, 2 serias 459, 3 seria 460, 4 seriam 461, 5 seriatz 462, 6 serien, serion 463, *pr. ind.* 1 sui 215, 421, 2 est 422, es 216, 422, 3 es 217, 218, 423, 4 em (*or* sem?) 424, 5 etz 425, 6 sun 31, 32, 426, *impf. ind.* 1 era 427, 2 eras 428, 3 era 429, 4 eram 430, 5 eratz 431, 6 eren, eron 432, *pr. subj.* (and *imper.* 452–6) 1 sia 472, 717, 2 sias 452, 473, 717, 3 sia 453, 474, 717, 3474, 4 siam 454, 475, 718, 5 siatz 455, 476, 718, 6 sian 456, 718, sien 477, sion 456, 477, 718, *pret.* 1 fui 433, 2 fust 434, 3 fo 435, 4 fom 436, 5 foz 437, 6 foren, foro 438, *cond.* 1 fora 458, 2 foras 459, 3 fora 460, 3238, 4 foram 461, 5 foraz 462, 6 foren, foro 463, *impf. subj.* 1 fos 480, 2 fosses 481, 3 fos 482, 4 fossem 483, 5 fossetz 484, 6 fossen, fosson 485, *p. part.* estat 439–44, 465–70, 487–9, 495–500, *v. intr.*, to be

essilhar, *pr. ind.* 3 essilha 3410, *v. tr.*, to exile

essugar 928, *v. tr.*, to dry

estacar, *pr. subj.* 2 estacs 1547, *v. tr.*, to tie up

estancar, *pr. ind.* 3 estanca 3452, *pr. subj.* 2 estancs 1760, 3111, estanques 3111, *v. tr.*, to shut 1760; to hinder 3111, *more exactly*: to dam, hold back (water) 3452

estancs 1761, *sb.*, pool

estandartz 1810, *sb.*, military standard, banner

estar 921, *v. intr.*, to stand

estela 3294, *sb. f.*, star

estendre 1293, *p. part.* estendutz 3065, *v. tr.*, to stretch, extend

estenher 1268, *pret.* 3 esteis 588, *v. tr.*, to extinguish

esterns 2282, *sb.*, track, footprints

esters aiço 1522, *adv.*, besides, moreover

esterzer, *pret.* 3 esters 618, *v. tr.*, to wipe

esteus, *adv.*, self; eu esteus 210, I myself

esthonir 1393 (*conjectured*), *v. tr.*, **to make (s.o.) tremble, to terrify** (?)

esthornir 1393 (*conjectured*), *v. tr.*, **to make (s.o.) tremble, to terrify** (?)

estivals 1574, *adj.*, pertaining to summer

estoiar 959, *v. tr.*, to put away, lay aside

estorcs 2794, *meaning uncertain*

estorser, *pr. ind.* 3 estortz 2873, *p. part.* estortz 2872, 2874, *v. tr.*, to save from danger 2872, 2873; to set free (from bonds) 2874

estoutz 2933, *adj.*, irascible; foolish

estranh 98, *adj.* (*uninflected neuter*), strange

estrelha 3398, *sb. f.*, curry-comb

estrelhar: estrelha 3399, *without translation, no doubt* = *pr. ind.* 3 of estrelhar, *v. tr.*, to curry (a horse)

estremir 1393, *v. tr.*, to make (s.o.) tremble, to terrify

estrenher 675, 1275, *pr. ind.* 1 estrenh 530, *pr. subj.* 3 estrenga 3446, *pret.* 3 estreis 587, *p. part.* estreit 682, estretz 2420, *v. tr.*, to squeeze

estrons 2751, *sb.*, piece of dung

esvelhar, *pr. ind.* 3 esvelha 3384, *v. refl.*, to wake up

eu 100, 206, 262, 263, 362, etc., *obl. sg.* me 98, *pers. pron.*, I

fabregar 972, *v. tr.*, to forge, construct
fadeiar 971, *v. intr.*, to act stupidly
fadetz 2398, *adj.*, foolish

GLOSSARY

fadiar 969, *v. refl.*, to suffer a refusal, to be refused something
fais 171, 1599, *sb. m. indecl.*, burden
faiturar 970, *v. tr.*, to bewitch
falha 3370, *sb. f.*, torch
falha 3372, *sb. f.*, a game akin to trick-track or backgammon
falha 3373, *without translation, no doubt = sb. f.*, **buttocks (of horse)**
falhir 1395, *pr. subj.* 3 falha 3371, *p. part.* falitz 2597, *v. intr.*, to do wrong, to fail
fals 15, 161, *f.* falsa 17, *adj. m. indecl.*, false
falsartz 1813, *sb.*, short sharp sword (i.e. dagger?)
falsura 3134, *sb. f.*, falsity
falz 163, *sb. f. indecl.*, scythe
fams 1686, *sb. m.* and *f.*, hunger
fancs 1757, *sb.*, mud
far 968, *pr. ind.* 1 fatz 1874, *pr. part.* fazens 2101, *pret.* 1 fezi, fi 558, 2 fezist 558, 3 fetz 561, fes 2323, *p. part.* fathz 1899, *v. tr.*, to make, do
fars 164, 1770, *sb. m. indecl.*, stuffing
fatz 1873, *sb. f.*, face
fatz 1872, *adj.*, foolish
feira 3184, *sb. f.*, fair, market
fels 2019, *sb.*, gall, bile
femenils 2475, *adj.*, female, womanish, womanly
fems 174, 2082, *sb. m. indecl.*, dung
fencheire 74, *sb.*, pretender, hypocrite
fendalha 3377, *sb. f.*, fissure, cleft
fendre 660, 1287, *pr. ind.* 2 fens 2149, *pr. part.* fendens 2103, *pret.* 3 fendet 599, *p. part.* -ut 666, fendutz 3044, *v. tr.*, to split
fenher 673, 1271, *pr. ind.* 1 fenh, fenhi 527, 2 fehz, fenhes 528, 3 fenh 529, *pr. subj.* 3 fenga 3444, *pr. part.* fenhens 2158, *pret.* 1 feissi 559, 2 feissist 559, 3 feis 561, 586, 1999, *p. part.* feinht 683, *v. tr.*, to pretend
fenics 2457, *sb.*, phoenix
feniers 2225, *sb.*, pile of hay, haycock, haystack
fenir 1396, *pr. ind.* 1 fenisc, fenis 511, 2 fenisses 512, 3 fenis 513, *p. part.* finitz 2583, *v. tr.*, to finish; finitz 2583, dead
fenis 2526, *adj.*, physically weak

ferir 1398, *pr. ind.* 2 fers 2184, *pr. subj.* 3 feira 3185, *v. tr.*, to strike, beat
ferire 80, *sb.*, one who strikes
fermar 973, *v. tr.*, to make firm
ferrar 974, *v. tr.*, to fit with iron, to shoe (a horse)
fers 2182, *sb.*, iron
fers 2183, *f.* fera 3168, *uninflected neuter* fer 97, *adj.*, fierce, wild 2183, 3168; unpleasant 97
fes 2321, *sb. f.*, faith
fes 2322, *sb.*, hay
festucs 2985, *sb.*, blade of straw, stem
feus 2428, *sb.*, fief
fiar 975, *v. refl.*, to trust
ficar, *pr. ind.* 3 fica 3483, *v. tr.*, to fix, attach
fiçels 2012, *adj.*, faithful
fics 2447, *sb.*, wart
figa 3457, *sb. f.*, fig
figuiers 2250, *sb.*, fig-tree
fihtz 2616, *adj.*, fixed
filar 976, *pr. ind.* 3 fila 3302, *pr. subj.* 2 fils 2468, *v. tr.*, to spin (thread)
filha 3405, *sb. f.*, daughter
fillola 3323, *sb. f.*, god-daughter
fils 2467, *sb.*, thread
fis 2517, *adj.*, excellent
flacs 1541, *adj.*, soft, pliable
flagelar, *pr. subj.* 2 flagelz 2032, *v. tr.*, to scourge
flagelz 2031, *sb.*, flail
flars 1772, *sb.*, a bright light
flebeçhir 1401, *v. tr.*, to weaken
flechir 1400, *v. tr.*, to bend
flecmatics 2465, *adj.*, phlegmatic
fleis 1990, *sb.*, moderation
fleissar, *pr. subj.* 3 fleis 1991, *v. refl.*, **to be satisfied, to content oneself**
flocs 2643, *sb.*, monk's gown
florir 1402, *v. intr.*, to blossom
flors 2825, *sb. f.*, flower
focs 2642, *sb.*, fire
foira 3554, *sb. f.*, diarrhoea
foire, *pret.* 3 fos 631, *v. tr.* and *intr.*, to dig, dig up
foletz 2402, **adj., foolish**; *sb.*, sprite, goblin
folha 3432, *sb. f.*, leaf
folhar, *pr. ind.* 3 folha 3432, *v. intr.*, to grow leaves
folhz 2705, *sb.*, leaf; sheet of paper

follar 977, *pr. ind.* 3 fola 3335, *v. tr.*, to trample underfoot
folz 2689, *f.* fola 3312, *adj.*, foolish
fondre 1290, *pr. ind.* 2 fons 2743, *pr. part.* fondens 2105, *v. tr.*, to melt 1290, 2743; *v. intr.*, to melt 1290, 2105
fons 2757, *sb.*, bottom
fons 2742, *sb. f.*, fountain, spring
fora 3229, *adv.*, outside
forar, *pr. subj.* 2 fors 2811, *v. tr.*, to pierce
forbir 1406, *v. tr.*, to polish, furbish
forcar, *pr. subj.* 2 forcs 2793, *v. tr.*, **to pile up with a fork** (?)
forçhar 981, *v. tr.*, to force
forcs 2793, *sb.*, bifurcation (of a road)
formiers 2209, *sb.*, last-maker
formir, *p. part.* formitz 2576, *v. tr.*, to form (*more exactly*: to complete); to provide for
forniers 2210, *sb.*, baker
fornir 1403, *v. tr.*, to equip
forns 2915, *sb.*, oven
fors 2811, *adv.*, outside
fortmen 229, *adv.*, strongly
fortraire 1266, *p. part.* fortrahz 1916, *v. tr.*, to carry off 1916; to pilfer 1266
fortz 2863, *adj.*, strong
fossa 3526, *sb. f.*, pit
foteire 75, *sb.*, one who copulates frequently
fotre 663, *pr. ind.* 2 fotz 2964, *pret.* 3 fotet 600, *p. part.* -ut 666, *v. tr.*, to copulate with
franchamen 1474, *adv.*, frankly, freely
francs 58, 1753, *adj.*, free 58; noble, courtly 58; gentle 1753
franher, *pret.* 3 frais 641, *v. tr.*, to break
freiçir 1399, *p. part.* freisithz 2588, *v. tr.*, to cool 2588; *v. intr.*, to grow cold 1399
freidors 2832, *sb. f.*, cold, coldness
fremir 1397, *v. intr.*, to tremble
fres 2343, *sb.*, bit, bridle
fresca 3507, *adj. f.*, fresh
frethz 2409, *adj.* and *sb.*, cold
frire 1334, *p. part.* frihz 2617, *v. tr.*, to fry
fronçhir 1405, *v. tr.*, to wrinkle, pleat
fronir 1404, *v. tr.*, **to wear out**

frons 2752, *sb.*, forehead
fugiditz 2573, *sb.* and *adj.*, fugitive
fugir 1407, *p. part.* fugitz 2572, *v. intr.*, to flee
fumiers 2227, *sb.*, chimney
fums 2998, *sb.*, smoke
fus 200, 3091, *sb. m. indecl.*, spindle

gabar, *pr. subj.* 2 gabs 1524, *v. intr.* and *refl.*, to boast
gabs 1524, *sb.*, praise, flattery
gadanhar 987, *v. tr.*, to gain, win
gais 1601, *sb.*, jay
gais 1600, *f.* gaia 109, *adj.*, gay
gaita 112, *sb. m.* (*correctly*?), watchman
gaitar 988, *v. tr.*, to watch over, guard
galengaus 1854, *sb.*, galingale, a spice
galiotz 2947, *sb.*, pirate
galliar 993 (*BL*), *v. tr.*, to deceive
galobs 2626, *sb.*, gallop
galopar 984, *v. intr.*, to gallop
galz 1638, *sb.*, cock
gandir 1409, *p. part.* ganditz 2552, *v. intr.*, to flee
gans 1710, *sb.*, glove
garar 983, *pr. ind.* 3 gara 3162, *v. tr.*, to watch over, protect 983, 3162; to look at 983
gardar 982, *v. tr.*, to watch over, protect; to look at
garir 1411, *pr. part.* garens 2133, *p. part.* garitz 2549, *v. tr.*, to heal 1411, 2549; to watch over, protect 2133
garnir, *p. part.* garnitz 2550, *v. tr.*, to fortify
garz 1808, *sb.*, man of low rank and character, wretched fellow
gastar 985, *v. tr.*, to lay waste
gauç 19, *sb.*, joy
geis 1994, *sb.*, gypsum
gelar 989, *v. intr.* and *refl.*, to become frozen
gels 2020, *sb.*, frost
gençer 93, *adj.*, more beautiful
generals 1576, *adj.*, general
genolz 2721, *sb.*, knee
gensar, *pr. subj.* 3 gens 2111 (*conjectured*), *v. tr.*, to adorn
gens 2111, *adj. m.* and *f.* (*correctly*?), beautiful
gergons 188, 2754, *sb. m. indecl.*, thieves' slang, cant

GLOSSARY

ergons 188, *sb. m. indecl.*, jacinth (*conjectured*)
giquir 1416, *p. part.* giquitz 2554, *v. tr.*, to leave, abandon
girar, *pr. ind.* 3 gira 3217, *v. tr.*, to turn (sthg.) round
gisclar, *pr. ind.* 3 giscla 3559, *v. intr.*, to rain and be windy at the same time
gitar 992, *v. tr.*, to throw
glaçar 994, *v. tr.*, to freeze
glais 1602, *sb.*, sword; a plant (gladiolus or iris); *the third translation is corrupt*
glans 1707, *sb. m.* and *f.*, acorn
glatir 1410, *pr. ind.* 2 glatz 1871, *v. intr.*, to bay (of hounds)
glatz 166, 1869, *sb. m. indecl.*, ice
glatz 1870, *sb.*, baying of hounds
glaucs 1829, *adj.*, blue-green, glaucous
gles 147, 2344, *sb. m. indecl.*, dormouse
globs 2633, *sb.*, mouthful (of liquid)
glosa 3542, *sb. f.*, gloss, commentary
glotir 1412, *v. tr.*, to swallow
glotoneiar 997, *v. intr.*, to be gluttonous
glotz 2956, *adj.* and *sb.*, gluttonous, glutton
glutz 3029, *sb.*, glue
gola 3327, *sb. f.*, throat
golir 1414, *v. tr.*, to devour
gollarz 1807, *adj.*, gluttonous
gondir 1413, *v. intr.*, to grumble
gorcs 2795, *sb.*, abyss
gortz 2890, *adj.*, **stiff with infirmity**
gotar 996, *v. intr.*, to drip
governar 995, *v. tr.*, to direct, govern
graçir 1408, *v. tr.*, to thank
grams 1685, *adj.*, sad
graniers 2235, *sb.*, granary
grans 22, 23, 1706, *adj.*, big, great
graps 1529, *sb.*, **hooked claw** (?)
gras 157, 1923, *f.* grassa 3548, *adj. m. indecl.*, fat
gras 1937, *sb.*, grain, seed
gratar 986, *pr. subj.* 2 gratz 1875, *v. tr.*, to scratch
grazals 1558, *sb.*, bowl, deep vessel for serving food
graziz 2551, *adj.*, agreeable, pleasing
grenar 991, *v. tr.* and *intr.*, to glean
grens 2112, *sb.*, moustache
greps 2166, **adj., haughty**
greuger 94, *comp. adj.*, heavier

greujar 990, *v. tr.*, to burden, oppress
greus 2431, *uninflected neuter* greu 96, *adj.*, heavy, burdensome, grievous
gris 181, 2515, *adj. m. indecl.*, grey
grius 2611, *sb.*, griffin
grobs 2629, *sb.*, knot
grocs 2646, *sb.*, hook
grola 3334, *sb. f.*, old sole (of a shoe)
gronhz 2782, *sb.*, snout, muzzle of an animal
gronire 80, *sb.*, one who groans or grumbles frequently
grossa 3527, *adj. f.*, large
grupir 1417, *p. part.* gurpitz 2553, *v. tr.*, to leave, abandon
grus 3085, *sb.*, grape
grutz 3028, *sb.*, gruel
guers 176, 2173, *adj. m. indecl.*, squint-eyed
guidar 993, *v. tr.*, to give safe-conduct to
guila 3303, *sb. f.*, deception, guile
honors 2844, *sb. f.*, honour
humils 2472, *adj.*, humble

içalar 999, *v. intr.*, to run away from flies (of oxen)
ila 3299, *sb. f.*, island
ilh 101, *pers. pron. m.* and *f.*, he, she
ilha 3414, *sb. f.*, flanks
implir 1422, *p. part.* implitz 2569, *v. tr.*, to fill
infernals 1587, *adj.*, infernal
ins 2495, *adv.*, within
intrar 998, *v. intr.*, to enter
ira 3208, *sb. f.*, anger
iscla 3561, *untranslated; perhaps* = *sb. f.*, island
isnelz 2046, *adj.*, swift
issir 1421, *pr. ind.* 3 eis 1989, *p. part.* issithz 2590, *v. intr.*, to go out
ivernals 1573, **adj., pertaining to winter**

ja 1479, *adv.*, now, already, ever
jaians 1727, *sb.*, giant
jais 1616, *sb.*, joy
japs 1534, *sb.*, bark (of dog)
jatz 167, 1876, *sb. m. indecl.*, animal's lair
jauzir 1418, *p. part.* jauzens 2123, *v. tr.*, to enjoy 1418; *v. intr.*, to rejoice 2123

GLOSSARY

jazer, *pr. ind.* 3 jatz 1877, *pr. part.*
jaçens 2162, *v. intr.*, to lie down
jocs 2638, *sb.*, jest, game
jogar 1001, *v. tr.* and *intr.*, to play
joglars 1783, *sb.*, public entertainer or player, jongleur
joher 669, *pret.* 3 jois 626, *p. part.* jonht 681, *v. tr.*, to join
jornals 1583, *sb.*, area which can be ploughed in one day (unit of land-measurement)
jos 1494, jus 3089, *adv.*, down
jovenils 2478, *adj.*, youthful
jovenir 1419, *v. intr.*, to become young again
juçiar 1002, *p. part.* juciatz 1893, *v. tr.*, **to judge**
jurar 1000, *pr. ind.* 3 jura 3122, *v. tr.* and *intr.*, to swear
justiciar 1003, *v. tr.*, to pass sentence on

laborar 1009, *pr. ind.* 3 labora 3235, *v. tr.* and *intr.*, to work
labors 2817, *sb. m.* and *f.*, work
lahz 1903, *adj.*, ugly, nasty
lai 1493, *adv.*, there; de lai 1493, there, from there (*badly translated as* to that place)
laics 1553, *adj.* and *sb.*, lay, layman
lairar 1006, *pr. ind.* 3 laira 3518, *v. intr.*, to bark
lais 171, 1608, *sb. m. indecl.*, a kind of song, *lai*
laissar 1007, *pr. subj.* 2 lais, laisses 3114, 3 lais 1608, *v. tr.*, to leave
lams 1688, *sb.*, lightning
lans 1712, lanz 164, *sb. m. indecl.*, throw, action of throwing
lansar, *pr. subj.* 2 lans 1711, *v. tr.*, to throw
laps 1533, *sb.*, **flap or skirt of garment**
larcs 1795, *adj.*, broad
las 158, 1924, *f.* lassa 3549, *adj. m. indecl.*, tired
lassar 1008, *v. tr.*, to tire
latinar 1010, *pr. subj.* 2 latis 2518, *v. intr.*, to speak Latin
latz 166, *sb. m. indecl.*, knotted cord
lauçar 1064, *pr. subj.* 2 laus 1846, *v. tr.*, to praise
laupartz 1815, *sb.*, leopard
laura 3245, *adj. f.*, laurel-coloured
laurs 1859, *sb.*, laurel-tree

laus 169, *sb. m. indecl.*, praise
laus 169, *sb. m. indecl.*, lake
lausenga 3443, *sb. f.*, flattery; hypocritical or treacherous speech
lausengiers 2206, *adj.*, evil-tongued
l'autrer 1479, *adv.*, recently
lavar 1005, *v. tr.*, to wash
lebrers 2244, *f.* lebreira 3193, *sb.*, greyhound
lecar 1013, *pr. subj.* 2 lecs 1986, *v. tr.*, to lick
lecs 1979, *adj.*, greedy
lega 3488, *sb. f.*, league (measure of distance)
legar, *p. part.* legatz 1892, *v. tr.*, to bind, tie
legir, *cond.* 1 lesquera 3171, *p. part.* legit 679, *v. tr.*, to read
legors 2843, *sb. f.*, leisure, idleness
leials 1560, *adj.*, just, lawful
leis 1996, lethz 2412, *sb. f.*, law
leis 1992, *meaning uncertain*
lenga 3442, *sb. f.*, tongue
lenhiers 2258, *sb.*, wood-pile
lens 2113, *adj.*, slow
les 2342, *adj.*, smooth
lesca 3505, *sb. f.*, thin slice (of bread)
lethz 2377, *sb.*, bed
leuger 94, *comp. adj.*, lighter
leujar 1011, *v. tr.*, to make lighter
leus 2432, *adj.*, light
levar 1012, *v. tr.*, to raise
lezer, *pret.* 3 lec 579, *v. intr.*, to be permitted; *see also* liçers
liar, *pr. ind.* 3 lia 3470, *v. tr.*, to bind
liçers 2200, *sb.*, permission
lins 2496, *sb.*, boat
lipsar 1016, **lispar** 1016 (*L*), *v. tr.*, to polish
lis 193, 2520, *adj. m. indecl.*, smooth
listrar 1014, *v. tr.*, to adorn with stripes
liurar 1015, *v. tr.*, to give (*more exactly*: to hand over)
lo 22, 43, 44, *obl. sg.* lo 48–50, *def. art.*, the
lobs 2632, *sb.*, wolf
locs 2649, *sb.*, place
logar, *pr. subj.* 2 locs 2650, *v. tr.*, to hire, take on lease
loguiers 2273, *sb.*, recompense
loira 3556, *sb. f.*, otter
lonhar, *pr. subj.* 2 lonhz 2784, *v. tr.*, to remove to a distance

GLOSSARY 405

lortz 2889, *adj.*, **hard of hearing**
lotz 2939, *adj.*, slow
luitar 1017, *v. intr.*, to struggle
lums 2999, *sb.*, light
lus 3079, *sb.*, Monday
lutz 3030, *sb. f.*, light
luzir, *pr. ind.* 3 lutz 3031, *pr. part.* luçens 2152, *v. intr.*, to shine

maçeliers 2268, *sb.*, butcher
maçelz 2042, *sb.*, butcher's shop, slaughter-house
maçerar 1021, *v. tr.*, to knead (dough)
machar 1037, *v. tr.*, to strike
macips 2439, *sb.*, boy
madurar 1036, *v. tr.* and *intr.*, to ripen
maestre 88, 123, *sb.*, master
magorns 2903, *sb.*, stump (of leg after loss of foot)
maials 1572, *sb.*, **gelded pig**
maier 91, *comp. adj.*, bigger
mainera 3196, *sb. f.*, manner
mainera 3196, *adj. f.*, tame
mairolhz 2723, *sb.*, marrubium, hoarhound
mais 1611, *sb.*, month of May
mais 1496, 1611, *adv.*, more
maissela 3270, *sb. f.*, jaw
mala 3260, *sb. f.*, knapsack, valise
malamen 1468, 1472, 1473, 1476, malemen 1470, malamenz 1476, *adv.*, badly
malastrucs 2982, *adj.*, unfortunate
malaus 1849, *adj.*, ill
maldire, *pr. part.* maldizens 2157, *p. part.* maldithz 2622, *v. tr.*, to speak ill of, to curse
maldithz 2622, *sb.*, curse, malediction
malevar 1022, *v. tr.*, to go bail for, to stand surety for
malha 3345, *sb. f.*, chain-mail
malha 3348, *sb. f.*, albugo
malha 3350, *without translation*
malhar, *pr. ind.* 3 malha 3347, *v. tr.*, to make (a hauberk) in chain-mail
malhar, *pr. ind.* 3 malha 3349, *v. tr.*, to hammer
malhz 1653, *sb.*, mace (weapon)
mals 15, 1562, *obl. sg.* mal 1472, *f.* mala 17, 3259, *uninflected neuter* mal 96, *adj.*, bad, wicked; mals 23, *sb.*, evil
mamella 3271, *sb. f.*, breast

man 1482, *adv.*, in the morning
mancs 1755, *f.* manca 3454, *adj.*, one-handed
mandar, *pr. subj.* 2 mans 1719, *v. tr.*, to command
mandoliers 2251, *sb.*, almond-tree
manduirar 792, *v. intr.*, to play the mandora (a stringed instrument somewhat resembling a lute)
manjar 1018, *v. tr.*, to eat
mans 1718, *sb.*, command
mans 1720, *adj.*, gentle
mantelar, *pr. ind.* 3 mantela 3281, *v. tr.*, to cover, veil
mantelz 2056, *sb.*, cloak
mantener 1254, *pr. part.* mantenens 2122, *pret.* 3 mantenc 592, *v. tr.*, to support, maintain
maormen 1496, *adv.*, especially, principally
marcs 1797, *obl. pl.* marcs 399, 539, *sb.*, mark, a coin
maridar 1020, *v. tr.*, to give in marriage
marques 146, 2333, *sb. m. indecl.*, marquis
marrir 1423, *v. intr.*, to be sad, to become sad
mars 1777, *sb. m.* and *f.*, sea
martz 165, 1814, *sb. m. indecl.*, Tuesday; March
mas 1522, *conj.*, but
mas 158, 1927, *sb. m. indecl.*, farmhouse
mas 1941, *sb. m.* and *f.*, hand
mascarar 1023, *v. tr.*, to dye black with the aid of charcoal
massa 3551, *adv.*, a lot (of sthg.)
matar 1019, *v. tr.*, to kill, to mate (at chess)
matis 2532, *sb.*, morning
matz 1878, *adj.*, checkmated
mauca 3501, *sb. f.*, paunch
maurs 1863, *f.* maura 3246, *adj.*, black
meçeismes, meceismes 209, *adj.*; eu meçeismes 209, I myself
mechinar 1028, *v. tr.*, to give medical attention to, to treat (disease, patient)
meçola 3338, *sb. f.*, marrow (of bone)
meisser, *pr. ind.* 3 meis 2002, *pr. subj.* 3 mesca 3510, *pret.* 3 mesquet 597, *v. tr.*, to mix or prepare (a drink)

GLOSSARY

meitadar 1035, *v. tr.*, to make (sthg.) half of one colour, half of another
melher 90, *comp. adj.*, better
melhurar 1026, *pr. ind.* 3 melura 3131, *v. tr.*, to improve
mels 2018, *sb. m.* and *f.*, honey
menaçar 1025, *v. tr.*, to threaten
menar 1024, *imper.* 2 mena 48, *v. tr.*, to lead
menbrar 1031, *v. refl.* and *impers.*, to remember
mençoigniers 2264, *f.* mezoigneira 3197, *adj.*, untruthful
mendics 2453, *f.* mendiga 3463, *adj.*, indigent
mendigar 1029, *v.* ***intr.***, to beg
menre 92, *comp. adj.*, smaller
mens 1496 (*BL*), *adv.*, less
mentaure, *pret.* 3 mentac 606, *v. tr.*, to name
mentir 1424, *pr. ind.* 2 mens 2136, *v. intr.*, to tell a lie
mentre 1480, *conj.*, while
menutz 3041, *adj.*, small, minute
meraveilhar 1033, *v. tr.*, to marvel at
mercadar 1032, *v. intr.*, to trade
merir 1427, *pr. subj.* 3 meira 3206, *v. tr.*, to deserve
merz 2306, *sb. f.*, goods for sale
mes 144, 2326, *sb. m. indecl.*, month
mes 160, *sb. m. indecl.*, messenger (?); dish (of food) (?) (*conjectured*)
mescaps 160, *sb. m.* ***indecl.*** (*correctly?*), battle against great odds, i.e. military disaster (*B*; *without translation in A*)
mesclar 1034, *v. refl.*, to quarrel
mesdir 1426, *v. intr.*, to speak ill of s.o.
meselz 2035, *adj.* and *sb.*, leprous, leper
mesgabar 1030, *v. tr.*, to lose by ill-luck
mespoliers, nespoliers 2260, *sb.*, medlar-tree
mesprendre 1303, *pret.* 3 mespres 2336, *p. part.* mespres 2336, *v. intr.*, to do wrong 1303, 2336; *v. tr.*, to blame, reprove 2336
mesquis 2525, *adj.*, wretched
messurar 1027, *v. tr.*, to measure
mestiers 2218, *sb.*, weaver's loom
mesura 120, 3124, *sb. f.*, measure, moderation

meteis 2007, *adj.*; el meteis 2007, he himself
methz 2380, *adj.*, half
metre 661, 671, 1338, *pret.* 3 mes 594, 2327, *p. part.* mes 680, mis 2523, *v. tr.*, to put
meus 212, 2430, *f.* mia 3473, *poss. pron.* and *adj.*, my, mine
mezalha 3369, *sb. f.*, halfpenny
mia 3478, *sb. f.*, friend (female)
mielz 2062, melhz 173, *adv.*, better
mil 399, 539, *num. adj.*, thousand
miralhz 1649, *sb.*, mirror
mirar 1038, *pr. ind.* 3 mira 3209, *pr. subj.* 2 mirs 2506, *v. tr.*, to look at (sthg.) in a mirror 1038; to gaze at 2506, 3209
miravilha 3406, *sb. f.*, wonder, marvel
mocs 2657, *sb.*, nasal mucus
mohtz 2764, *sb.*, peck (measure for corn, etc.)
mola 3314, *sb. f.*, millstone
molhar, *pr. subj.* 2 molhz 2713, *imper.* 2 molha 3419, *v. tr.*, to soak, moisten
molhz 2712, *sb.*, hub of a wheel; **axle** (?)
moliniers 2211, *sb.*, miller
molis 2522, *sb.*, mill
molre, *pret.* 3 molc 629, *p. part.* moutz 2918, *v. tr.*, to grind in a mill
molz 2692, *f.* mola 3314, *adj.*, soft
molzer, *pr. ind.* 3 moutz 2931, *pret.* 3 mols 2685, *p. part.* mols 2684, *v. tr.*, to milk
monestar 1043, *v. tr.*, to advise
monestiers 2217, *sb.*, monastery, convent
mongils 2481, *adj.*, monastic
mons 2745, *sb.*, mountain; heap
montar 1042, *v. intr.*, to go up
mora 3237, *sb. f.*, blackberry
moralha 3357, *sb. f.*, catch (of lock), hasp
mordre, *pr. part.* mordens 2119, *pret.* 3 mors 2814, *p. part.* mors 2808, *v. tr.*, to bite
moriers 2259, *sb.*, mulberry-tree
morir 1429, *p. part.* mortz 2881, *v. intr.*, to die
morns 2912, *adj.*, sad
mors 189, 2815, *sb. m. indecl.*, bite
mortals 1578, *adj.*, mortal, deadly
mortz 2880, *sb. f.*, death
moschar 1040, *v. intr.* (or ***tr.***?), to drive away flies

GLOSSARY

moscidar 1041, *v. tr.*, to sniff
mossa 3533, *sb. f.*, moss
mostrar 1039, *v. tr.*, to show
motir 1428, *v. tr.*, to utter (a word, a sound); to designate
motz 2957, *sb.*, word
moure 1279, *fut. impf.* 1 mouria 353, *pr. ind.* 2 mous 2803, *pret.* 3 moc 574, *cond.* 1 mogra 353, *p. part.* mogutz 3060, *v. tr.* and *intr.*, to move
moutz 2930, *adj. m.*, *obl. pl.*, many
moyols 2667, *sb.*, glass goblet
muls 2993, *f.* mula 3341, *sb.*, mule
mundas 1947, *adj.*, of this world
murar, *pr. ind.* 3 mura 3150, *v. intr.*, to build a wall
murs 3015, *sb.*, wall
mutz 3035, *adj.*, dumb

nadals 1571, nadaus 1850, *sb.*, Christmas
nadar 1045, *v. intr.*, to swim
nafrar 1046, *v. tr.*, to wound
naisser, *pr. ind.* 3 nais 1605, *p. part.* natz 1879, *v. intr.*, to be born
naps 1525, *sb.*, goblet
nas 138, 1928, *sb. m. indecl.*, nose
nas 1940, *sb.*, dwarf
natura 3151, *sb. f.*, nature
naucs 1830, *sb.*, trough (for pigs)
naus 1852, *sb. f.*, ship
naveiar 1044, *v. intr.*, to navigate
neblar 1048, *v. refl.*, to be spoilt by the mist (of plants, etc.) (?); or *v. intr.* or *refl.*, **to be lost in the mist** (?)
necs 1967, *adj.*, having a defect of speech
negar 1047, *v. tr.*, to drown
negus 3088, *adj.* and *sb.*, no, none, no one
neis 1520, 2005, *adv.*, even
nelethz 2417, *sb.*, fault, transgression
nems 2085, *adv.*, too much, very much
nespoliers, *see* mespoliers
nevar 1049, *v. impers.*, to snow
ni 1518, *conj.*, neither, nor
no 230, 1468, *adv.*, not
nocalens 2094, *adj.*, improvident, negligent
noela 3267, *adj. f.*, new; noela 3268, *sb. f.*, news

noguiers 2252, *sb.*, walnut-tree
noirims 2489, *sb.*, nourishment (?); offspring, brood
noirir 1430, *p. part.* noirithz 2591, *v. tr.*, to feed
nomar 1052, *v. tr.*, to name
nombrar 1051, *v. tr.*, to count
noms 2732, *sb.*, name
nora 3226, *sb. f.*, daughter-in-law
nos 255, 424, etc., *pers. pron.*, *n. pl.*, we
nostre 103, 213, *poss. pron.* and *adj.*, our, ours
notar 1050, *v. tr.*, to note, denote
notz 194, 2963, *sb. f. indecl.*, nut
nous 2800, *adj.*, new
noveliers 2236, *sb.*, newsmonger
nozer, *fut. impf.* 1 noçeria 355, *pr. ind.* 3 notz 2949, *pret.* 3 noc 574, *cond.* 1 nogra 355, *v. intr.*, to harm
nualha 3353, *sb. f.*, idleness
nutz 3036, *adj.*, bare

o 1518, *conj.*, either, or
obezir 1431, *v. tr.* and *intr.*, to obey
oblidar 1063, *v. tr.*, to forget
obrar 1053, *v. tr.*, to construct, fashion
obrir 1432, *pret.* 3 ubri, uberc 615, *p. part.* overtz 2299, *v. tr.*, to open
ocaisonar 1059, *v. tr.*, to seek out (unjust) accusations against
ocs 2641, *adv.* and *sb.*, yes
odorar 1058, *pr. ind.* 3 odora 3242, *v. intr.*, to smell or sniff at something
odors 2842, *sb. f.*, odour
ofegar 980, *v. tr.*, to suffocate
offitials 1582, *sb.*, official, officer
ofrir 1433, *pr. part.* offrens 2114, *p. part.* offertz 2297, *v. tr.*, to offer
ogan 1481, *adv.*, this year
oi 1478, *adv.*, today
ola 3339, *sb. f.*, pot
oler, *pr. part.* olens 2124, *v. intr.*, to smell (of sthg.)
olhz 2703, *sb.*, eye
oliers 2233, *sb.*, potter
olivers 2245, *sb.*, olive-tree
om 540, hom 399, *sb.*, man
onceiar 1057, *v. intr.*, to crook or wriggle one's toes
ondeiar 1056, *v. intr.*, to undulate, billow

GLOSSARY

onher 669, *pr. ind.* 2 onhz 2774, *pret.* 3 ois 626, *p. part.* oinht 681, onhz 2773, *v. tr.*, to anoint
onrar 1054, *pr. ind.* 3 onora 3240, *v. tr.*, to honour
ops 185, obs 2624, *sb. m. indecl.*, what is needful or necessary
ora 3232, *sb. f.*, hour
orar 1055, *v. intr.*, to pray
orbs 2895, *adj.*, blind
orcs 2787, *sb.*, a sort of plant
organar 793, *v. intr.*, to sing in an ornamented or decorated manner (?)
orgolhar, *pr. ind.* 3 orgolha 3428, *v. refl.*, to be haughty
orientals 1584, *adj.*, eastern
ors 191, 2827, *sb. m. indecl.*, bear
ors 2807, *sb.*, edge of cloth, seam
ortz 2857, *sb.*, garden
osa 3541, *sb. f.*, leather boot
oscar 1060, *v. tr.*, to blunt
ossa 3529, *sb. f.*, bones (*collective*)
ostalar 780, 1062, *v. intr.*, to lodge, take a lodging
ostar 1061, *v. tr.*, to take away
ous 2798, *sb.*, egg
ovelha 3385, *sb. f.*, sheep

padela 3287, *sb. f.*, frying-pan
pagar 1067, *imper.* 5 pagatz 1891, *p. part.* pagatz 1890, *v. tr.*, to pay
pahz 1905, *sb.*, agreement, covenant
pahz 1905, *adj.*, stupid
paisser, *fut. impf.* 1 passeria 350, *pr. ind.* 3 pais 1606, *pret.* 3 pac 606, *cond.* 1 pagra 350, *v. intr.*, to graze
pala 3255, *sb. f.*, shovel for taking bread from the oven
palha 3358, *sb. f.*, straw
palhers 2226, *sb.*, pile of straw, strawrick
palhucs 2984, *sb.*, **a small straw** (?); chopped straw (?)
palms 1671, *sb.*, span (unit of measurement)
pals 1563, *sb.*, fence
palueçir 1436, *v. intr.*, to turn pale
palus 3093, *sb. f.*, marsh
panatiers, paniers 2215, *sb.*, pantler
panelz 2040, *sb.*, small loaf
panelz 2040, *sb.*, type of saddle
paniers 2214, *sb.*, basket
pans 1705, *sb.*, part, piece; piece of cloth; flap or skirt of a garment

pantaiar 1075, *v. intr.*, to dream
paors 2846, *sb. f.*, fear
paorucs 2983, *adj.*, timid
papa 113, 114, *sb.*, pope
paradis 181, 2516, *sb. m. indecl.*, paradise
parar 1064, *pr. ind.* 3 para 3159, *v. tr.*, to prepare
parens 2128, *sb.*, kinsman
parer, *pret.* 3 parec 578, *v. intr.*, to appear
parlar 1066, *v. intr.*, to speak
parliers 2205, *adj.*, loquacious
pars 1780, *adj.*, equal
partir 1434, *pr. ind.* 2 partz 1818, *v. tr.*, to share out
partz 1817, *sb. f.*, part, share
pas 138, 1929, *sb. m. indecl.*, pace, step
pas 1942, *obl. sg.* pan 227, *sb.*, bread
passar 1068, *pr. ind.* 3 passa 3550, *pr. subj.* 3 pas 1930, *v. tr.* and *intr.*, to cross
passeiar 1065, *v. intr.*, to stride
pastar 1070, *v. tr.*, to mix (flour) into a paste with water
pastre 89, *sb.*, shepherd
pastura 3138, *sb. f.*, pasture
pasturar, *pr. ind.* 3 pastura 3139, *v. intr.*, **to graze**
patz 167, *sb. f. indecl.*, peace
paucs 1831, *f.* pauca 3499, *adj.*, small
paus 1851, *sb.*, peacock
paussar 1069, *v. intr.* and *refl.*, to rest
peçeiar 1082, *v. tr.*, to break into small pieces
pechar 1081, *v. intr.*, to sin
pecs 1968, *f.* pega 3490, *adj.*, stupid
pectenar 1088, *v. tr.*, to comb
peçugar 1086, *pr. subj.* 2 pezucs 2979, *v. tr.*, to pinch
peier 90, *comp. adj.*, worse
peintura 3144, *sb. f.*, painting
peis 1997, *sb.*, fish
peitrals 1581, *sb.*, breast-strap (of horse); parapet
peiurar 1078, *pr. ind.* 3 peiura 3132, *v. intr.* and *refl.*, to become worse
pejurar 1094, *pr. ind.* 3 perjura 3123, *pr. subj.* 2 perjurs 3017, *v. refl.*, to perjure oneself
pelha 3393, *sb. f.*, rag
pellar 1079, *pr. ind.* 3 pela 3292, *v. tr.*, to pull the hairs from
pels 2025, *sb.*, a hair

GLOSSARY 409

pelutz 3040, *adj.*, hairy
pelz 2058, *sb. f.*, skin
penar 1076, *v. intr.*, **to suffer pain or punishment** (?); *v. tr.*, **to expiate** (?)
penartz 1811, *sb.*, pheasant
pencheire 74, *sb.*, painter
pendelhar, *pr. ind.* 3 pendelha 3391, *v. intr.*, to dangle
pendre 661, 1309, *pr. ind.* 2 pens 2141, *pret.* 3 pendet 599, *p. part.* -ut 666, pendutz 3057, *v. tr. and intr.*, to hang
penedir, *pr. part.* penedens 2131, *v. refl.*, to repent
penher 673, 1269, *pr. ind.* 1 penh 530, *pr. part.* penhens 2159, *pret.* 3 peis 587, 1998, *p. part.* peinht 683, *v. tr.*, to paint
penhurar 1077, *v. tr.*, to seize as a gage
pensar 1085, *pr. ind.* 1 pens 2142, *v. tr. and intr.*, to think
pentir 1437, *v. refl.*, to repent
pera 3179, *sb. f.*, pear
percebre 1282, *v. tr.*, to perceive
percolar, *pr. ind.* 3 percola 3318, *v. tr.*, to embrace
perdre, *pret.* 3 perdet 598, *p. part.* perdut 708, perdutz 3045, *v. tr.*, to lose
periers 2247, *sb.*, pear-tree
perilhar 1084, *v. tr.*, to endanger; *v. intr.*, to be in danger
perir 1438, *p. part.* peritz 1506, 2584, *v. intr.*, to perish, die
perjurs 3017, *adj.* and *sb.*, perjured, one who breaks his word
per mo vol, see vols
perponhz 2780, *sb.*, doublet, thick embroidered garment worn as part of armour
per que 1490, *interrogative adv.*, why?
pers 2181, *sb.*, a kind of cloth
persegre 1317, *pr. ind.* 2 persecs 1974, *pr. subj.* 3 persega 3496, *pret.* 3 perseguet 596, *v. tr.*, to pursue
pertener 1253, *v. intr.* and *refl.*, to pertain
pertrahz 1915, *sb.*, apparatus, equipment, materials
pertraire 1264, *pret.* 3 pertrais 644, *v. tr.*, to pull 644; to make the necessary preparations for (sthg., perhaps for work of construction) 1264

pertus 198, 3094, *sb. m. indecl.*, hole
pertusar 1089, *v. tr.*, to pierce
pervers 2179, *adj.*, perverse
pes 141, 2318, *sb. m. indecl.*, weight
pes 2313, *sb.*, foot
pesar 1087, *v. tr.*, to weigh; *v. intr.*, to be displeasing or annoying; *pr. part.* pesans 1737, heavy
peschar 1080, *pr. ind.* 3 pesca 3511, *v. tr.*, to fish
pesquiers 2238, *sb.*, fish-pond
pesucs 2987, *adj.*, heavy
petazar 1083, *v. tr.*, to mend, repair
pethz 2383, *sb.*, breast, chest
pethz 2384, *comp. adv.*, worse
petiers 2276, *f.* peteira 3205, *sb.*, one who breaks wind frequently
petz 2389, *sb.*, breaking of wind
petz 2390, *untranslated; no doubt = sb. f.*, pitch
pezolhz 2722, *sb.*, louse
pezucs 2978, *sb.*, pinch
picar 1098, *pr. ind.* 3 pica 3482, *pr. subj.* 2 pics 2450, *v. tr.*, to strike
pics 2448, *sb.*, woodpecker
pics 2449, *adj.*, pied, changeable
pifartz 1809, *adj.*, fat
pila 3300, *sb. f.*, hollowed-out stone receptacle
pila 3300, *sb. f.*, pillar of a bridge
pilar, *pr. ind.* 3 pila 3301, *v. tr.*, to pound, grind (in a mortar)
pis 2528, *sb.*, pine
pissar 1097, *v. intr.*, to micturate
pistar 1099, *v. tr.*, to crush, grind
piuçella 3275, *sb. f.*, girl, virgin
placeiar 1073, *v. intr.*, to walk about the streets
placher 1259, *fut. impf.* 1 plairia 349, *pr. part.* plasens 35, plasenz 1504, plaçens 36, plaisens 37, *pret.* 3 plac 606, *cond.* 1 plagra 349, *v. intr.*, to please
plaideiar 1071, *v. intr.*, to conduct a lawsuit
plais 1615, *sb.*, plashed hedge
planher, *pret.* 3 plais 641, *v. tr., intr.*, and *refl.*, to lament
plantar 1072, *v. tr.*, to plant
platz 1909, *sb.*, dispute between enemies, i.e. lawsuit; agreement between enemies, i.e. treaty
plazenteira 3198, *adj. f.*, pleasing, agreeable

plecs 1982, *sb.*, fold
plegar 1095, *pr. subj.* 2 plecs 1984, *v. tr.*, to fold
plethz 2415, *sb.*, fold
plevir 1439, *v. tr.* and *intr.*, to swear, take an oath
ploms 2734, *sb.*, lead
plorar 1105, *pr. ind.* 1 plori, plor 248, 3 plora 3236, *v. tr.*, *intr.*, and *refl.*, to weep, weep for
ploure 1328, *pr. ind.* 2 plous 2804, *pret.* 3 ploc 575, *v. intr.*, to rain
plovinar 1107, *v. intr.*, **to drizzle**
plus 196, 1496, 3097, *adv.*, more
podar 1103, *v. tr.*, to prune (vines)
poder 335, 665, *used as sb.* poders 2190, *fut. impf.* 1 poria 344, *pr. ind.* 2 potz 2943, *pret.* 3 poc 574, *cond.* 1 pogra 344, *p. part.* pogut 677, 708, *v. intr.*, to be able
pohz 2769, *sb.*, peak, mountain
poiar 1104, *v. intr.*, to go up
poirir 1441, *p. part.* poiritz 2595, *v. intr.*, to rot
poliers 2261, *sb.*, poulterer
polir 1440, *p. part.* polithz 2594, *v. tr.*, to polish
pols 185, 2677, *sb. m. indecl.*, pulse
pols 2679, *sb. m.* and *f.*, dust
polsar 1109, *pr. subj.* 3 pols 2678, *v. tr.*, to push, beat 2678; *v. intr.*, to pant 1109
polz 2699, *sb.*, young bird, chicken
polz 2698, poutz 187, *sb.* (*m. pl.*?) *indecl.*, gruel
pomelar 1108, *v. intr.*, to throw a ball into the air (?)
pomelz 2038, *sb.*, small ball, knob
pomiers 2248, *sb.*, apple-tree
poms 2737, *sb.*, knob on top of a tent
ponçeiar 1102, *v. intr.* (?), **to reject a favour** (?)
ponher 669, *pr. ind.* 2 ponhz 2779, *pret.* 3 pois 626, *p. part.* poinht 681, ponhz 2778, *v. tr.*, to prick
ponhtar 1110, *v. tr.*, to punctuate
ponhz 2777, *sb.*, fist
ponhz 2779, *sb.*, point, moment
ponre 1320, *v. tr.* and *intr.*, to lay an egg
pons 2750, *sb.*, bridge
ponzilar 1101, *pr. ind.* 3 ponzilha 3413, *v. tr.* (*or* **intr.**?), **to set up a wooden contrivance** (i.e. some sort of siege-engine) **against a wall** 1101, 3413; **to destroy walls by this method** 1101
porcelz 2034, *sb.*, piglet
porcs 2786, *sb.*, pig
porquiers 2208, *sb.*, swineherd
pors 2809, *sb.*, leek
portar 1100, *pr. subj.* 2 portz 2876, *v. tr.*, to carry
portelz 2043, *sb.*, little gate
portz 2875, *sb.*, port, harbour
potz 195, 2960, *sb. m. indecl.*, well
potz 2941, *sb.*, lip
praticar 1074, *v. intr.*, to practise (as doctor, lawyer, etc.)
pratz 1880, *sb.*, meadow
preçar 1093, *v. tr.*, to esteem, prize; *pr. part.* presans 26, 27, 1738, presantz 1503, praiseworthy; arrogant, conceited 1503
preçicar 1090, *v. tr.* and *intr.*, to preach
pregar 1092, *v. tr.* and *intr.*, to pray
premer, *pret.* 3 preus 639, *v. tr.*, to press
prendeire 76, *sb.*, one who takes or accepts freely
prendre 366, 658, 671, 1300, *pr. ind.* 2 prens 2137, *pr. part.* prendens 2129, *pret.* 3 pres 594, 2335, *p. part.* pres 148, 680, 2334, *v. tr.*, to take
preons 2760, *adj.*, deep
pres 2316, *adv.*, near
prescentar 1091, *v. tr.*, to present
presenteira 3204, *adj. f.*, bold of speech
prestar 1096, *v. tr.*, to lend
prestre 88, *sb.*, priest
prims 2487, *adj.*, sharp; delicate, subtle
princols 2682, *sb.*, wine from first pressing
priorils 2479, *adj.*, pertaining to a prior
proar 1106, *v. tr.*, to prove
prometre 1339, *v. tr.*, to promise
propheta 112, 114, *sb.*, prophet
pros 58, 136, *adj.*, worthy
prosa 3543, *sb. f.*, liturgical prose
pruir 1443, *v. intr.*, to itch (*badly translated as* to scratch)
pruniers 2249, *sb.*, plum-tree
pudir 1442, *pr. ind.* 2 putz 3037, *pr. part.* pudens 2125, *v. intr.*, to stink

GLOSSARY

pudors 2829, *sb. f.*, stench
purgar 1111, *v. tr.*, to cleanse, purge
purs 3012, *f.* pura 3119, 3149, *adj.*, pure
pustella 3286, *sb. f.*, pustule

quais 1514, *adv.*, as if, as it were, almost
quan 1521, *conj.*, when
quar 1521, *conj.*, for, because
quarar 1112, *pr. ind.* 3 quaira 3520, *v. tr.*, to square (timber, stone)
quartar 1115, *v. tr.*, to take a fourth part of (as a due)
quartz 1824, *sb.*, fourth part
quazerns 2281, *sb.*, gathering (of leaves in a manuscript)
que 1521, *conj.*, that
quecs 1980, *pron. adj.*, each, every; *see also* usquecs
querer 1323, *pret.* 3 ques 594, *v. tr.*, to seek
quetz 2394, *adj.*, quiet, silent
qui 101, *rel. pron.*, who
quins 2492, *adj.*, fifth
quintar 1114, *v. tr.*, to take a fifth part of (as a due)
quitar 1113, *v. tr.*, to exempt (from payment, service, etc.)

raçims 2486, *sb.*, grape
raçonar 1118, *v. tr.*, to explain
radeire 73, *sb.*, barber
raiar 1122, *v. intr.*, to shine forth
rainartz 1820, *sb.*, fox (?)
raire 1319, *pret.* 3 ras 1925, *p. part.* ras 139, 1925, *v. tr.*, to shave, scrape
rais 1614, rathz 1907, *sb.*, ray
ramponar 1119 (= **ramponhar** ?, *cf.* ranponhar *L*, rampoignar *D*), *v. tr.*, to jeer at
rancura 3120, *sb. f.*, complaint
rancurar 1117, *pr. ind.* 3 rancura 3121, *pr. subj.* 2 rancurs 3018, *v. refl.*, to lament, complain
rancs 1763, *sb.*, rock which stands out above the water, reef
rancs 1762, *adj.*, lame
ranqueirar 1123, *v. intr.*, to limp
rara 3157, *adj. f.*, rare
rasclar 1121, *v. tr.*, to scrape with a wooden implement
rasors 2833, *sb.*, razor
raspalhz 1667, *sb.*, chaff

raubar 1116, *p. part.* raubatz 1881, *v. tr.*, to rob, plunder
raubir 1444, *p. part.* raubitz 2586, *v. tr.*, to carry off, steal
raucs 1833, *f.* rauca 3502, *adj.*, hoarse
rauquezir 1445, *v. tr.*, to render hoarse
raus 169, 1853, *sb. m. indecl.*, reed
raustir 1446, *v. tr.*, to roast
rautar 1120, *v. tr.*, to snatch
reborcs 2791, *adj.*, blunt, obtuse
recebre 1284, *p. part.* receubutz 3047, *v. tr.*, to receive
reclams 1678, *sb.*, complaint at law
reclams 1679, *sb.*, meat used as bait to recover a hawk
reclus 196, 3086, *sb. m. indecl.*, recluse
recobrir 1372, *v.* **refl.**, to become covered again (*perhaps intended with reference to the sky*)
recolhir 1375, *pr. ind.* 2 recolhz 2709, *pr. subj.* 3 recolha 3427, *v. tr.*, to gather up 1375; to receive, give protection to 2709, 3427
reconoisser, *pret.* 3 reconoc 624, *p. part.* reconogutz 3071, *v. tr.*, to recognize
recozer, *p. part.* recohtz 2766, *v. tr.*, to recook
recreire, *p. part.* recreütz 3054, *v. refl.*, to desist from, give up (good deeds)
recular, *pr. ind.* 3 recula 3342, *v. intr.*, to go backwards
refar, *p. part.* refathz 1900, *v. tr.*, to remake; *p. part.*, fattened up
refiudar 1125, *v. tr.*, **to renounce possession of (a fief, in another's favour)** (?)
refiudar 1125, *v. tr.*, to refuse (?)
refranher, *pret.* 3 refrais 642, *v. tr.*, to console
refrire 1335, *v. intr.*, **to reverberate**
regarar, *pr. ind.* 3 regara 3164, *v. tr.*, to look at
regardar 1126, *v. tr.*, to look at
regirar, *pr. ind.* 3 regira 3218, *v. tr.*, to turn (sthg.) round and round
regotz 2945, *sb.*, curl (in the hair)
reials 1567, *adj.*, royal
reis 44, 57, 2004, *obl. sg.* rei 46, 48, 50, *sb.*, king
rejovenir 1420, *v.* **intr.**, **to become young again**
relha 3394, *sb. f.*, ploughshare
remembrar 1031, 1133, *v. tr.*, to remember

GLOSSARY

remirar 1127, *pr. ind.* 3 remira 3210, *pr. subj.* 2 remirs 2507, *v. tr.*, to gaze at 1127, 3210; to gaze again at (?) 2507

remolhar, *pr. ind.* 3 remolha 3420, *v. intr.* or *refl.*, to become damp

rendre, *pr. ind.* 2 rens 2147, *v. tr.*, to give back

renoelar 1129, *pr. ind.* 3 renovela 3269, *v. tr.*, to refresh, renew

renous 2801, *sb.*, usury, interest on money

repairar, *pr. ind.* 3 repaira 3523, *v. intr.*, to return home

reparar 1128, *v. tr.*, to repair

reprendre, *pr. ind.* 2 reprens 2139, *pr. part.* reprendens 2130, *pret.* 3 repres 2338, *p. part.* repres 2337, *v. tr.*, to blame, reprove

requerer, *pr. subj.* 3 requeira 3201, *v. tr.*, to ask for, demand

rescodre, *p. part. f.* rescossa 3538, *v. tr.*, to thresh (?)

resorzer, *pret.* 3 resors 2855, *p. part.* resors 192, 2854, *v. tr.* and *intr.*, to raise again, rise again

respalhar, *pr. subj.* 2 respalhz 1668, *v. intr.*, to collect straw after threshing

respethz 2382, *sb.*, respite, delay; expectation

respirar 1131, *v. intr.*, to breathe

resplandir, *pr. part.* resplandens 2156, *v. intr.*, to shine brightly

respondre 662, 1286, *pret.* 3 respondet 597, 603, *p. part.* -ut 666, *v. tr.* and *intr.*, to reply

restaurar 1124, *pr. ind.* 3 restaura 3251, *v. tr.*, to repair, restore

retalhar, *pr. ind.* 3 rethalha 3361, *pr. subj.* 2 retalhz 1659, *v. tr.*, to cut again

retalhz 1658, *sb.*, small piece of cloth

retener 1251, *p. part.* retengutz 1505, *v. tr.*, to retain, hold back

retornar, *pr. subj.* 2 retorns 2914, *v. intr.*, to return

retorser, *pr. ind.* 3 retortz 2870, *pret.* 3 retors 637, *p. part.* retortz 2871, *v. tr.*, to twine (thread)

retrahz 1913, *sb.*, expression of ingratitude, undeserved reproach

retraire 1265, *pret.* 3 retrais 643, *v. tr.*, to recount

revelar 1130, *pr. ind.* 3 revela 3283, *imper.* 2 revela 3283, *v. intr.* and *refl.*, to rebel

revelhar 1132, *pr. ind.* 3 revelha 3383, *v. tr.*, to awaken, rouse

revendre 1298, *v. tr.*, to resell

revenir 1459, *p. part.* revengutz 3069, *v. tr.* and *intr.*, to restore to health, regain health

revers 2180, *adj.*, back to front

revestir 1464, *v. tr.*, to clothe again

revirar, *pr. ind.* 3 revira 3216, *v. tr.*, to turn (sthg.) round and round

revolver, *pret.* 3 revols 635, *p. part.* revoutz 2920, *v. tr.*, *intr.*, and *refl.*, to turn round

ribar 1135, *v. tr.*, to clinch (nails)

ribeira 3190, *sb. f.*, flat river bank

ricors 2847, *sb. f.*, riches

rics 540, 2460, *f.* rica 3486, *adj.*, rich

rimar 1134, *v. tr.*, to compose in rhyme

rips 2441, *sb.*, point of a nail

rire 1336, *pr. subj.* ria 3479, *pret.* 1 ris 610–11, 3 ris 609, *v. intr.*, to laugh

ris 183, 2530, *sb. m. indecl.*, laugh

rius 2608, *sb.*, stream

robis 2510, *sb.*, ruby

rocegar 1144, *v. tr.*, to drag behind horses

rocs 2651, *sb.*, rook (at chess)

rodar 1136, *v. intr.*, to go round in a circle

rofiols 2673, *sb.*, a food made of flour-paste and eggs

roflar 1139, *v. intr.*, **to rattle (in the throat)** (?); **to sob, groan** (?)

rogeiar 1143, *v. intr.*, to turn reddish-yellow, to glow

roïlha 3407, *sb. f.*, rust

roïlhar 1142, *pr. ind.* 3 roïlha 3407, *v. tr.*, to make rusty 1142; *v. intr.* and *refl.*, to rust 3407

roiols 2674, *sb.*, a sort of fish (small gudgeon)

roire, *pret.* 3 ros 633, *v. tr.*, to gnaw

roizir 1447, *v. intr.*, to turn red

rolhz 2715, *sb.*, wooden instrument for cleaning an oven

romeus 2433, *sb.*, pilgrim

romiar 1137, *v. tr.*, to ruminate, chew

rompre, *pr. ind.* 2 roms 2736, *p. part.* romputz 3038, rotz 2959, *v. tr.* and *intr.*, to break

GLOSSARY 413

roms 2735, *sb.*, a sort of fish (*probably* turbot)
ronchar 1140, *v. intr.*, to snore
ronciniers 2243, *sb.*, knight who owns only a nag
roncis 2514, *sb.*, nag
rons 2755, *sb.*, wrinkle
ronsar, *pr. subj.* 2 rons 2756, *v. tr.*, to wrinkle
rosa 3540, *sb. f.*, rose
rosiers 2256, *sb.*, **rose-garden**
rossa 3532, *adj. f.*, red, ruddy
rosseiar 1141, *v. intr.*, to turn red
rossinols 2661, *sb.*, nightingale
rotar 1138, *v. intr.*, to belch
rotiers 2277, *sb.*, one who belches
rotz 2940, *sb.*, belch

sabatiers 2234, *sb.*, shoemaker
saber 335, 665, 689, 1248, *used as sb.* sabers 2189, *pr. ind.* 1 sai 524, 2 saps 525, 1528, 3 sap 526, *imper.* 2 sapchas 690, *pr. part.* sabens 2153, *pret.* 3 saup 584, *p. part.* saubut 677, sabut 706, saubutz 3046, *v. tr.*, to know
saborar 1147, *v. tr.*, to savour, to give flavour to
sabors 2831, *sb. f.*, taste, savour
saçhir 1448, *p. part.* saziz 2568, *v. tr.*, to seize
sacrar 1154, *v. tr.*, to consecrate
sacrifiar 1155, *v. tr.*, to sacrifice
sacs 1542, *sb.*, sack
sadola 3326, *adj. f.*, sated, full (after eating)
sadolar 1146, *pr. ind.* 3 sadola 3333, *v. tr.*, to satiate
safirs 2503, *sb.*, sapphire
sagetar 1152, *v. tr.*, to shoot arrows at
sairar 1149, *v. tr.*, to close; to bolt
sala 3254, *sb. f.*, hall, palace
salar, *pr. ind.* 3 sala 3263, *v. tr.*, to salt
saleira 3195, *sb. f.*, salt-box
salhir 1449, *pr. ind.* 2 salhz 1665, *pr. subj.* 3 salha 3366, *p. part.* salithz 2598, *v. intr.*, to jump
salms 1670, *sb.*, psalm
sals 1565, *sb. m.* and *f.*, salt
sals 1565, *adj.*, safe, saved
saludar 1151, *pr. subj.* 2 salutz 3033, *v. tr.*, to salute, greet
salutz 3032, *sb. m.* and *f.*, salvation, salutation

salutz 3034, *sb. m.* and *f.*, health
salvar 1150, *v. tr.*, to save
sambucs 2969, *sb.*, elder-tree
samithz 2592, *sb.*, a kind of silk cloth
sanar 1148, *v. tr.*, to heal
sancs 1751, *sb. m.* and *f.*, blood
sancs 1752, *f.* sanca 3455, *adj.*, left-handed, left
sanglentar 1153, **sangletar** 1153 (*BD*), *v. tr.*, to stain with blood
sans 1730, *adj.* and *sb.*, holy, saint; *see also List of Proper Names, s.v.* Sang Danis
santatz 130, *sb. f.*, health
saps 1528, *sb.*, fir-tree
sarçir 1452, *v. tr.*, to patch, repair
sarralha 3356, *sb. f.*, lock (of door)
sas 1945, *adj.*, healthy
saücs 2970, *sb.*, elder-tree
saumaliers 2213, *sb.*, driver of a beast of burden
saumiers 2212, *sb.*, beast of burden (mule, ass, etc.)
saurs 1858, *f.* saura 3247, *adj.*, golden (in colour)
sautar 1145, *imper.* 3 saute 303, *v. intr.*, to jump
savais 1617, *adj.*, idle, good-for-nothing
savieza 119, *sb. f.*, wisdom
sebelir, *p. part.* sebelitz 2578, *v. tr.*, to bury
sebrar 1164, *v. tr.*, to separate
secar 1157, *pr. subj.* 2 secs 1985, *imper.* 5 secatz 1885, *p. part.* secatz 1884, *v. tr.*, to dry
secher 335, *fut. impf.* 1 seiria 348, *pret.* 3 sec 579, *cond.* 1 segra 348, *v. intr.*, to sit
secodre 1312, *v. tr.*, to shake
secs 1983, *adj.*, dry
segar 1160, *pr. ind.* 3 sega 3491, *imper.* 5 segatz 1883, *p. part.* segatz 1882, *v. tr.*, to cut
segons 2748, *adj.*, second
segre 1316, *pr. ind.* 2 secs 1973, *pr. subj.* 3 sega 3492, *pret.* 3 seguet 596, *v. tr.*, to follow
segurs 3006, *f.* segura 3146, *adj.*, sure, secure
seis 1993, *num. adj.*, six
sela 3277, *sb. f.*, saddle
selar 1159, *pr. ind.* 3 sela 3278, *v. tr.*, to saddle

GLOSSARY

selha 3395, *sb. f.*, bucket
seliers 2220, *sb.*, saddler
semar, *pr. subj.* 2 sems 2083, *v. tr.*, to diminish
semelhar, *pr. ind.* 3 semelha 3380, *pr. subj.* 2 semelhz 2078, *v. tr.* (*or intr.* ?), to resemble
seminar 1158, *v. tr.*, to sow
semitaurs 1862, *sb.*, half-bull, minotaur
sems 2083, *adj.*, incomplete, half-full
semtiers 2229, *sb.*, path
senblar 1163, *v. tr.*, to resemble
sener 89, segner 123, *sb.*, lord
senescals 1642, *sb.*, seneschal
senestriers 2272, *adj.*, left-handed
senhals 1575, *sb.*, sign, ensign
senhar 1156, *v. tr.*, to sign, brand, make the sign of the cross over
senhoreiar 1161, *v. tr.* and *intr.*, to rule
senhorils 2474, *adj.*, pertaining to a lord (?)
senhorius 2612, *sb.*, lordship
sens 2120, *sb.*, sense, meaning
sentir 243, 1453, senthir 563, *pr. ind.* 1 senti, sen 262, 2 sens 2134, *p. part.* sentit 756–60, scentit 755, senthiz 2579, *v. tr.*, to feel, perceive
seps 2165, *sb. f.*, hedge, fence
serps 2287, *sb. m.* and *f.*, snake
sers 2198, *sb.*, evening
sers 2171, *sb.*, servant
servir 1454, *pr. ind.* 2 sers 2172, *v. tr.* and *intr.*, to serve
sesca 3506, *sb. f.*, **cut bulrush** (i.e. gathered ready for use or sale)
setz 2391, *sb. f.* and *m.*, thirst
seus 212, 2429, *poss. pron.* and *adj.*, his, her(s), its
si 539, 707, 1520, se 1468, s' 398, 539, 706, 709, *conj.*, if
siblar 1162, *v. intr.*, to whistle
si cum 1514, *conj.*, just as
sirventes 142, *sb. m. indecl.*, satirical song
sitar 1182; *probably a scribal error for* suçar
sitot 1516, *conj.*, although
sivals 1516, *adv.*, at least (*concessive*)
soans 1724, *sb.*, scornful rejection, disdain
sobdar 1176, *v. tr.*, to come upon, or attack, unexpectedly
sobradaurar 886, *pr. ind.* 3 sobredaura 3249, *v. tr.*, to gild
sobranceiar 1177, *v. intr.*, to behave arrogantly
sobrar 1178, *v. tr.* and *intr.*, to conquer
sobreira 3191, *adj. f.*, proud, arrogant; pre-eminent
sobreprendre 1304, *v. tr.*, to blame, reprove; to seize
socore 1315, *pret.* 3 socors 2822, *v. intr.*, to help, succour
socors 190, 2824, *sb. m. indecl.*, help
soflar 1168, *v. intr.*, to blow through the nostrils
sofranher, *pret.* 3 sofrais 642, *v. intr.*, to be lacking
sofrir 563, *pr. part.* sufrens 1504, suffrens 2115, *pret.* 3 sufri, sofrec 615, *v. tr.* and *intr.*, to suffer
sogautar 1174, *v. tr.*, to strike across the mouth
sohanar 1170, *pr. subj.* 2 soans 1725, *v..tr.*, to disdain, reject
solachar 1172, *v. intr.*, to engage in badinage
solar 1173, *pr. ind.* 3 sola 3319, *v. tr.*, to sole (shoes)
solelhz 2069, *sb.*, sun
soler, *pr. ind.* 2 sols 2665, *v. intr.*, to be wont to
soletz 2396, *adj.*, alone
solhar, *pr. ind.* 3 solha 3437, *v. tr.*, to soil, pollute
solhelar 1180, *pr. ind.* 3 solelha 3386, *pr. subj.* 2 solelhz 2070, *v. tr.*, to dry or warm in the sun
soliers 2263, *sb.*, (top) storey (of a house); flat roof, balcony
solorius 2607, *adj.*, unique
sols 2664, *sb.*, soil, floor
sols 2676, *f.* sola 3332, *adj.*, alone
solver, *pret.* 3 sols 635, 2666, *p. part.* solz 2694, soutz 2925, *v. tr.*, to untie, set free
solz 2697, soutz 187, 2929, *sb. m. indecl.*, meat or fish pickled in vinegar
solz 2693, *sb.*, a coin
somnelhar, *pr. ind.* 3 somnelha 3381, *pr. subj.* 2 somnelhz 2077, *v. intr.* and *refl.*, to doze 2077, 3381; *v. tr.*, to dream 3381
somnhar 1166, *v. tr.* and *intr.*, to dream

GLOSSARY

soms 2733, *sb.*, dream (?)
soms 2733 (*B*), *sb.*, highest point, top
sonalhz 1654, *sb.*, small bell
sonar 1165, *pr. ind.* 1 soni, so 249, *v. tr.* and *intr.*, to sound
sons 2753, *sb. m.*, sleep
sopar 1167, *v. intr.*, to sup
sor 92, *sb. f.*, sister
sorbiers 2255, *sb.*, service-tree, rowan
sordeiar 1179, *v. tr.* and *intr.*, to make worse, become worse
sordeier 91, *adj.*, worse
sortz 2867, *sb. f.*, fate, destiny
sortz 2887, *adj.*, deaf
sorzer, *pr. ind.* 3 sortz 2892, *pret.* 3 sors 2852, *p. part.* sors 191, 2853, *v. tr.* and *intr.*, to raise, rise
sospendre, *p. part.* sospendutz 3059, *v. tr.*, to hang up
sospirar 1171, *pr. ind.* 3 sospira 3212, *pr. subj.* 2 sospirs 2505, *v. intr.*, to sigh
sospirs 2502, *sb.*, sigh
sostar 1175, *v. intr.*, to grant a delay or respite
sosteirar 1169, *v. tr.*, to bury
sostener, *pret.* 3 sostenc 592, *p. part.* sostengutz 3067, *v. tr.*, to support, sustain
sotz 2961, *sb. f.*, pigsty
sotz 2962, *prep.*, under, below
sotzmetre 1341, *p. part.* sothzmis 2524, *v. tr.*, to submit
sotztraire 1267, *pret.* 3 sostrais 644, *v. tr.*, to take away
soudadera 3202, *sb. f.*, paid woman
sovenir 1462, *pr. part.* sovinens 2118, *pret.* 3 sovenc 591, *v. impers.*, to remember
stola 3311, *sb. f.*, stole
suar 1181, *v. intr.*, to sweat
suaus 1848, *adj.*, sweet, pleasant
subtils 2476, *adj.*, fine, delicate, subtle
suçar 1182 (*conjectured*), *v. tr.*, to suck
sucs 2980, *sb.*, juice, sap
sugar 1182 (*B*), *v. tr.*, to wipe dry
sumrire, *pret.* 1 sumris 610–11, 3 sumris 609, *v. intr.*, to smile
sumsir, *p. part.* sumsitz 2577, *v. tr.*, to submerge
sus 1494, 3102, *adv.*, up

tabors 2818, *sb. m.* and *f.*, drum
tabustar 1193, *v. intr.*, to make a din
tacs 1543, *sb.*, a disease of pigs
tafurs 3015, *adj.* and **sb.**, rascally, rascal
tais 172, 1618, *sb. m. indecl.*, badger
tala 3256, *sb. f.*, damage, devastation
talar 1191, *pr. ind.* 3 tala 3257, *v. tr.*, to lay waste
talens 2160, *sb.*, inclination, desire
talha 3360, *sb. f.*, tax
talhar 1192, *pr. ind.* 3 talha 3360, *pr. subj.* 2 talhz 1657, *imper.* 5 talhatz 1886, *p. part.* talhatz 1886, *v. tr.*, to cut (with metal implement 1886)
talhiers 2266, *sb.*, meat-dish, trencher
talhz 1656, *sb.*, cutting down (of trees, etc.)
tals 1564, *adj.*, such
tamboreçar 1189, *v. intr.*, to play a drum or timbrel
tams 1689, *adj.*, **even** (of numbers) (?)
tanar, *pr. subj.* 2 tans 1733, *v. tr.*, to tan (leather)
tancar, *pr. ind.* 3 tanca 3451, *v. tr.*, to close
tancs 1759, *sb.*, **thorn** (?), splinter (?)
tanher, *pret.* 3 tais 645, 1620, *v. intr.* and *refl.*, to be appropriate
tans 1733, *sb.*, tan (bark of trees used in preparation of leather)
tans 1732, *adj. m.*, *obl. pl.*, so many
taps 1532, *sb.*, clay
tart 1481, *adv.*, late
tartalhar, *pr. ind.* 3 tartalha 3368, *v. intr.*, **to chatter at length and unnecessarily**
tastar 1194, *v. tr.*, to touch; to taste
taular 1183, *v. tr.*, to set out the board for (a game); *v.* **intr.**, **to be victorious** (in a game)
tauleiar 1190, *v. intr.*, to play small cymbals or castanets
taurs 1861, *sb.*, bull
taütz 3077, *sb. m.* and *f.*, bier
tavas 1944, *sb.*, horse-fly
tavecs 1969, *adj.* expressing an insult— *perhaps* foolish
taverniers 2271, *sb.*, innkeeper
teira 3186, *sb. f.*, series, line; a teira 3189, in a line
teiralhz 1650, *sb.*, piece of ground
tela 3293, *sb. f.*, cloth
telha 3396, *sb. f.*, bast, inner bark of lime-tree

telhz, telz 2071, *sb.*, lime-tree
teliers 2267, *sb.*, weaver's loom
temer, *pr. ind.* 2 tems 2088, *pret.* 3 teus 639, *v. tr., intr.*, and *refl.*, to fear
temerosamen 1474, *adv.*, timorously
temptar 1205, *v. tr.*, to tempt
tems 174, temps 2087, *sb. m. indecl.*, time; per tems 2089, at the appropriate time
tençar 1204, *v. intr.*, to quarrel, dispute
tendir 1457, *v. intr.*, to resound
tendre 242, 366, 658, 1292, *pr. ind.* 2 tens 2144, *pret.* 3 tendet 598, *impf. subj.* 1 tendes 375, 2 tendesses 376, 3 tendes 377, 4 tendessem 378, 5 tendessez 379, 6 tendessen, tendesson 380, *p. part.* -ut 666, tendut 708, 748–53, tendutz 3062, *v. tr.*, to stretch
teneire 76, *adj.*, tenacious
tener 240, 335, 665, 1250, *fut. impf.* 1 tenria 343, *pr. ind.* 1 tenh, teni 521, 2 tes, tenes 522, 3 te 523, *pr. part.* tenens 2121, *pret.* 1 tengui 556, 2 tenguist 556, 3 teng 561, tec 580, *cond.* 1 tengra 343, *p. part.* tengut 678, 707, 764–9, tengutz 3066, *v. tr.*, to hold
tenher 673, 1273, *pr. ind.* 1 tenh 530 (*mistranslated*), *pr. subj.* 3 tenga 3445, *pret.* 3 teis 586, 2000, *p. part.* teinht 683, *v. tr.*, to dye
terçar 1203, *v. intr.*, to take a third part of sthg. (as a feudal due, called the *tertz*); or *v. tr.*, to levy the *tertz* on (produce, etc.) (?)
terrenals 1589, *adj.*, earthly
terriers 2228, *sb.*, domain
tertz 2304, *adj.*, third
terzer, *imper.* 2 tertz 2305, *pret.* 3 ters 618, *v. tr.*, to wipe
tesauriers 2274, *sb.*, treasurer
tesaurs 1857, *sb.*, treasure
teus 212, 2434, *poss. pron.* and *adj.*, thy, thine
thez 2419, *sb.*, small roof
tins 2494, *sb.*, temple (of the head)
tirans 1736, *sb.*, tyrant; *adj.*, hard, cruel
tirar, *pr. ind.* 3 tira 3211, *v. tr.*, to pull, drag
toalha 3374, *sb. f.*, a cloth

tocar 1217, *pr. subj.* 2 tocs 2658, *v. tr.*, to touch
tolhz 2719, *sb.*, dog-fish
tolre, *pr. ind.* 2 tolz 2691, *pr. subj.* 3 tolha 3423, *pret.* 3 tolc 628, *p. part.* toutz 2924, *v. tr.*, to take away
tombar 1213, *pr. subj.* 2 toms 2738, *imper.* 3 tombe 304, *v. intr.*, to fall 304, 2738; to caper, turn a somersault 304, 1213
toms 2738, *sb.*, fall
tondeire 73, *sb.*, shearer
tondre 1329, *pret.* 3 tondet 603, *v. tr.*, to shear, clip
tonelz 2054, *sb.*, cask
torbar 1214, *v. tr.*, to disturb
tornar, *pr. subj.* 2 torns 2911, *v. intr.* and *refl.*, to turn, return
torns 2911, *sb.*, lathe
tors 2810, *sb.*, piece of fish
tors 2838, *sb. f.*, tower
torser, *pr. ind.* 3 tortz 2869, *pret.* 3 tors 637, 2812, *p. part.* tortz 2869, *v. tr.*, to twist
tortelz 2037, *sb.*, small loaf
tortitz 2603, *sb.*, torch
tortz 2888, *sb.*, thrush (bird)
tortz 2868, torz 229, *sb.*, injustice 229; violence offered to s.o. 2868 (*more generally*: harm, wrong)
tosetz 2397, *sb.*, boy
tost 1468, 1470, 1473, *adv.*, soon
tostar 1215, *v. tr.*, to roast
totz 2958, *adj.*, all, whole
totztems 1482, *adv.*, always
trabs 1526, *sb.*, sort of tent
trahir 1456, *p. part.* traïtz 2580, *v. tr.*, to betray
traïnar 1185, *v. tr.*, to drag (at the horse's tail); to draw (s.o.) on by wiles, to lure on
traire 1262, *pret.* 3 trais 643, *p. part.* trahz 1910, *v. tr.*, to pull, drag 1262, 1910; to shoot (arrow) 643
traïre 78, *sb.*, traitor
trametre 1342, *v. tr.*, to send, transmit
transgitar, *imper.* 5 transgitatz 1888, *p. part.* transgitatz 1889, *v. tr.*, **to deceive (of magicians or mountebanks)**, i.e. **to perform tricks by sleight of hand** (?)
transitz 2581, *adj.*, half-dead
transpas 1932, *sb.*, moment

GLOSSARY

transpassar 1068, *pr. ind.* 3 traspassa 3550 (*B*), *pr. subj.* 3 transpas 1931, *v. intr.*, to cross over
trapaussar 1069, *untranslated; no doubt* = *v. tr.*, to carry over
trasbucar 1188, *pr. subj.* 2 trasbucs 2972, *v. tr.*, to throw down 1188 (?), 2972; *v. intr.*, to fall to the ground 1188 (?)
trasdossa 3528, *sb. f.*, whatever is carried on a horse's back, e.g. pack
trassalhir 1450, *v. tr.*, to jump across
traucar 1195, *pr. subj.* 2 traucs 1832, *v. tr.*, to pierce
traucs 1832, *sb.*, hole
traus 1847, *sb. m.* and *f.*, wooden beam
travar 1186, *v. tr.*, to hobble (a horse)
travers 2177, *adj.*, oblique
traversar 1196, *v. tr.*, to cross
traversiers 2237, *adj.*, transverse, oblique
trebailhz 1651, *sb.*, work
trebalha 3351, *sb. f.*, work
trebalhar, *pr. ind.* 3 trebalha 3352, *pr. subj.* 2 trebalhz 1655, *v. intr.*, to labour
treblar 1202, *v. tr.*, to stir up (water or other liquid)
trebucs 2971, *sb.* m., leggings
trega 3494, *sb. f.*, truce
trelha 3400, *sb. f.*, climbing vine
tremblar 1198, *v. intr.*, to tremble
trencar 1200, *imper.* 5 trençatz 1887, *p. part.* trençatz 1887, *v. tr.*, to cut
trepar 1201, *pr. subj.* 2 treps 2168, *v. intr.*, to play (*more exactly*: to caper) 2168; **to caress** (?) 1201
treps 2167, *sb.*, game
tresca 3515, *sb. f.*, sort of round-dance
trescar 1199, *pr. ind.* 3 tresca 3516, *v. intr.*, to perform a round-dance
trevar 1206, *v. intr.*, to frequent
triar 1208, *pr. ind.* 3 tria 3469, 3472, *v. tr.*, to choose 1208, 3469; to discern 3472
tribolar 1211, *v. tr.*, to afflict
tribs 2440, *sb.*, tribe
trichar 1209, *v. tr.* and *intr.*, to cheat
trics 2451, *sb.*, **entanglement, difficulty** (?)
trigar, *pr. ind.* 3 triga 3458, *v. intr.*, to delay
trissar 1210, *v. tr.*, to grind
tristors 2850, *sb. f.*, sadness

tritz 2582, *adj.*, ground (by grinding)
trobar 1216, *pr. subj.* 2 trobs 2627, *v. tr.*, to find
trolhar 1221, *pr. ind.* 3 trolha 3431, *v. tr.*, to press (in a wine-press or oil-press)
trolhz 2708, *sb.*, wine-press
trombar 1218, trumbar 795, *v. intr.*, to blow trumpets
tronar 1212, *v. intr.*, to thunder
trons 2749, *adj.*, **blunt**
trossa 3534, *sb. f.*, pack, load
trossar 1220, *pr. ind.* 3 trossa 3535, *v. tr.*, to tie on (baggage)
trotar 1219, *imper.* 4 trotem 308 (Lat.), 5 trotaz 308, 6 troten 311, *v. intr.*, to trot
trotiers 2204, *sb.*, messenger, runner
trotz 2944, *sb.*, trot
truans 1731, *sb.*, vagrant
trufar 1222, *v. refl.*, to speak frivolous or empty words, i.e. to mock, jeer; *v. tr.*, to deceive
tu 100, 206, 252, etc., *obl.* te 398, 1468, *pers. pron.*, thou

ucar 1240, *pr. subj.* 2 ucs 2967, *v. tr.*, to call (s.o.) by holloing 1240; *v. intr.*, to cry out 2967
ucs 2966, *sb.*, cry, shout
udolar 1238, *v. intr.*, to howl
umas 1946, *adj.*, human; friendly, kind
umbralhz 1647, *sb.*, shade
umors 2836, *sb. f.*, moisture, humour (in medical sense)
upar 1239, *v. intr.*, to sing (in some specific manner which cannot be guessed from the text) (?)
urtar 1242, *v. intr.*, to collide face to face
us 3081, l'us 3080, *num. adj.* and *indef. art.*, one, a
us 3082, *sb.*, door
us 200, 3083, *sb. m. indecl.*, usage, custom
usar 1243, *v. tr.* and *intr.*, to use
usclar 1241, *v. tr.*, **to singe (hair)**; to burn
usquecs 1981, *indef. pron.*, each, every one

vabors 2835, *sb. f.*, steam
vacs 1544, *adj.*, unoccupied, idle

GLOSSARY

vairar 1224, *pr. ind.* 3 vaira 3519, *v. tr.* and *intr.*, to change, vary
valer 1261, *fut. impf.* 1 valria 352, *pr. subj.* 3 valha 3365, *cond.* 1 valgra 352, *v. tr.* and *intr.*, to be worth, to be of value
valors 2834, *sb. f.*, valour, merit
valz 1638, *sb. f.*, valley
vantar 1223, *v. refl.*, to boast
varar 1225, *v. tr.*, to launch (a ship)
vars 1784, *adj.*, variegated, changeable
vas 139, 1926, *sb. m. indecl.*, sepulchral monument, tomb
vas 1950, *adj.*, vain, empty
vec, *interj.*, here is, here are; veus me 1486, here I am; vel vos 1486, here he is
veçer 670, vecher 1325, *pr. ind.* 1 vei 50, 215, 216, *p. part.* -ist 670, *v. tr.*, to see
vedar 1227, *v. tr.*, to forbid
vegada, *sb. f.*, time, occasion; a la vegada 1480, at times
veirolhz 2720, *sb.*, bolt (of door)
vela 3291, *sb. f.*, sail
velhar 1228, *pr. ind.* 3 velha 3382, *pr. subj.* 2 velhz 2074, *v. intr.* and *refl.*, to stay awake, be wakeful
vellzir 1466, *v. intr.*, to become worthless, debased
venals 1570, *adj.*, venal
vencher 1281, *pr. ind.* 3 vens 2135, *pret.* 3 venquet 596, *v. tr.* and *intr.*, to conquer
vendre 1297, *pret.* 3 vendet 600, *v. tr.*, to sell
vengar 1232, *v. tr.*, to avenge
venials 1585, *adj.*, venial
venir 1458, *fut. impf.* 1 venria 356, *pret.* 3 venc 591, *cond.* 1 vengra 356, *p. part.* venguth 218, 3068, vengutz 23, 44, 215-17, *v. intr.*, to come
ventalha 3375, *sb. f.*, part of a coat of mail which protected the face, ventail
ventar 1226, *v. tr.*, to expose to the wind
ventrelhz 2076, *sb.*, stomach
vera 3180, *adj. f.*, true
veramen 1468, 1469, 1488, *adv.*, truly, indeed
verçiers 2246, *sb.*, orchard, garden
verdeiar 1233, *v. intr.*, to turn green
verdors 2837, *sb. f.*, greenery

vergar 1235, *v. tr.*, **to stripe, make (sthg.) in stripes** (?)
vergonhar 1229, *v. refl.*, to be ashamed, to blush
vermelhz 2065, *f.* vermelha 3379, *adj.*, scarlet
verms 2290, *sb.*, worm
vernhissar 1230, *v. tr.*, to varnish (a weapon—no doubt a shield—after painting)
verns 2284, *sb.*, alder
verolhar, *pr. ind.* 3 verolha 3438, *v. tr.*, to bolt (door)
verps 2288, *meaning uncertain*
vers 2199, *sb.*, truth
vers 133, 2174, *sb. m. indecl.*, verse
vers 2175, *sb.*, springtime
versificar 1234, *v. tr.*, to versify
vertz 2308, *adj.*, green
vescoms 2727, vescons 41, *sb.*, viscount
vescomtals 1569, *adj.*, pertaining to a viscount
vespertinar 1231, *v. intr.*, to sup
vestir 1463, *p. part.* vestithz 2599, *v. tr.*, to clothe
vethz 2379, *sb.*, penis
vetz 2392, *sb.*, fault, defect, bad quality (*apparently attested only in the expression* mal vetz)
vetz 2393, *sb. f.*, occasion, time
vianans 1729, *sb.*, traveller
vidals 1577, *adj.*, pertaining to life
vielhz 2061, *f.* velha 3402, *adj.*, old
vila 3298, *sb. f.*, town
vilas 1938, *adj.*, rustic; ignorant, uncultivated
vims 2485, *sb.*, osier
viola 3321, *sb. f.*, violet
violers 2257, *sb.*, bed of violets (?)
virar 1237, *pr. ind.* 3 vira 3215, *v. tr.*, to turn round
vis 184, 2534, *sb. m. indecl.*, face
vis 2533, *obl. sg.* vin 227, *sb.*, wine
visitar 1236, *v. tr.*, to visit
viular 789, *imper.* 2 viula 298, *v. intr.*, to play the viol
viure 366, 1280, *v. intr.*, to live
vius 2609, *adj.*, alive
vohtz 2763, voitz 2771, *adj.*, empty
volar, *pr. subj.* 2 vols 2662, *imper.* 2 vola 3322, *v. intr.*, to fly
volbs 2636, *sb. f.*, fox
voler 335, 359, 1258, *fut. impf.* 1 volria 228, 337, 2 volrias 338,

GLOSSARY 419

3 volria 339, 4 volriam 340, 5 volriatz 341, 6 volrien 342, *pr. ind.*
1 voilh 231, 2 vols 2662, *pr. subj.*
3 volha 390, 472, 546, 3422, vola 494, *pret.* 3 volc 628, *cond.* 1 volgra 337, 2 volgras 338, 3 volgra 339, 4 volgram 340, 5 volgraz 341, 6 volgren 342, *v. tr.*, to wish
vols 2662, *sb.*, will, desire; per mo vol 458, 465, 479, would that (*introducing phrases exemplifying the optative mood*)
volver, *pret.* 3 vols 635, 2662, *p. part.* voutz 2919, *v. tr., intr.*, and *refl.*, to turn
volz 2700, voutz 2928, *sb.*, wooden image

vorms 2905, *untranslated; no doubt* = *sb.*, glanders, a disease of horses
vos 257, 443, etc., *pers. pron.*, you
vostre 103, 213, *poss. pron.* and *adj.*, your, yours
voutitz 2593, *adj.*, changeable

yverns 2279, *sb.*, winter

zai 1493, *adv.*, here; de çhai 1493, here, from here (*badly translated as* from there)
zocs 2656, *sb.*, **base of a chessman** (?)
zo es a saber 1516, *adv.*, namely, to wit
zoira 3557, *sb. f.*, old dog
zucs 2981, *sb.*, skull, cranium

PRINTED IN GREAT BRITAIN
AT THE UNIVERSITY PRESS, OXFORD
BY VIVIAN RIDLER
PRINTER TO THE UNIVERSITY